# Words Their Way®

# Words THEIR WAY Digital

*Words Their Way* is a developmental approach to phonics, vocabulary, and spelling instruction. Guided by an informed interpretation of spelling errors and other literacy behaviors, *Words Their Way* offers a systematic, teacher-directed, child-centered plan for the study of words from kindergarten through high school. Step by step, the chapters explain exactly how to provide effective word study instruction. The keys to this research-based approach are knowing your students' literacy progress, organizing for instruction, and implementing word study.

We are excited to announce the new *Words Their Way Digital* website—an online platform that provides automatically scored spelling inventories, 130+ interactive sorts, 40+ word study games, and the ability to monitor student progress.

**New edition ordering ISBN: 9780135174623**

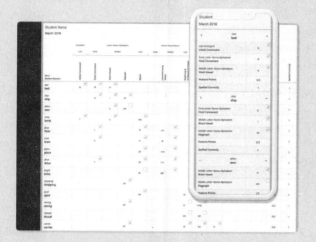

Automatically Scored Feature Guides

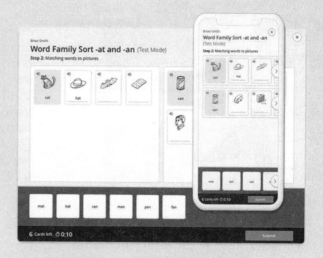

Interactive Word Sorts

**Visit the preface of this book for more information about what is new to the 7th Edition!**

**To learn more, visit: www.pearsonhighered.com | www.wtwdigital.pearson.com**

# Other available titles from the *Words Their Way* series

## Word Sort Supplements

*Words Their Way: Letter and Picture Sorts for Emergent Spellers,* 3e © 2019, ISBN: 9780134773674

*Words Their Way: Word Sorts for Letter Name-Alphabetic Spellers,* 3e © 2018, ISBN: 9780134529790

*Words Their Way: Word Sorts for Within Word Pattern Spellers,* 3e © 2018, ISBN: 9780134575681

*Words Their Way: Word Sorts for Syllables and Affixes Spellers,* 3e © 2018, ISBN: 9780134530710

*Words Their Way: Word Sorts for Derivational Relations Spellers,* 3e © 2019, ISBN: 9780134773667

## Companion Titles

*Words Their Way for PreK-K* © 2015, ISBN: 9780132430166

*Words Their Way: Vocabulary for Middle and Secondary Students,* 2e © 2015, ISBN: 9780133431032

*Words Their Way for Struggling Readers: Word Study for Reading, Vocabulary, and Spelling Instruction: Grades 4-12* © 2011, ISBN: 9780135135211

*Words Their Way: Vocabulary for Elementary Mathematics* © 2017, ISBN: 9780133376074

*Words Their Way: Vocabulary for American History, The World Before 1600 to American Imperialism (1890-1920)* © 2017, ISBN: 9780132790154

*Words Their Way for Parents, Tutors, and School Volunteers* © 2018, ISBN: 9780132882637

## English Learners

*Words Their Way with English Learners: Word Study for Phonics, Vocabulary, and Word Study* © 2012, ISBN: 9780136119029

*Words Their Way: Emergent Sorts for Spanish-Speaking English Learners* © 2019, ISBN: 9780132421430

*Words Their Way: Letter-Name Alphabetic Sorts for Spanish-Speaking English Learners* © 2009, ISBN: 9780132421034

*Words Their Way: Within Word Pattern Sorts for Spanish-Speaking English Learners* © 2014, ISBN: 9780137028726

**To learn more, visit:** www.pearsonhighered.com | www.wtwdigital.pearson.com

# About the Authors

**Donald R. Bear** is Professor Emeritus in Literacy Studies at Iowa State University and University of Nevada, Reno where he directed reading centers and taught at all levels. He is a former classroom teacher, and an author and co-author of numerous articles, chapters, and 17 books. He is involved in innovative professional development activities, and his work in assessment and word study is used widely. Donald is involved in studies that examine literacy learning, particularly studies of orthographic development in different and second languages.

**Marcia Invernizzi** is the Henderson Professor Emerita of Reading Education at the University of Virginia. As a founder of *Book Buddies*, a nationally recognized reading tutorial for struggling readers, and *PALS*, a literacy screening and diagnostic tool, Marcia's research interests continue to revolve around evidence-based practices for the prevention of reading and writing difficulties. A former English and reading teacher, Marcia continues to collaborate with school districts and organizations seeking progressive change.

**Shane Templeton** is Foundation Professor Emeritus of Literacy Studies in the College of Education at the University of Nevada, Reno. A former classroom teacher at the primary and secondary levels, his research focuses on the development of orthographic and vocabulary knowledge. He has written several books on the teaching and learning of reading and language arts and is a member of the Usage Panel of the *American Heritage Dictionary*.

**Francine Johnston** is a former first-grade teacher and school reading specialist. She retired from the School of Education at the University of North Carolina at Greensboro, where she coordinated the reading master's program and directed a reading clinic for struggling readers.

for developmental instruction—in word study specifically and in literacy more generally. This understanding is now being applied to instruction in vocabulary—in particular, *generative* instruction based on an understanding of how morphology works to generate most of the words in the English language, as well as general academic vocabulary and domain-specific vocabulary.

### Francine

Students learn best when they are working with content that is in their "zone of proximal development" or window of opportunity. *Words Their Way* offers an assessment-driven developmental guide for word study that helps teachers differentiate instruction to meet children's needs and provides the resources to do so.

Bring your colleagues and come join us in the most active edition of *Words Their Way*® yet. We wish you happy sorting with your students!

Sincerely,

**Donald R. Bear   Marcia Invernizzi   Shane Templeton   Francine Johnston**

# Letter from the Authors

**Dear Educator,**

It is an honor for the authors of *Words Their Way:® Word Study for Phonics, Vocabulary, and Spelling Instruction* to present the seventh edition of this seminal text on word study. Accompanying this edition is a new online resource, *Words Their Way® Digital* featuring a student input assessment that automatically scores and suggests word study groups. *WTW Digital* also contains more than 130 interactive digital sorts and printable games across the five stages. Additionally, the enhanced eText version of the book includes more than 40 classroom videos and a wealth of printable resources for the classroom all in one place. These tools will help you to effectively implement word study instruction.

Here the authors highlight a few key ideas presented in *Words Their Way*.

## Donald

*Words Their Way* presents a developmental approach that makes word study more efficient and students more responsive. This approach to word study integrates phonics, spelling, and vocabulary because of the reciprocal nature of literacy: what students learn in spelling transfers to reading, and what they learn in reading transfers to spelling and vocabulary. These are not, therefore, three separate and unrelated areas of instruction. Integrating phonics, vocabulary, and spelling instruction with a developmental approach contributes, we hope, to deep and rewarding learning and teaching.

## Marcia

*Words Their Way* has gotten teachers to think about phonics, spelling, and vocabulary instruction from a completely different point of view. Teachers welcome our student-centered, minds-on, active approach that considers word study not only as an integral part of literacy development, but also as an integral vehicle for fostering critical thinking. Effective word study lessons pose questions and involve students in solving problems through careful analysis, reflection, and discussion. The questions teachers pose during words study—such as, "Why do some words end in a silent *e*?"—encourage an investigative mindset and give purpose for engaging in word study activities such as word sorts. The language we use when we talk with students about words has a powerful influence on their self-efficacy as learners. This is in sharp contrast to most phonics and spelling programs that merely ask students to memorize relationships, rules, and words.

## Shane

*Words Their Way* helps teachers provide their students with the breadth and depth of exploration necessary to construct knowledge about words over time—from individual letters to sound, from groups of letters to sound, and from groups of letters to meaning. The awareness and appreciation of how children construct this knowledge empowers and emboldens many teachers to advocate

This book is dedicated to
the memory of our teacher,
Edmund H. Henderson.

Donald R. Bear
Marcia Invernizzi
Shane Templeton
Francine Johnston

*Director and Publisher:* Kevin Davis
*Portfolio Manager:* Drew Bennett
*Managing Content Producer:* Megan Moffo
*Content Producer:* Yagnesh Jani
*Portfolio Management Assistant:* Maria Feliberty
*Managing Digital Producer:* Autumn Benson
*Digital Studio Producer:* Lauren Carlson
*Development Editor:* Carolyn Schweitzer
*Executive Product Marketing Manager:* Krista Clark
*Procurement Specialist:* Deidra Headlee
*Cover Design:* Pearson CSC, Jerilyn Bockorick
*Cover Art:* Jim Atherton
*Full Service Vendor:* Pearson CSC
*Full Service Project Management:* Pearson CSC,
*Editorial Project Manager:* Pearson CSC, Heather Winter
*Printer-Binder:* Menasha
*Cover Printer:* Phoenix
*Text Font:* PalatinoLTPro-Roman

Credits and acknowledgments borrowed from other sources and reproduced, with permission, in this textbook appear on appropriate page within text.

**Library of Congress Cataloging-in-Publication Data**
Bear, Donald R.
   Words their way: word study for phonics, vocabulary, and spelling instruction/Donald R. Bear, Iowa State University, Marcia Invernizzi, University of Virginia, Shane Templeton, University of Nevada, Reno, Francine Johnston, University of North Carolina at Greensboro. —Seventh Edition.
       pages cm
   Rev. ed. of: Words their way / Donald R. Bear … [et al.]
   Includes bibliographical references and index.
   ISBN 978-0-13-520491-7—ISBN 0-13-520491-7   1. Word recognition.   2. Reading—Phonetic method.
3. English language—Orthography and spelling.   I. Invernizzi, Marcia.   II. Templeton, Shane.
III. Johnston, Francine R.   IV. Bear, Donald R. Words their way.   V. Title.
   LB1050.44.B43 2015
   372.46'2—dc23
                                                                                2015008892

5 2022

ISBN-10:    0-13-520491-7
ISBN-13: 978-0-13-520491-7

# Words Their Way®

## Word Study for Phonics, Vocabulary, and Spelling Instruction

**SEVENTH EDITION**

### Donald R. Bear
*Iowa State University & University of Nevada, Reno*
*Professor Emeritus of Literacy Studies and Literacy Center Director*

### Marcia Invernizzi
*University of Virginia*
*Edmund H. Henderson Professor Emerita of Education*

### Shane Templeton
*University of Nevada, Reno*
*Foundation Professor Emeritus of Literacy Studies*

### Francine Johnston
*University of North Carolina, Greensboro*
*Associate Professor Emerita*

 Pearson

# Brief Contents

# Contents

**CHAPTER 1** Developmental Word Knowledge     2

**CHAPTER 2** Getting Started     24

## CHAPTER 5   Word Study for the Letter Name–Alphabetic Stage   146

**CHAPTER 6**    **Word Study for the Within Word Pattern Stage**    **206**

**CHAPTER 7**   Word Study for the Syllables and Affixes Stage   256

**CHAPTER 8**   Word Study for the Derivational Relations Stage   294

## CHAPTER 9   Implementation of Word Study Instruction: Schedules, Routines, Materials, and Effective Practices   344

## APPENDICES   371

# Activities

# Preface

*I see and I forget. I hear and I remember. I do and I understand.*

—Confucius

Word study involves "doing" things with words—examining, manipulating, comparing, and categorizing—and offers students the opportunity to make their own discoveries about how words work. When teachers use this practical, hands-on way to study words with students, they create tasks that focus students' attention on critical features of words: sound, pattern, and meaning.

*Words Their Way* is a developmental approach to phonics, vocabulary, and spelling instruction. Guided by an informed interpretation of spelling errors and other literacy behaviors, *Words Their Way* offers a systematic, teacher-directed, child-centered plan for the study of words from kindergarten to high school. Step by step, the chapters explain exactly how to provide effective word study instruction. The keys to this research-based approach are knowing your students' literacy progress, organizing for instruction, and implementing word study.

## New to This Edition

Two new digital tools accompany *Words Their Way*, seventh edition. Together with the text, these resources provide the tools you need to understand and carry out word study instruction that will motivate and engage your students and help them succeed in literacy learning.

*Words Their Way*® *Digital* provides students and teachers the opportunity to engage in interactive word study. Features include:

- **Automatically scored spelling inventories** generate student word study groups based on inventory results. Students can input spellings directly into the website, or the teacher may choose to key in students' spellings from an assessment administered on paper.

- **130+ interactive online sorts** span all five developmental stages. Sorts are also available in a printable PDF format for in-class or take-home use. Users can also create their own interactive or printable picture and word sorts.

- **40+ word study games and templates** in a printable PDF format are available for all five developmental stages.

- **Data reporting and administrator oversight** allows literacy coaches or specialists to view and track student progress across multiple teachers' classrooms. Student assessment data can viewed at the whole class and individual student level.

The **Enhanced Pearson eText** provides online access to the full book and includes the following multimedia features to help teachers implement word study instruction:

- **Video examples** feature real teachers and students using *Words Their Way* in the classroom.
- **Teacher Resources** are links to PDFs that include directions for various assessments and activities to be used as part of word study instruction.

**Note:** Access codes for *WTW Digital* and the Enhanced Pearson eText are included with each new copy of the package ISBN: 9780135174623.

## Key Content Changes

This edition incorporates the following updates:

- Chapter 3 has been revised to focus on the word study lesson, teacher-student interactions, and follow-up activities whereas a new Chapter 9 addresses the larger issues involved in organizing word study in the classroom.
- Sample lesson plans are included in each chapter to demonstrate how teachers guide thoughtful discussions about words. For example, Chapter 5 provides three lesson plans, including one to introduce word families in picture sorts.
- "Ten Indicators of Effective Word Study Classrooms" in Chapter 9 have been added to guide evaluation and professional development.
- Activities have been added, and many have been revised in Chapters 3–8. In Chapter 8, for example, vocabulary activities are categorized according to being *generative* and *word-specific*, and additional activities such as *Operation Examination* and *Word Challenge: Words from Myths and Legends* are provided.
- Progress monitoring and goalsetting materials are available in Appendix B.
- A new term, *focused contrasts*, is introduced to highlight the importance of comparing and contrasting letters and spelling patterns related to speech sounds and meaning units or morphemes.
- References throughout the book with the latest research pertaining to word study have been updated.
- English learner callouts provide more information about comparisons between English and other languages.
- Visually enhanced, full-color design breaks the content into more manageable sections that highlight Teacher Tips and boxed text supplements in the main text. The design facilitates easy interaction between the printed text and the eText.

## Knowing Your Students

Chapter 1 provides foundational information on word study and the research in orthography and literacy development that led to this word study approach. Chapter 2 presents assessment and evaluation tools, walking you step by step through the process of determining your students' instructional level and focusing your word study instruction appropriately. After you administer one of the spelling inventories, you will be able to compile a feature guide for each of your students that will help you identify the stage and the word study features they are ready to master. The classroom composite will identify which students have similar instructional needs, allowing you to plan wisely and effectively for word study grouping.

## Organizing for Instruction

Chapter 3 describes key activities for small groups, partners, and individuals that can be incorporated into weekly routines We also describe a continuum of support that will help you plan and implement lessons to maximize classroom time. Tips are provided to help guide discussions about words. Chapter 9 will help you establish a word study routine and manage leveled groups at all grade levels. It also introduces ten indicators of effective word study classrooms as a guide to professional development.

## Implementing Word Study

After you have assessed your students, created leveled groups, and developed routines for word study, the information and materials in Chapters 4 through 8 and the Appendices will guide your instruction. Chapters 4 through 8 explore the characteristics of each particular stage, from the emergent learner through to the advanced reader and writer in the derivational relations stage of spelling development. Each of these chapters covers the research and teaching principles that drive instruction and details an appropriate scope and sequence of word study skills. Suggestions are offered for differentiated instructional pacing.

Activities described in each chapter include concept sorts, word sorts, games, and activities that will help you focus instruction where it is needed to move students into the next stage of development. These word study activities promise to engage your students, motivate them, and improve their literacy skills. The activities sections have shaded tabs for your convenience, creating a handy classroom resource. This edition extends our emphasis on vocabulary strategies and activities for each developmental level.

Importantly, as you work to address the English Language Arts standards for which you are responsible, you will see how *Words Their Way* supports the reading foundational skills and language standards across all the grades. The depth and breadth of word knowledge developed through *Words Their Way* also supports most standards' emphasis on students reading and exploring more complex literary and informational texts.

The Appendices at the back of the book contain most of the assessment instruments described in Chapter 2, as well as sound boards, word sorts, word lists, and game templates you will need to get your own word study instruction under way.

# Companion Volumes

Since the last edition of this book, the stage-specific companion volumes have been revised and updated with expanded step-by-step directions for each lesson. These supplements provide you with a complete curriculum of reproducible sorts:

- *Words Their Way:*® *Letter and Picture Sorts for Emergent Spellers* (3rd ed.), by Donald R. Bear, Marcia Invernizzi, Francine Johnston, and Shane Templeton
- *Words Their Way:*® *Word Sorts for Letter Name–Alphabetic Spellers* (3rd ed.), by Francine Johnston, Donald R. Bear, Marcia Invernizzi, and Shane Templeton
- *Words Their Way:*® *Word Sorts for Within Word Pattern Spellers* (3rd ed.), by Marcia Invernizzi, Francine Johnston, Donald R. Bear, and Shane Templeton
- *Words Their Way:*® *Word Sorts for Syllables and Affixes Spellers* (3rd ed.), by Francine Johnston, Marcia Invernizzi, Donald R. Bear, and Shane Templeton
- *Words Their Way:*® *Word Sorts for Derivational Relations Spellers* (3rd ed.), by Shane Templeton, Francine Johnston, Donald R. Bear, and Marcia Invernizzi

Other related volumes are designed to meet the needs of English learners and students across all grade levels:

- *Words Their Way*® *for PreK–K*, by Francine Johnston, Marcia Invernizzi, Lori Helman, Donald R. Bear, and Shane Templeton
- *Words Their Way*® *with English Learners: Word Study for Phonics, Vocabulary, and Spelling* (2nd ed.), by Lori Helman, Donald R. Bear, Shane Templeton, Marcia Invernizzi, and Francine Johnston
- *Words Their Way:*® *Emergent Sorts for Spanish-Speaking English Learners*, by Lori Helman, Donald R. Bear, Marcia Invernizzi, Shane Templeton, and Francine Johnston
- *Words Their Way:*® *Letter Name–Alphabetic Sorts for Spanish-Speaking English Learners*, by Lori Helman, Donald R. Bear, Marcia Invernizzi, Shane Templeton, and Francine Johnston
- *Words Their Way:*® *Within Word Pattern Sorts for Spanish-Speaking English Learners*, by Lori Helman, Donald R. Bear, Marcia Invernizzi, Shane Templeton, and Francine Johnston
- *Words Their Way: Vocabulary for Middle and Secondary Students* (2nd ed.), by Shane Templeton, Donald R. Bear, Marcia Invernizzi, Francine Johnston, Kevin Flanigan, Dianna Townsend, Lori Helman, and Tisha Hayes
- *Words Their Way*® *with Struggling Readers: Word Study for Reading, Vocabulary, and Spelling Instruction, Grades 4–12*, by Kevin Flanigan, Latisha Hayes, Shane Templeton, Donald R. Bear, Marcia Invernizzi, and Francine Johnston
- *Words Their Way*® *for Parents, Tutors, and School Volunteers*, by Michele Picard, Alison Meadows, Marcia Invernizzi, Francine Johnston and Donald Bear.

# Acknowledgments

We would like to thank the many reviewers who, over the years, have helped to make each edition of *Words Their Way* grow and continue to be responsive to teachers' needs and expectations. Colleagues and friends are too numerous to mention here, but those who have in recent years worked with and taught us include Kelly Bruskotter, Sharon Cathey, Shari Dunn, Kevin Flanigan, Michelle Flores, Kristin Gehsmann, Ashley Gotta, Amanda Grotting, Tisha Hayes, Lori Helman, Ryan Ichanberry, Darl Kiernan, Sandra Madura, Alison Meadows, Kara Moloney, Sarah Negrete, Molly Ness, Ann Noel, Michelle Picard, Leta Rabenstein, Kelly Rubero, Alisa Simeral, David Smith, Regina Smith, Kris Stosic, Dianna Townsend, and Alyson Wilson. We would like to thank the video production team from the University of Nevada, Reno, for their excellent work on the videos accompanying this book, as well as many photos in the book. The team includes Mark Gandolfo, Theresa Danna-Douglas, Maryan Tooker, and Shawn Sariti. We would also like to thank Michelle Murray and Kristen Braatz for a number of videos and photos that appear in Chapter 8, and Ann Marie Howard for the photo that appears in Chapter 9.

Special thanks to the following teachers for their classroom-tested activities: Cindy Aldrete-Frazer, Tamara Baren, Margery Beatty, Telia Blackard, Cindy Booth, Karen Broaddus, Wendy Brown, Janet Brown Watts, Karen Carpenter, Carol Caserta-Henry, Jeradi Cohen, Fran de Maio, Nicole Doner, Allison Dwier-Seldon, Marilyn Edwards, Monica Everson, Ann Fordham, Mary Fowler, Elizabeth Harrison, Esther Heatley, Lisbeth Kling, Pat Love, Rita Loyacono, Barry Mahanes, Carolyn Melchiorre, Colleen Muldoon, Liana Napier, Katherine Preston, Brenda Riebel, Leslie Robertson, Geraldine Robinson, Elizabeth Shuett, Lauren Sloop, Jennifer Sudduth, Charlotte Tucker and Krista Wieser.

Finally, a very special "thank you" to the following individuals: Drew Bennett, who joined us in this new edition to navigate new terrains and ways of presenting word study; and content producer Yagnesh Jani.

# chapter 1

# Developmental Word Knowledge

For students of all ages and language backgrounds, the key to literacy is knowing how their written language represents the language they speak. Central to this knowledge is understanding how written words represent sound and meaning. The *Words Their Way* approach to developing this knowledge supports students' thinking, problem solving, and making sense of words.

## How Children Learn about Words

During the preschool years, most children:

- Acquire word knowledge aurally, from the language that surrounds them within their everyday experiences.
- Develop a speaking vocabulary through listening to and talking about everyday events, life experiences, and stories.
- Begin to make sense of their world as they have opportunities to use language to describe it and negotiate it.
- Begin to experiment with pen and paper when they have opportunities to observe parents, siblings, and caregivers writing for many purposes. They gradually come to understand the forms and functions of written language.
- Learn their first written words, usually their own names, followed by those of significant others. Words such as *Mom*, *cat*, and *dog* and phrases like *I love you* represent people, animals, and ideas dear to their lives.

As students grow as readers and writers:

- The language of books and print becomes a critical component to furthering their literacy development.
- Vocabulary is learned when purposeful reading, writing, listening, and speaking take place.
- Even more words can be learned when children explicitly examine printed words to discover consistencies among them, and come to understand how these consistent patterns relate to oral language—to speech sounds and to meaning.

### The Braid of Literacy

Literacy is like a braid, beginning with the intertwining threads of oral language and stories that are read to children (Bear, Invernizzi, & Templeton, 1996). As children experiment with putting ideas on paper, a writing thread is entwined. All along the way, vocabulary is acquired. Then, as children move into reading, the threads of literacy begin to bond. Students' growing knowledge of spelling or **orthography**—the ways in which letters and letter patterns in words represent sound and meaning—strengthens that bonding. The size of the threads and the braid itself become thicker as this orthographic knowledge grows (see Figure 1.1).

A major aim of this book is to demonstrate how word study can lead to the lengthening

**FIGURE 1.1   Braid of Literacy**

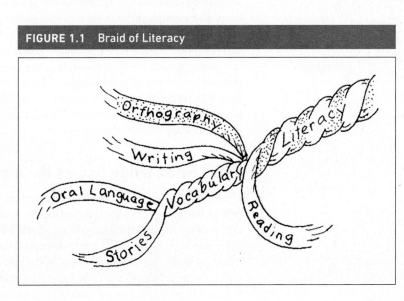

and strengthening of the literacy braid. Teachers' understanding of the ways in which these threads intertwine to create this bond will empower them to direct children's attention to words *their* way.

## Children's Spellings: A Window into Developing Word Knowledge

In the early 1970s Charles Read (1971, 1975) and Carol Chomsky (1971) took a serious look at preschoolers' attempts to spell. Their work introduced the world of literacy to the notion of "invented spelling" and the idea that children could write before they had formal reading instruction. Through linguistic analyses, Read explained how young children's attempts were not just random collections of letters, but instead provided a window into their developing word knowledge. These inventions revealed a systematic logic to the way some preschoolers selected letters to represent speech sounds.

At about the same time, Edmund Henderson and his colleagues at the University of Virginia had begun to look for similar logic in students' spellings across ages and grade levels (Beers & Henderson, 1977; Henderson & Beers, 1980). Read's findings provided these researchers with the tools they needed to interpret the errors they were studying. Building on Read's discoveries, Henderson discerned an underlying logic to students' errors that changed over time, moving from the spelling of single letters and letter groups or patterns to the spelling of meaning units such as suffixes and Latin roots. The Virginia spelling studies corroborated and extended Read's findings upward through the grades and resulted in a comprehensive model of developmental word knowledge (Henderson, 1990; Henderson & Templeton, 1986; Templeton & Bear, 1992). Subsequent studies confirmed this developmental model across many groups of students, from preschoolers (Ouellette & Sénéchal, 2008) through adults (Massengill, 2006; Worthy & Viise, 1996), as well as across socioeconomic levels, dialects, and other alphabetic languages. The power of this model lies in the diagnostic information contained in students' spelling inventions that reveal their current understanding of written words (Bahr, Silliman, & Berninger, 2009; Treiman, Stothard, & Snowling, 2013).

## Conceptual Development Grows through Categorizing

There are similarities in the ways learners of all ages expand their concepts and their knowledge of the world. It seems that humans have a natural interest in finding order and patterns, comparing and contrasting, and paying attention to what remains the same despite minor variations. For example, infants learn to recognize Daddy as the same Daddy with or without glasses, with or without a hat or whiskers. Through such daily interactions, all learners categorize their surroundings. Similarly, our students expand their vocabularies by comparing and contrasting one concept with another. Gradually, the number of concepts they analyze increases, but the process is still one of comparing and contrasting. Young children may first call anything with four legs "doggie" until they attend to the features that distinguish dogs, cats, and cows, and later terriers, Labrador retrievers, border collies, and greyhounds. In the process, they learn the vocabulary to label the categories.

## Word Knowledge Grows through Categorizing and Reflecting

Word study, as described in this book, occurs in hands-on sorting and matching activities that reflect basic cognitive learning processes: categorizing, comparing and contrasting words by different word features, and talking about and reflecting on what they notice. For example, when teachers engage students in **focused contrasts** such as categorizing words according to whether or not they end in a "silent" *e*, students can discover a consistent spelling pattern: words ending with a "silent" *e* usually have a long vowel sound (ā as in *cake*) whereas those without a final *e* have a short vowel sound (ă as in *cat*). When students examine, categorize, discuss, and think about words under the guidance of a knowledgeable teacher, the logic of the spelling system is revealed.

## Why Is Word Study Important?

Becoming fully literate depends on the quality of the mental representations of words in an individual's **lexicon**, or "dictionary in the head" that every individual constructs in his or her mind. For each word, **lexical quality** (Invernizzi, 2017; Perfetti, 2007) includes knowledge of pronunciation (**phonology**), meaning (**semantics**) and use (**syntax**). When this information in each word's mental representation is merged with the word's spelling, its orthography, this supports

Emma sorting words—silent *e* versus no silent *e*

- The immediate, accurate recognition of words in texts that facilitates comprehension in reading
- The immediate, accurate production of words in writing that allows writers to focus their attention on making meaning

Henderson and his colleagues used the term **word study** to refer to the teaching of spelling and how it merges with pronunciation, meaning, and use. They also showed how, through an informed analysis of students' spelling attempts, teachers can differentiate and provide timely instruction in phonics, spelling, and vocabulary—instruction that is essential to move students forward in reading and writing.

Planning and implementing a word study curriculum that explicitly teaches students necessary skills, and that engages their interest and motivation to learn about words, is a vital aspect of any literacy program. However, some approaches to phonics, spelling, and vocabulary do not engage and motivate: They primarily involve repeated practice involving drill, memorization, and an emphasis on teaching rules. Students have little opportunity to discover spelling patterns, manipulate word concepts, or apply critical thinking skills.

Word study should be embedded within purposeful reading and writing. In that context, effective, engaging, and motivating word study provides:

- A systematic, developmentally based scope and sequence
- Multiple hands-on opportunities to manipulate words and features in ways that allow students to look at and analyze words, generalizing beyond individual words to entire groups or families of words
- Opportunities for active, critical thinking about words that lead to an ever-deepening understanding of how spelling works

## What Is the Purpose of Word Study?

Word study helps students:

- Actively explore and understand the nature of the spelling system, developing a **general** knowledge of the regularities, patterns, and conventions needed to read and spell
- Develop **specific** knowledge of the spellings, meanings, and uses of individual words

*General word knowledge* is what we use when we encounter a new word, when we do not know how to spell a word, or when we do not know the meaning of a specific word. The better our general knowledge of the system, the better we are at decoding unfamiliar words, spelling correctly, or guessing the meanings of words. For example, primary students who have general knowledge about short vowels and consonants would have no trouble attempting the word *brash*

### Phonics: Analytic vs. Synthetic? Both!

There is an ongoing debate in literacy teaching between *analytic* and *synthetic* phonics. Actually, research settled the debate a long time ago—both are needed (International Literacy Association, 2018; National Reading Panel, 2000). In *analytic phonics* students break known words down to analyze the individual sounds and letters within them; in *synthetic phonics* students build words up by blending the individual sounds and letters. The problem with relying on synthetic approaches exclusively is that students may not recognize the word as one they know even after they blend all the individual sounds correctly. This is particularly true of English learners and even native speakers with limited vocabularies. Analytic phonics instruction helps children learn how to use the spelling patterns in known words to then figure out unknown words that have similar spelling patterns. Most children need *both* types of instruction—when, how, and how much depend on where they are developmentally. For example, a child who is just on the cusp but not yet beginning to read would have difficulty trying to blend all the consonants and vowels within a word because full segmentation of all the sounds within a word is a more advanced skill; very beginners are solidifying their knowledge of beginning and ending consonants. Nevertheless, even beginners *synthesize* sounds as they write: Listening for sounds in what they want to write and trying to match letters to those sounds is a great application of synthetic phonics.

*for* **English learners**

**Enhanced eText**
**Video Example 1.1**
In this video, author Marcia Invernizzi and several classroom teachers discuss word study and why word study is important.

even if they have never seen or written it before. The spelling is straightforward, like so many single-syllable short vowel words. For intermediate students who have general knowledge that words that are similar in spelling are related in meaning, such as *compete* and *competition*, would be more likely to understand the meaning of an unfamiliar word like *competitively*. Additional clues offered by context also increase the chances of reading and understanding a word correctly.

*Specific word knowledge* enables us to remember the correct spelling and meaning of individual words. For example, the word *rain* might be spelled *rane*, *rain*, or *rayne*; all three spellings are theoretically plausible. However, only specific knowledge helps us spell it correctly. Likewise, only specific knowledge of the spelling of *which* and *witch* makes it possible to know which is which! The relationship between specific knowledge and general knowledge of the system is *reciprocal*—each supports the other—as is their application in reading and spelling. Conrad (2008) expressed this idea in noting that "the transfer between reading and spelling occurs in both directions" (p. 876) and that "the orthographic representations established through practice can be used for both reading and spelling" (p. 869).

## Alphabet, Pattern and Meaning: The Basis for Developmental Word Study

Word study evolves from decades of research exploring developmental aspects of word knowledge with children and adults. This research has documented specific kinds of spelling errors that tend to occur in clusters at different points throughout development and which reflect students' uncertainty over certain spellings or orthographic conventions. These "clusters" have been described in terms of

- errors dealing with the **alphabetic** match of letters and sounds (FES for *fish*)
- errors dealing with **letter patterns** (SNAIK for *snake*) and **syllable patterns** (POPING for *popping*)
- errors dealing with words related in **meaning** (INVUTATION for *invitation*; a lack of knowledge that *invite* provides the clue to the correct spelling of the second vowel in *invitation*)

The same cluster types of errors have been observed among:

- Students with learning disabilities and dyslexia (Bear, Negrete, & Cathey, 2012; Sawyer, Lipa-Wade, Kim, Ritenour, & Knight, 1997; Templeton & Ives, 2007; Worthy & Invernizzi, 1989)
- Students who speak a variant dialect (Cantrell, 2001; Dixon, Zhao, & Joshi, 2012; Stever, 1980)
- Students who are learning to read in different alphabetic languages (Helman, 2004; Helman et al., 2012; Ford, Invernizzi & Huang, 2018)

Longitudinal and cross-grade-level research has shown that essentially the same developmental progression occurs for all learners of written English, varying only in the rate of acquisition (Invernizzi & Hayes, 2004; Templeton & Bear, 2018; Treiman, Stothard, & Snowling, 2013).

**FIGURE 1.2  Developmental Word Study Instruction**

Word study also builds on the history of English spelling. Developmental spelling researchers have examined the three layers of English orthography in the historical evolution of English spelling and compared this evolution to students' developmental progression from *alphabet* to *pattern* to *meaning* layers. Figure 1.2 illustrates how each of the three layers of the English spelling system is built on the one before: to the straightforward alphabetic base of Old English was added the more abstract letter patterns in Middle English, and to that layer were added the Greek and Latin meaning units such as prefixes, suffixes, and roots in early Modern English. From the intermediate grades and up, word study includes students' examining the interactions among these three layers.

## Alphabet

The **alphabetic layer** in English spelling is the first layer of information at work. Our spelling system is alphabetic because it represents the relationship between letters and sounds. In the word *sat*, each sound is represented by a single letter; we blend the sounds for *s*, *a*, and *t* to read the word *sat*. In the word *chin*, we still hear three sounds, even though there are four letters, because the first two letters, *ch*, function like a single letter, representing a single sound. So we can match letters—sometimes singly, sometimes in pairs—to sounds from left to right and create words.

The alphabetic layer of English orthography was established during the time of Old English, the language spoken and written by the Anglo-Saxons in England between the Germanic invasions of the fifth century c.e. and the conquest of England by William of Normandy in 1066 (Lerer, 2007). Old English was remarkably consistent in letter–sound correspondence and used the alphabet to systematically represent speech sounds. The long vowels were pronounced close to the way they are in modern Romance languages today, such as Spanish, French, and Italian; for example, *e* is pronounced as long A as in *tres*; *i* is pronounced as long E as in *Rio*.

The history of the alphabetic layer reflected in the story of Old English is relevant to teachers today because beginners spell like "little Saxons" as they begin to read and write (Henderson, 1981). Armed with only a rudimentary knowledge of the alphabet and letter sounds, beginning spellers of all backgrounds use their alphabet knowledge quite literally. They rely on the sound embedded in the names of the letters to represent the sounds they are trying to represent (Invernizzi, 1992; Read, 1971; Young, 2007). This strategy works quite well for consonants when the names do, in fact, contain the correct corresponding speech sounds; for example *Bee, Dee, eF, eS*, and so forth. It works less well for letters that have more than one sound: (*C:/s/* and */k/*), and it does not work at all for consonants with names that do not contain their corresponding speech sounds (*W: double you; Y: wie;* and *H: aitch*). Short vowel sounds are particularly problematic for young spellers because there is no single letter that "says" the short vowel sound. As a result, beginning readers choose a letter whose name, when pronounced, sounds and feels closest to the targeted short vowel sound (Beers & Henderson, 1977; Read, 1975). For example, beginning readers often spell the short *e* sound in *bed* with the letter *a* (BAD) and the short *i* sound in *rip* with the letter *e* (REP).

**Enhanced eText**
**Video Example 1.2**
The authors describe the three layers of English spelling: alphabet, pattern, and meaning, and how the five stages of development build on these layers.

## Pattern

Why don't we spell all words in English "the way they sound"—at the alphabetic level, in other words? If we did, words like *cape*, *bead*, and *light* would look like *cap*, *bed*, and *lit*—but these spellings, of course, already represent other words. Therefore, the **pattern layer** overlays the alphabetic layer. Because there are 42 to 44 sounds in English and only 26 letters in the alphabet, single sounds are sometimes spelled with more than one letter or are affected by other letters that do not stand for any sounds themselves. When we look beyond single letter–sound match-ups and search for **patterns** that guide the groupings of letters, however, we find surprising consistency (Hanna, Hanna, Hodges, & Rudorf, 1966; Venezky, 1999). For example, consider the *ain* in *rain*: We say that the silent *i* is a **vowel marker**, indicating that the preceding vowel letter, *a*, stands for a long vowel sound. The *i* does not stand for a sound itself, but "marks" the vowel before it as long. The *ai* group of letters follows a pattern: When you have a pair of vowels in a single syllable, this letter grouping forms a pattern that often indicates a long vowel. We refer to this as the "AI pattern" or as the consonant-vowel-vowel-consonant (CVVC) pattern—one of several high-frequency long-vowel patterns. Overall, knowledge about orthographic patterns within words is considerably valuable to students in both their reading and their spelling.

Where did these patterns originate? The simple letter–sound consistency of Old English was overlaid by a massive influx of French words after the Norman Conquest in 1066. Because these words entered the existing language through bilingual Anglo-Norman speakers and writers, some of the French pronunciations and spelling conventions were adopted, too. Old English was thus overlaid with the vocabulary and spelling traditions of the ruling class, the Norman French. This complex interaction of pronunciation change on top of the intermingling of French and English spellings led to a proliferation of different vowel sounds represented by different vowel patterns. The extensive repertoire of vowel patterns today is attributable to this period of history, such as the various pronunciations of the *ea* pattern in words like *bread* and *thread*, *great* and *break*, *meat* and *clean*. It is uncanny that students in this pattern stage of spelling spell like "little Anglo-Normans" when they write *taste* as TAIST or *leave* as LEEVE.

Students sort by the patterns of long *a*

## Meaning

The third layer of English orthography is the **meaning layer**. When students learn that groups of letters can represent meaning directly, they will be much less puzzled when encountering unusual spellings. Examples of these units or groups of letters are prefixes, suffixes, and Greek and Latin roots. These units of meaning are called **morphemes**—the smallest units of meaning in a language.

One example of how meaning functions in the spelling system is the prefix *re-*: Whether we hear it pronounced "ree" as in *rethink* or "ruh" as in *remove*, the morpheme spelling stays the same because it directly represents meaning. Why is *sign* spelled with a silent *g*?

Because it is related in meaning to *signature*, in which the *g* is pronounced. The letters *s-i-g-n* remain in both words to visually preserve the meaning relationships that these words share. Likewise, the letter sequence *photo* in *photograph, photographer,* and *photographic* signals spelling–meaning connections among these words, despite the changes in sounds that the letter *o* represents.

The explosion of knowledge and culture during the Renaissance required a new, expanded vocabulary to accommodate the growth in learning that occurred during this time. Greek and Latin were used by educated people throughout Europe, so new words could be built out of elements that came from classical Greek and Latin: for example, Greek roots *auto* + *graph*; *bio* + *sphere*; Latin roots, prefixes, and suffixes (*inspect*, *spectator*, and *respectable*). So, a third layer of meaning was added to the orthographic record of English (Upward & Davidson, 2011).

The spelling–meaning relations among words brought into English during the Renaissance have important implications for vocabulary instruction today as students move through the intermediate grades and beyond (Templeton 2011/2012, 2012). When students explore how spelling visually preserves meaning relationships among words with the same derivations (for example, note the second b in *bomb* and *bombard*), they see how closely related spelling is to meaning and vocabulary. The seemingly arbitrary spelling of some words—in which silent letters occur or vowel spellings seem irrational—is in reality central to understanding the meanings of related words. For example, the silent *c* in *muscle* is "sounded" in the related words *muscular* and *musculature*—all of which come from the Latin *musculus*, literally a little mouse. (The rippling of a muscle reminded the Romans of the movements of a mouse!) Such words, through their spellings, carry their history and meaning with them (Venezky, 1999; Templeton et al., 2015).

## How History Speaks to Instruction

Organizing the phonics, spelling, and vocabulary curriculum according to historical layers of alphabet, pattern, and meaning provides a systematic guide for instruction. It places the types of words to be studied in an evolutionary progression that mirrors the development of the orthographic system itself. Anglo-Saxon words, the oldest words in English, are among the easiest to read and the most familiar. Words like *sun, moon, day,* and *night* are high-frequency "earthy" words that populate easy reading materials in the primary grades. Anglo-Saxon words survive in high-frequency prepositions, pronouns, conjunctions, and auxiliary verbs (for example, *have, was, does*) although the pronunciation is now quite different. More difficult Norman French words like *chance, chamber, royal, guard,* and *conquer* frequently appear in books suitable for the elementary grades. The less frequent, more academic vocabulary of English—words like *atonement, epigraph, antecedent, immunology, disingenuous,* and *rectilinear*—are Latin or Greek in origin and appear most often in student reading selections beginning in the upper elementary grades and beyond.

Alphabet, pattern, and meaning represent three broad principles of written English and form the layered record of orthographic history. As students learn to read and write, they appear to reinvent the system as it was itself invented. As shown in Table 1.1, beginners invent the spellings of simple words phonetically, just as the Anglo-Saxons did more than a thousand years ago. As students become independent readers, they add a second layer by using patterns, much as the Norman French did. Notice in Table 1.1 the overuse of the silent *e* vowel marker at the ends of all of Antonie's words, much like Geoffrey Chaucer's! Intermediate and advanced readers invent conventions for joining syllables and units of meaning, as was done during the Renaissance when English incorporated a large classical Greek and Latin vocabulary (Henderson, 1990; Templeton, Bear, Invernizzi, & Johnston, 2010). As Table 1.1 shows, both Julian, age 14, and Queen Elizabeth I in 1600 had to deal with issues of consonant doubling in the middle of words.

**TABLE 1.1** Comparison of Historical and Students' Development across Three Layers of English Orthography: Alphabet, Pattern, and Meaning

| Alphabet | Historical Spelling<br>Anglo-Saxon<br>(Lord's Prayer, 1000) | Students' Spelling-by-Stage<br>Letter Name–Alphabetic<br>(Tawanda, age 6) |
|---|---|---|
| | WIF (wife)<br>TODAEG (today)<br>HEAFONUM (heaven) | WIF (wife)<br>TUDAE (today)<br>HAFAN (heaven) |
| Pattern | **Norman French<br>(Chaucer, 1440)** | **Within Word Patterns<br>(Antonie, age 8)** |
| | YONGE (young)<br>SWETE (sweet)<br>ROOTE (root)<br>CROPPE (crop) | YUNGE (young)<br>SWETE (sweet)<br>ROOTE (root)<br>CROPPE (crop) |
| Meaning | **Renaissance<br>(Elizabeth I, 1600)** | **Syllables & Meaning<br>(Julian, age 14)** |
| | DISSCORD (discord)<br>FOLOWE (follow)<br>MUSSIKE (music) | DISSCORD (discord)<br>FOLOWE (follow)<br>MUSSIC (music) |

*Source:* Adapted from "Using Students' Invented Spellings as a Guide for Spelling Instruction That Emphasizes Word Study" by M. Invernizzi, M. Abouzeid, & T. Gill, 1994, *Elementary School Journal, 95(2)*, p. 158. Reprinted by permission of The University of Chicago Press.

## TEACHING TIPS

### Learning and Integrating the Layers of English Orthography

Word knowledge advances as students develop orthographic understandings at the alphabetic, pattern, and meaning levels. This happens when they read and write purposefully and are also provided with explicit, systematic word study instruction by knowledgeable teachers. How can word study give students the experiences they need to progress through and integrate these layers of information? The following examples illustrate the emphasis at each layer:

- For students who are experimenting with the alphabetic match of letters and sounds, teachers can focus on contrasting aspects of the writing system that relate directly to the representation of sound. For example, words spelled with short *e* (*bed, leg, net, neck, mess*) are contrasted with words spelled with short *o* (*hot, rock, top, log, pond*).

- For students experimenting with pattern, teachers can contrast patterns as they relate to vowels. For example, words spelled with *ay* (*play, day, tray, way*) are compared to words spelled with *ai* (*wait, rain, chain, maid*).

- For students experimenting with conventions of syllables, affixes (prefixes and suffixes), and other meaning units, teachers can help students see that words with similar meanings are often spelled the same, despite changes in pronunciation. For example, *admiration* is spelled with an *i* in the second syllable because it comes from the word *admire*.

# The Development of Orthographic Knowledge

When we say word study is developmental, we mean that the study of specific word features must match the level of the learner's word knowledge. Word study is not a one-size-fits-all program of instruction that begins in the same place for all students within a grade level. Rather, it is an approach that uniquely emphasizes the critical role of differentiating instruction for different levels of word knowledge.

Word study instruction must match the needs of the child. This construct, called **instructional level**, is a powerful determinant of what may be learned. Simply put, we must teach within each child's zone of understanding (Harré & Moghaddam, 2003; Vygotsky, 1962). To do otherwise results in frustration or boredom and little learning in either case. Just as in learning to play the piano—when students must work through book A, then book B, and then book C—learning to read and spell is a gradual and cumulative process. Word study begins with finding out what each child already knows and starting instruction there.

One of the easiest and most informative ways to know what students need to learn is to look at the way they spell words. Recall that students' efforts to spell provide a direct window into how they think the spelling system works. By interpreting what students do, educators can target a specific student's instructional level and plan word study instruction that this student is ready to learn. Furthermore, by applying basic principles of child development, educators have learned how to engage students in learning about word features in a child-centered, developmentally appropriate way.

When students are instructed within their own zone of understanding or **zone of proximal development (ZPD)**—studying words *their* way—they are able to build on what they already know, to learn what they need to know next, and to move forward. Zone of proximal development was first described by Vygotsky (1962): The "zone" refers to the span between what a learner knows and is able to do independently, and what she is able to do with support and guidance. With explicit instruction and ample experience reading, writing, and examining words, spelling features that were previously omitted or confused become incorporated into an ever-increasing reading and writing vocabulary.

## Stages of Spelling Development

As we have described, students move from easier one-to-one correspondences between letters and sounds, to more abstract relationships between letter patterns and sounds, to even more sophisticated relationships between meaning units as they relate to sound and pattern. Developmental spelling research describes this growth as a continuum or a series of chronologically ordered *stages* or phases of word knowledge: Emergent, Letter Name-Alphabetic, Within Word Pattern, Syllables and Affixes, and Derivational Relations (Henderson, 1990; Ehri, 2005; Nunes & Bryant, 2009).

Stages are marked by broad, qualitative shifts in the types of spelling errors students make as well as changes in the way they read words. The names of the stages or phases represent the predominant type of orthographic information—alphabetic, pattern, meaning—used by learners in the spelling and reading of words (Berninger, Abbott, Nagy, & Carlisle, 2009; Bryant, Nunes, & Bindman, 1997; Ehri, 1997, 2006; Templeton, 2003).

In this book we use the word *stage* as a metaphor to inform instruction. In reality, as students grow in their general knowledge of the three layers of information in English and in their specific knowledge of word features, some overlap exists in the layers and features students understand and use. In fact, as students grow in their understanding of how spelling represents both sound and meaning, they become more flexible in their application of spelling strategies. For example, in figuring out an unfamiliar word they are able to do more than just "sound it out"—they may use analogies to other words with similar sounds, patterns, or meanings, or use spelling–meaning connections. There is a range of grades during which most students pass through these stages, and these are presented in Table 1.2.

| TABLE 1.2 | **Spelling and Reading Stages, Grade Levels, and Corresponding Instructional Chapters** |

*Alphabet* ⟶ *Pattern* ⟶ *Meaning*

**Emergent Stage**
**Emergent Reading**
*PreK to K*
*Chapter 4*

**Letter Name–Alphabetic Stage**
**Beginning Reading**
*K to Grade 2*
*Chapter 5*

**Within Word Pattern Stage**
**Transitional Reading**
*Grades 1 to 4*
*Chapter 6*

**Syllables and Affixes Stage**
**Intermediate Reading**
*Grades 2 to 6*
*Chapter 7*

**Derivational Relations**
**Advanced Reading**
*Grades 5 and up*
*Chapter 8*

Because word study is based on each student's stage of spelling, the word study activities presented in this book are arranged by stages of spelling development. This chapter presents a brief overview of these stages. As shown in Table 1.2, Chapters 4 through 8 explore each of these stages in depth. By conducting assessments throughout the year, as described in Chapter 2, teachers can determine the spelling stages of their students and monitor students' progress and development (Gehsmann, Spichtig, & Tousley, 2018).

For each stage, students' orthographic knowledge is defined by three functional levels that are useful guides for knowing when to teach what (Invernizzi et al., 1994):

- What students *know and use correctly*—an **independent** or easy level • What students *use but confuse*—an **instructional** level or zone of proximal development at which instruction is most helpful
- What is *absent* in students' spelling—a **frustration** level in which spelling concepts are too difficult

What students "use but confuse" helps to define each spelling stage.

**EMERGENT STAGE.** The **emergent stage** encompasses the writing efforts of children who are not yet reading conventionally and in most cases have not been exposed to formal reading instruction. Emergent writers typically range in age from 2 to 5 years, although anyone not yet reading conventionally is in this stage of development. Emergent writing may range from random marks to legitimate letters that bear some relationship to sound. However, most of the emergent stage is decidedly **prephonetic**, which means there is little if any direct relationship between a character on the page and an individual speech sound.

As we explore in Chapter 4, emergent writing may be divided into a series of steps or landmarks. Children move from producing large scribbles indecipherable from an accompanying drawing (as illustrated in Figure 1.3A, Haley's picture of birdies), to using something that looks like scribbles separate from the picture (see Figure 1.3B where the child labeled his drawing to the left as "cowboy"), and on to using letters to represent some sounds in words (Figure 1.3C where "Jasmin" has been written as JMOE). In between, emergent learners are learning and experimenting with various symbols such as numbers and letter-like forms (Cabell, Tortorelli, & Gerde, 2013). Moving from this stage to the next stage hinges on learning the **alphabetic principle**: understanding that speech can be divided into individual units of sound and matched to letters in a systematic way (Liberman, Shankweiler, & Liberman, 1989).

**LETTER NAME–ALPHABETIC STAGE.** The letter name–alphabetic spelling stage encompasses that period during which students are first formally taught to read, typically during kindergarten and early first grade. Most letter name–alphabetic spellers are between the ages of 4 and 7 years, although a beginning reader at age 55 also can be a letter name–alphabetic speller (Bear, 1989; Massengill, 2006; Viise, 1996). Early in this stage, "letter name" is students' predominant approach to spelling; that is, they use the *names* of the letters as cues to the sounds

**FIGURE 1.3 Emergent Writing**

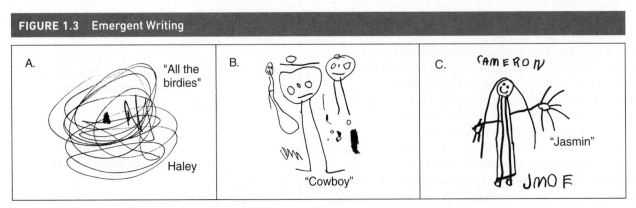

A. "All the birdies" — Haley

B. "Cowboy"

C. CAMERON — "Jasmin" — JMOE

*Source:* From dissertation by Janet Bloodgood (1996). Adapted with permission.

**FIGURE 1.4** Early Letter Name–Alphabetic Spelling: Ellie's Note to Her Sister, Meg—"When Are You Coming?"

**FIGURE 1.5** Late Letter Name–Alphabetic Spelling: Matt's Informational Writing about "Bears"

they want to represent (Read, 1975). In Ellie's early letter name–alphabetic spelling shown in Figure 1.4, she wrote YNRUKM: She used the letter *Y* to represent the /w/ sound at the beginning of the word *when*, because the first sound in the pronounced letter name *Y* ("wie") matches the first sound in the word *when*. The letter name for *N* includes the "en" sound to finish off the word *when*. Ellie used *R* and *U* to represent the entire words *are* and *you*, another early letter name strategy.

As students move through this stage, they learn to segment the individual speech sounds or **phonemes** within words and to match an appropriate letter or letter pairs to those sounds. Students in the later part of the letter name–alphabetic stage spell much like the sample in Figure 1.5. Matt, a class cut-up in his writing as well as in his behavior, shows mastery of most beginning and ending consonants. What clearly separates his spelling from Ellie's early letter name spelling is his consistent use of vowels. Long vowels, which "say their name," appear in TETH for *teeth* and MET for *meat*, but silent letters are not represented. He has spelled the high-frequency word *eat* correctly. *R*-influenced vowels in *bears* and *sharp* are challenging, but Matt has made a good effort to represent these sounds.

**WITHIN WORD PATTERN STAGE.** Students entering the within word pattern spelling stage can read and spell many words correctly because of their automatic knowledge of letter sounds and short-vowel patterns. This level of orthographic knowledge typically begins as children transition to independent reading toward the end of first grade. It expands for most students throughout second and third grade and into fourth. Although most within word pattern spellers typically range in age from 6 to 9 years, many low-skilled adult readers remain in this stage. Regardless, this period of orthographic development lasts longer than the letter name–alphabetic stage because the vowel pattern system of English orthography is quite extensive.

The within word pattern stage begins when students move away from the linear, sound-by-sound approach of the letter name–alphabetic spellers and begin to include patterns or chunks of letter sequences and silent vowel markers like final *e*. Within word pattern spellers can think about words in more than one dimension; they study words by sound and pattern simultaneously. As the name of this stage suggests, within word pattern spellers take a closer look at vowel patterns within single-syllable words (Henderson, 1990).

My teme won the scoer game.
I was the boll girl.
We had to use cons
for the gowl. Evre time
the boll wintdowe Hill
I Had to Throwe them a
nother boll.

Kim's writing in Figure 1.6 is that of an early within word pattern speller. She spells many short-vowel and high-frequency words correctly, such as *hill, had, them, girl,* and *won.* She also spells the common silent *e* long-vowel pattern correctly in words like *time* and *game.* Kim hears the long vowel sound in words like *team, goal,* and *throw,* but she selects incorrect patterns, spelling them as TEME, GOWL, and THROWE and she omits the silent *e* in *cones.* These are good examples of how Kim is using but confusing long-vowel patterns.

During the within word pattern stage, students first study the common long-vowel patterns (long *o* can be spelled with *o*-consonant-*e* as in *joke, oa* as in *goal,* and *ow* as in *throw*) and then less common patterns such as the VCC pattern in *cold* and *most.* The most challenging patterns are **ambiguous vowels** because the sound is neither long nor short and the same pattern may represent different sounds, such as the *ou* in *mouth, cough, through,* and *tough.* These less common and ambiguous vowels may persist as misspellings into the late within word pattern stage.

Although the focus of the within word pattern stage is on the pattern layer of English orthography, students must also consider the meaning layer to spell and use **homophones,** words such as *bear* and *bare, deer* and *dear,* and *hire* and *higher.* These words sound the same but have different spellings and meanings. Learning the correct spelling of homophones requires attention to sound, pattern, and meaning. Homophones introduce the spelling–meaning connection that is explored further in the next two stages of spelling development.

**SYLLABLES AND AFFIXES STAGE.** The syllables and affixes spelling stage is typically achieved in middle to upper elementary school when students are expected to spell many words of more than one syllable. This represents a new point in word study when students consider spelling patterns where syllables and meaning units such as **affixes** and **base words** join. A base word is a word to which prefixes and/or suffixes are added. Students in this fourth stage are most often between 8 and 12 years old, though many adults can also be found in this stage.

We went out west last sumer. We drove a littel camper bus. We stoped in alot of Nashal Parks and went hikeing in the mountins. It was relly cool.

In Figure 1.7, a fourth-grader in the early part of the syllables and affixes stage has written about his summer vacation. Xavier spelled most one-syllable short and long vowel words correctly (*went, west, drove, last*). Many of his errors are in two-syllable words and fall at the places where syllables and affixes meet. Xavier does not know the conventions for preserving vowel sounds when adding affixes such as -*ed* and -*ing*. He spelled *stopped* as STOPED and *hiking* as HIKEING. The convention of doubling the consonant to keep the vowel short is used in LITTEL for *little,* but is lacking in his spelling of *summer* as SUMER. Final syllables often give students difficulty because the vowel sound is not clear and may be spelled different ways, as shown in Xavier's spellings of LITTEL and MOUNTINS.

During the syllables and affixes stage, students explore the spelling of affixes that affect the meanings of words—for example, DESLOYAL for *disloyal* and CAREFULL for *careful.* Though studying simple affixes and base words as a decoding strategy begins earlier, studying base words and affixes more closely at this stage helps students construct the foundation for further exploration of word meanings in the next stage, derivational relations. At that stage, students study the spelling–meaning connections of related words (Templeton, 2004). By studying base words and derivational affixes, students learn more about English spelling as they enrich their vocabularies.

**DERIVATIONAL RELATIONS STAGE.** Some students move into the derivational relations spelling stage as early as grade 4 or 5, but most derivational relations spellers are found in middle school, high school, and college. This stage continues throughout adulthood, when individuals continue to read and write according to their interests and specialties. This stage of orthographic knowledge is referred to as *derivational relations* because this is when students examine in depth how many words may be *derived* from base words and word roots. Students discover that the meanings and spellings of meaningful word parts or morphemes remain constant across different but derivationally related words (Henry, 1988; Schlagal, 2013; Templeton, 2004) —for example *mandate/mandatory*, *human/humanity*, *custody/custodian*, and *define/definite/definitive*. Word study in this stage builds on and expands knowledge of a wide vocabulary, including thousands of words of Greek and Latin origin. We refer to this study as **generative** because as students explore and learn about the word formation processes of English they are able to *generate* knowledge of literally thousands of words (Harris, Schumaker, & Deshler, 2011; Kirk & Gillon, 2009; Templeton, 2012). Learning that the Latin root *jud* means "judge" and seeing how it combines with other word parts in *judgment*, *judgmental*, and *prejudice* helps students figure out the meaning of the unfamiliar words such as *adjudicate*, *judiciary*, and *injudicious* when they encounter them in context.

Early derivational relations spellers like sixth-grader Kaitlyn (Figure 1.8) spell most words correctly. However, some of her errors reflect a lack of knowledge about derivations. For example, *favorite* spelled FAVERITE and *different* spelled DIFFRENT do not reflect their relationship to *favor* and *differ*. Her errors on final suffixes, such as the *-sion* in *division* and the *-ent* in *ingredients* are also very typical of students in this stage.

The logic inherent in this lifelong stage can be summed up as follows: Words that are related in meaning are often related in spelling as well, despite changes in sound (Templeton, 1979, 1983, 2004). Understanding these spelling–meaning connections provides a powerful means of expanding vocabulary.

**FIGURE 1.8  Derivational Relations Spelling: Kaitlyn's Sixth-Grade Math Journal Reflection**

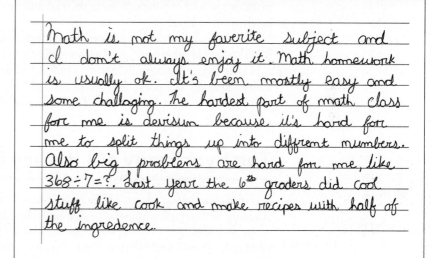

Math is not my faverite subject and I don't always enjoy it. Math homework is usually ok. It's been mostly easy and some challaging. The hardest part of math class for me is devision because it's hard for me to split things up into diffrent numbers. Also big problems are hard for me, like 368÷7=?. Last year the 6th graders did cool stuff like cook and make recipes with half of the ingredence.

## Stages of Spelling: A Perspective

As an educator, you should know that the concept of "stages" in the development of the ability to spell and read words has been debated for many years. It's important that you be aware of this debate because it has direct implications for instruction. A number of researchers have challenged a stage model, describing spelling development as "overlapping waves" (Sharp, Sinatra, & Reynolds, 2008), "nonlinear" (Bahr et al., 2012), "statistical" (Treiman & Kessler, 2006), or based on "multiple sources" (Masterson & Apel, 2010). There is considerable overlap between the stage model on which *Words Their Way* is based and these other perspectives, but they differ in the degree to which they emphasize alphabet, pattern, and meaning information at any point in development.

The critiques of the stage model of development are based on a literal interpretation of stages—that they limit what learners are exposed to and are capable of learning. In learning and instruction, for example, they assume that a stage model of spelling development implies that:

- Letter name–alphabetic learners are not exposed to or able to learn about words with long vowel spellings, or able to spell simple morphological endings such as -*ed* and -*ing*.
- Within word pattern learners are not exposed to or able to learn about words of more than one syllable.
- Syllables and affixes learners do not learn about Greek and Latin word roots.

Stage theorists have long argued that a developmental model does *not* mean that learners are limited in what they are exposed to or that they are incapable of learning about multiple aspects of words (Templeton, 2003). For example, in the world of print that surrounds them and in which they are immersed, letter name–alphabetic learners of course are exposed to words with long vowel patterns. By grounding instruction for such learners in what they are "using but confusing," however—short vowel spellings, consonant digraphs and blends—we are more effectively helping them develop the quality of their lexical knowledge to eventually better understand and accommodate those long vowel patterns. By grounding instruction for within word pattern learners in long vowel and other more challenging vowel patterns, we are supporting them in applying that knowledge to multisyllabic words they want to spell and need to read. And for all learners, as we will explore throughout this book, vocabulary learning and instruction will often focus on multisyllabic words and their meanings. However, though letter name and within word pattern children may learn the meanings of *pterodactyl*, *brontosaurus*, and *Jurassic* and be able to recognize these words in print, we would not expect them to read and spell other related multisyllabic words correctly forever after!

With the important exception of the literal interpretation of developmental stages, stage theorists would otherwise agree with much of what some other researchers are saying. There *is* overlap between stages in learning and instruction, and different aspects of words may be addressed at any one point in development. The key is in knowing *which* aspects, and *how much* they should be emphasized. *Words Their Way* provides you with that key.

## The Synchrony of Literacy Development

So far in this chapter we have seen how research supports the developmental progression in students' orthographic knowledge that underlies their ability to spell and to read words. The scope and sequence of word study instruction we present in Chapters 4 through 8 is based on this developmental relationship between spelling and reading behaviors. When teachers conduct word study with students, they address learning needs in all areas of literacy because development in one area relates to development in other areas. This harmony in the timing of development has been described as the **synchrony** of reading, writing, and spelling development (Bear, 1991b; Bear & Templeton, 1998). The word *synchrony* literally means "together in time," and we'll see how reading, writing, and spelling advance together in stage-like progressions that share important dimensions. Table 1.3 illustrates this synchrony and presents key examples in the following discussion of each reading stage.

Individuals may vary in their rate of progress through these stages, but most tend to follow the same order of development. The observed synchrony makes it possible to bring together reading, writing, and spelling behaviors to assess and plan differentiated instruction that matches each student's developmental pace. The following discussion centers on this overall progression, with an emphasis on the synchronous behaviors of reading and writing with spelling.

**Enhanced eText**
Teacher Resource:
The Synchrony of
Literacy Development

**TABLE 1.3**   The Synchrony of Literacy Development

# The Synchrony of Literacy Development
## Layers of the Orthography

ALPHABET/SOUND   PATTERN   MEANING

## Reading and Writing Stages:

| | Emergent | Beginning | Transitional | Intermediate/Advanced |
|---|---|---|---|---|
| Pretend read | | Read aloud; word-by-word, finger point reading | Approaching fluency, phrasal, some expression in oral reading, emergence of silent reading | Read fluently, with expression. Develop a variety of reading styles. Vocabulary grows with reading experience. |
| Developing concept of word | | Rudimentary–Firm concept of word | | |
| Pretend write | | Word-by-word writing; writing moves from a few words to paragraph in length | Approaching fluency, more organization, several paragraphs | Fluent writing, build expression and voice, experience different writing, styles and genre, writing shows personal problem solving and personal reflection. |

## Spelling Stages:

| | Emergent → | | | Letter Name–Alphabetic → | | | Within Word Pattern → | | | Syllables and Affixes → | | | Derivational Relations → | | |
|---|---|---|---|---|---|---|---|---|---|---|---|---|---|---|---|
| | Early | Middle | Late | Early | Middle | Late | Early | Middle | Late | Early | Middle | Late | Early | Middle | Late |
| Examples of spellings: | | | | | | | | | | | | | | | |
| bed | *(scribble)* | M3T | B | bd | bad | | <u>bed</u> | | | | | | | | |
| ship | *(scribble)* | TFP | S | sp | sep | shep | <u>ship</u> | | | | | | | | |
| float | *(scribble)* | SMT | F | ft | fot | flot | flote | flowt | floaut <u>float</u> | | | | | | |
| train | *(scribble)* | FSMP | G | jn | jan tan | chran tran | teran | traen | trane <u>train</u> | | | | | | |
| bottle | | | B | bt | botl | bodol | botel | botal | | bottel | <u>bottle</u> | | | | |
| cellar | | | S | slr | salr | celr | seler | celer | seler | celler | seller | <u>cellar</u> | | | |
| pleasure | | | P | pjr | plasr | plager | plejer | pleser | pleser | pleser | plesher | plesher | plesour | plesure | <u>pleasure</u> |
| confident | | | | | | | comfudate | | | confedent | confedent | confident | confident | | |
| opposition | | | | | | opasishan | opasishion | opasishan | | oposision | opasitian | oposition | oposition | <u>opposition</u> | |

## Emergent Readers

During the emergent stage, children may undertake reading and writing in earnest, but adults will recognize their efforts as more pretend than real. These students may "read" familiar books from memory using the pictures on each page to cue their recitation of the text. Chall (1983) called this stage of development *prereading* because students are not reading in a conventional sense. Emergent readers may call out the name of a favorite fast food restaurant when they recognize its logo, but they are not systematic in their use of any particular cue.

During the emergent stage, children lack an understanding of the alphabetic principle or show only the beginning of this understanding as they start to learn some letters. Emergent learners gradually acquire **directionality**—the understanding that print moves left-to-right, top-to-bottom—as they try to fingerpoint read, and in their writing. By the end of this stage, emergent learners will have learned many letters of the alphabet and they may even include a few letters to represent some speech sounds when they write.

## Beginning Readers

Understanding the alphabetic nature of our language is a major hurdle for readers and spellers. The child who writes *light* as LT has made a quantum conceptual leap, having grasped that there are systematic matches between sounds and letters that must be made when writing. Early letter name–alphabetic spellers have moved from pretend reading to the beginning of real reading, as they start to use systematic letter–sound matches to identify and store words in memory. Beginning reading is achieved when students have a **concept of word in text**, which is demonstrated by a child's ability to point accurately to a few lines of familiar text—a demonstration of the one-to-one correspondence between what they read and say (Clay, 1979; Morris, Bloodgood, Lomax, & Perney, 2003; Uhry, 1999, 2002).

Just as early attempts to spell words are partial, beginning readers initially have limited knowledge of letter sounds as they try to identify words by using the letter sounds they do know. The kinds of reading errors students make during this phase offer insights into what they understand about print. Using context as well as partial consonant cues, a child reading about good things to eat might substitute *candy* or even *cookie* for *cake* in the sentence, "The cake was good." Readers in this stage require support in the form of predictable, memorable texts or books that limit the number and nature of words.

The reading by beginning letter name–alphabetic learners is often disfluent—that is, choppy and often word-by-word, unless they have read the passage before or are otherwise familiar with it (Bear, 1992). If you ask them to read silently, the best they can do is to whisper. They need to read aloud to vocalize the letter sounds and usually fingerpoint as they read. Chall (1983) described children as being "glued to print" during this stage as they plod along slowly reading words, sometimes letter-by-letter, sound-by-sound. Beginning writers progress from writing a few words as they work to match letters and sounds to writing full stories. So much of their writing length at this stage will depend upon students' enthusiasm and the encouragement they receive.

## Transitional Readers

During the transitional stage, students' reading becomes more fluent because it is supported by a store of words that can be identified automatically "at first sight." These tend to be words they have read over and over again in meaningful contexts and words with frequently occurring letter patterns that they have mapped to speech sounds such as the consonant-vowel-consonant (CVC) pattern for short-vowel words. However, they "use but confuse" the various long-vowel patterns of English (Invernizzi, 1992).

During this stage, students integrate the knowledge and skills acquired in the previous two stages and they become more flexible in thinking about alphabet, pattern, and meaning. Advances in word knowledge affect students' writing, too. Their sizable sight word vocabulary allows them to write more quickly and with greater detail. Writing and reading speeds increase significantly from the beginning letter name–alphabetic stage to the transitional within word pattern stage, and over the course of this stage, oral reading is gradually replaced by silent reading as the preferred mode (Bear, 1992; Ehri, 2014; Invernizzi, 1992).

## Intermediate and Advanced Readers

The stages of word knowledge that characterize intermediate and advanced readers include syllables and affixes and derivational relations. Students in these stages have relatively automatic word recognition, leaving their minds free to think as rapidly as they can read. Intermediate students read most texts with good accuracy and speed, both orally and silently. Students learn to become *flexible, strategic readers* and ultimately become *proficient adult readers* (Spear-Swerling & Sternberg, 1997). Reading becomes an ever-more dominant mode of learning information and concepts. Intermediate and advanced readers are usually fluent writers. The content of their writing often displays more complex analysis and interpretation, reflecting a more sophisticated, discipline-specific vocabulary. The degree to which they write at this level often depends on the quality of the writing instruction they receive.

Vocabulary and word use play a central role in the connections that intermediate and advanced readers forge between reading and writing. From adolescence on, most of the new vocabulary students learn—except perhaps for slang—comes from reading, and reflects new domains of content-specific knowledge that students explore (Beck, McKeown, & Kucan, 2013; Zwiers, 2014). Studying spelling–meaning connections is central to maximizing this vocabulary growth (Nunes & Bryant, 2006; Templeton, 2011/2012).

Teachers often return to Table 1.3 to examine the integrated model of how reading, writing, and spelling progress in synchrony. In parent–teacher conferences, they often refer to it when they discuss a student's development. They explain to the parent how the child's spelling level corresponds to the characteristics of her reading level, as well as the types of writing to expect from a child at that particular developmental level.

# Words Their Way

Students acquire word knowledge implicitly as they read and write, and explicitly through instruction orchestrated by the teacher. An informed interpretation of students' reading and writing attempts shows us which words they can read and spell, and of those, which they might learn more about. There is more to pacing instruction than plugging students into a sequence of phonics or spelling features. Instructional *pacing* must be synonymous with instructional *placing*. That is, we must fit our instruction to what our students are using but confusing. How do we know what they are using but confusing? A good deal of what students understand about orthography is revealed in their uncorrected writing. Using the spelling inventories described in the next chapter as a guide, you will be able to place students and pace the content of word study.

Figure 1.9 illustrates the theory of developmental word knowledge and shows how word study links reading and writing. To help students explore and learn about words their way, instruction must be sensitive to two fundamental tenets:

1. Students' learning of phonics, spelling, and vocabulary is based on their developmental or instructional level.
2. Students' learning is based on the way they are naturally inclined to learn—through comparing and contrasting word features and discovering consistencies.

When these two tenets are honored, students learn *their* way—building from what is known about words to what is new. Rather than rote memorization activities designed only to

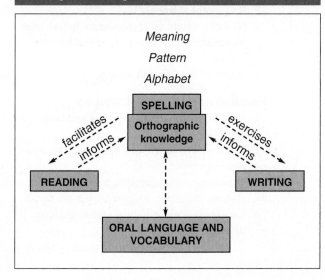

**FIGURE 1.9  The Integration of Word Study with Reading and Writing**

Word study is active and engaging

ensure repeated mechanical practice, word study encourages exploration and examination of word features presented in focused contrasts that are appropriate to a student's stage of literacy development. Word study is active, and by making judgments about words and categorizing words according to similar features, students construct their own understandings about how the features work. Engaging instruction and thoughtful practice helps students internalize word features and become automatic in using what they have learned.

The box on pages 20–22 provides a bird's-eye view of the terrain you will explore in *Words Their Way*: the characteristics of each spelling stage, the reading and writing contexts, and the instruction that is appropriate for each stage. After learning in Chapter 2 how to assess the developmental word knowledge of your students, Chapter 3 presents the key word study activities for all stages, and Chapters 4–8 provide detailed scope and sequences with specifics about planning and conducting word study instruction for each stage of development. As a bookend to Chapter 3, Chapter 9 presents routines, schedules and grouping strategies to help you implement word study in your classroom. As you delve into the instructional chapters, the box that follows can be a handy reference to check for how reading, writing, and word study are integrated at each developmental stage.

# Developmental Stages, Characteristics, and Word Study Instruction

## I. EMERGENT STAGE—CHAPTER 4

### Characteristics

1. Scribbles letters and numbers
2. No concept of word in text
3. No letter–sound correspondence at first; later, represents most salient sounds with single letters
4. "Pretend" reading and writing

### Reading and Writing Activities

1. Read to children and encourage oral language activities
2. Model writing for children, including dictations and charts
3. Encourage pretend reading from memory of rhymes, dictations, and simple pattern books
4. Encourage pretend writing and invented, or developmental, spelling

### Word Study Focus

1. Develop oral language with concept sorts
2. Play with speech sounds to develop phonological awareness
3. Teachers plan activities to learn the alphabet
4. Children sort pictures by beginning sound

## II. LETTER NAME–ALPHABETIC STAGE—CHAPTER 5
## EARLY LETTER NAME–ALPHABETIC STAGE

### Characteristics

1. Represents beginning and some ending sounds in writing
2. Uses letter names to create developmental spellings

3. Has rudimentary concept of word in text seen in fingerpointing
4. Reads word-by-word in beginning reading materials
5. Has a sight vocabulary of less than 15 words
6. Word by word writing

### Reading and Writing Activities

1. Read to students and encourage oral language activities
2. Develop concept of word in text reading in predictable books and simple rhymes
3. Model writing and record and reread individual dictations
4. Label pictures and write in journals regularly

### Word Study Focus

1. Collect known words for word bank
2. Categorize pictures and words by beginning sounds
3. Study word families that share a common vowel
4. Study beginning consonant digraphs and blends
5. Encourage developmental spelling

## MIDDLE TO LATE LETTER NAME–ALPHABETIC STAGE

### Characteristics

1. Correctly spells initial and final consonants and some blends and digraphs
2. Uses letter names and articulation as clues to spell vowel sounds
3. Spells phonetically, salient sounds in a one-to-one, linear fashion
4. Omits most silent letters and preconsonantal nasals in spelling (*bop* or *bup* for *bump*)
5. Has a firm concept of word; fingerpoints accurately and can self-correct when off track
6. Reads aloud slowly in a word-by-word manner
7. Adds sight words easily from extensive reading

### Reading and Writing Activities

1. Read to students
2. Encourage developmental spellings in independent writing, but hold students accountable for features and words they have studied
3. Collect two- to three-paragraph reading selections in books, poetry, and dictations. Read and reread beginning reading materials and dictations.
4. Encourage more expansive writing and consider some simple editing procedures for punctuation and high-frequency words

### Word Study Focus

1. Sort pictures and words by different short-vowel word families
2. Sort pictures and words by short-vowel sounds and CVC patterns
3. Continue to examine more difficult consonant blends with pictures and words
4. Study preconsonantal nasals, digraphs, and blends at ends of words
5. Sort pictures comparing short-and long-vowel sounds
6. Collect known words for word bank (up to 200)

## III. WITHIN WORD PATTERN STAGE—CHAPTER 6

### Characteristics

1. Spells most single-syllable short vowel words correctly
2. Spells most beginning consonant digraphs and two-letter consonant blends correctly
3. Attempts to use silent long-vowel markers
4. Reads silently and with more fluency and expression
5. Writes more fluently and in extended fashion
6. Can revise and edit

### Reading and Writing Activities

1. Continue to read aloud to students
2. Guide silent reading of simple chapter books
3. Write each day: writers' workshops, conferencing, and publication

### Word Study Focus

1. Complete daily activities in word study notebook
2. Sort words by long and short vowel sounds and by common long-vowel patterns
3. Compare words with *r*-influenced vowels
4. Explore less common vowels, diphthongs (*oi, oy*), and other ambiguous vowels (*ou, au, ow, oo*)
5. Examine triple blends and complex consonant units such as *thr, str, dge, tch, ck*
6. Explore homographs and homophones; vocabulary from reading

## IV. SYLLABLES AND AFFIXES—CHAPTER 7

### Characteristics

1. Spells most single-syllable words correctly
2. Makes errors at syllable juncture and in unaccented syllables

(*continued*)

3. Reads with good fluency and expression
4. Reads faster silently than orally
5. Potential to write responses that are more sophisticated and critical

### Reading and Writing Activities

1. Plan read-alouds and literature discussions
2. Include self-selected or assigned silent reading of texts from different genres
3. Begin simple note-taking and outlining skills, report writing, and work with adjusting reading rates for different purposes
4. Explore reading and writing styles and genres, developing a critical stance and independently backing up opinions with evidence to support them

### Word Study Focus

1. Study compound words
2. Study consonant doubling and inflectional endings including plurals
3. Study open and closed syllables and other syllable juncture features
4. Explore syllable stress and vowel patterns in the accented syllable, especially ambiguous vowels
5. Focus on unaccented syllables such as *er* and *le*
6. Explore unusual consonant blends and digraphs (*qu, ph, gh, gu*)
7. Study base words and affixes (prefixes and suffixes)
8. Focus on two-syllable homophones and homographs
9. Connect spelling and vocabulary studies; link meaning and spelling with grammar and meaning
10. Examine general and domain-specific vocabulary in texts

## V. DERIVATIONAL RELATIONS— CHAPTER 8

### Characteristics

1. Makes errors on low-frequency multisyllabic words derived from Latin and Greek
2. Reads with good fluency and expression
3. Reads faster silently than orally
4. Writes responses that are sophisticated and critical

### Reading and Writing Activities

1. Include silent reading and writing, exploring various genres
2. Develop study skills, including textbook reading, notetaking, adjusting rates, test taking, report writing, and reference work
3. Focus on exploring and analyzing the genres within literature and informational texts with more sophisticated responses
4. Read and analyze primary source material

### Word Study Focus

1. Join spelling and vocabulary studies; link meaning and spelling with grammar and meaning
2. Examine vowel and consonant alternations in derivationally related pairs
3. Examine common Greek and Latin word roots and their combination with affixes
4. Examine easily confused Latin suffixes (*ent/ant, ence/ance; ible/able*)
5. Explore less common Greek and Latin word roots
6. Learn about absorbed or assimilated prefixes
7. Focus on words that students bring to word study from their reading and writing
8. Explore etymology, especially in the various disciplines/content areas
9. Examine content-related foreign borrowings

# chapter 2

# Getting Started
## THE ASSESSMENT OF ORTHOGRAPHIC DEVELOPMENT

Effective teaching cannot begin until you understand what students already know about words and what they are ready to learn. Likewise, you cannot make changes to improve instruction until you evaluate the results of your teaching. This chapter presents an informal assessment process that will enable you to:

- Informally observe and interpret orthographic knowledge in writing and reading. (page 25)
- Select and administer a qualitative spelling inventory. (page 27)
- Score and analyze the inventory to identify features that students need to study as well as their developmental stage of word knowledge. (page 31)
- Group students for differentiated instruction. (page 38)
- Monitor students' progress and set realistic goals for their growth in orthographic knowledge over time. (page 45)
- Interpret the orthographic knowledge of your English learners. (page 48)

# Informal Observations to Assess Orthographic Knowledge

There is synchrony in the development of reading, writing, and spelling. Because of this synchrony, informal observations of what students do when they read and write provides information for planning word study instruction.

## Observe and Interpret Students' Writing

Daily observations of student writing reveal what students understand about words. The following example appears to be a menu, but Sarah posted it on the wall the way she had seen reviews posted in restaurants.

| What Sarah Wrote | How Sarah Read What She Wrote |
|---|---|
| 1. CRS KAM SAS | First course, clam sauce |
| 2. CRS FESH | Second course, fish |
| 3. CRS SAGATE | Third course, spaghetti |
| 4. CRS POSH POPS | Fourth course, Push Pops |

This writing tells us a lot about Sarah: She sees a practical use for writing and she enjoys displaying her work. She has a good grasp of how to compose a list and she is even beginning to understand menu planning! When we look for what Sarah knows about spelling, we see that she represents many consonant sounds and some digraphs (the /sh/ in *fish* and *push*), but blends are incomplete (using only K to spell the *cl* in *clam* or S for the *sp* in *spaghetti*). She is using vowels consistently (except in CRS for *course*); however, in spelling *fish* as FESH, Sarah confuses *e* and *i*. According to the sequence of development presented in Chapter 1, Sarah is considered a letter name–alphabetic speller who would benefit from instruction emphasizing short vowel sounds and blends.

**FIGURE 2.1** Jake's Writing Sample

### My Acident

Last year I scrapped my chian. I was shacking and my mom was too. My Dad met us at the docters offises. And I had to have stiches. Then my Dad bout me an ice crem cone. And we went home. I didn't go to school the nexs day. I was to tird.

**LOOK FOR WHAT STUDENTS KNOW AND WHAT THEY USE BUT CONFUSE.** In Figure 2.1, we see a writing sample from Jake, an older student. The writing is readable because many words are spelled correctly and the others are close approximations. When we look for what Jake knows, we see that he has mastered most consonant relationships—even the three-letter blend in SCRAPPED—but not the complex *tch* unit in STICHES. Most long and short vowels are spelled correctly, as in *had, have, went, cone, home,* and *day.* When we look for what Jake uses but confuses, we see that he confuses the -*ck* and -*ke* ending in SHACKING for *shaking.* He inserts an unnecessary extra vowel when he spells *chin* as CHIAN but omits some silent vowel markers where they are needed, as with CREM for *cream.* Based on the vowel errors, Jake is considered a within word pattern speller who would benefit from the study of vowel patterns. We will take another look at Jake's word knowledge when we examine his spelling inventory later in this chapter.

Student writing, especially unedited rough drafts, are a goldmine of information about their orthographic knowledge. Many teachers keep a variety of student writing samples to document students' needs and growth over time. The Qualitative Spelling Checklist in Appendix A, provides a systematic way to analyze your students' writing samples for specific orthographic features. However, over time as you become familiar with spelling features and stages you will become more adept at analyzing your students' writing samples "on the fly."

**THE LIMITATIONS OF WRITING SAMPLES.** Relying entirely on writing samples does have some drawbacks. Some students are anxious about the accuracy of their spelling and will only use words they know how to spell. Others will get help from resources in the room, such as word walls, dictionaries, and the person sitting nearby, and thus their writing may overestimate what they really know. On the other hand, when students concentrate on getting their ideas on paper, they may not pay attention to spelling and make excessive errors. Some students write freely with little concern about accuracy and need to be reminded to use what they know. Daily observations will help you to determine not only students' orthographic knowledge but also their habits and dispositions.

Assessing student's reading performance

## Observe Students' Reading

Important insights into orthographic knowledge can also be made when we observe students' reading. Reading and spelling are related but not mirror images because the processes differ slightly. In reading, words can be recognized with many types of textual supports, so the ability to read words correctly lies a little ahead of students' spelling accuracy (Bear & Templeton, 2000; Templeton & Bear, 2011). For example, within word pattern spellers, who are also transitional readers, read many two-syllable words like *shopping* and *bottle* correctly but may spell those same words as SHOPING and BOTEL.

Spelling is a conservative measure of what students know about words in general, so if students can spell a word, then we know they can read the word. It seldom works the other way around except in the emergent and early letter name stages, in which students might generate spellings they don't know how to read (Invernizzi & Hayes, 2010; Rayner, Foorman, Perfetti,

Pesetsky, & Seidenburg, 2001). When students consult reference materials such as a spell checker or dictionary, the spelling task becomes a reading task; we all know the phenomenon of being able to recognize the correct spelling if we just see it.

**RESPONDING TO READING ERRORS.** Like spelling errors, reading errors show us what students are using but confusing when they read, and certain errors can be expected of students in different stages. Teachers who understand students' developmental word knowledge will be in a good position to interpret students' reading errors and to make decisions about the appropriate prompt to use in reading with students (Brown, 2003). A student who substitutes *bunny* for *rabbit* in the sentence "The farmer saw a rabbit" is probably a very beginning reader and an early letter name–alphabetic speller. The student uses the picture rather than knowledge about sound–symbol correspondences to generate a logical response. For students in the partial alphabetic phase (Ehri, 2014), drawing attention to the beginning sound can teach them to use their consonant knowledge. The teacher might point to the first letter and say, "Can that word be *bunny?* It starts with an *r.* What would start with *rrrrr?*"

Later in development, assessments of oral reading substitutions show a different level of word knowledge. A transitional reader who substitutes *growled* for *groaned* in the sentence "Jason groaned when he missed the ball" is probably attending to several orthographic features of the word. The student appears to use the initial blend *gr,* the vowel *o,* and the *-ed* ending to come up with an approximation that fits the meaning of the sentence. Because this student has vowel knowledge, a teacher might direct the student's attention to the *oa* pattern and ask him to try it again.

**SOUND IT OUT?** Our response to reading errors and our expectations for correcting such errors depend on a number of factors, one of which is knowing where students are developmentally. For example, it is inappropriate to ask beginning readers in the early letter name–alphabetic stage to sound out the word *flat* or even to look for a familiar part within the word because they simply don't know enough to sound out words or apply analogies. They must use context clues and pictures to identify unknown words on the page (Adams, 1990; Johnston, 2000). In contrast, students in the latter part of the letter name–alphabetic stage could be expected to sound out *flat* because they know other written words that sound and look the same and they know something about blends and short vowels. Students reading at their instructional level read most words correctly and when they encounter unfamiliar words in text, their orthographic knowledge, combined with context, will usually help them figure out the words with adequate comprehension. As noted earlier, there are parallels between oral reading errors and the types of spelling errors students make but there is not a one-to-one match, for with the use of context, students can read more difficult words than they can spell.

# Qualitative Spelling Inventories to Assess Orthographic Knowledge

Although observations made during writing and reading offer some insight into students' development, assessments should also include an informal qualitative spelling inventory administered two or three times a year.

## The Development of Spelling Inventories

**Spelling inventories** consist of lists of words specially chosen to represent a variety of spelling or phonics features at increasing levels of difficulty. The lists are not exhaustive in that they do not test all features; rather, they include those that are most helpful in identifying a stage

Ms. Kiernan administers a spelling inventory to her class

**Enhanced eText**
**Video Example 2.1**
In this video, teachers discuss steps in the assessment process.

of development and planning instruction. Students take an inventory as they would a spelling test. The results are then analyzed to obtain a general picture of their orthographic development.

The first inventories were developed under the leadership of Edmund Henderson at the University of Virginia (Bear, 1982; Ganske, 1999; Invernizzi, 1992; Invernizzi, Meier, & Juel, 2003; Morris, 1999; Viise, 1994). The same developmental progression has been documented through the use of these inventories with learning-disabled students (Invernizzi & Worthy, 1989), students identified as dyslexic (Sawyer, Wade, & Kim, 1999), and functionally literate adults (Worthy & Viise, 1996). Spelling inventories have also been developed and researched for other alphabetic languages (Ford & Invernizzi, 2009; Helman, Delbridge, Parker, Arnal, Mödinger, 2016; Gill, 1980; Temple, 1978; Yang, 2005).

We start by focusing on the three inventories shown in Table 2.1: the Primary Spelling Inventory (PSI), the Elemetary Spelling Inventory (ESI), and the Upper-Level Spelling Inventory (USI). Each can be found in Appendix A.

## Using Inventories

Spelling inventories are quick and easy to administer and score, and they are reliable and valid measures of what students know about words. Many teachers find these spelling inventories to be the most helpful and easily administered literacy assessments in their repertoires. Using these spelling inventories requires the four basic steps summarized here and discussed in detail in the sections that follow.

1. Select a spelling inventory based on grade level and students' achievement levels. Administer the inventory much as you would a traditional spelling test, but do not let students study the words in advance.
2. Analyze students' spellings using a **feature guide**. This analysis will help you identify what orthographic features students know and what they are ready to study, as well as their approximate stage.
3. Organize groups using a **classroom composite form** and/or the **spelling-by-stage classroom organization chart**. These will help you plan instruction for developmental groups.
4. Monitor overall progress by using the same inventory two or three times a year. Weekly spelling tests and unit spell checks will also help you assess students' mastery of the orthographic features they study, and are excellent tools to monitor progress.

**SELECTING AN INVENTORY.** The three spelling inventories described in this chapter can cover the range of students from primary to high school and college. The best guide to selecting one is the grade level of the students you teach. However, you may find that you need an easier or more challenging assessment depending on the range of achievement in your classroom.

| TABLE 2.1 | *Words Their Way*® Spelling Assessments |

| Spelling Inventories | Grade Range | Developmental Range |
| --- | --- | --- |
| Primary Spelling Inventory (PSI) (p. 376) | K–3 | Emergent to late within word pattern |
| Elementary Spelling Inventory (ESI) (p. 380) | 1–6 | Letter name to early derivational relations |
| Upper-Level Spelling Inventory (USI) (p. 383) | 5–12 | Within word pattern to derivational relations |

Table 2.1 is a guide to make your selection. Specific directions are provided in Appendix A, but the administration is similar for all of them.

Some teachers begin with the same list for all students but shift to small-group administration of other lists. For example, a second-grade teacher may begin with the Primary Spelling Inventory and decide to continue testing a group of students who spelled most of the words correctly using the Elementary Spelling Inventory. A key point to keep in mind is that students must generate about five errors for you to determine a spelling stage.

**Primary Spelling Inventory (PSI).** The PSI found in Appendix A on page 376 consists of a list of 26 words that begins with simple CVC words (*fan, pet*) and ends with inflectional endings (*clapping, riding*). It is recommended for kindergarten through early third grade because it assesses features found from the emergent stage through the within word pattern stage. The PSI is used widely along with the accompanying feature guide and is a reliable scale of developmental word knowledge. The PSI validity was established using the California Standards Tests (CST) for English Language Arts (ELA) (Sterbinsky, 2007).

For kindergarten students or with other emergent readers, you may only need to call out the first five words. In an early first-grade classroom, call out at least 15 words so that you sample digraphs and blends; use the entire list of 26 words for late first grade, and second and third grades. For students who spell more than 20 words correctly, you should use the Elementary Spelling Inventory.

**Elementary Spelling Inventory (ESI).** The ESI found in Appendix A on page 380 is a list of 25 increasingly difficult words that begins with *bed* and ends with *opposition*. The ESI can be used in grades 1 through 6 to identify students up to the derivational relations stage. If a school or school system wants to use the same inventory throughout the elementary grades to track growth over time, this inventory is a good choice, but we especially recommend this inventory for grades 3 through 5. By third grade, most students can try all 25 words but be ready to discontinue testing for students who are visibly frustrated or misspell five in a row. Students who spell more than 18 words correctly should be given the Upper-Level Spelling Inventory.

The words on the ESI present a reliable scale of developmental word knowledge. As with the PSI, the validity of the ESI was established using the California Standard Tests (CST) for English Language Arts (ELA) (Sterbinsky, 2007). In this study with 862 students, the relationships between scores on the ESI teachers' stage analysis and standardized reading and spelling test scores were moderte to strong.

**Upper-Level Spelling Inventory (USI).** The USI found in Appendix A on page 383 consists of a list of 31 words, arranged in order of difficulty from *switch* to *succession*. It can be used with students in upper elementary to college. List words were chosen because they help identify—more specifically than the ESI—what students in the syllables and affixes and derivational relations stages are doing in their spelling.

The USI is highly reliable; for example, scores of 183 fifth-graders on the USI significantly predicted their scores on the Word Analysis subtest of the CST four months later (Sterbinsky, 2007). With normally achieving students, you can administer the entire list, but stop giving the USI to students who have misspelled five of the first eight words—the words that assess spelling in the within word pattern stage. The teacher should use the ESI with these students to identify within word pattern features that need instruction.

**PREPARING STUDENTS FOR THE SPELLING INVENTORY.** Unlike weekly spelling tests, these inventories are used for screening and are not used for grading purposes. Students should not study the list of words either before or after the inventory is administered. Set aside 20 to 30 minutes to administer an inventory. Ask students to number a paper as they would for a traditional spelling test. For younger children, you may want to prepare papers in advance with one or two numbered columns. (Invariably, a few younger students write across the page from left to right.) Very young children should have an alphabet strip on their desks for reference in case they forget how to form a particular letter.

**Create a Relaxed Atmosphere.** Children who are in second grade and older are usually familiar with spelling tests and can take the inventory as a whole class but sometimes it is easier to create a relaxed environment working in small groups, especially with kindergarten and first-grade students. If any students appear upset and frustrated, you may assess them individually at another time or use samples of their writing to determine an instructional level with the Qualitative Spelling Checklist.

**Explain the Purpose.** Students must understand the reason for taking the inventory so they will do their best. They may be anxious, so be direct in your explanation:

> "I am going to ask you to spell some words. You have not studied these words and will not be graded on them. Some of the words may be easy and others may be difficult. Do the best you can. Your work will help me understand how you are learning to read and write and how I can help you."

Once these things are explained, most students are able to give the spelling a good effort. You can use the model lesson below to prepare younger students for the assessment or to validate the use of developmental spelling during writing. Lessons like these are designed to show students how to sound out words they are unsure of how to spell.

**Copying.** Some students will try to copy if they feel especially concerned about doing well on a test. Creating a relaxed atmosphere with the explanation suggested earlier can help overcome some of the stress students feel. Arrange seating to minimize the risk of copying or hand out cover sheets. There will be many opportunities to collect corroborating information, so there is no reason to be upset if primary students copy. If it is clear that a student has copied, make a note to this effect after collecting the papers and administer the inventory individually at another time.

# Model Lesson for Spelling the Best You Can

To help young children feel more comfortable attempting to spell words conduct several lessons using the theme, "How to Spell the Best You Can." You might do this to prepare them for taking the inventory or to encourage them to write for many other purposes. If you want children to feel free to write about topics important to them, they need to take risks in their spelling. Hesitant writers who wait for the teacher to spell a word for them or avoid using words they can't spell lose the reward of expressing themselves.

**Talk about spelling:** Begin a discussion by saying something like, "We are going to do a lot of writing this year. When we want to write a word and we don't know how to spell it what can we do?" Students might respond with, "Ask the teacher, ask someone else, use the word wall, or use another word." If no one suggests the strategy of listening for the sounds, bring it up: "You can say the words slowly and listen for the sounds. Do you ever do that? Let's practice."

**Spell some words together:** Say, "Let's try spelling some words by listening for the sounds. Who has a word they want to spell?" A student might suggest something like *turtle*. The teacher can then respond, "That's a good one. Let's say it slowly and stretch out the sounds. *Turtle* has two syllables: turrr – till. What is the sound at the beginning of *turtle*? What letter do we need to spell that /t/ sound? Continue to stretch out the word and listen for more sounds. Depending on the level of the group you might generate a range of possible spellings: TL, TRTL, TERTL, and TERTUL. Write down what the children come up with.

**Spell it the best you can:** Explain, "This is not the way you would see *turtle* spelled in a book, but it has some of the right letters. In kindergarten (or __ grade) it is okay to spell *the best you can*. Sometimes all you can do is start with the sound at the beginning and write the first letter, but you are getting practice in spelling! At the end of the year you will be surprised by how much more you can write." Repeat this exercise several times or when you feel it is needed.

**If students criticize each other:** Occasionally a student might be critical about another student's attempt: "That's not right." Handle this firmly and say something like, "The important thing is that you have written down the word you need and spelled it the best you can. You and I can read it. Later you will learn how to spell it correctly, but for now this is a good try."

**ADMINISTER THE INVENTORY.** After setting up a relaxed atmosphere, you are ready to administer the inventory:

**Call the Words Aloud.** Pronounce each word naturally without drawing out the sounds or breaking them into syllables. Say each word twice and use it in a sentence if context will help students know what word is being called. For example, use *cellar* in a sentence to differentiate it from *seller*. Sentences are provided with the word lists in Appendix A. For most words, however, offering sentences is time-consuming and may even be distracting.

**Can You Read What Students Have Written?** Move around the room as you call the words aloud to observe students' work and behaviors. Look for words you cannot read due to poor handwriting. Without making students feel that something is wrong, it is appropriate to ask them to read the letters in the words that cannot be deciphered. Students using cursive whose writing is difficult to read can be asked to print.

**Know When to Stop.** As you walk around the room or work with a small group, scan students' papers to look for misspellings and look for signs of frustration to determine whether to continue with the list. With younger students who tire quickly, you might stop after the first five words if they do not spell any correctly. For older students in groups, who can usually take an entire inventory in about 20 minutes, it is better to err on the side of too many words than too few. Rather than being singled out to stop, some students may prefer to "save face" by attempting every word called out to the group even when working at a frustration level.

In Figure 2.2, you can see that Jake missed more than half the words on the inventory but continued to make good attempts at words that were clearly too difficult for him. However, his six errors in the first 15 words identify him as needing work on vowel patterns, and testing could have been discontinued at that point. Sometimes teachers are required to administer the entire list in order to have a complete set of data for each child. In this case, explain before you start that the words will become difficult but to do the best they can.

| FIGURE 2.2 | Jake's Spelling Inventory |
| --- | --- |

| Jake | | September 8 | 9/25 |
| --- | --- | --- | --- |
| 1. bed | | 14. caryes | *carries* |
| 2. ship | | 15. martched | *marched* |
| 3. when | | 16. showers | *shower* |
| 4. lump | | 17. bottel | *bottle* |
| 5. float | | 18. faver | *favor* |
| 6. train | | 19. rippin | *ripen* |
| 7. place | | 20. selar | *cellar* |
| 8. drive | | 21. pleascher | *pleasure* |
| 9. brite | *bright* | 22. forchunate | *fortunate* |
| 10. shoping | *shopping* | 23. confdant | *confident* |
| 11. spoyle | *spoil* | 24. sivulise | *civilize* |
| 12. serving | | 25. opozishun | *opposition* |
| 13. chooed | *chewed* | | |

**Enhanced eText**
**Video Example 2.2**
Tips for selecting and scoring the inventories are described in this video.

## Score and Analyze the Spelling Inventories

After you administer the inventory, collect the papers and set aside time to score and analyze the results. Scoring the inventories is more than marking words right or wrong. Instead, each word has a number of features that are counted separately. For example, a student who spells *when* as WEN knows the correct short vowel and ending consonant and gets points for knowing those features even though the complete spelling is not correct. The feature guides will help you score each word in this manner. This analysis provides *qualitative* information regarding what students know about specific spelling features and what they are ready to study next.

**SCORE STUDENT PAPERS.** Begin by marking the words right or wrong. It helps to write the correct spellings beside the misspelled words as was done in the sample of Jake's spelling in Figure 2.2. This step focuses attention on each word and the parts of the words that were right and wrong and makes it easier to share results with parents or other teachers. At this point you can calculate a raw score or **power score** by adding up the total number spelled correctly (nine words correct on Jake's paper in Figure 2.2). Table 2.2 can be used to get a rough estimate of the student's spelling stage. The table lists the power scores on the three major inventories in relation to estimated stages and their breakdown by early, middle, or late stage designations. As we can see, Jake's ESI power score of 9 places him in the late within word pattern stage.

**TABLE 2.2**  Power Scores and Estimated Stages

| Inventory | Letter Name | | | Within Word Pattern | | | Syllables and Affixes | | | Derivational Relations | | |
|---|---|---|---|---|---|---|---|---|---|---|---|---|
| | E | M | L | E | M | L | E | M | L | E | M | L |
| Primary Spelling Inventory | 0 | 1–3 | 4–6 | 7–10 | 11–15 | 16–19 | 20–22 | | | | | |
| Elementary Spelling Inventory | 0 | 1–2 | 3–4 | 5–6 | 7–8 | 9–10 | 11–13 | 14–16 | 17–18 | 19–25 | | |
| Upper-Level Spelling Inventory | | | | 1–2 | 3–6 | 7–8 | 9–10 | 11–15 | 16–18 | 19–22 | 23–25 | 26–31 |

**FEATURE ANALYSIS.** Feature guides help teachers analyze student errors and confirm the stage designations suggested by the power score. Every feature in every word is not scored; however, the features sampled are sufficient to identify the stages of spelling. The feature guides that accompany each inventory are included in Appendix A.

Jake's spelling inventory in Figure 2.2 will be used as an example for the feature guide in Figure 2.3.

**Complete a Feature Guide.**  Use the following steps to complete the feature guide.

1. To score by hand, make a copy of the appropriate feature guide for each student and record the date of testing. The spelling features are listed in the second row of the feature guide and follow the developmental sequence observed in research.
2. Look to the right of each word to check off features of the word that are represented correctly. For example, because Jake spelled *bed* correctly, there is a check for the beginning consonant, the final consonant, and the short vowel for a total of three feature points. Jake also gets a point for spelling the word correctly, recorded in the far-right column. For the word *bright*, which he spelled as BRITE, he gets a check for the blend *br* but not for the *igh* vowel pattern. Notice on Jake's feature guide in Figure 2.3 how the vowel patterns he substituted have been written in the space beside the vowel feature to show that Jake is using but confusing these patterns. Some teachers like to insert the actual errors a student made for each feature.
3. After scoring each word, add the checks in each column and record the total score for that column at the bottom as a ratio of correct responses to total possible features. (Adjust this ratio and the total possible points if you do not ask a student spell all the words.) Notice how Jake scored six out of six under Digraphs, seven out of seven for Blends, and four out of five under Long Vowels.
4. Add the total feature scores across the bottom and the total words spelled correctly. This gives you an overall total score that you can use to rank-order students and to compare individual growth over time.

**Common Confusions in Scoring.**  Questions often arise about how to score reversals and other errors.

**Reversals.**  Letter reversals or **static reversals**, such as writing *b* as *d*, are not unusual for young spellers. Reversals should be noted and there is a space in the boxes of the feature analysis to record them but they are not considered spelling errors. Reversals might be considered handwriting errors instead and should be seen as the letters they were meant to represent. Letter reversals occur with decreasing frequency through the letter name–alphabetic stage.

Confusions can also arise in scoring **kinetic reversals** when the letters are present but out of order. For example, beginning spellers sometimes spell the familiar consonant sounds and

**FIGURE 2.3** Feature Guide for the Elementary Spelling Inventory

## Words Their Way Elementary Spelling Inventory Feature Guide

Student's Name: Jake Fisher  Teacher: T. Atkinson  Grade: 5  Date: September

Words Spelled Correctly: 9 /25  Feature Points: 43 /62  Total: 53 /87  Spelling Stage: Late Within Word Pattern

| SPELLING STAGES → | EMERGENT LATE | LETTER NAME-ALPHABETIC MIDDLE | LETTER NAME-ALPHABETIC MIDDLE | LETTER NAME-ALPHABETIC LATE | WITHIN WORD PATTERN EARLY | WITHIN WORD PATTERN LATE | SYLLABLES AND AFFIXES EARLY | SYLLABLES AND AFFIXES MIDDLE | SYLLABLES AND AFFIXES MIDDLE | SYLLABLES AND AFFIXES LATE | DERIVATIONAL RELATIONS EARLY | | |
|---|---|---|---|---|---|---|---|---|---|---|---|---|---|
| Features → | Consonants Initial / Final | Short Vowels | Digraphs | Blends | Common Long Vowels | Diphthongs and R-influenced Vowels | Inflected Endings | Syllable Junctures | Unaccented Final Syllables | Advanced Suffixes | Bases or Roots | Feature Points | Words Spelled Correctly |
| 1. bed | b✓ d✓ | e✓ | | | | | | | | | | 3 | 1 |
| 2. ship | p✓ | i✓ | sh✓ | | | | | | | | | 3 | 1 |
| 3. when | | e✓ | wh✓ | | | | | | | | | 2 | 1 |
| 4. lump | l✓ | u✓ | | mp✓ | | | | | | | | 3 | 1 |
| 5. float | t✓ | | | fl✓ | oa✓ | | | | | | | 3 | 1 |
| 6. train | n✓ | | | tr✓ | ai✓ | | | | | | | 3 | 1 |
| 7. place | | | | pl✓ | a-e✓ | | | | | | | 2 | 1 |
| 8. drive | v✓ | | | dr✓ | i-e✓ | | | | | | | 3 | 1 |
| 9. bright | | | | br✓ | igh i-e | | | | | | | 1 | |
| 10. shopping | | o✓ | sh✓ | | | | pping | | | | | 2 | |
| 11. spoil | | | | sp✓ | | oi oy | | | | | | 1 | |
| 12. serving | | | | | | er✓ | ving✓ | | | | | 2 | 1 |
| 13. chewed | | | ch✓ | | | ew oo | ed✓ | | | | | 2 | |
| 14. carries | | | | | | ar✓ | ies | rr | | | | 1 | |
| 15. marched | | | ch✓ | | | ar✓ | ed✓ | | | | | 3 | |
| 16. shower | | | sh✓ | | | ow✓ | | | er✓ | | | 3 | 1 |
| 17. bottle | | | | | | | | tt✓ | le | | | 1 | |
| 18. favor | | | | | | or✓ | | v✓ | or | | | 1 | |
| 19. ripen | | | | | | | | p✓ | en | | | | |
| 20. cellar | | | | | | | | ll✓ | ar✓ | | | 1 | |
| 21. pleasure | | | | | | | | | | ure | pleas✓ | 1 | |
| 22. fortunate | | | | | | or✓ | | | | ate✓ | fortun | 2 | |
| 23. confident | | | | | | | | | | ent | confid | | |
| 24. civilize | | | | | | | | | | ize | civil | | |
| 25. opposition | | | | | | | | | | tion | pos | | |
| **Totals** | 7/7  5/5 | 5/5 | 6/6 | 7/7 | 4/5 | 5/7 | 3/5 | 2/5 | 2/5 | 1/5 | 1/5 | 43 | 10 |

Completing the feature guide by hand

then tag on a vowel at the end (for example, FNA for *fan*). This can be due to repeating each sound in the word *fan* and extracting the short *a* after having already recorded the FN. Regardless, give credit for the consonants and vowels that are present but do not give a point for correct spelling. However, when students reverse letters in vowel patterns, such as spelling *train* as TRIAN or *bright* as BRIHGT, do not give credit because this suggests they need more work on the pattern.

**Other Confusions.** There are a few unique errors to consider that can be confusing to score. Very young spellers sometimes spell part of the word and then add a random string of letters to make it look longer (for example, FNWZTY for *fan*). It is also not unusual for students to add silent vowel markers where they are not needed (as in FANE for *fan*) or to include two possibilities (as in LOOKTED for *looked* or TRAINE for *train*) to cover all bases. In these examples, students would not receive credit for the vowels, but we would make note of the strategies they might be using. Such errors offer interesting insights into their developing word knowledge. FANE for *fan* may be incorrect but it represents a more sophisticated attempt than FN.

**IDENTIFY FEATURES FOR INSTRUCTION.** The completed feature guide can be used to determine what phonics or spelling features students are ready to study. Looking across the feature columns from left to right, *instruction should begin at the point where a student first makes two or more errors on a feature.* Consider the totals along the bottom of Jake's feature guide. Ask yourself what he knows and what he is using but confusing. His scores indicate that he has mastery of consonants and short vowels, so he does not need instruction there. Jake only missed one of the long vowels (*igh* in *bright*) for a score of 4/5 and this can be considered an acceptable score. However, he missed two of the other vowels, so this is the feature that needs attention during instruction.

The features in the columns are presented in a general scope and sequence from beginning consonants to roots. However, there may be times when you vary the order of feature presentation. For example, some students may need more work on short vowels even when they have mastered blends and digraphs. In the upper spelling stages we sometimes see students ready to study a number of features at the same time. In this case, the order will not be as important, and this offers more flexibility in grouping.

If you think that an inventory has overplaced a student, go on to the next inventory. Usually the next inventory will place the student more conservatively. For example, you may have a few third graders who scored in the early derivational relations stage using the ESI but after administering the USI you find that they are in the syllable and affixes stage. Regardless, we may begin with word study in the syllables and affixes stage at a relatively fast pace to be certain these students understand syllable types including open and closed syllables, principles of accent, and syllabication.

**DETERMINE A DEVELOPMENTAL STAGE.** Knowing the developmental spelling stage of students is essential in planning instruction - where to start word study instruction and for forming instructional groups. Knowing the student's developmental stage is also useful for navigating this book. For example, in Jake's case, refer to Chapter 6 for more information.

The continuum of features at the top of the feature guide shows gradations for each developmental stage of *early*, *middle*, and *late*. A student who has learned to spell most of the features relevant to a stage is probably at the end of that stage. Conversely, if a student is beginning to use the key elements of a feature but still has some misspellings from the previous stage, the student is at an early point in that new stage. These gradations make assessing orthographic knowledge more precise than simply an overall stage designation, and this precision will be useful in designing a word study curriculum.

**Using the Feature Guide to Call a Level.** A student's developmental level should be circled in the shaded bar across the top of the feature guide that lists the stages. Using Figure 2.3 as an example, look at the bottom row of the feature guide. Jake spelled all the short vowels and most long vowel features correctly but missed more than one in the other vowels category. Looking up from that feature to the shaded bar we see that Jake falls in the later part of the within word pattern stage. This stage and gradation have been circled in the top row. Considering the first feature that needs instruction (he got five out of seven on other vowels) it seems safe to assign him to the late within word pattern stage and that has been written in the blank beside *Spelling Stage* at the top right of the feature guide.

**Confirming the Developmental Levels.** There are different ways to determine a developmental stage. While the spelling inventory is probably the most reliable, considering both the feature analysis and raw score, we recommend using multiple sources of information for a final call. For example, you may want to use The Qualitative Spelling Checklist, found in Appendix A, to analyze students' writing and compare the results from the checklist to the stage derived from the feature guide. Tables in each instructional chapter (Chapters 4 to 8) provide additional information about how to determine where students are within each stage. Spell Checks described later will also help to confirm the developmental level.

You do not need to make the discrimination within stages too weighty a decision. In regards to planning instruction, taking a step backward to choose word study activities at a slightly easier level than the stage determination may indicate is often best. Introducing students to sorting routines when they are working with familiar features and known words is more effective.

**Consider the Synchrony of Literacy Development.** Spelling inventory results should be compared to what we know about students' reading and writing. Use Table 1.3 or Table 2.3 to understand development by reading from top to bottom across the literacy behaviors of reading, spelling, and writing. Look for corroborating evidence to place students' achievement along the developmental continuum.

Referring back to Jake's writing in Figure 2.1, we see similar strengths and weaknesses revealed by the inventory. His mastery of short vowels and his experimentation with long vowels and other vowels is what we would expect of a student in the middle to late within word pattern stage of spelling. When Jake reads he may confuse words like *choose* and *chose*. These errors in word identification will be addressed in word study when he examines the other vowels. His spelling inventory, writing sample, and reading errors offer supporting evidence that we have identified his developmental stage and the features that need attention.

Some students are out of synchrony in their development, such as the student who is notoriously poor at spelling but is a capable reader. When there is a mismatch between reading and spelling development, you can help improve spelling and obtain synchrony by pinpointing the stage of spelling development and then providing instruction that addresses the student's needs.

## Sample Practice

The spelling examples of five students in Figure 2.4 can be used to practice analyzing student spellings and determining a developmental stage if you do not have a class of children to assess or if you want to try analyzing a broad spectrum of responses. Make a copy of the ESI feature guide for each student. Determine both the developmental stage of the speller and the place you would start instruction. After you are finished, check the results at the bottom of the page. Were you close in the stages you selected? If you scored the spelling in terms of the three gradations within a stage, you may find that although your assessment may differ by a stage name, it is possible that the difference is just between the latter part of one stage and the early part of the next. Also compute a power score for each student (number correct) and use Table 2.2 on page 32 to estimate the stage. Were your results similar?

**TABLE 2.3** Concordance of Grade Levels, Reading and Spelling

| Grade Level | Spelling Stage | Reading Phase | Reading Stage | Book Levels | | |
|---|---|---|---|---|---|---|
| | | | | Lexiles | Letters | Numbers |
| PreK-K | Emergent | Pre-alphabetic | Emergent | N/A | A, B | 1,2 |
| K to Early 1st | Early letter name | Partial alphabetic | Early beginning | N/A | C | 3,4 |
| Early 1st | Middle letter name | Partial alphabetic | Middle beginning | N/A | D, E | 4–8 |
| Mid 1st | Late letter name to early within word pattern | Full alphabetic | Late beginning | 200–400 | F, G | 10–12 |
| Late 1st to Early 2nd | Early within word pattern | Full alphabetic | Early transitional | 200–400 | H, I | 14–16 |
| 2nd | Middle within word pattern | Consolidated alphabetic | Middle transitional | 400–600 | J, K | 18–20 |
| Late 2nd | Late within word pattern | Consolidated alphabetic | Late transitional | 400–600 | L, M | 24–28 |
| Late 2nd to Early 3rd | Early syllables and affixes | Consolidated alphabetic | Early intermediate | 500–820 | N–P | 30–36 |
| 4th | Middle syllables and affixes | Automatic | Middle intermediate | 600–900 | Q–S | 40 |
| 5th | Late syllables and affixes to early derivational relations | Automatic | Intermediate to advanced | 740–1010 | T–V | 50 |
| 6th | Early derivational relations | Automatic | Intermediate to advanced | 800–1015 | W–Y | 60 |
| 7th | Early to middle derivational relations | Automatic | Early to middle advanced | 925–1185 | W–Z | 70 |
| 8th | Middle to late derivational relations | Automatic | Middle advanced to advanced | 1000+ | Z+ | 80 |

The grade levels are general ranges and averages; the actual match will vary. The single grade-level destinations are mid-year approximations. The book levels represent the most current systems used to level texts. The Lexile levels (Lexile Framework for Reading, 2013) reflect broad ranges using the "stretch" ranges presented in the Common Core State Standards, though other forms of text complexity should be considered. The letters and numbers approximate the leveling systems used for beginning reading materials.

**TEACHING TIPS**

## When Synchrony Is Not Observed

There are two common scenarios we have observed when there is a lack of synchrony between reading and spelling.

- Some students have very strong verbal skills and are quite bright, and when they read, they are able to use context better than most to comprehend what they read. However, when we listen to their oral reading, we see that they make many reading errors and their reading rate is significantly slower than you would expect. Such students will benefit from word study that requires them to analyze words at their developmental level as determined by a spelling inventory.

- English learners may have memorized how to spell many words, making their spelling development appear more advanced than their reading fluency and their comprehension. Such students will benefit from continued practice in reading and learning word meanings in English.

**Figure 2.4   Examples of Students' Spelling in September**

| Spelling Words | Greg (Grade 1) | Jean (Grade 1) | Reba (Grade 2) | Alan (Grade 3) | Mitch (Grade 5) |
|---|---|---|---|---|---|
| bed | BD | BED | bed | bed | bed |
| ship | SP | SEP | ship | ship | ship |
| when | YN | WHAN | when | when | when |
| lump | LP | LOP | lump | lump | lump |
| float | FOT | FLOT | flote | flote | float |
| train | | TRAN | trane | train | train |
| place | | PLAC | plais | place | place |
| drive | | DRIV | drive | drive | drive |
| bright | | BRIT | brite | brigt | bright |
| shopping | | SOPNG | shopen | shoping | shopping |
| spoil | | | spoal | spoale | spoil |
| serving | | | serving | serveing | serving |
| chewed | | | chud | choued | chewed |
| carries | | | cares | carres | carries |
| marched | | | marcd | marched | marched |
| shower | | | | shouer | shower |
| bottle | | | | bottel | bottle |
| favor | | | | favir | favor |
| ripen | | | | ripen | ripen |
| cellar | | | | seller | celler |
| pleasure | | | | | pleshur |
| fortunate | | | | | forchenet |
| confident | | | | | confedent |
| civilize | | | | | civilize |
| opposition | | | | | oposition |

**RESULTS:**

**Greg**   Early letter name–alphabetic; review consonants, study short vowel word families, digraphs, and blends.

**Jean**   Middle letter name–alphabetic; study short vowels.

**Reba**   Middle within word pattern; study long vowel patterns.

**Alan**   Late within word pattern; study long vowels and other vowel patterns.

**Mitch**   Middle syllables and affixes; study syllable juncture and unaccented final syllables.

Since Mitch spelled so many words on the ESI correctly, consider administering the USI.

# Group Students for Instruction

Your spelling analysis as discussed in the previous section will pinpoint students' instructional levels and the phonics and spelling features that are ripe for instruction. In most classrooms, there will be a range in students' word knowledge. For example, in a second-grade class most students will be in the within word pattern stage but there will also be students in the letter name–alphabetic stage who need to study short vowels and consonant blends, while others may be in the syllables and affixes stage and ready to study two-syllable words. After analyzing students individually, you can create a classroom profile by recording the individual assessment data on a single chart.

Experience shows that when students study a particular orthographic feature, it is best if they work with others who are ready to study the same feature. For example, studying long-vowel patterns is difficult when some of the students in the group still need work on digraphs or blends and may not even be able to read the words that contain the long-vowel patterns. When students are taught at their developmental levels in spelling (even when instruction is below grade level), they will make more progress than with materials that are too difficult for them (Morris, Blanton, Blanton, Nowacek, & Perney, 1995). Chapter 9 offers suggestions about how to manage multiple instructional groups.

We present two ways to record and analyze information about the class: a classroom composite chart for each of the inventories to group students by features, and the spelling-by-stage classroom organization chart to group students by developmental levels. These charts show you the instructional groups at a glance.

## Classroom Composite Chart

After administering an inventory and completing a feature guide for each student, transfer the individual scores to the Classroom Composite Chart to get a sense of the group as a whole. See an example in Figure 2.5. These charts can be found with the corresponding inventory in Appendix A. The following steps will help you do this.

1. Begin by stapling each student's spelling test and feature guide together.
2. Order student papers by the power score (or number of words correct) or by the total feature score, and record students' names from top to bottom on the composite form on the basis of this rank order. Next, record scores from the bottom row of each student's Feature Guide in the row beside his or her name on the Classroom Composite Chart.
3. Highlight cells in which students are making two or more errors on a particular feature and column to spotlight areas of need. For example, a student who spells all but one of the short vowels correctly has an adequate understanding of short vowels and is considered to be at an independent level. However, students who misspell two or three of the short vowels need more work on that feature. Do not highlight cells in which students score a zero because this indicates frustration rather than using but confusing a feature. Look to the left of any zero scores to identify features that need attention first.
4. Look for instructional groups. If you rank-order your students when completing the composite chart, you can find clusters of highlighted cells that can be used to assign students to developmental stages and word study groups. The fifth-grade class composite in Figure 2.5 shows that many students fall under the syllables and affixes stage of development because this is where they are making two or more spelling errors (students 3 through 12). Sarah (number 16) could also join this group. John, Maria R., and Patty (students 13–15) , who missed more than two words in vowel patterns, should go with other students who all need work on common long vowels and fall under the middle within word pattern stage (students 17 through 25). Mike (student 26) needs individualized help, beginning with short vowels as well as digraphs and blends. At the upper end of the class composite are two children who fall into the derivational relations stage. However, we suggest that any students who score more than 18 or better on the ESI be reassessed with the USI to gather more information about particular features to study.

**FIGURE 2.5** Classroom Composite Chart

## Words Their Way Elementary Spelling Inventory Classroom Composite

Teacher _____  School _____  Grade _____  Date _____

| SPELLING STAGES → | EMERGENT | LETTER NAME–ALPHABETIC | | | WITHIN WORD PATTERN | | | SYLLABLES AND AFFIXES | | | DERIVATIONAL RELATIONS | | |
| | LATE | EARLY | MIDDLE | LATE | EARLY | MIDDLE | LATE | EARLY | MIDDLE | MIDDLE | LATE | EARLY | | |
| Students' Names ↓ | Consonants | Short Vowels | Digraphs | Blends | Common Long Vowels | Diphthongs and R-influenced Vowels | Inflected Endings | Syllable Junctures | Unaccented Final Syllables | Advanced Suffixes | Bases or Roots | Correct Spelling | Total Rank Order |
|---|---|---|---|---|---|---|---|---|---|---|---|---|---|
| **Possible Points →** | **7** | **5** | **6** | **7** | **5** | **7** | **5** | **5** | **5** | **5** | **5** | **25** | **87** |
| 1. Stephanie | 7 | 5 | 6 | 7 | 5 | 7 | 5 | 5 | 5 | 4 | 3 | 23 | 82 |
| 2. Andi | 7 | 5 | 6 | 7 | 5 | 7 | 5 | 4 | 4 | 3 | 2 | 21 | 76 |
| 3. Henry | 7 | 5 | 6 | 7 | 5 | 7 | 5 | 4 | 3 | 3 | 2 | 20 | 74 |
| 4. Molly | 7 | 5 | 6 | 7 | 5 | 7 | 4 | 4 | 3 | 2 | 2 | 20 | 72 |
| 5. Jasmine | 7 | 5 | 6 | 7 | 5 | 7 | 3 | 3 | 3 | 2 | 2 | 19 | 69 |
| 6. Maria H. | 7 | 5 | 6 | 7 | 5 | 7 | 3 | 3 | 2 | 3 | 2 | 19 | 69 |
| 7. Mike T. | 7 | 5 | 6 | 7 | 5 | 6 | 3 | 3 | 2 | 2 | 1 | 17 | 64 |
| 8. Lee | 7 | 5 | 6 | 7 | 5 | 6 | 2 | 2 | 1 | 2 | 1 | 15 | 59 |
| 9. Beth | 7 | 5 | 6 | 7 | 5 | 7 | 2 | 2 | 1 | 1 | 2 | 14 | 59 |
| 10. Gabriel | 7 | 5 | 6 | 7 | 5 | 6 | 2 | 2 | 1 | 1 | 2 | 14 | 58 |
| 11. Yamal | 7 | 5 | 6 | 7 | 4 | 6 | 2 | 2 | 1 | 1 | 0 | 12 | 53 |
| 12. Elizabeth | 7 | 5 | 6 | 7 | 4 | 6 | 2 | 2 | 1 | 0 | 0 | 11 | 51 |
| 13. John | 7 | 5 | 6 | 7 | 3 | 5 | 2 | 2 | 1 | 1 | 0 | 10 | 49 |
| 14. Patty | 7 | 5 | 6 | 7 | 3 | 5 | 2 | 2 | 1 | 0 | 0 | 11 | 49 |
| 15. Maria R. | 7 | 5 | 6 | 7 | 3 | 4 | 2 | 2 | 1 | 0 | 0 | 11 | 48 |
| 16. Sarah | 7 | 5 | 6 | 7 | 4 | 4 | 2 | 1 | 0 | 1 | 0 | 9 | 46 |
| 17. Jared | 7 | 5 | 6 | 7 | 2 | 3 | 1 | 1 | 1 | 1 | 0 | 9 | 43 |
| 18. William | 7 | 5 | 6 | 7 | 3 | 3 | 2 | 0 | 1 | 0 | 0 | 8 | 42 |
| 19. Steve | 7 | 5 | 6 | 7 | 3 | 3 | 2 | 1 | 0 | 0 | 0 | 8 | 42 |
| 20. Anna | 7 | 5 | 6 | 6 | 4 | 3 | 1 | 1 | 0 | 0 | 0 | 8 | 41 |
| 21. Nicole W. | 7 | 4 | 6 | 6 | 3 | 3 | 1 | 1 | 1 | 0 | 0 | 8 | 39 |
| 22. Robert | 7 | 5 | 5 | 7 | 3 | 3 | 2 | 0 | 0 | 0 | 0 | 6 | 38 |
| 23. Celia | 7 | 4 | 6 | 6 | 2 | 3 | 1 | 0 | 0 | 0 | 0 | 7 | 36 |
| 24. Nicole R. | 7 | 4 | 5 | 6 | 2 | 3 | 2 | 0 | 0 | 0 | 0 | 7 | 36 |
| 25. Jim | 7 | 5 | 5 | 6 | 2 | 2 | 1 | 0 | 0 | 0 | 0 | 7 | 35 |
| 26. Mike A. | 7 | 3 | 4 | 5 | 1 | 0 | 1 | 0 | 0 | 0 | 0 | 4 | 25 |
| **Highlight for instruction\*** | 1 | 1 | 1 | 1 | 12 | 13 | 22 | 16 | 15 | 13 | 10 | | |

\*Highlight students who miss more than 1 on a particular feature; they will benefit from more instruction in that area.

## Spelling-By-Stage Classroom Organization Chart

When you know students' developmental stages, you can also form groups with the Spelling-by-Stage Classroom Organization Chart found in Appendix A on page 379. Some teachers find this easier to use than a class composite when planning groups. Students' names are recorded underneath a spelling stage on the chart, differentiating among those who are early, middle, or late. After the names are entered, begin to look for groups and circle them.

Figure 2.6 shows examples of ways to form groups at three different grade levels. You can see where teachers have used arrows to reconsider the placement of a few students. Inventory results are considered along with other observations of students' reading or writing. The arrows indicate students who might be placed slightly higher or lower as the groups take shape. Some of the group placement decisions might be based on social and psychological factors related to self-esteem, leadership, and behavior dynamics.

The first profile is of a first-grade class with many emergent spellers. Although the teacher might have formed three groups, the four circled groups are also the teacher's reading groups. The third-grade classroom has a large group of late within word pattern spellers and the arrows show how the teacher has tried to move some of the students into other groups for balance. The teacher in the sixth-grade classroom could consider running two groups at the upper levels or combining them as one group. The three students in the letter name–alphabetic stage will need special attention because they are significantly behind for sixth graders. Ideally, these students will have additional instruction with a literacy specialist or in a tutoring program with activities that are appropriate for the letter name–alphabetic spelling stage.

## Factors to Consider When Organizing Groups

The Classroom Composite Chart and the Spelling-by-Stage Classroom Organization Chart help to determine word study groups for instruction. Teachers often have questions about grouping.

**HOW DO I MANAGE GROUPS?** Ideally you want no more than three groups to keep things manageable. If this sounds difficult, be assured that students working on different features and with different words can still work side by side during most follow-up word study routines that occur across the week. Only the initial teacher-led discussion requires a separate time. Different schemes for managing class, group, and individual word study are discussed in Chapter 9. If three groups is overwhelming, start with two. A traditional spelling program has no grouping at all, so even two groups will get children closer to their instructional level. Sometimes a fourth or even fifth word study group can be formed when there are specialists like ESL and Title I teachers who work with small groups.

**HOW DO I FIT A DIVERSE CLASS INTO THREE GROUPS?** If a wide range of achievement exists, some students may not be placed exactly at their developmental stages. Although you will certainly try to accommodate them, your best spellers are not likely to be negatively affected with grade-level word study activities that might be a bit easy for them. However, your less able spellers such as Victoria, Juan and Mike in the 6th grade example will undoubtedly fall further behind if they do not get the instruction they need, so group your least able students as close as possible to their instructional level. In all cases student progress should be monitored, as described shortly, to adjust placement as needed.

**WHAT ABOUT THE OUTLIERS?** In many classrooms, there are students at each end of the developmental continuum who, in terms of word study and orthographic development, are outliers. For example, Zac, in the third-grade class in Figure 2.6, is the only student in the middle syllables and affixes stage, and placing him in a group by himself is impractical. He has been placed in the closest group for instruction or, because he is already above grade level and making progress independently, he might be exempted from word study. Less advanced students, such as Jon in the second group of sixth grade in Figure 2.6, may work with partners who can help them read and sort the group's words, such as one-syllable words with long-vowel patterns. English language learners also benefit from sorting with partners who can clarify word pronunciations and meanings.

**FIGURE 2.6** Examples of Spelling-by-Stage Classroom Organization Charts

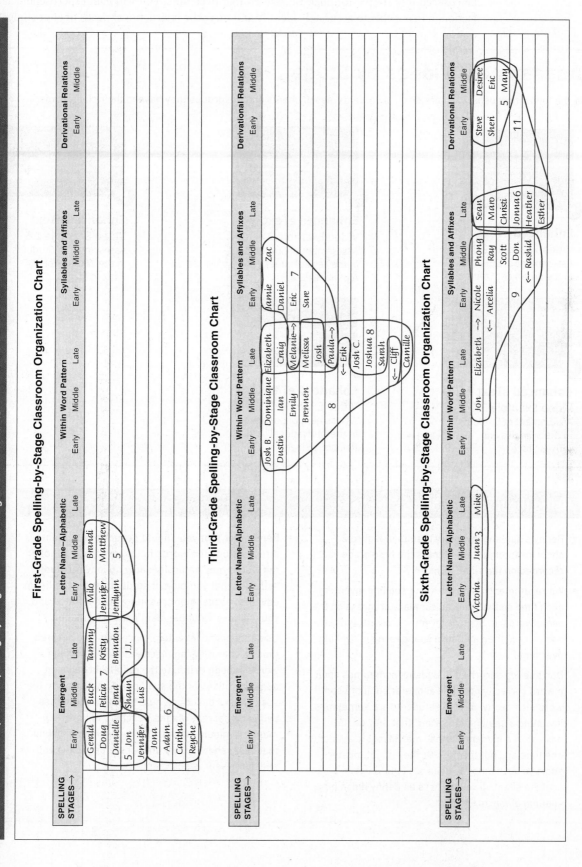

**IT TAKES PRACTICE.** Interpreting feature guides, determining stages, and then creating and monitoring groups involves ongoing assessment, observations, and teacher judgment. It cannot be reduced to a simple formula. Be assured that over time, you will gain expertise and satisfaction in being able to accurately identify and meet the instructional needs of your students.

## Assessment Videos by Stage

In the following videos, teachers discuss students' assessments and the groups they have in their classrooms.

**Enhanced eText**
Video Example 2.3
Assessment of Students in the Emergent Stage

**Enhanced eText**
Video Example 2.4
Assessment of Students in the Letter Name–Alphabetic Stage

**Enhanced eText**
Video Example 2.5
Assessment of Students in the Within Word Pattern Stage

**Enhanced eText**
Video Example 2.6
Assessment of Students in the Syllables and Affixes Stage

**Enhanced eText**
Video Example 2.7
Assessment of Students in the Derivational Relations Stage

## TEACHING TIPS

### Using the Inventory across the Year

- Benny's spelling inventory results in Figure 2.7 show inventory results across the first-grade year recorded on the same form.

- We recommend using the same spelling inventory each time so that you can compare progress on the same words. In Benny's inventory results, we can easily track the qualitative changes in his spelling over time.

- Don't be too surprised if students sometimes spell a word correctly one time and later spell the same word incorrectly. Because students are sometimes inventing a spelling for a word that they do not have stored in memory, they may invent it correctly one time and not the next. Or they might master short vowel sound matches but later use but confuse silent vowel markers as Benny did in his spelling of *fan* as FANE.

- Remember that you should never have students directly study the words in the inventory, although the words may naturally show up in word study activities that you plan. If students study the list in advance, assessment results will be inflated and you will lose valuable diagnostic information.

- Using the same inventory more than two or three times a year may familiarize students with the words enough to inflate the results. In between administrations of the spelling inventories, use the spell checks described next to monitor progress within and across stages. Teachers in upper elementary, middle school, and high school may find that using an inventory only at the beginning and end of the year is sufficient.

# Spelling Inventories for Formative and Summative Assessment

Students may be given the same spelling inventory up to three times during the year to assess what they have learned and to determine whether changes need to be made in groups or instructional focus. Figure 2.7 shows Benny's growth during the year, moving from early letter name–alphabetic spelling to the within word pattern stage. However, don't expect such dramatic progress in one year beyond the primary grades. Some students will take two years to master the within word pattern stage.

**FIGURE 2.7** Samples of Benny's Spelling Errors at Three Times in First Grade

|  | September | January | May |
|---|---|---|---|
| 1. fan | FNA | fan | fane |
| 2. pet | PT | pat | pet |
| 3. dig | DKG | deg | dig |
| 4. hope | HOP | hop | hope |
| 5. wait | YAT | wat | wayt |
| 6. sled | SD | sed | sled |
| 7. stick | SK | stek | stike |
| 8. shine | HIN | shin | shine |

## Benchmarks and Grade Level Expectations

Although it is true that all students do not develop at the same rate despite the very best instruction, it helps to articulate end-of-grade expectations in terms of developmental word knowledge so that you can identify students who are at risk of falling behind. Matching specific spelling stages to grade levels is impossible, but Table 2.4 captures the typical *range of development* within grade levels and where students should be (at the very least) at the end of the year if they are to succeed in subsequent grades and meet standards in reading and writing. Based on the model of synchrony development in Chapter 1 and illustrated in Table 1.3, Table 2.3 shows a concordance between developmental stages and instructional materials. For example, this table says that by mid-year, most third graders are in the early syllables and affixes stage and are early intermediate readers, reading in the 500–820 Lexile range.

**TABLE 2.4** Spelling Stage Expectations by Grade Levels

| Grade Level | Typical Spelling Stage Ranges Within Grade | End-of-Year Expectation |
|---|---|---|
| Pre-K | Early Emergent –Early letter name–alphabetic | Middle emergent |
| K | Emergent–Letter name–alphabetic | Middle letter name–alphabetic |
| 1 | Late emergent–Within word pattern | Early within word pattern |
| 2 | Late letter name–Early syllables & affixes | Late within word pattern |
| 3 | Within word pattern–Syllables & affixes | Early syllables & affixes |
| 4 | Within word pattern–Syllables & affixes | Middle syllables & affixes |
| 5 | Syllables & affixes–Derivational relations | Late syllables & affixes |
| 6 + | Syllables & affixes–Derivational relations | Derivational relations |

# Additional Assessments

Other assessments and forms are useful as supplements or alternatives to the inventories. For example, the Emergent Class Record and the Kindergarten Spelling Inventory are appropriate for young students. Spell Checks and Goal Setting Forms can help teachers fine tune placement

**TABLE 2.5** Additional Spelling Assessmenrts

|  | Grade Range | Developmental Range |
| --- | --- | --- |
| Qualitative Spelling Checklist | K–8 | All stages |
| Emergent Class Record | Pre K–K | Emergent to letter name–alphabetic |
| Kindergarten Spelling Inventory (KSI) | Pre K–K | Emergent to early letter name–alphabetic |
| McGuffey Qualitative Inventory of Word Knowledge (QIWK) | 1–8 | All stages |
| *WTW* Spell Checks | K–12 | Early letter name–alphabetic to early derivational relations |
| *WTW* Goal-Setting/Progress Monitoring Charts | K–12 | Early letter name–alphabetic to early derivational relations |

and closely monitor progress. These additional assessments described next and listed in Table 2.5 can be found in Appendix A and B.

## Qualitative Spelling Checklist

When you look at students' writing in their journals or in the first drafts of their reports and stories, you can use the Qualitative Spelling Checklist (page 373 in Appendix A to verify what types of orthographic features students have mastered, what types of features they are using but confusing, and the degree to which they are applying their spelling knowledge in actual writing. Through a series of 20 questions, you check off the student's progress through the stages. Consider what features are used consistently, often, or not at all in their unedited writing. The checklist is set up to be used at three different points during the school year and can serve as a record of progress over time. Collecting a variety of writing samples across the curricular areas is a great way to verify students' application and transfer of their word study instruction.

## Emergent Class Record

The Emergent Class Record is used to assess daily writing or spelling inventory results of pre-K children, kindergarten students, or other emergent spellers. Making a copy of the PSI feature guide for each student may seem like a waste of paper when at most they will only score a few initial and final consonants. The Emergent Class Record found in Appendix A on page 405 can be used as an alternative with the entire class represented on one form. It captures the pre-phonetic writing progression (from random marks to letters) that is missing from the other feature guides and covers the range from emergent through letter name–alphabetic spelling that is expected in many kindergarten classes at the beginning of the year. Other emergent assessments are described in Chapter 4 and are available in Appendix A starting on page 388.

## Kindergarten Spelling Inventory

The Kindergarten Spelling Inventory (KSI) has been used widely with thousands of children as part of Virginia's Phonological Assessment and Literacy Screening (PALS) (Invernizzi, Juel, Swank, & Meier, 2006). Children are asked to spell only five three-letter words that have been carefully chosen after extensive research. A feature guide is provided, but unlike the feature guides described so far, students get credit for identifying phonemes and representing those sounds with phonetically logical letters, even if those letters are actually incorrect. For example, *jet* spelled GD will earn two points because G has a letter name that starts with /j/ and D and T are voiced/ unvoiced pairs whose sounds are produced in exactly the same place in the mouth. As a result, the KSI is a reliable measure of phonemic awareness development, letter–sound correspondences, and their gradual development of conventional spelling (Invernizzi, Justice, Landrum, & Booker, 2005). KSI scores in kindergarten predict children's end-of-year reading standards scores as much as three years later (Invernizzi, Juel, Swank, & Meier, 2008).

## McGuffey Spelling Inventory

The McGuffey Qualitative Inventory of Word Knowledge (QIWK) (Schlagal, 1992) is useful for conducting individual testing and for obtaining grade-level information; see page 387 in Appendix A. The inventory spans grades 1 through 8, with 20 to 30 words in each level. After administering the grade-level list, use the list from the previous grade level with students who fall below 50 percent and use the list from the next higher grade level for students who score above 90 percent to determine an instructional spelling level (Morris, Blanton, Blanton, & Perney, 1995; Morris et al., 1986).

The QIWK is especially useful when you want to report spelling achievement in terms of grade levels. In addition, the words in these lists present plenty of opportunities to observe a student's spelling across a variety of features. For example, for teachers wanting to obtain a fuller assessment of prefixes, suffixes, and roots, Levels 5 and 6 offer a larger number of derivational words with prefixes and suffixes to analyze. However, a feature guide has not been developed for the McGuffey Inventory so you must analyze errors yourself to determine which features and patterns students know, and which they are using but confusing.

## Monitor Student Growth Over Time

**PROGRESS**
**MONITORING**

Monitoring students' progress in response to instruction with brief, ongoing assessments alerts us to the need to adjust the content and pacing of instruction to meet student needs, and arranging additional instruction for students who may need extra help meeting long-term goals. Teachers have been monitoring their students' progress for years through weekly spelling tests that provide immediate feedback regarding students' short-term retention of specific words they have studied. But few teachers consider long-term retention, the generalization of the spelling patterns students have learned relative to words they may not have studied, or the application of students' orthographic word knowledge in their writing. We offer several ways you can monitor progress in orthographic development in the short and long terms.

**WEEKLY SPELLING TESTS AND REVIEW TESTS.** We recommend weekly tests at most grade levels as a way to monitor mastery of the studied features, and to send a message to students and parents alike that students are accountable for learning to spell the words they have sorted and worked with in various activities all week. Students should be successful on these

Students can begin to take traditional weekly spelling tests once they are studying short vowels

weekly tests when they are appropriately placed for instruction. If they are misspelling more than a few words, it may mean that you need to adjust your instruction. They may either need to spend more time on a feature with follow-up activities, or they are not ready to study the feature and should work on easier patterns first. You may also want to periodically give a review posttest. Do not ask students to study for these tests in advance as that would not be a true test of retention. Simply select a sample of words from previous lessons and call them aloud as you would for any spelling test. Below we describe prepared spell checks designed to assess particular spelling features. These can be found in Appendix B.

**SPELL CHECKS.** Spell checks are mini-inventories that can be used over shorter periods of time than spelling inventories to assess students' mastery of specific features and words over and beyond what they may have demonstrated on weekly spelling tests. Like inventories, spell checks are organized by sequential groups of phonics features and spelling patterns, but each spell check includes more words for each feature. Because spell checks are more thorough, they can also be used to confirm the stage designation and placement determined by the spelling inventories. If students misspell only one or two words in a feature category on the inventory, you may want to do some further assessment using the spell checks. In Jake's case (see his feature guide in Figure 2.3), we might want to gather some more information about his knowledge of long-vowel patterns because he misspelled *bright*. If Jake were to spell 90% of the words correctly on the spell check for common long vowel patterns, you would have additional assurance that he is in the latter part of the within word pattern stage and needs no further work on common long vowels These spellchecks can be found in Appendix B and in the *Words Their Way* supplements where they are described as unit tests. Spell checks serve a variety of purposes.

**Pretests to Determine Need for Instruction.** A score of 30% to 70% on a spell check would suggest that a student is using but confusing a feature, making it an area ripe for instruction (we recommend taking a step back to an easier feature when possible if a student scores less than 50%) In Figure 2.3 Jake's inventory results showed that he spelled the *r*-influenced vowels in the words *serving, carries,* and *marched* correctly but missed several of the other vowel patterns. A spell check of more r-controlled vowels might reveal that he (1) needs thorough instruction if he scored less than 75%, (2) could use a quick review if he scored between 75% and 85% or (3) could skip the study of r-controlled vowels entirely if he scored at 90% or better. Pretesting students on particular features is helpful when you are concerned about pacing as it can identify features that students do not need to study in depth.

**Posttests to Monitor Progress.** Comparing the results on a posttest to a pretest is an excellent way to demonstrate progress. Figure 2.8 shows Omar's spell checks for short vowels and preconsonantal nasal sounds (the *m*'s and *n*'s that come before consonants at the end of words). The first is a pretest on which he scored 30 percent. The second, using a different form on which he scored 90 percent, was given after he had spent several weeks working on that feature in his word sorts. Several weeks later, his teacher assessed his retention of this feature by administering another form of the same spell check. Although Omar misspelled two words in the delayed posttest, eight out of ten words spelled correctly is still a good indication of mastery.

**Target Re-teaching.** Sometime a posttest will reveal that a student has not retained knowledge

---

**FIGURE 2.8   Omar's Spell Checks for Preconsonantal Nasals**

| Oct 10 | | Nov 7 | | Nov 29 | |
|--------|------|-------|------|--------|-------|
| 1. rug | rung | 1. bring | | 1. rung | |
| 2. lamp | | 2. camp | | 2. lamp | |
| 3. prin | print | 3. hunt | | 3. print | |
| 4. theng | think | 4. blend | | 4. thingk | think |
| 5. limp | | 5. wink | | 5. limp | |
| 6. stup | stump | 6. tent | | 6. stup | stump |
| 7. send | | 7. thank | | 7. send | |
| 8. plat | plant | 8. dup | dump | 8. plant | |
| 9. lag | long | 9. sang | | 9. long | |
| 10. jok | junk | 10. hand | | 10. junk | |
| 3/10 | 30% | 9/10 | 90% | 8/10 | 80% |

about spelling a particlar feature and re-teaching is needed. Rather than repeating all the lessons however, a careful analysis might reveal that only a review is needed or only a particular sound or pattern is problematic. Omar's teacher recorded his scores on the progress monitoring chart for late letter name–alphabetic spellers in (Figure 2.9). If Omar had scored less than 90% on the posttest, some targeted review would be needed. In his case, it appears that the *ump* pattern is a problem (he missed that pattern twice), so that pattern could be targeted by comparing words like *jump* and *stump* to words like *cup* and *pup* in which there is no preconsonantal nasal.

**Assess Generalizations and Meanings.** In some cases a posttest that uses words students have not studied is recommended. This is particularly important when a unit of study has focused on a broad generalization (or rules) such as how to add inflected endings (*-ed, -ing, -s, -es*). In other cases (that is, homophones, prefixes, or root words) it is just as important to assess meaning as spelling. Specialized pre- and posttests can be found in the *Words Their Way* supplements for certain features, and students in the derivational relations stage are often asked to define words as well as spell them.

## Expectations and Goal-Setting

Setting high expectations for students, setting realistic goals for making progress over time, and involving students in the process of setting goals are important. Generally speaking, long-term goals reflect your basic expectations for what stage your students must be in to succeed in the next grade level. (See Spelling Stage Expectations by Grade Level in Table 2.4) In contrast, short-term goals indicate the features necessary to study and learn to reach the basic long-term stage goal (Flanigan et al., 2011). Goal-setting forms make explicit what must be learned to reach the ultimate long-term goal and can be used to track student progress and to guide your conferences with specialists, parents, and students. Goal setting forms have been created for each of the developmental stages and can be found in Appendix B or in the *Words Their Way* supplements.

**Enhanced eText**
**Video Example 2.8**
Learn how word study is part of a family literacy program.

**USING THE FORMS TO RECORD PROGRESS.** The goals are stated for each feature or unit of study and a check box to the right corresponds to the spell checks with spaces for pre- and posttest results. Figure 2.9 is a sample that shows how Omar's teacher has checked off each feature he used correctly and put an X beside those he is missing. Different colors of ink can indicate different testing dates.

**INVOLVE STUDENTS IN GOAL SETTING.** It can be motivating for students to set goals and monitor their own progress. We recommend that you meet with students individually and share the results of the inventory or spell checks to set goals. The charts help student define a set of goals that are within reach – within their zone of proximal development. This is especially helpful for students who are struggling in the area of spelling and may feel overwhelmed with all they need to learn.

| FIGURE 2.9 Omar's Goal-Setting/Progress Monitoring Chart | |
|---|---|
| 10. Spell short vowels with preconsonantal nasals | ing ✓ ang ✓ ong ✗ ung ✗ amp ✓✓ ump ✗✗ imp ✓ <br><br> ant ✗ int ✗ ent ✓ unt ✓ and ✓ end ✓✓ <br><br> ank ✓ ink ✗✓ unk ✗ |
| Spell Check 10 | Pretest: 30% Date: 10/10    Posttest: 90% Date: 11/7 |

# Assessing the Spelling Development of English Learners

By assessing their orthographic knowledge using the assessments described in this chapter, teachers can determine whether English learners are applying the rules of phonology and orthography from the written form of their primary language to English, or vice-versa (Helman, 2004, 2010). Bilingual learners can often use knowledge of their primary language to spell words in a second language (Babayigit, 2014; Helman, 2004; Pasquarella, Chen, Gottardo, Geva, 2014). For example, Spanish speakers take the 22 sounds of Spanish and match them to the roughly 44 sounds of English, making some logical substitutions along the way.

Additional assessments in their primary or first language provide a more complete understanding of the word knowledge of English learners. A spelling inventory in students' spoken language can indicate their literacy levels in the primary language and more specifically, show which orthographic features they already understand. *Words Their Way™ with English Learners* discusses spelling development, assessment, and instruction for English learners in depth (Helman, Bear, Templeton, Invernizzi, & Johnston, 2012) and also provides inventories in several languages.

## The Influences of Students' Primary Languages

As you listen to the speech and oral reading of English language learners, notice the influences of their first languages on pronunciation and look for spelling errors that may be explained by a primary language or dialect. For example, one teacher learned about the influence of different East Indian dialects when she noticed confusions of /p/ for *f* and /sh/ for *s*. Another teacher noted her Korean students consistently confusing *r* for *l* and vice versa. In spoken Korean, /r/ and /l/ are not different sounds and are represented with the same letter in Hangul, the Korean writing system (Yang, 2005).

**FIGURE 2.10**
**Rosa's Spelling**

| | |
|---|---|
| 1. bed | bed |
| 2. ship | shep |
| 3. when | wan |
| 4. lump | lamp |
| 5. float | flowt |
| 6. train | trayn |
| 7. place | pleays |
| 8. drive | kids |
| 9. bright | brayt |
| 10. shopping | shapen |
| 11. spoil | spoyo |
| 12. serving | sorven |
| 13. chewed | shod |
| 14. carries | cares |
| 15. marched | marsh |
| 16. shower | showar |
| 17. cattle | cadoto |
| 18. favor | fayvr |
| 19. ripen | raypn |
| 20. cellar | sallar |

**PREDICTABLE CONFUSIONS.** English consonant sounds are often problematic for Spanish speakers, who make a variety of substitutions that can be traced to the influence of Spanish on their spelling (Bear et al. 2003). Examples include spelling *that* as DAT and *ship* as CHAP because the digraphs /th/ and /sh/ do not exist in Spanish. *Hot* may be spelled JAT because the silent *h* in Spanish can be spelled with a *j*. Short *a*, *e*, *i*, and *u* do not occur in Spanish, and the sound we call short *o* is spelled with the letter *a*. We can expect many confusions about how to represent these short vowel sounds such as using *a* for the short *o* in *hot*. Look in each of the instructional chapters for specific guidance on the interrelatedness of students' home languages and English.

**INVENTORY EXAMPLE.** Because students are expected to learn the orthography of English, administering one of the inventories from Table 2.1 to see what they know and are ready to learn is useful. The spelling sample of a second grader in Figure 2.10 shows how a student's spoken Spanish can affect her English spelling. Several of Rosa's attempts follow the logical substitutions that are seen from English-speaking students in the letter name–alphabetic stage; that is, SHEP for *ship* and WAN for *when*. Other errors make good sense in relation to Spanish letter–sound correspondences. For example, given the pronunciation of *a* as /ah/ in Spanish, her spelling of SHAPEN for *shopping* is understandable. She replaces the *ch* in *chewed* with *sh* (SHOD). Rosa is also trying to find a spelling for the long *i*, shown by her use of AY in two of her spellings (bright as BRAYT and ripen as RAYPN). The long *i*—when elongated—really sounds like two vowels ("eye-ee"—a diphthong). Rosa is using the *y*, pronounced as a long *e* in Spanish, to spell the second half of the vowel combination.

# Conclusion

Looking at a student's spelling gives us a window into that student's word knowledge, the information he or she uses to read and write words. The word *assessment* comes from the Latin word *assidere*—"to sit beside." Spend some time sitting beside your students and looking through the window that their spellings provide, and use inventories to assess what they know about how words work.

A summary of the developmental sequence can be found inside the front cover of this book, and each of the instructional chapters for this book offers detailed information about the stage, the features to study, and activities to enhance instruction. Remember that the inventories only sample the most common features. At each stage, there is a considerable body of knowledge that students should master before they move on to the next stage.

Keep your fingers on the pulse of development by monitoring progress over time using the spell checks and the goal-setting/progress-monitoring tools discussed in this chapter. The assessments in this chapter are a start because they let us know what each student is ready to learn, knowledge that is crucial to organizing word study instruction—the topic of Chapter 3.

# chapter 3

# Word Study Principles
# and Practices

After you determine the developmental level of each of your students, as described in Chapter 2, you are ready to implement word study for phonics, spelling, and vocabulary. In this chapter, we describe the basic activities for word study, how to lead thoughtful word-study discussions, and how to put word knowledge to use in reading and writing. We address related issues such as expectations for editing and grading, before ending with a summary of the guiding principles of word study and a table of resources. To illustrate the details that make up this chapter, let's first visit the classroom of Mrs. Zimmerman as she introduces a group of her students to *r*-influenced vowels.

Earlier in the year, Mrs. Zimmerman assessed her third-grade students and divided them into three instructional groups for word study. On most Mondays, she meets with each group for about 15 to 20 minutes to go over the words and help her students make discoveries and reach conclusions about the particular group of words she has chosen. After getting her students started on independent reading and journal writing, Mrs. Zimmerman calls her first group to a table. She has a set of words cards laid out on a table. She begins by saying, "Let's go over these words to be sure everyone knows how to read them and what they mean." After discussing *mare*, which Julio defines as a "mother horse," she picks up *bear* and *bare* and reads both. "Who remembers what words like these are called? That's right, they're homophones." She holds up *bear* and asks who knows what it means.

"It's an animal and I saw one last summer when we went camping," offers Shannon.

"What about this *bare*?" asks Mrs. Zimmerman, as she holds up the word. Rayshad explains that it means "having no hair, like being bald."

"Any other ideas?" asks Mrs. Zimmerman, to which Jessie adds, "You might go barefooted, without shoes."

Other examples are given and then Mrs. Zimmerman continues, "There is another set of homophones here. Can anyone find them?" Mason finds *hair* and *hare* and again they talk about the meaning of each. They recall that they have heard the word *hare* in the story *The Hare and the Tortoise*, which they read during a unit on fables.

Mrs. Zimmerman now moves into the heart of the lesson by using an open-ended question to get students thinking and observing, "What do you notice about our words for this week?" Rachel points out that all the words have A's and Samuel adds that they also have R's. "What else?" Mrs. Zimmerman probes, "Tell me more." Tiffany identifies the patterns of AR and AIR and Belle adds that there are also words with ARE. Mrs. Zimmerman responds, "So you are using your eyes to see how they are alike. What do your ears tell you about how they sound? Julio?" Julio says that he can hear /ar/ and / ār/. Mrs. Zimmerman affirms, "Yes, I hear those also. Does anyone hear any other sounds?

Mrs. Zimmerman then begins a teacher-directed sort by setting up categories with a focused contrast in vowel sounds. "Let's sort our words by sounds in the middle. I am going to put *cart* here as one of our key words and *care* over here for the other. Listen to the sounds in each: *caaarrrt, caaarrrre*." Then she picks up and reads the word *farm*. "Will this go with *cart* or *care*? *Farm* and *cart* sound alike in the middle—I hear the /ar/ sound in both—so we will put *farm* under *cart*. How about *chair*? Does it sound like *cart* or *care* in the middle?" After sorting several more words, Mrs. Zimmerman hands out the rest of the word cards and calls on students to read and categorize each word by its vowel sound. After sorting all the words, the students read down each column to verify that the words all have the same sound in the middle. The final sort by sound looks like Figure 3.1.

Next, Mrs. Zimmerman directs her students' attention to the spelling patterns: "When you look at these words, what do you notice about all the words in each column?" Lisa replies that

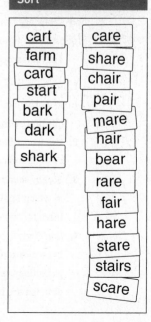

**FIGURE 3.1** Mrs. Zimmerman's Sound Sort

| | |
|---|---|
| cart | care |
| farm | share |
| card | chair |
| start | pair |
| bark | mare |
| dark | hair |
| shark | bear |
| | rare |
| | fair |
| | hare |
| | stare |
| | stairs |
| | scare |

**FIGURE 3.2** Mrs. Zimmerman's Pattern Sort

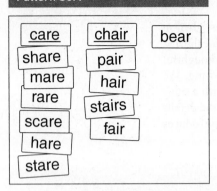

they all have an *a* and *r* in them. "Does everyone see that pattern? What else?" she prompts. William volunteers that under *care,* there is an *e* at the end or an *i* in the middle. "Shall we put these words into two separate categories by spelling pattern?" asks Mrs. Zimmerman. "What should we use as headers?" The students agree to keep *care* as one header and to use *chair* for the other, and these words are underlined. Mrs. Zimmerman passes out the word cards and students take turns placing each word under *care* or *chair* after reading it aloud.

"I have an oddball!" calls out Tan, and she places the word *bear* off to the right.

"Ahh," says Mrs. Zimmerman. "Why is it an oddball?"

"It is the only /ār/ sound spelled with an *EA*," explains Tan.

After sorting the words by pattern as shown in Figure 3.2, they read down each column of words to verify that they all have the same sound in the middle and the same spelling pattern. Mrs. Zimmerman then asks her students whether the patterns remind them of other words they have studied. Brian points out that *ai* and *a* with an *e* on the end are patterns that go with long *a.* "Are these long *a* words?" probes Mrs. Zimmerman. "Listen: caaaare, chaaair." The children agree that they can hear the sound of /ā / in those words. "What do you notice about the *a* in cart?" asks Mrs. Zimmerman. This time there is some discussion as students come to the conclusion that they cannot even hear a vowel! They only hear "R"! Mrs. Zimmerman tells the students that over the next few weeks they will look at more words with an *r* after the vowel and they should watch how the *r* influences the sound of vowels. To end the lesson, Mrs. Zimmerman asks students to reflect on what they have learned, and she records their summary: The sound /ār/ can be spelled two ways—*air* and *are.* The homophone *bear* is an oddball because the /ār/ sound is spelled *-ear.*

Before they return to their seats, Mrs. Zimmerman gives each student a handout for sorting independently. She reminds them to draw colored lines down the back to personalize their set of words and then underline the key words before cutting them apart. They are to categorize the words first by sound (naming each word quietly as they sort) and then by pattern as they did in their final group sort. Two volunteers agree to illustrate the homophones for the class homophone dictionary.

After Mrs. Zimmerman meets with another group, she quickly checks in with each student in the first group to look at his or her sort. As she moves around the room, she asks individual students to read a column of words and explain how they are alike. On Tuesday, she will ask all her students to sort their words once more and then to write the words by categories in word study notebooks along with a sentence or two about what they have learned. On other days, they will work with partners to sort again and to find more words from the books they are reading that fit the same sounds and/or patterns. On Friday, Mrs. Zimmerman assesses all three groups at one time by calling out a word in turn for each group to spell.

This classroom vignette illustrates five of the eleven key principles of developmental word study:

1. *A step backward is a step forward.* Students in this group had already studied the fairly consistent *ar* sound in words like *car* and *star.* In this sort, those sounds are reviewed with different words and a new sound is introduced that is spelled with two patterns.

2. *Use words students can read.* Mrs. Zimmerman began this lesson by going over the words, reading and discussing their meanings.

3. *Sort by sound and pattern.* Mrs. Zimmerman began by comparing two sounds before leading a visual contrast in which spelling patterns were compared. Even when students sort words by patterns it is important for them to "say it" as they "lay it."

4. *Don't hide exceptions.* In this sort, the word *bear* was included as an **oddball**, a word that has the same sound but a different spelling pattern. Words like *pear* and *wear* might have been included as well. These so-called exceptions reveal that there is a small subset of words with the /ār/ sound spelled with an *ear* pattern. Most of these are homophones.

**5.** *Teaching is not telling.* Mrs. Zimmerman is careful to use open-ended questions so that students have the opportunity to draw their own conclusions about the set of words. She expects her students to do the thinking for themselves. Mrs. Zimmerman provides guidance by calling attention to the *focused contrasts* between the sounds they hear and the patterns they see below the key words cart and *care.*

# Why Focused Contrasts?

Throughout this book you will see many examples of games and activities, but the simple process of contrasting words by sound, pattern, and/or meaning and sorting them into categories is at the heart of word study. A **focused contrast** is a set of deliberately targeted features that can be categorized. Making contrasts is one way to categorize, a fundamental way that humans make sense of the world. It enables us to find order and similarities among various objects, events, ideas, and words that we encounter. When students categorize words, they engage in the active process of searching, comparing, contrasting, and analyzing. Word sorts help students organize what they know about words to verbalize generalizations that they can then apply to new words they encounter in their reading or spell in their writing (Cartwright, 2012; Henderson, 1990; Templeton & Bear, 2018).

Because categorizing words by focused contrasts is such a powerful way to help students make sense of words, we will take some time here to discuss it in depth. The *focus* changes but the act of contrasting and categorizing remains the same across the grades and stages. At first, emergent and beginning readers contrast sounds at the beginnings of words by categorizing pictures, as shown in Figure 3.3 on page 55. By the time they are transitional readers, enjoying their first *Dyamonde Daniel* books (by N. Grimes), or the *Fox* series (by E. Marshall), students benefit from contrasting vowel sounds and vowel patterns. In later grades, students enhance their spelling and vocabulary as they group words by prefixes and suffixes. In middle school and high school, students sort words by Greek and Latin roots that share common meanings.

## Teaching Word Knowledge through Sorting

Word sorting offers the best of both constructivist learning and direct instruction. Begin by identifying a focus and "stacking the deck" with words that can be contrasted by sound, pattern, or meaning. During sorting, Mrs. Zimmerman's students will discover generalizations about how the English spelling system works to represent speech sounds and meanings. Over the next few weeks, they will focus on other *r*-influenced vowels through a series of contrasts. They will discover that *r* often "robs" the vowel of the sounds we normally associate with it. Rather than simply memorizing 20 words each week for a spelling test, students have the opportunity to construct their own word knowledge that they can apply to reading and writing. Through sorting, students acquire and integrate new word knowledge that is extended and refined through the activities we describe. In addition to learning how to spell, read, understand, and use new words, students develop productive habits of mind (Marzano, 1992).

One central goal of word study is to teach students how to spell and decode new words and to improve their word recognition and writing in general. To accomplish this goal, we teach students, through focused contrasts, how to examine words and talk about the regularities that exist in the spelling system. Picture sorts and word sorts are designed to help students learn how and where to look at and listen to words. It's not just the sorting that accomplishes these goals however; the talk that surrounds these sorting activities helps students form generalizations about how the spelling system words to represent pronunciations and meanings. Discussion about how words sound, how they look, and what they mean is essential for building the

Student sorts short *a* and -*ar* words

Student contrasts /ûr/ sounds spelled -*er*, -*or*, and -*ar*

word knowledge that underpins spelling, reading, and writing, for native speakers and English learners alike.

## Teaching Phonics through Word Study

Word study differs from other phonics approaches in some important ways. Students manipulate, see, say, and write words as they learn to spell them. The multisensory process of feeling where sounds are made in the mouth while pronouncing words during word study is an excellent way of building kinesthetic-tactile awareness, an essential component of multisensory approaches. The hands-on process of sorting words into categories requires students to pay attention to the look and feel of words and to make logical decisions as they place each one in a column. Consider the ancient proverb: "I hear and I forget, I see and I remember, I do and I understand." Word sorts help students learn by doing (Morris, 2013).

Second, students work with words or the names of pictures that they can already pronounce. In this way they are able to bring their tacit, subconscious understandings to explicit awareness. This is not possible if students cannot first name the words. Because learning to spell involves associating the spelling of words with their pronunciations and meanings, it is important that children know and can already pronounce most of the words to be sorted. Discussing the meanings of the words before, during, and after sorting them is also important.

A third way in which sorting differs from some other phonics approaches is that categorizing words is analytic, whereas many phonics programs take a predominantly synthetic approach. In both approaches, students are directly taught letter–sound correspondences. However, in a **synthetic-only** phonics approach, students are taught the letter–sound correspondences and then expected to sound out words phoneme by phoneme. This can make reading tedious, especially if the meaning of the words is totally unknown. An **analytic phonics** approach uses known words; students are asked to examine their parts listening for speech sounds, looking for the spelling patterns that go with them, and thinking about meaning. Analytic phonics supports the synthetic skills necessary to decode new words when reading and to encode words when writing. Word study involves both **analytic** and **synthetic phonics**.

A fourth way in which sorting differs from most phonics and spelling programs is that sorting does not rely solely on memorizing or reciting rules prior to understanding the underlying principles. During sorting, students are asked to determine similarities and differences in a focused collection of words as they use higher-level critical thinking skills to make categorical judgments. When students make decisions about whether the middle vowel sound in *cat* sounds more like the medial vowel sound in *map* or *top*, independent analysis and judgment are required. Memorization *is* necessary to master the English spelling system. One simply must remember that the animal is spelled *bear* and the adjective is spelled *bare*, but memorization is easier when served by knowledge and understanding of the principles of English spelling. Rules are useful mnemonics for concepts already understood.

Finally, because of the simplicity of sorting routines, teachers find it easy to differentiate instruction among groups of learners. Sorting is highly adaptable and the process of categorizing word features by focused contrasts lends itself to cooperative learning.

## Types of Sorts

The three basic types of sorts reflect the three layers of English orthography: sound, pattern, and meaning. These three types of sorts address how the alphabet reflects speech sounds and how spelling patterns reflect both sound and meaning.

## Sound Contrasts

Sound is the first layer of English orthography that students must negotiate to make sense of the alphabetic nature of English spelling. At different points in development, students sort words (and/or pictures of words) by rhyme, initial sounds, consonant blends or digraphs, rhyming word families, or vowel sounds. More advanced spellers may sort by syllable stress or the shifting sounds of vowels as affixes are added.

Pictures are naturally suited for **sound sorts**: The picture begs to be named, yet there is no printed form of the word for reference. As students sort each picture, they must pay attention to the individual speech sounds or **phonemes** contained in the word. Picture sorting is particularly suited for students who are still developing phonemic awareness and do not have extensive reading vocabularies. Students say the names of the pictures as they place them under the letters and the **key pictures** associated with the initial sound. Refer to Figure 3.3 where pictures have been sorted under letters and **key words** associated with the initial sound. For variety, small objects can be used instead of pictures, like a penny, pencil, and pin for sorting by beginning /p/ sound. English learners will need extra time and support to learn the names of the objects and pictures before sorting them by sound. Printed words, too, can be sorted for sounds, as Mrs. Zimmerman did using the key words *cart* and *care*. Because sound is the first aspect of a word that a speller has for reference, sound contrasts are very important. For example, only after the long *a* sound in *tape* is identified can the speller consider which of several spelling patterns might be used. (Is it *taip* or *tape*?) Not all word sorts involve a sound contrast, but many do.

### FIGURE 3.3 Beginning Sound Sort

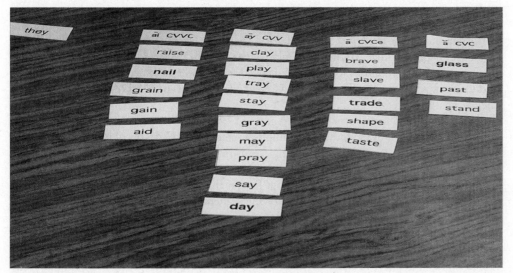

## Pattern Contrasts

Students use the printed form of the word to sort by spelling patterns or letter sequences. Letter name–alphabetic spellers sort words into **word families**, sometimes called **closed syllables**, **consonant-vowel-consonant patterns**, or **phonograms** (*hat, rat, pat* versus *ran, fan, tan*). Students in the within word pattern stage sort their words by vowel patterns (*wait, train, mail, pain* versus *plate, take, blame*). More advanced spellers will sort by the pattern of consonants and

Three different patterns of long-a contrasted with short a

**FIGURE 3.4** Word Sort by Final -*ch* and -*tch* Patterns

| wi<u>tch</u> | rea<u>ch</u> | rich |
| patch | coach | such |
| hutch | peach | |
| switch | teach | |
| hatch | roach | |
| fetch | speech | |
| match | | |

**FIGURE 3.5** Closed Sort Handout for -*tch* and -*ch* Patterns with Headers and Key Words

| **tch** | **ch** | |
| --- | --- | --- |
| **wi<u>tch</u>** | **tea<u>ch</u>** | catch |
| coach | each | patch |
| hutch | rich | switch |
| much | hatch | reach |
| fetch | much | match |
| peach | screech | sketch |

**Enhanced eText**
**Video Example 3.1**
In this video you can see examples of students engaged in a variety of sound, pattern, and meaning sorts.

vowels in the middle of the word at the syllable juncture (*button*, *pillow*, *ribbon* versus *window*, *public*, *basket*) or by patterns of constancy and change across derivationally related words (for example, *divine–divinity*, *mental–mentality*).

**Pattern sorts** often follow a sound sort as we saw in the lesson with Mrs. Zimmerman. The words under *care* were subdivided into two pattern groups: words spelled with *air* and words spelled with *are*. Because certain spelling patterns go with certain sound categories, students must be taught first to listen for the sound and then to consider alternative ways to spell that sound.

Sometimes a new feature is best introduced with a pattern sort to reveal a related sound difference. Consider the words in Figure 3.4 that have been sorted by the final *ch* or *tch* pattern. The final sound in all the words is the same, so a sound sort would not help to differentiate their spellings. However, now that the words are sorted by the final consonant patterns, read down each column to see whether you notice anything about the vowel sounds within each column. What did you discover? The *tch* pattern is associated with the short vowel sound whereas *ch* is associated with the long vowel sound. Exceptions are *rich* and *such*, which are moved to the oddball category. The spelling patterns of words are best remembered when associated with categories of sound.

Word sorts with printed word cards are the mainstay of pattern sorts and are useful for all students who have a functional sight word or reading vocabulary. Key words containing the pattern under study may be underlined or bolded (as in Figure 3.5) to label each category. Students categorize word cards by matching the spelling pattern in each word to the pattern in the key word at the top of the column. **Headers** are used to highlight the recurring spelling pattern (as shown in Figure 3.5, where *tch* and *ch* identify the focus of the sort). Students can sometimes create their own headers as part of the word sorting lesson to summarize a generalization. Because it is easier to sort words by visual spelling patterns, students can lose sight of the fact that certain patterns go with certain sounds. Sometimes mixing a few pictures in with a stack of word cards challenges students to be vigilant in their word analysis.

## Meaning Contrasts

Sometimes the focus of a contrast is on meaning. The two major types of **meaning contrasts** are concept sorts and meaning sorts related to spelling.

**CONCEPT SORTS.** Grouping objects, pictures, or words by similar concepts or meaning is a good way to link word study instruction to students' conceptual understanding and vocabulary. Concept sorts are appropriate for all ages and stages of word knowledge and can be used in the content areas. Pictures of mammals, mathematical formulas, geometric shapes, or social studies vocabulary words all can be sorted for greater understanding. The creative possibilities for using concept sorts are endless. As writing tools, they can be used to organize ideas before composing. Concept sorts are even useful for teaching grammar when words are sorted by parts of speech.

You can use concept sorts for assessing and building background knowledge before embarking on a new unit of study. For example, a science unit on states of matter might begin by having students categorize the following words into groups that go together: *steam*, *wood*, *air*, *ice cube*, *rain*, *metal*, *glue*, *paint*, *plastic*, *smoke*, *milk*, and *fog*. Discussing the reasons behind their conceptual groupings will be revealing. Revisit the sort as the unit progresses to review and assess core concepts and vocabulary. Having students categorize examples under the key words *solid*, *liquid*, and *gas* will help them sort out the essential characteristics for each state of matter. Concept sorts are effective for dealing with new words in novels, too. While reading *Stuart Little* (by E. B. White), a group of Mrs. Birckhead's third graders sorted some of the vocabulary they encountered and discussed what the words within a group had in common, as shown in Figure 3.6.

Concept picture sorts are particularly beneficial for English learners. Without knowing the English labels, they can sort pictures of a dog, a cat, a duck, and so on into an animal category. These can be contrasted with pictures of a flower, a tree, a cornfield, a pumpkin, and so on—all examples of plants. English vocabulary is learned as students repeat the sort, naming each picture and discussing categories with help from a teacher or peer. Like all children, English learners learn words by predicting relationships and building word meanings through knowledge networks and categories (Neuman & Wright, 2014).

*for* **English learners**

**SPELLING–MEANING CONTRASTS.** Students see that meaning influences the spelling of words when they first encounter soundalike **homophone** pairs like *by* and *buy* or *to* and *too*. Students enjoy homophones because they are interesting, and it makes sense that words with different meanings take different spelling patterns. When you discuss homophones while word sorting, students expand their vocabularies and learn about spelling patterns at the same time, as demonstrated by the discussion of *bear* and *bare* in Mrs. Zimmerman's class. **Homographs** are words that are spelled the same but pronounced differently, depending on part of speech: We *record* our sorts so that we have an ongoing *record* of them. By sorting homographs into grammatical categories by part of speech, students enrich their vocabularies while learning how to pay attention to syllable stress.

| FIGURE 3.6 | Concept Sort Based on *Stuart Little* |

| Weather | Boat Terms | Birds |
|---|---|---|
| squall | rigging | henbird |
| mist | bow | vireo |
| breeze | stern | wren |
| brisk | schooner | beak |
| ominous | helm | breast |
| cloudy | mainmast | |
| sunshiny | capsize | |

Advanced spellers learn how words that are related in meaning often share similar spellings. This spelling–meaning connection in derivationally related words provides a rich arena for meaning sorts that build on Greek and Latin elements. When the focus shifts to derivational relationships, students will sort words by similarities in roots and stems such as the *spect* in *spectator*, *spectacle*, *inspect*, and *spectacular* versus the *port* in *transport*, *import*, *portable*, and *port-o-john*. Derivational words can also be contrasted by word endings that signal grammatical parts of speech—educ**ate**, dict**ate** (verb), educat**ion**, dictat**ion** (noun-thing), educat**or**, dictat**or** (noun-person). By discussing the slight changes in meaning and use across these derived forms, students begin to generalize the spelling-meaning connections they observe.

Land and sea animals concept sort

A spelling-meaning sort contrasting prefixes dis-, mis-, and pre-

# The Word Study Lesson

Instruction in word study, as in comprehension and other areas of the curriculum, follows a gradual release model, an *I do, we do, you do* procedure (Fisher & Frey, 2008). A gradual release model begins with teacher modeling and explicit explanations (Duffy, 2009), moves to guided practice, and then proceeds to independent application. Each week, students get a new set of words and you decide how best to introduce those words so that students are led to form generalizations about how the contrasted features work.

## Levels of Support

Introductory lessons can range from teacher-directed sorts to student-centered sorts done independently or in buddy pairs. Which level of support you select depends on several factors:

1. How familiar students are with categorizing words according to focused contrasts
2. Whether a new feature is being introduced
3. The amount of time available for sorting, reflecting, and discussing
4. How well students can work independently

Different levels of support are summarized in Table 3.1 and described in the following subsections. Look across the top for the differing levels of teacher support and then down the side to see how the lesson components vary according to the amount of support students need. Open-ended questions that require students to think and form their own generalizations are used at all levels, but you should always be ready to model your own thinking when they are unable to articulate a generalization.

Mrs. Zimmerman chose a teacher-directed sort to introduce the new feature of *r*-influenced vowels in the vignette at the beginning of this chapter. Such a lesson can take 20 minutes or more. The next week when she gives them words contrasting the spelling patterns *er (her, per)*, *ear (hear, fear)*, and *eer (deer, cheer)*, she might assign a student-directed sort before they come to the group because they are experienced sorters. In this case she may only need five to ten minutes of group time in which the students quickly re-sort their words and reflect on what they discovered.

| TABLE 3.1 | Continuum of Support for Word Study |
|-----------|-------------------------------------|

| | For Novice Sorters Or To Introduce New Features | | For Experienced Sorters Or To Assess | |
|---|---|---|---|---|
| | **Teacher-Directed Closed Sort** | **Teacher-Directed Guess My Category** | **Student-Centered Closed Sort** | **Student-Centered Open Sort** |
| **Materials** | One set of words for group to focus on using a pocket chart, overhead, interactive whiteboard, or other method.<br><br>Students bring their own set of words to the group or are given a set at the end of group work to take back to their seats to cut apart and sort. | | Students get their own set of words with key words and/or headers. | Students get their own set of words with no key words or headers. |
| **Introduce the Sort** | Read through all the words and talk about any that students might not know.<br><br>Introduce each category with a header and a key word and explicitly describe the features students are to look for. | Read through the words and talk about any that are unfamiliar.<br><br>Set up the categories with key words but do not describe the feature or put up headers. | Read through the words and talk about any that are unfamiliar.<br><br>Students can also do this on their own, putting aside any words they don't know to discuss and sort later. | Students work on their own to read through words and put aside words they don't know. |
| **Sorting** | Demonstrate how to sort two or three words in each category and describe explicitly why each word goes there.<br><br>Students help to complete the sort and justify their placements. | Model by sorting several words in each category but do not explain the reasons.<br><br>Students are then invited to try sorting the rest of the words. | Students use headers and key words to set up categories and sort independently. | Students determine categories and sort their own words.<br><br>They explain to you or each other why they sorted as they did. |
| **Reflect** | Model how to check the columns and create a generalization with student help.<br><br>Be ready to model as needed to summarize what the sort has revealed. | Ask students to describe the features in each category and then check each column.<br><br>Create a generalization with students' help. Supply headers at this point or label key words. | Call group together or check in individually for students to describe the features and talk about any unfamiliar words.<br><br>Everyone checks. | Call group together to talk about categories.<br><br>"Close" the sort. Establish key words so everyone sorts the same way.<br><br>Check and talk about generalizations. Supply or label headers. |
| **Sort Again** | Students sort their own set of words in the group under your supervision or at their seats.<br><br>Remind students to check, and ask each student to state generalizations. | Students sort their own set of words using the key words and headers in the group or independently.<br><br>Monitor and check in during or after students sort. | Students sort independently. | Students sort independently. |

## Teacher-Directed Closed Sorts

The highest level of support and explicit instruction is offered in teacher-directed **closed sorts**. Closed sorts are a type of direct instruction in which you define the focused contrast in advance and make it clear how to conduct the sort (Gillet & Kita, 1979). In teacher-directed closed sorts you explicitly introduce the key words and set up the headers. For example, in a beginning sound phonics sort, you would isolate the beginning sound to be taught, make an explicit connection to the letter that represents it, and explicitly point out the key word, letter, and/ or picture used to designate the category. You might think aloud like this: "*Shhhhhoe, shhhhell.* I hear the same /*sh*/ sound at the beginning of *shoe* and *shell*, so I am going to put the picture of the *shell* under *shoe*. They both begin with /sh/, the sound made by the letters *s–h* together."

After modeling several words this way, gradually release the task to the students' control as they finish the sort under your supervision. After sorting, students reread and discuss the characteristics of the words in each column and develop a generalization based on the selected feature. Students may then sort independently or collaboratively in pairs under your guidance. This practice is carefully monitored and corrective feedback is provided.

The teacher-directed sort is the most commonly used approach to introduce a new sort to a group and provides a model of direct instruction that is explicit and systematic, yet sensitive to individual variation. The teacher-directed lesson plan includes four components:

1. Introduce the sort
2. Guide the reflection
3. Re-sort and check
4. Extend

**INTRODUCE THE SORT.** The four steps to introducing the sort are:

1. *Introduce the words and explore meaning.* Look over the words or pictures for items that are potentially difficult to identify or that may be unfamiliar to students. Students in the elementary grades and higher might be assigned a word to look up in advance. Display the pictures or words and quickly read or name them together. Give names of pictures as needed. ("This is a picture of a yard.") Students should already be able to read most of the words in a sort but any words students cannot identify should be set aside until later. Help students define unfamiliar words and discuss words with multiple meanings: "Does anyone know what a *hutch* is? It is a kind of wooden cage up on legs. Pet rabbits often live in hutches. It is also a piece of furniture." You might keep a picture dictionary handy to help explain different word meanings. Students who looked up selected words can be asked to report to the group. Revisit new word meanings and discuss these words throughout the week. Your English learners will especially benefit from picture dictionaries and vocabulary discussion. When there are many unknown words, as is often the case when we teach English learners, we may define and discuss only half of the pictures or words on the first day.

*for* **English learners**

2. *Establish the categories.* Display all the words and use open-ended questions to help students focus on the categories:
   * What do you notice about these words?
   * What do your eyes and ears tell you about these words?
   * How might we sort these words?

   If you stacked the deck with words that share common patterns or sounds and your students are familiar with categorizing, they should notice common features fairly quickly. If not, then define the categories for them. Display letter cards, key pictures, key words, or headers with spelling pattern cues to identify the categories. If you are working with contrasting sounds, you can emphasize or elongate them by stretching them out. If you are working with contrasting patterns, you can think aloud as you point out the spelling patterns in each category. If you are working with syllables, affixes, or derivational relations, you can explicitly point out the unit you are using to compare and contrast.

3. *Model how to sort several words and explain why.* "We are going to listen for the vowel sound in the middle of these words and decide whether they sound like the /ă/ sound in the middle of *map* or like the /ŭ/ sound in the middle of *duck*. I'll do a few first. Here is a rug. *Ruuuuug, uuuug, uuuuuuh.* Notice how I peel off the sounds before and after the vowel to make it easier to hear the vowel in the middle. *Rug* has the 'uh' sound (/ŭ/) in the middle, so I'll put it under *duck, uuuuck, uuuuh.* Here is a flag. *Flaaaaag, aaaag, aaaa.* I'll put *flag* under *maaaap. Flag* and *map* both have the /ă/ sound in the middle.

**4.** *Invite students to help with the sorting.* Display the rest of the pictures or words so students can select one they are sure of, or pass them out. Students should name the picture or read the word aloud and then place it in a category, explaining why it goes there. If students make a mistake at the very beginning, correct it immediately. Simply say: "*Sack* would go under *map.* Its middle sound is /ă/." Then model how to segment the phonemes to isolate the medial vowel: /s/–/ă/–/k/.

**GUIDE THE REFLECTION.** After sorting, read down the lists of words in each column to check for the sound or pattern. Now comes the most important part of the lesson where students are asked to verbalize what the words or pictures in each column have in common and arrive at some conclusion or generalization. Be sure to talk about why the oddballs are placed in another category and return to any words that students were not able to read.

Teacher introducing the sort

**1.** Begin with open ended questions such as the following ones listed and take responses from more than one student:
- What do you notice about our categories? Anyone else have an idea?
- How are the words alike in this column? What else?
- Why did you put these words together? Do you all agree?
- Are there any oddballs? What makes them odd?

**2.** Focus attention on sound, pattern, and/or meaning with probing questions such as:
- How are the sounds in these words alike?
- What kind of pattern do you notice? Have we seen this pattern before?
- Are any of these words similar in meaning?

**3.** Talk about *where* in the word the feature occurs, how often students encounter the feature in their reading, and other words that have those same word parts.
- **Position.** Some spelling patterns are found at the ends of words (like the *oy* in *toy* and *enjoy*) and others in the middle (like the *oi* in *soil* or *choice*). By asking students to reflect on *where* certain patterns occur within words, you can lead students to understand that certain patterns that represent certain sounds occur in certain positions. This insight will help them enormously as they learn to read and spell.
- **Frequency.** Frequency of occurrence is also worthy of reflection. For example, word hunts will reveal that words ending in *er* are much more common than words ending in *or* or *ar*. After students are clued into the frequency of certain spelling patterns, they can apply this insight by using a "best bet" approach to spelling and reading unfamiliar words.
- **Related words.** Reflecting on related words will extend students' insights to other words—a major goal of word study. Words with similar roots and affixes are related in both spelling and meaning. For example, the word *cover* is related to *discover, uncover, recover, discovery, recovery,* and so on. Such is the generative nature of word study.

**4. Reach conclusions.** Avoid telling rules, but help students shape their ideas into generalizations such as, "All of these words have the letter *u* in the middle and make the 'uh' sound," or "The words with an *e* on the end have the /ā/ sound in the middle." With the

**Enhanced eText**
**Video Example 3.2**
In this video, the authors outline the lesson plan format for word sorting.

generalization or "big idea" now explicitly stated, they may be able to apply it to the decoding of unfamiliar words. Use questions such as:

- What did you learn from this sort? Something else?
- How can this help you as a speller? As a reader?
- Are there any words that might be especially difficult to spell? Why?
- Can we apply what we have learned to read (or spell) these words?

During the reflection part of the lesson, students are asked to verbally declare and discuss their understanding about sound, pattern, and meaning.

**RE-SORT AND CHECK.** Ideally right after the discussion, or when time allows, ask students to re-sort. Leave up the headers and key words and scramble the rest and turn them face down in a pile. Students may enjoy the anticipation of turning over a card when it is their turn to draw. Students might also sort their own set of words cooperatively or independently under your supervision. Unless your students are in the last two levels of word knowledge (syllables and affixes or derivational relations), ask them to name each word or picture aloud as they sort.

During this second, repeated sort, do not correct your students, but when they are through, have them name the words or pictures in each column to check the sort. When students make mistakes, finding out why they sorted a picture or word in a particular way is sometimes useful. Simply asking, "Why did you put that there?" can provide further insight into a student's word knowledge. If mistakes are made, your students will learn more if you guide them to finding and correcting the mistake on their own. You might say, "I see one word in this column that doesn't fit with the others. Can you find it?"

**EXTEND.** Extensions consist of activities designed to reinforce and apply what students have learned after the group demonstration, sorting, and reflection. During the extension, students participate in a number of activities at centers, with partners, as seatwork, and for homework to link their understandings to reading and writing. They continue to sort a number of times individually and with partners for several days. They hunt for similar words in their books, draw and label pictures, add to word charts, complete word study notebooks, write words and play games. Extensions that link word study to reading and writing are described in more detail later in this chapter.

Extend activities: Games and books for word hunts

## Teacher-Directed Open Sorts

Teacher-directed open sorts are different from the teacher-directed closed sorts because in the open sort, the categories are not predefined. Although the sort still contains a focused contrast and the teacher is still leading the introduction, in the teacher-directed open sort the *students* are given more responsibility to figure out the categories as opposed to being told what they are by the teacher. In the teacher-directed open sort, students are required to do more thinking.

**GUESS MY CATEGORY.** When students are comfortable with sorts, you can use a variation of the teacher-directed sort called Guess My Category. After reviewing the words, set up key words or pictures as in a closed sort but do not offer any explanation of the categories. Rather, it is your students' job to develop hypotheses about how the things in each category are alike. The steps for conducting a Guess My Category activity are as follows:

- Begin by sorting two or three pictures or words into each column without any headers to give away the focus of the sort.
- Pick up the next object, picture, or word and invite someone to guess where it will go. Continue doing this until all the pictures or words have been sorted.
- Try to keep the students who have caught on to the attributes of interest from telling the others until the end.
- After sorting, read through the word, and guide a reflective discussion as you would for the earlier teacher-directed sort.
- Give students their own objects, pictures, or words to sort and assign follow-up activities to do throughout the week.

Look at the following words sorted under the key words *dead*, *street*, and *reach*. Can you guess the categories and decide where to sort *speak*, *bread*, and *sweet*?

| dead | street | reach |
|------|--------|-------|
| head | queen | dream |
| breath | trees | beach |

Guess My Category is particularly useful in small groups for exploring content-specific vocabulary while also stimulating creative thinking. Give small groups sets of words, pictures, or objects that might be grouped in various ways; ask each group to come up with its own categories. Allow them to have a miscellaneous designation for those things that do not fit the categories they establish. After the groups are finished working, let them visit each other's sorts and try to guess the categories that were used. For example, pictures of animals might be sorted into groups according to body covering, habitat, or number of legs. As with the sorts described previously, discussion of what's the same and what's different is critical for student learning.

**BRAINSTORMING.** Brainstorming can also be used to introduce a sort. You might ask students for words that have particular sounds, patterns, or roots and write them on the board. You can then write words in categories as they are given, as in the Guess My Category activity described earlier, or categories might be determined by discussion. These words can be transferred to word study sheets for weekly word sorting routines. After one student raised a question about why the word *sleeve* had an *e* on the end when it already had the *ee* pattern, Mrs. Zimmerman asked her students to think of other words that ended in either *ve* or *v*. After listing their brainstormed words on the board, students sorted them into two groups—those that had a long vowel sound and needed the *e* to mark the vowel (*stove*, *alive*, *cave*) and those that did not (*give*, *love*, *achieve*). Students could think of no words that ended in plain *v*, and they concluded that an *e* always came after *v*, whether it was needed to mark the vowel or not!

## Student-Centered Sorts

As students become sorting pros, student-centered sorts increase the cognitive demand and can reduce the amount of teacher-directed group time.

**CLOSED SORT.** In many classrooms, students are given their words for the week on Monday morning, and they sort their words independently in anticipation of the categories they will be sorting later in teacher-directed groups. The handout for a closed sort, such as the example shown

**FIGURE 3.7** Open Sort Handout for *tch* and *ch* Patterns

| | | |
|---|---|---|
| witch | teach | catch |
| coach | each | patch |
| hutch | rich | switch |
| much | hatch | reach |
| fetch | much | match |
| peach | screech | sketch |

earlier in Figure 3.5, provides the headers and key words students need to complete the sort on their own. They have some support, but they must still read each word and think about sounds and patterns as they make their own decisions about how to categorize. Remind students to watch out for oddballs. Oddballs present an enjoyable challenge for students that forces them to test the hypotheses they form about the words.

**OPEN SORT.** The student-centered **open sort** is really our favorite, demanding the highest level of independent effort and thought because students are not given any clues to the categories or features—only a set of words to sort. Open sorts are often the most satisfying for students as well because they present a puzzle to solve. To conduct an open sort:

1. Distribute a handout that has no headers or key words, such as Figure 3.7. If you are using prepared sorts that come with headers and key words, as in Figure 3.5, cut off the headers and key words to save for later.
2. Ask students to read over the words and create their own categories.
3. Have students compare their categories with a partner and come up with their own generalizations.
4. Bring the students together to talk about the meanings of any unfamiliar words. Review their sorts, and ask they what they noticed about the words and what conclusions they were able to reach on their own.

Even with student-centered sorts, this last step is very important. Ask the students to sort so you can check for accuracy and observe their thinking. You may find that some students have sorted the words in ways that do not reveal a generalization or the "big idea." For example, your students may sort the words in Figure 3.7 by the number of letters, by rhyming words, or by beginning consonants (with a blend or no blend). After acknowledging that the words could be sorted that way, you should "close the sort" by agreeing on the focused contrasts you had in mind. At this point you might give students the headers and key words that were cut off the handout, or have students create their own headers as a way for them to summarize the features as part of the reflection process. In the final sort (see Figure 3.4 on page 56), the *tch* and *ch* endings have been underlined to identify both key words and headers. The same headers should be used each time students sort.

Student-centered sorts are diagnostic in nature because they reveal what students know when they work independently. Open sorts provide opportunities for students to test their own hypotheses and they often come up with unexpected ways to organize words. These open sorts are interesting to observe and to discover what students already understand or misunderstand. Some of the most productive discussions about orthography come when students explain *why* they sorted the way they did in an open sort. Remember the kinds of questions to guide the reflection discussed on page 61. Broadly these questions probe:

- How are the words the same within each category?
- Are there any oddballs? What makes them odd?
- What can we learn from sorting these words in this way?

## Teacher Talk and Student Reflection

Peter Johnston has written extensively about how the language that teachers use with students can position them as problem solvers or as passive recipients (Johnston, 2004, 2012). Word study, as we describe it, offers valuable opportunities for students to be actively involved in making discoveries about the spelling system and developing vocabulary—but only if teachers facilitate group discussions that foster thoughtful interactions (Gehsmann, Millwood, & Bear, 2012). Classroom observations by Ganske and Jocius (2013) revealed that teachers often relied on a traditional initiate/respond/evaluate format during word study lessons: The teacher *initiates* a question to which he or she knows the answer, the student *responds*, and the teacher *evaluates* the response as right or wrong. Such interactions are more like interrogations dominated by the teacher than discussions in which students practice higher-level thinking skills and learn from each other.

Student reflection and discussion are critical parts of word study instruction, but teachers must carefully consider how it is done. The language we use when we talk with students has a powerful influence on their understanding and can cultivate a sense of self-efficacy and problem solving. Asking open-ended questions such as, "What do you notice about these words?" followed by "Who has another idea?" suggests there are multiple aspects of words worth considering and that there is no one right answer. When students are writing and ask how to spell a word, asking, "Do you know another word that has a similar sound at the beginning?" conveys the message that they can figure it out for themselves (Johnston, 2004). Table 3.2 presents examples of teacher talk that encourage students to solve problems, to reason and reflect, and to apply their growing word knowledge to other words.

Try to frame your response to their answers in ways that avoid judgment and will further the discussion. Instead of saying "Right" or "Good job," try,

- "Who agrees?"
- "Why?" or "Why not?"
- "Who can add to that?"

**TABLE 3.2**  Questions to Guide Critical Thinking during Word Study

| Problem Solving | Reflection | Application & Transfer |
|---|---|---|
| What do you notice about these words? Remember to use your ears and your eyes as you examine them. | What can you tell us about these words now that we have sorted them? How are they alike? | Let's go back to these words we were not sure about earlier. Can we read them now? Can we figure out what they mean? |
| How are these words alike? How are they different from this set over here? Tell us more. | Why did you put this word here? | What if we changed that prefix to another prefix? What would the word mean then? |
| Where in the word do you find the ___ (sound, spelling patterns, root)? Who can add to that? | What did we learn from this sort that might help us be a better reader or speller? | If you're not sure how to spell a word, how would you know which pattern to use? What would be your best try? Why? |
| How else could you figure that out? Does anyone have a different idea? | In your reading, which pattern do you see more frequently? Which pattern has the most words in your column? The fewest? | If you weren't sure what a word meant, what could you do to figure it out? |
| What are some ways we could figure out the meaning of that word? How could we check? | How did you figure that out? | Can you think of other words that have the same root or base word? |
| Which part of the word are you sure about? Which part are you not sure about? What do the rest of you think? | Tell me how your sorting went. What words were difficult? What were you sure of/unsure of? What problems did you come across in your sort? | One of the things people do when they aren't sure about a word is think of another word they know that has a similar base word or root. Let's try it. Let's say you don't know the meaning of *recital*. What other word might you think of that you do know? |
| Can you divide the word into parts? What is the base word? Are there any prefixes or suffixes? | What word parts did you use? Do the word parts give you information about the word's meaning? | What other word can you think of that has the same _____ (sound, pattern, root)? |
| How are you planning to go about this word sort? | Write down an observation about these words. | Let's try making some new words with these word parts. Let's see if we can guess the meaning. |
| Do you all agree? Why or why not? Any more ideas? | Do you think this will apply to other words like this? | How or when could you use this word? |

*Source:* Based on Palmer, J., and Invernizzi, M. (2014). *Not This, But That: No More Phonics and Spelling Worksheets.* Portsmouth, NH: Heinemann.

When you say, "I like your ideas" or "Who can add to Todd's comment?" you are giving students credit for their thinking rather than congratulating them on coming up with the answer you wanted to hear. Questions such as these can help you get meaningful conversations about words going in classrooms where students develop into confident thinkers.

# Extensions and Follow-Up Routines

After an introductory sort, assign students a variety of follow-up activities designed to reinforce generalizations and their memory of words, build speed and accuracy, and connect to reading and writing. Ideally, such activities develop productive habits of looking for and thinking about word attributes, while at the same time providing individual practice and experience manipulating and categorizing words. All of these activities can and should be introduced to the whole class through modeling before assigning them to be completed independently.

## Repeated Sorting

To become fluent readers and writers, students must achieve automaticity in reading (Samuels, 1988), the fast and accurate recognition of words in context, and automaticity in writing to produce fast and accurate spellings. The words they encounter in reading and use in writing are made of the same sounds, patterns, and meaning units they examine out of context in word study. One of the best ways to achieve automaticity in word recognition and spelling is to repeat a picture or word sort over the next several days. In Mrs. Zimmerman's class, students sort individually after the group lesson, again on Tuesday, and then on Wednesday with partners. They eagerly participate in timed or speed sorts and they are expected to take their words home to sort several days a week for homework. All this adds up to sorting (and checking) the same words six to eight times throughout the week. There are several types of sorts to assign.

## Buddy Sorts

Students love to work cooperatively. In a **buddy sort**, they work together to read the words or name the pictures in each column, place the words into categories, check the sort, and then talk to each other about the generalization covered by the sort. The sorting can take place in tan- dem, side by side with two sets of words, or alternating turns with one set of words. Buddy sorts can provide support for students who are not sure of how to name pictures (often the case for English learners) or read words. Two sorts that work well with buddies are blind sorts and blind writing sorts.

*for* **English learners**

## Blind Sorts

In a **blind sort**, headers or key words are used to establish categories, but then the teacher or a partner shuffles the word cards and calls each word aloud without showing it. The student indicates the correct category by pointing to or naming the header. The response is checked and corrected immediately when the printed word is revealed and put in place. Buddies can switch roles (reader or sorter) after going through the whole set of words or they can switch roles word by word. This sort is important for students who need to attend less to visual patterns and more to the sounds. Sometimes, you can use a blind sort as a way to introduce a sort when sound is particularly important, as in the study of short vowels. Note, however, that blind sorts do not present a challenge when sound is not an issue, as in the study of prefixes or root words.

## Writing Sorts

Writing words as a study technique for spelling is well established and is a highly recommended multisensory activity. Undoubtedly the motoric act of writing reinforces the memory for associating letters and patterns with speech sounds and meanings. However, the practice of assigning students to write words five or more times is of little value because it can become mindless copying. Where there is no thinking, there is no learning. In con-

Students take turns calling words out to each other

trast, writing words into categories demands that students attend to the sounds or patterns of letters and think about how those characteristics correspond with the key word or header at the top of the column. Writing sorts are essential if you want students to transfer their word knowledge to writing.

Start a **writing sort** by writing headers or key words for each category at the top of a paper. Students can record a sort that they complete with word cards or by turning over one word at a time from their collection and writing it under the correct header. Figure 3.8 shows how the words from a long *a* sort have been written under the key words *came, clay,* and *rain.* Students can also be asked to write a reflection about what they have learned from the sort as described later.

## Blind Writing Sorts

A combination of the blind sort and writing sort, a **blind writing sort** requires students to write each word in the correct category *before* seeing the word. In a blind writing sort, students must rely on the sounds they hear in the word as well as their memory for the letters associated with them, cued by the key word at the top of the column. This is what spelling is all about. Blind writing sorts are an established weekly routine in many classrooms after students have had the chance to practice the sort several times. Some teachers conduct them in a group using the document camera or interactive whiteboard, saying the word aloud and letting the students write it before they reveal the word for checking. Blind writing sorts done with a buddy or for homework are a good way to prepare for a weekly test by identifying which words need more attention. Partners take turns calling the words aloud for each other to write. It is important to immediately show the word to check the spelling and placement after each word is written. Writing sorts are also an instructionally sound way to construct weekly spelling tests. Key words are written and then students write and sort the words as they are called.

**FIGURE 3.8  Word Study Notebook**

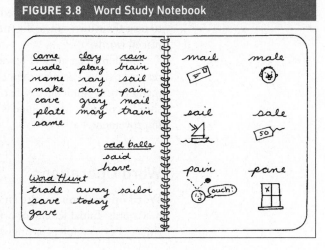

**Enhanced eText**
**Video Example 3.3**
In this video, the authors discuss the different kinds of sorting extensions. You can see examples of students engaged in writing sorts, word hunts, speed sorts, and blind sorts.

In this way, students are rewarded for the thinking that goes into writing words correct—not just for memorizing their spelling. Writing sorts and blind writing sorts connect word study to writing and to reading.

The following are some guidelines for conducting blind writing sorts:

- **Establish format.** Blind writing sorts can be recorded in the word study notebook, on loose writing paper, or on a whiteboard. Have students divide their notebook, paper, or whiteboard into columns and write the header and/or key words at the top of each one. The headers should match the headers from the sort.
- **Dictate words from the sort.** Working in buddy pairs, students take turns calling out words from the sort (without showing them) and asking their partner to write them under the appropriate header. After the partner writes a word, it should be shown and checked immediately. If an error is made, the partners should discuss what might have contributed to the mistake. The written word should be marked through and the card moved to the bottom of the collection to call again later.

## Written Reflections

Part of the introductory lesson is to help students draw conclusions about what they learned from the sort. This offers a good place to model how to write a reflection that summarizes what they learned from the lesson. Help students shape their ideas into a generalization such as, "The long *a* sound can be spelled with *a-e*, *ai*, and *ay* patterns." Or "*Dge* follows a short vowel and *ge* follows a long vowel." At first you may ask students to copy this group-generated reflection into their word study notebooks, but over time they should be given responsibility for writing it themselves. A good time to write this reflection would be after the writing sort or after a word hunt, especially following discussion.

## Speed Sorts

Students are highly motivated to practice their sorts to prepare for **speed sorts**. The easiest way to do speed sorts is a quick whole-class activity. Display a timer (laying a tablet or phone with a timer on a document camera is one way) or simply call the seconds aloud from the classroom clock. Students set up their headers, shuffle the rest of their words, then hold up the words to signal that they are ready (students in different groups will have different words). When you say "go," everyone begins to sort. As they finish, students record their times. After checking, the speed sort can be repeated immediately as well as on other days so students can attempt to beat their own times. To encourage accurate sorting, seconds may be added for incorrectly placed words.

Students can also be paired to time each other using a stopwatch and chart their progress over time. Partners then check for correctness using an answer sheet. We do not recommend pitting students against each other in a competitive mode, however; instead, students should compare their speeds with their own earlier speeds and work toward individual improvement.

## Word Operations

**Word operations** require students to change a letter (or letters) of a selected word to make new words. Initial letters, or orthographic units, might be substituted to create lists of words that rhyme. For example, starting with the word *black*, a student might substitute other consonant blends or digraphs to generate *stack*, *quack*, *track*, *shack*, and so on. Students studying more complex words might substitute prefixes, suffixes, or roots—for example, using *graph* to generate *autograph*, *biography*, *photograph*, and *photography*.

## Word Hunts

Students do not automatically see the relationship between spelling words and reading words. Word hunts help them make this important connection. In **word hunts**, students hunt through their reading and writing for words that are additional examples of the sound, pattern, or meaning unit they are studying and can develop an understanding of how many other words have the same feature. For example, they see that *le* is much more common at the ends of words than *el*. Some patterns are found in virtually every text again and again, whereas others are harder to find; thus, word hunts are more appropriate for some features than others. Before students are expected to do word hunts, you should model the activity.

Student recording words from a word hunt

**MODELING AND RECORDING WORD HUNTS.** Start with a portion of familiar text projected onto a whiteboard, a big book, or simply a book being used for instruction. Working line by line, demonstrate how to locate words that fit the categories under study and how to record those words into categories. Then, assign students to look in their own texts for other words that contain the same features. Add these words to written sorts under the corresponding key word. See Figure 3.8 for words added to the long *a* categories at the bottom of the notebook page. Ask the students to use familiar books or already-read portions of the books they are currently reading so they do not confuse skimming for words with reading for meaning.

Figure 3.9 shows an example of a word hunt conducted on a retelling of *The Three Billy Goats Gruff* by a group of students in Mrs. Fitzgerald's third-grade class. After working with the long *o* and short *o* in word study, students found more words that she underlined. Then, they organized the words by sound and patterns and recorded them in their word study notebooks. Three words, including *gobble*, were added to the short *o* column. *Groaned* and *goat* were added to the *oa* column, *home* to the *o*–consonant–*e* column, and *meadow* was added to the *ow* column. A new pattern of open, single, long *o* spellings was discovered with *so*, *go*, and *over*. Students debated where to put *too* and *who* before classifying them as oddballs.

This word hunt in *The Three Billy Goats Gruff* retelling added more examples for students to consider and created new categories. Word hunts not only link word study to reading but they also extend the reach to more difficult vocabulary such as *meadow* and *gobble*. With these words, students are able to generalize the pattern within one-syllable words to two-syllable words. Word hunts thus provide a step up in word power.

**STUDENT WORD HUNTS.** Word hunts can be conducted cooperatively in small groups, with partners, or individually for seatwork or homework. Figure 3.10 shows students gathered around a large sheet of paper on which key words have been written. Students skim and scan pages of books that they have already read, looking for words that match the key words according to the feature under study. Discussion may ensue as to whether a word contains the spelling feature in question and sometimes students consult the

**Enhanced eText**
**Video Example 3.4**
This video presents an introduction to sorting across the three layers of orthography: sound, pattern, and meaning.

**FIGURE 3.9** Word Hunt in Story Summary

The Three Billy Goats

The goats had to go over a bridge to get to the meadow on the hill. By the bridge lived an old troll. One day Little Billy Goat Gruff started over the bridge. Trip trap Trip trap went his feet. "Who is on my bridge?" the troll roared in his great big voice. Little goat said, "Oh, it is only I, the little Billy goat. I must go over the bridge to get to the meadow on the hill." "You can not cross over my bridge. I will eat you up," roared the troll. "Oh, don't eat me," said the little goat. "I am too little."

**FIGURE 3.10** Cooperative Group Word Hunt

dictionary, particularly to resolve questions of stress, syllabication, or meaning.

When conducting word hunts with emergent to beginning readers, have students scan texts that are guaranteed to contain the phonics features targeted in their search. Many core reading programs provide **phonics** or **decodable readers**, which are simple books organized around specific phonics features that repeat in the text. Other publishers offer phonics readers such as the *Ready Readers* by Pearson Learning Group or the *Learn to Read* series by Starfall. Phonics readers can also be downloaded from websites such as Reading A-Z. Although such controlled texts may not be the heart of your reading program, they offer beginning readers a chance to put into practice what they are learning about words and to see many words that work the same way. Simple poems and jingles such as those in *I Saw You in the Bathtub, And Other Folk Rhymes* (Schwartz & Hoff, 1991) also contain recurring sounds and patterns in their rhyme scheme.

Use the following guidelines to implement word hunts:

- **Establish format.** The word hunt is usually recoded in a word study notebook or on a chart. Students can either add the words they have hunted to their writing sorts or create new columns using the same headers.
- **Set expectations.** Provide guidance on the number of words to collect and/or the amount of time to spend hunting. In general students look back through books they have already read, scanning for words that fit the features in the sort, but sometimes you might provide special text that is filled with the spelling features under study.
- **Model how to hunt for words.** Figure 3.9 is an example of text used by the teacher to model a word hunt. Students in the emergent and letter name stages benefit from word hunts as a group activity directed by the teacher but students in the upper stages learn to do them independently. When studying initial sounds, students can hunt in alphabet books or beginning dictionaries.
- **Check and reflect.** Finish the word hunt by following the same process used in sorting. Read the words in each column to make sure they belong, reflect on their meaning, the spelling pattern, and the number of words found in each category. Encourage students to declare what they have learned about the spelling of these words and how their understanding of why they are spelled the way they are supports them as readers and writers. In many cases, reflecting on the patterns that are most common is especially useful, because this suggests which pattern is most likely to be used when spelling unknown words.

**BRAINSTORMING.** Although word hunts in text can extend the number of examples to consider, students may also supply additional examples through brainstorming. In this case, brainstorming might be considered a word hunt through one's own memory. You may want to ask for more words that rhyme with *cat*, words that describe people ending in *er*, or words that have *spir* as a root. Word hunts in current reading materials are not always productive when it comes to some features. For example, it is unlikely that a word hunt would turn up many words with the Latin root *spir*, but students may be able to brainstorm other words they already know that contain *spir*, such as *spirit*, *inspire*, or *perspire*. Words brainstormed by students can be added to established categories listed on the board, a chart, or a word study notebook.

## Draw and Label/Cut and Paste

**Draw and label** is a good activity at a variety of levels to demonstrate the meanings of words. See the second page of the word study notebook in Figure 3.8 (page 67) for an example. Multiple meanings for words like *block* can be illustrated (for example, as a toy, a section of a neighborhood, and a sports play). Homophones like *bear* and *bare* are made more memorable through drawings, and creating an ongoing class homophone book, as shown in Figure 3.11, is a popular activity. Even advanced spellers in the derivational relations stage enjoy drawing pictures to illustrate the meanings of words like *spectacles*, *spectators*, and *inspector*.

Drawing pictures of additional words that start with a particular sound is a good activity for emergent and letter name–alphabet spellers. Provide paper that is divided into columns headed by a key letter so that students can see where to draw, how big to draw, and how many to draw. It helps to begin by asking students to brainstorm other words before assigning them the drawing task. They might even look through alphabet books for ideas. After drawing pictures under the appropriate key letter, ask students to label the picture–spelling as best they can. Hold students accountable for spelling the initial sound correctly when that is the focus of the sort but encourage them to try the rest of the word as well.

**Cut, paste, and label** is a variation of draw and label that involves looking for pictures instead of written words, making it appropriate for emergent and letter name–alphabetic spellers. Students hunt through old catalogs and magazines for pictures beginning with a certain sound and then cut out the pictures to paste them in the appropriate column.

Many teachers have their students paste words or pictures from a sort into the correct categories as a culminating activity. When using pictures, the students are expected to label them spelling as best they can; the results can be used for assessment. See an example in Figure 3.12.

## Alternative Sorts

Skilled reading requires attention to many aspects of written words simultaneously. Some students have a hard time attending flexibly to multiple features of words, often focusing exclusively on either sound or the visual letter patterns. These students often lack the insight that words represent more than just pronunciations; they have a difficult time grasping the idea

**FIGURE 3.11   Class Homophone Book**

Ava's draw and label for two letter sounds. The correct spelling has been provided by the teacher.

**FIGURE 3.12** Paste and Label the Pictures

that words have both meaning and sound (Cartwright, 2010). To lessen this difficulty, students can be challenged to sort their words a different way as an added activity. For example, they might sort pictures by living and nonliving things, whether you would find them inside or outside, whether you could hold them in your hand, or things people can make or not make. Words intended for a short vowel sort might also be sorted by blends at the beginning or end. Other alternative categories might include parts of speech, or words that show action or objects. You might suggest an alternative sort based on the words in the sort, or students might simply be asked to select as many words as possible that are related to a semantic category (for example, shoes, socks, and slippers are things you wear on your feet). Coming up with categories that include all the words is not necessary. The important thing is to teach children how to think more flexibly about word features and to allow ample time to discuss their insights. This kind of flexible thinking about words will improve spelling, word identification, decoding, and comprehension (Cartwright, 2008). The *Words Their Way* companion books and *WTW Digital* include a number of concept sorts to promote students' flexibility in sorting.

## Games

At the end of each chapter that follows, you will find a number of games and other activities that provide additional practice with words and generalizations for each stage of spelling. Classrooms are busy places and there is not much time for games, but most of these are designed to move quickly in cooperative settings. You can use games during the week to reinforce a particular sort and keep them available over time to provide review. Review sorts can also be stored in manila folders and placed in centers for students to do independently, as shown in the picture on the next page.

Fifth grade students play word study game with assimilated prefixes

## Periodic Spell Checks

We recommend that you assess students' mastery of the spelling feature after completing the sort and other routines designed to extend the lesson over several days. Here are some things to consider:

- For children sorting pictures, the assessment can be the cut-and-paste activity shown in Figure 3.12. Students would be expected to spell the initial sound correctly although they should be encouraged to spell as much as they can. Beginning with the study of word families, students are expected to spell the entire word correctly on spell checks, which can be done using the traditional spelling test format.
- There is no need to call aloud all the words from the sort, especially when you have more than one group. A random sample of ten words will suffice.

- Consider conducting the periodic spell checks as a blind writing sort in which students are expected to group words that share common features in addition to spelling them correctly. One point can be awarded for correct spelling and an additional point for correct categorizing. Bonus points might be awarded to students who can provide a written reflection as to why they grouped the words as they did.

- Call out several words students have not studied to check for transfer. However, be aware that sometimes there is no easy generalization that governs which pattern to use. For example the /ār/ sound introduced by Mrs. Zimmerman is spelled with both *air* (chair) and *are* (care) so she could use a prompt such as, "If you know how to spell *care*, then you can spell *glare*."

- When students are appropriately placed in the word study sequence and have had adequate time working with the words you should see scores of 90% or better on weekly spell checks. If this is not the case, you may want to consider whether students are getting enough practice. You might also re-examine the spelling inventory results or unit spell checks to determine whether students have been properly placed.

Henry sorts independently using a file folder

## Guidelines for Preparing Word Sorts

After identifying spelling stages and grouping students for instruction, as described in Chapter 2, you must decide on what orthographic features to study and prepare collections of words or pictures with appropriate features to contrast. The particular feature you choose to study should be based on what you see students using but confusing on a spelling inventory or in their writing. No matter what the feature is, when preparing word lists for sorting, collect sets of words that offer a focused contrast between at least two sounds, patterns, or meaning categories. Compare *b* to *s*, compare long *o* patterns such as *oa*, *o-e*, and *ow* to short *o* patterns, or compare words with different prefixes. By carefully setting up focused contrasts in a collection of words, you are stacking the deck so that students can make discoveries and form generalizations as they sort. Sample word sort handouts are shown in Figure 3.13.

The spelling features introduced across grade levels in other phonics and spelling programs generally follow the same progression of orthographic features outlined in this textbook (for example, Templeton & Bear, 2011). One difference, however, is that some phonics or spelling programs present only one sound or spelling pattern at a time in lists that offer no contrasts. For example, one unit may be on words ending with the /ch/ phoneme spelled with the *tch* pattern (*patch, itch, fetch,* and so on). Without a focused contrast such as the one shown in Figure 3.4, students are not able to discover that the spelling of the final sound (*tch* or *ch*) is related to the medial vowel sound.

Chapters 4 through 8 have guidelines for features to study at each stage and Appendix D has a collection of sample sorts for different

**FIGURE 3.13   Sample Word Study Handouts**

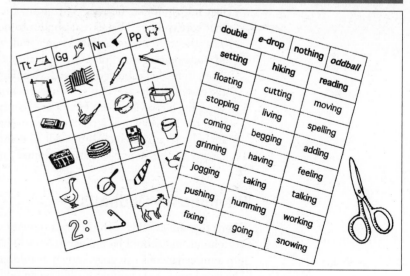

stages that can give you ideas about the kinds of focused contrasts to set up. The *Words Their Way*® companion books provide a complete curriculum for each stage, with prepared sorts and assessments for each unit. (See a list of these and other resources at the end of this chapter.) However, there are also times when you and your students many want to modify existing sorts or create your own. Only you can be sure of what words your students can already read and thus use for sorting. It is unlikely that any prepared collection of sorts or sequence of study will be just right for your students. To create your own sorts, consult the pictures and wordlists in the appendices.

Consider using online dictionaries to search for internal spelling patterns if you need more words. To search for an internal pattern, you usually use an asterisk or a question mark before or after the pattern. Using a question mark as in "??ar?" or "?ar??" would yield five-letter words with *ar* in the middle. Using an asterisk, as in "*ar*," would yield all the words in the dictionary with *ar* in them.

## Making Sorts More or Less Challenging

As you plan your focused contrasts, remember that students in different stages will be more successful with certain factors in mind. The difficulty of sorts can be adjusted in several ways:

*for* **English learners**

- You may use fewer words with English learners if students do not know the vocabulary. In such instances, limit the words you use when introducing a new sort. They may be learning new vocabulary at the same time they are learning to pronounce the words. Gradually introduce a few new words each day so that students can focus on both the sort and the new vocabulary. Concept sorting with these same words gives more exposure to the new vocabulary.
- The more contrasts that a sort provides, the more challenging it will be. If students are young or inexperienced, starting with two categories is a good idea. As they become adept at sorting, step up to three categories and then four. Even after working with four categories or more, however, you may want to go back to fewer categories when you introduce a new unit of study.
- The difficulty of the sort also depends on the contrasts you choose. For example, it is easier to compare the sounds for /b/ and /s/ than for /b/ and /p/ because the letter names *b* and *s* are made in different parts of the mouth. Likewise, it is easier for students to learn the short sound for *i* when it is contrasted with the short sound of *a* or *o* than with *e*. Start with obvious contrasts before moving to finer distinctions.
- The level of difficulty can be increased or decreased by the actual words within each category. For example, adding words with blends and digraphs (*black*, *chest*, *trunk*) to a short vowel sort can make those words more challenging than simple words like *tap* and *set*. Ideally, students should be able to read all the words in a word sort. In reality, however, this may not always be the case. The more unfamiliar words in a given sort, the more difficult that sort will be. This caveat applies to both being able to read the word and knowing what the word means. A fifth grader studying derivational relations will need easier words to study than a tenth grader in that same stage, simply because the fifth grader will have a more limited vocabulary. If there are unfamiliar words in a sort, try to place them toward the end of the deck so that known words are the first to be sorted. Unfamiliar words can be set aside, but revisit them later and encourage your students to compare the new spelling with the known words already sorted in the columns to arrive at a pronunciation.
- Including a miscellaneous or oddball column with "exception" words that do not fit the targeted letter–sound or pattern feature can also increase the difficulty of a sort.

## Planning for Oddballs

Words that are at odds with the consistencies within each category will inevitably turn up in word hunts and should be deliberately included in teacher-developed sorts. These words go into a miscellaneous category known as **oddballs**, rather than exceptions or irregular words. The word *work*, for example, would be an oddball in a sort with other *r*-influenced *o* words like *fork*, *corn*, and *sport*, but it fits a small—but regular—category of words that start with *wor*: *world*, *worm*, *worse*, and *word*. Oddballs are sometimes high-frequency words such as *have*, *said*, *was*, and *again*. Such words become memorable from repeated usage but are also memorable because they are odd. They stand out in the crowd. Such words should be included in the sorts you prepare, but not too many. One to three oddballs per sort are plenty, so that they do not overshadow the regularity you want students to discover.

The oddball category is also where students may place words if they are simply not sure about the sound they hear in the word. This often happens when students say words differently due to dialectical or regional pronunciations that vary from the "standard" pronunciation. For example, one student in Wise County, Virginia, pronounced the word *vein* as *vine* and was correct in placing *vein* in the oddball column as opposed to the long *a* group. To this student, the word *vein* was a long *i*. Sometimes students detect subtle variations that adults may miss. Students often put words like *mail* and *sail* in a different sound category than *maid*, *wait*, and *paid*, because the long *a* sound is slightly different before the letters *r* and *l*. *Mail* may sound more like /mā-ul/. The important thing is to discuss students' reasoning for placing words in the oddball category and to explore their reasoning.

## Using Word Study Notebooks

Word study notebooks provide a built-in, orderly record of the word study activities discussed previously and also provide a place to apply word study to writing and reading vocabulary. Many teachers rely on these student word study notebooks to organize the sequence of word study activities across the week (see Chapter 9). Students record the sorts for each week in their word study notebook and add to the categories as other words are found during word hunts and brainstorms. Students write generalizations and practice writing a few of the words into sentences. Common activities that students conduct in the word study notebook include:

**Enhanced eText**
**Video Example 3.5**
In this video, a fifth grade teacher discusses her students' use of word study notebooks throughout the week.

- **Writing sorts.** Students record the words into the same categories developed during hands-on sorting using the same key words or headers.
- **Written reflection.** Ask students to write a reflection that summarizes the generalization or the big idea about each word sort.
- **Draw and label.** Even older students enjoy the opportunity to illustrate words with simple drawings that reveal their meanings. Select five to ten words to draw and label. Ask students to illustrate homophones like *bear* and *bare* and the multiple meanings of homonyms like *park* or *yard*.
- **Word operations.** Students change a letter (or letters) of a selected word to make new words. This is a good way to encourage transfer.
- **Select five words to use in sentences.** Meaning and usage are important as students begin to study homophones, inflected words (*ride*, *rides*, *riding*), and roots and suffixes. Challenge students to use two or more words from their sort, especially derivationally related words. Words can be made into sentences such as "I will need new *spectacles* to *inspect* the *spectacular* new *specimen*" (González-Fernández & Schmitt, 2017; Schmitt, 2014; 2012).
- **Record words from word hunts.** Students add new words from their reading and writing to the written sorts in their notebooks.
- **Record times from speed sorts.** When students are timed early in the week and then again after repeated sorting, they are likely to show improvement.
- **Record a blind writing sort.** Led by a partner or the teacher, a blind writing sort is a good preparation for a final spelling assessment.

Many teachers grade the word study notebooks as part of an overall spelling grade. Figure 3.14 is an example of the kinds of expectations and grading criteria used by Kathy Gankse when she taught fourth grade. This chart can be reproduced and pasted inside the cover of the notebook. Classroom and homework assignments can be completed in the word study notebook. You may want to distinguish

**FIGURE 3.14   Expectations for Word Study Notebooks**

**Word Study Notebooks**

Weekly activities for this WS notebook include:
1. Record your Sort and Reflection
2. Draw and label six words
3. Make up sentences with five words
4. Record words from Word Hunt
5. Record times for Speed Sorts

You are expected to:
1. Use correct spelling of assigned words
2. Use complete sentences
3. Use your best handwriting
4. Make good use of word study time

You will be evaluated in this manner:
★ Excellent work
✓ Good work but could be improved
R You need to redo this assignment

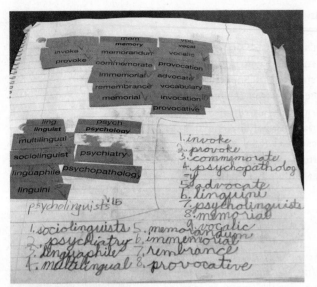

A sixth grader's word study notebook

required activities, such as recording the sort, and choice activities, such as draw and label. There is no need to do each activity every week and some are more valuable at times than others. Upon completing the study of the generalization underlying the categories, students can paste or write the words in their word study notebooks. Other ideas for word study notebooks are noted in the chapters that follow.

# Linking Word Study to Reading, Writing, and the Language Arts Curriculum

Word study reveals how our writing system reflects speech sounds and word meanings. As such, orthographic knowledge—knowledge of how words are spelled—is central to both reading and writing. Because of the essential role spelling plays in becoming fully literate, it is important to intentionally link the insights students gain during word study to their reading and writing, and even to their study of grammar. Students can return again and again to trade books they have already read to analyze the reading vocabulary. Poetry lessons might begin with reference to a word study lesson on syllable stress. In a writing lesson, students might discuss comparative adjectives from a previous word study lesson that focused on words ending in *er*. During a lesson on parts of speech, students can be asked to sort their week's spelling words into categories of nouns, verbs, and adjectives.

The orthographic features that students learn during word study can also be applied to decoding strategies during reading and to spelling strategies during writing. If students get stuck on a word while reading, prompt them with one of the appropriate features from the word study lesson. For example, remind them to look for the vowel pattern or to break a word into syllables. Point out the similarity between the orthographic features in a particular word and the spelling features they have been sorting. The more frequently you make such connections between word study and decoding strategies, the more often your students will use them. This is equally true for writing—many teachers use the features students are categorizing during word study for targeted proofreading., as described later.

Teachers and parents often complain that students get perfect scores on their spelling tests only to misspell those same words in their writing assignments the following week. To ensure transfer of the big ideas gained during word study, students must be engaged in activities that specifically require them to apply their growing word knowledge through wide reading and writing. Using the following techniques can promote further connections.

## Apply Spelling Generalizations to Read New Words

Words that students cannot read when a sort is first introduced can be revisited after the reflection to see if they can now apply the generalization. Likewise, display other words that have the same spelling features so that students can apply what they have been learning to reading additional words that were not included in the sort. For example, after working with the *r*-influenced vowels that Mrs. Zimmerman had her students sort, she might ask students to read the words *flare, blare, snare, flair,* and *lair*. These new words might be presented in sentences such as, "The cougar retreated to its lair."

## Apply to Writing

You might try the same thing with spelling unfamiliar words. Ask students to attempt writing the words *start, sharp,* or *smart*. In the case of the /âr/ sound there are two possible spellings, so begin with a clue such as, "You know how to spell *care*, so how would you spell *dare*?" Another way to link word study to writing is through dictated or silly sentences. Select several words from the weekly word sort and dictate a sentence for the student to write. For example, following an *at* and *an* rhyming family word sort, letter–name spellers might be asked to write, "*The fat cat sat in the tan van*" (Johnston, Invernizzi, Juel, & Lewis-Wagner, 2009). Or, following a sort examining how vowel sounds are altered when a suffix is added, derivational spellers might be asked to write, "*The competitor competed in the competition.*"

Student writes a sentence using words that start with consonant digraphs

## Promote Strategies for Independent Problem Solving

Students in the earliest stages of developmental word knowledge do not have a large enough repertoire of word knowledge to support independent writing to their satisfaction. They may want to rely on copying words or on asking an adult to tell them how to spell the words as they try to write them. Giving into these dependencies short changes the opportunity to learn strategies for independent problem solving and self-efficacy. Instead of doing the work for the student, encourage them to figure things out for themselves. A resource they might use is a **soundboard**—a one-page reference for letter–sound features (beginning consonants, digraphs, blends, and vowels) that pairs a key picture with each sound and letter. When beginners get stuck on how to write a sound, encourage them to refer to their soundboard to find the proper letter–sound match.

Examples of soundboards may be found in Appendix C. Place a copy of the appropriate sound board in each child's writing folder, as described in Activity 5.18 on p. 196.

## Brainstorm Relatives to Widen the Net

To link the big ideas behind the word study lesson to other words students may know, you might engage them in brainstorming lists of friends and relatives. We call this, *making relations among related relatives!* Provide a word root such as *divide* and ask students to write related words like *division, divisive, divisor,* or *dividend.* Interesting discussions about students' thinking as they spelled these related words are likely to follow, including lots of talk about the meaning as well as about sound and spelling patterns.

## Use Cover and Connect

Use the cover and connect strategy to link word study to decoding. Write a word on the board and demonstrate how to cover up word parts, saying the remaining portion and then connecting that segment with the rest of the word when it is uncovered (O'Connor, 2007). The parts that are covered vary according to developmental stage of word knowledge. For letter name–alphabetic spellers, consonant digraphs, consonant blends, or the short-vowel rhyming family can be covered and then connected (for example, *fl-at*). For within word pattern spellers, long-vowel patterns can be covered and connected to the remaining consonant blends or digraphs (for example, *sn-ake*). For syllables and affixes spellers, prefixes and suffixes can be covered and connected to base words, or syllables can be covered and connected one to the next (for example, *re-read-ing; in-ter-est-ing*). When students encounter a word they don't know in their reading, they can be prompted to use this cover and connect strategy for decoding.

## Proofread for Targeted Spelling Features

Although students might be encouraged to spell as best they can when they compose rough drafts, daily journal entries, or observation notes for a science experiment, there are times when writing products should be spelled as accurately as possible, especially in the upper grades. Proofreading involves identifying misspelled words, so it is not an easy task for younger students who are still spelling many words incorrectly. Proofreading needs to be handled judiciously in the

**TABLE 3.3** Writing Word Hunt/Editing Chart

| Target | oi | oy | ow | ou |
|---|---|---|---|---|
| Features (write two to four target features across the columns) | BOIL | BOY | HOW | SOUND |
| Words I spelled correctly | SPOIL FOIL NOISE | TOY | HOW | GROUND |
| Words I corrected | TINFOIL | | CLOWN DROWSY CHOWDER | |

*Source:* Adapted from Hayes, L., & Flanigan, K. (2014). *Developing word recognition,* p. 217. Guilford Publications.

lower grades and can be adjusted for students' development. After identification, the errors need to be corrected using a variety of spelling strategies (Turbil, 2000). Students should be explicitly taught how to execute this complex skill, not simply told to proofread. You can use your own or a student's writing samples (with permission) that contain errors to model the ideas below. Subsequent chapters have additional information about what spelling strategies and resources are appropriate for each stage, including the development of dictionary skills. Table 3.3 shows an example of a targeting proofreading sheet for students who had been studying the effect of position on the spelling of the /oy/ and /ow/ sounds words like *boil, toy, how,* and *sound.* Other guidelines for proofreading for spelling errors with intermediate students are listed in the box below.

## Allow Students to Write "As Best They Can"

**Invented spelling**, or spelling "as best you can," frees students to write even before they can read during the emergent stage, and they should be free to make spelling approximations when writing rough drafts at all levels. Most state standards encourage this and refer to this process as "phonetic spelling." Invented spelling, or as we like to call it, **developmental spelling**, also offers you

**TEACHING TIPS**

### Proofreading Tips with Intermediate Students

- Focus only on spelling. Don't expect students to edit for punctuation, spelling, and word choice all at the same time. Have students re-read with just spelling in mind as one step of the editing process.

- Reread carefully for errors. Proofreading one's own work is often hard because it is so familiar that we may not pay careful attention to the printed words. The key is to focus attention on spelling, and this can be done by reading aloud, pointing to each word with a pencil, reading each line backward, or getting someone else to read it for you, such as an assigned editing buddy. Waiting a few days to reread also seems to help.

- Give students tools such as colored pencils in blue or green (rather than red) to use for correcting, circling, or underling misspelled words. This way you can monitor their corrections and even talk with them about the strategies they used.

- Keep the task manageable. You might assign students to find and correct a certain number of errors so that they do not feel overwhelmed. Five might be reasonable for students who are still misspelling a large percentage. Or you might ask students to look for errors related to the feature they are currently studying, such as long vowels or inflected endings.

- Teach students to use resources such as a word wall or dictionaries to correct misspellings. A simple spelling dictionary is a list of words arranged alphabetically and may be only a few pages long. This is much easier to use as it does not have definitions or other information typically found in a dictionary.

- Teach students to use spellcheck as part of a word processing application.

- Sometimes we want a final draft to be absolutely perfect, especially if it will be published in a classroom collection, school newspaper, or other permanent place. This is the point at which teachers, parents, or other reliable sources should serve as the final copyeditor.

diagnostic information about what students know and what they need to learn. But that does not mean that you do not hold students accountable for accurate spelling. Knowing where students are in terms of development level and considering which word features they have studied enables you to set reasonable expectations for accuracy and editing. For example, you can expect third-grade students in the within word pattern stage to spell words like *jet*, *flip*, and *must*, but expecting them to handle multisyllabic words like *leprechaun* or *celebration* is unreasonable. Just as students are gradually held more and more accountable for conventions of writing such as commas and semicolons, so, too, are they gradually held more accountable for spelling accuracy.

A study by Clarke (1988) found that first graders who were encouraged to use developmental spellings wrote more and could spell as well at the end of the year as first graders who had been told how to spell the words before writing. A comprehensive review of research on spelling instruction (Graham & Santangelo, 2014) also underscored the importance of encouraging students to apply their knowledge of letter–sound relationships in their writing. This suggests that students are not marred by their own invented developmental spellings, nor do they persevere with errors over time. However, unless you communicate that correct spelling is valued, students may develop careless habits.

Writing as "best they can"

Many teachers wonder when they should make the shift from allowing students to write in invented developmental spelling to demanding correctness. The answer is "from the start." You must hold students accountable for what they have been taught; what they have not been taught can be politely ignored. For example, if a student has been taught consonant sound-to-letter correspondences, you would expect the student to spell those sounds correctly, as in PGS LK MD (*Pigs like mud*). However, if the student has not yet been taught the short vowel sounds needed in *pigs* and *mud*, these attempts should be allowed to stand as is. Because the sequence for phonics and spelling instruction is cumulative and progresses hierarchically from easier features such as individual letter sounds to harder features such as Latin-derived *tion*, *sion*, and *cian* endings, there will always be some features that have not yet been taught. Thus, students (and adults) will always invent a spelling for what they do not yet know. Use the scope and sequence of spelling features in Table 3.4 to determine

**Enhanced eText**
**Video Example 3.6**
See developmental spelling, writing and proofreading in action in a primary classroom.

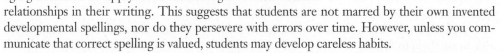

**TABLE 3.4** **Scope and Sequence of Spelling Features**

| Letter Name–Alphabetic | Within Word Pattern | Syllables & Affixes | Derivational Relations |
|---|---|---|---|
| 1. Beginning consonants | 8. CVCe long vowel patterns | 15. Inflectional endings: plural and past tense | 22. Sounded-silent spelling/meaning connections |
| 2. Ending consonants | 9. Other common long vowel patterns | 16. Consonant doubling, e-drop, & changing the *y* to *i* | 23. Consonant alternations in derivationally related pairs |
| 3. Short vowels | 10. Less common long vowel patterns | 17. Open & closed syllable patterns | 24. Greek roots |
| 4. Consonant digraphs | 11. Consonant-influenced vowels (*r,l,w*) | 18. Vowel patterns in accented syllables | 25. Latin roots |
| 5. Consonant blends | 12. Diphthongs & other vowel sounds that are neither long nor short | 19. Unaccented Final Syllables | 26. Predictable changes in derivationally related words |
| 6. Preconsonantal Nasals | 13. Complex consonant clusters | 20. Common prefixes | 27. Advanced suffixes |
| 8. R and L influenced CVCC words | 14. Homophones | 21. Common suffixes | 28. Absorbed or assimilated prefixes |

*Note:* There is an overlap in instruction across contiguous features.

where your students are in their development. They should be held accountable for everything earlier, but they shouldn't be penalized for what they haven't yet been taught or learned. So, if a student was learning feature 10, less common vowel patterns, she would be expected to spell features 1–9 correctly in her writing; all features 10 and above would be allowed to be spelled as "best she can."

# Caveats Regarding Tradition

## Traditional Spelling Activities

Many long-standing activities are associated with spelling that teachers often assign their students, such as writing words five times, listing them in alphabetical order, and copying definitions from the dictionary. Assignments like these do not fulfill the purpose of spelling instruction, which is not only to learn the spellings of particular words, but also to understand generalizations about the spelling system itself and to cultivate a curiosity about words. Writing a word five times is a rote, meaningless, and ineffective activity (Templeton & Morris, 2000), whereas writing words into categories requires recognizing common spelling features and using judgment and critical thinking. Writing words in alphabetical order may teach alphabetization, but it will not teach anything about spelling patterns. (Alphabetizing words might be assigned occasionally as a separate dictionary skill, but students will be more successful at it when they can first sort their word cards into alphabetical order before writing them.)

Students do need to associate meanings with the words they are studying so it is reasonable to ask them to discuss or look up the meanings of a few words they do not know or to find additional meanings for words. However, asking students to write out the definitions of long lists of words whose meanings they already know is boring and not likely to encourage dictionary use or a curiosity about words.

Writing words in sentences can also be overdone. You might ask students to choose 5 words (out of 20 to 25) each week to write sentences in their word study notebooks. For example, students like the challenge of using two or more in the same sentence. This is a more reasonable assignment than writing 20 isolated sentences with the weekly spelling list. Many teachers employ sentence writing to also work on handwriting, punctuation, and grammar (see the expectations in Figure 3.14 on page 75). Writing sentences is also more useful for some features than others. For example, sentences will help students show that they understand homophones or the tenses of verb forms when studying inflectional endings such as *ed* and *ing*. Writing words in short phrases also helps illustrate the multiple meanings of words; consider the following phrase collection for the word *condition: mint condition, pre-existing condition, good condition, air condition, medical condition*, etc.

Be wary of other traditional assignments that take up time and may even be fun but have little value in teaching children about spelling. Activities such as word searches and acrostics may keep students busy, but they impart little or no information about the English spelling system. Although it is exciting to see the interest generated for the yearly spelling bee broadcast on national television, it is still the case that spelling bees reward children who are already good spellers and quickly eliminate the children who need practice the most.

Word study can be fun, but make good use of the time available and do not overdo it. Remember that word study activities should be short in duration so that students can devote most of their attention and time to reading and writing for meaningful purposes.

| The following may be entertaining but will not improve spelling: | Be wary of overdoing the following: |
|---|---|
| • Word searches | • Writing words five times |
| • Acrostics | • Writing words in ABC order |
| • Rainbow writing | • Copying dictionary definitions of long lists of words |
| | • Using long lists of words in sentences |

## Word Walls

Traditional word walls display a relatively small set of words and can supplement systematic developmental word study, but just having words displayed on a wall won't teach your students how to spell. Word walls as originally conceived by Pat Cunningham (2000, 2013) are a display of alphabetically ordered, high-utility words that grows cumulatively across the school year. We provide a list of high-frequency words on page 467 but select words based on your students' needs. Cunningham recommends that five words needed for reading and writing be added each week, and students should engage in activities that help secure those words in memory—chanting the letters, writing the words several times, and playing games such as giving clues about the beginning sound and a rhyming word (for example, what word starts with *o* and rhymes with *mother*?). If you want to hold students responsible for using the word wall, then you need to add words gradually, plan quick daily activities, model using it, and review the wall regularly. We recommend that word walls for beginning readers provide separate column headers for consonant digraphs, like CH for *chick*, and SH for *shoe*, as opposed to including the words under C or S alone.

Word walls should not look the same at all grade levels. In kindergarten, they should begin with student's names, and then several high-frequency words might be added each week such as *the*, *can*, and *like* —words that students often use in their writing and see in their reading. By second grade, students should have mastered many of the most common words, but other words such as *because*, or homophones such as *their*, *there*, and *they're*, are good candidates for a word wall. You can easily find out which words students have already mastered by asking them to spell them. The list in Appendix F has high-frequency words ordered by the first hundred, second hundred, and third hundred.

**Enhanced eText**
**Video Example 3.7**
In this video, first graders learn how to use clues to find words on the word wall and spell them from memory.

## Word Displays

Word displays call attention to the richness and power of a versatile vocabulary and provide a ready reference for writing. Typically, thematic words are displayed in lists or groups on bulletin boards but there are other more creative options that serve various purposes. Charts of word families, syllable types, Latin roots, content vocabulary, word hunt results, and other word displays posted around the room announce to students, parents, and visitors that words are valued and celebrated. See the box below for more ideas such as illustrating lists of collective nouns (a *gaggle of geese*, *a batch of brownies*), idioms (*at the drop of a hat*; *pulling your leg*, and so on), or homophones (for example *pair*, *pare*, *mail*, *male*). Eponyms, or words associated with people's names, such as *pasteurization* (form Louis Pasteur) are a great way to build interest in vocabulary related to units of study. Students can create their own illustrated displays of alliteration (*big bad Bruce*) or palindromes (*mom*, *level*, *radar*).

# Word Displays

- Spelling demons (relevant, unparalleled)
- Onomatopoeia words (boo-hoo, cockadoodledoo)
- Sophisticated synonyms (tell=explain, enumerate, explicate, justify, illustrate)
- Oxymorons (plastic silverware)
- Multiple meanings (bat, run, draw)
- Brand names that now represent a generic product (Kleenex for tissue)
- Homophones and homographs (due/dew, wind/wind)
- Collective nouns (batch of brownies, gaggle of geese)

- Acronyms (LASER, SCUBA)
- Eponyms (Louis Pasteur—pasteurization)
- Spanish–English cognates (content—contento)
- Palindromes (mom)
- Idioms (pulling your leg)
- Puns (an artist who could really draw a crowd)
- Similes (smiling like an angel)
- Alliteration (big bad Bruce)
- Collection of phrases using key vocabulary
- Word webs of polysemous words

Involving students as much as possible in the creation of such word displays is important for the displays to be useful and meaningful. For example, in the activity *Said is Dead*, students help brainstorm lists of words (for example, *shouted, jeered, whispered, lisped*) to use in their writing instead of that overworked verb (*said*). Be mindful of referring to such displays on a regular basis if you want students to benefit from them. Continue to add to such lists to keep them fresh in students' minds and when you add a new word, go back over the list of previous words.

# Principles of Word Study Instruction

A number of basic principles guide the kind of word study described in *Words Their Way*® (you were introduced to some of these at the beginning of the chapter as they related to Mrs. Zimmerman's class). Many of these principles set word study apart from other approaches to the teaching of phonics, spelling, or vocabulary.

## 1. Look for What Students Use but Confuse

Students cannot learn things they do not already know something about. This is the underlying principle of Vygotsky's (1962) zone of proximal development (ZPD) and the motivating force behind the assessment described in Chapter 2. By analyzing invented developmental spellings, a ZPD may be identified and instruction can be planned to address features the students are using but confusing instead of those they totally neglect (Invernizzi et al., 1994). Take your cue from the students to teach developmentally.

## 2. A Step Backward Is a Step Forward

After you have identified students' stages of developmental word knowledge and the orthographic features under negotiation, take a step backward and build a firm foundation. Then, in setting up your categories, contrast something new with something that is already known. It is important to begin word study activities where students will experience success. For example, students in the within word pattern stage who are ready to examine long vowel patterns begin by sorting words by short vowels sounds, which are familiar, and long vowel sounds, which may be introduced for the first time. Then they move quickly to sorting by pattern. A step backward is the first step forward in word study instruction.

**FIGURE 3.15** Doubling Sort: Comparing Words That "Do" with Words That Don't"

| | |
|---|---|
| hopping | raining |
| planning | cleaning |
| skipping | nailing |
| batting | reading |
| hugging | sleeping |
| | peeling |
| | feeling |

## 3. Use Words Students Can Read

Analyzing words students can already pronounce is much easier to do than on ones they cannot pronounce. Known words come from any and all sources that students can read: language experience stories, recent readings from texts, poems, and phonics readers. As much as possible, choose words to sort that students can read out of context. Put any aside they cannot read to examine later.

## 4. Compare Words That "Do" with Words that "Don't"

To learn what a Chesapeake Bay retriever looks like, you have to see a poodle or a bulldog, not another Chesapeake Bay retriever. What something *is* is also defined by what it is *not*; contrasts are essential to students' building of categories. Students' spelling errors suggest what focused contrasts will help them sort out their confusions. For example, a student who is spelling *stopping* as STOPING will benefit from a sort in which words with consonants that are doubled before adding *-ing* are contrasted with those that do not take doubled letters, as in Figure 3.15.

## 5. Begin with Obvious Contrasts

When students start studying a new feature, choose key words or pictures that are distinctive. For example, when students first examine initial consonants, do not begin by contrasting *m* with *n*, which are both nasals and visually similar. It is better to begin by contrasting *m* with something totally different at first—*s*, for example—before working toward finer distinctions as these categorizations become quite automatic. Move from general, gross differences to more specific discriminations.

## 6. Sort by Sound and Pattern

Students examine words by how they sound and how they are spelled. Both sound and visual patterns are part of students' orthographic knowledge. Too often, students focus on visual patterns at the expense of how words are alike in sound. The following sort illustrates the way students move from a sound sort (by hard and soft *g*) to a visual pattern sort (by final *dge*, *ge*, and *g*). See what you can discover from this sort. (Hint: Pay attention to the vowel sounds.)

**First Sort by Sound of g**

| Soft | Hard |
|------|------|
| edge | bag |
| cage | twig |
| huge | slug |
| judge | drug |
| stage | leg |
| badge | flag |
| page | |
| lodge | |

**Second Sort by Pattern**

| dge | ge | g |
|-----|-----|-----|
| edge | cage | bag |
| judge | huge | twig |
| badge | stage | slug |
| lodge | page | flag |
| | | drug |
| | | leg |

## 7. Don't Hide Exceptions

Exceptions arise when students make generalizations. Do not hide these exceptions. By placing so-called irregular words in a miscellaneous or oddball category, new categories of consistency sometimes emerge. For example, in looking at long vowel patterns, students find exceptions like *give*, *have*, and *love*, yet it is no coincidence that they all have a *ve*. They form a small but consistent pattern of their own. True exceptions do occur (for example, *was*, *women*, *laugh*) and become memorable by virtue of their rarity.

## 8. Avoid Rules

Rules with many exceptions are disheartening and teach students nothing. They may have heard the long vowel rule, "When two vowels go walking, the first one does the talking," but this rule does not apply in phonetically regular words like *boot* or *soil*. Learning about English spelling requires students to consider sound and pattern simultaneously to discover consistencies in the orthography. This requires both reflection and continued practice. Students discover consistencies and make generalizations for themselves. Your job is to stack the deck and structure the focused contrasts to make these consistencies explicit and to instill in students the habit of looking at words, asking questions, and searching for order. Rules are useful mnemonics if you already understand the underlying concepts at work. They are the icing on the cake of knowledge. But memorizing rules is not the way students make sense of how words work. Rules are no substitute for experience.

## 9. Work for Fluency

Accuracy in sorting is not enough—accuracy *and* ease are the ultimate indicators of mastery. Acquiring automaticity in sorting and recognizing orthographic patterns leads to the fluency necessary for proficient reading and writing. Your students will move from hesitancy to fluency in their sorting. Keep sorting until they do.

## 10. Encourage and Participate in Student Talk

Picture sorts and word sorts are designed to help students learn how the spellings and word structures reflect spoken language and meaning. It's not just the sorting that accomplishes these goals, however. It's the student talk about their observations about the focused contrasts that helps students form generalizations.

## 11. Return to Meaningful Texts

After sorting, return to meaningful texts to hunt for other examples to add to the sorts. These hunts extend students' analysis to other words and more difficult vocabulary. For example, after sorting one-syllable words into categories labeled *cat*, *drain*, and *snake*, a student added *tadpole*, *complain*, and *relate*. Through a simple word hunt, this child extended the pattern-to-sound consistency in one-syllable words to stressed syllables in two-syllable words. Intentionally linking the features explored during word study to the words that students are reading and writing ensures the application of word knowledge in contexts that matter.

# Teaching Is Not Telling

These principles of word study boil down to one golden rule of word study instruction: *Teaching Is Not Telling* (James, 1958). In word study, students examine, manipulate, and categorize words by focused contrasts pertaining to sound, pattern, and meaning. For this to happen, you must create a systematic program of word study, guided by an informed interpretation of spelling errors and other literacy behaviors. This is a teacher-directed, student-centered approach to vocabulary growth and spelling development.

The next five chapters will show you exactly how to provide effective word study instruction for students at different stages of development. Chapter 9 describes various ways of managing word study in the primary, elementary, and secondary classroom.

# RESOURCES FOR IMPLEMENTING WORD STUDY *in Your Classroom*

Throughout this text you will see references to *WTW Digital®*, which includes interactive spelling assessments, interactive sorts, and games. The following companion books offer additional resources for teachers.

**Words Their Way Digital® (WTW Digital)**

**Words Their Way Digital®**, the website that accompanies this text, prepares you for word study by examining successful classroom instruction—from assessment to organization to implementation across grade levels. Find interactive sorts, digital assessments, games, and more.

***Words Their Way*® *with English Learners: Word Study for Phonics, Vocabulary, and Spelling*, Second Edition, by L. Helman, D. R. Bear, S. Templeton, M. Invernizzi, and F. Johnston**

Based on the same research and developmental model, this companion volume focuses on using word study to enhance literacy learning for English learners.

***Words Their Way*® *for PreK–K Learners* by F. Johnston, M. Invernizzi, L. Helman, D. Bear, and S. Templeton**

The literacy diet for Pre-K and K is presented in detail in separate chapters. Foundations of word study for each aspect are presented with ample activities for the classroom. The website includes activities and materials as well as videos for emergent and letter–name word study.

***Words Their Way*® *with Struggling Readers: Word Study for Reading, Vocabulary and Spelling Instruction, Grades 4–12*, by K. Flanigan, L. Hayes, S. Templeton, D. R. Bear, M. Invernizzi, and F. Johnston**

The needs of struggling readers in grades 4 to 8 are discussed with an emphasis on developmental instruction and presentation of reading and vocabulary activities for success in disciplinary studies. Numerous schedules for classroom organization are presented.

*Vocabulary Their Way: Word Study with Middle and Secondary Students,* Second Edition, by S. Templeton, D. R. Bear, M. Invernizzi, F. Johnston, K. Flanigan, D. Townsend, L. Helman, and L. Hayes

Supports discipline-specific instruction in the middle and secondary grades and addresses context-based instruction, word-specific instruction, and generative vocabulary/morphology instruction. Subject matter areas include English Language Arts, Social Studies, Mathematics, Science, and Art/Music/Physical Education/Career and Technical Education.

Each of the following stage-specific companion volumes provides reproducible sorts and unit assessments and progress monitoring forms. You'll find extensive background notes about the features of study and step-by-step directions on how to guide the sorting lesson. Organizational tips and follow-up activities extend lessons through weekly routines.

***Words Their Way*®: *Letter and Picture Sorts for Emergent Spellers*, (2018, Third Edition) by D. R. Bear, M. Invernizzi, F. Johnston, and S. Templeton**

Teachers in pre-K through grade 1 will find ready-made sorts as well as rhymes and jingles for emergent readers.

***Words Their Way*®: *Word Sorts for Letter Name–Alphabetic Spellers*, (2018, Third Edition), by F. Johnston, D. R. Bear, M. Invernizzi, and S. Templeton**

Primarily for students in kindergarten through grade 2, the 60 blackline masters include picture sorts for beginning consonants, digraphs and blends, word families (with pictures and words,) and word sorts for short vowels.

***Words Their Way*®: *Word Sorts for Within Word Pattern Spellers*, (2018, Third Edition), by M. Invernizzi, F. Johnston, D. R. Bear, and S. Templeton**

Teachers of grades 1 through 4 will find 59 reproducible word sorts that cover the many vowel patterns as well as other features such as complex consonants.

***Words Their Way*®: *Word Sorts for Syllables and Affixes Spellers*, (2018, Third Edition) by F. Johnston, M. Invernizzi, D. R. Bear, and S. Templeton**

This text includes 58 sorts for syllables and affixes spellers in grades 3 to 8. Prefixes and suffixes are introduced.

***Words Their Way*®: *Word Sorts for Derivational Relations Spellers*, (2018, Third Edition), by S. Templeton, F. Johnston, D. R. Bear, and M. Invernizzi**

Teachers of grades 5 to 12 will find 65 upper-level word sorts that help students build their vocabulary as well as spelling skills. Lots of additional words are provided to modify or create new sorts.

***Words Their Way*®: *Emergent Sorts for Spanish-Speaking English Learners.* By Helman, L., Bear, D. R., Invernizzi, M., Templeton, S., Johnston, F. (2009).**

***Words Their Way*® *Letter Name-Alphabetic Sorts for Spanish-Speaking English Learners.* By Helman, L., Bear, D. R., Invernizzi, M., Templeton, S., Johnston, F.**

***Words Their Way*®: *Within Word Pattern Sorts for Spanish-Speaking English Learners.* By Helman, L., Bear, D. R., Invernizzi, M., Templeton, S., & Johnston, F. (2014).**

Spanish speakers learning to read English benefit from word study that clarifies some of the contrasts between English and Spanish spelling. These supplements contain sorts and games with directions and assessments that explore the first three stages of English spelling development.

***Words Their Way*® *for Parents, Tutors, and School Volunteers* (2018) by Picard, M, Meadows, A. Invernizzi, M. Johnston, F, & Bear, D.R.**

Parents, tutors and school volunteers may be asked to participate in word study without any background knowledge of what word study is. This friendly book provides straightforward answers and practical advice such as "sort support" and "let's talk about it" that provides an ideal companion to the core text.

# chapter 4

# Word Study for the Emergent Stage

**Words THEIR WAY** *WTW Digital* is a new online tool that accompanies this core text, and it was designed to help you implement word study in an engaging and interactive way. Resources for this chapter include:

- **9 interactive sorts** that allow students to engage with word study in a digital environment.

- **3 word study games** in a printable format that present fun activities for students.

An access code for *WTW Digital* is included with each new copy of package ISBN: 9780135174623. Visit www.wtwdigital.pearson.com to get started.

The emergent stage is the beginning of a lifetime of learning about written language. This chapter describes literacy development during a period in which young children imitate and experiment with the forms and functions of print: directionality, the distinctive features of print, the predictability of text, and how all of these relate to oral language. Emergent children do not read or spell conventionally, and they score 0 on spelling inventories like those in Chapter 2 because they have only very tenuous understandings of how units of speech and units of print are related. Nevertheless, children are developing remarkable insights into written language, and with the help of caregivers and teachers they learn a great deal. Before we go into a thorough description of the emergent stage, let's visit a kindergarten classroom.

During a unit about pets, Ms. Regina Smith shares a big book, *Cat on the Mat*, by Brian Wildsmith. This simple patterned book opens with a cat sitting contentedly on a mat, but on each subsequent page bigger and bigger animals join as the cat becomes increasingly agitated. When an elephant joins, the cat hisses and all the animals run away. Ms. Smith introduces the book by pointing to the cover and asking, "Where is the cat?" Several children sing out, "on the rug." Then she says, "Let's look at the title here." As she reads she point to each word. "It says, Cat on the . . ." and she pauses while several children say, "on the rug." "Hmmm," says Ms. Smith. "The picture does look like a rug but this word (pointing to *Mat*) starts with *M* and *r-r-r-r*ug would start with *R*. What else could this be? I will give you a clue: It rhymes with cat. Listen, *Cat* on the *Mmmmmat*. We use mats at rest time, don't we?"

After asking the children what they think the book will be about she says, "Let's read and find out what happens." She points to the words in the single sentence for each two-page spread and by the third sentence the children are catching on to the repetitive pattern and saying the name of the new animal based on the illustrations. She pauses before the elephant appears and asks for predictions about what the next animal might be and why they think it might be that animal. On a second reading the children can all join in and "read" along chorally. Ms. Smith takes the time to ask about how the cat is feeling about sharing the mat with so many animals. The children suggest *mad* but she introduces several new vocabulary words (*annoyed, angry*, and *furious*) and uses them to describe the cat's growing discontentment leading up to the explosive hiss. She uses the cognate *furioso* as she points to the picture to bring her Spanish-speaking children into the discussion.

In this fashion, Ms. Smith shares a predictable book with her children that they can easily memorize and read along with her. We can see how she draws her students' attention to letters and sounds and models pointing to words as she reads. She also finds an opportunity to introduce new vocabulary. After the children enjoy the big book version, she plans a number of follow-up activities to further develop emergent literacy skills.

On the next day the story is re-read and the cat's feelings are described again with a reveiw of the newvocabulary words. Ms. Smith defines them. For example, *annoyed* is when you are feeling unhappy and bothered. She asks the children what would make them feel annoyed. "Would you feel annoyed getting the birthday present you've

Pointing with *Cat on the Mat*

always wanted?" "Would you feel annoyed if someone teased you? Can you show me how your face would look?" Discussions like these continue over several days so the children hear and use the words in different ways.

Ms. Smith has created a chart with the lines of patterned text. She has also written them on sentence strips and placed them in order in a pocket chart. After the children have read the sentences chorally on the chart, Ms. Smith passes out the strips. As a group they put the sentences back in order by comparing them to the chart. Then Ms. Smith calls on volunteers to point as they read sentences from the pocket chart and she observes carefully to see which children are beginning to accurately track the words as they recite. On another day, word cards for the animals are held up one by one as volunteers come up to match the words to the chart or sentence strips. When Abby matches *cat* to *cow* Ms. Smith says, "Yes they both start with *C* but look at the other letters. What do you hear at the end of *cat*?" She makes sure the book, chart, strips, and words are left out where everyone can practice freely with them during the day.

Ms. Smith's class pulls a small group to do a picture sort contrasting initial consonant sounds. She begins by holding up the letter *M* and asks the group to find a word in the story that begins with that letter. They quickly find *mat* at the end of every sentence. She repeats with *C*. The children find *cat* and then *cow*. Ms. Smith then brings out a collection of pictures to compare *M* and *C* and puts up a picture of a *cat* and a *mat* as headers along with the letters in a pocket chart. After naming all the pictures, she models the sort: "Here is a mouse. Listen to the first sound *mmmmmm*ouse. *Mouse* starts like *mat* so I will put it under *M*." After placing several pictures in this way she invites the children to take turns sorting the rest. This sort is repeated, and on subsequent days the children have a number of opportunities to sort on their own, to hunt for more pictures in alphabet books beginning with *M* and *C*, and to draw and label pictures with those sounds. After the children contrast M and C over several days, they compare *D* (dog) and *S* (sat) and then combine them for a four-category sort as shown in the opening picture of this chapter. The children work with all four letters and sounds for several days before moving on to a new contrast.

Ms. Smith uses a core book as the basis for teaching a variety of emergent literacy skills in a developmentally appropriate fashion. She starts with a whole text and works down to the parts (sentences, words, letters, and sounds) in a **whole-to-part lesson framework** that can be used to provide systematic literacy instruction in pre-K and kindergarten classrooms.

## From Speech to Print

Before we describe characteristics of the emergent stage, we offer a little background in the tasks faced by young children. Learning to read and spell is a process of matching oral and written language at three different levels: (1) the discourse level (2) the sentence level and (3) the level of sounds and letters within words and syllables. For someone learning to read, mismatches occur because of the fixed nature of print versus the flowing stream of speech it represents.

**THE DISCOURSE LEVEL.**  In oral language, the *discourse level* includes sentences or phrases. Within these phrases, speakers produce and listeners hear elements of **prosody** such as expression, intonation contours, and tone of voice, all of which communicate ideas and emotions. For example, a rising intonation at the end of a statement often indicates a question; precise, clipped words in a brusque tone may suggest irritation or anger.

*Oral language* is a direct form of communication accompanied by gestures and facial expressions that take place in a shared context, whereas *written language* is an indirect form of communication and must contain complete, freestanding messages to make meaning clear. Punctuation and word choice are often the reader's only cues to the emotions and intent of the writer. In addition, written language tends to be more formal and carefully constructed, using literary devices such as "happily ever after" to cue the reader. When children learn to read, they must match the prosody of their oral language to these more formal structures of written language.

## The Word Level

A second level that children must negotiate is the unit called *words*. In print, words are clearly set off with spaces between a string of letters. However, in speech, words are not distinct; there is no clear, separable unit in speech that equates perfectly to individual words. For example, the phrase "once upon a time" represents a single idea composed of four words and five syllables. Because of this, when children try to match their speech to print, they often miss the mark, as Lee does in her elephant story in Figure 4.1 where "once upon a time" is represented as though it were one word. It takes exposure, explanation, alphabet knowledge, and practice in both reading and writing to match words in speech to written words (Flanigan, 2007; Mesmer & Williams, 2015; Morris, Bloodgood, Lomax, & Perney, 2003; Uhry, 2002).

## Sounds in Words

Sounds and letters make up the third level of analysis. In learning to read, children must segment the speech sounds or **phonemes** within words and match them to the letters in print. In speech, the phonemes (consonants and vowels) are interconnected and cannot be easily separated (Liberman & Shankweiler, 1991). Yet letters of the alphabet and individual speech sounds must be understood as discrete units that match in systematic ways in order to master reading and spelling English. This understanding is called the **alphabetic principle**, the foundation of the English writing system (Liberman, Shankweiler, & Liberman, 1986).

---

**FIGURE 4.1   Lee's Elephant Story**

| | |
|---|---|
| 1spntm | Once upon a time |
| Lft. T. f | the elephant went to the fair. |
| pplsm. et. sk | The people saw him eating strawberry cake. |
| nobDSMg | And nobody saw him again. |
| VN | The end |

# Characteristics of the Emergent Stage

Our ideas about what young children can do in terms of reading and writing changed dramatically in the latter part of the twentieth century (Invernizzi & Buckrop, 2018). Instead of thinking about getting children "ready to learn" we now talk about how reading and writing "emerge" throughout the preschool years as children gradually acquire insights and knowledge from observations, explanations, modeling, and instruction. Dramatic changes occur across the emergent stage in their reading, writing, and spelling that can be characterized as early, middle, and late emergent behaviors, as summarized in Table 4.1.

## Emergent Reading

Can children in the emergent stage read? Yes, but not in a conventional way. They may attempt to match their oral language with written language in different ways depending on the context and their knowledge of how print works.

**Pretend reading** is basically a paraphrase or spontaneous retelling at the discourse level that children produce while turning the pages of a familiar book, usually without trying to point to the words. In pretend reading, children pace their retelling to match the sequence of pictures and orchestrate dialogue and the voice and cadence of written language (Sulzby, 1986).

**Memory reading** is more exacting than pretend reading and it might *sound* as though a child is actually reading. It involves an accurate recitation of the text and may be accompanied by pointing to the print in some fashion. Young children's attempts to touch individual words while reading from memory are initially quite inconsistent and vague but they gradually acquire directionality, realizing that they should move left to right, top to bottom, and end up on the last word on the page. However, the units that come in between are a blur until the systematic relationship between letters and sounds is understood. The ability to fingerpoint or track accurately

---

**TABLE 4.1**  Characteristics of Children in Emergent Stage

| | |
|---|---|
| **Early Emergent**<br><br>Drawing & Scribbling | May pretend to read but does not point to the print. |
| | Holds the writing implement and marks on the page. |
| | Scribbles and makes random marks in no particular direction. |
| | Does not distinguish between drawing and writing. |
| | Does not describe scribbles as "writing." |
| **Middle Emergent**<br><br>Letter-Like Forms & Random Letters | Recites text from memory and points to print in linear fashion (side to side and top to bottom) but not to words. |
| | Experiments with letter-like forms or mock linear writing. |
| | Distinguishes between writing and drawing and may identify work as "writing" |
| | Begins to use known letters and numbers in a "symbol salad." |
| | Does not attempt to match letters to sounds. |
| **Late Emergent**<br>SKP for *housekeeping*<br>D for *duck*<br>Partial Alphabetic | May identify a few words using a pre-alphabetic strategy |
| | Points to words left to right, reciting from memory, but gets off track as stressed units do not match words or syllables. |
| | Writes in a linear fashion but reversals are not unusual. |
| | Uses known letters to represent salient phonemes in partial alphabetic spelling. |
| | Does not leave spaces between words. |
| | Substitutes letters that sound, feel, and look alike: *B/P.* |
| | Uses letter names as a clue to represent sounds: Y (wie) for /w/. |

to words in print while reading from memory is a phenomenon called **concept of word in text (COW-T)**. It is a watershed event that separates the emergent reader from the letter name–alphabetic beginning reader (Flanigan, 2007; Henderson, 1981; Morris, 1992, 1993).

**Pre-alphabetic reading** is what Ehri (2014, Templeton, 1997) calls the phase children are in until they learn the relationships between letters and sounds. They may learn to identify a few words, such as their names and the names of friends and family. They might also identify signs in their environment, but their strategy is to look for nonalphabetic cues such as the shape and color of a stop sign. They may identify a large retail store because it starts with a big red *K*, but they are not systematic in their selection of any particular cue because they lack the alphabetic principle.

However, pre-alphabetic children do begin to notice letters in the world around them, especially letters that are most familiar. On entering preschool, Lee realized that other children's names on their cubbies had some of the same letters that were in her name. Perplexed and somewhat annoyed, she pointed to one of the letters. "Hey, that's MY letter!" she insisted. Walking around the grocery store, Lee pointed to the box of Cheer detergent and said, "Look, Mommy! There's my name!" Lee's special relationship with the letters in her name is a living embodiment of the pre-alphabetic strategy.

## Emergent Writing and Spelling

Like emergent reading, early emergent writing is largely pretend. Regardless of most children's cultural backgrounds or where they live, this pretend writing occurs spontaneously wherever writing is encouraged, modeled, and incorporated into play (Ferreiro & Teberosky, 1982). When children begin to represent speech sounds with letters of the alphabet, they are well on their way to acquiring the alphabetic principle. While we talk about children's pretend writing, it is only at this point we say they are attempting to *spell*. Their partial alphabetic efforts are truly something to celebrate and should be encouraged and supported.

**SCRIBBLING AND DRAWING.** Children first learn to hold a pencil, marker, or crayon and to make marks on paper (or windows, walls, or floors). These marks are best described as scribbles that lack directionality and may not serve a communicative function. Over time scribbles evolve into more representational drawings and children learn that print is distinct from drawing—a drawing of a flower does not actually say "flower." Writing is necessary to communicate the complete message. The top row of Figure 4.2 presents a progression of drawings and their accompanying utterances.

**LETTER-LIKE AND RANDOM LETTERS.** Children first approximate the most global contours of the writing system: the top-to-bottom linear arrangement and what has been called mock linear writing shown in the bottom row of Figure 4.2 (Clay, 1975; Harste, Woodward, & Burke, 1984). They experiment with letter-like forms that resemble the separate circles and lines of manuscript writing or the connected loops of cursive. The child may identify his or her efforts as "writing" and announce that it is a "note for Daddy." Parents may be challenged at this point when children come to them with their pretend writing and say, "Read this to me, Mommy" or "What does this say?" What is exciting and significant is that young children recognize that print carries a message that can be read by others. As letters of the alphabet and numbers are learned, they begin to show up in random strings or a "symbol salad," as in the spelling of *macaroni*.

**SALIENT OR INITIAL SOUNDS.** If children know some letters and understand the alphabetic principle, they will begin to match letters to the most salient or prominent sounds. At first, children rely on the feel of their mouths as they analyze the speech stream. Say the phrase "once upon a time" aloud while paying attention to what your tongue and lips are doing. The tongue touches another part of the mouth only for the /s/ sound of *once*, the /n/ sound of *upon*, and the /t/ sound of *time*. The lips touch each other twice: for the /p/ sound in the middle of *upon* and for the /m/ sound at the end of *time*. So it is not surprising that Lee wrote "once upon a time" as 1SPNTM in Figure 4.1. Late emergent spellers pay attention to those tangible points of an utterance in which one part of the mouth touches another, or to the most forcefully articulated sounds that make the most vibration or receive the most stress.

The initial sounds of words and syllables often show up first in children's tentative efforts as shown in the last box of Figure 4.2 where cat is spelled K and baby is spelled BB. However,

**Enhanced eText**
**Video Example 4.1**
A preschooler writes about butterflies using mock linear writing in this video.

**FIGURE 4.2** The Evolution of Emergent Writing

| Random Marks | Representational Drawing | Drawing Distinct from Writing |
|---|---|---|
| | "This is my sister." | "A flower for my Mom." |
| Mock Linear or Letterlike | Symbol Salad | Partial Phonetic |
| "A note for Daddy." | "Macaroni" | K "cat" <br> BB "baby" <br> ILU "I love you" |

in Lee's elephant story shown in Figure 4.1 we see that the phonemes represented by letters are not always at the beginnings of words; she spelled *went* as T and *him* as M. Lee is not yet able to isolate every phoneme and her spellings reflect this as in F for *fair* or TM for *time*. Notice her confusion with word boundaries and how she tries to mark them with periods. These spellings match letters to the most salient speech sounds, sometimes at the beginning and sometimes at the end of syllables. Ehri referred to such spelling as *partial alphabetic* and this matching of letters to sounds represents an important milestone in emergent literacy development (2014).

**PARTIAL ALPHABETIC LETTER NAMES.** Children often use letter names instead of letter sounds to represent speech sounds. Many letter names contain the sound of their associated letter sound in their name; for example: B (bee), D (dee), K (kay), M (em). Children will use these letter names to represent beginning and ending sounds in words and names like Katie (KT). But some letters do not contain the sound of their associated letter sound, and these can cause some confusions, such as in the early letter name example of YNRUKM ("When are you coming?") presented in Chapter 1. Because the name of the letter Y (wie) begins with the "wuh" (/w/) sound, it is often substituted for W in words like *when* spelled as YN. You will read more about these letter name substitutions in Chapter 5.

As children begin to achieve a concept of word, they become better able to pay attention to sounds that correspond to the beginnings and ends of word units. When letter names are coordinated with word boundaries—the beginning and endings of words—the child is no longer an emergent speller. Spelling that honors word boundaries consistently is spelling in the early part of the next stage, the letter name–alphabetic stage. Compare the late emergent writing in Figure 4.3 with the early letter name writing in Figure 4.4.

**FIGURE 4.3** Late Emergent Writing without Word Boundaries

IKSKP

"I like housekeeping"

**FIGURE 4.4** Early Letter Name–Alphabetic Spelling with Word Boundaries

i K hskpen

"I like housekeeping"

**DEVELOPMENTAL SPELLING.** Children's first tentative efforts at spelling represent a remarkable achievement that involves a number of important insights and skills and should be encouraged on a daily basis. Sometimes these efforts are called **invented spellings** but we prefer the term **developmental spellings** because over time they will change and mature as children learn more about letter sound correspondences. To summarize, even partial representations of sounds represent four critical insights and skills:

- To produce a spelling, children must recognize and know some letter names—not all, but enough to get started.
- They must isolate and analyze some of the sounds or phonemes within spoken words and syllables.
- They must know that letters represent speech sounds. If they know the names of the letters, they might use those as clues to the sounds they represent.
- They must know how to form the letters and write them in a linear fashion.

# Creating Classrooms for Early Literacy Learning

Some emergent children may have well-developed language skills and know a great deal about stories and books; others may not. However, a certain level of proficiency in oral language is *not* a prerequisite for learning the alphabet or seeing printed words tracked in correspondence to speech. To withhold these essential components of the learning-to-read process would put them in double jeopardy. Besides putting them behind in language and story development, they also would be behind in acquiring the alphabetic principle. Children can develop oral language, learn about stories, *and* learn about words, sounds, and the alphabet simultaneously as teachers model reading and writing and encourage children to imitate and experiment in the gradual release model outlined in the box below.

## Support Emergent Writing and Spelling

The mere act of leaving one's mark on paper has been called the "fundamental graphic act" (Gibson & Yonas, 1968)—an irresistible act of self-fulfillment. As described in the gradual release model, it is critical that teachers write *for* and *with* children to demonstrate and explain the forms and functions of print. This can take place as they record students' ideas in personal or group dictations or during interactive writing when they make the writing process explicit by talking aloud about how to spell, punctuate and compose (Williams, 2018; Button, Johnson & Furgerson, 1996). Outfitted and supported accordingly, writing will happen well before children can spell conventionally or properly compose (Chomsky, 1970; McGee & Richgels, 2012; Strickland & Morrow, 1989).

---

## Gradual Release Model

To make progress in the emergent stage, learners need lots of teacher-scaffolded experiences with reading and writing for real purposes. These experiences should progress from modeling and explaining by the teacher, to guided practice, and then to independent practice by the child in a gradual release model (Pearson & Gallagher, 1983; Duffy, 2014; Fisher and Frey, 2008):

1. *Modeling and explanation:* Look for opportunities to introduce new vocabulary, identify rhyming words, talk about letters and sounds, write for children, and point to words in enlarged text as you read and model writing.
2. *Guided practice:* Ask children to sort pictures by beginning sounds, clap the syllables in words, recite poems and songs from memory, and add a question mark to a sentence, all under your supervision. Write with children, asking them to add letters, words or punctuation that they have seen you model.
3. *Independent practice:* After modeling and guided practice, children can then be expected to produce rhyming words, re-sort pictures in centers or for seatwork, write letters in attempts to spell, and fingerpoint-read short, memorable selections of text. The most important condition for emergent literacy to blossom is the opportunity to practice, and children's approximations must be encouraged and celebrated. Pretend writing and pretend reading come first, and as they evolve, real reading and real writing will follow.

## Writing

Engaging children in the writing process is the first step and this acts as an incentive for learning more about the process.

- Provide ready access to writing materials—markers, crayons, pencils, chalk—and a variety of paper) and model how to use them as you write for and with children every day.

- Provide writing materials in play centers and model how writing serves a variety of functions:
  - A grocery store play area where grocery lists are drawn and labeled
  - A restaurant where menus are offered and orders are written
  - A block center with cardboard shapes for making signs

- Provide journals and encourage children to write in them daily. Figure 4.1, Figure 4.3 and Figure 4.4 show samples of Lee's daily preschool journal entries. For many young writers, their first efforts may be drawings accompanied by labels such as Kaitlyn's kindergarten journal entry in Figure 4.5.

- Model and encourage writing for a variety of purposes. Record classroom news as a Morning Message (See Activity 4.38.) Create charts with students' help for rules, reminders, directions, and so on. Children might record their observations of seeds growing, write about a field trip, or record a prediction.

- Identify where children are in their writing development and provide scaffolding to move them to the next level (Cabell, Tortorelli, & Gerde, 2013). For example, children at the drawing and scribbling level should be prompted to use letters, even random letters, while children who use random letters should be encouraged to think of letters to represent the most prominent sounds. Teachers should model for children who already represent one sound how to listen for and represent additional sounds by saying words slowly and drawing out the sounds. Table 4.2 describes different prompts according to children's early writing development.

- Always praise something specific about attempts to write no matter where students are on the writing continuum. At the same time, always encourage them to do more. *"What else can you say about that? What other sounds do you hear?"*

**TABLE 4.2**   Scaffolding Children's Writing Development in the Emergent Stage

| What Children Use | Teacher Prompts to Move Them to Next Level |
| --- | --- |
| Drawing and Scribbling | Prompt to incorporate some letters they might know to label their picture. "I love your picture of your brother. This would be a good place to write his name so we'll know who he is!" Explain that when we write, we use letters, but accept any attempt. |
| Letter-like Forms or Random Letters | If using letter-like forms, prompt to use actual letters: "Can you use some letters like the ones on the alphabet chart? Can I show you how to make the one you want?" If using random letters with no connection to sound, prompt to match a letter name to a salient sound by elongating that salient sound. "R**O**-bot" I hear an O in R**O**-bot!" |
| Partial Alphabetic | If representing salient sounds, call their attention to the other sounds "Great job putting down an R for that last sound *car*. Can you tell what letter might be at the beginning of that word? *Car.*" Accept a K. If already representing beginning sounds with letter names, prompt them to represent ending sound. "Good listening for that /K/ sound at the beginning of car. What sound do you hear at the end?" |

## Support Emergent Reading

There are two kinds of reading formats for emergent learners: *reading to* students, which includes interactive read-alouds with children's literature, and *reading with* students. Both formats involve lots of modeling by the teacher and provide a supportive social context with opportunities to talk about the forms and functions of print.

**INTERACTIVE READ-ALOUDS.** Reading *to* children is a long standing tradition but how it is done can make a dramatic difference in children's understandings about literacy and their oral language development. Barrentine (1996) describes interactive read-alouds where teachers read aloud to children and pause to invite their questions and responses. The interaction serves as a way to promote oral language and new vocabulary and builds ideas, and concepts related to the content and genre of a book. Read more about this in Activity 4.1.

**SHARED READING.** During **shared reading** (Holdaway, 1979) teachers read *with* students from enlarged texts like big books and charts on which children can see the print and join in chorally on re-readings. Shared reading, in which students' attention is directed to enlarged print, is particularly powerful for cultivating awareness of important aspects of how print works. Teachers can use **print referencing** (Justice & Sofka, 2010), such as where to begin to read on the page, or demonstrate left-to-right directionality and the return sweep at the end of each line—conventions of written language known as **concepts about print (CAP).**

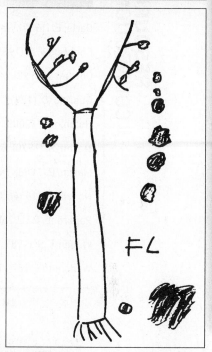

**FIGURE 4.5** Kaitlyn's Kindergarten Journal in October

Although children in the emergent stage are heavily supported by memory in their first efforts to read, these attempts are nonetheless valuable. The best way to create a reader is to make reading happen, even if it is just pretend. The whole-to-part lesson framework (McCracken & McCracken, 1995) used by Ms. Smith in the opening vignette begins with the shared reading of familiar rhymes and jingles (whole texts). Then follow-up activities move to the parts (sentences, words, letters, and sounds) as children rebuild the text with sentence strips in pocket charts, and match word cards to individual words on the sentence strips as an explicit way to direct attention to words in print. The smallest parts involve sorting pictures and words by beginning sounds to draw attention to letter–sound correspondences. Read more about the whole-to-part model on page 116.

Practicing handwriting

**PREDICTABLE READING MATERIALS.** Emergent readers need support in the form of memorable or predictable text that features repetition of simple lines and illustrations that cue changes in the text. The reading materials best suited for shared reading include predictable books (see some classic examples under "Resource Connections"), familiar nursery rhymes, poems, songs, jump rope jingles, and children's own talk written down. Many publishers offer leveled little books that are highly predictable. Recording students' own language in the form of picture captions and dictations nurtures the notion that print is talk written down. The ownership that comes with having one's own experiences recorded in print is a powerful incentive to explore the world of written language. See the Language Experience Approach (LEA) described in Activity 4.39.

## Classic Predictable Books to Use for Shared Reading

Carle, E. (1997). *Have You Seen My Cat?* Aladdin.

Christelow, E. (1989) *Five Little Monkeys Jumping on the Bed*. HMH Books for Young Readers.

Cowley, J (1997). *Mrs Wishy Washy*. Wright Group.

Guarino, D. (1997). *Is Your Mama a Llama?* Scholastic.

Hutchins, P (2005). *Rosie's Walk*. Aladdin.

Martin, B. (1970). *Brown Bear, Brown Bear, What Do You See?* Henry Holt & Co.

Martin, B (1998). *Here Are My Hands*. Henry Holt & Co.

Neitzel, S. (1994). *The Jacket I Wear in the Snow*. Greenwillow.

Paparone, P. (1995) *Five Little Ducks*. Scholastic

Williams, S. (1989). *I Went Walking*. HMH for Young Readers.

Wildsmith (1982). *The Cat on the Mat*. Oxford.

## The Literacy Diet for the Emergent Stage

The sections that follow are devoted to describing the most important elements of what we call the "literacy diet" (Invernizzi, 2002). Through reading and writing activities and word study instruction teachers of emergent learners aim toward the development of six fundamental components:

1. Oral language, concepts, and vocabulary
2. Phonological awareness (PA)
3. Alphabet knowledge
4. Letter–sound knowledge or phonics
5. Concepts about print (CAP)
6. Concept of word in text (COW-T)

Just like any diet, all the components need to be addressed concurrently in as integrated a fashion as possible. All of these components can be incorporated into a shared reading lesson such as the one Ms. Smith does with *Cat on the Mat*. At the same time, the English Language Arts standards that all teachers are expected to address are met. The literacy diet and activities are covered more thoroughly for early childhood educators in *Words Their Way for PreK–K* (Johnston, Invernizzi, Helman, Bear, & Templeton, 2015).

## Oral Language, Concepts, and Vocabulary

Most children have an oral vocabulary of 13,000 words by the time they enter kindergarten (Justice, 2006) and have mastered the basic subject–verb–object word order of the English language. But children come to school with widely varying language experiences (Biemiller, 2010). In a classic study, researchers estimated that by 3 years of age, some children had heard 3 million more words than other children, and by the time they enter school, some children have heard 30 million more words than others (Hart & Risley, 1995). Many children come from multilingual backgrounds and their vocabularies include their first language at home and the English they are learning at school (Genishi & Dyson, 2009; Vasquez, 2014).

To help children develop the deep and wide vocabulary knowledge they will need to succeed in their future studies, vocabulary and language learning must become an integral part of all aspects of the early childhood classroom (Biemiller, 2001, 2004). There are many strategies to build a language-rich environment. Here we describe how daily classroom interactions can be a context for word learning—how to get children talking and using language, how to use read-alouds, and how to develop big ideas and language through concept sorts. Activities 4.1 through 4.7 in the activities section that follows provide more ideas.

## Classroom Interactions for Language Development

Adults should engage children in conversation at every opportunity and consciously use language that includes new vocabulary and complex sentences. Sit with small groups at snack time, at lunchtime, in centers and on the playground, and engage them in conversations. Give children lots of opportunities to talk with each other. Children with less language skill benefit from conversation with children who have better language skills (Mashburn, Justice, Downer, & Pianta, 2009) and peer interactions are particularly important for children learning English.

**SOPHISTICATED SYNONYMS.** Although simplifying your language may be tempting, and necessary for English learners, thoughtfully exposing children to less familiar words and phrases is also very important. Be on the lookout for, gradually teach, and consistently use more sophisticated synonyms for the common language of everyday routines as well as for topical interests. For example, children can be asked to *distribute* or *allocate* materials. During discussions, encourage *participants* to *contribute* and *elaborate* their ideas and those of others. Children may be asked to *assemble adjacent to* the wall, and then to *proceed* in an *orderly* fashion. Lane and Allen (2010) describe how a kindergarten teacher begins the year by asking the "weather watcher" to report to the class using terms such as *sunny*, *cloudy*, or *warm* but she gradually introduces new terms—the appointed "meteorologist" is expected to *observe* the weather *conditions* and report the *forecast* using words such as *overcast*, *brisk*, or *frigid*.

**LANGUAGE IN CENTERS.** Centers provide a stimulus for new vocabulary and concept development. Sand is *gritty* and *moist* and can be *sifted* with *sieves*. In the block center, encourage children to *construct*, *erect*, and *dismantle* their creations. McGee and Richgels (2012) suggest keeping a list of words posted in centers as a reminder of vocabulary to use with students. Add to the lists as more words occur to you and save them from year to year.

**READ-ALOUDS** Books expose children to new words and more complex sentence structures, and they provide background and conceptual knowledge that children may not have experienced firsthand. Read from a variety of genres and select storybooks that offer rich language and themes appropriate for young children. For example, nonfiction about seasons, weather, transportation, and how seeds grow provides new vocabulary and develops background information, especially when read for units of study. Folktales offer strong plots that help children develop a sense of story, and poetry offers rhyme and playful language.

*Targeting Vocabulary.* Reading aloud to children exposes them to a wide range of new words, but teachers also need to develop the meanings of particular words in more depth to ensure vocabulary growth. When new words are introduced with a simple explanation, children should be asked to repeat them and say them in phrases and sentences. After reading about how a little bear *hustled* after his mother (*Blueberries for Sal* by Robert McCloskey), you might pause briefly to draw attention to the word and then follow up later with more discussion: "*Hustle* means to walk very quickly. Say the word *hustle*. Would you hustle to catch the bus? Would you hustle to bed? Would you hustle fast or hustle slow? Tell your partner how you would fill in this sentence: I hustled to_____." Beck, McKeown, and Kucan (2008, 2013) describe how to plan repeated exposure to words in different contexts to help children learn the meanings and uses of new vocabulary words. For example, you might urge the children to hustle as they line up to go inside. Although you may focus on many words as they occur in the context of the book, pull English learners aside before a read-aloud to preteach particularly important words to ensure their understanding.

*Selecting Words for Vocabulary Development.* Preview books to select vocabulary to teach. Simply looking for hard words is easy and tempting, but those may not be the words children are most likely to retain and use on their own. Four criteria are important in selecting target words:

1. *Utility.* When thinking about utility, consider words that can be used regularly in the classroom or words that will show up in other books. For example, the book *Corduroy* by Don Freeman includes *amazing, admiring,* and *enormous.* After talking about these words during the read-aloud, make a point of using them in other contexts. Instead of saying, "I like the drawing you did," substitute with "I admire your drawing. The colors are amazing and that house is enormous!"

2. *Concreteness.* Concrete words are more likely to be illustrated in the story (such as the *elevator* in *Corduroy*). Many denote concepts that children can act out, like *hustled.* Abstract words like *imagined* will take more work to develop.

3. *Repetition in Text.* Words that are used more than once in the story are good candidates because these will offer repeated exposure in a meaningful context. The word *hustled* occurs several times in *Blueberries for Sal* (McCloskey, 1948).

4. *Thematic or Topical Relatedness.* When considering thematic or topical relatedness, choose words that can be clustered in a semantic category (Whitehurst, 1979). The words *buds, blooms,* and *blossoms* all relate to the growing seeds motif in *The Tree* (A First Discovery Book). From the same book, other concrete selections that form clusters for repetition include *seed, roots,* and *sapling.*

*Make it Interactive.* As mentioned above, reading to children should be an interactive process that stimulates lots of oral language as children ask questions and comment on the content and illustrations (Barrentine, 1996). Ideas for planning and conducting an interactive read-aloud with a focus on vocabulary development can be found in Activity 4.1. To increase opportunities to talk, you might want to use the "turn and talk" technique described in Activity 4.3. Children talk with assigned partners to answer a question, share a response, or make a prediction. Turn and talk techniques multiply the opportunities for individuals to articulate their own ideas and are especially beneficial for children who are shy or learning to speak English.

*Experiences and Extensions.* Reading aloud to children provides virtual experiences that can stimulate oral language and vocabulary learning, but real experiences with cooking, science experiments, special visitors, classroom pets, and field trips are engaging and provide direct opportunities for verbal interactions. These experiences will be particularly important for English learners, but the immediacy of real life is engaging for all young children. It is easy to think that experiences and conversations just happen, and to a certain extent they do, but *planned* experiences with careful attention to vocabulary, language, and concepts are more likely to be fruitful (Neuman & Roskos, 2012). Even better, combining read-alouds with experiences supports the necessary repetition of targeted vocabulary and promotes linkages that facilitate learning. Because encountering new words and concepts in different contexts is important for children, planning experiences that promote vocabulary learning and help maintain that vocabulary over time is critical.

Follow-up activities to a read aloud offer opportunities for children to interact with peers and apply their understanding of concepts and vocabulary through cooperative learning formats or centers (Wasik, Bond, & Hindman, 2006). Reread favorites and then always keep the books available so children can pick them up during free time to explore on their own.

*Thematic Units.* Many concepts as well as vocabulary are taught through thematic units. Let's say you develop a unit on pets that includes a series of read-alouds on animals that make good pets, and you decide to get a hamster for the classroom. Some of the concepts and vocabulary include *hamster, male, female, habitat, nutrition, diet, exercise, bedding, gnaw,* and *nocturnal.*

Children can then use these words in their daily conversations about hamsters. Use the same criteria outlined earlier to select words: utility, concreteness, opportunities for repetition, and relatedness.

An experience like caring for a classroom pet can lead to writing activities as well. You might create labels with the students' help for the *cage*, *water bottle*, *exercise ball*, and so on. Children might dictate their observations and insights about hamsters in the language experience approach described in Activity 4.39 or participate in an interactive writing activity described in Activity 4.38. In addition, you might ask children to illustrate and write about hamsters in their own journals.

***Retellings.*** Prompting children to retell what they heard in the read-aloud encourages them to use new words and more complex sentence constructions in hands-on, engaging activities (Ward, 2009). Retellings should be

Acting out *Five Little Ducks* with simple props

modeled for students: "When you have a chance to look at this book on your own, try to retell the story. Watch how I do that by looking at the pictures." Proceed to retell the story using the pictures and your memory of the words. An intervention known as **dialogic reading** described in Activity 4.2 is a well-researched approach that is designed to stimulate oral language and dialogue while enhancing students' ability to retell stories (Doyle & Bramwell, 2006; Whitehurst, Arnold, Epstein, Angell, Smith, & Fischel, 1994). Simple predictable books such as the ones listed in "Resource Connections" on page 96 might be used with English learners because the repetitive sentence structures support retellings.

***Dramatic Play.*** Children love to act out simple stories or parts of stories. Brainstorm with children about which characters are needed and what each one will do, and then walk through the dramatization by posing questions and prompting oral responses. You can also stimulate retellings by supplying props like puppets, flannel board cutouts, and other objects used in the story. Stick puppets are easy to make by simply copying pictures of characters or objects from the book, adding some color, cutting around them, and gluing them to popsicle sticks. After modeling the use of props or puppets as a group activity, they can be placed in a center or made available during free time.

## Concept Sorts

The human mind appears to work by using compare-and-contrast categorization to develop concepts and relationships among objects and attributes. By recognizing similarities among items, it is possible to create groups or categories according to meaningful associations, the foundation of critical thinking (Gillet & Kita, 1979). The ability to categorize demonstrates maturing hierarchical and associative thinking, but needs to be coupled with conversation about why and how objects and pictures are being categorized (Carpenter, 2010).

The concept sorts described in Activities 4.4 to 4.7 are appropriate for children in the emergent stage, but concept sorts can be used at all levels of development as children categorize objects, pictures, words, or phrases. Concept sorts are a surprisingly simple way to expand students' word knowledge, and they are also a good way to engage English learners and get them involved in verbal interactions (Bear & Helman, 2004). For example, the concept sort for wild animals and pets in Figure 4.6 could be done successfully by children who do not know all the words to name the animals. However, in the course of discussion and repeated sorting, they are exposed to those words along with the picture to support word learning.

**Enhanced eText**
**Teacher Resource:**
Concept Sorts

**FIGURE 4.6  Concept Sort for Wild Animals and Pets**

### LEARNING TO CATEGORIZE AND TALK ABOUT SORTS.

Concept sorts can develop deeper understanding about words and how they relate to other words within a semantic field. For example, most 5-year-olds know about tables, chairs, sofas, beds, ovens, refrigerators, microwaves, and blenders, but in their minds, these may be all undifferentiated "things in a house." Teachers can help to expand students' understanding of "things in a house" by introducing two different conceptual categories—furniture (tables, chairs, sofas, and beds) and appliances (refrigerators, ovens, microwaves, and blenders). Discussion can focus on how appliances are different from furniture, such as the fact that appliances require "electricity" and need to be plugged into "receptacles."

To ensure vocabulary development, ask children to name the pictures as they sort and to justify their placements as they describe their categories ("Why did you put a bear with the wild animals?"). If the pictures used in concept sorts reflect words that are new to students, they need to be explicitly taught. Talking about the meanings of words and using them repeatedly each time they appear in sorting is important. It might be an opportune time to discuss the meaning of *claw* or *hoof* when sorting pictures of birds and animals. English learners may need to learn the names of more common objects, like *bird* or *cow*.

### EXTEND CONCEPT SORTS.

You can use concept sorts to extend interactive read-alouds and provide additional exposure to new vocabulary. For example, after listening to Ruth Heller's book *Chickens Aren't the Only Ones*, provide children with picture cards to sort into groups of birds, mammals, and reptiles. In this way, they build on a simple conceptual understanding of where eggs come from to include other attributes of the animal kingdom.

In addition to basic sorting, concept development activities are generally followed by draw-and-label or cut-and-paste procedures, as described in Chapter 3. As always, we recommend having children write at every possible opportunity during or following the concept sorts. For example, as a culminating activity for a unit on animals, one kindergarten teacher helped her children create their own books in which they drew pictures of their favorite animals. When asked to label these pictures or write briefly about the animals, her children's efforts ranged from random letters to readable approximations such as "I LIK THE LINS N TGRS."

### ASSESSING AND MONITORING VOCABULARY GROWTH.

Use instructional activities that extend interactive read-alouds, such as retellings and concept sorts, to measure progress in students' vocabulary growth. Note increases in word use or tally the number of ideas, facts, or concepts children express when retelling or explaining the sort. Retell assessments are authentic, valid, and reliable means of assessing understanding (Fuchs, Fuchs, & Maxwell, 1988). Noting the number of objects, pictures, or items sorted into conceptual categories also yields a reliable means of assessing depth of receptive vocabulary (Ward, 2009). Other developmentally appropriate ways of assessing receptive vocabulary growth in emergent learners include pointing to pictures that answer direct questions (for example, "Which picture is the veterinarian?") or answering sets of yes/no questions (for example, "Is an acorn a seed?" "Do plants grow from seeds?" "Do all seeds look the same?").

## Phonological Awareness

The ability to pay attention to, identify, and reflect on various sound segments of speech is known as **phonological awareness** (**PA**). It is the umbrella term for a range of understandings about speech sounds, including syllables, rhyme, and a sense of alliteration. **Phonemic awareness** is a subcategory of phonological awareness and refers to the ability to identify and

**Enhanced eText**
**Video Example 4.3**
This video contains several examples of concept sorts.

**PROGRESS**
**MONITORING**

reflect on the smallest units of sound: individual phonemes. The ability to segment *sit* or *thick* into three sounds (/s/-/i/-/t/ or /th/-/i/-/ck/) is an example of phonemic awareness. Children can hear and use individual phonemes easily at a tacit level—they can talk and can understand when others talk to them. But it is not easy to bring tacit, subconscious awareness of abstract individual phonemes to the surface to be examined consciously and explicitly.

Phonological awareness and phonemic awareness are widely identified as critical understandings needed to progress in literacy (Ball & Blachman, 1988; Ehri & Roberts, 2006; National Reading Panel, 2000). This is because children need a certain amount of phonemic awareness to grasp the alphabetic nature of English and understanding beginning sounds will get them started. Thereafter, phonemic awareness, word recognition, decoding, and spelling continue to develop in a symbiotic fashion. Growth in one area stimulates growth in another (Ehri, 2006; Morris et al., 2003; Perfetti, Beck, Bell, & Hughes, 1987).

## Development in PA During the Emergent Stage

Phonological awareness develops gradually over time and progresses from a sensitivity to big chunks of speech sounds, such as syllables and rhyme, to smaller parts of speech sounds, such as individual phonemes (Pufpaff, 2009; Pullen & Justice, 2003; Ziegler & Goswami, 2005). Early emergent learners might participate in activities that focus attention on syllables and rhyming words, whereas middle emergent learners work on alliteration by sorting pictures that begin with the same sound.

Children achieve partial phonemic awareness near the end of the emergent phase of literacy development when they can isolate the most salient consonant sounds at the beginnings, and sometimes ends, of words and syllables. They develop full phonemic awareness during the letter name–alphabetic stage as they learn to separate all the sounds in a word, including blends and medial vowels (step = /s/-/t/-/e/-/p/). We can see the development of phonemic awareness in children's spelling of *step* as it moves from partial (S or SP) to developing (STP) to full (STEP).

The following sections discuss different aspects of phonological awareness. You can find related activities for each in the activity section (Activities 4.8 to 4.19) at the end of the chapter.

Using a variety of instructional strategies that are identified as successful and effective, phonological awareness activities can be engaging whole-group language activities that benefit all students (Blachman, 1994, 2000; Lundberg, Frost, & Peterson, 1988; Smith, Simmons, & Kame'enui, 1995). These activities need not be conducted as isolated tasks, nor do they need to take up a lot of time. According to some estimates, an entire year of phonemic awareness instruction need not exceed 20 hours (Armbruster, Lehr, & Osborn, 2001).

In addition to planned instructional activities look for opportunities throughout the day to talk about a variety of speech units—have children line up by the number of syllables in their own name or listen for the beginning sound in the title of a book. As you draw children's attention to units of sound, familiarize them with terms such as *word*, *rhyme*, *syllable*, and *beginning sound*.

## Syllables and Words

Young children are concrete thinkers, so it is not surprising that they associate the length of a word with the size of its referent. Although *caterpillar* is a fairly long word, it refers to a relatively small insect, and so young children may think the word *caterpillar* is smaller than the word *cat*, because cats are bigger than caterpillars (Papandropoulou & Sinclair, 1974; Templeton & Spivey, 1980). This is no "small" confusion because to learn to read it is necessary to pay attention to the word's sound independently of its meaning.

The sound unit to address first with young children is the syllable, because syllables have a physical reality other units lack: Each syllable is a release of breath that can be felt. Clapping or tapping syllables is fairly easy for young children to master. However, words can be one syllable or multiple syllables, and until students actually learn to read, they will confuse them.

## Syllables

- A first step in leading children to an awareness of spoken words as a unit is to take two concrete "short" words and make them into one "long" *compound word* (for example, *snow, man, snowman*).
- Rhythm activities like marching, tapping, singing, clapping, and playing drums to the rhythm of songs and ditties helps children establish syllable segmentation. (Corriveau & Goswami, 2009; Goswami, et al., 2010).

## Rhymes

Rhyming activities are an appealing way for children to play with words and to begin to focus on speech sounds. Many children develop a sense of rhyme easily, whereas others need more structured activities that draw their attention specifically to rhyming.

**Enhanced eText**
**Video Example 4.4**
Jackie introduces rhyme to preschoolers in this video.

## Rhyme

- Fill students' ears with the sounds of rhyme by sharing jingles, nursery rhymes, poems and books that feature rhyming words. Some books lend themselves to an activity in which you simply pause and let the children supply the second rhyming word in a couplet. A picture book such as *Is Your Mama a Llama?* by Deborah Guarina or *"I Can't," said the Ant* by Polly Cameron have illustrations and clues to help children name the rhyme. Some other favorite rhyming books are listed in Activity 4.10.

- Follow up read-alouds with picture sorts for rhymes. For example, an extension to *"I Can't," said the Ant* is matching pictures of objects named in the book with other rhyming pictures. To make it easier for beginners, lay out just two pictures that rhyme along with one that does not. This odd-one-out setup, shown in Figure 4.7, enables children to identify more readily the two rhyming pictures.

- Songs are naturally full of rhythm and rhyme and hold great appeal for children. Several songs recorded by Raffi, a popular singer and songwriter for children, are particularly well suited for language play. For example, rhyme features prominently in the song "Willoughby Wallaby Woo" from the collection *Singable Songs for the Very Young*. The song features a rhyme starting with *W* for everyone's name and can be easily adapted for the children in your class. Sing the initiating phrase, changing the first letter of a name to *W* ("Willoughby Wallaby Wackie"), then children sing the next phrase, naming the appropriate classmate ("An elephant sat on Jackie"). You can pass a stuffed elephant to the child to add to the fun. Change the song to focus on alliteration by holding up a particular letter to insert in front of every word. *B*, for example, results in "Billaby Ballaby Boo," and *F* produces "Fillaby Fallaby Foo."

- As children become more adept at listening for rhymes, they can play a variety of sorting and matching games. Traditional games such as Bingo, Lotto, and Concentration, in which picture cards are matched to other picture cards that rhyme, are always winners.

English learners may not understand rhyming in English. In Spanish, for example, rhyming focuses on the stress and vowels in words of more than one syllable, whereas in English rhyming focuses more on one-syllable word endings. Expect that developing a sense of rhyme in English may take a little longer to master for English learners than native speakers.

*for* **English learners**

**FIGURE 4.7** Odd-One-Out with Rhyming Words

## Alliteration and Beginning Sounds

Children must become aware that words can be divided into smaller segments of sound—phonemic awareness—before they will advance far in learning to read. They must also learn some of the terminology used to talk about these sounds. Without this knowledge, instruction in phonics will have little success. Children have no trouble hearing sounds, but directions such as "Listen for the first sound" may mystify them. In response to the question, "What sound does *cow* start with?" one puzzled child tentatively replied, "Moo?" Without a stable concept of word in text, "first sound" is a relative notion. Phonological awareness activities at the emergent level help children attend to sounds, and learn to label and categorize these sounds in various ways.

### Alliteration and Beginning Sounds

Activities that play with **alliteration** focus students' attention on the beginning sounds.

- Start with ABC books such as *Dr. Seuss's ABC*, which celebrates alliteration in the famous Seuss style. Others that include alliteration are *A My Name is Alice* by Jane Byer and *Animalia* by Graham Base.

- Play beginning-sound games with puppets or stuffed animals. Use games such as I Spy or I'm Thinking of Something to accentuate the initial sound. "This thing I'm thinking of begins with *mmmmm*. This thing is small and gray. It is an animal." As the children respond "mouse" or "mole," ask them to exaggerate the beginning sound. As children become proficient at playing this game, they create their own riddles.

- Alliteration is further developed as children sort pictures by beginning sound, an activity that will be described in detail shortly. At this point, oral language activities designed to teach phonemic awareness cross over into learning letter–sound correspondences, or phonics.

## Assessing and Monitoring Phonological Awareness

You can find a collection of assessments that cover different aspects of phonological awareness in Appendix A: syllable, rhyme, and phonemic awareness of initial consonants (alliteration). In general, a score of 80 percent is considered sufficient mastery of a task.

Phonological awareness tasks similar to these have been scientifically validated by Invernizzi and her colleagues, with thousands of children screened in Virginia with *Phonological Awareness Literacy Screening* (PALS) assessments at the preschool and kindergarten levels (Invernizzi et al., 2006). Monitoring the development of phonological awareness during kindergarten helps to identify children who need additional instruction.

**PROGRESS MONITORING**

# Alphabet Knowledge

Among the reading readiness skills that are traditionally studied, letter naming appears to be the strongest predictor of later reading success (NELP, 2008; Snow, Burns, & Griffin, 1998).

## Lots to Learn About Letters

There is a great deal to learn about the alphabet. Letters have names, a set sequence, sounds, and upper- and lowercase forms. They must be written in particular ways, and directional orientation is vital. In the three-dimensional world, a chair is a chair whether you approach it from the front or the back, from the left or the right. Not so with letters: A *b* is a *b* and a *d* is a *d*. Print is one of the few things in life in which direction makes a difference, and young children lack this directionality. They also confuse letters that share visual features: *S* may be mistaken for *Z*, *E* for *F*, *h* for *n*, and so forth (Clay, 1975; Ehri & Roberts, 2006). In addition, children must learn to recognize the distinguishing but stable characteristics of letters across different fonts, sizes, shapes, and textures, as shown in Figure 4.8. Children form a concept of *B* from seeing such variations and encountering *B* in many contexts.

**Enhanced eText**
**Teacher Resource:**
Font Sorts

Learning the names of the letters is an important first step toward learning the sounds associated with the letters. Most of the letters have names that include a sound commonly associated with it and can serve as mnemonic devices for remembering the sounds (Huang, Tortorelli & Invernizzi, 2014; Kim, Petscher, Foorman, & Zhou, 2010; Treiman & Broderick, 1998). *B* (bee), *K* (kay), and *Z* (zee) have their sounds at the beginnings of their names, whereas *F* (eff), *L* (ell), and *S* (ess) have their sounds at the end. The names of the vowels are their long sounds. Only *H* (aitch), *W* (double you), and the consonant *Y* (wie) have no sound association, and not surprisingly, these letters are often the most difficult to learn. Letter names serve as the first reference point many children use when writing and explain some of the interesting developmental spellings they create during the letter name–alphabetic stage, discussed more in Chapter 5.

Most children take five years to acquire all this alphabet knowledge at home and in preschool. Magnetic letters on the refrigerator door, alphabetic puzzles, and commercial alphabet games are staples in many homes (Adams, 1990). There is an increasingly broad range of apps many parents use to develop alphabet and letter–sound knowledge. Attentive parents model letter formation and speech segmentation as they encourage their children to write a grocery list or a note to Grandma. Other children have less preparation, and their parents benefit from instruction and encouragement in how to interact with their children (Sinclair, McCleery, Koepsell, Zukerman, & Stevenson, 2018). The best way to share five years of accumulated alphabet knowledge with children who have not had these experiences is to teach it directly, in as naturalistic, fun, and game-like a manner as possible in pre-K and kindergarten classrooms (Delpit, 1988).

**FIGURE 4.8  Different Print Styles**

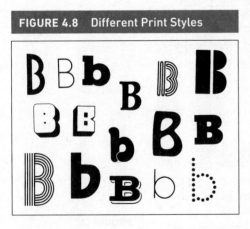

## Teaching the Alphabet

Teachers often ask, "How do I know what order to follow in teaching the alphabet?" and "Which letters are the easiest and which are the hardest to learn?" The answers are not simple because a number of factors influence the answers. Table 4.3 summarizes some of the research findings and the implications for instruction based on a synthesis by Invernizzi and Buckrop (2018).

Activities planned by teachers should develop all aspects of alphabet knowledge, including letter naming, letter recognition (both uppercase and lowercase), letter writing, and letter sounds.

**ASSESSING AND MONITORING GROWTH IN ALPHABET KNOWLEDGE.** A variety of tasks are needed to assess alphabet knowledge, and these can be found in Appendix A. Ask children to point to and recite the letters in order as a first step. Watch how they handle *LMNOP*—because of the way these letters are sung in the alphabet song, sometimes they become one letter! Present upper- and lowercase letters in random order to assess letter recognition. You can easily assess letter production by calling out letters, in or out of order, for children to write.

According to research conducted with hundreds of thousands of kindergartners in Virginia, kindergartners are able to recognize and name an average of 20 lowercase letters, presented in random order in the fall of the year and nearly all of them by the end of kindergarten (Invernizzi et al., 2006). Longitudinal research suggests that kindergarten children who name fewer than 12 lowercase letters in the fall of the year would benefit from additional instruction to prevent falling further behind. Alphabet learning is easy to monitor; assess children regularly to plan instruction for those who are not making progress.

**Enhanced eText**
**Video Example 4.5**
Jackie uses children's names to teach alphabet and a variety of concepts about print in this video.

**BACKGROUND I EMERGENT STAGE**

**TABLE 4.3** Research Findings and Instruction for Teaching the Alphabet

| Research Findings | Implications for Instruction |
|---|---|
| **Some letters take longer to learn than others, so instruction needs to vary depending upon a number of factors.** | **Link alphabet instruction to meaningful print: children's names, environmental print, picture books, alphabet books, big books, and charts.** |
| 1. The easiest letters for children to learn are those in their name, particularly the first letter of their name. | Begin instruction with children's names using activities such as Name of the Day and name puzzles. Display names along with the alphabet and refer to them often when writing. |
| 2. Lowercase letters that look like corresponding capital letters (Cc, Ss) are easier to learn than those that are different (Aa, Rr). | Expect to spend more time teaching lowercase letters that do not match capitals. Font sorts and matching games like Alphabet Eggs (Activity 4.26) and Concentration (Activity 4.27) are recommended. |
| 3. Some lowercase letters are easily confused (u/n, t/ f/ j, or b/p/ d /q), which makes them harder to learn. | Avoid comparing similar letters at first. Contrast them with other letters and later with each other along with their sounds. Use matching games like Letter Spin (Activity 4.28) or Font Sorts (Activity 4.30). |
| 4. Letters that are seen frequently in print are easier to learn than those that are not. Q is one of the hardest to learn because it is rarely seen. | Expect to spend more time teaching letters that are not commonly seen. Compare and contrast their shapes, names and sounds in sets of two three or four. |
| 5. Learning the names of the letters make it easier for children to learn the sounds because many letter names contain the sound. Those that do not are more difficult to learn (W or H). | Begin letter sound instruction with letters that have the associated sound at the beginning (B = "bee") or at the end (F = "eff"). Use initial sound sorts that include letters as headers. |

Based on Invernizzi, M. & Buckrop, 2018.

**TEACHING TIPS**

## Alphabet

Here are some general routines for teaching children about the forms and functions of the alphabet. See Activities 4.20–4.30 in the activities section for more detail.

- Teach the letter sequence by singing the alphabet song daily until children know it by heart. In addition, point to the letters as they sing and then give children a copy of an alphabet strip so they can practice pointing and finding letters as they are named.

- Share alphabet books with students, pointing out the capital and lowercase forms and naming the pictures that begin with a letter. Children typically learn capital letters first, but by kindergarten lowercase letters are needed; teach them together along with the sounds associated with them. Make alphabet books available for children to explore on their own but model for children how to use them independently: "Here is the capital *B* and the lowercase *b*. *Bear* and *bowl* begin with *b*." (See a list of alphabet books in the activity section.)

- Begin with the children's names and ask them to build it with letter tiles, cut it out of playdough, or match it letter-for-letter with a second set. Writing or copying their own names and the names of other family members or friends is alluring to emergent writers, making a great introduction to the alphabet as well as to writing. Letters take on personalities: *M* is Manuel's letter, and *T* is Tonisha's letter.

- Name of the day is a popular activity first described by Pat Cunningham (2005) as a way to provide a meaningful context for leaning letters (see Activity 4.23). Studying a name each day is a more appropriate pace than letter of the week in kindergarten classrooms. To make this even more meaningful, children should *use* their names to participate in daily activities, such as signing in each day for attendance and lunch choices, or signing up for centers or popular tasks like feeding the fish. Start by providing preprinted name cards but move toward expecting children to write out their names.

- Point out letters on signs, in book titles, on charts, and all around the school. The modern world is full of letters, but you need to draw students' attention to them and name them. When you read and write with children, there are endless opportunities to talk about letters; this helps them understand the many functions letters serve.

- Create an alphabet center where children have access to puzzles and games that change on a regular basis. Provide an alphabet strip and a variety of writing implements (markers, chalk, rubber stamps) and writing surfaces (paper, card stock, chalkboards, whiteboards, magnetic drawing boards, and so on) to encourage children to write and form their letters. Make learning the letters into a sensory experience by forming them out of clay or pipe cleaners, rubbing over textured letters or tracing them in trays filled with sand.

- Handwriting is an important and often neglected component of early literacy instruction (Graham, Harris, & Fink, 2000). When writing for children, model proper letter formation and be consistent about spatial matters such as where to start and directionality. Have children vocalize these movements as they form their letters (for example, "up, down, up, down" for *M*; "around" for *O*) and also repeat the letter names as they trace them.

# Letter–Sound Knowledge and Phonics

During the emergent stage, children learn their letters, develop phonological awareness, and begin to make connections between letters and sounds as they come to understand the alphabetic principle in spelling. Toward the end of the emergent stage, many children will begin producing partial phonetic spellings. Picture sorts designed to contrast beginning sounds secures these tentative efforts and moves children along in acquiring more knowledge of letter–sound correspondences through a game-like, manipulative phonics activity.

## Selecting Contrasting Initial Consonants

Just like learning the alphabet, there are multiple factors to consider when planning the introduction of initial consonant sounds. Although there is not one "right" sequence for introducing and contrasting letter sounds, the principle of word study, *begin with obvious contrasts first*, is a good general rule to follow. In considering obvious contrasts, think about how the sounds are produced or ***articulated*** in the mouth, how easily they may be confused with other sounds, and how frequently they may occur in classroom materials.

**ARTICULATION.** Choosing sounds that feel very different when producing them makes it easier for children to focus on the sound contrast while sorting. Letters such as *M* and *S* are appropriate for students' first consonant contrast because both letter names contain the associated letter sound (for example, the letter name *em* contains the /m/ sounds) and both letters have **continuant** sounds that can be isolated and elongated without undue distortion (*mmmmoon* and *ssssun*). Talk about how the sounds feel in the mouth as well as where in mouth they are produced. The sound for *B* (/b/) cannot be elongated or isolated without adding a vowel to it (*buh*), but it is still fairly easy to learn, perhaps because it has a distinctive feel as the lips press together and also because it is one of the earliest consonantal phonemes acquired during oral language development (Pense & Justice, 2008). However, contrasting *B* and *P* in an early sort would be confusing because they are both articulated or produced the same way (Purcell, 2002). The only difference is that the /b/ sound causes the vocal cords to vibrate whereas /p/ does not. Try placing two fingers on your larynx and feel the difference in **voiced** /b/ and **unvoiced** /p/ as you say *bay* and *pay*.

Table 4.4 shows a pronunciation chart of consonants. Read across each row saying the sound of the letter (that is, /p/, /b/, /m/) to see how those sounds share the same place of articulation (that is, lips together). Compare the voiced and unvoiced pairs such as /f/ and /v/ or /t/ and /d/. Notice how the nasal sounds of /m/, /n/, and /ng/ pass through the nose rather than the mouth. As teachers, learning about articulation may seem unnecessarily complicated, but it explains so many of the interesting things children do in their developmental spellings during the emergent and letter name–alphabetic stages. Use the chart to see the logic in the spelling of JP for *chip*, VN for *fan*, and PD for *pet*. In each case, the substitutions vary only because one is voiced and the other is unvoiced. Otherwise, they are articulated exactly the same way. Knowing about articulation helps you make decisions about setting up picture sorts. The letters in any row will feel very much alike and are best not contrasted in the very first letter–sound sorts. It is important to begin with obvious contrasts.

**ENGLISH LEARNERS.** Students leaning English are often unfamiliar with some of the sounds and will substitute sounds and letters closest to their primary languages and alphabets. They will not articulate some sounds at first, but their substitutions are logical. For example, Spanish speakers may use the letter *v* to represent the /b/ sound because these sounds are the same in Spanish. The logic behind the misspellings of English learners was discussed in Chapter 2, and more detail will be provided in Chapter 5. See Table 5.6 in Chapter 5 for potential consonant confusions.

*for* **English learners**

When sorting with English learners at this stage, use fewer pictures and those that are most familiar. Focus on a few new high-utility words to teach by holding up the picture and talking about it or dramatizing it. Ask students to repeat the words and be ready to supply the names of the pictures and review them as needed before, after, and during sorting. Be sure students name words aloud as they sort and pair up English learners with a partner who can supply the names of the pictures when they sort independently.

**TABLE 4.4** Pronunciation Chart of Consonant Sounds

| Unvoiced | Voiced | Nasals | Other | Place of Articulation |
|---|---|---|---|---|
| p | b | m | | lips together |
| wh | w | | | lips rounded |
| f | v | | | teeth and lips |
| th (thin) | th (the) | | | tip of tongue and teeth |
| t | d | n | l | tip of tongue and roof of mouth |
| s | z | | | tongue and roof of mouth |
| sh | | | y | sides of tongue and teeth |
| ch | j | | r | sides of tongue and roof of mouth |
| k | g | ng | | back of tongue and throat |
| h | | | | no articulation—breathy sound |

## Introducing Focused Contrasts for Beginning Sounds

Word study in the emergent stage is designed to teach students the letter sound matches for beginning consonants by contrasting two or more sounds at a time. Whenever possible choose several sounds that represent key words from a familiar rhyme, patterned book (such as M and C from *Cat on the Mat*), or student dictation. A new sound sort is introduced on day 4 of the whole-to-part lesson plan outlined on page 116. Start with two obvious contrasts and then add one or two for up to four categories. The lesson in the box on page 109 describes the steps to introduce students to a picture sort.

## Assessing and Monitoring Growth in Letter–Sound Knowledge

There are several ways to assess students' abilities to match beginning consonant sounds to the appropriate letters. The first step is observing children to see how quickly and accurately they sort. Then monitor children's daily writing efforts using developmental spelling for ongoing and authentic assessment. A number of assessments for letter sound knowledge can be found in Appendix A, starting on page 388.

- The Emergent Class Record helps you analyze children's writing across the emergent stage.
- There is also a Beginning Consonant Sounds and Letters assessment that asks children to circle a picture that begins with a given letter.
- A simple five-word spelling assessment such as the Kindergarten Spelling Inventory (KSI) is particularly appropriate for late emergent spellers.
- You might also call out five of the words on the Primary Spelling Inventory described in Chapter 2.

Focused contrast with initial consonants

Assess children formally at least three times a year, and informally all the time, using daily writing. For children receiving additional instructional interventions, we recommend more frequent monitoring to gauge their progress (Invernizzi, 2009). Longitudinal research indicates that kindergarten children should be aware that letters are associated with speech sounds and be able to provide at least four letter sounds in the fall of the year and at least 20 letter sounds in the spring (Invernizzi et al., 2005) in order to succeed without additional instruction or intervention. On average, kindergartners can accurately produce 14 letter sounds in the fall and nearly all of them in the spring (Invernizzi et al., 2014).

# LESSON ON BEGINNING SOUNDS

Here is a sample lesson that introduces a focused contrast with two consonants sounds: B and F.

1. ***Prepare materials for sorting.*** After reading a selection such as *Oh A-Hunting We Will Go*, focus on two sounds that are very different in articulation, such as B and F. Prepare a collection of pictures from Appendix D or other resources that can be sorted on a tabletop or pocket chart. Also prepare headers with the words and cards with both the capital and lowercase letters. You will also need a handout for each child of the sort or place the sort in a center for children to do independently.

2. ***Connect to the reading section.*** Hold up a card and say, "Here is capital B and lowercase b. Let's look back at our rhyme to look for words that start with B." Reread the rhyme if necessary to find the word *box*. say, "*Box* starts with B and here is a picture of a box." Repeat with F and identify *fox* as a word that start with F. Display the letters, words, and pictures as headers for the sort.

3. ***Introduce the pictures.*** Display the rest of the pictures in random order and say, "Let's name these pictures together." Have the children repeat the names after you, especially if you have English learners. Talk about any picture that might not be familiar ("Here is a picture of a *fist*—"When you clench your fingers into a ball, you make a fist. Make a fist with me.")

4. ***Introduce the sort.*** Say, "Here is the letter B. *Box* start with B. Here is the letter F. Fox starts with F. Now let's find more pictures we can match to B and F. I'll start. Here is a *fish*, Ffffish and fffffox both begin with F so I will put the *fish* under the *fox*. Here is a *bed*. *Bed* and *box* begin with B, so I will put *bed* under *box*." (Note: Although you can elongate the sound of F without distorting the sound, you cannot elongate the sound of B. Just emphasize it without adding /uh/ to it.)

5. ***Involve students in the sort.*** After modeling a few pictures and how to compare a new picture to the header, ask students to help you sort the rest of the pictures. Let them chose a picture and encourage them to say something like, "This is a bear. *Bear* and *box* begin with B." Guide students to sort correctly the first time through.

6. ***Review the sort.*** After sorting say, "Let's name all the pictures under the letter B and listen for the first sound in each picture." Read down the column, emphasizing the first sound and ask, "How are these words all alike? They all begin with B." Repeat with F.

7. ***Re-sort and check.*** Leave up the letters and pictures of *fox* and *box* and mix up the rest of the pictures. You might turn them face down in a pile and let children take turns drawing a picture, naming it, and identifying the letter it begins with. This time let mistakes go. After sorting say, "Let's name the pictures in each column and listen for the first sound to check our work." If a word has been misplaced say, "One of these does not sound the same at the beginning. Can you find it?"

8. ***Extend.*** Children should sort independently several times over the next few days using their own set of pictures or pictures in a center. Observe to see how quickly and accurately they sort. If you give students their own handout of pictures be sure to model how to cut apart the pictures after scribbling over the back in an assigned color so that lost pieces can be returned. These can later be glued into categories for a final assessment.

## Word Study for Initial Sounds

Here are a few things to keep in mind as you plan word study for children in the emergent stage who are sorting pictures by beginning sounds.

- *Resources for sorting.* You can find pictures for sorting in Appendix D that can be enlarged for group modeling. See the resources on page 430 for prepared sorts or how to create your own. Use easily identified pictures that do not start with consonant blends or digraphs. Single-syllable words are better than two-syllable words, because they have fewer sounds that need attention. The same key picture and a letter should be used each time to help children associate the letter and the sound. Suggestions for key pictures are on the sound boards in Appendix C.

- *Vary the sorting.* Start by putting out all the pictures face-up and let children choose one that they feel confident in naming and sorting correctly. Another time, pass out the pictures and call on children to come up and sort the card they were given. Then turn the pictures face-down in a stack or spread them out on the floor and let children turn over the picture they will sort. Children enjoy the anticipation of not knowing which picture they will get. Children can also sort with a partner as they take turns choosing a picture. This is helpful for English learners. Look for fast and accurate picture sorting. Be ready to drop back to fewer categories if a child has difficulty.

- *Plan plenty of time for individual practice and follow-up activities.* After the group lesson, put sets of pictures in centers or create copies of picture sets for children to cut apart for more sorting over several days. Cut-and-paste, draw-and-label, and word hunts through familiar chart stories, nursery rhymes, or little books are helpful follow-up activities described in Chapter 3. They require children to recognize, or recall, the same beginning sounds and to judge whether they fit the category.

- *Encourage pretend writing and developmental spelling.* In the process of writing, children exercise their phonics knowledge in a meaningful activity (Clarke, 1988; NRP, 2000; Snow et al., 1998). To get children started, demonstrate how to use letters to represent sounds as you write with children during interactive writing (see the Morning Message described in Activity 4.38). Asking children to label their drawings or to write just a sentence about something is a good way to get writing started (see Figure 4.5).

**Enhanced eText**
**Video Example 4.6**
This video shows how letter sounds are assessed in kindergarten.

Two students take turns sorting pictures by initial consonants

# Concepts About Print (CAP)

Children are surrounded by print on signs, package labels, magazines, computers, and television, even on the clothes they wear. However, unless adults talk about the purposes print serves and the special ways in which the visual forms of print are organized, children may not develop what is known as **concepts about print**. There are many ways to draw their attention to print and how it is used. For example, when you print the words to "Where Is Thumbkin?" on chart paper and point to them as the children sing along, you are helping them understand concepts of print. It happens when you stop to point out the *X* in the exit sign and explain what it means. It happens when you show a book cover and remind children that they have heard other stories written and illustrated by Tomie dePaola. The key is to be conscious of the many ways we use print and to "think aloud" as we draw children's attention to it in explicit ways. Justice and Ezell (2004) call this **print referencing**.

**Enhanced eText**
**Video Example 4.7**
Jackie uses the nursery rhyme *Humpty Dumpty* to develop concepts about print in this video.

## Print Referencing

Table 4.5 provides a list of the functions and forms of print and offers examples of print referencing that you might use. Reading with children during interactive or shared reading and writing with children during interactive writing and as you take dictations, provides abundant

**TABLE 4.5**  **CAP and Print Referencing Examples**

| Functions and Forms of Print | Print Referencing During Reading and Writing |
| --- | --- |
| Print is speech written down, and once written down it does not change. | I'm going to write down what you say, and then we can read it back. |
| Print is different from illustrations. | You look at the picture while I read what it says over here. |
| Print carries a message. | Here are the words to "Humpty Dumpty." Can you find the box that says "scissors"? |
| Print serves many purposes. | Here is the recipe for cookies. Let's read and find out what ingredients we need. |
| Book-handling skills—Start with the cover and turn from front to back. | Let's look at the cover of the book to see what it is about. |
| Directionality—Print is oriented left to right with a return sweep and top to bottom. | This is the top of the page where I will start reading. Then I will go to the next line. Show me where to go next. |
| Language related to units of print—Letters (capital and lowercase), numbers, words, sentences, lines. | There are four letters in this word. Let's name them. The first letter is a capital because it is a person's name. |
| Language related to books—Title, author, illustrator, title page, dedication, poem, song, beginning, end. | We have read another book by this author. Where do we look for the author's name? |
| Language related to phonological sensitivity—Syllable, sound, beginning and ending sound. | This is a long word. Let's clap the syllables in *caterpillar*. Can this word be *rug*? What is the first sound in *rug*? |
| Punctuation and special print—Periods, question marks, exclamation marks, quotation marks, bold print, italics. | Listen to how I read this sentence. It ends with an exclamation point so I want it to make it sound exciting. |
| Concept of word in text—Words are composed of a string of letters; words are separated by spaces. | Watch while I point to the words in this sentence. We need to leave a space here before we write the next word. |
| Word identification—Words can be identified in different contexts. | Here is the word *cat*. Can you find the word again on this page? What will you look for? |

*Source:* Adapted from Justice et al., 2009.

opportunities to develop concepts about print. When you use a print referencing style such as naming and pointing out letters or asking questions about print and pointing to words as you read, children show growth on measures of concepts about print, letter recognition, and name writing (Justice, Kaderavek, Fan, Sofka, & Hunt, 2009).

Reference specific print forms and functions during tasks that encourage children to write their own names, such as sign-up procedures. When you incorporate print into dramatic play centers such as restaurants, doctors' offices, and so on, children use writing as they pretend to be waiters writing down a dinner order, doctors writing a prescription, and the like. In the process, they learn that print takes many forms and serves many functions. You can find some specific activities (Activities 4.35 to 4.38) at the end of this chapter.

## Assessing and Monitoring Growth in CAP

Marie Clay (1985) first developed a formal protocol for assessing concepts about print using a series of questions while sharing a book with a child. Many variations of this exist; in fact, state and local standards for early literacy may include a checklist of questions regarding children's development in CAP. You can also see concepts about print in children's efforts to write their names. Their efforts, which may range from scribbles to letter-like forms mixed with numbers to recognizable signatures, can predict later literacy achievement (Welsch, Sullivan, & Justice, 2003).

- We provide several assessments in Appendix A that help you interpret name writing and other writing.
- Concepts about print can be informally assessed all the time as you read and write with children by posing questions such as "Who can point to a capital letter *D*?" or "What do we put at the end of a sentence?"

# Concept of Word in Text (COW-T)

The ultimate concept about print is achieving a **concept of word in text** (COW-T)—the ability to fingerpoint or track accurately to printed words in text while reading from memory. Reaching this milestone depends on a student's ability to isolate the beginning consonant sounds of spoken words and knowledge of letter–sound correspondences—skills that help the beginning reader find words on the page. Figure 4.9 shows the progression of finger pointing accuracy in relation to writing development during the emergent to early letter name–alphabetic stage of word knowledge. Incorporating concept of word activities into daily literacy practice not only strengthens students' speech-to-print matching, but it also solidifies their alphabet knowledge, emerging phonemic awareness, and knowledge of words in print. There is an interaction between alphabetic knowledge, the ability to match speech to print, and phonemic awareness (Flanigan, 2007; Morris et al., 2003; Tunmer, 1991). However, achieving a concept of word in text is not an all-or-nothing affair—there is a developmental continuum.

## COW-T Continuum

The concept of word continuum includes *developing*, *rudimentary*, and *firm* levels. During the emergent stage, learners move from the developing level to a rudimentary concept of word. Children with a firm concept of word in text are letter name–alphabetic spellers, described in Chapter 5.

To determine where your children are on the concept of word continuum, examine the accuracy of their fingerpoint reading to memorized rhymes and jingles, their ease with identifying words in context, and their ability to remember words in isolation that were viewed previously in context (Blackwell-Bullock, Invernizzi, Drake, & Howell, 2009; Flanigan, 2007; Morris, 1993).

**FIGURE 4.9** Voice-to-Print Match in Relation to Spelling Development

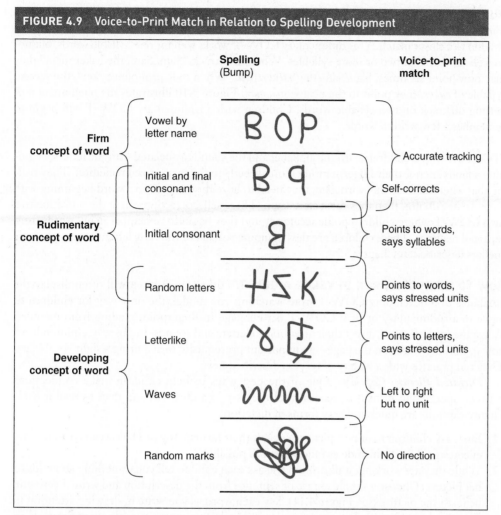

Spelling
(Bump)

Voice-to-print
match

| Firm concept of word | Vowel by letter name | | Accurate tracking |
| | Initial and final consonant | | Self-corrects |
| Rudimentary concept of word | Initial consonant | | Points to words, says syllables |
| Developing concept of word | Random letters | | Points to words, says stressed units |
| | Letterlike | | Points to letters, says stressed units |
| | Waves | | Left to right but no unit |
| | Random marks | | No direction |

*Source:* Gill (1992). Focus on research: Development of word knowledge as it relates to reading, spelling, and instruction. *Language Arts, 69,* 6, 444–453. Adapted with permission.

**DEVELOPING COW-T.** Children who are just developing a COW-T will have some orientation to the page, moving from the top to the bottom and linearly side to side (but perhaps not from left to right). What they point to on the page as they recite does not coincide with printed word units at all. The pre-literate child may punch at the page in a rhythmic recitation of the memorized text, but with little attention to word boundaries.

Through your demonstrations, top-to-bottom and left-to-right movement becomes habitualized. As they note white spaces, children begin to track rhythmically across the text, pointing to words for each stressed beat. For example, when tracking the traditional five-word ditty, "Sam, Sam, the baker man," they may point four times: Sam/Sam/the-baker/man. An article (*the, a, an*) may be treated as part of the word that follows it. The child pointing to "One, two buckle my shoe" can be seen to point off-track.

Child with a developing COW-T points to the words as she reads

**RUDIMENTARY COW-T.** As children become aware that print has something to do with sound units such as syllables, their fingerpointing becomes more precise and changes from a gross rhythm to a closer match. This rudimentary COW-T works well for one-syllable words, but not so well for words of two or more syllables. When they track "Sam, Sam, the baker man," they may now point six times: Sam/Sam/the/ba/ker/man. When they pronounce /ker/, the second syllable of *baker*, they point to the next word, *man*. Figure 4.10 illustrates the phenomenon of getting off track on two-syllable words. Children with a rudimentary COW-T will begin to remember a few written words.

**FIRM COW-T.** As children learn the alphabet and the sounds associated with the letters, beginning sounds anchor their fingerpointing more directly to the memorized recitation. They realize that when they say the word *man*, they need to have their finger on a word beginning with an *m*. If they do not, then they must start again. These self-corrections mark the transition to a firm COW-T where children point accurately and they begin to remember many words from repeated readings. These children are the beginning readers or the early letter name–alphabetic spellers described in Chapter 5.

**HOW TO HELP CHILDREN DEVELOP A COW-T.** Although children will often display the attributes of a developing COW-T from watching you model, the only way for children to move to a rudimentary or firm COW-T is to engage in fingerpoint reading from memory. When they get off track, direct their attention to letters and sounds. In this way, children learn how to find the words on the page—an important prerequisite to acquiring a sight vocabulary. They can practice with a variety of texts as described next.

*Dictated Picture Captions.* One of the best ways to help children make connections between speech and print is to record what they say in a dictation and then to read it back. Picture captions are quick and easy forms of dictation.

1. First, ask children to draw a picture, such as their favorite toy or Halloween costume, and encourage them to include as much detail as possible.
2. While they are working, walk around and ask each child to tell you something about his or her picture. Choose a simple phrase or sentence from the description and write it verbatim beneath the picture (see Figure 4.11). Say each word as you write it, drawing attention to the sounds and letters and involving the child when appropriate with questions such as, "What sound do you hear first?"

**Enhanced eText**
**Video Example 4.8**
Regina talks about her kindergarten students who at are different places in their development of COW in this video.

**FIGURE 4.10  Trying to Match Voice to Print**

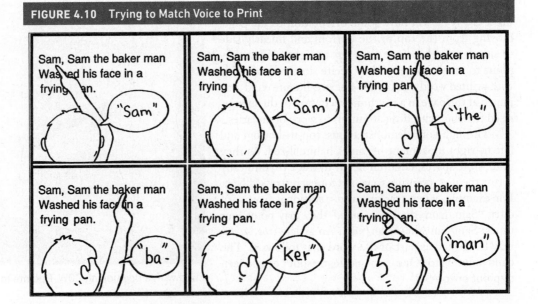

**3.** Read the caption by pointing to each word. Ask the child to read along with you and then to read it alone while pointing. Later, the child may attempt to reread the caption to a buddy.

*Group Dictations.* Like picture captions, spoken or dictated accounts of students' experiences also help them link speech to print. This approach is described in more detail in Activity 4.39 and is traditionally referred to as the Language Experience Approach (**LEA**), (Stauffer, 1970; Labbi, Eakle, & Montero, 2002). The LEA is based on the premise that what you say can be written and what you write can be read. The motivation and engagement that results from using students' self-generated language has revitalized an interest in LEA, especially for emergent learners and for children learning English as another language (Dorr, 2006). Experience is the best teacher!

*Rhymes for Reading.* Familiar rhymes, songs, or jingles are easily memorized texts that students can use to practice fingerpointing after a shared reading experience. Rhythmic texts are particularly appealing to use when children are developing a COW-T but may throw them off in their tracking. Eventually moving to less rhythmic, less predictable texts may be in order (Cathey, 1991).

**1.** *Memorize.* First help children learn the rhyme, song, or jingle "by heart," because developing a COW-T is all about matching oral speech to print. It helps to use pictures for prompts, as shown in Figure 4.12. To teach your children to memorize the rhyme, point to each picture frame while singing or reciting the line that goes with it, repeating as needed. Some children may only be able to memorize two lines, whereas others can handle four or six. "Resource Connections: Traditional Rhymes and Jingles" on the next page lists some collections of traditional rhymes and jingles. They can also be found by searching online. Many nursery rhymes, songs, and jump rope jingles are illustrated in *Words Their Way:® Letter and Picture Sorts for Emergent Spellers* (Bear, Invernizzi, Johnston, & Templeton, 2018).

**2.** *Introduce the print.* After children memorize the rhyme, display it on a whiteboard, chart paper, or on sentence strips printed in text large enough for everyone to see. Model how to fingerpoint and invite children to "read" with you chorally (in unison) or using echo reading (you read a line, then they read the same line again, fingerpointing). If you used a song, it is time to slow it down and read it at this point.

**3.** *Individual copies.* Giving children their own copy of the rhyme on a single sheet of paper is very important so that they can get more practice pointing to the words as they read chorally and individually. These texts should be printed in the largest possible font (26-point or better) and for children with a developing COW-T, you may keep to two lines and insert an extra space between words. You might also give them sentence strips to cut apart and rebuild the text.

**4.** *Words.* Begin to focus on words in the text. After several rounds of fingerpoint reading, see whether children can identify one or two targeted words per line. Point to a word and ask, "What's this word?" If a child doesn't know the word, show him or her how to start at the beginning of the line to reread or **voice point** up to the word in question. Alternatively, you can ask children to find a word in a particular line by providing a beginning sound: "I'm thinking of a word in this line that starts just like the word *ball*. What word am I thinking of? Can you point to it? How did you know that was the word I was thinking of? Yes! *Box* and *ball* both begin with the /b/ sound. They both begin with the letter *b!*" When children have their own copies of the rhyme, they can highlight or underline the words you ask them to find.

Learners with limited English will benefit from practicing fingerpointing using materials in their primary languages. Rhymes and jingles in Spanish can be found in *Words Their Way:®️ Emergent Sorts for Spanish-Speaking English Learners* (Helman, Bear, Invernizzi, Templeton, & Johnston, 2009) and *Words Their Way:® Letter Name–Alphabetic Sorts for Spanish-Speaking English Learners* (Helman, Bear, Invernizzi, Templeton, & Johnston, 2009).

*for* **English learners**

**FIGURE 4.11  Drawing with Dictated Caption**

This is a firetruck going to the house.

**FIGURE 4.12  Rhymes for Reading**

There was a little turtle.

He lived in a box.

He swam in the water.

He climbed on a rock.

**BACKGROUND | EMERGENT STAGE**

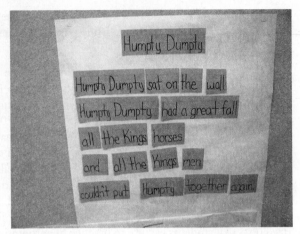

Children rebuild a favorite rhyme and compare their work with a chart

**RESOURCE CONNECTIONS**

**Traditional Rymes and Jingles**

Cole, J. (1989). *Ann Banana: 101 jump-rope rhymes.* New York: Scholastic.

Cole, J., & Calmenson, S. (1990). *Miss Mary Mack and other children's street rhymes.* Illustrated by Alan Tiegreen. New York: Morrouno.

Ratisseau, S. (2014) *Jumping Joy: A book about jump rope rhymes.* Seattle, WA: Laughing Elephant

Schwartz, A. (1989). *I saw you in the bathtub.* New York: HarperCollins.

Sierra, J., & Sweet, M. (2005). *Schoolyard rhymes: Kids' own rhymes for rope jumping, hand clapping, ball bouncing, and just plain fun.* New York: Knopf.

# The Whole-to-Part Five-Day Lesson Framework

Kindergarten children practice finger pointing to familiar text in small group

The whole-to-part, five-day lesson plan includes all aspects of the literacy diet: vocabulary, phonemic awareness, alphabet, letter sounds, and concepts of print in the service of developing a concept of word in text. You can use the five-day format with any kind of text—poems, rhymes, jingles, songs, language experience dictations, or parts of a simple pattern book. The key is to limit the text to no more than two to eight lines that children can memorize after repeated readings. The procedures move from introducing a whole text to the parts with a gradual release of responsibility. Activities on days 2 to 5 can vary, depending on the skill of your children and the time you have.

# The Five Day Whole-to-Part Lesson Framework

*MATERIALS*

You will need:

- chart paper
- a pocket chart
- sentence strips
- envelope
- word cards

Record a copy of the text on chart paper using print large enough for all to see and/or prepare two sets of sentence strips with individual lines from the text and have word cards ready to record selected words. In addition, prepare a handout with several lines from the text. Glue these into personal readers made from newsprint or blank white paper stapled together as described in Chapter 5. Leave out the chart, sentence strips, and word cards for children to use independently as a center activity after they have been introduced in the group.

*PROCEDURES*

**Day 1. Introduce the whole text.**

1. *Memorize.* Have children memorize a rhyme, poem, song, or jingle or a patterned refrain from a storybook introduced during shared reading. Use simple pictures if possible to help them memorize the lines by heart. If children have difficulty memorizing four or five lines, cut back to two. Talk about any unusual or unfamiliar vocabulary. For example, in the nursery rhyme of "Jack and Jill" the word *fetch* should be discussed. Talk about rhyming words and allow children to supply the ending rhymes as you recite.

2. *Introduce the print.* Introduce the printed text on chart paper or a pocket chart—one sentence per line. (Or start with this step if you are using a simple book like *Cat on the Mat* described in the opening vignette.) Model how to read the text by using your finger or pointer to touch every word as you say it. Include print referencing as you talk about how you are starting with the first *word* on the left and touching each *word* in the *sentence* as you say it. Touch multisyllabic words several times and explain why. Point out special punctuation and the use of capital letters.

3. *Read together.* Ask the children to read each sentence exactly as you do after you have read it. Then invite the children to say it with you (chorally) as you point to each word; this is the third reading. Then ask individual children to come up and recite as much of it as you think they are capable of while

pointing to each word. Be prepared to guide as needed to ensure accurate pointing.

**Day 2. Work with the parts (sentences).**

1. *Review.* Review the text by repeating steps 2 and 3 from day 1. Add more print referencing and ask children to find some of the things you talked about previously. For example, "Can someone find the question mark?"

2. *Sentence strips.* Hand out sentence strips and ask children to find the sentence it matches in the pocket chart and place it there. Discuss how they knew it was the same—prompt for specifics like "starts with" or "the word . . . ." Rebuild the text with and without a model for reference. Simple pictures like those in Figure 4.12 on page 115 can help children get the sentence strips in order.

3. *Individual Copies for Fingerpointing Practice.* Pass out individual copies of the rhyme. Read this together as every child tracks the print. Keep this copy in their personal readers (see Chapter 5 for more details). Pair children with a buddy and have them practice reading the rhyme to each other while fingerpointing. Ask the non-reading buddy to make sure his or her partner is saying and pointing to each word. Have each partner read twice.

**Day 3. Work with the parts (words).**

1. *Reread.* Ask children to fingerpoint-read their own copies to review the text.

2. *Match words.* Pass out individual word cards and have children come up and find a word on the chart or sentence strips and place it on top of its match in the pocket chart. Limit this to one sentence at first. Discuss how they knew it was the same word. (Prompt for letters and beginning sounds.)

3. *Cut up sentence strips.* Pass out the sentence strips along with envelopes containing that particular sentence cut up into individual words. Have children rebuild the sentence word by word. See Cut-Up Sentences (Activity 4.40) and Be the Sentence (Activity 4.41). See Figure 4.20.

4. *Rhyme.* If the text you are using includes rhyming words, you can ask students to find them and talk about how they are alike (they end the same way). You might want to do a rhyme sort or invent other rhymes as described in Activities 4.11 to 4.14.

**Day 4. Work with the parts (letters and sounds).**

1. *Find words that begin with a sound.* Use the chart copy or pocket chart to reread the text and then ask children to find words that start with particular

letters or sounds. Say something like, "I'm thinking of a word in this line that starts with the same sound as _____. What word am I thinking of? How did you know?"

2. *Reread.* Have children reread their own copies. Name words (or letters for children still learning the alphabet) for them to find and talk about how they found it (what letter or sounds they used). They can highlight or underline the words you ask them to find. Children can also call out words for each other to find.

3. *Word study for initial sounds.* Select two to four letter sounds to use as the basis for a picture sorting lesson described on page 112. Model the sort with the group and then assign students to do it independently with their own set of pictures or in centers.

**Day 5. Review the whole and assess the parts.**

1. *Reread.* Have the children reread the text using the chart or personal copies. Select words for a word bank as described in Chapter 5 for children who have at least a rudimentary COW-T. Have children illustrate their rhymes in their personal readers as a reward for all their hard work.

2. *Word Study Review.* Ask children to re-sort pictures used for the initial sound sort under your supervision. Repeat the sort over the next few days and complete extensions.

3. *Assess COW-T.* Assess children's ability to track using the guidelines described on pages 114 and 144. Ask individual children to read the rhyme as they point to the words. Observe how accurately they track and whether they self-correct when they get off track. Point to a few words for a child to name, or hold up word cards in isolation to name.

4. *Reread over time.* Periodically have children reread charts done throughout the year and all the pages in their personal readers. Personal readers can go home so children can share their developing skills. Be sure that parents understand that they will read from memory but should try to touch each word as they read.

The exact activities you do each day in the whole-to-part framework will vary depending on where your students are in terms of their literacy development. Although the whole group can participate in the first or second day, you may want to form small groups for subsequent days. Later we describe how to organize for small group instruction that meets individual needs.

## Assessing and Monitoring Growth in COW-T

You can easily assess concept of word in text by asking children to point to individual words in a familiar piece of text, such as a nursery rhyme or jump rope jingle. "One, Two, Buckle My Shoe" or "Humpty Dumpty" work well because they have words of more than one syllable. Observe how children point to words on the page. Do they move left to right and top to bottom? Do they point to words as they say syllables or stressed beats? Do they get off track on two-syllable words? Do they self-correct when they get off track? You can find assessment directions and forms in Appendix A starting on page 373.

After several rounds of fingerpoint reading, ask children to name the words that you point to in context or more randomly, as described previously, and observe their strategies. Do they reread an entire line and count up the memorized words to identify it? Or do they identify it immediately? Ask, "How did you find that word?" or "How did you know that word?" Children who can tell you that a word starts with a *w* are using developing letter–sound knowledge to track words in text. This is a necessary precursor to acquiring sight words, which is discussed in Chapter 5.

## Word Study Routines and Management

The research in emergent literacy suggests that a comprehensive approach to instruction and early intervention is the most effective procedure (Pressley, 2006). A comprehensive approach includes attention to the six components of the emergent literacy "diet" described in this chapter done, not sequentially, but simultaneously. These essential components can be integrated into major organizational time units during which you *Read To, Read With, Write With*, do *Word Study*, and *Talk With* (RRWWT) children.

- During *read to* time, you read aloud literature that offers exposure to new vocabulary and literary language.
- During *read with* time, children engage in shared reading and rereading of familiar texts and print referencing is easy when you use enlarged text.
- When you model how to write by stretching out the sounds in words and matching them to letters, you are *writing with* children, who will, in turn, write for themselves.
- *Word study* includes direct instruction in phonological awareness, the alphabet, and letter sounds.
- Finally, a comprehensive program provides children with ample opportunities to *talk with* you and their peers about the books and experiences they share.

Combining these activities into a cohesive RRWWT routine is important so that the activities and materials flow together in a logical way and serve multiple purposes. Recall how Ms. Smith introduced an engaging core book and used it to draw attention to letters and sounds, to highlight vocabulary, to offer children practice tracking familiar text, and to sort pictures by rhyme and beginning sounds. *Words Their Way:® Letter and Picture Sorts for Emergent Spellers* (Bear et al., 2019) offers examples of how these components can be integrated and provides ready-to-print rhymes and jingles for reading as well as prepared sorts.

## Emergent Literacy Daily Management Plan

The daily management of emergent literacy instruction should include whole groups, small groups, and literacy centers, as outlined in Table 4.6. In a whole group, Ms. Smith modeled finger-point reading and other concepts about print, and then called a small group together to introduce a picture sort of initial sounds that children later practiced independently. They worked from a whole text, then with sentences, words, letters, and sounds in the whole-to-part framework.

**WHOLE GROUP.** Whole-group activities emphasize reading to and with students, teacher modeling, listening, and vocabulary development. Print referencing opportunities arise during whole-group instruction. Read-alouds serve many purposes and you can plan two or more whole-group sessions during the day for emergent children where they listen to read-alouds from a variety of genres, including information books related to thematic studies, alphabet books, and books with language play such as rhyme. Use whole-group time to sing songs while pointing to the words, practice the alphabet song, model writing, and introduce shared reading activities designed to facilitate CAP and COW-T. This is where the "whole" of a whole-to-part model takes place, with some attention to the parts.

**Enhanced eText**
Video Example 4.9
Regina combines support reading and word study of initial consonants in this video.

**SMALL GROUPS.** Children can participate actively under close supervision while in small groups or during circle time. This is when to implement differentiated instruction according to assessed needs. You can form small groups initially based on alphabet knowledge and phonological awareness but also on concept of word (developing versus rudimentary). For example, some children will need to focus on alphabet recognition and look for letters in familiar texts, whereas children who already know their letters and have a rudimentary COW-T may be ready to acquire some sight words from repeated readings of familiar text. The small group is where the "parts" of the whole-to-part lesson format are addressed in depth, such as rhyming picture sorts or picture sorts for beginning sounds.

**Enhanced eText**
Video Example 4.10
Regina explains how she organized her kindergarten classroom in this video.

**SEAT AND CENTER.** Independent work provides additional practice. After children are introduced to activities and sorts in small groups, they can work independently, with partners, in centers, or at their seats. Betty Lee's word study routines described in Chapter 3 are designed for independent work. Games and puzzles, such as those described in the activities section in this chapter, should be first introduced and modeled in groups and then placed in centers. Writing can be an independent activity as children work in journals or draw and label pictures based on sorts.

**TABLE 4.6** Emergent Literacy Plan

| Whole-Group Activities | Small-Group/Circle Time Differentiated Activities | Seat/Center Differentiated Activities |
|---|---|---|
| "Read To": Read-alouds for thematic units and vocabulary work<br><br>Introduce concept sorts | Concept sorts<br><br>Retelling, dramatization, rhythm | Practice concept sorts<br><br>Retell using picture books, puppets, and so on |
| "Read With": Shared reading of big books, rhymes, songs, dictations<br><br>Memorize "whole" texts such as nursery rhymes and jingles | Reread familiar texts until memorized<br><br>"Parts"—Work with sentence strips, word cards, and so on | Partner or individual work with sentences and words |
| "Word Study": Sing and recite alphabet<br><br>Share alphabet and language play books<br><br>Name of the Day | Introduce differentiated sorts: rhyme, font, initial consonants | Practice sorts<br><br>Letter and sound hunts<br><br>Games and puzzles for rhyme, alphabet, initial consonants |
| "Write With": Modeled and interactive writing<br><br>Morning Message | Language experience dictations | Picture caption dictations<br><br>Draw and label<br><br>Journal writing |

*Note:* "Talk With" happens throughout all the activities.

# RESOURCES CONNECTIONS — IMPLEMENTING WORD STUDY *in Your Classroom*

A number of materials are available to help you implement word study with children in the emergent stage:

1. *Words Their Way for PreK–K* (Johnston et al., 2015) offers a more thorough coverage of the literacy diet described in this chapter, as well as more activities and lesson plans. It is recommended for early childhood teachers working with children in the emergent and letter name–alphabetic stages.

2. Pictures to create sound sorts for rhyme and initial sounds can be found in Appendix D and can be used with the template on page 502 to create your own sorts. See the directions and lists of rhyming pictures on pages 430–431.

3. Prepared sorts and games are available at WTWD. There are also resources to create your own picture sorts.

4. *Words Their Way:® Letter and Picture Sorts for Emergent Spellers* (Bear et al., 2019, 3rd edition) offers a complete curriculum of sorts including concept sorts, rhyme sorts, alphabet font sorts, and beginning consonant sorts. There are also numerous reading selections—ready-to-print illustrated copies of short rhymes and jingles to use for developing concept of word.

5. *Words Their Way:® Emergent Sorts for Spanish-Speaking English Learners* (Helman et al., 2009) provides many prepared sorts to develop concepts and vocabulary as well as sound sorts with different contrasts.

6. Two of many websites to support emergent literacy learning are *PALS* Virginia and *Webbing into Literacy* Curry School of Education, both from the University of Virginia. You need not register to take advantage of the resources at PALS.

## ACTIVITIES for the Emergent Stage

This section provides specific activities arranged by the six components of early literacy. Within each, the activities are roughly in order of increasing difficulty. However, concept sorts do not have to precede sound awareness, which in turn must precede alphabet. In reality, these develop simultaneously and constitute the "literacy diet" during the emergent years, with many activities that cut across the categories. Some of the games are generic to all stages of developmental word knowledge as indicated by the Adaptable for Other Stages symbol used throughout the book.

*WTW Digital* **activities and interactive digital sorts**. There are a dozen sorts and a variety of game templates and materials to print and package for student use. Each sort includes clear directions and questions to encourage discussion.

**Multisensory learning.** Many word study activities have multisensory properties that involve the senses through seeing, saying, listening, and feeling. Specifically, in this & and Chapter 5, students see the letters, say their names, hear their associated speech sounds, feel how they are made or articulated in their mouths, and how they are formed with their hands and fingers. These visual, auditory, kinesthetic and tactile (VAKT) experiences solidify their knowledge of letter names, letter sounds, and letter shapes as they say the words aloud, sort them into categories, and write them during word study games and activities. Students articulate speech sounds; write them; engage in word bank activities; check and reflect on their sorts; and tap, clap, dance, and sing to the rhythm of familiar songs, rhymes, and lines from stories. On the reflective side, we teach students that "after you say, explain" why they categorized words or pictures the way they did.

# Oral Language, Concepts, and Vocabulary

Oral language, concept and vocabulary are developed throughout the day in many different ways. Earlier in this chapter we described some generic ideas, and here we offer some more specific ones.

### 4.1 Using Interactive Read-Alouds to Develop Vocabulary

Books provide the best exposure to new vocabulary for young children, but simply reading to them is not enough. You need to draw attention to words and plan ways to ensure that new words are acquired and used. Interactive read-alouds take additional time to implement because you want children to have the opportunity to engage in a lot of oral language. At the same time, excessive interruptions can disrupt the flow of the text, so striking a balance between stopping and reading is important. Sometimes you may want to read a book with few, if any, interruptions and sometimes you may use a second reading to focus on words and invite responses.

**PROCEDURES**
1. Select a book with rich language that is age-appropriate for your listeners. Preview the book, looking for new vocabulary and conceptual understandings that will extend students' background knowledge. For example, rural or small-town children might not be familiar with the escalator mentioned in *Corduroy* by Don Freeman. Select three to five words based on (1) utility, (2) concreteness, (3) repetition, and (4) relatedness to themes or topics of study (see criteria on page 98). Prepare child-friendly definitions. (You might occasionally model using a picture dictionary, and even use it yourself to develop definitions, but dictionaries often do not provide clear examples or explanations.)
2. Introduce the book by reading the title and naming the author and illustrator. Look at the cover and at least the first few pages to elicit a prediction ("What do you think this book will be about?") and to set a purpose for reading. Build background knowledge as needed and try to introduce the target words conversationally, perhaps pointing to a picture or supplying a brief definition. Ask the children to listen for the words as you read.
3. Make the read-aloud interactive by inviting comments and questions from the children during reading. Encourage them to connect with the characters and theme ("Have you ever

worn overalls like Corduroy's?"). Expand on children's brief utterances ("lost button") with complete sentences to model more complex language ("Yes, Corduroy had lost a button but he did not realize it."). Point out the targeted words when they occur in context and have children say the words with you.

4. After reading, invite children to respond to the story in personal ways and then revisit the targeted words as you model their use, pose questions, and elicit children's responses. Use the new words in questions about the story and ask children to use them in sentences, act them out, or find other applications for them to engage the children. ("Why do you think Corduroy admired the furniture in the store?" "What is something that you admire?" "Turn to your partner and use the word *admire* in a sentence.")

5. Always make books you read aloud available for children to look at on their own. Encourage them to retell it in their own words (see the next activity) and/or talk with a friend about the pictures to elicit oral language.

## 4.2 PEER—Retellings through Dialogic Reading

Studies of dialogic reading have demonstrated growth in expressive and receptive language when used by parents and teachers of at-risk preschoolers (Whitehurst et al., 1994; Justice & Pullen, 2003; NELP, 2008). In this gradual release of responsibility activity, children learn how to talk about and retell a familiar book after seeing it modeled by adults. Parents can be trained in this technique and you can send books home that have been read and discussed in school. Adults can use the PEER sequence (Morgan & Meier, 2008) to stimulate oral language and help the child become the storyteller.

**PROCEDURES** Begin by reading a book aloud and then follow up with small-group or individual rereadings before engaging in a prompted discussion. You might find that children are even happier to do a retelling when they can record themselves and listen to it afterward. Repeat the prompt sequence several times using the PEER guidelines:

**P Prompt** the child to say something about the book using open-ended questions. (Point to a picture of a mouse and say, "What is he doing?" The child says, "Running.")

**E Evaluate** the child's response. ("That's right!")

**E Expand** the response by rephrasing or adding information to it. ("The mouse is running away from the cat.")

**R Repeat** the prompt and ask the child to expand on it. ("What is the mouse doing?" The child says, "He is running away from the cat.")

Use additional prompts such as the following to stimulate talk:

1. Ask what, when, where, why, and how questions.
2. Leave a blank at the end of a sentence for the children to fill in.
3. Ask children to retell what has happened so far or to retell the ending.
4. Ask children to describe what they see happening in pictures.
5. Ask children to make connections with their own experiences.

## 4.3 Turn and Talk

A good way to increase the opportunities for oral interaction and vocabulary use in your classroom is to ask children to turn and talk to an assigned partner during a discussion. Rather than calling on one child, everyone has a chance to respond to a question, to share an experience, to make a prediction, to summarize, and so on. Turn and talk is a good way to encourage children who might be reluctant to speak in front of the whole group. This includes English learners as well as shy or less verbal students.

**PROCEDURES**

1. Model your expectations for "turn and talk" with another adult. Demonstrate how both partners need a chance to speak and suggest ways to encourage a reluctant talker. ("Tell me what you think. It's your turn now" or "You go first this time.") You can also ask two

children who do a particularly good job together to model for the rest of the group. Children should not move about during turn and talk but instead turn "knee to knee and eye to eye" and talk softly so they do not disturb others. Signal cards such as an ear for listening and a mouth for talking can be mounted on tongue depressors or popsicle sticks.

2. Select partners before the read-aloud or other shared experience begins. You may allow children to pick their own partners on the way to the group and then sit down together. Or you may select partners, taking into consideration childrens' language competence and confidence. A more verbal child may provide a model for a less verbal child, but he or she might also dominate the conversation, so watch to see how pairs work out and be ready to intervene with suggestions about ways to give the less verbal child an equal opportunity. Use the same partners for a week or longer to save organizational time.

Children have signal cards to use during Turn and Talk

3. Bring turn and talk time to a close by offering a countdown warning. One way to do this is to silently hold up five fingers and then lower each finger in turn. As children notice, they should imitate you down to the final fist when everyone should be done talking. How much time you allow will vary, but bring turn and talk time to a close before children lose their focus and get off the assigned topic.

4. As partners talk to each other, listen in to monitor their conversations. When the group is back together you might call on one or two children to report what they talked about. Because less verbal or shy children have had a chance to rehearse their ideas, they should be better able to speak before a larger group after turn and talk time.

## **4.4** Paste the Pasta and Other Concrete Concept Sorts

Categorizing pasta by size, shape, and color is a good hands-on activity that introduces the idea of sorting to young children. Many early childhood curricula include the study of pattern, but being able to categorize by particular attributes must come first. Staying focused on a single attribute of interest is difficult for young children. They may begin sorting by color and then switch to shape in midstream. They will need many activities of this kind, sorting real, concrete objects that have different features.

**MATERIALS** You need three to six types of pasta of various sizes and shapes. You may want to use pasta of various colors or you can dye your own by shaking the pasta in a jar with a tablespoon of alcohol and a few drops of food coloring, then lay it out on newspaper to dry. If you dye your own, make sure that any one color encompasses a variety of shapes and sizes. Two or three colors are enough. Children can sort onto paper divided into columns, as shown in Figure 4.13 or simply into piles.

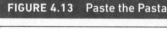

**FIGURE 4.13 Paste the Pasta**

**PROCEDURES**
1. Prepare a mixture of the dried pasta and give each child a handful and a sorting paper.
2. Begin with an open sort, in which you invite the children to come up with their own way of grouping. This gives you an opportunity to evaluate which children understand attribute sorting and which need more guidance. Ask the children to share their ideas and show their groups. Discuss the different features or attributes by which they can sort.
3. Ask children to re-sort using a category different from their first one. You might end this activity by letting the children glue the pasta onto their sorting sheets by categories and then labeling their chosen sorts.

**VARIATIONS** There is no end to the concrete things you can sort with your children as you explore the different features that define your categories, as in the following suggestions

- Children—male/female, hair color, eye color, age, favorite color
- Shoes—sandals/sneakers, right/left, tie/hook and loop/buckle/slip-on
- Clothing—mittens/gloves, types of headwear, short-sleeved tops/long-sleeved tops, coats with or without hoods, coats that button or zip
- Buttons—two holes/four holes/no holes, shape, color, size
- Bottle caps—size, color, plastic/metal, plain/printed, ribbed/smooth
- Blocks—shape, color, size, length
- Toys—size, color, purpose, plastic/wood/metal
- Food—sweet/sour/bitter/salty, fruits/vegetables/grains, healthy/not healthy.

**GUESS MY CATEGORY** It is fun to sort children by different attributes in a guess my category activity. Begin by calling on a child to stand to one side to start the categories (such as child with long sleeves and a child with short sleeves) without telling what the contrasting feature is. Then sort a few more before pausing to ask, Where will Jill go? Watch to see who is catching on to the categories but don't let them tell until the end. Of course, objects can be sorted this way also.

## 4.5 Concept Books and Concept Sorts

Simple concept books designed for young children make great beginnings for concept sorts. Examples include *Is It Red? Is It Yellow? Is It Blue?* and other books by Tana Hoban, and *My Very First Book of Shapes* by Eric Carle. Topics include shapes, colors, textures, positions, types of clothing, animals, opposites, and so on.

**PROCEDURES**

1. Because concept books have little text, engage children in discussing what they see and supplying appropriate labels. "This is a book about colors. Here is a picture of a toy dump truck. What color is the dump truck? Yes, the dump truck is red. Now it's your turn. Tell me what you see here."

2. Collect objects or pictures of objects that can be used for sorting. In the case of colors, you can probably find real objects around the room such as books, markers, toys, and so on. Explain to the children that they are going to help you sort the objects by color. Use complete sentences to model: "Here is a red ball. I will put the ball with the other things that are red." After sorting, help children make generalizations such as "How are all these things alike? Yes, all the things in this category are red."

3. Make labels for each category of your sort with help from the students: "I am going to write *red* on this card to label this category. Listen, *rrrr-ed*. What letter do I need to write down first?"

4. Put sorts where children can use them on their own and encourage them to talk as they sort. Children can look for more pictures in magazines or catalogs that fit the categories or they can draw pictures, cut them out, and paste them into categories. Encourage them to label their own sorts spelling as best they can.

**VARIATIONS** You can develop other concept sorts along the same lines. The following list of categories represents opposites or antonyms that are frequently confused by young children and can be better understood through sorting.

- Real/imaginary
- Smooth/rough
- Big/little
- Hard/soft

Of course, books can be the starting point for a concept sort. In Chapter 5, we describe a food sort based on *Gregory the Terrible Eater* by Marjorie Sharmat.

## 4.6 All My Friends Photograph Sort

Another example of an open-ended sort involves guessing each other's categories.

**MATERIALS** Take digital pictures of your students and create a composite so that they are all on one page. Each small group gets a set of pictures to cut apart and sort. The children also need a sheet of construction paper to divide into columns for sorting.

**PROCEDURES** Brainstorm with the children some of the ways that the pictures might be grouped (hair length, hair color, clothing, boys/girls, facial expressions). Have children work in groups to sort by these or other categories they discover. After pasting their pictures into the columns on their paper, each group can hold up their effort and ask the others in the class to guess their categories. The category labels or key words should then be written on the papers.

**VARIATIONS** Children can sort photographs from home according to places (inside/outside, home/vacation), number of people in the photograph (adults, sisters, brothers), number of animals in the photograph, seasons (by clothing, outside trees/plants), age of people in the photograph, and so forth. As children learn to recognize their classmates' names, have them match the names to the pictures.

## 4.7 Transportation Unit

Teachers of young children often organize their curriculum into thematic units of study. Such units frequently lend themselves to concept sorts, which review and extend the understandings central to the unit goals. The following example uses a transportation theme.

**MATERIALS** You need a collection of toy vehicles (planes, boats, cars, and trucks) or pictures of vehicles. Books featuring transportation, such as *My Truck Is Stuck* by Kevin Lewis, can introduce the sort. An interactive version of a transportation sort is included on the WTW Digital website.

**PROCEDURES**

1. Lay out the pictures on the floor or table and invite the children to think of which ones might go together. Encourage them to think up a variety of possibilities that will divide everything into only two or three categories. This is an open sort because the children are providing the categories.

2. After each suggestion, sort the vehicles by the identified attributes, talking about the categories and how things are sorted: "A truck has wheels so I will put it with the car and the bicycle." Record the ideas for different sorts on a chart or chalkboard. Some possibilities include plastic/metal, big/little, old/new, one color/many colors, windows/no windows, wheels/no wheels, and land/air/water.

3. After exploring this open sort thoroughly, have the children select the category they like the best. They can then be given construction paper to label their categories and draw or cut out pictures for each. As always, encourage them to label the pictures and the categories with developmentally appropriate spelling, as shown in Figure 4.14.

**FIGURE 4.14** Transportation Draw and Label

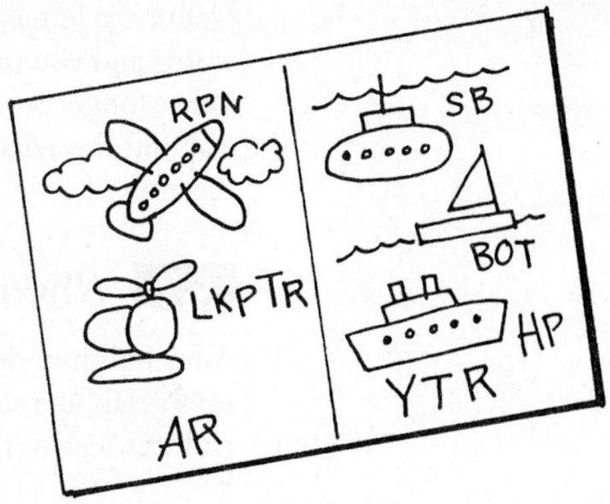

# Phonological Awareness (PA)

Phonological awareness consists of an array of understandings about speech sounds that includes a sensitivity to syllables, rhyme, alliteration, and phonemes. Syllables, rhyme, and alliteration are the best places to start with emergent learners and many activities for developing these are included here. The Morning Message (Activity 4.38) and Start with Children's Names (Activity 4.23) also include phonological awareness instruction in the context of reading and writing.

## 4.8 Two for One! Long Words, Short Words

Emergent learners have difficulty separating the sound structure of a spoken word from its meaning. One way to sensitize children to the phonological aspects of words is to build compound words. The following activity focuses on the concept that some words are long and some are short, and the difference between long and short words has nothing to do with the size of the referent.

**MATERIALS** Consult the list of compound words in Appendix F. Pick concrete, two-syllable compound words that you can easily illustrate. The words *bedroom, blackbird, cowboy, doorbell, fingernail, fireman, football, doghouse, lipstick, mailman, pancake, raincoat, sandbox, snowman,* and *snowball* are good choices for starters. Pictures for many of the words can be found in Appendix D.

**PROCEDURES**
1. Take a picture of snow and another picture of a man. After discussing the meaning of each word separately, place the two pictures side by side and ask children to say each word in succession: "snow-man." Talk about how the one word, *snowman,* is made of two words, *snow* plus *man.*
2. Replace the two separate pictures of snow and a man with one picture of a snowman and discuss again how the word *snowman* is made up of two words: *snow* and *man.* However, because a *snowman* might not be "as big" as a real man, it is necessary to take this exercise one step further to develop the idea of word size in terms of sound as opposed to meaning.
3. Hold up the picture of snow and ask children to clap as they say the word *snow.* Next, hold up the picture of the man and ask the children to clap as they say the word *man.* Finally, hold up the picture of the snowman and ask the children to clap for each word in *snowman.*
4. Discuss how the word *snowman* is longer than either the word *snow* or the word *man* because *snowman* has two syllables, whereas *snow* and *man* have only one! *Snowman* has more syllables, so it is a longer word.

**VARIATIONS** Hold up the printed word *snow* and compare it to the printed word *snowman.* Count the letters and talk about which word has more letters. Say, "I'm going to say two short words and you tell me what long word those two short words make. Ready? *Bed* (pause) *room.* What longer word do those two smaller words make? Yes, they make the word *bedroom!* Let's clap out the syllables in *bedroom* (clap, clap). Ready for another one?" Repeat with other concrete words.

## 4.9 Whose Name Is Longer? Let's Clap to Find Out!

After children develop sensitivity to syllables through clapping out compound words, move on to clapping out the syllables in everyone's names. Tie this in with Activity 4.23 (start with children's names).

**PROCEDURES** Choose two children whose first names differ in the number of syllables. Say each name and have your children clap to each syllable as they pronounce it. "Whose name is longer? Which name has more claps? *Shamika* has three claps; *Charles* has only one." Go around the classroom clapping out the syllables in everyone's name. Have children move into groups by the number of claps in their names.

### 4.10 Rhyme in Children's Books

Filling children's heads with rhyme is one of the easiest and most natural ways to focus their attention on the sounds of the English language. Books written with rhyme provide one way to do this. As you read and reread these books aloud, pause to allow the children to guess the rhyming word. *"I Can't," said the Ant* is an old favorite that invites child participation, with each line cued by an illustration.

Here are some more of our favorites:

- Bluemie, E. (2012). *How Do You Wokka Wokka?* Somerville, MA: Candlewick.
- Cameron, P. (1961). *"I Can't," Said the Ant*. New York: Putnam Publishing.
- Crews, D. (1986). *Ten Black Dots*. New York: Greenwillow.
- Degan, B. (1983). *Jamberry*. New York: Harper.
- Dewdney, A. (2005). *Llama Llama Red Pajama*. New York: Viking Juvenile. Look for more books in this series, including *Llama Llama Mad at Mama* (2007), *Llama Llama Misses Mama* (2009), and *Llama Llama Time to Share* (2012).
- Gray, K (2014) *Frog on a Log?* New York: Scholastic.
- Guarina, D. (1989). *Is Your Mama a Llama?* Illustrated by Steven Kellogg. New York: Scholastic.
- Raffi. (1999). *Down by the Bay*. New York: Crown Books. Look for other titles by Raffi.
- Rinker, S. D. (2011). *Goodnight, Goodnight, Construction Site*. San Francisco, CA: Chronicle Books.
- Seuss, Dr. (1965). *Hop on Pop*. New York: Random House. Also see *There's a Wocket in My Pocket* and *Fox in Socks*.
- Shaw, N. E. (1997). *Sheep in a Jeep*. Boston, MA: Houghton Mifflin. Look for other books in this series, including *Sheep Out to Eat* (1995).
- Slate, J. (1996). *Mrs. Bindergarten Gets Ready for Kindergarten*. New York: Scholastic.
- Thomas, J. (2009). *Rhyming Dust Bunnies* San Diego: Beach Lane Books. Also *Here Comes the Big Mean Dust Bunny!*
- Wilson, K. (2002). *Bear Snores On*. New York: Little Simon. Look for more titles in this series, including *Bear Wants More* (2003), *Bear's new friend* (2006), and *Bear Says Thanks* (2012).
- Wilson, S. (2003). *Nap in a Lap*. New York: Henry Holt.
- Wood, A. (1995). *Silly Sally Went to Town*. Boston, MA: Houghton Mifflin Harcourt.

### 4.11 Match and Sort Rhyming Pictures

After reading rhyming books aloud, follow up with an activity in which the children sort or match rhyming pictures.

**MATERIALS** Appendix D in this book contains pictures grouped by initial sounds and by vowels. These can be copied, colored lightly, and glued to cards to make sets for sorting. The lists on pages 430 and 431 will help you find rhyming sets. You can create sets of matching pairs or sets of three or more pictures that can be sorted by rhyme.

**PROCEDURES** Display a set of pictures and model how to sort them by rhyme. Say something like, "Let's look for rhyming words. *Boat* rhymes with *coat*, so I will put it with the picture of the coat. Can you find two pictures that rhyme?" To make it easier for beginners, put out three pictures at a time: two pictures that rhyme and one that does not. Name the pictures and ask children to find the two that rhyme: "Listen. *Boat, train, coat*. Which pictures rhyme?" After sorting pictures as a group, put the pictures in a center for child to match on their own or create a rhyming sort handout so that each child can have his or her own sort.

## 4.12 Rhyming Books as a Starting Point to Invent Rhymes

Making up your own rhymes is quite an accomplishment and it is likely to come after the ability to identify rhymes. Younger children need support to create rhymes, and a good place to start is pure nonsense. Jan Slepian and Ann Seidler's *The Hungry Thing* (2001) tells of a creature who comes to town begging for food but has trouble pronouncing what he wants; *shmancakes* (pancakes), *feetloaf* (meatloaf), and *hookies* (cookies) are among his requests. Only a small boy can figure out what he wants.

**PROCEDURES**  After reading the book, children can act it out. As each takes the part of the Hungry Thing, they must come up with a rhyming word for the food they want, such as *mough-nut*, *bandwich*, or *smello*. The story continues in *The Hungry Thing Returns*.

**VARIATIONS**  No one was a greater master of nonsense than Dr. Seuss. *There's a Wocket in My Pocket* (1974) takes readers on a tour of a young boy's home in which all kinds of odd creatures have taken up residence. There is a *woset* in his closet, a *zlock* behind the clock, and a *nink* in the sink. After reading this to a group, ask children to imagine what animal would live in their cubby, under the rug, or in the lunchroom. Their efforts should rhyme, to be sure, but anything will do: a *rubby*, *snubby*, or *frubby* might all live in a cubby.

## 4.13 Making Up Rhymes

Children who need more explicit instruction in rhyme will benefit from making up rhymes.

**MATERIALS**  Pictures of rhyming objects such as *rose*, *nose*, *hose*, and *toes* (see the list of rhyming pictures at the beginning of Appendix D).

**PROCEDURES**
1. Introduce a rhyming element. Explain that you are going to make words that have *ose* in them. Ask your children to say *ose*. Hold up a picture of a *rose* and ask children to say the word *rose* and listen for the *ose* at the end. Emphasize the rhyme in a whole word. Say *rrr-ooose*, emphasizing the *ose*.
2. Hold up a picture of a *nose*. Ask your children to tell you what it is. Tell them that *n-ose* has *ose* in it. Hold up other pictures (*hose* and *toes*) and ask if they can hear the *ose* at the end.
3. Ask children whether they can tell what sound is the same in *rose*, *nose*, *hose*, and *toes*. Emphasize the *ose* at the end of each word makes them rhyme.
4. Ask children to brainstorm other words that rhyme with rose: *goes*, *chose*, and *blows*, for example. Make other rhymes in a similar fashion.

## 4.14 Use Songs to Develop a Sense of Rhyme and Alliteration

Earlier, we mentioned how appropriate works by the singer/songwriter Raffi are for young children. Teaching these songs by Raffi, some of which are available in books, can lead to inventive fun with rhymes and sounds.

- "Apples and Bananas" (from *One Light, One Sun*)
- "Spider on the Floor" (from *Singable Songs for the Very Young*)
- "Down by the Bay" (also available from *Singable Songs for the Very Young*)

Another song that features names, rhyme, and alliteration is "The Name Game," originally sung by Shirley Ellis. It has apparently passed into the oral tradition of many neighborhoods and may be known by some children in your class. Sing the song over and over, substituting the name of a different child on every round, as in the following two examples:

Sam Sam Bo Bam, Banana Fanna Bo Fam, Fee Fi Mo Mam, Sam!
Kaitlyn Kaitlyn Bo Baitlyn, Banana Fanna Bo Faitlyn, Fee Fi Mo Maitlyn, Kaitlyn!

Encourage children to share with you any playground songs and chants they might already know. Generations of children have made up variations of "Miss Mary Mack" and a new generation with a taste for rap is creating a whole new repertoire. You can take an active role in teaching these jingles to your students—or letting them teach you! Write them down to become reading material.

## 4.15 Rhyming Bingo

You can adapt bingo to many features like rhyming and initial consonant.

**MATERIALS**

**Game boards.** Prepare enough Bingo game boards for the number of children who will participate (small groups of three to five children are ideal). An appropriate game board size for young children is a 3-by-3 array; for older students, the game board can be expanded to a 4-by-4 or 5-by-5 array. A ready-to-use version is available at the *WTW Digital* website.

Copy sets of pictures from Appendix D and form rhyming groups such as those listed on pages 430 and 431. Paste all but one of each rhyming group in the spaces on the game boards and then laminate them for durability. Each game board must be arranged differently.

**Deck of Pictures.** Prepare a complementary set of cards on which you paste the remaining picture from each rhyming group. These will become the deck from which rhyming words are called aloud during the game.

**Markers.** You will need some kind of marker to cover the squares on the game board. These may be as simple as two-inch squares of construction paper, plastic chips, bottle caps, or pennies.

**PROCEDURES**
1. Give each child a game board and markers to cover spaces.
2. You, or a designated child, act as the caller, who turns over cards from the deck and calls out the name of the picture.
3. Each child searches the game board for a picture that rhymes with the one that has been called out. Children cover a match with a marker to claim the space.
4. The winner is the first child to cover a row in any direction or the first child to fill his or her entire board.

## 4.16 Rhyming Concentration

This game for two or three children is played like traditional Concentration or the more current Memory game.

**MATERIALS** Assemble a collection of six to ten pairs from the pictures in Appendix D. There is a list of rhyming pictures on pages 430 and 431. Paste the pictures on cards and laminate for durability. Be sure the pictures do not show through from the backside.

**PROCEDURES** Shuffle the pictures and then lay them face-down in rows. Children take turns flipping over two pictures at a time. If the two pictures rhyme, the child keeps the cards to hold to the end of the game. A child who makes a match gets another turn. The winner is the child who has the most matches at the end of the game.

**VARIATIONS** This can be adapted to use with beginning sounds. Put letters on one set of cards and paste a picture of something that begins with that letter on another.

*Adaptable* **for Other Stages**

ACTIVITIES I EMERGENT STAGE

## 4.17 Pamela Pig Likes Pencils: Beginning Sounds and Alliteration

Sensitivity to beginning consonant sounds is essential for children to move out of the emergent phase and begin to learn to read, and alliteration is a good way to get started. (Alliteration is the occurrence of two or more words having the same beginning sound.) The following activity helps children focus their attention on beginning consonant sounds in sequences of spoken words. You might introduce this by reading *A My Name Is Alice*, by Jane Bayer and illustrated by Steven Kellogg.

**MATERIALS** You will need a variety of animal puppets that can be named with matching beginning consonant sounds, such as Bob Bear, Donald Dog, Cass Cat, or Pamela Pig. Try to pick names and animals beginning with just one single consonant sound—not a blend or consonant digraph. Although Charles starts with the letter *C*, it doesn't start with the initial *c* sound (/s/ or /k/); it sounds with a /ch/ sound instead. You want both the name and the animal to have the same beginning sound. Puppets may be store-bought, but they can also be simple pictures of an animal like a bear or a cat cut out and fastened to the end of a stick to hold up.

**PROCEDURES**

1. Hold up your puppet and introduce it. Emphasize the beginning consonant sound as you introduce the name and the animal name. Say something like, "This is Pamela. She is a pig named Pamela. We call her Pamela Pig."
2. Explain that Pamela Pig likes things that start with the same sound as her name, /p/. So Pamela likes *pencil*s because *pencil*s start with the /p/ sound just like *Pamela* and *pig*.
3. Display various pictures (see Appendix D) or objects, some of which start with a /p/ sound ( *pen*, *paper*, *paint*, *pan*, *pin*, *pear*) and some of which don't. Pick two at a time (one that starts with a /p/ sound and one that doesn't) and ask, "Which one would Pamela Pig pick?"

**VARIATION** Have children brainstorm other things that Pamela Pig would like. They may volunteer such things as parties, plays, or parks. Have children jump rope to the familiar jump rope jingle that plays on alliteration: "(letter) my name is (child's name) and my friend's name is (name). We live in (place) and we sell (item)."

## 4.18 It's in the Bag—A Phoneme Blending Game

**MATERIALS** You will need a paper bag (gift bags are attractive) and an assortment of small objects collected from around the classroom, from outside, or from home: chalk, pen, paper clip, tack, key, rock, stick, and so on. You might use a puppet to add interest.

**PROCEDURES** Lay out a dozen or so objects and name them with the students, explaining that you will use them to play a game, and then introduce the puppet. The puppet will name an object in the bag, saying it very slowly (by syllables: *pa-per-clip*, or phonemes: *rrr-oooo-ck*), and the children will guess what it is saying. Let children take turns using the puppet to practice saying words slowly.

**VARIATIONS** Use objects or pictures related to a topic of study. For example, if you are teaching a unit on animals, you could put toy animals or pictures of farm animals in the bag. This can be a sensory activity by letting children reach into the bag, figure out an object by touch, and then say it slowly for the other children to guess. Objects that begin with the same beginning sounds can also be put into the bag to sort.

## 4.19 Incorporate Phonological Skills into Daily Activities

Teachers of emergent children can incorporate sound play into many daily activities and routines.

1. Lining up, taking attendance, or calling children to a group: Call each student's name and then lead the class in clapping the syllables in the name. Announce that everyone whose name has two syllables can line up, then one syllable, three, and so on. Say each student's name slowly as it is called. Make up a rhyme for each child's name that starts with a sound of interest: Billy Willy, Mary Wary, Shanee Wanee, and so on. Substitute the first letter in everyone's name with the same letter: Will, Wary, Wanee, Wustin, and so on.

2. During read-alouds: Pause to let children fill in a rhyming word, especially on a second or third reading. If they have trouble, say the first sound for them with a clue: "It rhymes with cat and starts with *m*." Draw attention to a long word by repeating it and clapping the syllables: "That's a big word! Let's clap the syllables: *hip-po-pot-a-mus*, five syllables!" You can also pause while reading and say a key word very slowly before asking the children to repeat it fast: "The next day his dad picked him up in a red . . . *jeeeep*. What's that? A jeep, right." Point to the letters as you do this.

# Alphabet Knowledge

The following activities are designed to develop all aspects of alphabet knowledge, including letter recognition (both uppercase and lowercase), letter naming, letter writing, and letter sounds. You may notice that these activities address more than one letter at a time: In kindergarten, one letter per week is much too slow a pace and it does not address the needs of children who come to school already knowing their letters.

## 4.20 The Alphabet Song and Tracking Activities

Every early childhood classroom should have an alphabet strip or chart at eye level. Too often these strips are put up out of the children's reach. The best locations for the strips are desktops or tabletops for easy reference. Use the following activities to make active use of these charts.

**MATERIALS** Use commercial or teacher-made alphabet strips for both wall display and for individual students.

**PROCEDURES**
1. Learn the ABC song to the tune of "Twinkle, Twinkle, Little Star." Sing it many times.
2. Model, pointing to each letter as the song is sung or the letters are chanted. Then ask the children to fingerpoint to the letters as they sing or chant.
3. Play "find the letter" by naming a letter for children to touch on their strip. Ask them to name the letter that comes before or after the target letter.
4. When children know about half of the alphabet, they can work on putting a set of letter cards, tiles, or linking letters in alphabetical order. Use uppercase or lowercase letters, or pair the two (see Figure 4.15). Keep an ABC strip or chart nearby as a ready reference.

**FIGURE 4.15** Alphabet Link Letters

**4.21** Share Alphabet Books

Share alphabet books with a group as you would other good literature and plan follow-up activities when appropriate. Some books are suitable for toddlers and merely require naming a letter and a single accompanying picture, such as Eric Carle's *ABC* (2007). Others, such as Graeme Base's *Animalia*, will keep even upper-elementary children engaged as they try to name all the items that are hidden in the illustrations. Look for the alphabet books in the list that follows by Base, Bayer, Berenstein, Cole, and Suess to draw attention to beginning sounds through alliteration. Many ABC books can be incorporated into thematic units, such as Mary Azarian's *A Farmer's Alphabet*. Other alphabet books present special puzzles, such as Jan Garten's *The Alphabet Tale*. Invite children to predict the upcoming animal by showing just the tip of its tail on the preceding page.

**RESOURCE CONNECTIONS**

## ALPHABET BOOKS

Here are some outstanding ABC books for school-age children but there are many more.

- Azarian, M. (1981). *A Farmer's Alphabet*. Boston, MA: David Godine.

- Baker, K. (2010) *LMNO Peas*. San Diego, CA: Beach Lane Books.

- Base, G. (1986). *Animalia*. New York: Harry Abrams.

- Bayer, J. (1984). *A My Name Is Alice*. Illustrated by Steven Kellogg. New York: Dial.

- Berenstain, S., & Berenstain, J. (1971). *The Berenstain's B Book*. New York: Random House.

- Cole, J. (1993). *Six Sick Sheep: 101 Tongue Twisters*. New York: Morrow.

- Ernst, L. C. (1996). *The Letters Are Lost*. New York: Scholastic.

- Fain, K. (1993). *Handsigns: A Sign Language Alphabet*. New York: Scholastic.

- Falls, C. B. (1923). *ABC Book*. New York: Doubleday.

- Folsom, M. (2005). *Q Is for Duck: An Alphabet Guessing Game*. San Anselmo, CA: Sandpiper.

- Gág, W. (1933). *The ABC Bunny*. Hand lettered by Howard Gág. New York: Coward-McCann.

- Hague, K. (1984). *Alphabears: An ABC Book*. Illustrated by Michael Hague. New York: Holt, Rinehart & Winston.

- Horenstein, H. (1999). *Arf! Beg! Catch! Dogs from A to Z*. New York: Scholastic.

- Jay, A. (2005). *ABC: A Child's First Alphabet Book*. New York: Dutton Juvenile.

- Lewis, Betsie (2016). *My Alphabet Animals: Learning Letters and Sounds with Critters from A to Z*.

- McPhail, D. (1989). *David McPhail's Animals A to Z*. New York: Scholastic.

- Miranda, A. (2001). *Alphabet Fiesta*. New York: Turtle Books.

- Musgrove, M. (1976). *Ashanti to Zulu: African Traditions*. Illustrated by Leo and Diane Dillon. New York: Dial.

- Seuss, Dr. (1963). *Dr. Seuss's ABC*. New York: Random House

- Shannon, G. (1996). *Tomorrow's Alphabet*. Illustrated by Donald Crews. New York: Greenwillow.

- Sobel, J. (2006). *B is for Bulldozer*. New York: HMH Books for Young Readers.

- Tyron, L. (1991) *Albert's Alphabet*. New York: Atheneum.

- Zuckerman, A. (2009). *Creature ABC*. San Francisco, CA: Chronicle Books.

**PROCEDURES**

1. Discuss the pattern of the books, solve the puzzle, and talk about the words that begin with each letter as you go through the books a second time.

2. Focus on alliteration by repeating tongue twisters and creating a list of words for a particular letter. Brainstorm other words that begin with that letter and write them under the letter on chart paper or an interactive whiteboard.

3. Look up a particular letter you are studying in several alphabet books or a picture dictionary to find other things that begin with that sound. This is an excellent introduction to using resource books.

## 4.22 Chicka Chicka Boom Boom Sort

Martin and Archambault's *Chicka Chicka Boom Boom* (1989) is a great favorite and provides a wonderful way to move from children's books to alphabet recognition. Letters can be sorted by capitals and lowercase and by beginning sounds (see Figure 4.16). Some teachers create a large coconut tree on the side of a metal filing cabinet so that children can act out the story and match uppercase and lowercase forms using magnetic letters.

**FIGURE 4.16** *Chicka Chicka Boom Boom* **Board**

## 4.23 Name of the Day

Names are an ideal point from which to begin studying alphabet letters because children are naturally interested in their own names and their friends' names.

**MATERIALS** Prepare a card for each child on which his or her name is written in neatly executed block letters. Put all the names in a box or gift bag. Have additional blank cards ready to be cut apart as described. A pocket chart is handy for displaying the letters.

**PROCEDURES**

1. Each day, with great fanfare, draw a name—it becomes the name of the day. Begin with an open-ended question: "What do you notice about this name?" Children will respond in all sorts of ways depending on what they know about letters: "It's a short name." "It has three letters." "It starts like Taneesh's name." "It has an *o* in the middle."

2. Next, children chant or echo the letters in the name as you point to each one. A cheer, led by you, is lots of fun:

> Teacher: "Give me a *T*." Children: "*T*"
> Teacher: "Give me an *O*." Children: "*O*"
> Teacher: "Give me an *M*." Children: "*M*"
> Teacher: "What have we got?" Children: "*Tom!*"

3. On another card, write the student's name as the children recite the letters again. Then cut the letters apart and hand out the letters to children in the group. Challenge the children to put the letters back in order to spell the name correctly in a pocket chart or on a chalkboard ledge. After several repetitions, put the cut-up letters into an envelope with the child's name and picture on the outside to create a name puzzle. Add the envelope to the collection in a center. Children love to pull out their friends' names to put together.

4. All the children in the group should attempt to write the featured name on individual whiteboards, chalkboards, or pieces of paper. This is an opportunity to offer some handwriting instruction, as you model for the students. Discuss the details of direction and

Children enjoy reading the name of friends

movement of letter formation as the children imitate your motions.

5. Each day, add the featured name to a display of all the names that have come before. Compare the names with sorting activities:
   - Sort the names by the number of letters or syllables.
   - Sort the names that share particular letters; for example, find all the names with an *e* in them.
   - Sort the names that belong to boys and girls.
   - Sort the names by alphabetical order.

**VARIATIONS** Create a permanent display of the names and encourage children to practice writing their own and their friends' names. If you have a writing center, you might put all the names on index cards in a box for reference. Encourage children to reproduce names not only by copying the names with pencils, chalk, and markers, but also with rubber stamps, foam cutout letters, link letters, or letter tiles. The names display is an important reference tool during writing time.

**FIGURE 4.17** Brandon's Name Puzzle

### 4.24 One Child's Name

Learning the letters in one name is a good starting point for children in the early emergent stage. Use the following approach: Spell out a child's name with letter cards, tiles, foam, or plastic letters using both uppercase and lowercase. Spell it with uppercase letters in the first row and ask the child to match lowercase letters in the row below, as shown in Figure 4.17. Ask children to touch and name each letter. Scramble the top row and repeat. Play Concentration with the set of uppercase and lowercase letters needed to spell a child's name.

### 4.25 Alphabet Scrapbook

**MATERIALS** Prepare a book for each child by stapling together blank sheets of paper. (Seven sheets of paper folded and stapled in the middle is enough for one letter per page.) Children can use this book in a variety of ways (see Figure 4.18).

**FIGURE 4.18** Alphabet Scrapbook

**PROCEDURES**
1. Have children practice writing uppercase and lowercase forms of the letter on each page.
2. Have children cut out letters in different fonts or styles from magazines and newspapers and paste them into their scrapbooks.
3. Have children draw and label pictures and other things that begin with that letter sound.
4. Have children cut and paste magazine pictures onto the corresponding letter page. These pictures can be labeled, too.
5. Have children add sight words as they are learned to create a personal dictionary.

## 4.26 Alphabet Eggs

These are simple puzzles designed to practice pairing uppercase and lowercase letters. Children can put the letter puzzles together at their seats or in centers.

**MATERIALS** On posterboard, draw and cut out enough four-inch egg shapes for each letter in the alphabet. Write an uppercase letter on the upper half and the matching lowercase letter on the lower portion. Cut the eggs in half using a zigzag line. Make each zigzag slightly different so the activity is self-checking. Children should say the letters to themselves and put the eggs back together by matching the uppercase and lowercase form.

**VARIATIONS** Many other shapes can be cut in half for matching. For example, use pumpkin shapes in October or heart shapes in February. There is no end to matching possibilities. Acorn caps can be matched to

Matching capital and lower case letters

bottoms, balls to baseball gloves, frogs to lily pads, and so on. You can also create matching sets to pair letters and a picture that starts with that letter, rhyming words, contractions, homophones, and so on.

## 4.27 Alphabet Concentration

This game works just like Concentration with rhyming words, as described in Activity 4.16. Create cards with uppercase and lowercase forms of the letters written on one side, using both familiar and not-so-familiar letters. Be sure they cannot be seen from the backside. Do not try this with all 26 letters at once, or it may take a long time to complete; eight to ten pairs are probably enough.

**VARIATIONS** To introduce this game or to make it easier, play it with the cards face-up. As children learn the letter sounds, matching consonant letters to pictures that begin with that letter sound can change the focus of this game.

## 4.28 Alphabet Spin

This fast-paced game helps children practice upper- and lowercase letter recognition.

**MATERIALS** Make a spinner with six to eight spaces, and label each space with a capital letter. If you laminate the spinner before labeling, you can reuse it with other letters. Print the letters with a grease pencil or nonpermanent overhead transparency pen. Write the lowercase letters on small cards, creating five or six cards for each letter (see Figure 4.19). See Appendix G for tips on making a spinner. A ready made version of this game is available on the WTW Digital website.

**PROCEDURES**
1. Lay out all the lowercase cards face-up.
2. Each student, in turn, spins and lands on an uppercase letter. The child then picks up one card that has the corresponding lowercase form, orally identifying the letter.
3. Play continues until all the letter cards have been picked up.
4. The child with the most cards when the game ends is the winner.

**FIGURE 4.19** Alphabet Spin Game

*Adaptable* **for Other Stages**

**VARIATIONS** Ask children to name and write the uppercase and lowercase forms of the letter after each turn. You can adapt this game to any feature that involves matching—letters to sounds, rhymes, vowel patterns, and so on.

### 4.29 Alphabet Cereal Sort

Alphabet cereal or other three-dimensional letters made from foam, plastic, or wood are used in this sorting activity.

**MATERIALS** You will need enough letter shapes to give each child a handful. Prepare a sorting board by dividing a paper into 26 squares. Label each square with an uppercase or lowercase letter as shown in Figure 4.20.

**FIGURE 4.20** Cereal Sort

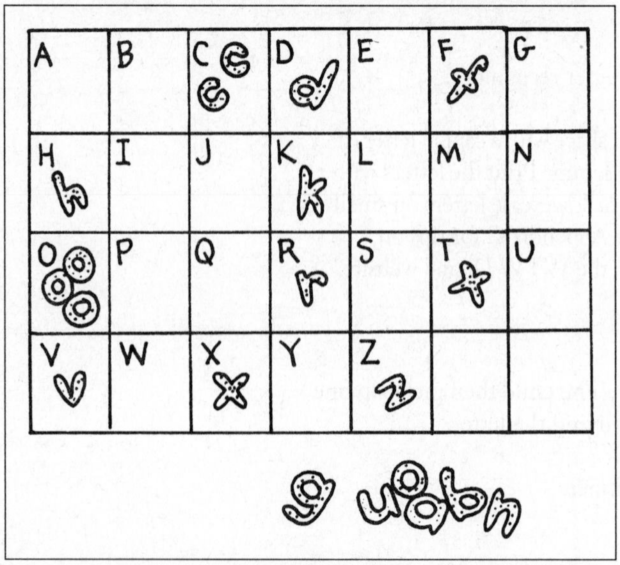

**PROCEDURES**
1. Allow the children to work individually or in teams to sort their cereal or letter shapes.
2. After the children finish, they can count the number of letters in each category. This could become a graphing activity.
3. Finally, eat the cereal! (Or glue it down.)

**VARIATIONS** Have the children spell their names or other words using the cereal.

### 4.30 Font Sorts

Children need to see a variety of print styles or fonts to identify their ABCs in different contexts. Draw children's attention to different letter forms wherever you encounter them. Environmental print is especially rich in creative lettering styles. Encourage children to bring in samples from home—like the big letters on a bag of dog food or cereal—and create a display on a bulletin board or in a class big book.

**MATERIALS**  Cut out different styles of letters from newspapers, catalogs, magazines, and other print sources. You can also search your computer fonts and print out letters in a large size. Cut the letters apart, mount them on small cards, and laminate for durability. Sample font sorts can be found on the *WTW Digital* website. Use both capitals and lowercase, but avoid cursive styles for now (see Figure 4.21).

**PROCEDURES**  After modeling the sort with a group of students, place the materials in a center where the children can work independently. Avoid putting out too many different letters at one time—four or five are probably enough, with 8 to 12 variations for each.

**VARIATIONS**  If you created alphabet scrapbooks (Activity 4.25), children can paste in samples of different lettering styles.

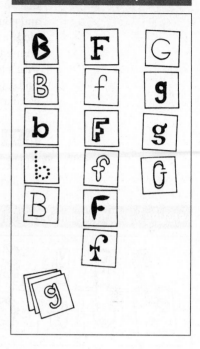

**FIGURE 4.21  Sorting Letters with Different Print Styles**

# Letter–Sound Knowledge

Specific guidelines for creating and using picture sorting for initial sounds are described earlier in this chapter, and general guidelines are presented in Chapter 3. Picture and word sorts are at the heart of word study and the procedures are revisited throughout this book. Use other games and activities to review beginning sounds after children have already practiced categorizing targeted sounds in basic picture sorting activities.

## 4.31  Use Alphabet Books to Enhance Beginning Sounds and Introduce Dictionary Skills

Alphabet books can be a child's first introduction to reference materials such as dictionaries. They can be used to introduce an initial sound or they can be a resource for a word hunt as children go searching for more words that start with targeted letters. Watch out for the choices authors and artists sometimes make, however. The *C* page may have words that start with the digraph *ch* (*chair*), hard *c* (*cat*), and soft *c* (*cymbals*), which may be confusing. Children will eventually need to sort out these confusions, but not at this time. It's best to limit the *C* page to just hard *C* exemplars for starters.

**MATERIALS**  A variety of alphabet books (see list in Activity 4.21), picture dictionaries, and word books. The *Busy Bee Kids Printables* website has an ABC book you can download and print, and you may find others.

**PROCEDURES**
1. Before studying individual sounds, see whether children can find different letters among letters placed in alphabetical order, as on an alphabet strip. After children can recite the alphabet in order, select a letter and challenge them to name the letters that follow, in order. Even young children first learning the alphabet and beginning sounds are ready to use the most basic of dictionary skills—alphabetical order.
2. When studying a particular beginning sound, pass out alphabet books to pairs of children and ask them to find a letter and report what is pictured there. Begin by naming the letter, pointing to where it falls in the alphabet, and deciding where in the books to look—in the first, middle, or last part. Otherwise, children may start at the beginning and look through the entire book to get to Z!
3. Create a chart of words or pictures that children find beginning with a particular letter.
4. Read the list to children several times to emphasize the beginning sound and challenge them to find more words over the next week or so. This will reinforce the idea that there are many words that begin with a particular letter.

**VARIATIONS** Picture dictionaries and wordbooks such as those by Richard Scarry or Roger Priddy, in which pictures are thematically arranged and labeled with words, are another resource that young children enjoy. They are an excellent way to encourage vocabulary growth as adults and young children take turns pointing, questioning ("What's that?"), and naming the colorful pictures on the pages. However, young children may ignore the printed labels unless they are pointed out. Challenge children to look through such books on a word hunt for things that start with a particular letter. For example, if you look on the body parts page of such a book you will find several words that start with *H—hand, head,* and *hair.* Show children how to use the printed word as a clue in addition to naming and listening for the beginning sound.

## 4.32 Soundline

This center activity is a way to review the beginning consonant matches children learned in the picture sorts.

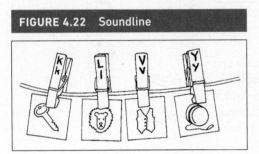

**FIGURE 4.22** Soundline

**MATERIALS** Use heavy string or a piece of rope and wooden clothespins. Write uppercase and lowercase letters on the top of the clothespins. Glue a picture beginning with each letter on a square of tagboard and laminate. Prepare two or three for each letter that has been studied.

**PROCEDURES** Introduce this as a group activity before putting it in a center where children can do it independently. Children match the picture card to the clothespin and hang it on the rope (see Figure 4.22). Add new letters and sounds as children learn them.

## 4.33 Letter Spin for Sounds

This is a popular game to review up to eight beginning sounds at a time. It is a variation of the letter spin described in Activity 4.28.

**MATERIALS** You will need a spinner divided into four to eight sections and labeled with beginning letters to review; you can use a large cube, like a die, instead of a spinner. You will need a collection of picture cards that correspond with the letters, with at least four pictures for each letter. Follow the procedures for the letter spin activity.

**PROCEDURES**
1. Lay out all the pictures face-up.
2. Two to four children take turns using the spinner, selecting one picture that begins with the sound indicated by the spinner. After selecting, the student's turn is over and the next child spins. If there are no more pictures for a sound, the child must pass.
3. Play continues until all the pictures are gone. The winner is the one with the most pictures at the end.

## 4.34 Initial Consonant Follow-the-Path Game

This game is simple enough that even preschoolers can learn the rules and use it to practice a variety of features. You will see this game adapted in many ways in Chapter 5 and Chapter 6.

**MATERIALS** Copy the two halves of a follow-the-path game board, found in Appendix G. Keep the game in a folder that can be easily stored: paste each half on the inside of a manila folder (colored ones are nice) leaving a slight gap between the two sides in the middle (so the folder can still fold). Add some color and interest with stickers or cutout pictures to create a theme such as "Trip to the Pizza Parlor" or "Adventures in Space." The photo shows a

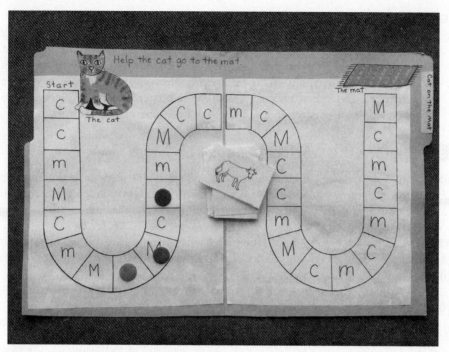

Follow-the-path game for *Cat on the Mat*

game that goes along with *Cat on the Mat*. Label each space on the path with one of the letters you want to review, using both uppercase and lowercase forms—sets of three to six letter sounds work best. Reproduce a set of picture cards that correspond to the letters. Copy them on card stock or glue cutout pictures to cards. You will need two to four game pieces to move around the board; flat ones, like bottle caps or plastic disks, store well. Keep the pictures and playing pieces in a labeled plastic zip-top bag inside the folder.

**PROCEDURES**
1. Turn the picture cards face-down in a stack.
2. Each child draws a picture in turn and moves his or her playing piece to the next space on the path that is marked by the corresponding beginning consonant.
3. The winner is the first to arrive at the destination.

**VARIATIONS**  Place pictures in each space for a Follow-the-Pictures game. Children roll a die or spin a spinner marked with letters to move to the appropriate space.

A variety of games can be played in the emergent stage using the blank Follow the Path template in Appendix G.

*Adaptable* **for Other Stages**

# Concepts About Print (CAP)

Concepts about print are best learned in the context of reading and writing. Put songs that you sing, poems and jingles that you learn, and portions of longer books with catchy memorable refrains (such as "I'll huff, and I'll puff, and I'll blow your house down") on charts for easy reference. Use them for print referencing and to develop concept of word.

### 4.35  Who Can Find?

This works best with a big book, chart story, or poem you have read several times. It can also be used after creating a dictation or other writing.

**PROCEDURES**

1. After reading a piece of text several times, ask children questions about conventions of print such as, "Who can find a period? Who can find a capital *A?* Who can find the last word in the first sentence? Who can find the title? Who can find a word that rhymes with *can?*"
2. Call children forward to point to the features of print your name. It is easy to differentiate this activity for children at various points of development so that it offers just the right challenge. Ask some children to find letters, and ask others to find words.

## 4.36 Explore the World of Logos

Children can learn to "read" their environment in the pre-alphabetic or logographic stage in which they use shapes, colors, and logos to distinguish words. Draw students' attention to these forms of print to emphasize the many functions print serves and the different forms it can take.

**MATERIALS** Collect commercial labels and logos from cereal boxes, advertisements, signs, and so on. Encourage children to bring in examples from home. Mount these on card stock.

**PROCEDURES**

1. Hold up an example, such as the label on a fast food bag, and ask children whether they can "read" it. Talk about what it says and where it came from.
2. Create a sentence strip for a pocket chart printed with: "I can read _____." Insert the logo in the empty space.
3. Put these in a center for children to use on their own after introducing it in a group.

## 4.37 What Were You Saying?

Many concepts about print can be directly taught by writing in speech bubbles—especially speech bubbles connected to students' own pictures.

**MATERIALS** You will need a digital camera to take photos of your students. If you don't have a digital camera, find pictures of children engaged in an activity such as kicking a ball to a friend or licking an ice cream cone.

**PROCEDURES**

1. Print or project a picture that shows children. Ask questions to engage your children in recounting the event.
2. Draw a speech bubble coming out of one child's mouth. Explain that the pictures only *show* what is happening, but you can *write* what the child actually said in the speech bubble. Prompt by saying something like, "What do you think she is saying in this picture?"
3. Write down what the children say in the speech bubble. You can reference various aspects of print, such as letter–sound matches, capitals, and punctuation.
4. Read what it says in the speech bubble while pointing to individual words. Point out once again that the picture *shows* what happened, but the writing in the speech bubble tells what was actually *said*. Ask individual children to come up and read their own speech bubbles.

**VARIATIONS** Read comic strips, comic books, and children's books that feature speech bubbles, such as one of the following.

Using speech bubbles to teach concepts about print

- Peggy Rathman's *10 Minutes till Bedtime* (1999) and *Goodnight Gorilla* (1994). New York: Scholastic.
- Susan Meddaught's *Martha Speaks* (1992). Boston: Houghton Mifflin.
- Mo Willems's *Don't Let the Pigeon Drive the Bus* (2003), *Knuffle Bunny* (2004), and their sequels. New York: Hyperion Books.
- Easy-to-read comics known as TOON books. New York: RAW Junior, LLC.

## 4.38 Interactive Writing and Morning Message

The act of writing with children offers you the opportunity to model the use of the alphabet, phonemic segmentation, letter–sound matching, concept of word, and conventions such as capitalization and punctuation, all in the context of a meaningful group activity. As you write on the chalkboard, chart paper, or an interactive whiteboard, children see their own ideas expressed in oral language transformed into print, allowing many opportunities for print referencing. During interactive writing, children share the pen and are invited to come forward to add a letter, a word, or a period. Such writing can take place any time of the day and for any reason; for example, to list class rules, make a shopping list, record observations from a field trip, create a new version of a familiar text, or list questions for a classroom visitor.

Morning Message is a favorite form of group writing in which you and your children compose sentences that report on daily home and school events that are important to the class. Each morning, talk with the entire group to discover bits of news that can be part of the morning message. In preschool or early kindergarten, this may be only one sentence. Keep a lively pace and be sure all children are engaged.

**MATERIALS** It is important that everyone can see the print. Many teachers use a large sheet of chart paper, markers, and white tape for covering mistakes. To involve students, give each one a lap-sized whiteboard, chalkboard, or clipboard so they can participate in listening for sounds, handwriting, and the use of punctuation.

**PROCEDURES**
1. Chat with children informally, sharing news from home or the classroom. This is a time for generating lots of talk so do not rush through this step too quickly.
2. Select a piece of news to record in the form of a single sentence such as, "We will go to PE." Recite the sentence together with the children to decide how many words it contains, holding up one finger for each word. Then draw a line for each word on the board or chart (see Figure 4.23).
3. Repeat each word, emphasizing the sounds by stretching them out, and invite the group to make suggestions about what letters are needed: "The first word we need to write is *we*. Wwwweeee. What letter do we need for the first sound in *wwweee?*" A child might suggest the letter *Y*. "The name of the letter *Y* does start with that sound. Does anyone have another idea?" Clap the syllables in longer words, spelling one syllable at a time. Every letter in every word need not be discussed at length. Focus on what is appropriate for the developmental level of your students.
4. Model how to use resources in the room such as an alphabet chart or a display of children's names and point out concepts about print such as left to right, return sweep, capitalization, punctuation, and letter formation. Start by modeling (I need to end the sentence with a period.) and gradually release responsibility as children learn the conventions: "What do we need at the end of the sentence?" And then, "Who can come up and make a period here?"
5. Let children take turns coming forward to write, usually just one child per letter or word at this level. You can do the writing in the beginning, but as children learn to write their letters you can share the pen. Use white tape to cover any mistakes made on paper.
6. After the sentence is completed, read it aloud to the group, touching each word, and then have the children read with you. If your sentence contains a two- or three-syllable word,

**FIGURE 4.23** Morning Message

touch it for every syllable, helping children see how it works. Invite children to come forward and fingerpoint as they read.

7. Repeat steps 2 to 5 for another sentence. Keep in mind children's attention span when deciding how many sentences to write. One sentence may be enough at the beginning.

**VARIATIONS** Leave up the morning message all day and encourage children to read it on their own. You might want to use it for some activities in the next section, such as Cut-Up Sentences, Be the Sentence, or for the whole-to-part lessons. You can send home a collection of all the morning messages for a week on Friday as a summary of class news that most children will be able to proudly read from memory to their parents.

# Concept of Word in Text (COW-T)

When children are learning about letters and sounds at the same time or they are fingerpoint-reading from memory, there is a complementary process at work. Learning one gives logic and purpose to learning the other. Fingerpoint-reading familiar rhymes and pattern books followed by deliberate attention to words in and out of context is the best way to achieve a COW-T. See page 116 for a description of the whole-to-part framework.

### 4.39 The Language Experience Approach (LEA)

Language experience accounts are one of the best ways to integrate the six components of the emergent literacy diet. Teachers write down student accounts of these experiences and use them to develop emergent word knowledge, meeting many of the standards for Kindergarten Language Arts.

Children practice pointing to their dictation

**MATERIALS** All students must be able to see as your write. Much like the Morning Message, use a large sheet of chart paper, markers, and white tape for covering mistakes.

**PROCEDURES**

1. Plan a language experience. Field trips, cooking activities, science experiments, playground events, changes in weather, and class pets provide opportunities for shared experiences in which new vocabulary and the students' own language abounds. The children dictated their experiences studying rocks. Help the students to generate lots of oral language about their observations and ideas. Introduce new vocabulary, use it several times,

and encourage children to use it. Then suggest writing down their ideas. Take multiple ideas and help shape the dictation into a coherent account as needed. For example, ask a child to hold an idea until later if it comes too early in a sequence of events. Don't call the dictation a *story* unless it has elements of a narrative.

2. Record statements on a chart. You may want to write "said" next to each student's name during a group dictation, as shown in Figure 4.24. This makes it easy for children to find what they said. Students' own language should be recorded as closely as possible so that they will be able to read it back. The child should approve any grammar corrections with prompts like, "Good idea, can we say it this way?" While writing, include print referencing: capitalization, punctuation, and so on and take the time to ask children to listen for some sounds in words much like you do in interactive writing. However, during LEA the teacher does the writing.

3. When the dictation is completed, it should be read and reread over time. With this format, attention to words and sentences can be highlighted in a meaningful context. For example, a child may be asked to locate his or her own name in the group dictation or to find a word that starts with the same letter as his or her own name.

4. If you want to use the dictation in the whole-to-part framework give each child a copy of the dictation to practice voice-pointing while reading together chorally and from memory. These copies can be typed in 26-point, illustrated, and collected into a notebook called a *personal reader* (described in more detail in Chapter 5). You can cut up a second copy of the dictation into sentence strips or individual words to match back to the original.

5. Children in the late emergent stage with a rudimentary COW-T can begin to select words to include in a word bank of known words. Word banks are described in Chapter 5.

**VARIATIONS** When time allows, children can dictate individual accounts. You can also use dictations to write variations on a text. For example, after sharing the predictable book *Cat on the Mat*, children can be asked to compose a new version starring a different set of characters (*Monkey on the Mat*).

**FIGURE 4.24  Dictated Language Experience Chart**

The Fire Station
Amanda said, "We went to the fire station yesterday."
Jason said, "We rode on a big orange bus."
Clint said, "I liked the ladder truck. It was huge!"
D.J. said, "The firemen told us how to be safe."
Beth said, "Firemen wear big boots and a mask."

## 4.40  Cut-Up Sentences

The spaces between words are not always obvious to emergent students, so cutting sentences into words is a concrete way to show this. This activity is an important routine in the whole- to-part framework described on page 116.

**MATERIALS** Write a sentence from a familiar piece of text on a sentence strip. Sentences should come from a familiar book or a poem the group has read together. A pocket chart is handy to hold the sentences. Prepare a second copy to cut into words.

**PROCEDURES**
1. Gather a small group of children with similar needs and read the sentence several times, pointing to the words.
2. Cut the sentence into words, snipping off each word as you read it aloud. Explain to the group that you need their help to rebuild the sentence because the words are all mixed up. Pass out the words to children in the group and then, pointing to the words in an intact copy of the sentence, ask who has each word as they are named from left to right.
3. Give children clues about how to find the words in order to rebuild the sentence: "What letter would you expect to see at the beginning of *swam?*" The child holding the

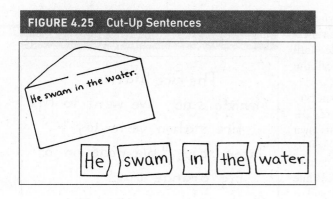

**FIGURE 4.25**  Cut-Up Sentences

word should come forward and display the word under the target word for comparison, checking each letter before leaving it in place.

4. Give each child a copy of the sentence strip and scissors. Under your guidance, have them cut off each word as it is named and then help them to reassemble the sentence. The words can be pasted down under a drawing done by the child or put into an envelope with the sentence written on the outside (see Figure 4.25). These can be sent home with the students.

5. Leave the word cards and model sentence strip with a pocket chart in a center for children to practice in their spare time.

## 4.41  Be the Sentence

Children can also rebuild familiar sentences by pretending to be the words themselves. Write a familiar sentence on a chart or on the board. Start with short sentences such as "Today is Monday" or "I love you." Then write each word from the sentence on a large card. Give each word to a student, naming it for him or her. "Stephanie, you are the word *Monday*. Lorenzo, you are the word *is*." Ask the children to work together to arrange themselves into the sentence. Have another child read the sentence to check the direction and order. Try this again with another group of children and then leave the words out for children to work with on their own.

## 4.42  Stand Up and Be Counted

As children build a repertoire of known songs, nursery rhymes, and jump rope jingles, post them around the room and use them for oral concept of word activities that integrate phonological awareness with concept of word in print.

**MATERIALS**  You will need a memorized nursery rhyme or jump rope jingle posted on the wall at an appropriate level. Be sure there is some floor space for everyone to sit in a circle.

**PROCEDURES**
1. Sitting in a circle, recall the nursery rhyme or jump rope jingle and recite it as you point to the written copy on the wall or chart.
2. Go around the circle, having children stand up for each word in the nursery rhyme. One child will stand up for *Hey*, another for *Diddle*, and a third for the next *Diddle*, and so on. Watch to see whether two children stand up for a two-syllable word like *Diddle* or *over*.
3. After everyone is finished standing up for each word, have everyone sit down, and say, "I think we made some mistakes. Did anyone notice?" Some children will notice. Ask them to explain.
4. Say to the students, "Yes, two people stood up for the word *over* but *over* is one word. It has two syllables, but it means one thing—over (motion with your hands jumping over something). Let's clap the word *over*. See? *Over* has two claps, but it's only one word. Go to the chart or wall poster and point out the word *over*. (You might note that it starts with an *o*.)
5. Repeat the exercise.

**VARIATIONS**  Have children recite a sentence or rhyme and add a LEGO or Unifix cube for each word as it is recited. Count the cubes (words). Compare sentences or lines. Ask the students, "Which sentence is longer? How can you tell?" (Longer sentences have more words—that is, LEGO or Unifix cubes.)

The word study activities for the emergent stage promote concept and vocabulary development, awareness of sounds, concepts about print and of word, and the alphabetic principle. These activities spring from and return to children's books and are extended through writing. After children achieve a concept of word in print and can segment speech and represent beginning and ending consonant sounds in their spelling, they are no longer emergent but beginning readers. This is also when they move into the next stage of spelling, the letter name–alphabetic stage. Word study for the letter name–alphabetic speller/beginning reader is described in Chapter 5.

# Word Study for the Letter Name–Alphabetic Stage

## Chapter 5: Letter Name—Alphabetic STAGE

*WTW Digital* is a new online tool that accompanies this core text, and it was designed to help you implement word study in an engaging and interactive way. Resources for this chapter include:

- **Automatically scored qualitative spelling inventories** suggest each student's approximate stage of spelling development. Word study groups are also automatically generated based on inventory results.
- **31 sorts** that allow students to engage with word study in a digital environment
- **17 games** in a printable format that present fun activities for students to build their phonics and spelling knowledge.

An access code for *WTW Digital* is included with each new copy of package ISBN: 9780135174623. Visit www.wtwdigital.pearson.com to get started.

The letter name–alphabetic stage of literacy development is a period of beginnings. Students begin to learn words and read text without the support of memory, and their writing becomes readable to themselves and others. This period of literacy development needs careful scaffolding because students know how to read and write only a small number of words. The reading materials and activities you choose should provide contextual support that relates to students' language, experience, and interests. In word study, the earliest activities use pictures; later, students work with words in families and known words. In the following discussion of reading and writing development and instruction, we look closely at the support teachers provide and the way word knowledge develops during this stage.

First let's visit the first-grade classroom of Mr. Richard Perez to see how he implements word study. During the first weeks of school, Mr. Perez observed his first graders as they participated in reading and writing activities, and he used the PSI inventory described in Chapter 2 to collect samples of their spelling for analysis. The spelling of three students is shown in Figure 5.1 Like most first-grade teachers, Mr. Perez's class has a range of abilities, so he manages three instructional groups for reading and word study and uses students' spellings as a guide to plan phonics and spelling instruction. Some days he uses part of small-group time for teacher-directed word study.

Take a look at three students, Tony, Cynthia, and Maria, and the word study in their respective groups. Cynthia is a typical student in the early letter name–alphabetic group who writes slowly, often needing help sounding out a word and still confusing some consonants such as *y* and *w* and *d* and *t*. Her spelling is limited primarily to consonants with a few vowels. Cynthia has memorized jingles, such as *Five Little Monkeys Jumping on the Bed*, but sometimes gets off track when she points to the words as she reads.

Deciding to take a step back with this group, Mr. Perez plans a quick review of beginning sounds. Every three days, he introduces a set of four initial consonants, such as *b, m, r,* and *s*. After modeling the picture sort and

### FIGURE 5.1 Spellings of Three First Graders

| Word | Cynthia | Tony | Maria |
|------|---------|------|-------|
| fan | FN | fan | fan |
| pet | PD | Pat | pet |
| dig | DK | dkg | deg |
| wait | YAT | Wat | wat |
| sled | SD | Sd | slad |
| stick | SK | Sek | stik |
| shine | CIN | Sin | shin |

practicing it in the group, he gives each student a handout of pictures to be cut apart for individual sorting practice, as shown in Figure 5.2(A). The next day, Mr. Perez observes how quickly and accurately they sort the pictures into columns. During seatwork time or center time, the students draw and label pictures beginning with those sounds, paste and label the pictures, and go on word hunts—all extend and follow-up routines described in Chapter 3.

Each day when Mr. Perez meets with Cynthia's group, they read and reread chart stories, jingles, and books with predictable text. To help the students in this group develop a sight vocabulary, Mr. Perez has a collection of known words, a **word bank**, for each student. To create the word bank, he took the words students could quickly identify from their reading and wrote them on small cards. The students in this group add new words from their reading several times a week and review them regularly on their own and with partners.

Tony is part of a large group in the middle letter name–alphabetic stage who can spell the beginning and ending consonants of words but shows little accuracy when spelling digraphs and blends, as shown in Figure 5.1. He is *using but confusing* vowels in some words. Tony points to the words as he reads *Five Little Monkeys* and immediately self-corrects on the rare occasion he gets off track with words that have more than one syllable, such as *jumping* and *mama*.

In a small group, Tony and his group sort pictures of digraphs (*sh, ch, th,* and *wh)* for several weeks and then begin the study of same-vowel word families such as *op, ot,* and *og.* Mr. Perez takes 10 to 15 minutes during group time to introduce new word families. The students then receive their own set of words, shown in Figure 5.2(B), to cut apart for sorting. They work alone and with partners to practice the sort, writing and illustrating the words, and then they play follow-up games. Students at this developmental level have typically learned to read more than 100 words automatically, and do not need a personalized word bank, like Cynthia.

Maria represents a third group of students in the late letter name–alphabet stage who correctly spells single consonants, as well as many digraphs and blends, as shown in Figure 5.1. This group also uses some short vowels accurately. Maria reads many books independently and is quickly accumulating a large sight vocabulary, the result of lots of reading. With this group, Mr. Perez reviews different-vowel word families for several weeks, making an effort to include words with digraphs and blends, but he soon discovers that the word family sorts are too easy and decides to move to the study of short vowels in nonrhyming words.

Each Monday, he introduces a collection of words that can be sorted by short vowels into three or four sets. This group also receives a sheet of words, as shown in Figure 5.2(C), to cut apart and use for sorting. Maria and her partners work in pairs for buddy sorts, writing sorts, word hunts, and games on other days of the week.

**FIGURE 5.2** Word Study Handouts for Letter Name–Alphabetic Spellers in Three Different Instructional Groups

A. Beginning Consonant Sort

B. Word Family Sort

| pot | dog | cot | hop |
|-----|-----|-----|-----|
| log | frog | top | jog |
| mop | dot | hot | pop |

C. Short Vowel Sort

| pig | cup | oddball |
|-----|-----|---------|
| zip | bit | but |
| big | jug | pin |
| tub | rip | will |
| him | cut | rub |
| hum | win | fun |
| six | nut | run |
| put | did | gum |

# Literacy Development of Students in the Letter Name–Alphabetic Stage

Many components of the literacy diet described for the emergent stage continue to develop during the letter name–alphabetic stage. Vocabulary, oral language, and concepts grow throughout all the stages described in this book, but phonological awareness and concept of word in text will reach maturity. At the beginning of this stage, students may only segment and spell the most prominent beginning and final consonant sounds, demonstrating only partial phonemic awareness. By the end of the stage, they have full phonemic awareness and are able to isolate the medial vowel and to pull apart the tightly meshed blends. As they learn to segment these sounds, they also learn the correct letter correspondences that represent them, including initial and final consonants, digraphs, blends, and short vowels. A new component becomes critical during the letter name–alphabetic stage—acquiring a reading vocabulary of **sight words** that can be recognized automatically in any context. It is fast and ever-growing word recognition that fuels fluency and comprehension.

**Enhanced eText**
**Video Example 5.1**
This video provides a description of letter name–alphabetic spelling, word study, and beginning reading.

## Reading

During the letter name–alphabetic stage, students transition from simple, **predictable** reading materials they read with support from shared reading and their memory for language, to less predictable beginning reading materials. With less predictable materials they must rely on their sight vocabularies and their abilities to figure out unfamiliar words using a variety of strategies, including decoding, analogy, and prediction. This transition in reading material is accompanied by word study instruction that continues to develop letter–sound correspondences and other phonics features such as consonant digraphs and blends, and short vowels.

The literacy diet described in Chapter 4 is continued during this stage. Teachers should develop new concepts and vocabulary, point out concepts about print, and encourage students to use their growing knowledge of phonics as they read. A key development in this stage happens as students acquire a firm concept of word in text described next.

**Enhanced eText**
**Teacher Resource:**
Continuum of Development in Ms. Kiernan's First Grade Classroom

**CONCEPT OF WORD IN TEXT (COW-T).** **Concept of word in text** is the ability to point to words in a memorized text. After students are past the developing level of concept of word in text in the emergent stage, there are two levels: rudimentary and firm COW-T (Blackwell-Bullock & Invernizzi, 2012; Flanigan, 2006, 2007; Morris, 1981; Morris, Bloodgood, Lomax, & Perney, 2003).

**Rudimentary COW-T.** Students with a rudimentary concept of word can point to and track the words of a memorized text left to right using their knowledge of consonants as clues to word boundaries. However, they may get off track with two-syllable words (see Figure 4.10), and when they are asked to find words in what they read, they are slow and hesitant. They may **voice point** by returning to the beginning of the sentence or line to get a running start with memory as a support to read and locate the requested word. Students like Tony, who have a rudimentary concept of word, are able to remember a few words from familiar stories and short dictations that they have reread several times. They begin

Rosa points to the words in her dictated sentence after a language experience.

Mrs. Smith's students reread familiar text and practice finger pointing

to understand how the letters at the beginning and ends of words match to sounds and this knowledge helps them store these words in memory as sight words. However, sight words grow slowly and it is common to "know" a word one day, but not the next.

**Firm COW-T.** Students with a firm concept of word can fingerpoint-read accurately, and if they get off track, they can quickly correct themselves without voice pointing or starting over. When asked to find words in the text, students can find them quickly using their knowledge of letters and sounds. They remember many words after several rereadings of familiar text, and these words are becoming recognized "at first sight." With increasing word knowledge, words begin to stick more readily.

**SIGHT WORD LEARNING.** **Sight words** are **known words** students can recognize automatically and consistently in text and in isolation. A large store of sight words makes it possible to read fluently and to devote attention to comprehension rather than to figuring out unknown words. Sight words also provide a spring board from which students make generalizations about phonics principles and how the spelling system works. However, sight word development among beginning readers depends on their knowledge of letters and sounds.

**Partial Alphabetic Readers.** Early on in this stage, students may be **partial alphabetic readers** (Ehri, 2000) because what they remember about words may be incomplete. Typically, they know something about consonants, but they lack the vowel knowledge needed to sound out words completely or store them in memory. For example, as they read, early letter name–alphabetic spellers may substitute *lion* for *leopard* in a story about big cats at the zoo. Or, in a familiar rhyming book, like *Five Little Monkeys Jumping on the Bed* by Eileen Christelow, children might identify the word *monkeys* by virtue of several letters in the word (*m-k* or *m-y* perhaps) but in another context, these partial phonetic cues alone will not suffice. *Monkeys* might be confused with other words, like *Mike* or *many*.

**Full Alphabetic Readers.** Later in this stage students advance to **full alphabetic readers** (Ehri, 2006) who know vowel and consonant sounds and can fully connect spelling to pronunciation and meaning in memory. It is this "orthographic mapping" between spellings and pronunciations that facilitate the development of sight words (Ehri, 2013).

**Common Misunderstandings about Sight Words.** The term *sight words* is often confused with **high-frequency words**. High-frequency words are the most commonly occurring words in print like *was, the, to, was, can,* and *these,* and they account for almost 50 percent of connected text for beginners. A list of Fry's top 300 high-frequency words can be found in Appendix F. Even though a reader's store of sight words will include many high-frequency words, students' sight words are not limited to high-frequency words; any word can be a sight word if it recognized "at first sight."

Another common misunderstanding about sight words is that they are phonetically irregular words children cannot sound out and therefore must be learned as unanalyzed wholes or "by sight." Although there are some high-frequency words that lack dependable letter–sound correspondences (of = /uv/ and was = /wuz/), most high-frequency words are more regular than not, especially in the consonant features that are most likely to be partially understood. For example, the high-frequency word *from* is 75 percent regular; only the *o* in the middle is irregular. The question in instruction often becomes how to teach students to read these words.

There is no evidence that readers learn these words in a different way. Repeated exposure to words and the word study described here is what students need to improve their sight-word vocabularies.

**READING FLUENCY.** All beginning readers read slowly, except when they are reading well-memorized texts. They are often described as word-by-word readers because they do not have enough sight words to read fluently and their reading rates may be painfully slow (Bear, 1989, 1991b). For example, a beginning reader may read as slowly as 30 words per minute, depending on the familiarity, difficulty, and genre of the text (Invernizzi & Tortorelli, 2013). Although fluency is an important goal of learning to read, a focus on getting beginning readers to "read fast" is misplaced. Beginning readers are "glued to the print" (Chall, 1983/1996) and need to pay careful attention to the words on the page if they are going to store words fully in memory to build their sight vocabularies.

Most beginning readers point to words when they read, and they read aloud to themselves. The pointing and reading aloud gives them time to hold the word in memory, read the next word and fit the words together into a phrase. This helps them to keep their place and buys them processing time. While they hold the words they have just read in memory, they read the next word, giving them time to fit the words together into a phrase. If you visit a first-grade classroom during independent reading, you are likely to hear a steady hum of voices. Finger-pointing, dysfluency, and reading aloud to oneself are natural reading behaviors to expect among beginning readers.

## Beginning Writing and Spelling

There is a similar pattern of dysfluency in beginning writing because students often write words slowly, sound-by-sound (Bear, 1991a), which limits the length of their compositions. Unlike emergent writers, students in the letter name–alphabetic stage can usually read what they write depending on how completely they spell, and their writing is often readable to anyone who understands the logic of their letter-name strategy.

A first grader shares her thoughts about winter in the example shown in Figure 5.3. Ellie spells most beginning and ending single consonants, as in her spelling of LK for *like* and WR for *wear*, but the SN blend in *snow*, spelled SO, is incomplete. Many vowels are missing, although she does include some long vowels that "say their name" as in MAK for *make* and SO for *snow*. She substitutes *a* for short *i* in *mittens* and *i* for short *o* in *hot*. Notice how she uses the letter *h* to represent the *ch* digraph in *chocolate* (spelled HIKLT) because the name of the letter (*aitch*) has the sound she is trying to represent. Correctly spelled words like *Mom* and *the* are probably sight words for Ellie. See more detailed information about spelling development under "Orthographic Development in the Letter Name-Alphabetic Stage" beginning on page 153.

## Vocabulary

Children's vocabularies continue to grow rapidly throughout this stage, but the quality and quantity of this growth depends on the richness and frequency of verbal interactions with peers and adults. Talking about the meanings of words or doing lots of reading helps but is not enough to enhance the vocabulary learning of those students who need it the most (Beck, McKeown, & Kucan, 2013). It is very important for you to be mindful and systematic about teaching students new words in the early childhood years, as a way to close the tremendous oral vocabulary gap that exists between children

| **FIGURE 5.3** Ellie Writes about Winter |
| --- |

I LK WNT. I MAK a SOMN in the SO I WR MATS. Mom Mask Me hit hiklt

I like winter. I make a snowman in the snow. I wear mittens. Mom makes me hot chocolate.

who come from literate homes and those who do not (Avineri, Johnson, Brice-Heath, McCarty, Ochs, et, al., 2015; Biemiller, 2005; Kuchirko, 2017). Observations of kindergarten and first-grade classrooms reveal that the current focus on teaching phonics in high-risk settings has resulted in measurable progress in decoding skills, but without attention to vocabulary these students are still at risk in later grades when knowing word meanings is critical for comprehension (Juel, Biancarosa, Coker, & Deffes, 2003).

## Win My casin FeL OFF her Bed

*Writing with agency.* Writing about what you know and have experienced increases agency and motivation. Over three days, Alyssa wrote about her cousin's accident with detail and power. The Tell a Story activity (Activity 5.6) encourages extended storytelling as a basis for writing.

See what you think of her development as you read her story. Does her writing help you determine her spelling stage? What word study would you assign? Try using the Qualitative Spelling Checklist in Appendix A to answer these questions.

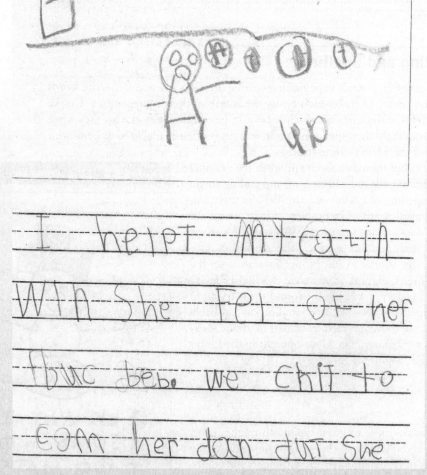

**Alyssa read back what she had written:** *When my cousin fell off her bed. I helped my cousin when she fell out of her bunk bed. We tried to calm her down but she / wouldn't calm down. I screamed for my Aunt Jackie she said. She ran upstairs. I was sad. Then we took Anabelle to the hospital. She said can I go home. No said me and Maddie. / And we went home and rest. Anabelle got her cast off on Nov. 14th.*

# Orthographic Development in the Letter Name–Alphabetic Stage

Students in the letter name–alphabetic stage provide a wonderful example of how learners construct knowledge in an attempt to make sense of the world of print. Without prior knowledge of how to spell words, children carefully analyze the sound system and make surprisingly fine distinctions about the ways sounds and words are formed in the mouth. They match the phonemes they can segment to the letter names of the alphabet in ways that may seem curious and random to the uninformed adult, but the important point is that they are on their way to acquiring the **alphabetic principle**, the insight that individual speech sounds can be represented by letters of the alphabet.

## Letter Names

Letters have both sounds and names, and students in the letter name–alphabetic stage use their knowledge of names of the letters in the alphabet to access sound as they spell phonetically or alphabetically. For example, students in the early part of this stage are likely to spell the word *jeep* as GP, selecting *g* as the first letter because of its name ("gee"). The letter name "gee" contains the phoneme /j/ in the first part of the pronounced name. According to letter name logic, there is no need to add the vowel because it is already part of the letter name for *g*. Sometimes early letter name–alphabetic spellers do include vowels, especially when they spell long vowels that "say their name," as Ellie did when she spelled *snow* as SO. This phenomenon accounts for the reason the stage is called *letter name–alphabetic*. Spellers in this group operate in the first layer of English—the alphabetic layer.

A few letter names do not cue students to the sounds they represent. For example, the letter name for *w* is "double u" and the name for *h* is "aitch." Neither offers a clue to the sound it represents. However, when you say the name of the letter *y* you can feel your lips moving to make the shape of the /w/ sound and the name for *h* does end with the /ch/ sound. Consequently, early letter name–alphabetic spellers may spell *witch* as YH. Read through the letter names in Table 5.1 to see what they offer students in terms of sound matches. Most consonants offer a clue to the sound they represent either at the beginning ("bee") or the end ("ef") of the letter name.

## Letter Sounds

Learning the letter-sound correspondences or grapho-phonics relationships constitutes a major achievement in this stage. Children appear to learn the letter sounds for letters that include the sound in their names (*b, d, f*) more easily than letters whose names have no relationship to their sound (*w, y, h*). Letters that are associated with more than one sound (*c, g,* and all the vowels)

**TABLE 5.1**   Names of the Letters of the Alphabet

| A | ay | H | aitch | O | oh | V | vee |
|---|----|---|-------|---|----|---|-----|
| B | bee | I | ie | P | pee | W | doubleyoo |
| C | see | J | jay | Q | kyoo | X | ecks |
| D | dee | K | kay | R | are | Y | wie |
| E | ee | L | el | S | es | Z | zee |
| F | ef | M | em | T | tee | | |
| G | gee | N | en | U | yoo | | |

or letters that share a sound with another letter (*k, c, s, g, j*) require more instructional time and attention (Huang, Tortorelli, & Invernizzi, 2014). The initial sounds associated with letters should be examined, compared and contrasted, and sorted through carefully sequenced word study routines. These routines must guarantee frequent practice in distributed cycles of review. The word study must include attention to letter names, letter sounds, and letter formation (Jones, Clark, & Reutzel, 2013). Importantly though, until students are required to segment their own speech *on their own*, and match those segmented speech sounds to appropriate letters, they will not easily acquire the alphabetic principle and their reading will be delayed. Students themselves must do the heavy lifting, and this is best done through daily writing and word study.

Children who demonstrate phonological awareness are better able to learn letter sounds (Piasta & Wagner, 2010) and we can see this in their attempts to spell. During the early part of the letter name–alphabetic stage, when students have only partial phonemic awareness, spelling efforts may be limited to the most prominent sounds in syllables, usually the beginning and ending consonants. As phonemic awareness improves in the middle part of this stage, students' spellings gradually include a vowel in each stressed syllable, and they spell short vowels by matching the way they articulate the letter names of the vowels (discussed later in this chapter). By the end of the letter name–alphabetic stage, students have learned how to spell many words with short vowels correctly, and with full phonemic awareness, they also spell blends. Table 5.2 summarizes characteristics of the letter name–alphabetic stage.

**TABLE 5.2**    Characteristics of Letter Name–Alphabetic Spelling

| Gradations of Stage with Examples of Spelling | What Students Do |
|---|---|
| **Early Letter Name–Alphabetic** | Rudimentary concept of word in text |
| B, BD for *bed* | Partial phonemic awareness |
| S, SP for *ship* | Use letter names sound matches (Y for /w/) |
| YN for *when* | Represent prominent sounds, usually beginning and sometimes ending consonants |
| L, LP for *lump* | Spell consonants based on articulation confusing affricates and voiced and unvoiced sounds (*j/dr, b/p*) |
| FOT for *float* | |
| G, J, JR, GF, JF, or GV for *drive* | Vowels generally missing |
| | Partial spelling of consonant blends and digraphs |
| | Spell a few sight words correctly |
| **Middle Letter Name–Alphabetic** | Firm concept of word in text |
| BAD for *bed* | Further development of phonemic awareness |
| SEP or SHEP for *ship* | Accurately represent single beginning and ending consonants in spellings |
| LOP for *lump* | Include short vowels spelled by place of articulation |
| FOT for *float* | Spell occurring short vowel words (*cat, dog*) |
| GRIV, JRIV for *drive* | |
| **Late Letter Name–Alphabetic** | Full phonemic awareness |
| *bed*   *ship*   *lump* | Spell many short vowels and most beginning consonant blends and digraphs correctly |
| STEK for *stick* | |
| FLOT for *float* | Learning to spell final blends including preconsonantal nasals (*bump*). |
| DRIV for *drive* | Spell many sight words, including some containing frequently occurring long vowel words (*like, come*). |
| BAKR for *baker* | |

# How Consonants are Made and Articulated in the Mouth

Knowing something about phonetics (the science of sounds) will help you understand and appreciate what young students do as they attempt to represent sounds with letters. When they spell, letter name–alphabetic students rely not only on what they hear in the letter names, but also on **articulation**, or how sounds are formed in the mouth. This can lead to predictable confusions. In addition, many sounds are not easy to isolate.

**Affricates.** When students try to spell the *dr* in *drive*, they are misled in their spelling by the similarity in sound and mouth movements between *dr* and *jr*, and they may spell *drive* as JRV. Say "drive" and "jrive." Do they sound and feel alike? Linguists call these sounds **affricates**, which are formed by forcing air through a small closure at the roof of the mouth to create a feeling of friction. (*Fric*tion, af*fric*atives—see the meaning connection?) English has several other letters and letter combinations that create the affricate sound and these are often substituted for each other: *j, g, ch, dr, tr,* and the letter name for *h* (aitch). Try saying "jip / chip," and then "trip / drip" several times to feel the similarity and help you understand why young students confuse these affricates.

**Voiced and Unvoiced Pairs.** The voiced and unvoiced consonant pairs discussed in Chapter 4 and listed in Table 4.4 account for other confusions experienced by letter name–alphabetic spellers. Students may spell *brave* as BRAF or *oven* as OFN. Both *v* and *f* are articulated in exactly the same place on the lips, but one is **voiced** and the other is **unvoiced**. When phonemes are voiced, the vocal cords vibrate. You can feel in your mouth the difference in the first sound of *van* compared to *fan*.

**Isolating Sounds.** When talking about letter sounds with students, it is important to realize that some sounds are rather difficult to say in isolation. Try to say the sound for *b*. What vowels did you attach to the *b*? If you said the letter name ("bee"), then you used the long *e* vowel. If you said "buh," the sound associated with *b*, you attached the **schwa** sound (/ə/ = "uh"). Now try to say a /b/ sound without a vowel. Try to whisper *b* and cut your breath short in a whisper. The whisper is as close as you come to separating the vowel from the consonant sound. Consonant sounds that cannot be held like these are known as **stop consonants** (*b, d, g, k, p, t*). Other consonants, known as **continuants** (*f, l, m, n, r, s, v, z*), can be said slowly without adding a vowel. You may find there are times when saying the sound in isolation draws attention to the feature of interest, but asking students to say "D says duh, duh, duh" is not the goal of word study lessons. D says "duh" only in words like *duck* and *dump*; it says "dee" in words like *deal* or *deed*. The goal of word study is to extrapolate the sound of D across many different exemplars (*day, dad, deer, desk,* . . . ).

**TEACHING TIPS**

## Mastering Sounds

- Students in the letter name–alphabetic stage benefit from saying the words aloud or naming the pictures aloud as they are sorting by focused contrasts so that they can feel the sound differences. How it feels in the mouth is as helpful as hearing the sounds in this stage.

- When you first teach these sounds, avoid contrasting voiced and unvoiced pairs: *b/p, d/t, g/k, z/s, v/f,* and *j/ch* (Purcell, 2002), as suggested by the sixth principle described in Chapter 3, " begin with obvious contrasts." Only when most consonant sounds are mastered should students focus attention on these finer distinctions. This is especially true for English learners, who may not have one of the contrasting sounds in their primary language.

## Vowels in the Letter Name–Alphabetic Stage

Vowels pose special problems for letter name–alphabetic spellers, who rely on the names of letters and how sounds feel in the mouth. Try saying the word *lip*. You can feel the initial consonant as your tongue curls up toward your palate and you can feel the final consonant as it explodes past your lips, but did you feel the vowel? Unlike consonants—articulated by tongue, teeth, lips, and palate—vowels are determined by more subtle variations in the shape of the mouth. In addition, they are tightly wedded to the consonants around them.

**WHAT ARE VOWELS?** Where consonants are the noise of language, vowels are the music. Vowels are sounds produced with an unobstructed flow of air through the vocal track and are represented by the letters *a*, *e*, *i*, *o*, *u*, and sometimes *y*. Vowels are categorized in many ways but the major difference is described linguistically as **tense** and **lax**. The vocal cords are tense when producing the **long** *a* sound (ā as in *ate*), but relax a bit in producing the **short** *a* sound (ă as in *at*). The vowels we call "long" are no longer in duration than short vowels but these are the traditional terms used to describe them. Long vowels are marked with a macron (ā in *bait*, ē as in *beet*, ī as in *bite*, ō as in *boat*, and ū as in *use* or *boot*) whereas short vowels are marked with a breve (ă as in *bat*, ě as in *bet*, ĭ as in *bit*, ŏ as in *bot*, and ŭ as in *but*).

**SPELLING THE VOWEL SOUNDS.** Spellers in the early to middle letter name–alphabetic stage use their knowledge of the alphabet to find a letter name to represent the vowel sounds. Long vowels say their letter name, so the letter choices are obvious. Students spell *line* as LIN, *rain* as RAN, and *boat* as BOT. Perhaps what is most interesting about the letter name–alphabetic stage is the way students spell the short vowels. They turn to the names of the letters, but find no clear letter–sound matches for the short vowel sounds. For example, there is no letter name that says the short *i* sound in *bit* or the "uh" sound in *cup*. (Very early letter name–alphabetic spellers occasionally use *f* ("ef") or *s* ("ess") for short *e* because the letters' names start with the short *e* sound.) Selecting a letter to represent the short vowel sound involves issues related to both articulation and letter names.

**HOW THE VOWELS ARE ARTICULATED IN THE MOUTH.** You may have never analyzed sounds at this level, so let's take a moment to consider the vowels, and where and how they are made in the vocal tract. In Figure 5.4, the vowels are placed to mimic the general area where you can feel their place of articulation. Vowels are subtly differentiated by the shape of the mouth, the openness of the jaw, and the position of the tongue when a word is said. They are all voiced because it is impossible to articulate a vowel sound without vibrating the vocal cords. Compare the vowels in this figure by saying the following words in sequence several times and trying to identify where the vowel sound is produced:

| | | | | | |
|---|---|---|---|---|---|
| beet | bit | bait | bet | bat | bite |
| but | bot | ball | boat | book | boot |

Do you feel how producing the vowels moves from high in the front of the oral cavity (*beet*) to low in the oral cavity (*bite*) to the back of the oral cavity (*bot*), down the front, back, and up (*boot*)? Also contrast the way your lips feel when you say the rounded vowel in *boot* with the high front vowel sounds in *beet* or *bit*.

**THE LETTER NAME STRATEGY TO SPELL SHORT VOWELS.** Students in the letter name–alphabetic stage often confuse the short vowels, spelling *bed as* BAD and *bit* as BET. Without being

**FIGURE 5.4** Vowels in the Mouth

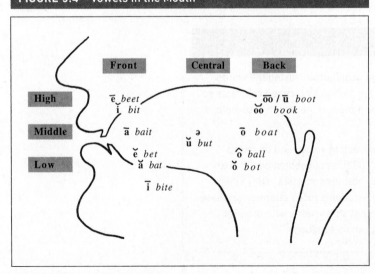

consciously aware that they are doing this, students in this stage use their knowledge of letter names and the feel of the vowels as they are produced in the vocal tract to select erroneous, but logical, substitutions. There are five letter names from which to choose: *a, e, i, o,* and *u*. How would an alphabetic speller spell the short vowel in the word *bed*?

By isolating the medial short vowel in *bed*, the letter name speller identifies the sound as short *e* but there is no letter in the alphabet that has that letter name. What letter name is closest to the short *e* sound in bed? Try saying *bed/bead* and *bed/bait* to compare how the short vowel sounds and the long vowels or letter names feel in your mouth. Repeat the pairs several times and pay attention to how your mouth is shaped. Look at Figure 5.4 to see how close the short *e* is to the long *a*. The short *e* sound is *closer in place of articulation* to the long *a* or letter name for *a* (ā) than it is to the letter name for *e* (ē) so spelling the word as BAD seems logical. Students might spell *bit* as BET for a similar reason—the short *i* sound is closer to the letter name for *e* (ē) than the letter name for *i* (ī).

Table 5.3 will help you remember how the letter names of vowels are typically substituted for the short vowel sounds beginning readers try to spell. Say the word pairs in Table 5.3 and compare them to the placement of vowels in the mouth. An easier way to think about this is that letter name–alphabetic spellers often confuse the front vowels (*a, e,* and *i*) or the back vowels (*o* and *u*). The amazing thing about these letter name substitutions for short vowels is that they are so predictable. Read (1975) found that nearly all students go through a period when they substitute the short vowels with other letter names closest in articulation.

| **TABLE 5.3** | **Letter Substitutions for Short Vowels** |
| --- | --- |
| **Spelling Attempt** | **Logical Vowel Substitution** |
| BAT for *bat* | None, short *a* is close to *a* |
| BAT for *bet* | *a* for short *e* |
| BET for *bit* | *e* for short *i* |
| PIT for *pot* | *i* for short *o* |
| POT for *put* | *o* for short *u* |

**LEARNING TO REPRESENT SHORT VOWELS CORRECTLY.**  Although these developmental spellings are interesting, students in the late letter name–alphabetic stage need systematic word study to learn the correct letter sound matches. Through word sorts they learn that short vowels follow a specific pattern—a consonant-vowel-consonant (CVC) or closed syllable pattern. Regardless of how many consonant letters are on either side of the single vowel (*cat, clap, clack,* or *strap*), one vowel letter in the middle signals the short vowel sound. The CVC pattern is introduced in the late letter name–alphabetic stage and is contrasted with long vowel patterns in the early within word pattern stage.

Sometimes students in the letter name–alphabetic stage may spell *bent, bet, bat,* and *bait* the same way as BAT. But letter name–alphabetic spellers are also readers, and when they reread their own spelling of *bait* as *bat*, a word that they know spells something else, they experience disequilibrium (Bissex, 1980). This forces them to find other ways to spell a word like *bait*,

**TEACHING TIPS**

## Learning about Vowels

- The simplest way to talk about vowels is probably the best. Descriptions like "the sound in the middle" may suffice to draw students' attention to the vowels at first, but students have no trouble learning *long vowel* and *short vowel*; such terms make word study discussions easier.

- Short *a* poses little problem for spellers because the letter name for *a* is already close in place of articulation. This is a good reason to teach short *a* first. However, because short *e* is close to short *a*, these pairs are not good contrasts for first introducing short vowel sounds.

perhaps as BATE. When students are able to spell basic short vowel patterns and also begin to experiment with long vowel patterns, they have entered the next spelling stage: the within word pattern.

**Do dialects influence how students learn and sort?.** The way a word is pronounced may vary by dialect, and this would include students who are learning English. For example, many people say *caught* and *cot* the same way. Some rhyme *roof* with *hoof* whereas others rhyme *roof* with *poof*. Although these dialectical differences do not interfere with learning to spell, being aware of these differences when students sort and talk about words enhances word study. Everyone speaks a dialect, but we all learn to read and write the same orthography. Later, you will see how students' first language influences their spelling in English.

## Other Orthographic Features

In addition to short vowels, students work through four other features during the letter name–alphabetic stage: (1) consonant digraphs, (2) consonant blends, (3) preconsonantal nasals, and (4) influences on the vowel from certain surrounding consonants (see Table 5.4). These phonics features are taught explicitly and sequentially, though different students may start at different places in the sequence depending on what they already know (see Chapter 2).

**CONSONANT DIGRAPHS AND BLENDS.** Letter name–alphabetic spellers take some time to learn the consonant units known as digraphs and blends.

**Digraphs.** A **digraph** is composed of two letters that represent a single sound. Digraphs are generally easier than blends because they only require segmenting and attending to a single phoneme. The digraphs studied in this stage include the bold letters in **th**in, fi**sh**, ea**ch**, and **wh**en. They can come at the beginning or end of words.

The digraph *th* actually represents two different sounds that are the same in articulation but different in voicing. The *th* in *bath* and *thin* is unvoiced whereas the *th* in *bathe* and *then* is voiced. Most children (and adults) ignore this difference—if they are aware of it at all. However, English learners may need to have the differences discussed. Listen as they try to pronounce words with *th* and offer help as needed.

**Blends.** A consonant **blend** is slightly different. A blend is a spelling unit (sometimes called a *consonant cluster*) of two or three consonants that retain their identity. Each sound in a blend can be heard, but they are tightly bound and not easily segmented into individual phonemes, making blends difficult for students to spell accurately. This is why the *t* in the *st* blend may be omitted in *stick*, as in the spellings SEK or SEC. Blends can occur at the beginning or end of syllables, as shown by the bold letters in the following words: **bl**ack, **cl**ap, **tr**ap, ju**st**, li**sp**, and

---

**TABLE 5.4**   Features Studied in the Letter Name-Alphabetic Stage

| | | |
|---|---|---|
| Consonant Digraphs | A unique single sound represented by two letters at the beginning and end of syllables | *ch, sh, th,* and *wh* |
| Consonant Blends | A combination of sounds represented by two letters at the beginning and end of syllables | *bl, rl, cl cr, dr, fl, fr, gl, gr, pl, pr, sc, sk, sl, sm, sn, sp, st, sw, tr, tw, qu* |
| Preconsonantal Nasals | A special final blend of a nasal sound followed by consonant | *-mp, -mb, -nd, -nk, -ng* |
| Consonant-Influenced Vowels | Vowels whose sound is neither long nor short before certain consonants | r-influenced: *-ar, -or* <br> l-influenced: *-all* |

ma**sk**. If you have trouble remembering these terms it may help to note that *blend* begins and ends with the blends *bl* and *nd*, whereas *digraph* ends with *ph* (a digraph representing the /f/ sound studied in later stages).

**PRECONSONANTAL NASALS.** Some final blends are especially difficult, deserving special mention. The nasal sounds associated with *m*, *n*, and *ng* are made by air passing through the nasal cavity in the mouth. Nasals that come right before a final consonant, such as the *n* in *pink*, are known as **preconsonantal nasals**. Try saying *bad* and *band* as you pay attention to way the sounds feel in your mouth. You cannot feel the *n* in *band* because it passes out through the nose on the way to the *d*, but it is definitely there! Preconsonantal nasals are often omitted by spellers during the letter name–alphabetic stage (*pink* may be spelled PEK and *jump* may be spelled JOP). When students begin to spell words with preconsonantal nasals correctly, they are usually at the end of the letter name–alphabetic stage, having achieved full phonemic awareness. Some students from Asian language backgrounds need more time to learn to spell and hear differences in the various nasal sounds at the ends of words, like /ng/, /n/ and /nk/.

**CONSONANT INFLUENCES ON THE VOWEL.** The letters *r*, *w*, and *l* influence the vowel sounds they follow. For example, the vowel sounds in words like *bar*, *ball*, and *saw* are not the same as the short vowel sounds in *bat* and *fast* even though they have the CVC pattern. The consonant sounds /r/ and /l/ are known in linguistics as **liquids** because they roll around in the mouth and have vowel-like qualities. Both can change the pronunciation of the vowel they follow. These spellings are often known as ***r*-influenced** (or *r*-controlled) and ***l*-influenced** (or *l*-controlled). The *w* also has an effect on vowels that follow it in words such as *want*, *was*, *wash*, *word*, and *war* but these are not studied until the within word pattern stage.

Spelling *r*-influenced vowels by sound alone can be difficult. For example, *fur*, *her*, and *sir* have the same vowel sound (represented as /ər/) yet are spelled three different ways. In addition, it is impossible to isolate the vowel from the *r* that follows in words like these. The *r*-influenced vowels that follow a CVC pattern (*car*, *for*) are examined during the late letter name–alphabetic stage and can be compared with short vowels in word sorts. Students might also contrast consonant blends with an *r* (*fr*, *tr*, *gr*) and *r*-influenced vowels (for example, *from/form*, *grill/girl*, *tarp/trap*) as a way to compare exactly where the *r* falls.

*for* **English Learners**

**Enhanced eText**
**Video Example 5.2**
Take a look at how a 2nd and 4th grade teacher engage their students in word hunts, games, and sorting to examine short vowels and consonant digraphs.

## Developmental Spelling Strategies

Young writers spell few words from memory, so if we want them to express their ideas in writing, we need to encourage them to spell as best they can. Children in the letter name–alphabetic stage benefit from trying to figure out how to spell words as they write independently using what has been called "invented spelling." We prefer to call this "developmental spelling" because it changes over time as children's word knowledge grows. This involves analyzing individual sounds or phoneme that make up the word, then matching letters to those sounds. This active analysis and application of growing skills is much more beneficial than simply being given a spelling to copy (Clarke, 1988). In addition, waiting for the teacher to come by and provide the spelling can slow down a student's production.

Some students might resist spelling as best they can and are anxious that every word is spelled correctly. While we want students to develop a desire to spell correctly, such over-concern at this stage in their development will likely severely limit what they can write about, while also reducing much needed practice. For example, one of the authors had a first grader, T.J., who spelled every word correctly using beautiful handwriting. But T.J. wrote almost the same thing in his journal every day. It was a cause for celebration when T.J began to misspell as he took risks and wrote about a wider variety of topics.

These ideas for teaching guide you in how to introduce sounds, involve parents, develop word banks, present academic vocabulary charts, and dictionaries to use in word study and writing.

**TEACHING TIPS**

## Encouraging Developmental Spelling

- Model how to analyze the sounds in words. Break words into syllables and slowly stretch out the sounds to match to a letter. Do this during interactive writing and other times when you write for and with students. It is best to select words that have regular letter sound matches (e.g., *flat* but not *laugh*) to model. See a model lesson for introducing how to spell as best you can on page 30 in Chapter 2.

- Parents need to understand the rationale behind developmental spelling, so be ready to communicate with them about the value of letting children spell as best they can, and how they can support their children's efforts.

- Although we want students engaged in developmental spelling, you should also model and teach students how to use resources in the room, such as their word banks, word walls, or other word displays. If children are writing about a specific topic, like autumn, you can brainstorm and post a word bank of special words they could use (like *leaves*, *cool*, *falling*, and *down*). Such a word bank can often help reluctant writers get started.

- Hold students accountable for what they have learned. For example, Sabina wrote about playing with her sister: "I like to PLA WIT mi STR." Her teacher complimented her on spelling "like" correctly and asked how she knew it. Sabina replied that she had used the word wall. The teacher then pointed to *with* and said, "Here's a word that is almost correct. Listen to the end of the word '*with*.' Do you hear that special sound that needs two letters? It is the sound you hear at the beginning of *thumb* (referring to a sound board with digraphs). You sorted words with TH several weeks ago. Can you fix that word?" In this way, the teacher helped Sabina apply what she knew. Other words (*play* as PLA and *sister* as STR) were left as her best efforts based on her current word knowledge.

- This is a good time to introduce students to the delights of age-appropriate picture dictionaries and wordbooks where they might find labeled pictures arranged thematically as a source of ideas for writing. Refer to Activities 5.16 and 5.17 for ideas about how to teach beginning dictionary skills and a list of resources. Don't ask students in the letter name–alphabetic stage to look up words in a dictionary, but we recommend that you keep a dictionary handy and occasionally model how you use one.

# Word Study Instruction for The Letter Name–Alphabetic Stage

This section starts with a discussion of how to support beginning readers as they acquire a firm concept of word in text and build a sight word vocabulary. Next are ideas for supporting writing and developing vocabulary. This section ends with considerable detail about planning and implementing the kind of focused contrasts that make up word study in this stage.

## Reading Instruction

Beginning reading should focus on solidifying a concept of word in text so that students can begin to amass a sight word vocabulary by reading and rereading familiar texts and by analyzing known words out of context, in word study. Through rereading, students see the same words over and over again, thereby increasing the number of words they can recognize automatically.

**MOVING TOWARD A FIRM CONCEPT OF WORD IN TEXT.** To develop a firm concept of word children need to do lots of fingerpoint reading in familiar simple text.

**SUPPORT READING.** Without a large sight vocabulary, beginning readers cannot read very much without some kind of support. Support can come from two sources: the text and the teacher. Predictable text has repetitive patterns, rhyme, and simple language that make it memorable when students have recited or sung it, or read or heard it, many times. Texts are also easy to read when the words are about an event students have experienced firsthand. The individual and group dictations created using the language experience approach (LEA) described in Chapter 3 and extended in this chapter (see Activity 5.9) builds on this assumption. Teacher support comes from shared reading and encouraging students to read in unison (**choral reading**) or immediately after you read (**echo reading**). Or, you might provide a book introduction or book walk that uses the language of the text and anticipates difficult words and concepts (Clay, 1991). In a book walk, teachers preview the book by turning the pages to look and comment on the pictures while using some of the language students will later encounter in the text.

Tension lies between these two forms of support. The more predictable a text is, the less teacher support is needed. Conversely, the less support provided from recurring elements of the text, the more scaffolding will be required from the teacher. During the letter name–alphabetic stage, students move from reading primarily predictable books to texts that are more controlled in terms of high-frequency words and decodability (Mesmer, Cunningham, & Heibert, 2012). As students develop a sight vocabulary and more automatic phonics knowledge, they will need less support. For a sense of the reading levels for beginning readers in the early, middle, and end of this stage, refer to Table 2.3 on page 36.

**SIGHT WORD LEARNING.** Repeated readings of text are the first step in helping students acquire a sight vocabulary, but after text is highly familiar, there may be diminishing returns. Taking words they first encounter in context to examine *out of context* makes a difference in how well students learn those words (Ehri & Wilce, 1980), and how many words they learn over time (Johnston, 1998, 2000). Other things that influence word learning include the nature of the words themselves. For example, words that have concrete referents (for example, nouns and adjectives like *moon* or *green*) or that are easily visualized (for example, action verbs like

Students reread a familiar book

## Draw Attention to Words in Text

TEACHING TIPS

- Encourage children to point to words as they read aloud. This helps them keep their place on the page and encourages them to look carefully at the words, which in turn helps them remember the words.

- When young readers get off track, offer explanations (*Touch this word* rabbit *two times for each syllable*) and raise questions (*Where is the word* hopped? Or *Could this word be* hopped? *Why not?*) to scaffold their learning.

- After reading, ask children to go back and find targeted words. Teach them to voice-point to find a word (starting at the beginning of the sentence and reading up to the word) but also pose questions to get them thinking about the sounds and letters that can help them find the word: *What sound do you hear at the beginning of* hopped?

Student reviews words from his word bank

*run*) are easier to learn than abstract prepositions, articles, or adverbs (such as *from* or *when*), which have no meaning by themselves (Mesmer et al., 2012). The whole-to-part model described in Chapter 4 offers ideas about how to isolate words. Here word banks and personal readers are described as an effective and engaging way to focus attention on words.

**Word Banks.** Students are actively involved in the process of determining which words they want to remember by selecting words from familiar reading materials that are written on small cards to make a **word bank**. These known words are reviewed in isolation, analyzed for grapho-phonic correspondences, and used in word study activities (Stauffer, 1980). The words in a word bank come from many sources that students read and reread: predictable books, preprimer readers, leveled books, poems, and individual and group dictations. We discuss how to develop word banks in some detail in Activities 5.10–5.13. Words are reviewed regularly and can also be used for focused sound contrasts in word study. The key is to encourage students to look more thoroughly at the words and note the letter–sound correspondences that will help to secure the words in memory.

Why do students need to review words they already know? The answer is they do not know them the same way more mature readers do; they know them only partially and tentatively. Letter name–alphabetic students who are partial alphabetic readers may confuse *ran* and *run*, *stop* and *ship*, and *lost* and *little* because they have them stored in memory as *r_n*, *s_p* or *l_t*. They may read *gingerbread* correctly every time because it is the only long word they know that starts with *g*, but when you ask them to spell it (GRBRD) you get a better idea of what they really know about the word.

Word banks are motivating for students because they offer tangible evidence of a growing sight word vocabulary (Johnston, 1998). Word banks take extra work for a few months, but are well worth the effort, particularly for students early in this stage. At first students may only collect a few words per week; middle letter–name students may collect several words a day. When the word bank contains between 150 and 200 words and the student is at the end of the letter name–alphabetic stage, the word bank is discontinued. An alternative to individual word banks is a group word bank, in which case the teacher identifies the most useful words for students to learn and uses them in word study Activities 5.12 to 5.15.

Child rereading group experience story in her personal reader

**Personal Readers.** Collect copies of familiar rhymes and jingles, group or individual dictations, or selected passages from books that children have read in a **personal reader** (Bear, Caserta-Henry, & Venner, 2004); see Figure 5.5. Students are enormously proud of their personal readers and they reread the selections many times before taking them home to read some more. Text selections in personal readers are ideal sources from which students can collect words for their word banks. They simply underline the words they know best and then these are transferred to small cards. A number can be written on each word card that matches the numbered stories.

The student's word bank can be a plastic bag that is stored in the personal reader and little books for rereading fit inside the front pocket. In addition, a small chart of sounds called a soundboard (see Appendix C) can be included for reference in word study and writing.

## TEACHING TIPS

### Personal Readers and Word Banks

There are several ways to manage personal readers and word banks. Here are a few ideas with more in Activities 5.10 to 5.15.

- Make copies of reading selections in a large font and leave an extra space between words when possible. These pages can be numbered, hole-punched, and added to folders or notebooks to form a personal reader. Have a supply of blank word cards ready for recording words for students' word banks. It is probably best to write the words on the word bank cards for the children rather than asking them to do it and add the number of the selection. Do not expect children to learn every word from the reading selection!

- As they study initial sounds through picture sorts, ask students to then find words in their word banks that begin with those same sounds. This helps them make connections between the pictures they sort and the words they read.

- Create a page of words for each selection that are good candidates for sight words. After several rereadings, ask students to identify the words they know from the list that can be added to their word bank. This can also be used as an assessment tool to see how well students are acquiring at least a few words from each selection.

- By using words from familiar readings and numbering the stories and rhymes to correspond to word cards, you can encourage students to return to the primary source to find a forgotten word or match the word bank card to its counterpart in print.

## Supporting Writing

Children need encouragement and instruction in the letter name stage to grow as writers. Because children are working hard to listen to sounds, match them to letters, and remember how to form those letters, their work is often slow and labored. Typically, they will only produce a few sentences at a time. The Teaching Tips on the next page will guide your writing instruction with beginning writers.

## Supporting Vocabulary Development

There are many ways you can enhance vocabulary development in the letter name–alphabetic stage. Activities from Chapter 4 (Activities 4.1 to 4.7) continue to play an important role in stimulating oral language and encouraging the use of new vocabulary. Throughout the week look for times to:

- Highlight, read, and discuss several words from a read-aloud.
- Engage in interactive read-alouds that encourage students to talk and ask questions.

**FIGURE 5.5  Personal Reader with Word Bank**

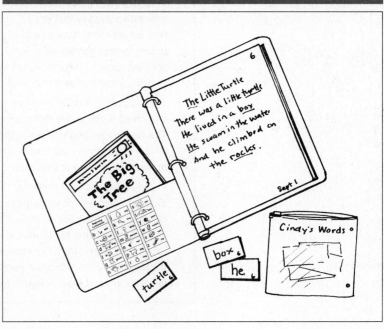

Students writing with teacher support

- Use "Turn and Talk" during any discussion time to increase the amount of oral language.
- Ask children to retell stories and act them out using simple props.

In the Activities section (Activities 5.1 to 5.7), we highlight several vocabulary strategies such as anchored word instruction (Juel et al., 2003), think-pair-share, and using dramatization. Routines to incorporate in daily practice in the classroom are presented here: use sophisticated synonyms, enrich simple text, and assign concept sorts.

## TEACHING TIPS

### Encourage a Variety of Writing

- Interactive writing provides an opportunity to model writing and use print referencing to further develop concepts about print as described in Chapter 4. Teach children directly about conventions such as when to use capitals letters and appropriate punctuation.

- Model a variety of writing experiences using the gradual release model described in Chapter 4 on page 93. Journal writing, letters to friends, observations, directions, predictions before reading, and written responses after reading are authentic writing activities that offer students opportunities to express themselves.

- Be sure that students write for themselves as they spell "the best they can." Teachers often guide students in their writing by asking, "What sounds do you hear when you say that word?" and then offering support as needed to write letters. Be sure they have an alphabet strip handy for reference. Asking students to simply copy sentences or words is of little value. It is in the hard work of transcribing speech into print where they exercise their phonemic awareness and growing understanding of how spellings represent speech sounds and meaning.

- The support writing in the photo on the next page illustrates an activity for beginning writers that also creates patterned material for repeated reading. The support writing you see in the photo only required the student to insert one or two words in the sentence frames. The picture and the repeated text will make it easier for the students to reread their stories.

- In the early phases of the letter name–alphabetic stage, you may sometimes dictate sentences for students to write. This removes the burden on students of trying to remember what they were trying to write so that they can concentrate on writing for sounds and using the phonics features they have been learning in word study. For example, Tony's group might be asked to write, "Put the top on the hot pot." after working with word families for *-op* and *-ot*. Watch for accuracy and fluency in this brief dication experience.

**USE SOPHISTICATED SYNONYMS.** This practice illustrates how to systematically expand the vocabulary you use with students. Opportunities exist throughout the day for you to model sophisticated words for familiar concepts as a way to promote vocabulary growth. Lane and Allen (2010) describe how a kindergarten teacher began the year by asking the "weather watcher" to report to the group using terms such as *sunny, cloudy,* or *warm.* However, as the teacher introduced new terms over several months, the appointed "meteorologist" was expected to *observe* the weather *conditions* and report the *forecast* with terms such as *brisk, frigid,* or *overcast.* Lane and Allen suggest that teachers look for, gradually teach, and consistently use synonyms for the common language of everyday routines. Students can be asked to *distribute, replenish, dispense,* or *allocate* materials. During group discussions *participants* are encouraged to *contribute, articulate, verbalize,* and *elaborate* their ideas. The class can be asked to line up *adjacent* to or *parallel* to the wall and *proceed* in an *orderly* fashion. Students are complimented for being *amiable, agreeable, courteous, proficient, gracious,* and *considerate.* Rather than "dumbing down" our language to children, we should consciously elevate our language and provide appropriate explanations, repeated exposure, and opportunities for them to use that same language.

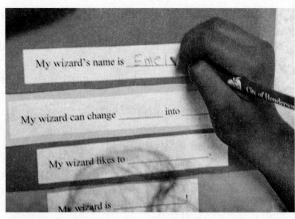

Support writing about a wizard story

**ENRICH SIMPLE TEXT.** Most beginning readers and writers are not able to grow their vocabularies through their own reading because the simple predictable texts they use for reading instruction rarely include words whose meanings they do not know. However, you can infuse more vocabulary as you discuss the story and illustrations using alternative words. For example, *Cat on the Mat* by Brian Wildsmith, described in Chapter 4, is written with very simple, predictable language. However, the cat experiences a range of emotions, from *contented* to *uneasy* to *agitated* to *furious,* as more and more animals gather on the mat. Part of your discussion should focus on how the cat feels, offering the opportunity for you to introduce many synonyms for *happy, sad,* and *mad*—the words children are likely to suggest. Discussing illustrations will especially benefit English learners, who rely on the illustrations to understand much of the story. You might ask students to share synonyms in their home language. *Content* and *furious* turn out to be *contento* and *furioso* in Spanish! Studying **cognates** (words descended from the same ancestral root) is addressed more in later chapters, but it can begin in the early stages as well.

**ASSIGN CONCEPT SORTS.** Use objects, pictures, and known words in concept sorts to expand children's vocabulary and to encourage rich verbal interactions. For example, after reading about and discussing concepts related to weather, students can sort pictures of mittens, boots , jackets, and caps under the headings of *sunny, rainy,* and *snowy.* In your modeling, use the language of comparison/contrast: "warmer than, cooler than, not as hot as," and so forth. This explicit attention to language helps students "unpack" what they tacitly know about the concepts underlying the labels, which becomes part of their own discussions about words and concepts. Students categorize words and pictures multiple times over several days. They might sort in multiple categories—you can see this when they contrast things *I like* with those *I don't like,* animals

Weather concept sort

that live *in the water* or *on land*, and so on. Vocabulary is learned best when it is used many times in phrases and sentences.

Concept sorts for English learners are particularly worthwhile because objects (such as plastic animals) or pictures can be sorted into categories without students needing to know the English terms. At the same time, English-speaking partners can supply unknown words and, while talking about the sort, students practice using and hearing the vocabulary they hear from you and their classmates. In a concept sort about weather with English learners, Ms. Polanski introduced three new vocabulary words and asked the students to explain to a partner why they paired two pictures from the sort. One child who spoke Hmong as her primary language made a novel pairing for this weather sort with moon and sun, explaining that "when the sun go down and the moon come up." Picture concept sorts makes it easy for English learners to show their thinking. Concept sorts are included in the activity section that follows and in the *WTW Digital* online materials.

Search the Internet for images of objects to compare in concept sorts. For example, in a search of dogs there are a wide variety of pictures to examine and talk about by breed, size, ears, tails, and color.

*for* **English Learners**

**Enhanced eText**
**Video Example 5.3**
This video depicts a concept sort with English learners.

**TEACHING TIPS**

### Developing Vocabulary

Here are some high-utility, research-based, vocabulary activities:

- Evidence suggests that linking a word's spelling to its pronunciation and meaning is more effective than vocabulary instruction that does not link spelling to pronunciations and meaning (Rosenthal & Ehri, 2008). Write targeted vocabulary words on cards even though you do not expect students to learn them as sight words. Saying the words aloud greatly increases their knowledge of them (Ehri, 2013).

- Be deliberate about using key vocabulary in sentences and phrases; use body movements as you talk; read supporting books and display objects and illustrations.

- Ask and answer interesting questions. Be an active listener and be responsive to what students say and want to know (Hamre, Downer, Jamil, Pianta, 2012). Often, teachers ask questions and respond to individual students. Instead, facilitate discussion among students by asking open-ended questions, questions that cannot be answered yes or no.

- Find cognates between English and students' primary languages. Online resources and print resources will provide cognates that will help students learn English. In Spanish, there are close to 15,000 words that are English cognates. When introducing vocabulary, you may ask students if there is a similar word in their first languages.

- Create charts of interesting words and phrases, including thematic words; general academic vocabulary; and domain, theme, or unit vocabulary.

## Word Study

In the whole-to-part model we propose, students learn to read big books, poems, and jingles at the same time they study letter–sound correspondences through focused contrasts with pictures and words. This **analytic phonics** approach begins with known words that are broken down into letters and sounds that students can compare and examine. As students begin to generalize these letter–sound correspondences across words, they can be expected to segment and blend those sounds to decode other words as they read in text and to encode words as they write for themselves. Word study entails both analytic and **synthetic phonics** approaches. Students are taught to sound out words, as in synthetic instruction, but we start by analyzing known words to ensure that by the time students get through the heavy lifting of segmenting and blending each grapheme and phoneme, they come up with a word they know in the end. Learning to blend letters and sounds together is addressed in the study of short vowels (see Activities 5.23 to 5.24 for examples).

**Sequence.** Our recommended word study sequence for this stage is outlined in Table 5.5 and is based on research on the developmental order in which phonics features are typically mastered. Initially, students use beginning consonants in their writing, so this is the place to begin word study in the early letter name–alphabetic stage. As their ability to segment phonemes becomes more complete later in the stage, they begin to use but confuse consonant digraphs, short vowels, and consonant blends. This is the time to study those features.

**Pacing.** The pace is not the same for every student because they progress at different rates. In Table 5.5, you can see how to modify instruction for students who are working at an introductory, moderate, or advanced and review pace. However, there is no time to waste—you must set as fast a pace as possible during the letter name–alphabetic stage because success in beginning reading depends on learning the basic phonics elements that comprise written English. Pacing should be tied to ongoing assessment to determine whether instruction is effective. We discuss progress monitoring for this stage on pages 178 and 179. **Early, Middle, or Late**

**Placement.** Placing students in the early, middle, or late parts of this stage using the spelling inventory depends primarily on how well they spell short vow- els. If students do not attempt vowels, they are in the early part of the stage. If they use but confuse vowels, perhaps getting one or two correct on an inventory, they are in the middle of the stage. If they spell half or more of the short vowels on an inventory, they are in the late letter name–alphabetic stage. If students are spelling most short vowels, as well as most digraphs and blends correctly, they are ready to move to studying long vowels in the within word pattern stage, in which the spelling of short vowels are reviewed as long vowel patterns are introduced. Table 5.5 helps you identify instruction for students in the early, middle, or late part of the stage.

## The Study of Consonant Sounds

Focused contrasts in the early letter name–alphabetic stage begin with picture sorts to draw attention to initial consonant sounds. Picture sorts help students continue to develop their phonemic awareness as they isolate beginning sounds and learn to pull apart consonant blends.

You can find pictures for sorts in Appendix D and prepared sorts on *WTW Digital* and in the other books in the *Words Their Way* series. Chapter 3 identified follow-up activities, such as draw and label or cut and paste, and many of the games described for beginning consonants (Activities 4.32 to 4.34) in Chapter 4 can be easily adapted for this stage. There are also ideas in the Activities section for this chapter (Activities 5.18 to 5.22) and *WTW Digital* provides games that are ready to print and use.

**INITIAL CONSONANTS.** Mr. Perez, whom we met at the beginning of this chapter, was wise in deciding to take a step back to firm up Cynthia's understandings of consonants. Many students benefit from a fast-paced review of consonants at the beginning of first grade to secure tentative letter–sound matches. There is no particular order to the sequence of beginning sounds, but we recommend starting with frequently occurring initial consonants, in which the contrasts or differences are clear both visually and phonologically. You might find that the sequence listed in Table 5.5 is effective for a review, but bear in mind that some beginning sounds are easier than others, depending on the relationship of

Student sorting pictures by initial consonants

**TABLE 5.5** Pacing and Sequence Guide for Letter Name–Alphabetic Spellers

| | Introductory Pace | Moderate Pace | Advanced Pace or Review |
|---|---|---|---|
| *Focused Contrasts for Early Letter Name–Alphabetic* | | | |
| **Picture Sorts for Initial Consonants**[*] | Contrast two sounds that are very different in place of articulation, such as /m/ and /s/. Contrast up to four sounds when students are able. A suggested sequence is:<br>**1.** *b m r s*<br>**2.** *t g n p*<br>**3.** *c h f d*<br>**4.** *l k j w*<br>**5.** *y z v* | Review all initial consonants sounds (four at a time) and then, as needed, contrast easily confused consonants: *w/y/; g/j; c/s; b/p; d/t* | Review initial consonant sounds only as needed. Use progress monitoring spell checks to determine which consonants need attention. |
| **Picture and Word Sorts for Same-Vowel Word Families** | Start out slowly, spending as much as one week on a set: *at; an/ad; ap/ag; op/ot/og; un/ut/ug; ip/ig/ill; op/ot/og; et/eg/en* | Use the same sequence but move more quickly after students catch on to how word families work | Use progress monitoring to determine which families need attention. |
| **Picture Sorts for Digraphs** | *s/h/sh; c/j/ch; h/sh/ch; t/th; th/wh; sh/ch/wh/th* | *s/h/sh; sh/ch/h; th/wh; wh/sh/ch/th* | *wh/sh/ch/th* |
| **Pictures Sorts for Blends** | Contrast single sound to blends first (e.g., *s/t/st* or *s/p/sp*) then compare blends (*sp/sk/sm; sc/sn/sw; p/l/pl; pl/sl/bl; cr/cl/fr/fl; bl/br/gr/gl: pr/tr/dr; k/wh/; qu/tw*) | *s*-blends; *l*-blends; *r*-blends | *r*-blends others as needed |
| *Focused Contrasts for Middle Letter Name–Alphabetic* | | | |
| **Word Sorts for Mixed-Vowel Word Families** | *at/ot/it/; an/un/in; ad/ed/ab/ob; ill/ell/all; ag/eg/ig/og/ug; ick/ack/ock/uck; ish/ash/ush* | *an/un/in; ag/eg/ig/og/ug; ill/ell/all; ick/ack/ock/uck; ish/ash/ush* | Use progress monitoring spell checks to determine which families need attention |
| **Picture Sorts for Short Vowels** | *a/o; i/u; e/o; e/i/o/u* | *a/o; i/u; e/i/o/u*<br>Combine with word sorts | Skip unless needed |
| *Focused Contrasts for Late Letter Name–Alphabetic* | | | |
| **Word Sorts with Short Vowels in CVC Words** | *a/o; i/u; e/i/o/u* with easy words | *a/o; i/u; e/i/o/u* with easy words | *a/e/i/o/u* with harder words |
| **Word Sorts for Short Vowels with Blends and Digraphs** | Ex: *drop trip dish* | Ex: *drag dash sled* | Use progress monitoring to determine what needs attention |
| **Word Sorts for Preconsonantal Nasals** | *rag/rang; lip/limp; win/wind; ram/rap/ramp; sad/sand/sank; ng/mp; nt/nd/nk* | *rag/ran/rang; win/wig/wing; ng/mp; nt/nd/nk* | *ng/mp; nt/nd/nk* as needed |
| **Word Sorts for *R*-Influenced** | *a/ar o/or* | *a/ar o/or* | Move on to next stage |

[*] When using picture sorts, add words if students can read them. Do not use words students cannot read.

the sound to the letter name. Because of this, some contrasts will take more time than others (Invernizzi & Buckrop, 2018). Some students may still be confused with certain letter sounds based on letter name mix-ups (for example, *y* and *w*) or voiced and unvoiced pairs (for example, *b* and *p*), and therefore benefit from specific word study activities that contrast those pairs. Many children delayed in language development will benefit from a slower pace of instruction that is coordinated with the language specialist.

Figure 5.6 is an example of a sort with focused contrasts for initial consonants *l*, *k*, *j*, and *w*. Chapter 4 offers suggestions for how to plan and carry out picture sorts for initial sounds starting on page 107. You can also contrast pictures with ini- tially occurring short vowels (for example, *igloo*, *octopus*, *apple*) as a way to introduce those letter–sound correspondences.

**FINAL CONSONANTS.** Beginning consonants are reviewed and ending consonants are targeted in same-vowel word families. This is because the only difference between *mat* and *man* is the final consonant sound, so contrasting same-vowel word families alerts students to looking for and listening to the final phoneme. Most students do not need to study ending consonant sounds with picture sorts, perhaps because after they develop the phonemic awareness to attend to final

**FIGURE 5.6   Sample Sort for Initial Consonants**

## Word Study with English Learners

English learners benefit from word study that addresses confusions that arise because of sounds that are missing or that are different in their native language. Focused sound contrasts using pictures can clarify beginning consonant sounds in English that may not exist in other languages like those sounds described in Table 5.6. Here are some examples to consider:

- Spanish speakers may benefit from sorting a series of pictures that begin with /j/ or /h/ to clarify the differences in these sounds in English, but that do not occur in Spanish.

- English learners will use what they know in their native languages to spell both consonant blends and digraphs. Spanish speakers also benefit from studying *s*-blends, a combination that does not exist in Spanish. Spanish speakers may substitute the affricate sound *ch* for the *sh* digraph, another sound that does not exist in Spanish.

- Arabic speakers may sort pictures that begin with a voiced /g/ as in *goat* and a voiceless /k/ as in *coat*. They may also be unfamiliar with many of the blends in English and insert a vowel between the letters in the blend.

- For Chinese and other from Asian language speakers, it helps to spend time studying nasal sounds to compare /n/ and /ng/.

- Take a look at prepared sorts and word lists in the appendices, the sorts online, and other *WTW* materials for English learners (Helman, Bear, Invernizzi, Templeton, & Johnston, 2011).

- English learners whose native language does not have many ending consonants may need more sorts with final consonant sounds.

**TABLE 5.6**    Consonant Confusions for English Learners

| Sound | Potential Confusion |
|-------|---------------------|
| b | The voiced *b* is confused with the unvoiced *p* and is difficult in final position. |
| c | Is often confused with hard *g*. Many languages do not have a hard *c*. |
| d | Is confused with /th/ in Spanish, so *dog* may be pronounced /thŏg/. |
| f | Is confused with *v*, especially in Arabic. In Japanese, it is confused with /h/. |
| g | The hard *g* sound may be confused with *k* by speakers of Arabic, French, or Swahili. |
| h | Is silent in Spanish, and in Chinese it sounds more like /kh/ as in *loch*. |
| j | May be confused with *h* in Spanish and may also be pronounced /ch/. |
| k | May be confused with hard *g* by Spanish speakers. |
| l | May be confused with *r*. Final *l* may be especially difficult. |
| m | May be dropped at the ends of words. |
| n | Is difficult for speakers of Chinese, especially at the ends of words. May be confused with *l*. |
| p | Is easily confused with its voiced mate *b*. |
| r | Is rolled in Spanish and may be spelled with *w*. It is confused with *l* in many Asian languages. |
| s | Is difficult to perceive in final position. |
| sh | Is a sound that does not exist in many languages and is confused with *ch*, *g*, and *j*. |
| s-blends | Blends in Spanish such as *st*, *sk*, and *sp* are separate syllables that begin with *e* as in *español*. |
| t | Is confused with the voiced sound of *d* by Spanish speakers and not pronounced at the ends of words. |
| v | May be confused with *b* in Spanish and Korean. It does not exist in many languages. |
| w | Is a letter that does not exist in many languages and may be confused with *v*. |
| y | May sound more like /ch/ in Spanish. |
| z | May be confused with *s* and not voiced in Spanish. |

**Enhanced eText**
**Video Example 5.4**
In this video, Darl models
a CVC short vowel sort.

sounds, they transfer their knowledge of letter–sound matches at the beginning to spell those final consonants as well. Some students may have a few problems even when they know most consonant matches, but do not hesitate to move on if they are beginning to represent vowels in their developmental spelling.

After students know their consonant sounds, they are ready to learn about consonant digraphs and blends. The goal is to not only master letter–sound correspondences, but also to help students see these two-letter combinations as single orthographic units in the CVC closed syllable pattern.

**DIGRAPHS.** Digraphs are introduced before blends because there is only one phoneme to deal with, but most students are ready to study both at about the same time. The suggestions in Chapter 4 for picture sorts apply to digraphs and blends as well as single conso- nants. The consonant digraphs to study in the letter name stage are *ch*, *sh*, *th*, and *wh*. (We do not include *ph* at this point because there are few words that beginning readers will encounter that begin with *ph*.) There are several things to keep in mind when setting up focused contrasts for digraphs sounds. First, consider the confusion students show in their spelling attempts. Some students substitute *j* for *ch*, as they spell words like *chin* as JN, or they may confuse the letter name of *h* (aitch) with *ch* and spell *chin* as HN. Consider a contrast to study *ch* or *sh* that compares pictures that contrast the digraphs with single consonants, such as *h*. You can compare *th* to single *t*, *sh* to single *s*, and *ch* to single *c*. However, a focused contrast with *w* and *wh* would be quite difficult because many words beginning with *wh* do not have a distinctive sound. (Which witch was which?) Compare *wh* to *th*, *sh*, and *ch* in a culminating digraph sort. Add known words such as *who*, *what*, *when*, and *why* to the picture sort. Table 5.5 contains a suggested sequence and possible contrasts for studying digraphs. Digraphs are revisited in the study of word families and short vowels in both initial and final positions.

**BLENDS.** You can group beginning consonant blends into three major and one minor categories as follows:

> S-blends: *sc, sk, sl, sn, sm, sp, st, sw*
> L-blends: *bl, cl, fl, gl, pl, sl*
> R-blends: *br, cr, dr, fr, gr, pr, tr*
> Blends with /w/: *qu, tw*

The easiest group to learn seems to be the *s*-blends, perhaps because *s* is a continuant that you can hold without distorting the sound (*sssss*). Blends with the "slippery" *l* or *r* are harder; some r-blends are sometimes confused with affricative sounds such those made by the letter names *g* or *j* (this explains why *trip* and *trap* are often spelled *JRP* by so many beginners). Finally, the hardest group includes *qu* and *tw*. In *qu*, the *u* is acting as a consonant representing the /w/ sound. Three-letter blends (*spr, str, squ, thr, shr*) are less commonly encountered in early reading material so are not studied until the within word pattern stage.

To study initial consonant blends, begin with focused contrasts that compare pictures of a single initial consonant with its blend. This is the problem for spellers such as Tony, who spell *stick* as SEK. To help Tony listen for the sounds in the blend, contrast *st* with pictures that begin with *s*. After studying several blends in this fashion, pick up the pace and introduce other blends in groups such as the s-blends contrast in Figure 5.7. See Table 5.5 for a suggested sequence of sorts and how to pace them. After students catch on to how blends work and learn to segment and blend the individual sounds in a consonant blend, they may move quickly through a sequence of study or even skip some contrasts altogether if you find they have quickly generalized. The procedures and routines for studying digraphs and blends using picture sorts are the same as for other beginning sound sorts, as described in Chapter 4.

Students in the early part of the letter name–alphabetic stage do not need to master consonant blends and digraphs completely because they will be revisited throughout the stage by studying word families and short vowels. Research by Johnston (2003) and others shows that blends, digraphs, and short vowels all begin to appear in students' spelling about the same time, so there should be some interplay among these features in the instructional sequence, as shown in Table 5.5. Consonant blends and digraphs that create an affricate sound (**trip**, **drip**, **chip**) take longer to master because their sounds are so similar.

**Final consonant blends** (*last, lisp, task, left, kept, felt, shelf,* and **help**) are not studied with pictures, due to a lack of examples, but words containing final consonant blends should be included toward the end of the stage in the study of short vowel words. Other ending blends that include an *r*, like *rd, rt,* and *rp,* in words like *bird, art,* or *chirp,* are studied with *r*-influenced vowels.

**Preconsonantal nasals,** a particular type of final blend that includes *mp, nt, nd,* and *nk,* are also studied at the end of the letter name stage. We add the digraph *ng* as well, which may be studied in word families, as there are many words spelled with *ang, ing, ong,* or *ung.* Many students find this feature particularly difficult and will need explicit routines for making words with and without the nasal, changing *rag* into *rang* or *hug* into *hung,* for example. The building, blending, and extending exercises described in Activity 5.23 can be adapted for this.

**FIGURE 5.7   Sample Sort for S-Blends**

## The Study of Short Vowels

After letter name–alphabetic spellers have a solid, if not complete, mastery of beginning and ending consonant sounds, they are ready to study medial short vowels. Students need full phonemic awareness to isolate the elusive vowel, but if vowels are still missing or used only occasionally in their spelling, start with word families as Mr. Perez did with his middle group. After students are using (though still confusing) short vowels consistently, ask them to compare short vowels in word sorts that examine the CVC pattern across a variety of vowels, as Mr. Perez did with his highest group. Appendix E contains lists of words spelled with short vowels that you can use to create handouts similar to those used by Mr. Perez in Figure 5.2(C). Appendix E has suggested sorts, and prepared games and more sorts are on the website and in *Words Their Way®: Word Sorts for Letter Name–Alphabetic Spellers.*

**WORD FAMILIES.** Word families, which are sometimes called **phonograms**, consist of groups of rhyming words like *cat, mat, sat,* and *bat* that all follow a CVC short vowel pattern and are spelled similarly. They offer an easy and appealing way to introduce short vowels within closed syllables; that is, one syllable short vowel words ending in a consonant. This supports students in their first efforts to analyze the vowel because the vowel and the ending letter(s) are presented as a chunk or pattern called a **rime** (for example, the *at* in *cat* and *mat*). What comes before the vowel is the **onset**. Examples of onset-rime breaks are *m-an, bl-and, m-at,* and *th-at*. It is easier and more natural for students to divide and blend words into onsets and rimes than divide them into individual phonemes (Goswami, 2008; Treiman, 1985).

Studying word families makes sense for several other reasons. First, 37 rimes can be used to generate 500 different words that students encounter in primary reading materials (Wylie & Durrell, 1970). In addition, these same rimes are familiar chunks in thousands of multisyllabic words: The *an* chunk can be found in *canyon, fantastic,* and *incandescent*. Second, vowel sounds are more stable within families than across families (Adams, 1990; Wylie & Durrell, 1970). For example, the word *dog* is often presented as a short *o* word in phonics programs, but in some regions of the United States, it is pronounced more like *dawg*. If you say it that way, then you probably pronounce *fog* as *fawg, frog* as *frawg,* and *log* as *lawg*. When studying word families, the actual pronunciation of the short vowel does not matter; it is the *og* chunk that is examined and compared.

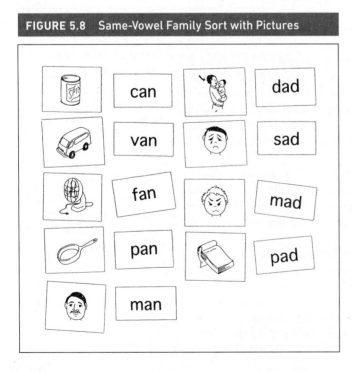

**FIGURE 5.8** Same-Vowel Family Sort with Pictures

can | dad
van | sad
fan | mad
pan | pad
man

**SAME-VOWEL WORD FAMILIES.** Early letter-name spellers and very beginning readers pay attention to beginning and ending consonants in order to read and spell words. Studying same-vowel word families reviews those features. The phonological awareness of the rime unit (for example, *-at,-an*) also lays the foundation for future vowel study when students begin to look inside the word for common short vowels across families. We suggest studying same-vowel word families before blends and digraphs, but students are usually ready to study all three at about the same time, so you might decide to do blends and digraphs first.

There is no particular order to study word families, but a good choice is to start with short *a* families (*at, an, ad, ap, ag)* because these words abound in early reading materials, and students are likely to already know several words from these families by sight. In addition, short *a* is the least likely short vowel to be confused when students try to make matches based on letter names and place of articulation. Compare other same-vowel word families in a similar way (*in, it, ip* or *ot, op, og,* and so on).

Table 5.5 suggests contrasts and a sequence for studying word families under three possible pacing guides.

However, it is just a suggestion for planning your own course of study. Consider the words that your students know as sight words, and the kinds of words they encounter in their reading. If you are reading a story with lots of short *u* words, then study a few short *u* families.

# Introduce Word Families with Pictures

**SAMPLE LESSON**

Apply the following procedure when introducing a word family sort with pictures (see Figure 5.8).

1. **Start with just the pictures for a rhyming sort.** Use pictures as headers for each column (for example, *can* and *dad*), name them, and then pick up another picture. Say to students, "*Van*. Does *van* rhyme with *can* or *dad*—*van, can: van, dad?* I will put it under the *can*." Model several and then have students help you finish the sort. Name all the pictures in each column and talk about how they rhyme.

2. **Now lay out the word cards.** Name a header such as *can*, and say, "Who can find the word *can*? What letters would you look for at the beginning and end?" Repeat for *dad*, and then ask students to find the word for each picture.

After all the words are sorted and matched to the pictures, read down each column. Ask the students how the words are alike; they should note that they all end with the same two letters. Explain that the words are in the same family (the *an* family or *ad* family) and they all rhyme.

3. **Remove the words and shuffle them.** Give them out to the students to match to the pictures again. Read each column, and then remove the pictures to see whether the students can use just the initial sound and the rime to read each word in the column.

4. **Give students their own set of pictures and words to sort for seatwork.** Follow up with other word family activities such as Build, Blend, and Extend, described in Activity 5.22.

# Introduce a Mixed-Vowel Word Family

**SAMPLE LESSON**

1. **Lay down a known word as a header for each family.** Choose words you are sure students can read, such as *big*, *dog*, and *bag*. Explain that the rest of the words are to be sorted under one of these headers.

2. **Pick up another word such as *frog* and say, "I am going to put this word under *dog* because it ends in *o* and *g*."** Then read the words: "Listen: *dog, frog*." Continue to model one or two words in each category, always *sorting first* and then reading down, starting with the header.

3. **Ask students to sort the next word.** They should sort first and then read from the top of each column to help them identify the new word. They are not expected to sound out the word first and then sort. Instead, their sense of rhyme will support them as they read the new word, by simply changing the first sound of a word they already know. The final sort might look like the following:

| big | dog | bag |
|-----|------|------|
| dig | frog | wag |
| pig | hog | rag |
| wig | fog | flag |
|     | log | tag |

4. **After all the words are sorted, read down each column and lead a discussion to focus students' attention on the common features** (sounds and letters): "How are the words in this column alike?" After giving students a chance to discuss what they notice about the words, summarize by explaining that the words in each column are in the same family because of the two ending letters and sounds that rhyme.

5. **Provide students with individual sorts.** Conclude with follow-up activities that include students working with partners to do blind sorts as described in Chapter 3. Flip charts and word wheels are just some of the follow-up activities that are found in Activities 5.23 to 5.28).

**MIXED-VOWEL WORD FAMILIES.** The difference between *top*, *tip*, and *tap* lies in the medial vowel, and it is through such contrasts that students are forced to listen to the vowel sound itself and look carefully at the vowel in the middle of a word. Students in the middle

**Enhanced eText**
**Video Example 5.5**
In this video, Darl
Kiernan models a mixed-
vowel short *e, i, o,* and *u;*
*rock, bed, pig, cup.*

letter-name stage should be ready to study mixed-vowel word families where the sorts do not have the support of pictures. Students should already know how to read several words in each family. Include words with blends and digraphs after they have been studied with picture sorts. For example, the *ag* family can be expanded to include words such as *flag, brag, drag, shag,* and *snag.*

**THE STUDY OF SHORT VOWELS IN THE CVC PATTERN.** After students are spelling about half of the short vowel words correctly on a spelling inventory and working with mixed-vowel word families easily and accurately, they are ready to study short vowels in nonrhyming words outside of word families. This asks them to look at words in a new way, not as two units with various rimes (*m-ad, fl-ag, tr-ack*), but as three units with the same CVC pattern (*m-a-d, fl-a-g, tr-a-ck*), one vowel surrounded by consonants. This ability to see words as patterns is the key feature of the next stage, the within word pattern stage. While studying short vowels, students come to see that CVC is the basic pattern for all short vowels across variations that include VC (e.g., *at*), CCVC (e.g., *flat*), CVCC (e.g., *fast*), and CCVCC (e.g., *blast*).

*R-INFLUENCED VOWELS.* Words like *car* and *for* look as though they follow the CVC pattern, but they do not have the short sounds of *a* or *o*. Instead, the vowel sounds are subsumed by the *r* that follows and are known as r-*influenced vowels* (or r-*controlled vowels*). Do not expect students to segment a vowel sound separately from the *r* but instead teach *ar* and *or* as patterns or chunks. Because words spelled with *ar* and *or* are common in beginning reading materials, it is worthwhile to introduce them at the end of this stage. The *r*-influenced vowels form a major subcategory of vowels that will be examined more extensively during the next stage. The following is a sort that compares the *r*-influenced *o* sounds with short *o*. Read down each column so you can hear the difference. What is odd about *word* and *work*? How are they different from the other *r* words? How are they similar to each other?

| o | or | *Oddballs* |
|------|------|---------|
| fox | for | word |
| shop | sort | work |
| spot | fort | |
| trot | horn | |

Student pasting two-way sort by vowels

# Contrast Two or More Short Vowels

**SAMPLE LESSON**

1. **Collect a set of word cards** that feature two or more short vowels to model on a tabletop, pocket chart, interactive whiteboard, or document camera. See lists and sorts in Appendix E & F and at *WTW Digital* and other *WTW* materials. Read through the words before sorting to be sure students know the words and talk about the meaning of any that might be unclear or have multiple meanings. For example, talk about the word *block* in Figure 5.9 which can mean something you build with, the action of stopping, or a section of a street. If students cannot read a word put it aside to revisit later.

2. **Model the sort with one vowel.** Begin by laying down a known word as a key word for each vowel. Read each word and isolate the vowel: "Here is the word *cap*. Listen: *cap, ap, /ă/. Cap* has the short *a* sound in the middle. Let's listen for other words that have the same vowel sound in the middle." Repeat for the short *i* and short *o* categories.

3. **Model comparisons.** Pick up a new word such as *fast* and say, "I am going to say this word slowly to listen for the vowel in the middle, /f-a-a-a-st/. Where should I put *fast*? Listen: *ca-a-ap, f-a-a-ast.* They have the same vowel sound in the middle so I will put *fast* under *cap.*" Continue to model one or two words in each category, reading each new word, saying the medial vowel slowly, and comparing it to the key word.

4. **Model an oddball.** Hold up an oddball, like *for* or *was*. Ask students if they hear the same vowel sound in the middle. Model how to place it in the oddball category because it does not have the same vowel sound. Ask your students to help finish the sort.

5. **Discuss the sort.** After the words are sorted, read down each column to check and discuss how the words are alike in sound and spelling. Ask: "How are the words in each column alike? How are the words alike under *cap*? Yes, they have the same vowel sound in the middle spelled with a. We call this the short *a* sound. How are the oddballs different? What is odd about them?" Help students identify the CVC pattern by labeling the units in *cap, pig,* and *hot.* Point out that *hill* and *trap* are also CVC words because *ll* and *tr* are consonant units on each side of the single vowel. At this point revisit any unknown words. Ask the students to put each in the correct column and sound it out.

6. **Sort a second time.** Have students sort a second time. Leave mistakes to the end and check them by reading down the columns.

7. **Follow-up activities:** Give students their own set of words to sort at their seats, with partners, or at home across several days and have them write the words into categories. Because it is easy to sort the words visually by attending to the vowel letters, the blind sort described in Chapter 3 is important as a follow-up activity. One partner reads each word aloud while the other partner indicates where it goes without seeing the word. Model this first in a small group and then let partners work together. See other word family activites (5.23–5.29). Assess student mastery by calling out at least 10 words to spell.

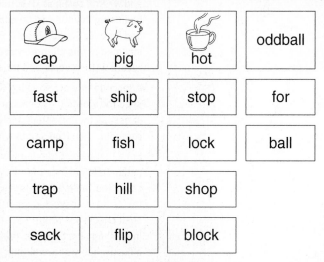

**FIGURE 5.9    Short Vowel Sort across Families**

| cap | pig | hot | oddball |
|-----|-----|------|---------|
| fast | ship | stop | for |
| camp | fish | lock | ball |
| trap | hill | shop | |
| sack | flip | block | |

**TEACHING TIPS**

## Word Families

As you study word families, keep these thoughts in mind.

- When studying word families, it is appropriate to modify one of the principles of word study described in Chapter 3, "Use words students can read." When working with word families, students probably cannot read *all* the words initially. However, because the words are in rhyming families, students are supported with pictures and with headers that are familiar. Students sort visually by the rime spelling first, and then read unknown words by blending different onsets with the header rime.

- Include words with digraphs and blends after they are introduced. Studying the *ack* family pays bigger dividends when you include *black, clack, track, shack, quack, stack, snack,* and *crack*.

- Supply supplemental reading materials that feature word families. With the publication of research about onsets and rimes, and renewed interest in word families, there has been a flood of reading materials for students that feature a particular family or short vowel. Some of these little books are engaging and well-written, offering students support in the form of patterned or rhyming text. Other books are contrived and nonsensical, as in *Nan and Dan Sat in the Pan*. Use well-written books as a starting point or as a follow-up for word study, and students can use the books to go on word hunts for additional words that follow the same phonics features. However, choose books carefully; text featuring sentences such as "The tan man ran the van" make reading into an exercise in word calling rather than comprehension. Although some phonics readers are better than others, they shouldn't constitute the sole reading materials used at this level.

- Plan follow-up activities. There are many activities and games to use when studying word families. Follow-ups to sorting include re-sorting, blind sorts, and writing sorts, as described in Chapter 3. Board games designed to study beginning sounds can be adapted to word families. Activities like Build, Blend, and Extend; Sound Wheels; Flip Charts; and Show Me are favorites and are included in this chapter's activities. Use word study notebooks for students to record writing sorts and the results of word hunts or brainstorming sessions.

- After students are working with word cards you should expect students to spell the words they sort correctly and you can administer short spelling tests to assess their mastery. Include dictated sentences that feature a family (for example, "The frog sat on a log in the fog").

- Set a fast pace. Studying word families can take a long time if you feel compelled to study every family in a thorough fashion, but this should not be the case. See Table 5.5 for ideas about how to modify the pace based on assessments such as weekly spelling tests, the qualitative checklist for writing, and spell checks for progress monitoring. Although students may still make errors in spelling short vowels, many quickly pick up the notion that words that sound alike probably share similar rimes and are spelled alike. They will also be able to use this knowledge to figure out new words by analogy; for example, noting the *and* in *stand*, they quickly decode it.

## TEACHING TIPS

### The Study of Short Vowels in CVC Words

As you study short vowels in CVC words, keep these points in mind:

- If students are still making some errors in the spelling of digraphs and blends, which is likely, include words with those features in the short vowel sorts. At this time, they have many more sight words that contain beginning and ending consonant digraphs and blends.
- You might plan a two-way sort as shown in Figure 5.10 —first by vowel sounds and second by digraphs or blends. This encourages flexibility in word analysis, a desirable trait (Sharp, Sinatra, & Reynolds, 2008).
- Consider doing a third sort, perhaps sorting by action words (*crash*, *drag*, *trim*) versus things (*crumb*, *truck*, *crib*); take time to discuss words that could be used as both, depending on context (for example, "We will trim the tree," or "We added trim to the valentine."). Cartwright (2006, 2008) shows that having students think about words by different attributes builds cognitive

flexibility, an important component of reading comprehension. Discussing the different meanings and uses of words also makes students aware of the multiple meanings or **polysemy** of words, an important aspect of vocabulary development (Templeton et al., 2015).

- Plan short vowel contrasts that are distinct from each other. We recommend that students first compare short *a* to short *i* or short *o*. Wait until later to compare short *a* to short *e*, or short *e* to short *i* as those sounds students are most likely to confuse.
- Use words and pictures. Most sorts are with printed words, but occasionally use pictures to focus attention on the vowel sounds. Use pictures for column headers, such as the sound board pictures for vowels in Appendix C or the pictures in Appendix D, also found in *WTW Digital*. Consider what words students already know from familiar texts and word banks as you select words for sorts.

---

### FIGURE 5.10 Two-way Sort by Vowel and Blends

| First Sort by Vowel Sound | | | Second Sort by Blends | | |
|---|---|---|---|---|---|
| 🐱 | ⛰️ | 🥥 | *tr* | *dr* | *cr* |
| trap | trick | drug | trap | drag | crack |
| crack | drill | crumb | track | drip | crash |
| drag | trim | truck | trick | drum | crush |
| crash | drip | drum | trim | drill | crumb |
| track | crib | crush | truck | drug | crib |

*(Continued)*

- Establish the oddball, or miscellaneous category. Good words to use for oddballs in this stage are high-frequency words students may already know as sight words, such as *for*, *put*, *was*, and *what*. *Was* will be odd in a short *a* sort despite its CVC spelling because it doesn't have the short *a* sound. Other oddballs have a short vowel sound but are spelled in unusual ways (for example, *laugh*, *head*). You can find examples in the word lists in Appendix F.
- The oddball category can be used to accommodate variations in dialect and spelling. Some students may hear a short *o* in *lost*, but others will hear a sound closer to "aw." Some students hear a different vowel in *pin* and *pen*, but others consider them homophones. Rather than forcing students to doubt their own ear, the oddball category offers an alternative and acknowledges that not everyone speaks the same way, nor does spelling always match pronunciation.
- Plan word hunts and other follow-ups. It is fairly easy to find words with short vowels in just about any beginning reading material because they are, by their nature, common in English. Encourage students to look for two-syllable words with a CVC syllable, such as *funny* or *kitten*.
- Pacing is important. Be prepared to spend some time on short vowels, as they pose special problems for young spellers and can persist as problems beyond first grade. Start with simple three-letter words that include many of the words studied in word families (for example, *bag*, *can*, *pat*) but then move to more complex words with blends and digraphs at the beginning and end (for example, *brag*, *than*, *path*). However, short vowels will be reviewed when they are compared to long vowels in the next stage, so do not expect complete mastery. Move on to the study of long vowel patterns if students have blends and digraphs under good control but seem to have reached a plateau on short vowels.

This chapter has presented examples of focused contrasts for all the basic phonics features through explicit, teacher-directed sorts or closed sorts. As in direct instruction, in a teacher-directed, closed sort the teacher selects the words and leads a group sorting activity accompanied by a discussion of the features of interest. We recommend teacher-directed sorts when you introduce a new feature. Offer clear explanations when introducing a new feature but gradually release responsibility to students to sort independently. Table 3.1 outlines the support different groups will need. Open sorts, as described in Chapter 3, ask students to establish their own categories and offer you diagnostic information that will help to determine how much students understand the generalization that underlies the activity.

## Assess and Monitor Progress in The Letter Name–Alphabetic Stage

**PROGRESS**
**MONITORING**

It is critical that you monitor student progress in attaining a firm concept of word in text (COW-T), and the fundamental phonics/spelling features that support the automatic recognition of a basic reading vocabulary, or sight words. Without attaining these fundamentals, students will not progress in reading. Assess students regularly to determine whether they need more practice or are ready to move on.

### Assess and Monitor Progress in Concept of Word

Over the course of this stage, students move from a rudimentary to a firm concept of word in text (COW-T). Not only should students point accurately to words in familiar text without getting off track on two-syllable words, but they should also be acquiring sight words from the texts that they read and from analyzing them in word sorts. The ultimate litmus test of a firm concept of word in text is a student's ability to identify some words seen previously in context when shown in isolation. So, to the COW-T assessment procedures we described in Chapter 4 we add a procedure for assessing word recognition in isolation. After fingerpoint-reading a text accurately, we ask students to identify words in the middle of some of the lines and then, as you can see in the Concept of Word in Text assessment using "Humpty Dumpty" in Appendix A, we make a randomized list of the words from the text and present them to see how many words the students remember and recognize after reading a simple text. Students with a firm concept of word will be able to read many if not most of the words on the list; they will pick up several words as sight words after several rereadings.

## Assess and Monitor Progress in Phonemic Awareness, Phonics, and Spelling

Phonemic awareness, phonics, and spelling are all highly related; therefore, frequent spelling assessments scored by features are an easy way to monitor student progress. You can administer the spelling inventories described in Chapter 2 several times a year to track progress. As shown in Figure 5.11, Zack began the year as an early letter name speller, often omitting vowels and blends, which suggested that his phonemic awareness was only partial. By February, he was in the middle letter name stage, including a vowel in each word and spelling many vowels, blends, and digraphs correctly. He had full phonemic awareness, fully segmenting each word into sounds. By May, his correct spelling of short vowels as well as his use of silent *e* showed that he was transitioning into the within word pattern stage. Zack made solid progress over the course of the year in phonemic awareness, phonics, and spelling.

Ongoing assessment can be as simple as observing how quickly and accurately students sort pictures, or you can have students paste the pictures they have sorted into categories and label them. Weekly assessment in the middle to late part of this stage may involve a brief spelling test of five to ten words. In addition, we provide a series of spell checks in Appendix B for letter name–alphabetic spellers. We recommend that you use these as a pretest before introducing

| FIGURE 5.11 Zack's Spelling | | | |
| --- | --- | --- | --- |
| | September | February | May |
| fan | ✓ | ✓ | ✓ |
| pet | PAT | ✓ | ✓ |
| dig | DK | deg | ✓ |
| rob | ✓ | ✓ | ✓ |
| hope | HOP | hop | ✓ |
| wait | YAT | wat | wate |
| gum | GM | ✓ | ✓ |
| sled | SLD | slad | ✓ |
| stick | STK | stik | ✓ |
| shine | SIN | shin | ✓ |
| dream | GREM | drem | dreme |
| blade | BAD | blad | ✓ |
| coach | KOH | coh | coche |
| fright | FRIT | frit | frite |

a feature, and after spending a few weeks or so on a feature you can use them as a post-test. Progress monitoring or goal-setting forms are also available in Appendix B.

### Assess and Monitor Progress in Sight Word Development

After students achieve a firm concept of word in text, they should remember some words they have seen in context, out of context. Although students cannot be expected to remember all the words they have read in context, they should be able "pick up" a handful of words after several readings to add to their sight vocabularies. Frequently assessing students' word recognition in isolation should provide the feedback you need to determine whether or not to back up or move forward in reading levels, spelling features, or instructional support. If students are not progressing, make sure they receive texts that they can read successfully.

The easiest way to monitor progress in sight word development is to keep track of the number of known words in students' word banks. Early in this stage we have a page of students' sight words that have been collected from the selections in the personal readers. The number of known words, or sight words, should grow steadily across the early middle to late letter name–alphabetic phase when students are given regular opportunities to select and review words out of context that they have read in context. You will know that a student is developing a solid sight word vocabulary when his or her word bank exceeds 200 known words.

You can also note progress in sight word development as students are able to read increasingly difficult levels of reading materials with less support in the form of shared reading. By the middle to late letter name–alphabetic stage, less predictable reading materials require young readers to carefully focus on print. By the middle of this beginning reading phase, students should rely more on word recognition and less on memory of the language. Use running records to monitor word recognition accuracy in context (Clay, 2009) in addition to your assessments of word recognition in isolation.

**Enhanced eText**
Video Example 5.6
In this video, the assessment of students in the Letter Name–Alphabetic Stage is discussed.

# Word Study with English Learners in The Letter Name–Alphabetic Stage

*for* **English learners**

In general, most other languages do not have as many single consonants or blends as we do in English. English learners may need more time to master these sounds because they will have to learn how to hear and pronounce the sounds, segment the sounds, and learn the letter correspondences. Table 5.6 on page 170 lists the sounds that English learners may omit or mispronounce.

For example, Spanish-speaking students may confuse words that begin with *d* and *th*, pronouncing *dog* with a *th* sound, more like "thog." *Jump* may be pronounced "chump." It is important to create sorts that make these comparisons clear (*d* and *th* or *j* and *ch*) after the other beginning sounds are established. Refer to *Words Their Way with English Learners*, *Words Their Way®: Emergent Sorts for Spanish-Speaking English Learners*, and *Words Their Way®: Letter Name–Alphabetic Sorts for Spanish-Speaking English Learners* (Helman et al., 2012) for additional sorts to help students learn these distinctions.

**Consonant Confusions.** Only a handful of consonants occur in the final position in Spanish (*d, n, l, r, s, z*), so it is common for English learners to omit the ending consonant sounds in words like *hard*, which may be spelled HAR. Final consonant picture sorts may be needed to bring attention to these sounds. Sorting words by rhyme or word families like *bag, rag, tag* can also be more of a challenge for English learners. Contrasts in which the vowel and the final consonant differ (*at, op, un*) are a better starting place. In Spanish, the *s*-blends work differently. In many Spanish words, the *sp* blend is split between two syllables. The *s* is given a vowel (*es*) and *p* starts the second syllable, as in *Es-pañol*.

Still, there are many consonants shared by Spanish and English (*b, d, f, g, k, l, m, n, p, r, s, t, w, y*), and Spanish-speaking students can begin studying consonants with these. Spanish picture sorts can be found in the toolkit for *Words Their Way for English Learners* (Helman et al., 2012) under both the Emergent and Letter Name categories and in *Palabras a Su Paso: El Estudio de Palabras en Acción* (Pearson Schools, 2013). Explain the different sounds in English and Spanish, and acknowledge students' confusion as logical. See Table 5.6 for more examples of predictable confusions. Because students might not be able to name the pictures, you might pair them with an English-speaking partner who can supply the English names.

**Vowel Confusions.** As with consonants, other languages do not have as many vowel sounds as we do in English. Spanish has only one short vowel sound (short *o*), and it is spelled with the letter *a* as in *gracias*. Expect students to substitute vowels in their own language that are close in point of articulation for these short English vowels when they say and spell English words. Short *e* may be pronounced like the long *a* (*pet* as PAIT), short *i* like the long *e* (*tip* as TEEP), and short *a* and short *u* like the short *o* (*cat* and *cut* as *cot*) (Helman et al., 2012). See Chapter 6 for more information about vowel confusions for students learning English.

Picture sort and word study notebook to help Spanish speakers clarify short a and short o sounds

*for* **English learners**

## Word Study *Routines and Management*

The letter name–alphabetic stage easily spans kindergarten through second grade. A handful of students in third grade and even a few students in the upper elementary grades will still need to work on the features that characterize this stage. It may be tempting to rush through, but word study in the letter name–alphabetic stage helps to build a solid foundation for the study of long vowels and other vowel patterns in the next stage.

**RRWWT.** A balanced literacy program includes these five activities: **R**ead To, **R**ead With, **W**rite With, **W**ord Study, and **T**alk With (RRWWT). During *read to* time, teachers read aloud literature that offers exposure to new vocabulary and literary language. During *read with* time, students meet in large groups for shared reading and small groups for instructional-level reading. Teachers model how to compose ideas and spell words as they *write with* students, who, in turn, write for themselves. *Word study* includes explicit instruction in letter–sound correspondences, phonics, and spelling patterns. Finally, a comprehensive program provides students with ample opportunities to *talk with* teachers and peers about the books and experiences they have shared. Whole-group read-alouds continue to be the best place to focus on vocabulary, but you should look for other opportunities throughout the day to highlight new vocabulary words. Concept sorts can be developed for science, social studies, and math to teach new vocabulary.

**Differentiate instruction.** To differentiate instruction, you need small groups. In first-grade classrooms, teachers like Mr. Perez often find that reading groups and word study groups are virtually the same. Word sorts can be introduced toward the end of the reading group, using words taken from the selection as exemplars for introducing new features. Students practice categorizing words for seatwork and in centers with partners or individually after they learn the routines. Other teachers have a separate word study time, meeting with small groups initially to introduce a sort, but then expecting follow-up routines to be done independently or with partners. We prefer the former arrangement so that connections can be made between

**Enhanced eText**
**Video Example 5.7**
This video is about Weekly Schedules and Activities in the Letter Name-Alphabetic Stage.

**Enhanced eText**
**Teacher Resource:**
Ms. Kiernan's Word Study Schedule

the phonics and spelling features learned in word study to the same features encountered while reading.

Word study during the letter name–alphabetic stage begins with picture sorts for initial sounds and ends with word sorts for short vowels in nonrhyming words. During this transition, there are various routines and generic activities to help students explore and study features in depth. Betty Lee's schedule discussed in Chapter 9 is particularly appropriate in the early letter name–alphabetic stage for students who are doing picture sorts and keeping their materials in two-pocket folders. Later in the stage when students are sorting words, other routines that involve writing sorts in word study notebooks are more effective. Table 5.7 summarizes routines for this stage. Games and activities are described in detail in the section that follows.

**Pacing is important.** There are many blends and many word families, and if every blend were studied for a week, it could take many months. You might want to create two- or three-day cycles. For example, you might introduce two word families on Monday, another two on Wednesday, and then combine them for several days. Be ready to pick up the pace by combining a number of blends or families into one sort (up to four or five) or by omitting some features. The progress monitoring assessments provided in Appendix B will help you to know what students can do. Ultimately, your own observations dictate the pace that is appropriate for your students. Remember Table 5.5 offers three pacing guides that you may use to identify shortcuts for achieving students or more in-depth study for struggling students.

**Enhanced eText**
**Video Example 5.8**
Ms. Kiernan demonstrates how to teach students the tricks of cutting and pasting word and picture cards.

**TABLE 5.7**  **Sample Weekly Schedules for Word Study in the Letter Name–Alphabetic Stage**

|  | Picture Sorting | Word Sorting |
|---|---|---|
| Day 1 | Small-group sort: Introduce the sort and discuss the features | Small-group sort: Introduce the sort and discuss the features |
| Day 2 | Seatwork or center: Repeat the sort, check | Seatwork or center: Repeat the sort, check, write the sort in word study notebook |
| Day 3 | Seatwork: Repeat the sort, draw and label | Seatwork, partner work: blind sort, writing sort, word study notebook extensions |
| Day 4 | Small group or seatwork: Repeat the sort, word or picture hunts in magazines, ABC books, and familiar texts | Seatwork: Repeat the sort<br><br>Small group: Word hunt in familiar texts |
| Day 5 | Assessment and games, paste and label pictures used for sorting during the week | Assessment and games |
|  | Homework: Students take pictures home to sort again and hunt for more pictures that begin with the sound | Homework throughout the week: Repeat the sort, blind sort, writing sort, word hunts |

# RESOURCES FOR IMPLEMENTING WORD STUDY *in Your Classroom*

Several sources are available to help you implement word study with students in the letter name–alphabetic stage. These materials to use in the activities that follow can be found both in the Appendices in the book as well as on *WTW Digital.*™

1. The pictures in Appendix D and word lists in Appendix F as well as suggested sorts in Appendix E are available for use with the templates in Appendix G to create your own picture sorts.
2. Prepared sorts and games that can be used cross platform are also available on *WTW Digital.* Also on *WTW Digital,* a Create Your Own feature enables you to create your own sorts. Look for the List of Available Images on *WTW Digital* to find what pictures can be selected. The files can be downloaded to your computer to drag and drop pictures into your own templates.

3. *Words Their Way for PreK–K* provides a comprehensive description of word study and other literacy activities for the emergent and letter name stage: oral language, vocabulary, and concept development; alphabet recognition and production; phonological awareness; concepts about print and writing; concept of word in text; and word study for phonics and spelling.
4. *Words Their Way®: Word Sorts for Letter Name–Alphabetic Spellers 3rd Edition* provides a complete curriculum of sorts beginning with a review of initial consonants, picture sorts for blends and digraphs, word family sorts, and short vowel sorts. This book offers detailed directions for implementing the sorts and spell checks are supplied for each of the units.
5. *Words Their Way®: Letter Name–Alphabetic Sorts for Spanish-Speaking English Learners* provides contrasts and additional practice geared to contrasts that are important for Spanish speakers.

# ACTIVITIES for the Letter Name–Alphabetic Stage

Students play word study games

In this section, specific activities for students in the letter name–alphabetic stage are organized into the following categories:

1. Vocabulary activities
2. Phonemic awareness activities
3. Development and use of personal readers and word banks
4. Dictionary skills
5. Study of initial consonant sounds
6. Study of word families
7. Study of short vowels

***Adaptable for other stages.*** Some of the games and activities are adaptable, using a variety of features at different stages. These are indicated by the Adaptable for Other Stages icon.

Many of the activities that follow use the sound board in Appendix C, pictures in Appendix D, and game templates in Appendix G. Some of these materials can also be found online at *WTW Digital*.

# Vocabulary Activities

These activities are designed to help students develop their oral vocabularies. The vocabulary activities in Chapter 4 are also relevant here (Activities 4.1 to 4.7).

## 5.1 Anchored Vocabulary Instruction

Printing words on cards that are the focus of vocabulary instruction during a read-aloud is a way to anchor the meaning of the word to its sounds and spelling (Juel et al., 2003). These vocabulary cards will also serve as a reminder to review the words over time and in different contexts.

**MATERIALS** Children's books to read aloud and a supply of 2-by-6-inch (or larger) cards. Print words neatly with markers.

**PROCEDURES**

1. Preview a book that you plan to read aloud and select a few words whose meanings may not be known to all of your students. Focus on words that are important to the meaning of the story but are also words that are likely to come up again in other stories. Juel et al. (2003) provide the examples of *pond*, *mill*, and *haystack* from *Rosie's Walk* (by P. Hutchins) as words urban children would probably not know. Write the words you select on cards in neat block letters.
2. Before reading the story, introduce the words. You might begin by asking students if they can supply a definition and then back that up with your own. At times you might model using a picture dictionary to look up the meaning of a word. If a concrete word like *haystack* is in the story, show a picture of a haystack. You can supply your own picture, photo, or bring in concrete objects. Even a quick sketch can help and might be added to the card. Always try to use "kid-friendly" definitions with accessible language. For example, a new word like *community* may be defined as a "neighborhood" or *vacant* as "empty." As students develop decoding skills, you might begin by asking them to figure a word out before telling them. Students in the late letter-name stage, for example, would probably be able to read *mill* or *pond* but might not know exactly what they are.
3. To help anchor the word in memory, point to the word as you say it slowly, stretching out the sounds as you touch the letters, and then have the students repeat it with you. You might point out the beginning or ending sound, the length and number of phonemes or syllables, or other letter–sound characteristics of the word, depending on what your students might need. For example, students whose home language is Spanish might have a hard time with double *l*s at the end of a word like *mill*, because that combination (*ll*) has

*for* **English learners**

a different letter–sound correspondence in Spanish. You could point out the double *l*s in *mill* and have the students say it with you, emphasizing the final sound. Students are not expected to learn these as reading vocabulary, but Juel's research shows that seeing the words can help students remember them as meaning vocabulary.

4. When you come to the word during the read-aloud, hold up the card and briefly draw attention to it to remind students of its meaning and letter–sound properties. Ask someone to point to the word on the book page.

5. After reading, go through the word cards once more and ask students to say each word, define it, and perhaps use the word in a sentence that also recalls events in the story. For example, you might hold up *pond* and say, "Who can tell me where the fox got all wet? Yes, he fell in the pond." Ask questions that use the words, such as "Would you rather land in a pond or in a haystack? Tell me why."

6. Add new word cards to a growing set to be reviewed over time. Keep them handy to pull out when you have a few minutes to spare and go through them. It is this continued exposure that will ensure that the words are retained over time. If students use the words or notice the anchored words in new contexts, make it a cause for great celebration. You can be deliberate in selecting new read-alouds with these same words, such as *The Little Red Hen*, in which the hen takes grain to the mill, or *In the Small, Small Pond* by Denise Fleming.

## 5.2 Think-Pair-Share

In Chapter 4, we described "turn and talk" (Activity 4.3) as a way to give more students the opportunity to engage in oral language and use new vocabulary. Instead of calling on one student to talk, all students are asked to talk with a partner. Turn and talk can be used with all ages but think-pair-share is a variation that provides more "think time" and ends with the opportunity to share ideas in the larger group. Both activities give less verbal children and English learners a chance to articulate their ideas in a less threatening situation.

### PROCEDURES

1. *Think*. During a read-aloud or discussion, instead of raising hands to answer questions, make predictions, share experiences, define words, or use in sentences, ask students to think of their own response for a few moments.

2. *Pair*. Students then turn and talk to a partner or discuss in small groups. You can assign partners or groups in advance and have them stay together for a week or more. Students can also count off to form groups. Observe the pairs or groups to make sure all students are participating.

3. *Share*. After everyone has had a chance to talk, call on individuals or groups to report back to the larger group. By listening in on the groups, you might identify ideas or examples that seem particularly worthwhile.

## 5.3 Books and Concept Sorts

Books make great beginnings for concept sorts. As an example to get you started, *Gregory, the Terrible Eater* by Marjorie Sharmat tells the story of a young goat who wants to eat real food while his parents constantly urge him to eat "junk food." In this case, the goats' favorite foods really are junk from the local dump: tires, tin cans, old rags, and so on.

**MATERIALS** You will need a copy of the book to read aloud. Collect real objects or pictures of items suggested by the story; for example, fruits, vegetables, newspaper, shoelaces, spaghetti, and pieces of clothing.

### PROCEDURES

1. After enjoying this story together, introduce the students to a concept sort. Gather the students on the rug around a large table or pocket chart, and challenge them to group

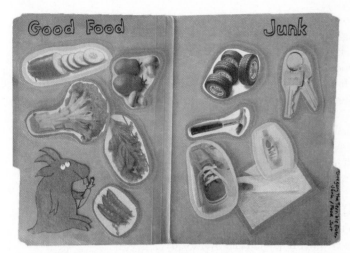

*Gregory the Terrible Eater* concept sort

the items by the things Gregory likes and the things he dislikes. Encourage them to talk about the items in complete sentences such as, "Carrots are food that Gregory likes."

2. After deciding where everything should go, ask the students to describe how the things in that category are alike. Decide on a key word or descriptive phrase that will label each category. *Good Food* and *Junk* are obvious choices, but your students might be more inventive. As you print the selected key words on cards, model writing for the students. Say each word slowly and talk about the sounds you hear in the words and the letters you need to spell them. You might give all the students in the group a card and ask them to label one of the individual items using invented spelling.

3. Plan time for individual sorting. Keep the items and key word cards available so that students will be free to redo the sort on their own or with a partner at another time, perhaps during free time or center time. Encourage them to talk as they sort.

4. Follow the sorting with draw-and-label or cut-and-paste activities. This may be done as a group activity, in which case a section of a bulletin board or a large sheet of paper is divided into two sections and labeled with the key words. If students work independently, give each student a sheet of paper folded into two sections. Ask the students to draw items, or give them a collection of magazines or catalogs to search for pictures to cut out and paste into the correct category (seed catalogs are great for fruits and vegetables). Again, encourage students to use developmental spelling to label the pictures.

**EXTENSIONS** *Gregory, the Terrible Eater* serves as an excellent introduction to studying healthy eating. The same pictures the students have drawn or cut out can serve as the beginning pictures for categories such as meats, grains, fruits and vegetables, and dairy products.

**VARIATIONS** Other books can also be used as the starting point for concept sorts of many kinds, as in the following:

*Noisy Nora* by Rosemary Wells. Sort pictures that suggest noisy activities or objects with pictures that suggest quiet activities or objects.

*Town Mouse, Country Mouse* by Jan Brett and various authors. Sort pictures of things you would see in the country and things you would see in the city.

*Alexander and the Wind-Up Mouse* by Leo Lionni. Sort pictures of real animals and toys or imaginary animals.

*Amos and Boris* by William Steig. Sort pictures of things that Amos would see on the land and things that Boris would see in the ocean.

*Tops and Bottoms* by Janet Stevens. Sort pictures by the vegetables that are found aboveground (peas and beans) compared to vegetables below (potatoes and carrots).

## 5.4 Thematic Unit on Animals as a Starting Point for Concept Sorts

Teachers of young students often organize their curriculum into thematic units of study. Such units frequently lend themselves to concept sorts, which review and extend the understandings central to the goals of the unit. Studying animals particularly lends itself to concept sorts and can be used as a way of introducing a unit.

**MATERIALS**  Plastic animals or animal pictures.

**PROCEDURES**  Lay out the collection of animals and ask students to think of ways that they can be grouped together. Such an open sort will result in many different categories based on attributes of color, number of legs, fur or feather coat, and so on. A lively discussion will arise as students discover that some animals can go in unexpected categories.

The direction you eventually want this activity to go depends on the unit goal. If you are studying animal habitats, then you will eventually guide the students to sorting the animals by the places they live. If you are studying classes of animals, then the students must eventually learn to sort them into mammals, fish, amphibians, and birds. If you are focusing on the food chain, your categories may be carnivores, herbivores, and omnivores.

## 5.5  Creative Dramatics

Creative dramatics is a way to encourage students' self-expression as well as vocabulary development (Honig & Shin, 2001; Mages, 2008; Lobo & Winsler, 2006). Students enjoy reciting what they hear and appreciate the rhythm of language as they act out memorable scenes from familiar stories. In creative dramatics, props are not necessary but add to the fun. For example, after hearing the story *Caps for Sale* (by E. Slobodkina) students march around the room singing, "Caps for sale, caps for sale. Red and white and blue and green. The finest caps you've ever seen." Students can also act out the part of the story when the monkeys steal the caps from the peddler after he falls asleep under a tree and then mimic the peddler with "Chi, chi, chi, chi."

**MATERIALS**  Many picture books can work, as well as classic folk tales. There are a number of anthologies to consider including:

De Las Casas, D. (2011). *Tell along tales!: Playing with participation stories*. Santa Barbara, CA: Libraries Unlimited.

Mayesky, M. (2008). *Creative activities for young children*. Boston: Cenage Learning.

Siks, G. B. (1958). *Creative dramatics: An art for children*. New York: Harper & Row, Publishers.

Ward, W. (1981). *Stories to dramatize* (Reprint ed.). Anchorage, KY: The Children's Theatre Press.

**PROCEDURES**

1. After they listen to a story, ask students to select a character and think about how that particular character acts, like crawling on all fours and roaring like a lion as in *Leo the Lion* or stirring a pot of food after hearing a version of *Stone Soup*.
2. Reread a short scene and have three or four students act out the scene with its movement and a few of its lines. Props are not typically used, and everyone is given a chance to participate.
3. Ask students who were watching to comment on what they liked and how they might improve the next time.
4. Have another three or four students try the same scene.

**EXTENSIONS**  Prepare copies of key lines from the scene in 26-point text that students place in their personal readers to reread, as in Figure 5.12. Note in the figure how Kari has underlined words for her word bank and also how she has recorded her rereadings with tick marks. Have students draw pictures of the scene they dramatized and bring the stories they have written to the group to dramatize a scene.

**FIGURE 5.12   Caps for Sale for Student Rereading**

<u>Caps</u> for <u>sale</u>
Caps for sale
<u>Red</u> and <u>white</u> and blue and green
The <u>finest</u> caps <u>you</u> have ever seen.

Caps for sale
Caps for sale
Red and white and blue and green
The finest caps you have ever seen.

卄 卄 卌 卅

## 5.6 Tell a Story to Get a Story

Tell-a-Story activity is a way to encourage students to tell personal narratives about events in their lives (McCabe, 1997). You can conduct this activity as a whole class, in small group, or while students are in line waiting for lunch.

1. Begin by telling students a two- or three-sentence story about a not-too-serious experience that happened to you; maybe a story about an insect sting, a broken arm, a cooking accident, or a time you were sick. Other examples of topics teachers have used can be found in McCabe (1997) and McCabe and Bliss (2003).
2. Ask an open-ended question to encourage students to tell a story about something that happened to them: "Has something like this ever happened to you?"
3. To encourage students to say more, nod, and ask "What else?" or repeat their last phrase.

These personal narratives give teachers, and speech pathologists insight into children's language development. A scoring quide (see link to the left) can be used to analyze students' narrative and language development. It comes from *Words Their Way with English Learners* (Helman, et al., 2012).

**Enhanced eText**
Teacher Resource:
EL Language and
Literacy Survey

## 5.7 Acting Out Meanings

Young children love any type of movement activity. As they encounter new words through read-alouds and your use of sophisticated words (see page 165), take advantage of opportunities to act out words so your students can develop understanding.

**MATERIALS** Any children's picture book can work, but choose a picture book that lends itself to action. Morales' *Niño Wrestles the World* or Knutson's *Love and Roast Chicken: A Trickster Tale from the Andes Mountains* are two excellent examples.

**PROCEDURES**
1. After reading *Love and Roast Chicken: A Trickster Tale from the Andes Mountains* aloud, discuss the meaning of the word *scurried*. You might demonstrate the terms *scurry*, *scramble*, *dash*, or *hustle*.
2. Invite the students to do these actions. In so doing, you are supporting their developing awareness of the shades of meaning, or nuances, among these words. Common verbs such as *march*, *stroll*, or *walk* are good starting points because they are the easiest for students to distinguish.

**EXTENSIONS**
1. Try acting out adjectives, which are just a bit more challenging. Begin with frequently occurring ones like *happy*, *sad*, *tiny*, and *enormous*, and invite students to demonstrate them through facial expressions and body movement. This is particularly effective with English learners.
2. Explore antonyms in the same way. Begin by sharing concept books such as Eric Carle's *Opposites* or Tana Hoban's *Exactly the Opposite*, both of which feature colorful illustrations. Then engage students in acting out antonyms as they follow along with your discussion and modeling. You might play "Simon Says" using directives such as, "Simon says walk *fast*. Simon says walk *slow*. Simon says put your hand *over* your head. Simon says put your hand *under* your chin." Other action-filled multicultural choices might include:

Brown, M. (2013). *Marisol McDonald and the clash bash: Marisol McDonald y la fiesta sin egual*. New York: Lee and Low. (Latino; bilingual; story)

Look, L. (2004). *Uncle Peter's amazing Chinese wedding*. New York: Atheneum. (Asian; story)

McKissack, P. (1986). *Flossie and the fox*. New York: Dial. (African American; folktale)

Rodgers, G. (2014). *Chufki rabbit's big bad bellyache: A trickster tale*. EI Paso, TX: Cinco Puntos Press. (Native American/American Indian; folktale)

Roth, S. L., & Abouraya, K.L. (2012). *Hands around the library: Protecting Egypt's treasured books*. New York: Dial. (Middle Eastern; nonfiction)

Woodson, J. (2012). *Each kindness*. New York: Nancy Paulsen Books. (African American; story)

# Phonemic Awareness

Phonemic awareness continues to develop from partial to full across the letter name–alphabetic stage. Students' developing awareness is exercised by sorting pictures and words for sounds—first for single consonants, then for blends, followed by onset and rime in word families, and finally all the sounds in short vowel sorts. Routines such as interactive writing and morning message, described in Activity 4.39 and Activity 4.40 in Chapter 4, should continue in this stage, providing you with the opportunity to model phonemic segmentation as you stretch out the sounds in words to write. Students will get this same practice as they write for many different purposes, spelling the best they can. Students who need extra help developing full phonemic awareness will benefit from the following activities.

### 5.8 Beginning-Middle-End: Find Phonemes in Sound Boxes

Sound Boxes provide a concrete way to demonstrate how words are made of smaller pieces of sound; some call these Elkonin boxes for the developer (1973). The following variation is a song the teacher and children sing as they try to find the location of each sound in the word.

**MATERIALS** You will need large letter cards and a three-pocket holder, such as the one shown in Figure 5.13.

**PROCEDURES**

1. Place the letters needed to spell a three-letter word in the pocket backwards so the children cannot see the letters. Announce a CVC word, such as *sun*. Choose words from a familiar book, poem, or dictation when possible. Words that start with continuant sounds such as /m/, /s/, or /f/ work well because they can be said slowly.

2. Sing the song to the tune of "Are You Sleeping, Brother John?"

    *Beginning, middle, end; beginning, middle, end.*

    *Where is the sound? Where is the sound?*

    *Where's the ssss in sun? Where's the ssss in sun?*

    *Let's find out. Let's find out.*

3. Children take turns coming forward to pick the position and check by turning the letter card.

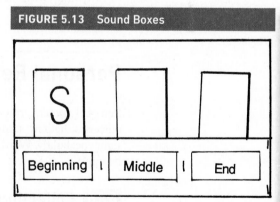

**FIGURE 5.13  Sound Boxes**

### 5.9 Push It Say It

This activity is a good way to teach students how to blend sounds as they move letter tiles or little cards around, as shown in Figure 5.14. Throughout the letter name stage, students learn to manipulate the sounds in words by exchanging one letter for another to make a new word. This skill will eventually help them sound out or decode unfamiliar words as they read by blending sounds and word parts together.

**FIGURE 5.14  Push It Say It**

**MATERIALS** You will need a large set of tiles or cards containing the letters of the alphabet, the consonant digraphs, and rimes for word families (such as *at, ill, ock*) for modeling and smaller sets so students can work along with you. Model with the cards on a desktop with a small group or prepare magnetized cards to use on a board.

**PROCEDURES**

1. Choose the rime card that matches the sort you are about to do or the features from a previous sort that need reviewing. If you are working with the *at* and *an* families, cut out these rime cards as well as an assortment of beginning sounds such as *f, m,* and *r*. Two or three rime cards and two or three consonant cards are enough for one lesson. Continuant consonants such as *f, m,* and *r* are easier to elongate than the stop consonants (*b, t, g*) so start with these. Students will need practice with all the consonants eventually.

2. First, identify the rimes as the *at* or *an* family, and have your students repeat them after you. Next, push a beginning letter such as the *f* card up while saying "f-f-f-f." Then, push the *an* card up while saying "an." Say the word *fan* as you push the cards together, as shown in Figure 5.14.

3. Tell your students that you can take the *an* away and change the word to *fat*. Push the *f* card up a little further while saying "f-f-f-f." then push the *at* card up next to it while saying "at." Then say *fat* as you push them together.

4. After modeling this procedure, ask your students to push and say *fan* with their own cards. Ask them how they might change *fan* into *fat*. Repeat with one or two other beginning sounds to change *fan* into *man, man* into *ran,* and *ran* into *rat,* and so on.

**EXTENSIONS**

1. Add consonant blends and digraphs as they are studied. Note that digraphs such as *sh,* are written on *one* card (not separated into a *s* card and an *h* card), while blends should be on separate cards. Follow the preceding procedures, using the digraphs and blends and exchanging different-vowel rimes. Model how to change *ship* into *shop, shop* into *chop, chop* into *chip,* using digraphs or *top* into *stop* into *slop* using blends.

2. The "Push It Say It" routine for medial vowel, CVC words is slightly different for the non-rhyming words because you will use a separate vowel card and push three or four cards. Change *pat* to *pet, pet* to *pit, pit* to *pot, pot* to *hot, hot* to *hit,* and so on.

# Personal Readers and Word Banks

Personal readers are collections of dictations and other short pieces of text that serve many purposes, helping students develop a concept of word and concepts about print as well as a sight vocabulary. Word banks take words out of context for close study and enhance sight word learning.

## 5.10 Collecting Individual Dictations and Group Experience Stories

Recording students' individual or group dictations as they talk about personal or group experiences is a key feature of the language experience approach, or LEA (Stauffer, 1980). The text created makes especially good reading material for beginning readers because it is inherently familiar and easy to remember. It is ideal to have every student in a group contribute a sentence, but dictations need to be kept to a reasonable length to be sure beginning readers can read them back. This activity is described in Activity 4.39 on page 142 in Chapter 4. Here we offer a description of using group dictations across a four-day sequence to collect words for a word bank. This can be accomplished in fewer days with smaller groups.

**MATERIALS** You will need chart paper, an overhead projector, a computer, or another way to record dictation so that students can observe you write. You will also need to make copies of the dictation for each student. See the See the discussion on pages 162–163 for more direction in how to develop personal readers.

## PROCEDURES

***Day 1.*** Share an experience and collect dictations, as described in Activity 4.39. When it is complete, read the entire dictation as you point to the words. Then have students repeat after you, sentence by sentence using echo reading, as you point to each word. Reread it again as the students read along with you in a choral reading fashion.

Before day 2, make a copy of the dictation for each student in the group to add to their personal reader. Computers make it easy to create these copies. Select a font that has the type of letters easily recognized by young readers (Geneva or Comic Sans MS work well) and enlarge it as much as possible. It is also easy to make copies by writing neatly in your best manuscript handwriting.

Ms. Bussey conducts a word hunt in students' group experience chart

***Day 2.*** Reread dictations and underline known words.

1. Choral read the original dictation and then again as students follow along on their own copies, pointing to words as they read. Call on individual students to read a sentence.
2. After students can read the dictation successfully, ask them to underline known words to harvest for their word bank, as described in Activity 5.11. Point to the underlined words randomly to make sure they know the words they underline. Students might make an illustration to go with the dictation.

***Day 3.*** Choral read and harvest known words.
Students can work together or individually to read the dictation again. Make word cards for underlined words that are recognized accurately and quickly.

***Day 4 and on.*** Choral read and review new word cards.

1. Have students continue to reread their dictations, review the words in their word banks, and complete their pictures.
2. Start a new dictation or story cycle when students can read the previous dictation with good accuracy and modest fluency.
3. Students can take their personal readers home where they reread the stories, review their word banks, and sort pictures and words.

## EXTENSIONS

1. Include personal readers in targeted interventions with the literacy specialist and Title I teachers. Students have additional opportunities to reread their entries to promote fluency, for phonics instruction, and the development of a sight vocabulary. Make an extra copy of the entries, share digital copies, and have the personal readers accessible to students when they meet with their teachers. (Bear et al., 2004; Johnston, Invernizzi, Juel, & Lewis-Wagner, 2009).
2. Bilingual entries in the personal readers are particularly useful during the early part of the letter name–alphabetic stage (Helman et al., 2012). These bilingual stories are written in both the first and second languages. Initially, dictations are just one or two sentences long. A school aide or parent can help with the translations. Shari Dunn and her students

*for* **English learners**

developed bilingual class readers that included students' individual pages about pets and other themes, like weather and health.

3. Develop digital personal readers that include digital photographs to accompany the students' dictations.
4. Incorporate software into the dictation process. Use voice recognition, drawing, and animation software in the dictation process to help students create their own language experience stories (Labbo, Eakle, & Montero, 2002).
5. Extend your language experience dictations into student-generated writing by using an author's computer chair (Labbo, 2004).

## 5.11 Support Reading with Rhymes and Pattern Stories

Rhymes and jingles and predictable, patterned texts make good reading materials because they provide support for beginning readers and can then be used to harvest known words for word banks. (See pages 116–118 in Chapter 4 for a complete guide to the whole-to-part lesson plan and supporting activities.) **MATERIALS** Find a rhyme, jingle, song, or predictable story that

students will find memorable and readable. You can focus on one major pattern or verse, such as the refrain in *The Gingerbread Man*. Find a big book, make a chart, or project a copy of the text electronically for group work, and make copies of the rhymes and patterns for students' personal readers.

### PROCEDURES
*Day 1.* Introduce and read the text.

1. Talk about the title and cover and look at the pictures (if applicable) with the students.
2. Read the rhyme or story while fingerpointing the text. Read fluently and with expression, but not too fast. Stop periodically to discuss and enjoy the story.
3. Reread the text and invite students to choral or echo read the entire text if it is short; or read parts of the text.
4. Decide which parts of the text will be compiled for personal readers. Type the text onto a single page that can be duplicated for each student. Number and date this entry.

*Days 2, 3, and 4.* Reread the rhyme or story and harvest words for word banks as described in Activity 5.12. Use the same procedures described in Activity 5.10 for dictations as follow-ups for rhymes and predictable text. Write sentences from the text can on sentence strips, and have students work to rebuild the text in a pocket chart as described in Activities 4.40 and 4.41 in Chapter 4. In Figure 5.12, you see a sample of a rhyme adapted from the story *Caps for Sale* (by E. Slobodkina).

## 5.12 Harvesting Words for Word Banks

Student circles sight words from a selection in her personal reader

Students need to have a stock of sight words that they can read with ease. These can be harvested from books, familiar rhymes, or dictations, and stored in a word bank to be reviewed over time. Although word bank words are traditionally chosen by the students, you can encourage young readers to include high-frequency words (*will, this, want*) that they need to learn, or words containing the spelling features being examined during word study. Favorite words are those that interest the reader (*dinosaur, chocolate, birthday*); these longer concrete nouns may be more memorable to the student than the high-frequency words! The following activities help students develop and maintain a word bank.

**MATERIALS** You will need copies of personal readers, dictations, familiar books, and so on. Prepare a collection of blank word cards. Tagboard and index cards can be cut to a size that is large enough to hold easily, yet small enough so that students can work with them on a desktop when sorting (4 by 1.5 inches is about right). You can also create a sheet of words for a particular story or poem read by a group of students. Reproduce and cut apart the sheets and the words, which you can hand out as students identify them.

Have students store their words in envelopes, plastic bags, small margarine containers, or small gift bags. Plastic and metal index card file boxes work well—words can be sorted with dividers. You can start with plastic bags for the first 50 words and then move to a box.

**PROCEDURES** Harvesting words may vary depending on the sources:

1. **From personal readers**. If students have an individual copy of dictations, jingles, parts of stories, and so on, simply ask them to underline the words they know. Many students will be tempted to underline every word, but over time they will begin to understand the procedure and realize they need to be selective and underline only words they really know. Suggesting that they scan through the text backwards can help some students find known words more accurately. You, your assistant, or a classroom volunteer can point to the underlined words in a random fashion to check whether the student can indeed name the word quickly (without rereading the sentence in which it occurs). Write known words on word cards. Writing the word for the student will ensure that it is neat and accurate. Ask the student to spell it aloud as you or another adult writes, to focus their attention on all the letters. On each card, usually on the back, write the number of the page in the personal reader. This makes it possible for students to go back and use context clues to name the word if they forget it. Then ask students to write their initials on the back of each card in case words get mixed up during word bank activities.

2. **From familiar books**. Students can also collect sight words independently from books they have read. Select words from the book that seem useful or interesting, write them on cards and store them in a library pocket in the back of the book. After reading the text, teach students to read through the words in the pocket to see which ones they know at sight. Have students write the words they know onto their own cards and place them in their word banks. They can match unknown words back to their counterparts in the text.

3. **From any text**. The easiest procedure for harvesting words is to simply ask the students to point to words in a book or from a chart that they would like to put in their word bank. After several words are written on cards, you or a helper can hold up the words to check for recognition.

**TIPS** To ensure that unknown words do not enter students' word banks, develop a short-term word bank for words that students recognize from the latest stories and dictations stored inside their personal readers (see Figure 5.5). Periodically, work with students in small groups to have them read through the words in their short-term word banks. Words they know from memory go into the permanent or long term word bank which can be stored in a different plastic bag, in a file card box, or a similar container.

Create a group word bank to use instead of or in addition to individual word banks. The group agrees on the words to add (with some gentle prodding by you to add high-frequency words that will show up in other stories) and the words can be reviewed in the group. Also make them available for individuals or partners to use in the word bank activities described in Activities 5.13–5.15.

## 5.13 "I Know It": Reviewing Word Bank Words

Reading through their words banks is a common activity with your supervision in circle time, with a partner or classroom volunteer, or independently. Have students review their word banks regularly as an important way to secure those words in memory as sight words. In this sort, students simply go through their word cards, say the words they know and put them in one pile, and place unknown words to the side. Have students try to move quickly reading through the pile. The words students put in the "I know" pile are words you and they can use in other sorts.

You can discard the unknown words, but this can be a touchy point for some students who are hesitant to throw away words. There is no harm in letting a few temporarily unknown words remain, but working with a lot of unknown words makes students' work hesitant, prone to errors, and frustrating. Students in the early letter name–alphabetic stage do not have the word knowledge they need to sound out many unknown words, so you should show them how to figure out an unknown word by using context. Referring to the number on the card, the students return to their personal reader to find the word and figure it out in context. Because this procedure can be time-consuming, it is important that only a small percentage of words in a word bank are unknown.

## 5.14 Other Ways to Work with Word Bank Words

There are other ways to review and work with words in the word bank.

1. **Pickup**. Lay out a collection of five to ten words face-up. Words that the student does not know or frequently confuses are good candidates. Someone calls out the words randomly for the student to find and pick up. This simple activity requires the student to use at least partial alphabetic cues to find the words but does not require him or her to sound out the word.

2. **I Am Thinking Of**. This activity is similar to Pickup, but the student is given clues instead of words: "I am thinking of a word that rhymes with *pet*" or "I am thinking of a word that starts like *play*."

3. **Concentration**. Make a second set of words and play this classic game as described in Activity 4.16 in Chapter 4. Work with no more than ten sets of words at a time so that the activity moves quickly.

4. **Word hunts**. Have students look through their word banks for words that have a particular feature; for example, words that start with *t*, words that end in *m*, or words that have an *o* in them.

5. **Alphabetize words**. Make and laminate a large alphabet strip up to six feet long. Students place their words under the beginning letter. Sort pictures by beginning sounds as well.

6. **Build sentences**. When students have nouns and verbs included in their word banks, they can start to build sentences. It's fun to add the names of friends and family to their word bank so they can build sentences like "Devon can run." During writing time, encourage students to use their word banks as a resource for words they might want to use. Sentence starter frames such as "I like to . . . " might get them started if they can't think of anything to write about.

7. **Sort words**. After students have 50 or more words in their word banks, they can use them to sort in various ways: by conceptual groups (such as animals, people, things we do), by beginning sounds, by alphabetical order, and so on.

## 5.15 Read It, Find It

This simple and fun game for two players reinforces the identification of words.

**MATERIALS** You will need 30 pennies, or as many pennies as there are words on the game board. Prepare a game board by creating a 5 by 5 or 6 by 6 grid. Write each word into one of the spaces on the grid. Prepare a set of word cards that have the same words as those on the board and place them face down. It is okay if some words repeat. You can take words from word banks or from previous word sorts.

**PROCEDURES**
1. One player flips a penny for heads or tails position. Each player chooses 15 pennies. One player will be heads and turns all his or her pennies to the heads side. The other will be tails and turns the pennies to the tails side.
2. The player who did not flip begins by taking a card from the pile and reading it. The player then finds the word on the board and covers it with a penny. If the player cannot read the word or reads it incorrectly, he or she cannot cover the word. The game proceeds as each player draws one card per turn.
3. The first player to cover 15 words, using up all his or her pennies, is the winner.

# Dictionary Skills in the Letter Name–Alphabetic Stage

Children can begin to use simple dictionaries and learn some basic skills, even in kindergarten and first grade.

## 5.16 Alphabetical Order

Alphabetical order is a skill that students in this stage can begin to master after they know their letters. Begin with activities that students can complete with relative ease. You may want to demonstrate whole class and then guide facilitated practice in differentiated groups.

- Develop flexibility with the alphabet. Help children learn to recite the alphabet in order starting at any point and going forward.
- Ask students to quickly find a letter on an alphabet strip to develop a sense of where letters fall in sequence; before *M* or after *M* is a good starting point.
- Keep a collection of alphabet books handy and ask students to find a page for a particular letter or beginning sound, and to look for pictures of other things that begin with that sound. Get them to think about where to look in the book—beginning, middle, or end to find the letter.
- Ask students to find words on a word wall. As a partner center activity, students call out words for each other.
- Look for opportunities to order words alphabetically: students' first names, color words, pictures with their names printed on them.
- Students with at least 50 words enjoy using index card boxes with alphabet dividers to organize their word bank words in by the first letter.
- At first, have students use alphabet strips as a guide. These strips can be a size that fits on their desks, or they can be large strips on the floor. Have students place their word bank words beside the letters, and have them use pictures in the same way.
- When large numbers of words end up under the same letter, introduce the idea of ordering them by the second letter. Model how to do this as you add words to a word wall where you will need to go to even the third or fourth letter to alphabetize words like *them*, *then*, and *they*.

## 5.17 Picture Dictionaries and Illustrated Word Books

When you teach young children, keep a simple dictionary handy and occasionally model how to look up words. Letter name–alphabetic spellers can begin to use these resources as well. The following are some ideas about how to use picture dictionaries along with a list of dictionaries and word books for young children.

- *Word books* are wonderfully illustrated collections of words that are fun for browsing but can also be used for word hunts and to get ideas for writing. In Richard Scarry's *Best Word Book Ever* you can find words arranged thematically, usually in the form of labeled pictures. Others like *My First Dictionary* by DK are arranged alphabetically with each word illustrated.
- Students studying beginning blends and digraphs often find words that begin with those sounds. They would find *chair*, *change*, *chicken*, *choose* and *chopstick* in *Curious George's Dictionary*.
- In addition, picture dictionaries can be used to for vocabulary development. Because he is so active and expressive, Curious George can be used to vividly illustrate words such as *afraid*, *before*, *curious*, *peek*, and *scamper* and each entry word is accompanied by a sentence defining that word. Suggestions for supporting young children's exploration of this

## Dictionaries for Beginning Readers

*Richard Scarry's Best Picture Dictionary Ever* (1998)

*Richard Scarry's Best Word Book Ever* (1999)

*Richard Scarry's Best First Book Ever!* (1979)

*Scholastic First Picture Dictionary* (2009)

*My First 1000 Words* (2005)

*My First Dictionary* (by DK) (2012)

*The Cat in the Hat Beginner Book Dictionary* (1964)

*Curious George's Dictionary* (2008)

*The American Heritage Picture Dictionary* (2006)

dictionary and engagements with print more generally are provided in the dictionary's Foreword (Templeton, 2008).
- Websites such as Enchanted Learning have simple alphabet books and picture dictionaries to download and print (see above for a list of dictionaries in "Resource Connections").

# Initial Consonant Sound Word Study

A number of activities or games in Chapter 4 are appropriate for students in the letter name–alphabetic stage who are working to master single consonants, digraphs, and blends: Soundline (4.32), Letter Spin for Sounds (4.33), and Initial Consonant Follow-the-Path Game (4.34). Concentration is another adaptable game. Any two pictures that begin with the same sound(s) make a match that can be claimed.

### 5.18 Sound Boards

Sound boards are references for letter–sound features (beginning consonants, digraphs and blends, and vowels).

**MATERIALS** You can find examples of sound boards in Appendix C. They provide a key word and picture for each letter–sound match, helping students internalize the associations.

**PROCEDURES** Place a copy of the sound boards at the front of students' writing folders or personal readers. These boards make it easy for students to find letters to stand for the sounds they want to use. Tape reduced copies of relevant sound boards to students' desks; you can also post charts of various letter–sound features. Chart printers have made it possible to take the individual sound boards and enlarge them to poster size. Add a little color and display them in a prominent place for reference. Keep sound boards in students' word study folders (see Figure 9.1) to serve as a record of progress. Students can lightly color the letters they have studied.

Use sound boards to generate more words to add to a word family. Write the family rime on a small card and slide it down beside the beginning sounds. In Figure 5.15 the word family *ack* has been expanded by adding many different blends and digraphs.

### 5.19 Hunting for Words and Pictures

Word hunts, described in Chapter 3, are conducted several different ways and at different times in the letter name–alphabetic stage.

1. **Picture Hunts**: In the early letter name–alphabetic stage, students can hunt for pictures that correspond to beginning sounds in magazines or catalogs, and paste them onto individual papers, onto group charts, or into alphabet scrapbooks. To save time,

**FIGURE 5.15 Expanding a Word Family Using a Sound Board**

you, an aide, or a student helper can rip out pages on which there are pictures that contain the feature being hunted. Have students label the pictures they find by spelling as best they can. Students can also hunt for pictures in alphabet books and record their findings as drawings.

2. **Word Hunts**: Students can also search for words that begin with the particular initial consonants, blends, or digraphs in familiar reading materials such as their personal readers or by going through their own word banks. After they begin studying vowels, picture and word hunts will help them attend to those medial sounds and letters. Note that hunting for additional word family words can be challenging for certain families unless you have books that have been specially written, but words with most short vowels should be plentiful in the materials they are reading (short-*u* words can be harder to find than the others).

At first students will need to be supervised as they work in small groups to find words and you, an aide, or a helper can serve as a scribe to record their findings. By the late letter name–alphabetic stage, students can work independently and record results of word hunts in their word study notebooks.

### 5.20 Initial Sound Bingo

In this version of Bingo, students discriminate among the initial sounds. This is another activity that can be adapted to single consonant, blends, digraphs, and word families.

**MATERIALS** Make Bingo cards with 9 or 16 squares. In each square, write a letter(s) that features the sounds students have been studying in sorts. Figure 5.16 shows a game prepared to review the *s*-blends. Note that each card must be different. You also need markers (bottle caps, pennies, or squares of paper work well) and picture cards to match sounds. A copy of this game can be found at *WTW Digital*.

**FIGURE 5.16 Blend Bingo Cards**

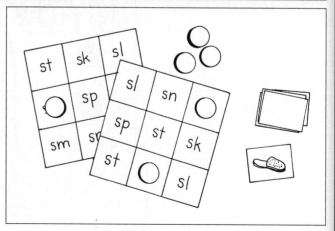

*Adaptable* **for Other Stages**

**PROCEDURES** Work with small groups of two to four students. Give each student a Bingo card and markers. Have students take turns drawing a card from the stack and calling out the picture name. Students place a marker on the corresponding square. Play continues until someone gets Bingo (three or four in a row) or the board is filled.

## 5.21 Gruff Drops Troll at Bridge

This is a special version of the basic follow-the-path game, described in Activity 4.34 in Chapter 4, that reinforces *r*-blends. This game was developed after reading Paul Galdone's *The Three Billy Goats Gruff*, which was part of a class study of books about monsters. Many of the books yielded a great crop of consonant-plus-*r* words such as *growl*, *groan*, and *fright*.

**MATERIALS** Prepare a game path filled in with *r*-blend combinations, as shown in Figure 5.17 (or whatever features you want to review). You will also need markers and pictures. A copy of this game board as well as other follow the path games can be found online at *WTW Digital*. Appendix G has blank templates.

**PROCEDURES** Each student selects a marker. Students turn over picture cards and move the marker to the correct space. In this game, the winner drops the troll from the bridge by turning up a picture that begins with *dr* (for *drop*) or *tr* (for *troll*) for the last space.

## 5.22 Match!

*Adaptable* **for Other Stages**

In this game, similar to the game of Slap Jack, students look for pairs that match by beginning sounds.

**MATERIALS** Create a set of cards that feature pictures with four to eight different beginning sounds. Include at least four pictures for each sound. Pictures can be copied from Appendix D glued on card stock, and laminated.

**PROCEDURES** Each student has half the deck of pictures. Students turn a picture card face-up from their deck at the same time. If the pictures begin with the same sound, the first person to recognize and say "Match!" gets the pair. If the pictures do not match, another set is turned

**FIGURE 5.17** Game Board for Gruff Drops Troll at Bridge

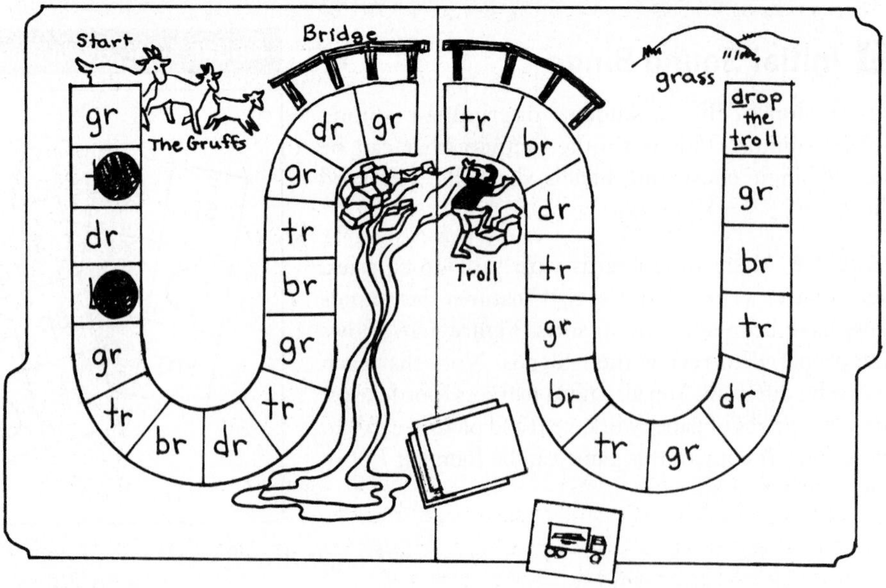

over until a match occurs. There can be penalties for calling out "Match" carelessly, such as losing a turn.

# The Study of Word Families

After students begin studying word families, they are expected to read and spell the words they sort. Many word games can be adapted, such as Match! (Activity 5.22). Some activities are especially designed to enhance students' understandings of how families work.

### 5.23 Build, Blend, and Extend

This series of teacher-led activities is designed to reinforce phoneme segmentation, phoneme blending, and using analogy as a spelling strategy ("If I can spell *cat*, then I can spell *fat*") as students work with onsets and rimes. This should follow sorting lessons in which students have worked with a collection of word families.

**MATERIALS** Prepare a set of cards to use in a pocket chart. Write the targeted onsets and rimes on these cards, keeping the letters of the rime together. For the *at* family, you would have cards with *at*, *b*, *c*, *f*, *h*, *m*, *p*, *r*, and *s*. As students study digraphs and blends, add those as well, such as *th*, *ch*, and *fl*; see Figure 5.18. Give students similar materials to use individually after you model for them.

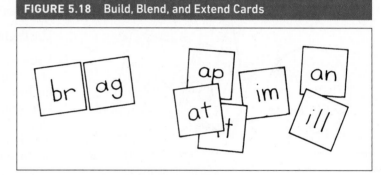

**FIGURE 5.18   Build, Blend, and Extend Cards**

**PROCEDURES**
1. **Building**. This procedure reinforces the *spelling* of word families. Explain that you are going to build or make a word such as *bag* and display two cards (*b* and *ag*). Then ask what letter needs to change the word to *rag*. Replace the *b* in *bag* with the *r* to make the new word. Model several words and then have students build additional words that you call out: *sag*, *tag*, and *brag*.
2. **Blending**. This activity reinforces the *reading* of word families. It is similar to building except that you start by displaying a word the students all know, such as *cat*, and then substitute a different beginning letter. Model how to blend the new onset with the familiar rime to read the word: "*Mmmmmm, aaaaaat, mat*. The new word is *mat*." Ask students to use the two parts of the onset and rime to sound out the word just as it was modeled.
3. **Extending**. During the extending part of this activity, find words that are not included in the sort to demonstrate to students that they can read and spell many more words after they know how to spell several words in a family. You may want to demonstrate using unusual words like *vat* or challenging words with digraphs and blends such as *chat*, *flat*, or *scat*.

**VARIATIONS**
1. Students work with small cards at their seats as you lead the activity, or ask students to write the words on paper, small whiteboards, or chalkboards.
2. Add more digraphs and blends as they are studied. There are many words you can make with families such as *ack* and *ick*.
3. For the study of short vowels and the CVC pattern, the vowel is separated from the rime (*at* is cut apart into *a* and *t*).

Build, Blend, and Extend to make word families

### 5.24 Word Family Wheels and Flip Charts

Wheels and flip charts are fun for students to play with independently or with partners. Use the wheels and flip charts to reinforce blending the onset with the rime to read words in word families they have sorted. Several flipbooks and word family wheels can be found at *WTW Digital*

**PROCEDURES**  To make word family wheels, follow these three steps.

1. Cut two 6-inch circles from tagboard. Cut a wedge from one circle, as shown in Figure 5.19, and write the vowel and ending consonants or rime to the right of it. Make a round hole in the center.
2. On the second tagboard circle, write beginning sounds that form words with that family. For example, the *op* family can be formed with *b, c, h, l, m, p, s, t, ch, sh, cl,* and *st.* Space the letters evenly around the outside edge so that only one at a time will show through the "window" wedge.

3. Cut a slit in the middle of the second circle. Put the circle with the wedge on top of the other circle. Push a brass fastener through the round hole and the slit. Flatten the fastener, making sure the top circle can turn.

Use the following steps to make flip books:

1. Use a piece of tagboard or lightweight cardboard for the base of the flip book. Write the family or rime on the right half of the base.
2. Cut blank pieces of paper that are half the width of the base piece and staple to the left side of the base. Write beginning sounds or onsets on each one. Have students draw a picture on the backside of the pages to illustrate the word.

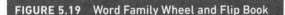

**FIGURE 5.19**  Word Family Wheel and Flip Book

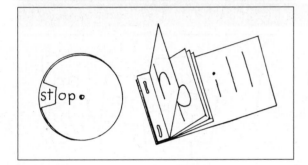

### 5.25 Show Me

This activity is a favorite with teachers who are teaching word families and short vowels.

**FIGURE 5.20**  Show Me Game

**MATERIALS**

- Make each student an individual three-pocket folder to hold letter cards. To make the folder, cut paper into approximately 7-by-5-inch rectangles. Fold up a 1-inch section along the 7-inch side, and then fold the whole thing into overlapping thirds. Staple at the edges to make three pockets (see Figure 5.20).
- Cut additional paper into 1.5-by-4-inch cards to make 14 for each student. Print letters on the top half of each card, making sure the entire letter is visible when inserted in the pocket. A useful assortment of letters for this activity includes the five short vowels and *b, d, f, g, m, n, p, r,* and *t.* Too many consonants can be hard to manage. A copy of this activity can be found at *WTW Digital.*

**PROCEDURES**  Each student gets a folder and an assortment of letter cards. When you or a student helper call out a word, the students put the necessary letters in the spaces and fold up their pockets. When "Show Me" is announced, all students open their pocket folders at once for you to see.

**VARIATIONS**  Start with words having the same families, such as *bad, sad,* or *mad,* in which the students focus primarily on changing the initial consonants. Move on to a different family and different vowels. For example, you could follow this sequence: *mad, mat, hat, hot, pot, pet.* Add cards with digraphs or blends to spell words such as *sh-i-p* or *f-a-st.*

### 5.26 Word Maker

Students match blends and digraphs with word families to make words.

**MATERIALS** Create a collection of cards that have onsets on one half (single consonants, blends, and digraphs) and common short vowel rimes on the other, such as *at*, *an*, *it*, *ig*, and so on (similar to the cards shown in Figure 5.18). For students in the later letter name–alphabetic stage, include rimes with ending blends, digraphs, and preconsonantal nasals, such as *ish*, *ang*, *ast*, *amp*, and *all*.

**PROCEDURES**
1. Each student begins by drawing five cards from the deck. With the five cards face-up, each student tries to create words, as shown in Figure 5.18.
2. After the students have made one or two words from their first five cards, they begin taking turns drawing cards from the deck. Every time they make a word, they can draw two more cards. If they cannot make a word, they draw one card.
3. Play continues until all the letter cards are used up. The player with the most words is the winner.

**VARIATIONS** Have students work independently with the word maker cards to generate and record as many words as possible. Students can write words they make onto word cards to add to their word banks.

## 5.27 Roll the Dice

This game for two to four players reinforces word families.

**MATERIALS** You need a cube on which to write four to six contrasting word families, (for example, *an*, *ap*, *ag*, and *at*). One side can be labeled "Lose a Turn," and "Roll Again" (see Figure 5.21). You will also need a blackboard, paper, chart board, or generic interactive whiteboard for recording words.

**PROCEDURES** The first player rolls the die. If it lands on a word family, the student must come up with a word for that family and record it on the chalkboard or paper. Students keep their own lists and can use a word only once, although someone else may have used it. If a player is stumped or lands on Lose a Turn, the die is passed to the next person. The person who records the most words at the end of the allotted time wins.

**VARIATIONS** Play with two teams for a relay. The first person of each team rolls the die and writes a word on the board. The player hands the die to the next player and goes to the end of the line. No word can be repeated by either team. This game can also be used with blends, digraphs, and vowel patterns.

**FIGURE 5.21** Cube for Roll and Dice Game

## 5.28 Rhyming Families Game

Use this is variation of the follow-the-path game to reinforce word families.

**MATERIALS** Prepare a game board as shown in Figure 5.22. You will also need a single die or a spinner, pieces to move around the board, pencils, and paper for each player. Directions for making game boards and spinners as well as game board templates are in Appendix G and a ready-to-print Follow The Families game is at *WTW Digital*. Write a word from each word family you have been studying in each space on the board. You can also write in special directions such as Roll Again, Go Back Two Spaces, and Write Two Words.

**FIGURE 5.22** Game Board for Word Families

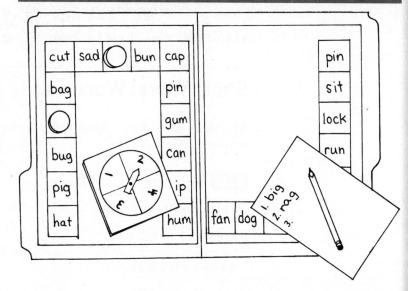

**PROCEDURES** The object is to make new words to rhyme with words on the game board that differ from the other players' words.

1. Spin to determine who goes first. The first player spins and moves the number of places indicated on the spinner. The player reads the word in the space where he or she lands. All players write a rhyming word by changing the initial letter(s). Players number their words as they go. Play continues until someone reaches the end of the path.
2. Beginning with the player who reaches the end first, each player reads the first word on his or her list. Players who have a word that is different from anyone else's gets to circle that word. Continue until all words have been compared.
3. Each circle is worth one point; the player who reaches the end first receives two extra points. The student with the most points wins the game.

**VARIATIONS** Label each space on the game board with the rime of a family you have studied (*at, an, ad, ack*). Use no more than five different rimes and repeat them around the path. Prepare a set of cards that have pictures corresponding to the families. Students move around the board by selecting a picture and moving to the space it matches. For example, a student who has a picture of a hat would move to the next space with *at* written on it.

*Adaptable* **for Other Stages**

### 5.29 Go Fish

This version of the classic game can be used as a review of word families.

**MATERIALS** Create a deck of 32 cards with four words from eight different word families written on them (for example, *that, bat, fat,* and *hat*). Write each word at the top left of the card so that the words are visible when held in the hand, as shown in Figure 5.23. A prepared set of cards can be found at *WTW Digtial.*

**FIGURE 5.23** Playing Cards for Go Fish

**PROCEDURES**

1. Deal five cards to each player and place the remainder in the middle as a draw pile.
2. The first player asks any other player for a match to a card in his or her hand: "Do you have any words that rhyme with *hat*?" If the player receives a matching card or cards, he or she may ask for another rhyming word. If the other player does not have the card requested, he or she tells the first player to "Go fish," which means that the first player must draw a card from the "fish pond." The first player's turn is over when he or she can no longer make a match.
3. After a player has a set of four rhyming words, she can lay the set down. Play continues until one player runs out of cards. Award points to the first person to go out and to the person who has the most sets of cards.

**VARIATIONS** Go Fish can be adapted for beginning sounds and blends using pictures.

## Short Vowel Word Study

After short vowels have been explored through word sorts and weekly routines, games can provide additional practice.

### 5.30 Hopping Frog Game

This game is for two to four players to review the five short vowels.

**MATERIALS**
• Create a game board like the one shown in Figure 5.24. A prepared game board can be found at *WTW Digital.*

**FIGURE 5.24** Frog Marker and Hopping Frog Game

- Cut green circle lily pads for each space and write CVC words students have used in word sorts on each one (for example, *pin, get, hot, bad, leg, run, bug, wish*).
- You will need four frog markers (in different colors) or some other playing pieces.
- The spinner is marked into five sections, with a vowel in each one. Add pictures to cue the sound: *a*, apple; *e*, ten; *i*, fish; *o*, frog; *u*, sun. See Appendix G for directions on how to make a spinner.

**PROCEDURES** Each student selects a marker. Players take turns spinning and moving their markers to the first word that matches the vowel sound on which they land (for example, *e, get*). They then pronounce this word and must say another word with the same vowel sound to stay on that space. The next player then spins and plays. The first player who can finish the course and hop a frog off the board wins.

**VARIATIONS** Label the spaces with *a, e, i, o,* or *u*. Make a collection of short vowel pictures on tagboard using the short vowel pictures in Appendix D. It is important that the pictures do not show through the card. On several additional cards write commands such as Skip a Turn, Go Back Two Spaces, and Move Ahead Three Spaces. The players move around the board by turning over a picture and moving their playing piece to the next free space on the board that has the corresponding short vowel.

### 5.31 Making-Words-with-Cubes Game

Short vowel words are built with letter cubes in this game. It can be used for other vowels as well.

#### MATERIALS
- Letter cubes can be found in commercial games or made from blank wooden cubes.
- Write all the vowels on one cube to be sure that a vowel always lands face up. (The sixth side can be a star that indicates that the player can select the vowel.)
- Put a variety of consonants on five or six other cubes. (You can write pairs like *qu* and *ck* together.)
- The students need a sand clock or timer, paper and pencil, and a record sheet such as the one shown in Figure 5.25

**FIGURE 5.25** Making-Words-with-Cubes Game

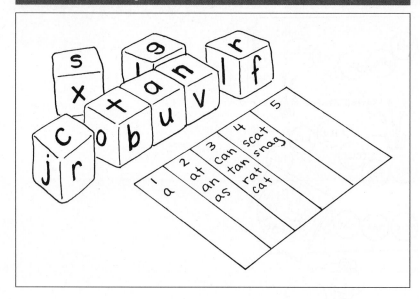

**PROCEDURES**

1. In pairs, students take turns being the player and the recorder. The recorder writes the words made by the player.

2. A player shakes the cubes just once or twice given the class noise this can make, spills them out onto the table, and then starts the timer. Whatever letters land face up are used to make words. The word maker moves the cubes to create words and spells them to the recorder. The cubes can then be moved around to make more words. Ignore errors at this point. Write the words in columns by the number of letters in the words.

3. When the time ends, the students review the words and check for accuracy. Score words by counting the total number of letters used. Students soon realize that the bigger the words they make, the greater their score.

**VARIATIONS** Students in the within word pattern stage should work with two vowel cubes. On a second cube, write vowel markers such as *e* (put two or three), *a*, *i*, and *o*. By this time, students may be able to use multiplication to total the letters (for example, four three-letter words is 12).

## 5.32 Follow-the-Pictures Spelling Game

This variation of the basic follow-the-path game works as a follow-up to word sorts for short vowel words.

### MATERIALS

- Copy pictures from Appendix D for medial short vowels, then cut apart and paste them onto a follow-the-path template that you copy from Appendix G. You may need to adjust the size to fit.

- Use two to five short vowels at a time. You will also need playing pieces to move along the path and a spinner or single die. In some spaces you can write Roll Again, Go Back Two Spaces, and other directives.

- Include an answer card on which all the words are written in the same order they are pasted on the board to settle any arguments about spelling.

**PROCEDURES** Students take turns spinning for a number. Before they can move to the space indicated by the spinner, they must correctly spell the word pictured. If they cannot spell the word, they must stay where they are for that turn. The student who reaches the end first is the winner.

**VARIATIONS** Paste pictures on the game board. Use long vowel pictures for students in the within word pattern stage.

Students play the Follow-the-Path game with short vowel words

## 5.33 Slide-a-Word

Ask students to list and then read all the CVC words they are able to generate using a slider, as shown in Figure 5.26. As different short vowels are studied, the central vowel letter can be changed.

**FIGURE 5.26   Slider for Slide-a-Word**

**MATERIALS** Supplies include tagboard or poster board, ruler, marker, single-edge razor blade, and scissors. Cut a piece of tagboard or poster board into 8.5-by-2.5-inch strips. Using the razor, cut a pair of horizontal slits on each end 1.5 inches apart. Write a vowel in the center. Cut two 12-by-1.5-inch strips for each slider. Thread them through the slits at each end and print a variety of consonants, blends, or digraphs in the spaces as they appear through the slits. Turn the strips over and print additional beginning and ending sounds on the back. A prepared slide-a-word can be found at *WTW Digital*.

**PROCEDURES** Students slide the strips to generate as many words as they can, listing each word as they find it.

**VARIATIONS** Students using word banks can add known words to their word banks.

## 5.34 Put in an *m* or *n*: Preconsonantal Nasals

The difference between *rag* and *rang* is real but it is subtle, so these contrasts can help learners understand how the preconsonantal nasals work.

**MATERIALS** Create word pairs like the following on word cards.

| rag | rang | rig | ring | sag | sang | tag | tang |
|-----|------|-----|------|-----|------|-----|------|
| cap | camp | rap | ramp | trap | tramp | bag | bang |
| dig | ding | pup | pump | hag | hang | lip | limp |
| rug | rung | gag | gang | bet | bent | wig | wing |
| sprig | spring | pin | ping | hug | hung | lap | lamp |
| swig | swing | | | | | | |

**PROCEDURES** Three or four students can play. Shuffle and deal all the word cards. Have players look for pairs (for example,, *rag/rang* or *cap/camp*) in their hands and lay them down before play begins. Students then take turns laying down a word from their hand. The student who has the match to the pair takes the card, matches it to the word in his or her hand, reads the words aloud, and adds the two cards to his or her pile. The student with the most cards is the winner.

# 6

# Word Study for the Within Word Pattern Stage

## Chapter 6: Within Word Pattern STAGE

*WTW Digital* is a new online tool that accompanies this core text, and it was designed to help you implement word study in an engaging and interactive way. Resources for this chapter include:

- **Automatically scored qualitative spelling inventories** suggest each student's stage of spelling development. Word study groups are also automatically generated based on inventory results.
- **37 interactive sorts** that allow students to engage with word study in a digital environment
- **13 word study games** in a printable format that present fun activities for students to build their phonics and spelling knowledge.

An access code for *WTW Digital* is included with each new copy of package ISBN: 9780135174623. Visit www.wtwdigital.pearson.com to get started.

Orthographic development and word study instruction during the within word pattern spelling stage helps students build on their knowledge of the sound layer of English orthography as they begin to explore the pattern layer. Before we discuss development, let's visit the classroom of Ms. Watanabe, a second-grade teacher working with a group of eight students in the early part of this stage of development.

On Monday morning, after meeting briefly with a reading group to share responses to *Fox and His Friends* by James Marshall, Ms. Watanabe takes time to introduce a new sort. She has prepared a word study sheet, like the one in Figure 6.1, and has written the words on index cards that she will use to model in a pocket chart. The students have already studied the common long *a* patterns (CVCe in *cake*, CVV in *say*, and CVVC in *chain*), and this lesson will introduce long *e* patterns. Notice how she guides the discussion so that students are led to make discoveries and connect with a previous sort.

Ms. Watanabe begins by saying, "Let's read these words together." As she reads each of the words, Ms. Watanabe places it randomly at the bottom of her pocket chart. There is some discussion of the homograph *read* when Jason points out that it can be read two ways. They agree for now to pronounce it as "reed." She then says to the group, "Turn and talk to your partner about the sounds and patterns in these words. What do you notice when you use your ears and eyes?" After a few minutes she calls on several students to share. Troy explains that they all have *e*'s in them and Ms. Watanabe responds with, "Tell me more." The group continues discussing the sounds and the fact that some words have one *e*, two *e*'s, or an *e* and an *a*.

Ms. Watanabe continues: "Let's start with a sound sort listening for long and short vowels." She puts up pictures of a web and a queen as headers for the sounds they are to listen for: "We'll place all the words with short *e* in the middle under this picture of a web. We'll put words with the long *e* sound under this picture of a queen. Let's place words that do not fit either under the oddball column. Jean, get us started. Where would you put this word?"

Jean places the word *bed* underneath the picture of the web while she says, "Web. Bed."

**FIGURE 6.1** Long *e* and Short *e* Word Study Sheet

| 🕸️ | 👦 | Long E Short E Sort 1 |
|---|---|---|
| web | queen | team |
| seat | bed | seen |
| yes | jeep | read |
| meal | tree | leg |
| treat | bell | sheep |
| jet | cream | seed |
| eat | been | feel |

**FIGURE 6.2** Long *e* and Short *e* Pattern Sort

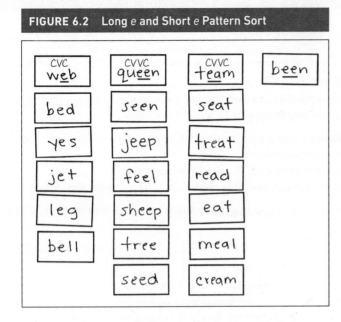

"Jean, why did you put *bed* under the web?"

"Because they sound alike in the middle. They both say 'eh' in the middle."

"Thank you! David, where would this word go?" Ms. Watanabe hands David the word *team*. David takes the word card and talks himself through the task as he has seen Ms. Watanabe model: "Team, web . . . Team, queen. *Team* has a long *e* sound." He places the word *team* underneath the picture of the queen.

Further into the sort, the students struggle with the vowel sound in the word *been* but agree it does not sound like a long or *a* short *e* so they put it in the odd-ball column. After all the words are sorted, Ms. Watanabe and the students check each category by reading the words from top to bottom as they listen for the medial vowel. Then Ms. Watanabe begins the reflection part of the lesson with the question, "How are the words in each column alike?"

David notes that the words under the picture of the web all have one *e*. Jean points out that the words in the second column all have two vowels. This leads to Ms. Watanabe's next question: "Do you see some words in the second column that look alike or are spelled alike?" Ms. Watanabe invites Tomas to come up, and he quickly pulls out all the words spelled with *ee* and puts them in a new column, leaving behind the words spelled with *ea*. Once more, Ms. Watanabe asks the students how the words in each column are alike. She helps them come to the conclusion that short *e* is spelled with a single *e*, whereas long *e* is spelled with two vowels—either *ee* or *ea* (refer to the final sort in Figure 6.2). Ms. Watanabe wants the students to make connections with a previous sort, when she introduced the use of initials C (for consonant) and V (for vowels) to talk about the patterns; she asks, "These words with *ee* and *ea* remind me of a long *a* pattern we labeled CVVC. Does anyone else notice that?"

The children think for a few moments then Troy begins waving his hand. "Both of these columns have the CVVC pattern!" said Troy. Ms. Watanabe asks him to explain and he adds that the words have two vowels in the middle just like the *ai* pattern. "Do the rest of you agree with Troy? Could we say that another way?" asks Ms. Watanabe. Sylvia responds by saying, "Long *e* has two different CVVC patterns—*ea* and *ee*."

Ms. Watanabe continues with, "And what about the short *e* words?" The students agree that they have the CVC pattern—just like short *a*. After labeling the key words headers with C and V to show the patterns, they revisit the oddball word *been* to talk about how it has the CVVC pattern but not the long *e* sound.

Ms. Watanabe ends the lesson by giving each student a copy of the word study sheet in Figure 6.1. Under her direction, the students underline the patterns in the key words and label them with C and V to use as headers. The students return to their seats, cut apart the words, and sort them independently while Ms. Watanabe checks in with another group. Later, Ms. Watanabe moves among the students and asks them, "Why did you put these words together?" This prompt gets individual students to reflect again on the categories and explain why they sorted as they did. Students store their word cards in plastic bags to sort throughout the week. The next day they will sort again, and Ms. Watanabe will watch to see how accurately and easily they sort. Later they will write the sort in their word study notebooks, work with partners to do a writing sort, and go on a word hunt for more words that have the same vowel sounds and patterns.

# Literacy Development of Students in the Within Word Pattern Stage

The within word pattern stage is a transitional stage of literacy development between the beginning stage when students' reading and writing are quite labored, and the intermediate stage when they can read and write a variety of genres quite fluently. We think of transitional readers as the "Wright Brothers" of reading: They have taken flight but have limited elevation in their reading, and it does not take much to bring them down to frustration level or to cause them to be less fluent in their reading. You will find transitional students in the middle-to-late part of first grade, but most are in second- and early third-grade classrooms. You will also find struggling readers in middle school and high school who are in this stage (Flanigan, Hayes, Templeton, Bear, Invernizzi, & Johnston, 2011).

## Reading in the Within Word Pattern Stage

Transitional readers read most single-syllable words accurately when they read at their instructional level, and they also read many two- and three-syllable words when there is enough contextual support. During this stage, students move from the **full alphabetic phase** to the **consolidated alphabetic phase** (Ehri, 2000), in which they begin to recognize patterns and chunks to analyze unfamiliar words. Instead of processing a word like *chest* as four speech sounds to match to letters (*ch-e-s-t*), they process it as two chunks (*ch-est*). This enables them to decode and store words more readily and their sight word vocabulary grows quickly. This, in turn, enables them to read in phrases and with greater expression (Templeton & Bear, 2011). Most fingerpointing from the beginning stage disappears, and transitional readers read orally at rates of more than 60 words per minute (Bear, 1992; Morris, 2013; Morris et al., 2013). All of these factors account for a transitional reader's increasing fluency compared to the dysfluent, word-by-word reading in the beginning stage of literacy.

Students generally read out loud at the beginning of the transitional period, but by the end they can manage substantial periods of silent reading during independent reading at school and at home. They can now read without support and this makes it possible to use reading group time to share reactions to a selection and to reread sections to find support for ideas. Transitional readers can discuss text in greater depth than they did as beginning readers, partly because what they read is longer and more complex.

Books for transitional readers cover a wide range of levels, from late first-/early second- through third-grade materials. In the early part of this stage, transitional readers read and reread familiar text from several sources—core reading programs, picture books, and favorite poems. They can read beginning chapter books such as the *Frog and Toad* books (by A. Lobel) and the *Henry and Mudge* books (by C. Rylant). By the end of this stage, students can read easy chapter books such as *The Time Warp Trio* series (by J. Scieska), the *Nikki & Deja* series (by K. English), or the *Magic Tree House* series (by M. P. Osbourne). Transitional readers also explore different genres, and informational text is more accessible. For example, they read informational books from the *Let's Find Out* and *I Can Read* series, and magazines such as *Ranger Rick*.

Lots of reading experience is crucial during this stage. Students should read **instructional-level** and **independent-level** materials for at least 30 minutes each day. They need this practice to propel them into the next stage; otherwise, they will stagnate as readers and writers. You can promote fluent and expressive reading, which is an important goal during this stage, by rehearsing (through repeated readings) for activities such as reader's theater, poetry readings, and reading famous speeches (Rasinski, 2010; Samuels, 1979; Therrien, 2004). However, fluent, expressive reading relies on automatic word recognition and extensive word knowledge (Bear, 1989). Simply trying to increase reading rates without building the underlying word knowledge is a shortsighted goal.

**Enhanced eText**
**Video Example 6.1**
Ms. Flores discusses how she integrates word study that includes spelling and vocabulary in the reading lesson.

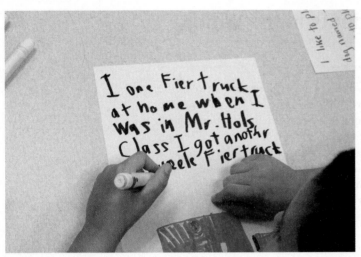

Using but confusing long vowel patterns in writing

## Writing in the Within Word Pattern Stage

Just like reading, writing also becomes more fluent during this period because students know how to automatically spell many words. They write with greater speed and less conscious attention (Bear, 1991a; Nagy, Berninger, Abbott, Vaughan, & Vermeulen, 2003; Graham, McKeown, Kiuhara & Harris, 2012). This added fluency gives transitional writers more time to concentrate on ideas, which may account for the greater sophistication in the way they express their ideas. Cognitively, they compose with a better sense of the reader's background knowledge and with a greater complexity in the story line or informational piece. Nevertheless, they often use but confuse the many ways of representing long vowel sounds as they work through their compositions.

Excerpts of Yolanda's two-and-a-half-page, single-spaced story about a squirrel named Nuts (see Figure 6.3) show how much students know about written language and spelling in the later part of the within word pattern stage. Yolanda, a second-grader, has a rich language base, and she writes with a strong voice. In terms of orthographic knowledge, Yolanda spells most long vowel patterns and *r*-influenced words correctly (*woke, search*). But her word knowledge is not stable, as seen in her later spelling of *searches* as SERCHES and her overgeneralization of patterns (BREAKFEAST for *breakfast* and HOWL for *whole*). Later in the story, Yolanda spelled *thought* as TOOUGHT but then went back and wrote in an *h*. She also confuses homophones (*there/their*). Yolanda is a late within word pattern speller who should be placed in a word study group in which students are studying diphthongs and ambiguous vowels.

| FIGURE 6.3 Yolanda's Squirrel Story | |
|---|---|
| Twelve year old Chistine was glad it was Fially Satarday alltow she loved school Epspshelly math she loved taking her pet Squrrle Nuts to the park even more.<br><br>(Nuts runs away and)<br><br>Christine orginizes a search. She looked evrywhere. Christine climbd a tree Nuts wasnt there.<br><br>(Nuts returns and the next day)<br><br>Christine and Nuts woke up they went down stairs and there breakfeast was ready it was all difrent kinds of pancake animals. | (Later)<br><br>Christine thought Nuts ran away but he didn't because Nuts went tawa difrent park. Christine serches the howl park.<br><br>(The story ends with Christine)<br><br>niting a sweter for Nuts the colors where red, white and blue. |

## Vocabulary Learning in the Within Word Pattern Stage

Estimates vary, but students in the early grades can add, on average, 10 to 15 new words a week to their oral vocabularies (Biemiller, 2005). During the transitional stage of literacy, you need to take an active and deliberate role in making sure this vocabulary growth happens for all students. You can make words interesting in many ways and in so doing help students become "wordsmiths"—children who are curious about words, their sounds, meanings, and usage. This type of attitude toward words raises students' **word consciousness** or word awareness, which is a critical aspect of vocabulary growth (Blachowicz & Fisher, 2009; Scott, Skobel, & Wells, 2008).

Do not confuse vocabulary instruction with spelling or phonics instruction (Gehsmann & Templeton, 2013). When we refer to vocabulary we are referring to *meaning* and *concepts*. We have observed that sometimes teachers assign spelling words in elementary classrooms that are really vocabulary words (for example, *butterfly* or *antenna*). Although students in the within word pattern stage can read and learn the meanings of many multisyllabic words (*glimmer, strategy, gesture*), they should not be expected to spell those words. This difference reflects the slant of development in word learning during the elementary years; the words students may read and study for meaning are more complex than those they study in spelling. For example, with context you can probably identify the partially spelled word in this sentence, "The caterpillar changes into a butterfly during the time it spends in the c-r-sa-lis." However, spelling *chrysalis* is a challenge for even adult spellers. Spelling a word is more exact than reading a word, as every letter must be represented accurately.

# Orthographic Development in the Within Word Pattern Stage

Students in the within word pattern stage "use but confuse" vowel patterns (Invernizzi, Abouzeid, & Gill, 1994). They no longer spell *boat* sound by sound to produce BOT but as BOTE, BOWT, BOOT, or even BOAT as they experiment with the possible patterns for the long *o* sound. When spellers begin including silent letters, they are ripe for instruction in long vowel patterns. In Eduardo's early within word pattern writing in Figure 6.4, we see that he knows a good deal about short vowels, spelling *with, pick, on, it,* and *up* correctly and *blanket* as BLANCKET. But Eduardo is experimenting with long vowel patterns, as in PLAED for *played* and TOOTHE for *tooth.*

> **FIGURE 6.4** Eduardo's Tooth Story
>
> My toothe came
> Owt beckus I plaed tugwoure
> with a blancket with botes on it
> and the tooth fairy
> came tw pick it up.

Table 6.1 summarizes students' orthographic development across the within word pattern stage. Short vowels, blends, and digraphs are nearly mastered and should only require some review. Their phonemic awareness is well developed and students should be able to isolate the vowel sounds in the middle of words. However, learning the various ways the sounds within those words can be spelled with patterns is the challenge—and accounts for the name selected to label this stage.

## The Pattern Layer

Students in this stage explore the **pattern layer** of English spelling. This requires a higher degree of abstract thinking because they face two tasks at once. They must not only isolate the phonemes to determine the sounds they need to represent, but must also choose from a variety of patterns that represent the same phoneme, which usually involves silent letters as part of the vowel spelling (*cute, through, suit*) or special consonant patterns (*lodge, itch*). There are several reasons why the same phoneme may be spelled with different patterns.

**Enhanced eText**
**Video Example 6.2**
This is an overview of the Within Word Pattern stage.

- *How words are spelled may depend on their histories and origins.* English has been enriched with vocabulary from many different languages over hundreds of years and has also imported diverse vowel sounds and spelling patterns. In addition, certain patterns represent sounds that have changed over the centuries. For example, *igh,* as in *knight,* once sounded quite different from long *i* (the word was pronounced *k-n-ict* in early Middle English). Over time, pronunciation is simplified but spelling tends to stay the same. Therefore, one vowel sound may be spelled many different ways (Vallins, 1954).
- *How vowel sounds are spelled may depend on their position within a word.* Comparing words such as *say* and *rain* reveals that, in single-syllable words, long a is usually spelled *ay* at the end of a word (but rarely in the middle) and often *ai* in the middle (but never at the end). Similarly, *oy* and *ew* usually occur at the ends of words or syllables whereas *oi, ui,* and *ou* occur in the middle of words.
- *How some sounds are spelled may depend on the letters next to them.* Examining words such as *ridge* and *cage* reveals that the /j/ sound is usually spelled *dge* when it follows a short vowel and *ge* when it follows a long vowel.

**TABLE 6.1**    **Characteristics of Within Word Pattern Spelling**

| Gradations of Stage with Examples of Spelling | What Students Spell Correctly | What Students Use but Confuse | What Is Absent |
|---|---|---|---|
| *Early Within Word Pattern* | | | |
| *ship, when, jump*<br>ROBE *for rob*<br>FLOTE *for float*<br>TRANE *for train*<br>BRITE *for bright* | Consonants, blends, digraphs<br>Preconsonantal nasals<br>Short vowels in CVC words<br>R-influenced CVC words: *car, for*<br>Known sight words | Silent letters in long vowel patterns<br>*-k, -ck,* and *-ke* endings: SMOCK *for smoke,* PEKE *for peak*<br>Substitutions of short vowels for ambiguous vowels: COT *for caught* | Vowels in unaccented syllables: FLOWR *for flower*<br>Consonant doubling: SHOPING *for shopping*<br>E-drop: DRIVEING *for driving* |
| *Middle Within Word Pattern* | | | |
| *float, train*<br>FRITE *for fright*<br>TABUL *for table* | All the above plus:<br>Common long vowel patterns (CVCe, CVVC)<br>*-k, -ck,* and *-ke* endings | R-influenced vowel patterns: TERN *for turn;* LIER *for liar.*<br>Less common and ambiguous vowel patterns: THOWGHT *for thought.*<br>*-ed* and other common inflections: MARCHT *for marched,* BATID *for batted* | Consonant doubling<br>E-drop |
| *Late Within Word Pattern* | | | |
| *bright*<br>SPOYLE *for spoil*<br>CHOOD *for chewed*<br>SURVING *for serving* | All the above plus:<br>Long vowel patterns in one-syllable words<br>R-influenced vowel patterns<br>Ambiguous vowels | Complex consonant units: SWICH *for switch,* SMUGE *for smudge*<br>Homophones: CLOSE *for clothes*<br>Plural Endings: MONTHES *for months*<br>Irregular Verbs: SWEEPED *for swept*<br>Vowels in unaccented syllables: COLER *for color* | Consonant doubling<br>E-drop<br>Changing *y* to *i:* CAREES *for carries* |

- *How vowel words are spelled may depend on the meaning of the word.* Although the long vowel sound in /pān/ may be spelled *a*-consonant-*e* or *ai*, the appropriate spelling is determined by *meaning*. Are you writing about the glass in a window (*pane*) or extreme discomfort (*pain*)? The meaning carries with it a consistent spelling: the /sāl/ on a boat is always spelled *sail*; the /sāl/ where products are sold is always spelled *sale*. For homophones like these, we hang our memory for spelling on a meaning hook.

## The Complexities of English Vowels

Studying vowel patterns characterizes much of the word study during the within word pattern stage. Short vowels pose a problem for letter name–alphabetic spellers because they do not match a letter name. However, after students learn to associate the five common short vowel sounds with *a, e, i, o,* and *u,* the relationship is usually one letter to one sound. In contrast, mastering the spelling of other vowel sounds is challenging due to the following factors.

1. There are many more vowel sounds than there are letters to represent them. Each designated vowel, including *y,* represents more than one sound. Listen to the sound of *a* in these words: *hat, car, war, saw, father, play.* To spell so many sounds, vowels are often paired (for example, the *ai* as a long *a* in *rain,* or *au* for the sound in *caught);* a second vowel or consonant is used to mark or signal the previous vowel sound. The silent *e* in *came,* the *y* in *play,* and the *w* in *saw* are all silent **vowel markers**.

2. Not only are there more vowel sounds than vowels, most of those sounds are spelled a number of different ways, as indicated in Table 6.2. However, some spelling patterns are far more likely to occur than others. For example, there are more instances of the *a*-consonant-*e* pattern (VCe) for the long *a* sound in the middle of a syllable than for any of the other patterns, and there aren't many words in which long *a* is spelled *ei,* as in *eight.*

3. In addition to short and long vowel sounds, there are **"other" vowel** sounds, all of which are spelled with various patterns. These other vowel patterns involve either a second vowel, or the vowel is influenced by a consonant letter that has some vowel-like qualities, such as *l, r,* or *w* (*bald, bird, crowd*). Other vowels include r-influenced vowels (*car, sir, earn*), **diphthongs** that blend two vowel sounds (*brown, toy*), and **ambiguous vowels**. Ambiguous vowels represent a range of sounds and spellings. For example, the vowel sound is the same in *cause, lawn,* and *false,* but is spelled three different ways (*au, aw, al*). The *ou* spelling pattern has four different sounds in *shout, touch, through,* and *thought.* These variations are often cited as examples of the irregularity of English spelling, but word sorting allows students to see that they form consistent categories just like other vowel patterns (Johnston, 2001).

**TABLE 6.2** Vowel Patterns

| Long Vowels | | Other Vowels | |
|---|---|---|---|
| *Common and Less Common Long Vowels* | | *Consonant-Influenced Vowels* | *Diphthongs and Ambiguous Vowels* |
| ā: Common long *a* patterns: | *a-e (cave), ai (rain), ay (play)* | R-influenced vowels | *oo (moon) and (book)* |
| Less common: | *ei (eight), ey (prey)* | /är/: *a* with *r: ar (car)* | *oy (boy), oi (boil)* |
| ē: Common long *e* patterns: | *ee (green), ea (team), e (me)* | /â/: *are (care), air (fair)* | *ow (brown), ou (cloud)* |
| | | /ôr/: *o* with *r: or (for), ore (store), our (pour), oar (board)* | *aw (crawl), au (caught)* |
| Less common: | *ie (chief), e-e (theme)* | | *o (dog)* |
| ī: Common long *i* patterns: | *i-e (tribe), igh (sight), y (fly)* | /ər/: *e* with *r: er (her), ear (learn)* | *ough (though, fought)* |
| | | /îr/: *e* with *r: eer (deer), ear (dear),* | |
| Less common: | *i* followed by *nd* or *ld (mind, child)* | /ər/: *i* with *r: ir (shirt)* | |
| ō: Common long *o* patterns: | *o-e (home), oa (float), ow (grow)* | /ir/: *i* with *r: ire (fire)* | |
| | | /ər/ *u* with *r: ur (burn)* | |
| Less common: | *o* followed by two consonants *(cold, most, jolt)* | /yoor/ *u* with *r: ure (cure)* | |
| | | *W* influences vowels that follow: *wa (wash, warn), wo (won, word)* | |
| ōō: Common long *u* patterns: | *u-e (flute), oo (moon), ew (blew)* | *L* influences the *a* as heard in *al (tall, talk)* | |
| Less common: | *ue (blue), ui (suit)* | | |

4. English is a language of multiple dialects, and the dialect differences are most noticeable in the pronunciations of vowels. In some regions of the United States, the long *i* sound in a word like *pie* is really more of a vowel diphthong as in *pi-e* (can you hear both a long *i* and a bit of a long *e* at the end?). *House* may be pronounced more like *hoose* in some areas, and *roof* may sound like *ruff*. Sometimes the final *r* in r-controlled vowels is dropped, as in Boston where you "pahk the cah" (*park the car*). In other regions, a final *r* is added to words, as in the "hollers" (hollows) of southwest Virginia. Such regional dialects add variety and interest to the language, but some teachers worry about how speakers of such dialects will learn to spell if they cannot pronounce words "correctly." Rest assured that *all* students speak a dialect and that *all* students will learn to associate certain letter patterns with their own pronunciations. Over time, the associations students make between their own pronunciations and spelling will sensitize them to the sound patterns of Standard American English (Cantrell, 2001). The value of *Words Their Way* word study over more inflexible phonics programs is that students can categorize word spellings according to their own pronunciations, and a miscellaneous or oddball column can be used for variant pronunciations.

5. Many words in English do not match even one of the patterns listed in Table 6.2. These words are sometimes called "exceptions to the rule." We prefer to put them in the miscellaneous or **oddball** category. When students study words in the within word pattern stage, the oddball category will get a lot of use. Sometimes these words are true exceptions (*was*, *build*, and *been*); at other times they are not exceptions, but rather part of a little-known category. For example, in *dance*, *prince*, and *fence* the words may look like they should have long vowel pronunciations because of the final *e*. But in these words, the e is there to signal or mark the "soft" /s/ sound of *c* (consider the alternative: *danc*, *princ*, and *fenc*). Do not ignore the exceptions; in fact, deliberately include a few such words in your sorts. They become memorable as deviations from the common patterns.

## Teaching Vowels to English Learners

*for* **English learners**

English vowels pose special challenges for English learners as they compare vowels in their primary language with English. Students may find that some vowel sounds in English do not exist in their native language, and even if they do, they may not be spelled the same way. The long *a* sound in Spanish, for example, is spelled with an *e*, so it might not be unusual for Spanish speakers to spell the word *train* as TREN. Drawing explicit attention to such differences whenever possible is helpful (Bear, Templeton, Helman, & Baren, 2003; Helman, 2004).

Unlike English, Spanish vowels have only one sound for each letter. Some are the same as English, but others are different. For example, *o* and *u* represent long *o* and long *u*, as in *uno*. However, *i* represents the long *e* sound (*amigo* or *sí*) and *e* represents a sound that is close to long *a* (*tres*, /trās/). The letter *a* is the only vowel in Spanish that is close to a short vowel sound in English: "ah" (/ö/) as in the vowel in *hot*. Table 6.3 shows these comparisons and some of the spelling errors students who are literate in Spanish might make, such as spelling *job* as JAB.

**TABLE 6.3** Vowels in Spanish and Predictable Spelling Errors

| Letters | Comparable Sound in Spanish | Spanish Examples | Possible Spelling Errors in English |
|---|---|---|---|
| a | / ä / "ah" | papa, madre, casa | job as JAB |
| e | / ā / "ay" | tres | lake as LEK or LEIK |
| i | / ē/ "ee" | si, mi, amigo | reach as RICH |
| ai | / ī / "eye" | aire | night as NAIT |
| o | / ō/ "oh" | uno, loco | float as FLOT or FLOUT |
| u | / ū / "oo" (never "yoo") | uno, tu, mucho | tune as TUN |

*Source:* Adapted from *Words Their Way with English Learners: Word Study for Phonics, Vocabulary, and Spelling Instruction* (2nd ed.), by Helman, Bear, Templeton, Invernizzi, and Johnston. Pearson/Allyn & Bacon.

For students who have learned to spell in Spanish there will be some predictable confusion with long vowels, such as using *i* for long *e* (RICH for *reach*). Students literate in Spanish expect each vowel sound to be represented. What English speakers think of as a single long vowel is actually sometimes pronounced as a diphthong or glide, as in "pi-ee" (*pie*) or "lay-eek" (*lake*)—depending on one's dialect. Spanish speakers may be more sensitive to these glides and attempt to spell both of the vowel sounds they hear. For example, when you pronounce the English long *i* slowly, you can feel and hear how the long *i* is a combination of the bottom vowel "ah" and the "ee" formed at the top of the mouth. The "ah" sound in English may be spelled with a short *o*, but in Spanish, this sound is spelled with an *a* and the long *e* sound is spelled with an *i*, so *pie* might be spelled PAI and *night* as NAIT. See Table 6.3 for more examples.

Other Romance languages, such as French, also represent long *a* with *e* (*tres*) and long *e* with *i* (*merci*). Four to five hundred years ago, English strayed from the original continental pronunciation of vowels and has, over time, changed or dropped the pronunciation of one vowel in combinations such as *ai, oa, ea, or ui*, so that the second vowel is now silent.

Despite the complexity of vowel spellings, by the end of the within word pattern stage, students who have experienced systematic word study have a good understanding of vowel patterns in one-syllable words. This knowledge is required to examine the way syllables are joined during the next stage of development, the syllables and affixes stage. For example, when students understand the patterns in words like *bet* and *beat*, they are ready to understand why *betting* has two *t*s and *beating* has only one.

## The Influence of Consonants on Vowels

In English, vowel patterns often consist of two vowels, one of which signals or marks a particular sound for the other vowel. Common examples are the silent *e* in words such as *bake* and *green*; however, consonants can also serve as vowel markers, such as the *gh* in *night* and *sigh*, which signals the long *i* sound. Students who associate the CVC pattern with short vowels may be puzzled by *saw, joy, hall,* or *car*. In those words, *w, y,* and *l* no longer act as consonants but take on vowel-like qualities. The consonant sound of *l* is lost in a word like *talk*—it has become part of the vowel sound, which is neither long nor short. When *w* precedes *a, ar,* and *or* the vowel takes on a different sound, as in *wand, war,* and *word*. These words may look like they are exceptions, but they are, in fact, simply additional patterns that are very regular. This is why it is important to learn patterns that relate to sound and meaning as opposed to memorizing rules. The influence of *r* is particularly common and deserves further discussion.

**THE *R*-INFLUENCED VOWELS.** As our friend, Neva Viise, says, "*R* is a robber!" The presence of an *r* following a vowel robs the sound from the vowel before it. The terms ***r*-influenced** or ***r*-controlled** both refer to this situation. Listen to the sound of *a* in *car*—it sounds quite different from short *a* in *cap*. The influence of *r* in *er, ir,* and *ur* makes them indistinguishable in some cases (*herd, bird, curd*). Even long vowel sounds before the robber *r* are pronounced differently than the same vowels preceding other consonants (*pair* versus *pain*). Young students sometimes confuse *r*-blends with *r*-influenced vowels, as in the spelling of *girl* as GRIL or *bird* as BRID. They can hear an *r* but are not sure of its location.

**Enhanced eText**
**Video Example 6.3**
Ms. Grotting discusses *r*-influenced vowels with her student and then reflects on her lesson.

## Triple Blends, Silent Initial Consonants, and Other Complex Consonants

Several other consonant issues pose challenges for within word pattern spellers who already know basic beginning and ending consonant blends and digraphs. For example, three-letter blends and blend-digraphs combinations often require further study: *spr (spring), thr (throw), squ (square), scr (scream), shr (shred), sch (school), spl (splash),* and *str (string)*. Because words that contain these triplets have a variety of vowel patterns, they are specifically studied toward the end of the stage but you can include them in sorts throughout the stage when appropriate. There are also several silent consonants to study in one-syllable words: *k (knife), w (wrong),* and *g (gnaw)*.

**TABLE 6.4** Complex Consonants Patterns

| tack | take | | fetch | peach | | fudge | huge |
|------|------|--|-------|-------|--|-------|------|
| lick | like | | notch | roach | | badge | cage |
| rack | rake | | patch | poach | | ledge | siege |
| smock | smoke | | sketch | reach | | ridge | page |

**Enhanced eText**
**Video Example 6.4**
Watch Ms. Wilson discuss complex consonant patterns with her students.

Another pattern of special interest is related to vowel sounds. Based on Venezky's (1970) work, Henderson (1990) called these **complex consonant patterns**. For example, students in the within word pattern stage can examine words that end in *ck (kick)*, *tch (catch)*, and *dge (ledge)*. Contrasting these pairs helps students make interesting discoveries. Say the word pairs in Table 6.4 and listen to the vowel sounds. What do you notice about the vowel sounds in the *ck*, *tch*, and *dge* patterns? What about the vowel sounds in the *ke*, *ch*, and *ge* patterns? By now you've probably figured out that *ck (tack)*, *tch (fetch)*, and *dge (fudge)* are associated with short vowel sounds, whereas *ke (take)*, *ch (peach)*, and *ge (huge)* are associated with long vowel sounds.

The consonants *g* and *c* have two different sounds that are influenced by vowels. When *g* and *c* are followed by *a*, *o*, and *u*, they have a "hard" sound, as in *gate* and *cake*. When they are followed by *i*, *e*, or *y*, they have a "soft" sound (/s/ or /j/) as in *ginger* or *cent*. (*C* is more regular than *g* because the *g* is hard in many words like *girl* and *gill*.) Similarly, words ending in *ce (dance)*, *ge (edge)*, *ve (leave)*, and *se (sense)* have a silent *e* associated with the consonant rather than the vowel. These patterns illustrate that how sounds are spelled often depends on other sounds next to them.

## Homophones, Homographs, and Other Features

Homophones will inevitably turn up when students study vowel patterns and you can include them in the word sorts you plan even at the beginning of this stage. However, we also recommend an intensive look at homophones at the end of this stage as they summarize the two big ideas of the within-word pattern stage:

- Homophones illustrate the role of meaning in determining spelling patterns; and
- The many vowel patterns that appear in homophones summarize the pattern-to-sound principle of the within word pattern stage.

Note the contrasts involving sound, pattern and meaning in the following long *o* homophone sort:

**Long *o* homophones**

| *oa* | *o-e* | *ow* | *oddballs* |
|------|-------|------|-----------|
| loan | lone | | |
| groan | | grown | |
| | throne | thrown | |
| | toe | tow | |
| | rose | rows | |
| | role | | roll |
| | close | | clothes |

At this point, students know most of the vowel patterns and are ready to focus on the meanings of the words. The different spellings of homophones (*Mary/marry/merry*) and the different pronunciations of homographs (*wind* up string, listen to the *wind*) may at first seem confusing, but they reflect the historical origins and may even make reading easier and meaning clearer (cf., Taft, 1991; Templeton, 1992).

Pairs of homographs and homophones sometimes differ grammatically as well as semantically. For example, when you discuss the homophones *read* and *red*, it makes sense to talk about the past tense of the verb *to read* and the color word *red*. Take the opportunity to explore the interaction of sound, pattern, and meaning of irregular or "strong" verbs. Many of these verbs differ by vowel sounds (*drink/drank*), spelling patterns (*pay/paid*), or both (*sweep, swept*). Studying contractions presents students with a new series of features to examine that are rooted in the pattern and meaning layers of the orthography. For example, we examine grammatical constructions and meaning when we compare *its* and *it's* or *we're* and *were*.

**Enhanced eText**
**Video Example 6.5**
Ms. Grotting discusses homophones with her second-graders.

## Word Study Instruction for the Within Word Pattern Stage

Carefully planned contrasts are a systematic way to guide students' mastery of the complexities of vowel and consonant patterns in the within word pattern stage. Principles of instruction were previously outlined in Chapter 3 but here we highlight five that are particularly applicable to this stage:

1. *Use words students can read.* Be sensitive to the difficulty of words in the sort and make sure students can read most of them easily. Words starting with consonant blends, like *blame* or *frame*, are harder than words starting with single consonants like *came* or *name* even though they share the same CVCe spelling pattern. If there are words that students cannot read set them aside and revisit them later in the sort when they can apply what they have learned to sound out the word.

2. *Look for what students use but confuse.* A spelling inventory will give you a good idea of what students know and what they are ready to learn. However, it is also important to look in your students' personal writing and reading materials for words to include in sorts. The words students can already read and spell are still useful when they are looking for patterns across words to form generalizations.

3. *Sort by sound and pattern.* Many word study lessons first ask students to contrast vowels by how they sound. Long vowels should be first introduced by comparing them to their corresponding short vowel sounds, as Ms. Watanabe did in the vignette at the beginning of this chapter. Sound sorts are important because sound is the first clue that spellers have to use and because certain patterns go with certain vowel sounds. You can use long and short vowel pictures for sound sorts, but most sound sorts at this stage are done with words. Consider using pictures as the column headers for your initial sound sort. After sorting by sound, sort by sight—look for the visual orthographic spelling patterns used to spell each sound category.

4. *Avoid teaching rules—instead, have students find reliable patterns.* Traditionally, students were taught rules about silent *e* and jingles like "when two vowels go walking the first one does the talking." However, rules are often unreliable. For example, the rule about two vowels works for *oa* and *ai* in *boat* and *rain*, but does not work for *oy* or *oi* in *boy* or *join*, yet *oy* and *oi* are regular spelling patterns (Johnston, 2001). We prefer to talk about patterns rather than rules. The time to talk about rules is when students have already

Sorting first by short and long vowel sounds before subdividing by pattern

observed a pattern, can think of other examples that fit the pattern, and understand the pattern as demonstrated in their reflections. Consider rules as useful mnemonics for something already understood; they are not for teaching.

5. *Don't hide exceptions.* Include two or three oddball words in sorts when appropriate. For example, include *love* and *some* in a long *o* sort, which look as though they fit the CVCe pattern but whose vowel sounds are not long. However, don't overdo it. Too many oddballs placed in a sort can make it difficult for students to find the pattern. The best oddballs are high-frequency words like *done* or *come* that students already know how to read. High-frequency words (both regular and irregular) are listed in Appendix F and marked with asterisks in the word lists. Help students see that even the oddballs are *mostly* predictable in terms of sound–spelling correspondences, it is often the vowel sound or spelling that is "odd." Students enjoy the challenge of finding the oddballs in a sort and the oddballs often serve as the real test of whether students are sorting carefully.

Ms. Wilson introduces the sort

## The Word Study Lesson Plan in the Within Word Pattern Stage

Word sorts often begin as a teacher-directed activity and then offered as individual practice throughout the week. Teacher-directed closed sorts are helpful when students are new to sorting or when they start studying a new feature. Most sorts will follow the standard format presented in Chapter 3 and are reviewed here.

**INTRODUCE THE SORT.** Follow these four steps to introduce a **teacher-directed** or **closed sort** for the within word pattern stage.

*for* **English learners**

1. *Read the words and explore word meanings.* When starting a sort, go over the words with students to be sure they can read the words and talk briefly about the meanings of unfamiliar words or multiple meanings of polysemous words like *park* or *train*. If there are more than a few words whose meanings students do not know, which is often the case for English learners, continue to talk about the meanings throughout the week. Be sure to keep a picture dictionary close by for English learners. Set aside any words students were not able to read and revisit them after the generalization has been established as a chance to apply what they have learned.

2. *Establish the categories.* As described in Chapter 3, there are many ways to introduce a sort. Some teachers set up the categories with **key pictures** or **key words**, as Ms. Watanabe did with short *e* and long *e*. Other teachers like to establish the key words as part of the group discussion with students, then highlight them. In a teacher-directed closed sort, introduce your headers, whether they are key pictures or key words, or in some cases, the short vowel and long vowel symbols as shown in the table. After going over the words, begin the sort with an open-ended question such as, "What do you notice about these words?"

3. *Model how to sort several words.* Model how to sort at least one word or picture into each column, stretching out the vowel sound in the middle to emphasize its sound. For example, you might say, "We're going to listen for the vowel sound in the middle of these words and decide whether it sounds like the /ĕ/ sound in the middle of *bed*, or like the ē sound in the middle of *feet*. I'll do a few first. Here is a *net. Net-et-ĕ.* Notice how I peel off the sounds before and after the vowel to make it easier to hear the vowel in the middle. *Net* has the "eh" sound (/ĕ/) in the middle, so I'll put it under *bed-ed-ĕ.* Here is a *jeep. J-ee-p.* I'll put *jeep* under the picture of *feet. Jeep* and *feet* both have the /ē/ sound in the middle; the /ē/ sound is made by two *ees.*"

**4.** *Invite students to help with the sorting.* Continue with the children's help. Encourage them to say the word slowly and compare the vowel sound to the headers, using the terms *long* and *short*. Students should name the picture or read the word aloud, then place it in a category and explain why it goes there. If a student makes a mistake at the very beginning, correct it immediately by saying, "*Wheel* would go under *feet* because it has the long *e* sound in the middle—it sounds like /ē/ in the middle." Then model how to segment the phonemes to isolate the medial vowel: /wh-ē-l/. Be sure to model the discovery and placement of the oddballs. "Listen to the sound in the middle of *been*: /b-ĭ-n/. Does *been* have the long *e* sound we have been listening for in words with the *ee* pattern today? It's an oddball because it has the *ee* pattern but it doesn't have the /ē/ sound."

**Enhanced eText**
**Video Example 6.6**
Ms. Flores describes her three groups and how she introduces the sorts.

**GUIDE THE REFLECTION.** After sorting have students read down the lists of words in each column to check for the sound or pattern. Ask them to verbalize what the words or pictures in each column have in common and to arrive at some conclusion or generalization. Begin with open ended questions presented on page 61 in Chapter 3 such as:

- How are the words in this column alike?
- Why did you put these words together? Do you all agree?

Focus attention on the contrasts in vowel sounds, pattern, and/or meaning. Use probing questions such as,

- What do your ears tell you? What do your eyes see?
- Are there any oddballs? What makes them odd?

Talk about *where* in the word the spelling pattern occurs, how often they have seen that spelling pattern in their reading, and other words they know that have those same patterns. By paying attention to the position of a spelling pattern within a word, students can often determine which spelling pattern occurs most often. For example, *aw* and *oy* usually occur at the ends of words or syllables (*straw, boycott*), whereas *au* and *oi* are found within syllables (*fault, voice*).

Help your students formulate their ideas into generalizations such as, "All of these words have the letter *e* in the middle and make the 'eh' sound," or "The words with two *e*s in the middle have the /ē/ sound in the middle." With the generalization or "big idea" now explicitly stated, they may be able to apply it to the decoding of unfamiliar words. Refer to Table 3.2 on page 65 for a menu of other questions that can help your students reach conclusions. During the reflection part of the lesson, students are asked to verbally declare and discuss their understanding about sound, pattern, and meaning. Encourage them to "turn and talk" to their classmates about what they learned from the sort. If students seem just to mimic other students, you can ask them to say it another way or ask, "What else did you notice about the words we sorted?"

**RE-SORT AND CHECK.** After guiding the reflection, have your students re-sort again. Insist that they say each word aloud as they sort it, to "say it as they lay" it down. Teach them how to check their sort by reading down each column to listen for sounds or to look for patterns that reflect on what the sort reveals. When there are errors in the sort, offer gentle hints such as, "One word in this column does not sound (or look) right. Can you find it?" Students can check each other's work in a similar fashion. A sort is successful when students sort accurately and easily and can discuss why they sorted as they did.

**EXTEND.** After a group sort, it is important for students to work independently or with partners using their own sets of words across the week in repeated sorts and other extensions. Some teachers create

Ms. Grotting guides the reflection after the sort

**FIGURE 6.5** Long Vowel Sorts: Student Sorts by Sound

reusable sorts in manila folders with the key words or pictures at the top and the words stored in a plastic bag inside the folder. Figure 6.5 shows a student isolating the long *e* sound in *leaf* before placing it in the column with the picture of the feet at the top. Saying the words aloud and comparing them in this way is a necessary strategy when students begin to sort independently.

Word study is extended through activities that students complete at their seats, in word study notebooks, at a word study center, or at home. Several word study extensions and follow up routines are discussed in detail in Chapter 3, but we particularly recommend those activities that link word study to reading and writing:

1. **Word hunts** (see page 69) in previously read material, provide opportunities for students to make connections between what they are learning in word study and the words they read in books. Often students will find more difficult two-or-three syllable examples of a spelling feature they have been studying in one-syllable words. For example, they might find *retreat*, *ordeal*, or *creature* as examples of the long *e* sound (/ē/) spelled with an *ea*. Word hunts help students generalize what they are studying to other words.

2. **Blind sorts** and **blind writing sorts** (see pages 66–67), in which students sort words by sound as a partner reads them aloud, help students distinguish the vowel sound, associate it with a visual spelling pattern, and then reinforce this link through the multisensory act of writing. Be careful not to assign blind sorts until after students have already had plenty of opportunities to sort and discuss the words.

3. **Word operations** (see page 68). Exchanging spelling features in various word positions give students an opportunity to apply what they are learning in their word study lessons to read, write and decode new words. Typically, consonants, blends, and digraphs are exchanged for other consonants at the beginning of words (for example, *make-bake-brake-flake*) or end (*mad-math—mash-mask*). Within word pattern spellers can exchange the vowel or vowel pattern in the middle to create new words (for example, *drive-drove; give-gave; braid-breed*). Students can record their word operations in their word study notebooks.

4. **Build, blend, and extend** is another type of word operation that is described in Chapter 5 but is also recommended in this stage. To build words, give students the vowel pattern (*-ime*) then name words for them to spell by changing the initial letter (*dime, crime, shine*). To blend, write the vowel pattern and substitute different beginning letters to create new words for students to read. Extend involves spelling and reading words that were not part of the original sort. See Activity 5.23 for more details.

5. **Games** are an enjoyable way to practice reading the words and think about their spelling patterns. Many games are described in the activities section at the end of this chapter, or can be adapted from games in Chapter 5.

**Enhanced eText**
Video Example 6.7
Ms. Flores discusses the word study extensions she implements across the week.

Racetrack game for R-Influenced vowels

## Picture Sorts to Contrast Long and Short Vowels

Students in the early part of the within word pattern stage who still have problems distinguishing spoken vowel sounds benefit from picture sorts that contrast the short and long vowel. Picture sorts develop phonemic awareness and focus attention on the sound without the support of the printed word. Use picture sorts for just one day and then follow up with word sorts. See an example of a teacher-directed sort in the sample lesson in the following box.

# Contrasting Short and Long *u* in a Teacher-Directed Lesson

**SAMPLE LESSON PLAN**

1. **Prepare the sort.** Use a prepared sort as shown in Figure 6.6 or select 10 to 14 pictures for one short vowel and its corresponding long vowel from the picture sets that come with this book. Arrange them in a template that students can later use to sort on their own. Prepare headers with a picture that will be a key word. Headers such as *cup* and *tube* are good, are used in many sorts, and can be found on the sound board in Appendix C. Include one or two words that do not have the sounds as oddballs.

2. **Introduce the sort.** Set up the headers and explain, "Today we will be listening to the vowel sound in the middle of words. Some of the words have the short *u* sound, as in *cup*. (Isolate the vowel by peeling off the initial consonant and then the final consonant: *cup, up, ŭ*). Some words will have the long *u* sound, as in *tube* (*tube, ube, ū*)."

3. **Sort.** Model several pictures: "Here is a cube. Listen to the vowel: *c-yū-b*. Will I put that under *cup* or *tube*? Yes, *cube* has the long vowel sound in the middle just like *tube*. They both have the /oo/ sound in the middle." (Note that there is a slight difference between the long *u* in *tube* (/ū/ or /oo/) and *cube* (/y/ū/ or /yoo/). The long *u* sound seldom really "says its name" ("yoo"), except in a few words like *cube, mule, use,* and *huge*. Adults tend to lump these variations together, but children can sometimes be more sensitive to the differences. They could be sorted into a different category but students should understand that both are long u and both have the /oo/ sound.) Find the oddball *skate* and place it in a third column.

4. **Check and discuss.** Have students sort the remaining pictures. Then check the sort by naming the pictures in each column to be sure they have the same sound. Then ask. "How are the words under *cup* alike? (They have short u in the middle). How are the words under *tube* alike? (They have long *u* in the middle). You might point out that long *u* is not really "longer" than short *u* but that is just what the vowels are called. Ask, "What was the oddball and why?" (*Skate* has a long *a* sound.)

5. **Sort again.** Repeat the sort in the group if time allows and encourage students to name each picture as they sort and identify it as having short *u* or long *u*, saying something like: "This is a bug and it has the short *u* sound in the middle."

6. **Extend.** Give the students their own set of pictures to sort and observe them to see how accurately they sort. Do not expect students to spell these words because they have not been working with the printed forms.

**FIGURE 6.6    Picture Sort for Short and Long *u***

## Teacher-Directed Sorts for Long Vowel Patterns

After students can isolate the vowel sound in the middle of words and distinguish a long vowel sound from a short one, it's time for them to associate the spelling patterns with each category of sound. One basic procedure is a two-step sort that begins with sound and moves to patterns. The example in the box is similar to the sort done by Ms. Watanabe but contrasts short *a* and long *a* sounds first, and then contrasts short *a* and long *a* spelling patterns second.

You can find prepared sorts in Appendix E, on the website for *WTW Digital*, and in the supplemental book *Words Their Way Word Sorts for Within Word Pattern Spellers*.

# Teacher-Directed Two-Step Sort for Long *a* by Sound and Pattern

1. **Prepare the sort.** Use a prepared sort or create your own sort for students. To create your own sorts, use the word lists for this stage in Appendix F and select about seven short *a* words, seven long *a* words that are spelled with the *ai* pattern (*rain, pail*), and seven with the *a-e* pattern (*cake, tape*). Include one or two oddballs that do not fit the expected sound or pattern (for example, *was* or *said*). Use short *a* and long *a* pictures (such as, *cat* and *cake*) as sound headers. Prepare word cards or write the words randomly on a word study handout template for students to cut apart. This teacher-directed sort starts with one set of words that everyone uses, after which students use their own sets at their seats.

| cat | cake | rain |
|-----|------|------|
| paint | late | flat |
| snap | paid | shade |
| tax | said | state |
| was | nail | black |
| flame | plan | pail |
| wave | train | plate |

Handout for short *a* and long *a* with *a-e* and *ai* patterns

2. **Introduce the words.** Begin by reading the words together and talking about any whose meaning may be unclear. If there are homophones (like *tale* and *tail*), talk about what each means. Set aside any words students cannot read. Invite students to make observations about the words: "What do you notice about these words? How are they alike? Do they all have the same vowel sound in the middle?"

3. **Introduce the sound sort.** Display the *cat* and *cake* key words or pictures for the sound sort. Say, "Listen to the vowel sound in the middle of *cat*. What vowel sound do you hear? *Cat* has a short *a*—*it makes the* / ă / *sound in the middle.*" Repeat with *cake*. Then model how to sort a few words by the sound of the vowel in the middle and then ask the students to help you finish the sort. Warn

them that there are oddballs with neither a short nor long vowel sound and challenge students to be on the lookout for them. When they are found, set them to the side or put under the oddball header. Read all the words in each column to check them and verify that they all have the same vowel sound.

4. **Introduce the pattern sort.** After discussing the two sound categories, ask students to look for patterns in the long *a* column and separate them into two subcategories. Talk about how the words in each column have different spelling patterns and why the oddballs don't fit. Help students see that the words with a silent *e* fit the CVCe pattern: a consonant, a vowel, another consonant, and the silent *e*. Repeat for the CVVC pattern and contrast with the CVC words in the short vowel category. Decide on key words for new headers from among the word cards and label them CVC, CVCe, and CVVC.

**Enhanced eText**
**Video Example 6.8**
Watch Ms. Flores working with her second-graders to sort short and long *a*.

5. **Sort again and reflect.** Keep the headers in place and scramble the words to sort a second time. Do not make any corrections until the end. Check each column by reading the words and review how the words in each column are alike by sound and by pattern. If a mistake has been made, ask the students to find it. Ask, "What did you learn about long *a*?" (It can be spelled with the *a-e* or *ai* patterns.) Talk about why the oddballs don't fit. (They have the pattern but not the sound). Revisit any words students could not read and apply the generalization to sound out the words. The final categories will look something like this:

| CVC | CVCe | CVVC | |
|-----|------|------|---|
| cat | cake | rain | |
| flat | late | paint | said |
| snap | shade | paid | was |
| tax | state | nail | |
| black | flame | pail | |
| plan | wave | train | |
| | plate | | |

6. **Extend.** Students need their own sheet of words to cut apart and sort again. Remind students to scribble on the back or draw three stripes in a color they can recognize if they lose a word card. Label the headers with CVC, CVCe, and CVVC and ask students to sort words while you observe. After sorting, check and reflect, and then ask students to shuffle the words and store them for activities on subsequent days.

Students sort their word cards by short and long vowel patterns

## Open Sorts

After students understand the process of sorting, use open sorts to require more analytic thinking and encourage problem solving. The open sort starts with everyone sorting their own set of words with no key words or headers. Students are challenged to determine their own categories and explain why they sorted the way they did. After sorting, get students together to talk about the distinguishing features of the contrast. See Table 3.2, "Questions to Guide Critical Thinking during Word Study," on page 65. You might start with, "What can you tell us about these words now that we have sorted them? How are they alike? How are they different from this set over here?"

Some vowels are called ambiguous because they are used to spell several sounds with different patterns. Listen to the sounds of *ow* in *snow* and *clown* and to *ou* in *shout*, *through*, and *thought*. The open sort described on the next page contrasts some of these patterns and sounds.

## Spelling Strategies

Students in the within word pattern stage have a growing store of known words they can spell accurately, including many high-frequency words, but there are still many words they don't know how to spell. Accept students' best spelling efforts but make it clear that they are also accountable for spelling word features they have formally studied, and that they should use a variety of strategies to spell words they do not know.

**ENCOURAGE STUDENTS TO TRY A WORD SEVERAL WAYS.** Teach students to attempt spelling a word before they ask for help and offer positive feedback on what they try. Australians Parry and Hornsby (1988) described this popular strategy as "have-a-go," and various forms have been developed. See Activity 6.6 for an example and procedures.

**USE AVAILABLE RESOURCES.** Model for students how to use the Sound Board for Long and Short Vowels found in the Appendix C on page 429, the word wall (described in Chapter 3), homophone charts, and other word sources in the classroom. Modeling the use of these resources as you write with students is essential if you want them to use the

# Open Sort for Ambiguous Vowels: *ou* and *ow*

1. **Introduce the sort.** For an open sort that asks students to really think about sound and pattern, you should cut off the headers and even the bolded key words. See Figure 6.7 for the handout we would recommend for this open sort. Give students a copy of the words and say, "I want you to read these words and use your eyes and ears to think about patterns and sounds. What categories can you find? Sort these words by yourself. Set aside any words you could not read and look out for several oddballs!"

2. **Discuss the sort.** Call the students together and ask them to sort their words where you can see them. Some students may have sorted by sound alone whereas others sorted by pattern alone. Ask, "What categories did you find? How are the words alike in each column?" Call on different students to describe the rationale for their sort. Probe with questions such as, "What sounds did you find in these words? How would you describe the patterns in the words you sorted? What oddballs did you find and why were they odd? Were there any words you had trouble reading?"

3. **Close the sort.** Hand out copies of the headers (*ow = ō*, *ou*, and *ow*) and key words (*show*, *out*, and *how*). Ask everyone to sort under them and check the sort by reading down each column to listen for the sound. Take time to talk about the meaning of any words that might be unfamiliar. Ask, "Does the position of the pattern matter?" (Yes, words that end with a single consonant are more likely to be spelled with *ow* than *ou*, and only *ow* can come at the end.) "Do certain ending consonants tend to go with certain patterns?"

(Yes, *t* and *d* go with *ou*, whereas *n* and *l* go with *ow*.) "What are the oddballs and why?" (They are spelled with *ou* but have a different sound.) The final sort will look like this:

| *ow = ō* | *ou* | *ow* | oddball |
|---|---|---|---|
| **show** | **out** | **how** | |
| glow | cloud | down | rough |
| crow | round | growl | through |
| | ground | clown | |
| | found | owl | |
| | shout | brown | |
| | count | frown | |
| | mouth | gown | |
| | south | plow | |

4. **Reflect.** Summarize by asking, "What did you learn from this sort?" Help students conclude that both *ou* and *ow* can spell the same sound, while *ow* can also spell another sound. Ask, "What makes these words hard to spell?" (Sound does not offer a clue.) "If you hear sound at the end as in *brow* or *stow* what would be your best guess for spelling that word? Why?" (*ow* is likely to come at the end of a word whereas *ou* does not.) "What could help you spell an unfamiliar word like *snout*?" (Think of known words like *out* or *shout*.)

5. **Extend.** Students should sort again over several days and work with partners to do a blind sort. Help them write a reflection that covers some of the ideas about how the sound is spelled two ways but position and ending consonants offer clues to the most likely pattern.

**FIGURE 6.7** Handout for Open Sort

| cloud | clown | growl |
|---|---|---|
| round | down | ground |
| brown | owl | found |
| shout | rough | frown |
| gown | mouth | plow |
| south | glow | town |
| count | through | crow |

resources for themselves. Have students keep a sound board in their writing folder and model how to locate the pictures associated with a given long vowel sound. If you write the sentence "Today is the first day of October," remind students that the name of the month is on the calendar. Or if you need to spell "through," identify it as a word wall word and model how you first listen to the beginning sound and then check out the words under *TH*. Challenge students to master words that they use frequently to wean them from the word wall or to add additional columns to the Sound Board for Long and Short Vowels as less common patterns are learned.

**USE SPELLING DICTIONARIES TO LOOK UP WORDS.** Spelling dictionaries or personal dictionaries are simply alphabetic lists of words (without definitions) commonly needed by young writers. This can be as simple as a blank book made by folding several sheets of paper (put two or three letters on each page). You can also download printable versions or buy commercially prepared books like those listed next. These usually have one or two pages for each letter with a list of the most common words as well as space for students to add more words.

- *My Dictionary*, available from Sunshine Books International (65 pages), also has words organized thematically
- *My Word Book*, published by Primary Concepts (35 pages)
- *Words I Use When I Write* (different grade levels), available from Educators Publishing Service

Add words from the word walls to spelling dictionaries as they are introduced. Students might also request words that they want to use in their writing on a regular basis. Model for students how to use a spelling dictionary by narrowing down the beginning sound and first letter before thinking about where in the alphabet that letter would be—the beginning, middle, or end. Personal dictionary words can also be organized thematically by colors, food, action words, word wall words, and content area words that students might need for writing about a topic of study.

**REMIND STUDENTS WHAT THEY KNOW.** Students often forget to use what they already know to figure out something new. Here are reminders to use when students ask you how to spell a word, or during conferencing when you see they have made a mistake:

1. *Use rhymes to make analogies.* One easy way to encourage students to puzzle out the spelling of a new word on their own is to ask them if they know how to spell another word that rhymes. For example, if a student is unsure of how to spell the name of the country *Spain* ask her if she knows how to spell *rain, drain,* or *brain.* Of course, not all words that rhyme are spelled the same (for example, *mane* also rhymes with *Spain*), but thinking of a known rhyming word will work more times than not. Prompt students by saying something like, "If you know how to spell *night,* then you can spell *slight.*"
2. *Use word chunks.* Encourage students to spell chunks of the word that they are sure of first, then tackle the next part. Getting down the initial consonant chunk, whether it is a single consonant, a blend, or a digraph, leaves the vowel and what follows as the chunk to ponder. Using Word Operations (explained in Chapter 3) as a routine in the word study notebook will encourage this strategy.
3. *Use the "best guess" strategy.* While sorting and studying vowel patterns, students will notice that one pattern invariably has more examples than another. For example, there are always more long *u* words spelled *u-consonant-e* than long *u* words spelled with *ui*. Prompt students to think about the most common pattern they know first, and then use some of the other strategies such as thinking of rhyming words they know.
4. *Refer to their word study notebook.* Students don't always make the connection between spelling and word study unless you remind them. If they ask you how to spell a word that follows a sound or pattern that you have studied and recorded in the word study notebook, refer them back to their word study notebook.

## Word Sorting with English Learners

Word sorting lessons are an explicit way to draw English learners' attention to both the similarities and differences between languages in terms of sounds and spelling, while simultaneously helping them to build vocabulary. For English learners, the following suggestions can enhance the effectiveness of the word study lessons described earlier:

1. Search online resources to learn about similarities and differences in the sound and spelling systems of languages spoken by your students.
2. Use concrete, highly imageable words that can easily be visualized, drawn, or acted out—concrete nouns, imageable adjectives, action verbs. These words will be easier to learn than prepositions, conjunctions, or helping verbs.

**FIGURE 6.8** Simple Drawings Help English Learners Associate Meaning with Spelling

3. Discuss the meanings of the words in the introductory lesson and review throughout the week as needed. Act out words when appropriate and supply photographs or drawings to develop meaning. Students can illustrate words in their word study notebooks or add a small drawing or definition to the word cards to remind them of meaning (see Figure 6.8).
4. Reduce the number of words in a sort so students will not be overwhelmed with too many new vocabulary words. Spend extra time reading the words in columns aloud as students check their sorts.
5. Pair words and pictures when possible. Long and short vowel pictures are included in the pictures that come with this book; more images can be downloaded from the Internet (for example, from Google images).
6. Pair English learners with native English speakers who can supply pronunciations during partner sorts.
7. Model careful pronunciation but do not be overly concerned if English learners do not master the correct pronunciations.

For further information on these recommendations, refer to *Words Their Way*® *with English Learners.*

**Enhanced eText**
**Video Example 6.9**
Ms. Wilson discusses adjustments she makes for English learners in the within word pattern stage.

# Sequence and Pacing of Word Study in the Within Word Pattern Stage

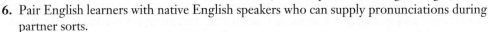

The sequence of word study in the within word pattern stage begins by taking a step back with a review of short vowel sounds as they are compared with long vowel sounds in CVCe words. If students have not completely mastered short vowels, they have another chance to study them in a different context. Then the focus shifts to the spelling of other vowel sounds that are neither long nor short—sounds like the /ô/ sound in *paw* or the /oi/ sound in *spoil*, and the spelling of *r*-influenced vowels like the û in *turn*. Complex consonant patterns (such as _tch versus ch; _dge versus _ge) are studied toward the end of the stage along with an intense study of homophones (*sail-sale; beet-beat*), contractions (*we'll-we will; we've-we have*), plurals (*babies-monkeys*), and irregular verbs (such as *keep-kept; sweep-swept; tear-tore; wear-wore*).

## Early, Middle, or Late Placement

Identifying whether students are in the early, middle, or late part of the stage (refer to Table 6.1, page 212) will help you target where in the sequence of features to begin word study instruction. After administering a spelling inventory, consider your students' scores in the different categories of vowels.

**EARLY.** In the early within word pattern stage, students know blends and digraphs and spell most short vowels correctly. They often experiment with silent letters that mark long vowels. The final silent *e* is the most common pattern and the most likely to turn up first. Students might use it but confuse it when spelling short vowels (*job* as JOBE) or long vowel patterns (FLOTE for *float*). If students spell fewer than two of the CVCe long vowels correctly, they are probably in the early part of the stage. They will begin comparing short and long vowel sounds and learning the consonant-vowel-consonant-e (CVCe) pattern across all five vowels. Other common and less common long vowel patterns, such as the consonant-vowel-vowel-consonant pattern (CVVC), are systematically studied across all five vowels.

**MIDDLE.** By the middle of this stage, students are spelling the most of the long vowels with the CVCe and CVVC patterns correctly but still make mistakes on other vowels such as *r*-influenced and ambiguous vowels. Short and long vowel patterns are reconsidered in the context of *r*-influenced words where AR words (*start, sharp, chart*) are contrasted with ARE and AIR words (*stare, fare, rare* versus *stair, hair, fair*). Similar contrasts are examined for the other *r*-influenced vowels. Students also will encounter other vowel sounds, such as the /oi/ sound in *noise* or *joy* or the /aw/ sound in *taught* or *crawl*, and these other vowel patterns are methodically examined at the end of the middle within word pattern stage.

**LATE.** By the end of this stage, students will have mastered the long vowel patterns and most spellings for *r*-influenced vowels like the û in *turn* and other vowel sounds such as the /ô/ sound in *saw* or the /oi/ sound in *boil*. They may be using but confusing patterns related to meaning differences so an intense examination of homophones (such as *side* versus *sighed*; *close* versus *clothes*) is appropriate for the late within word pattern stage. They also may be using but confusing some of the complex consonants (such as *-tch, -dge*) as well as the conventions for making singular nouns plural (for example, *eyes* versus *coaches*) and/or for representing the present and past tenses of irregular verbs (for example, *break-broke; speak-spoke*). Contractions, especially those that overlap with homophones (for example, *who's* versus *whose*), are also problematic for within word pattern spellers right up through the late end of the stage.

## Pacing

Table 6.5 suggests focused contrasts and a sequence of word study under three possible pacing guides in the early, middle, and late part of this stage. You can adjust pacing by adding more categories to a single sort (up to four or five) or by dropping back to fewer categories when students are confused. Because there is a lot to cover in this stage, two years is not too long to address the range of features for students of average achievement.

Pacing depends on several factors:

- Developmental level
- Grade level
- Rate of progress

For early within word pattern spellers in late first or early second grade, we recommend an introductory pace. Start with some picture sorts to focus attention on the different short and long vowel sounds, and then study the common CVCe pattern across four long vowels (the CVCe pattern is not studied among long *e* words because the CVCe pattern is rare in one-syllable words). During this introductory pace, students may be using word study notebooks for the first time and learning new sorting routines as described in Chapter 3.

If you teach students beyond the primary grades who are still in the early part of this stage, there is a greater sense of urgency to catch them up with peers. The moderate pace is a good place to start but monitor progress through observation and assessments to determine whether to go faster or slower. The first few vowels may take more time than those studied later. Students in the middle within word pattern stage might benefit from the fast pace outlined in the last column of Table 6.5: a quick review of long vowels before going on to *r*-influenced and ambiguous vowels.

**TABLE 6.5** Pacing and Sequence Guide for Within Word Pattern

| Slow Introductory Pace | Moderate Pace | Advanced Pace or Review |
|---|---|---|
| *Early Within Word Patterns*: Common and Less Common Long Vowels | | |
| Compare long and short vowels in picture and word sorts: short *a*, *a-e*; short *i*, *i-e*; short *o*, *o-e*; short *u*, *u-e*.<br><br>Review all CVC vs. CVCe<br><br>Contrast final *-k*, *-ck*, *-ke*.<br><br>Compare short and common long vowel patterns: short *a*, *a-e*, *ai*; short *o*, *o-e*, *oa*; short *u*, *u-e*, *oo*, *ui*; short *e*, *ee*, *ea*.<br><br>Review all CVVC patterns<br><br>Compare all long vowel patterns: *a*, *a-e*, *ai*, *ay*; *e*, *ee*, *e*; *o*, *o-e*, *oa*, *ow*; *u*, *u-e*, *ew*, *ue*; *i*, *i-e*, *igh*, *y*; VCC in *il*, *in*, *ol*, *os*. | Long and short vowel in word sorts: short *a*, *a-e*; short *i*, *i-e*; short *o*, *o-e*; short *u*, *u-e*.<br><br>Contrast final *-k*, *-ck*, *-ke*.<br><br>Compare short and common long vowel patterns: short *a*, *a-e*, *ai*; short *o*, *o-e*, *oa*; short *u*, *u-e*, *oo*, *ui*; short *e*, *ee*, *ea*.<br><br>Compare all long vowel patterns: *a*, *a-e*, *ai*, *ay*; *e*, *ee*, *ea*; *o*, *o-e*, *oa*, *ow*; *u*, *u-e*, *ew*, *ue*; *i*, *i-e*, *igh*, *y*; VCC in *il*, *in*, *ol*, *os*. | Compare all vowel patterns: *a*, *a-e*, *ai*, *ay*; *e*, *ee*, *ea*; *o*, *o-e*, *oa*, *ow*; *u*, *u-e*, *ew*, *ue*; *i*, *i-e*, *igh*, *y*; VCC in *il*, *in*, *ol*, *os*. |
| *Middle Within Word Pattern*: R-influenced Vowels, Diphthongs, and Ambiguous Vowels | | |
| Contrast short *a* and *o* with with *ar* and *or*.<br><br>Contrast *r*-influenced vowels: *a-e*, *are*, *air*; *er*, *ere*, *eer*, *ear*; *i-e*, *ire*, *ier*; *o-e*, *oar*, *ore*, *oor*; *ur*, *ure*, *ur-e*; *or*, *ur*, *ir*; *w+or*, *w+ar*.<br><br>Review *ar*, *er*, *ir*, *ur*, *or*. | Contrast *r*-influenced vowels: *a-e*, *are*, *air*: *er*, *ere*, *eer*, *ear*; *i-e*, *ire*, *ier*; *o-e*, *oar*, *ore*, *oor*; *ur*, *ure*, *ur-e*; *or*, *ur*, *ir*; *w+or*, *w+ar*. | Contrast *r*-influenced vowels: *a-e*, *are*, *air*; *er*, *ere*, *eer*, *ear*; *i-e*, *ire*, *ier*; *o-e*, *oar*, *ore*, *oor*; *ur*, *ure*, *ur-e*; *or*, *ur*, *ir*; *w+or*, *w+ar*. |
| Contrast long *o*, *oi*, and *oy*.<br><br>Contrast diphthongs and ambiguous vowels: *oo*; *ou*, *ow*; *oi*, *oy*, *ou*, *ow*; *al*, *aw*; *al*, *au*, *aw*, *wa*, *al*, *ough*.<br><br>Review *ow*, *ew*, *aw*. | Contrast diphthongs and ambiguous vowels: *oo*; *ou*, *ow*; *oi*, *oy*, *ou*, *ow*; *al*, *aw*; *al*, *au*, *aw*; *wa*, *al*, *ough*. | Contrast diphthongs and ambiguous vowels: *oi*, *oy*, *ou*, *ow*; *al*, *au*, *a*; *wa*, *al*, *ough*. |
| *Late Within Word Pattern*: Complex Consonants and Homophones | | |
| Contrast complex consonants: *kn*, *wr*, *gn*; *sh*, *shr*, *th*, *thr*, *scr*, *str*, *spr*, *spl*, *squ*; *dge*, *ge*; *ch*, *tch*; *ce*, *se*, *ve*, *ge*.<br><br>Contrast hard/soft *c* and *g*.<br><br>Homophones. | Contrast complex consonants as needed:<br><br>Compare *dge*, *ge*; *tch*, *ch*.<br><br>Contrast hard/soft *c* and *g*.<br><br>Homophones. | Contrast complex consonants as needed:<br><br>Compare *dge*, *ge*; *tch*, *ch*.<br><br>Contrast hard/soft *g* and *c*. |
| *Miscellaneous*: Contractions, Plurals, and Irregular Vowels | | |

Many teachers are expected to use their school district's adopted phonics or spelling program and/or their district's core reading program. Although these published programs may follow a developmental sequence similar to the one in Table 6.5, they often set a pace that is too fast for low-achieving students and do not supply enough practice to master the features. To differentiate instruction at students' developmental levels, you must monitor progress and adjust the lessons by adding extra sorts for students who need a slower pace or skip some sorts to increase the pace when possible.

Keep in mind that studying vowel patterns in single-syllable words lays a critical foundation for studying two-syllable words in the next stage and cannot be shortchanged. Perhaps 25 percent of the adult population in the United States is stunted at this point of literacy proficiency. Even community college and university students who are poor spellers benefit from beginning their word study by reviewing vowel sounds and their spelling patterns (Massengill, 2006). It is important to take a step back and conduct word study activities that help students cement their knowledge of vowel patterns in single-syllable words to get a running start as they study two-syllable words. For many of these students, the fast pace in the third column of Table 6.5 may be appropriate.

## The Study of High-Frequency Words

A few spelling programs feature high-frequency or high-utility words. The authors of these programs argue that spelling instruction should focus on a small core of words students need the most, such as *said, because, there, they're, friend,* and *again,* and because such words are irregular they simply must be memorized. Unfortunately, this narrow view of word study ignores the relationship between reading and spelling, and it offers students no opportunity to form generalizations that can extend to reading and spelling of thousands of unstudied words (Miles, Rubin & Frey, 2018).

There are high-frequency words that do not follow common spelling pattern-to-sound conventions, and they should be included in within word pattern sorts as oddballs. For example, *said* is usually examined with other words that have the *ai* pattern, such as *paid, faint,* and *wait.* It becomes memorable because it stands alone in contrast to the many words that work as the pattern would suggest. Most students are more likely to spell it correctly after noting its difference with *paid* and *wait.* Note that most of the top 300 most frequently occurring words listed on page 467 (Dolch, 1942; Fry, 1980; Zeno, Ivens, Millard, & Duvvuri, 1996) are covered in the suggested word sorts by the end of the within word pattern stage. See Appendix F for a list of high-frequency words compiled by Fry.

There are also some words that students need to write frequently in the lower grades that are not included in the weekly word study lessons designed to meet their developmental needs. An example is *because,* which occurs often in the writings of first graders. Many teachers accept students' inventions for such words (BECUZ, BECALZ, BECAWS), but some teachers grow tired of and concerned about such errors, especially beyond the primary grades. Although we feel confident that such errors will be worked out over time with developmentally appropriate instruction, there are good reasons to address them sooner.

However, asking students to memorize high-frequency words as whole words without any attention to their internal sounds and spelling patterns is not the answer (Mesmer & Duke, 2016). Instead, the teaching of high-frequency words should follow the same procedures for instruction in word decoding in general.

High-frequency word "give" in word study notebook under oddball column

As you discuss high-frequency words with your students, be sure to ask,

- "What part of this word do you *already* know how to spell?"
  (For *friend*, within word pattern spellers will already know how to spell the *fr*.)
- "What part of this word might be hard to remember and why?"
  (For *friend*, focus on the fact that it has a silent *i*.)
- "What might help you remember how to spell this word?" (Students might note that it ends with *end*.)

## TEACHING TIPS

### Teaching High-Frequency Words

Consider the following suggestions when teaching high-frequency words at the within word pattern stage:

1. Analyze the words. Ask students to listen for the sounds within high-frequency words and note the individual letter–sounds and spelling patterns that are consistent and inconsistent with each those sounds. Break down a word like *said* into its three phonemes (that is, /s/-/ĕ/-/d/) and discuss which sounds are consistent with its corresponding spelling and which ones aren't. In the case of *said*, only the *ai* is inconsistent with the phoneme /ĕ/. Ask students to say how the word *said* should be pronounced if it followed the generalization for the *ai* pattern (/s/-/ā/-/d/). This kind of discussion builds a phonological representation of the word, which supports the learning of its spelling pattern (Ehri, 2004).

2. Play Friends and Enemies. In Friends and Enemies, students use high-frequency words like *take* as a springboard for categorizing other CVCe words into groups of friends and enemies. *Make, take, came, made, name*, would all be *take's* friend—but the word *have* would be *take's* enemy. After a while, students can note which high-frequency words have more friends than enemies, or vice versa. The high frequency word *play* has many friends with the AY pattern (*may, say, way*, and so on) but quite a few enemies that use the EY pattern instead (*they, prey, grey, hey*) (Rawlins & Invernizzi, 2019).

3. Teach high-frequency words in groups that have similar spelling patterns. For example, instead of teaching the word *above* as a rule breaker, show how it is similar to *love, shove,* and *glove*. The first syllable of *because* might be pronounced like /buh/, but so is the first syllable of is *begin, before, between*, and *behind* (Warley, Invernizzi & Drake, 2015). You might not pronounce the second syllable of *because* exactly like *pause*, but noting the similarities helps remember the spelling.

4. Help students use high-frequency words they know to figure out words they don't know. If students know the word *could*, they can figure out the words *should* or *would*. If they know the word *own*, they can figure out the words *shown* or *grown*. Ehri, Satlow, & Gaskins (2009) demonstrated that students who were taught to analyze the letter-sound relationships within high-frequency words were better able to generalize from those words to new words. They could say, "If I know *found*, then I know *around*." Engaging in word operations in the word study notebook, as described in Chapter 3 (page 68) helps students learn to generalize in this way.

5. Practice reading high-frequency words in isolation and in context. Miles and Ehri (2017) found that the students in their study learned word meanings better with practice in context but they learned letter-sound associations better with practice in isolation. Therefore, to unite the meaning, pronunciation, and spelling of a word, both contextual and isolated practice are necessary.

# Vocabulary Instruction

There are many ways you can help students develop a deeper, richer oral vocabulary. Use sophisticated language in daily interactions (see page 165), and develop the habit of commenting on and making observations about words throughout the day. Read-alouds, word sorts, and concept sorts provide opportunities to discuss new words and focus on multiple meanings. Students in this stage should start using a dictionary as a reference tool and begin studying common prefixes and suffixes and how they affect the meaning of the base words to which they attach. See other vocabulary activities in chapter 5 (5.1-5.7)

## Read Alouds

Good children's literature and informational texts are the best starting place for vocabulary instruction and are much richer sources than television or adult daily conversation (Cunningham, Stanovich & West, 1994; McKeown & Curtis, 2014). Picture books and chapter books are full of new, rich vocabulary that is wrapped in complex sentences. Discussion is the key to unpacking the meanings of new words from read-alouds, and with your help, students can learn to use context to infer the meanings of new words. During and after listening to books read aloud, encourage students to talk about what they heard. Use the think-pair-share strategy described in Chapter 5 (Activity 5.2) to maximize the opportunity for everyone to use oral language.

## Repeated Exposure

When learning new vocabulary during this stage, students benefit from repeated exposure to words and from seeing the words in print as they hear them (Beck, McKeown, & Kucan, 2013; Rosenthal & Ehri, 2008). To help students, record words on cards, charts, and webs; post them for everyone to see; and refer to them as a reminder to use them in conversation throughout the day. It takes many exposures, over several weeks and in multiple contexts for students to learn a new word, so be deliberate when using new words and encouraging students to use them as well. Refer to Chapter 5 for anchored vocabulary instruction in Activity 5.1 (Juel, Biancarosa, Coker, & Deffes, 2003).

## Word Sorts and Vocabulary

Always take the time to read through words in a spelling sort to be sure students know the meanings. Most of the words will be familiar ones, unless students are English learners, but there are still opportunities to explore the meaning layer of English, most specifically in the case of homophones, homonyms, and polysemous words, or words with more than one meaning.

Homophone pear/pair tree

**HOMOPHONES.** Students will encounter many **homophones** during this stage—these words that sound the same but are spelled differently provide rich fodder for vocabulary development. Why is *thrown*, the verb, spelled with an *ow*? Because the vowel-consonant-*e* pattern is already taken for the noun *throne*—the chair occupied by kings and queens. The spelling pattern reflects the different meaning! Share with students that we spell these words differently because they mean different things! This insight provides a fun and interesting approach to both spelling and vocabulary instruction.

**HOMONYMS.** English is also rich in **homonyms**—words that sound the same and are also spelled the same despite the fact that they have different meanings. You can *park* (verb) the car or play in the *park* (noun). You might *tire* (verb) easily while climbing up a mountain but have to change the *tire* (noun) when it's flat. Discussing the multiple meanings of these words leverages vocabulary learning and leads the way to an understanding of the polysemy of words—their multiple meanings. Consider a simple homonym like *block*—something you build with, something you run around in the neighborhood, something you might do during a soccer game, or something you might do to your calendar to save a portion of time.

**HOMOGRAPHS.** There are also **homographs**—words spelled alike but pronounced differently, depending on their verb tense or part of speech. You can *read* a book or discuss one that you *read* yesterday. You can *wind* the string around a stick or lose your hat in the *wind*. Look for these words in word sorts and take the time to explore their multiple meanings through discussion, illustration, and examples in sentences.

**TEACHING TIPS**

## Teaching About Homophones

1. Create an ongoing collection, such as a Homophone Pear/Pair Tree, as a whole-class activity in second- or third-grade classrooms that goes on all year long. When students discover a homophone pair, ask them to write it on a pear shape and then add it to the branch of a tree posted on a bulletin board. This encourages students to always be on the lookout for homophones. They will truly become wordsmiths as they collect hundreds of homophones, such as the ones on page 477 in Appendix F. Usually there is one homophone in a pair that is familiar (*bear*), while the other one (*bare*) is what Beck and colleagues (2013) call a Tier 2 word. These are words that students can use in multiple contexts and are part of the *general academic* vocabulary that students need to acquire throughout the school years (Templeton et al., 2015). As teachers, we can never *rest* until we *wrest* every ounce of meaning from word study!
2. A class homophone book is shown in Figure 3.11. Students can be invited to add drawings to the book when homophones turn up.
3. Look for games in the Activities section. Homophone Win Lose and Draw (6.22), Homophone Rummy (6.23) and Concentration (6.26) are favorites.
4. Share books that feature homophones and homonyms such has those listed in the Resource Connections. Our favorites are *The King Who Rained* and others by Fred Gwynne.

**RESOURCE CONNECTIONS**

## Books that Celebrate Homophones, Homonyms, and Homographs

*The King Who Rained (1988)*, *A Chocolate Moose for Dinner* (1988) and *A Little Pigeon Toad* (1988) by Fred Gwynne

*Eight Ate: A feast of Homonym Riddles* by Marvin Turban

*Dear Deer: A Book of Homophones* (2010), *Zoola Palooza: A Book of Homographs* (2011), *The Bat Can Bat: A Book of True Homophones* (2018), and *The Bass Plays the Bass and Other Homographs* (2018) by Gene Barretta

*How Much Can a Bare Bear Bear?* (2007) by Brian Cleary and Brian Gable

*The Dove Dove: Funny Homograph Riddles* (2008) by Marvin Terban

*If You Were a Homonym or a Homophone* (2007) by Nancy Loewen and Sara Gray

**POLYSEMOUS WORDS AND IDIOMS.** **Polysemous** words and phrases share meaning in their origin, like *bed*, a place for sleeping and the place where a stream runs, or the two meanings of *head*, a part of the body or the chief of an organization. But even simple words like *run* can have more than one meaning. There can be a *run* on the stock market, or a *run* in your stocking; your nose can *run*, and a salmon *run* is when they migrate upstream. Be sure to point out how context helps to determine which meaning should be taken into account and include **idiomatic expressions** in your discussions. What does it mean to *run against the grain*? What is a *dry run*? What does it mean if something *runs in your family*? Are you giving me *the run around*? So much of comprehension depends on these more abstract, often metaphorical uses of word meanings. Native speakers and English learners alike benefit from spending time discussing the multiple meanings of words and the context clues that tell us which meaning is relevant.

*for* **English learners**

**CONCEPT SORTS.** Studying subjects such as math, science, and social studies exposes students to many new ideas and vocabulary that they can explore through concept sorts. In Activity 6.1, we describe a concept sort with math terms related to addition (*plus, combine, increase*) and subtraction (*take away, difference, decrease*) and also offer other examples. To prepare concept sorts, preview the vocabulary in textbooks or other curricular materials looking for the key terms, and then write them on cards or sorting templates like the one in Appendix G. Work with students to brainstorm words on a particular topic (for example, words related to outer space, government words, or key vocabulary words from other content areas) that can then be sorted into categories.

Plan a concept sort for the beginning of a study unit as an informal assessment of background knowledge. Begin by going over the words to be sure students can read them and are familiar with the meanings of the words (they will develop deeper understanding with repeated exposure). Students can sort the words as an **open sort** either individually or with a partner. This enables you to see what students know about a topic and get a sense of the difficulty of the reading. Similarly, at the end of a study unit, ask students to complete the sort again and add related words to show what they learned.

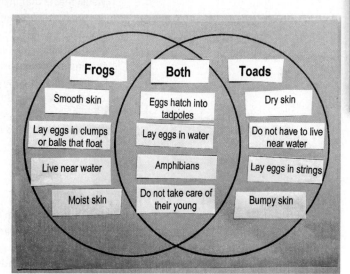

Concept sort for frogs and toads

## Dictionary Use

All kinds of dictionaries and thesauruses are important resources for within word pattern stage students. Students in the beginning of this stage can start using dictionaries to check word meanings. This does not mean students should be assigned to look up ten definitions to fulfill a seatwork or homework requirement—a strategy sure to make them dislike dictionaries. Instead, use a dictionary as a resource during reading groups, class discussions, word study lessons, and content area study to answer questions, resolve disagreements, and/or to provide information. For example, the dictionary can help students understand what *vent* means in the sentence "Josh had to vent when he got outside with his friends."

## Teaching Basic Morphology: Prefixes and Suffixes

Students learn to spell prefixes and suffixes in the next stage—syllables and affixes. However, they are taught simple affixes as meaning vocabulary beginning in late first and early second grade, when most students are developmentally in the within word pattern stage of spelling. Understanding how simple affixes combine with base words lays the foundation for more extensive exploration in forming words later on. But words with affixes are explored first as vocabulary words that students encounter during reading and content studies. They should not be treated as spelling words until students know how to spell the base words on which they are built.

## Teach Dictionary Skills

1. Model the use of dictionaries. Keep dictionaries handy and use them often to look up definitions, to check spellings, or to answer questions such as, "Do many words begin with *QU*?" Model for students how interesting and informative dictionaries can be and show them how they are organized.

2. After students have some skill using alphabetical order and guide words, take turns assigning a student each day to be the "dictionary meister" responsible for looking up any word that the class is curious about. Or, when introducing a new sort, ask students to each look up one word and report what they found out, particularly the multiple meanings of homonyms like *drive*, or *fudge*.

3. Children's dictionaries are most appropriate for second to fourth grade, where you will find most within word pattern spellers. Modern dictionaries, such as the *Merriam-Webster Children's Dictionary* published by DK, are visual feasts that invite students to browse.

4. See Activities 6.7 and 6.8 for resources and ideas about teaching dictionary skills.

5. Over the course of this stage, build a word reference area in your class library that includes thesauruses; various dictionaries (like rhyming dictionaries); Spanish and other language dictionaries; and books of antonyms, synonyms, and homophones. Although students' spelling focuses on the single-syllable word patterns, students can use these references to learn more about the meaning of two- and three-syllable words.

The most common prefixes in the English language are *un-* (meaning "not"), *re-* ("again"), *in-* ("not"), and *dis-* ("not"), and account for about 58 percent of all prefixes (White, Sowell, & Yanagihara, 1989). Some state standards mandate studying the prefixes *un-* and *re-* as well as the suffixes *-ly*, *-ful*, *and -y*, and the comparatives *-er/-est* in second grade. Use frequently occurring and easily understood words to walk students through a discussion of, for example, *small/smaller/smallest* versus *tall/taller/tallest* to learn how suffixes are added to a base word to change the meaning. Beginning with the base word *care*, talk about being *careful* and watching over a baby brother or sister *carefully*. Appendix F has lists of words with prefixes and suffixes.

# Assess and Monitor Progress in the Within Word Pattern Stage

By the end of second grade, most students should be well into the middle of the within word pattern stage or beyond. Students who are not should be getting carefully planned systematic word study in supplemental interventions. There are several ways to monitor students' progress in the within word pattern stage.

## Weekly Spelling Tests

In this stage, we recommend weekly spelling tests as a way to both monitor progress and to make students accountable for their learning. Select at least ten words from the sort and call them out in a traditional way. Many teachers also call out one or two transfer words—words that fit the features but that were not included in the sort. Prompt students to use analogy by saying something like, "If you know how to spell *rain*, then you can spell *stain*." When students are appropriately placed they should score 90 to 100 percent on these weekly assessments. If they do not, you should reconsider the placement or pacing of instruction. Also consider whether students are getting enough practice with the words across a week. We also recommend designing your weekly spelling test as a **blind writing sort**, having students sort the words into categories as they write them. This rewards the kind of thinking about sound, pattern, and meaning that is the whole point of word study. Give one point for the correct spelling and a second point for the correct grouping.

## Monitoring Progress and Setting Goals

Teachers often observe that students study for weekly tests and then forget the words when they need them for real writing (Gill & Scharer, 1996; Graham et al., 2008; Schlagal, 2013). For this reason, we recommend periodic unit spell checks to determine whether the words and features are retained over time. Spell checks have been developed for each of the major units of study and can be found in Appendix B or in *Words Their Way®: Word Sorts for Within Word Pattern Spellers, 3rd edition.*

You can easily create your own spell checks to use every three to six weeks by selecting words from the word sorts to assess retention of studied words and perhaps including additional transfer words to see whether students can apply their growing knowledge of sounds and patterns to unstudied words. Use these spell checks to monitor progress and fine-tune your instructional pacing. Depending on results, you may find you need to drop back to a slower pace or ratchet up to a quicker pace, as suggested in Table 6.5.

Students in the within word pattern stage can be involved in setting their own goals, using the forms described in Chapter 2 and found in Appendix B. This is especially beneficial for older students who struggle with spelling and need to see their own progress.

**Enhanced eText**
**Video Example 6.10**
Ms. Flores discusses assessing and monitoring progress with her second graders.

## Strategies for Assessing and Monitoring Progress of English Learners

When setting goals and planning word study with English learners it is important to know something about their native languages and what literacy experiences they have had. As discussed in "Teaching Vowels to English Learners" on page 214, students who are literate in their first language may spell the sounds they hear in English with the letter–sound correspondences they know from their first language, or if the sounds do not exist they will substitute close approximations. Knowing something about students' native languages and writing systems is helpful so you can guide comparisons and understand the difficulties English learners face.

*for* **English learners**

Some English learners can memorize many words, but their strategies for spelling unknown words often indicate that their orthographic knowledge could be deeper. For example, a student memorized the spelling of *rain* but continued to spell unknown long *a* words with an e (*train* as TREN), using the Spanish spelling of the long *a* sound as shown in Table 6.3. The spelling errors in uncorrected writing and spelling inventories described in Chapter 2 reveal what word knowledge English learners bring to the task of reading and writing English.

There may be times when you want to assess students' spelling development in their primary languages. Inventories for Spanish, Chinese, and Korean are available in *Words Their Way® with English Learners*. Inventories such as the *Spanish Spelling Inventory* will help you find out what students know about their own written language (Ford, Invernizzi & Huang, 2018). The more literate students are in their first language, the more information there is to transfer to learning to read in English (Proctor, August, Carlo, & Snow, 2006).

**Enhanced eText**
**Teacher Resource:**
Spanish Spelling Inventory

# Word Study Routines for Within Word Pattern Spellers

The within word pattern stage easily spans a number of grade levels, usually from first to fourth grade and beyond that for struggling students. A typical third-grade class will have students in the middle and late within word pattern stage, as well as students in the next stage, syllables and affixes. Differentiation occurs when students meet in small groups in which sorts are introduced and discussed under your guidance. However, after that, everyone can engage in the same weekly routines described in Chapter 3 (blind sorts, writing sorts, word hunts, speed sorts, word operations, homework). Table 9.4 (page 354 in Chapter 9) shows a weekly schedule for students in the within word pattern stage, and Table 9.5 (page 355 in Chapter 9) offers a variation on this. After students learn the schedule and the routines, they can work independently, with partners, or in small groups on most days of the week, freeing you to meet with reading groups. As in the letter name–alphabetic stage, you might find that reading groups are usually the same as the word study groups.

When word study follows the small-group reading lesson, more connections can be made between reading, writing, spelling, and vocabulary. Although vocabulary instruction usually takes place in whole-group settings, during read-alouds, and during content area instruction, conducting word study at the end of a small-group reading lesson creates additional opportunities to link to similar vocabulary. You might be learning about *dictators* in social studies, but in the reading group you might encounter the word *predict* and look it up in the *dictionary*. This is a great opportunity to discuss the meaning of the root *dict*, which means to say or to speak. A *dictionary* is a book that speaks about words. People who a ruled by a *dictator* have no say in what happens in their county. The prefix *pre-* means "before." To *predict* is to say what might happen or what might have happened before you really know. Now that links have been made between a content-area vocabulary word, *dictator*, and a word encountered and discussed in the small reading group, *predict*, students may be more equipped to figure out the meaning of other words with *dict* in them, such as *diction*, or *edict* (Templeton et al, 2015). Including word study in the reading group time extends the study of words beyond phonics and spelling to include the vocabulary that students are seeing and hearing, which typically exceed their level of spelling development.

Word study notebook

## Word Study Notebooks

A word study notebook is an essential tool in the within word pattern stage and provides an organizational structure and documentation of student work. It is used across the week for a number of activities (see Chapter 3) and students should have ready access to it throughout the day. Ask students to bring their notebook to small-group sessions, along with reading materials and response journals or logs. We recommend using sturdy stitched composition notebooks with a hard-marbleized cover or 3-brad folders with notebook paper and dividing them into several sections set off with a tab or sticky note. Word cards can be stored in a library pocket or envelope glued to the back cover and replaced each week. The sections might serve different purposes, as described next:

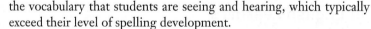

1.  Students record their weekly sort, word hunt, and other activities such as Word Operations in the word study section. Ask students to summarize what they learn from their sorts in their own words as shown in Figure 6.9.
2.  Students record words from their reading or from content area instruction in the vocabulary section. For example, when reading *Stuart Little* encourage students to make lists of boat terms (*rigging, bow, stern*) or weather-related words (*squall, breeze, mist*). These words can be shared and then combined and sorted into semantic categories or added, where possible,

to the spelling sorts (for example, add *breeze* to a long *e* category of *ee* patterns). Students might create a science web on pandas, make a list of concepts related to immigration, or compare and contrast geometric terms.

3. A third section might be an ongoing list of homophones, homographs, idiomatic expressions, and polysemous words, with sentences or pictures to illustrate the different meanings.

Incorporating the use of the word study notebook into the English language arts and other content area instruction encourages students to truly become word conscious—always on the lookout for interesting words that can be analyzed by sound, pattern, and meaning. Used in the ways described here and in Chapter 3 (pages 67–76), word study notebooks play a critical role in vocabulary learning across the content areas and increases students' awareness of how the spelling of words is also critical to their understanding of word meanings, something they will study in even greater depth in the next two stages.

**FIGURE 6.9** Written Reflection below a Writing Sort in a Word Study Notebook

| flag | ca**ge** | bri**dge** |
| plug | huge | smudge |
| drug | page | lodge |
| drag | stage | ridge |
| blog | | pledge |
| | | fudge |

GE at the end of a word is soft like J. DGE comes after a short vowel.

## Homework

Homework provides another opportunity to practice analyzing how the spelling patterns in words represent pronunciations and meaning. In addition to much needed practice, homework also serves an important role in communicating with parents and caregivers. Not only do word study notebooks provide an organizational structure for your daily word study instruction, but they also provide a record of student work and document what they are learning. For these reasons, we recommend that word study homework be conducted in the word study notebook and that the expectations for doing so be incorporated into your word study notebook routines. This means that the word study notebook will be sent back and forth between home and school, with parents signing off that they have read through the notebook each week.

Many teachers review their students' work in the word study notebook on a weekly if not daily basis and provide a weekly grade. Grading expectations are described in further detail in Chapter 9, as well as the details of a parent letter describing homework routines for each day of the week. To preview here, parents deserve to be informed of the daily routines expected to be completed in the notebook—such as sorting words into categories (on Monday), completing a writing sort (on Tuesday), going on a word hunt (on Wednesday), doing a blind sort (on Thursday), or a similar routine that are the same every week for at least a marking period. These routines are especially appropriate for within word pattern spellers for whom homework will provide much needed extra practice.

It's also important to communicate clearly with parents that their children will be held accountable for what they've been taught in phonics and spelling, but, at the same time, they won't be penalized for what they haven't yet been taught (see Table 3.3 in Chapter 3). The word study notebook provides the perfect vehicle for communicating what has been taught.

## RESOURCES FOR IMPLEMENTING WORD STUDY *in Your Classroom*

A number of materials are available to help you implement word study with students in the within word pattern stage that have been mentioned throughout this chapter. Here is a summary.

1. Suggested sorts in Appendix E can be used with the template on page 502, and the word lists in Appendix F can be used to create your own sorts.

2. Prepared sorts and games are available on the website for *WTW Digital*. With the Create Your Own feature, you can make your own sorts.

3. *Words Their Way®: Word Sorts for Within Word Pattern Spellers* provides a complete curriculum of sorts divided into ten units. The spell checks that are supplied for each unit can be used for pretesting to better identify what students are ready to study and for post-testing to monitor progress.

4. *Words Their Way: Within Word Pattern Sorts for Spanish-Speaking English Speakers* helps students to focus on English vowel sounds and grow their vocabularies.

# ACTIVITIES for the Within Word Pattern Stage

Several vocabulary activities are described first in this section followed by some dictionary activities. The remaining games and activities are designed to extend and reinforce spelling sorts.

## Vocabulary Activities

Refer to vocabulary activities in Chapter 5 (5.1 to 5.5) that are also appropriate for this stage.

### 6.1 Concept Sort for Math

Concept sorts are an excellent way for students to work with vocabulary related to units of study. In this example, students categorize terms related to addition and subtraction that they are likely to encounter in word problems.

**MATERIALS** Prepare a set of word cards with the terms to sort on the front and sample word problems on the back using the terms. For example, "*Take away*. If I have three books and you *take away* two, how many will I have?" If you want students to work with these terms individually, use a blank template and write the terms in the boxes in random order. Set off the headers in bold or underline.

**PROCEDURES**
1. Remind students that there are many words that mean the same thing as "add" and "subtract" and that these words will show up in written word problems.
2. Set up the headers, *Add* and *Subtract*. Introduce each new term in a simple problem sentence. "*Lost*. I had 10 pencils and I *lost* three so how many do I have left?" Or "*Difference*. What is the *difference* between six goals and three goals? Do I add or subtract to get the answer?"
3. Continue to sort all the terms, discussing where the terms should go and why. The final sort will look something like the following set of lists. Put the words in a student activity center for students to sort independently or give students their own sheets to cut apart and sort.

| add + | | subtract − | |
|---|---|---|---|
| and | plus | minus | difference |
| in all | more | take away | leave/left |
| combine | sum | lost | less |
| increase | join | decrease | delete |
| together | | fewer | reduce |

Challenge students to write their own word problems using the terms.

**VARIATIONS** You can add terms for multiplication and division. Many content area terms and concepts can be sorted in a similar manner. Simply write words into a template or onto cards, draw a simple figure, or use an online search engine to find pictures and images you can download. A book of mathematics sorts is also available across the elementary grades (Helman, Cramer, Johnston, and Bear, 2016). Use both pictures and words when appropriate. Here are more examples:

1. Geometric shapes: quadrilaterals, hexagons, right triangle, equilateral triangle
2. Open and closed figures

3. Objects that will or will not be attracted to a magnet
4. Food groups: protein, fruits, vegetables
5. Parts of speech: nouns, verbs, adjectives, adverbs (see Figure 6.10)
6. Animals by carnivores, herbivores, or omnivores; mammals, birds, reptiles, and amphibians
7. Things we can and cannot recycle
8. States of matter: solids, liquids, and gas
9. Simple machines: lever, pulley, wedge, inclined plane, wheel, screw
10. Fact and opinion statements
11. Habitats and the plants and animals that live there
12. Equivalent fractions
13. Objects you would or would not see used by settlers or Native Americans of the Old West

**FIGURE 6.10** Sorting Words by Part of Speech

## 6.2 Semantic Brainstorms

This small-group activity focuses on the meanings of the words and serves as a great activity for content studies.

### PROCEDURES

1. Choose a topic related to an area of study. Start with easy, familiar topics such as sports (or countries, animal life, clothes, furniture, or modes of transportation).
2. Have students brainstorm related words and then record them using chart paper or an interactive whiteboard.
3. Ask students to share their findings and see whether they can come up with subcategories from their brainstorming. Categories can be circled by color or written over into columns.

**VARIATIONS** Look in magazines, newspapers, and catalogs. Circle words that express feelings, colors, people's names, or parts of speech. Use organizing software to record these brainstorms electronically, to be moved about on an interactive white board; use software for drawing graphics the same way. You can record student responses within circles and rectangles using the drawing toolbar in PowerPoint software.

## 6.3 Semantic Sorts

Students work with content-related words to compare and contrast. In Figure 6.11, terms related to bees have been sorted into categories.

### PROCEDURES

1. Look through a chapter or unit in a textbook and make a list of the key terms; they are often listed at the end of a unit. Make word cards for the words or fill in a template such as the one in Appendix G.
2. Have students work alone or with partners to sort the words in an open sort, establishing their own categories. Then bring everyone together to compare and defend their groupings.
3. When doing a sort to introduce a unit of study, do not evaluate student groupings as right or wrong. Let disagreements or errors be the basis for questions to be answered with further study. For example, students might logically put royal jelly under "benefits" of honeybees. Rather than telling them where it should go, say something like, "I see that there is some disagreement about where to put royal jelly. As we read about honeybees we will pay special attention to this term."
4. Have students sort words again after a unit of study is finished. They can copy the sorts into word study notebooks in a separate section for that content area, and be used as one way to evaluate student learning.

**FIGURE 6.11** Honey Bee Semantic Sort

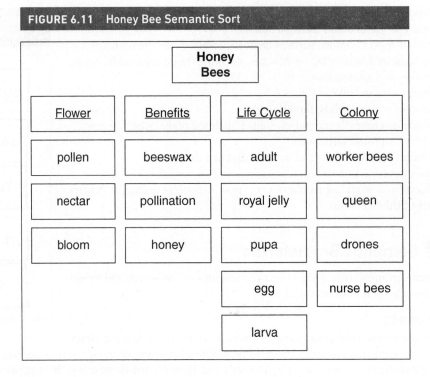

## 6.4 Shades of Meaning

This small-group activity focuses on the nuances of meaning among words in the same semantic category. It is useful for nurturing word consciousness in writing as well as reading. The activity focuses on the discussion and not on whether the order is right or wrong.

### PROCEDURES

1. Choose a vocabulary word that is essential to understanding a particular book or topic of study. For example, you might choose *stampede* from Scieszka's *The Good, the Bad, and the Goofy*, because this term describes so much of the action in this book.
2. Come up with other words that are similar to a *stampede* (noun): a *charge, rush, flight, mad dash*, and so on. Students can also contribute words.
3. Have students place the words along a continuum of strength (*move, rush, flight, mad dash, charge, stampede*) and then discuss the reasoning for their arrangement. Students might say that a charge is more forceful than a *rush*, or a *stampede* is even stronger than a *charge*.

## 6.5 "Said Is Dead" and "Good-Bye Good"

As students increase their writing fluency their word choices should reflect a more extensive and vivid vocabulary. These two activities are frequently used across the grades to help students add spice to their writing.

**MATERIALS** You will need a thesaurus for every small group, as well as chart paper, a projector, and models of either exemplary or tired writing. Some teachers use chart paper cut in the shape of a headstone. You can find prepared posters of "Said Is Dead" and other word lists online, but it is better to have students create their own and add to them.

### PROCEDURES

1. Begin with a piece of writing (a student sample or something that you create) and project it for all to see. Look through the selection for overused words, such as the verb *said* or the adjective *good*. Then project a piece of literature with a variety of words for contrast.

2. Create a vocabulary chart that students may use for their own writing and brainstorm other words to use in place of *said or good*. Students can refer to a thesaurus for related words. Post the chart where students can refer to it and continue to add to it over time. A brief list of words developed by students to replace *said* might include the following:

| | | | | |
|---|---|---|---|---|
| yelled | declared | laughed | ordered | scolded |
| remarked | screamed | blurted | demanded | argued |
| exclaimed | cried | boasted | requested | whispered |
| chuckled | explained | asked | muttered | suggested |

3. Another list to replace *good* might include the following:

| | | | | |
|---|---|---|---|---|
| fantastic | awesome | wonderful | lovely | superb |
| cool | joyful | fabulous | super | excellent |
| exciting | terrific | perfect | beautiful | pleasant |
| marvelous | enjoyable | great | honorable | compassionate |

# Spelling Strategies and Dictionary Skills

## 6.6 Have-a-Go Sheets

Asking students to try spelling a word several ways is an important strategy because identifying the vowel sound and then thinking of different possible patterns is one of the key goals of instruction in the within word pattern stage.

**MATERIALS** Prepare blank forms like the one in Figure 6.12. While these forms are not necessary—students can write the word in the margin of their paper or on a scrap of paper—they help when first introducing the strategy to students. Keeping a special form in a writing folder can serve as a reminder and also a record of a student's efforts.

**PROCEDURES**

1. Students can use the Have-a-Go sheets any time they are writing, and keep them in their writing folders. However, the sheets might be used specifically when students are editing pieces that will be taken to a finished state.

**FIGURE 6.12   Have-a-Go Sheet**

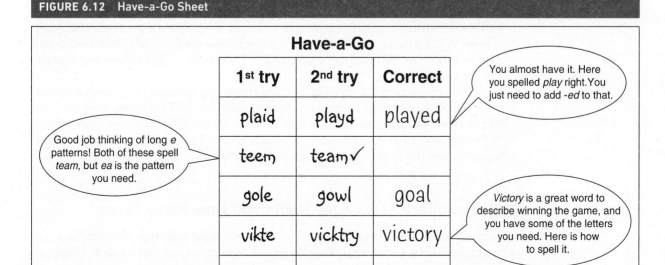

*Source:* Based on Parry, J., & Hornsby, D. (1988). *Write On: A Conference Approach to Writing.* Portsmouth, NH: Heinemann.

2. Expect students to make two attempts to spell a word they need and consider which one might "look right." Only then can they go to you to ask for help.

3. You can then see where the students need assistance, compliment them on what they figured out, and make suggestions about what else is needed, supply the correct spelling, or even confirm that they got it right! Figure 6.12 contains examples of the kinds of feedback you can use.

## 6.7 Dictionary Skills for Within Word Pattern Spellers

During the within word pattern stage, students can learn some essential dictionary skills and begin to use simplified dictionaries to look up the meanings of words.

**MATERIALS** You will need beginning dictionaries or elementary dictionaries that are best for students first learning to look up words. These look like traditional dictionaries but include the most common words with brief entries. However, they are not as limited as the picture dictionaries described in Chapter 5. If you do not have sets available in your classroom check with your school librarian, who might have sets that you can borrow. We recommend the following:

*DK Children's Illustrated Dictionary*
*Merriam-Webster Children's Dictionary*
*Scholastic Dictionary of Spelling*

**PROCEDURES**

1. Teach alphabetical order up to the second or third letter. Occasionally ask students to put their word sort for the week into alphabetical order before copying it down in their word study notebooks. To start, supply students with an alphabet strip to use as a guide and only require alphabetizing by the first letter. Next, take away the strip and then move on to using the second and even third letter to put words in order.

2. To help with dictionary searches, divide up the alphabet into early, middle, and late sections so students develop a sense of where a letter appears in the alphabetical sequence. Divide an alphabet strip into thirds then model how to think about where a letter falls (for example, "The letter *N* comes close to *M* so I know it is in the middle"). You can ask students to sort their weekly words into thirds by setting up headers such as A–G, H–R, and S–Z.

3. Teach students to use guide words. After students can alphabetize to two or three places, you can introduce the guide words at the top of the dictionary page that will help them narrow down the location of a word. Begin with lots of modeling and think-alouds as you do this using your own dictionary.

4. Teach students how to interpret definitions. Project a page of a dictionary and point out the bolded entries and the kinds of information they can find. Of particular interest at the within word pattern stage are the multiple meanings of even simple words like *beat*, *track*, or *lodge*. When introducing the words in the sort for the week you might ask several students to look up the definition(s) of selected words and to be ready to report to the group on their findings.

5. Model at every opportunity. You may find that a beginning dictionary is somewhat limited and you need to use a more advanced dictionary. Think out loud as you use the dictionary: "If I want to look up *contagious*, I first need to figure out the first few letters—*con*—I think that would be C-O-N. C comes early in the alphabet so I will open the dictionary to the beginning and flip to the C pages. Now to find some C-O words using the guide words at the top of the page . . . ."

## 6.8 Dictionary Scavenger Hunts and How Many Turns

As you teach basic dictionary skills, you can conduct scavenger hunt type activities for just a few moments each day by asking students to get out dictionaries and find words as quickly as possible. Students can also do this in small groups or with partners, taking turns naming words to find and keep track of the time or the number of pages they turn.

**MATERIALS** Students should all have similar dictionaries appropriate for primary or elementary grades.

**PROCEDURES**
1. Call out a word and write it for all to see. When appropriate, prompt students to consider the first and second letter (start with single consonants), to think about where to look in the dictionary (early, middle, late), and to use guidewords.
2. Challenge students to count the number of times they need to turn a page to find the word. De-emphasize competition, but winners might be allowed to call out the next word.

# Spelling Games and Activities

Many games from Chapter 5 can be used with the features covered in this stage. Look for *Match, Go Fish, Making Words With Cubes*, and *Follow the Path Spelling Game*. The Adaptable for Other Stages logo in each chapter indicates games that work for a variety of features and stages.

### 6.9 Word-O or Word Operations

Students can complete this activity in their word study notebooks. It is especially appropriate for the within word pattern stage because it shows students how analogy can help them spell.

**PROCEDURES** Give students a word (such as *cart*) and then ask them to add, drop, or change one or two letters at a time to create a new word. Typically, consonants, blends, and digraphs are exchanged at the beginning (*part, chart, smart*) or the end (*card*), but vowels can also be exchanged (*green, groan, grain*). Model this activity and show students how to use sound boards, as in Appendix C, for ideas. Challenge students to see how many words they can form. Here is an example starting with the word *space*:

| | | | | | | | |
|---|---|---|---|---|---|---|---|
| space | pace | place | lace | race | trace | | |
| track | rack | crack | clack | lack | slack | sack | Mack |
| mask | ask | task | bask | | | | |
| base | vase | case | | | | | |
| cast | last | | | | | | |
| lass | glass | grass | brass | | | | |
| brash | trash | crash | cash | | | | |

### 6.10 Train Station Game

Use this board game to emphasize automaticity with common long vowels.

*Adaptable* **for Other Stages**

**MATERIALS** Use the basic follow-the-path board found in Appendix G, decorated as in Figure 6.13. Write in words that students have studied in word sorts as well as words that share the same feature. Incorporate four special squares into the game board: (1) Cow on the track. Lose 1 turn. (2) You pass a freight train. Move ahead 2 spaces. (3) Tunnel blocked. Go back 1 space. (4) You lost your ticket. Go back 2 spaces.

**PROCEDURES** This game can be played with up to four students. Each student selects a game piece. The first student then spins or rolls the die and moves the appropriate number of spaces. Students pronounce the word they land on and identify the vowel. If students have studied the long vowel pattern within each long vowel, ask them to say the pattern. For example, "*Nail* is a long *a* with a CVVC pattern." In addition, students must say another word containing the same vowel sound to stay on that space. Play continues in this fashion until someone reaches the station.

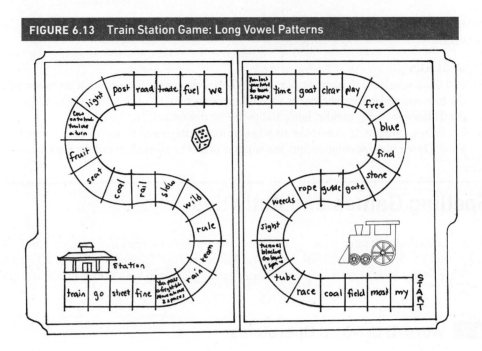

**FIGURE 6.13  Train Station Game: Long Vowel Patterns**

**VARIATIONS**  Divide a spinner into five sections and label each with a vowel. Students move to the next word with the vowel sound they spin.

### 6.11 Turkey Feathers

In this game, two players compare patterns across a single long vowel.

**MATERIALS**  You will need two paper or cardboard turkeys without tail feathers (see F igure 6. 14), 10 construction paper feathers, and at least 20 word cards representing the long vowel (for example, for long *a*: *a-e*, *ai*, and *ay*).  A ready made version of this game is available on the WTW Digital website.

**PROCEDURES**
1. One player shuffles and deals five cards and five feathers to each player. The remaining cards are placed face-down for the draw pile.
2. Each player puts down pairs that match by pattern. For example, *cake/lane* is a pair, but *pain/lane* is not. Each time a pair is laid down, the player puts one feather on his or her turkey.

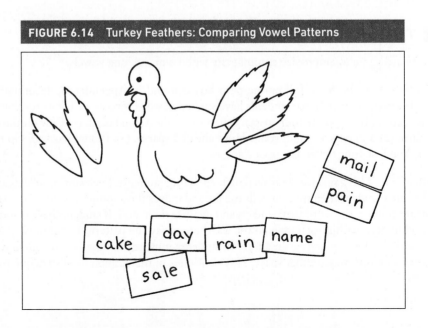

**FIGURE 6.14  Turkey Feathers: Comparing Vowel Patterns**

3. The dealer goes first, saying a word from his or her hand, and asks whether the second player has a card with the same pattern.

4. If the second player has a matching pattern, the first player gets the card and lays down the pair and a feather; if not, the first player draws a card. If the player draws a card that matches any word in his or her hand, the pair can be discarded, and a feather is earned. The next player proceeds in the same manner.

5. The player using all five feathers first wins. If a player uses all the cards before earning five feathers, the player must draw a card before the other player's turn.

## 6.12 The Racetrack Game

Darrell Morris (1982) developed this game, which has become a classic. It can be used for any vowel pattern and serves as a good review of the many patterns for the different vowels.

*Adaptable* **for Other Stages**

**MATERIALS** This game, for two to four players, is played on an oval race track divided into 20 to 30 spaces, which you can find in Appendix G. Five different versions of this game can be found at *WTW Digital*: one for each long vowel (see Figure 6.15 for an example). Different words following particular patterns are written into each space, except for a star drawn in two spaces. For example, you can use *night, light, tie, kite, like, my, fly, wish,* and *dig* on a game designed to practice patterns for long and short *i*. Prepare a collection of 40 to 50 cards that share the same patterns. A number spinner or a single die is used to move players around the track.

**PROCEDURES**
1. Designate one player as the dealer, who shuffles the word cards and deals six to each player; the remaining cards are turned face down to become the deck. Playing pieces are moved according to the number on the spinner or die.

2. When players land on a space, they read the word and then look for words in their hands that have the same pattern. For example, a player who lands on night may pull sign and *right* to put in his or her point pile. If players move to a space with a star, they dispose of any oddballs they might have (such as *give*) or choose their own pattern.

3. Any cards played are replaced by drawing from the deck. A player who has no match for the pattern must draw a card anyway.

4. The game is over when there are no more cards to play. The winner is the player who has put down the most word cards.

---

**FIGURE 6.15** Racetrack Games are Popular, Easy to Make, and Simple to Play

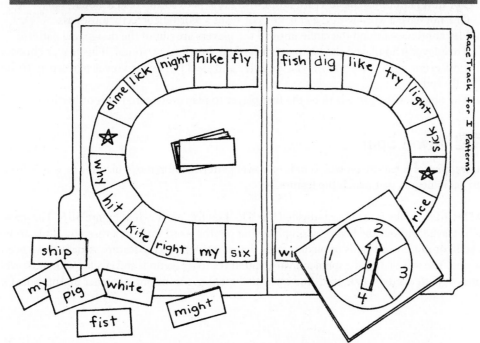

## 6.13 The Spelling Game

This game for two to four players can be used for any feature and is easily changed from week to week by simply replacing the word cards.

**MATERIALS**  Use a follow-the-path game board, but leave the spaces blank, except for several spaces where you may write directions such as Go Back 3 Spaces, Lose a Turn, and Go Ahead 2 Spaces. Add playing pieces and a spinner or die. Students use their own collections of words for the week.

**PROCEDURES**
1. Students each roll the die or spin the spinner. Whoever has the highest number will start and play proceeds clockwise.
2. The second player draws from the face-down stack of word cards. The player says the word to the first player, who must spell the word aloud. If players spell correctly, they can spin or roll to move around the path. Players who misspell the word cannot move.
3. The winner is the first one to get to the end of the path by landing on the space.

**VARIATIONS**  Use this game with word families, short vowels, and multisyllabic words, as well as the many one-syllable words explored in the within word pattern stage. You can also ask students to spell words on a dry erase board before claiming their space.

## 6.14 "I'm Out"

This card game is a favorite for two to five players; three is optimal.

**MATERIALS**  Prepare a set of 20 to 30 cards from a study unit, such as words with *a*, *a-e*, *ay*, and *ai*. Write the words at the top of cards for easy visibility as students fan them out in their hands. Students can also simply use the words they cut out for sorting.

**PROCEDURES**
1. Select one student to be the dealer, who deals all the cards so that each player gets the same number. The person to the right of the dealer begins.
2. The first player places a card down, reads the word, and designates the vowel pattern to be followed—for example, *rain–ai*.
3. The next player must place a card down with the *ai* pattern and read it aloud. A player who does not have a word with the *ai* pattern or reads a word incorrectly must pass.
4. Play continues around the circle until all the players are out of the designated pattern.
5. The player who played the last pattern card begins the new round. This player chooses a different card, places it in the middle, and declares what vowel pattern is to be followed.
6. The object of the game is to be the first player to play every card in his or her hand.

## 6.15 Vowel Spin

Players spin for a feature (vowel sounds or vowel pattern) and remove pictures or words from their game boards that match the feature.

**MATERIALS**  Make game boards divided like Tic-Tac-Toe, as shown in Figure 6.16. The game can be played without the board by simply laying out the word cards in a three-by-three array. Make 30 or more word cards or picture cards that correspond to the feature students have been studying. You will also need a spinner divided into three to six sections and labeled with the vowel sounds or patterns to be practiced. You can find directions for making a spinner in Appendix G.

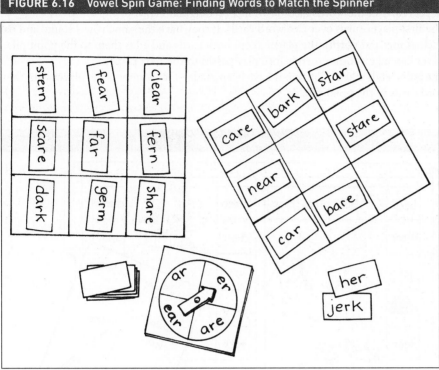

**FIGURE 6.16** Vowel Spin Game: Finding Words to Match the Spinner

## PROCEDURES

1. Put the cards in a deck face down. Players draw nine cards and turn them face up on their boards or in a three-by-three array.
2. The first player spins and removes the picture or word cards that fit the sound or pattern indicated by the spinner. The cards go into the player's point pile. That same player draws enough cards from the deck to replace the gaps on the playing board before play moves to the next player.
3. Play continues until a player is out of cards and there are no more to be drawn as replacements. The player who has the most cards in his or her point pile wins.

**VARIATIONS** Players prepare boards as described, but turn a winning card face down as in a tic-tac-toe game instead of removing it. The winner is the first player to turn down three in a row. Blackout is a longer version, where players must turn over all their cards to win. A large die (one-inch square) can be made instead of a spinner. Use sticky dots to label the sides with the different features.

## 6.16 Vowel Concentration

This game is played the traditional way, but students look for pairs of words with the same sound and pattern.

*Adaptable* **for Other Stages**

**MATERIALS** Prepare a set of word cards for a particular vowel pattern. Students can use the set of words they cut out for the week but they should not be able to read the word through the back of the card. Remove oddballs because they are not likely to make a pair and use an even number of words for each pattern so none are left over.

**PROCEDURES**

1. Players turn all the words face-down in a rectangular array.
2. The first player turns over two word cards. If they have the same vowel sound and pattern (such as *fort* and *north*), the player keeps both cards and adds them to the point pile. The player can take another turn before play passes to the next player.
3. The game ends when all matches have been made. The winner is the player with the most word cards in the point pile.

**FIGURE 6.17** Board Game for *Sheep in a Jeep*

### 6.17 Sheep in a Jeep Game

Students should be familiar with *Sheep in a Jeep* (by N. Shaw, illustrated by M. Apple). In this game, players examine the *ee* and *ea* patterns.

**MATERIALS** Prepare a game board using a follow-the-path template, as shown in Figure 6.17. Write long *e* words from the book as well as other words with the same patterns in each space. You will need a spinner with numbers 1 through 4 (see directions for spinners in Appendix G), playing pieces to move around the board, and a pencil and small piece of paper for each player.

**PROCEDURES** One player spins and moves that number of spaces on the board. The player reads the word on the space and "adds a sheep to the jeep" by saying or writing a word that rhymes with that word. A player who reads the word incorrectly must move back a space. Players alternate turns. The first player to the finish wins.

**FIGURE 6.18** Word Jeopardy Game

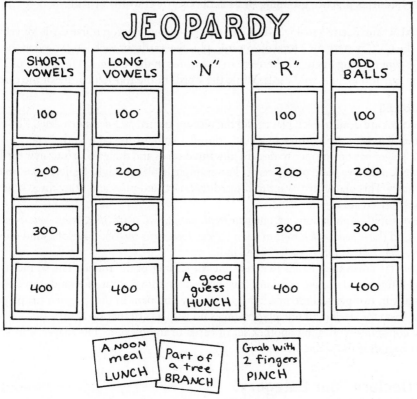

**Enhanced eText**
**Video Example 6.11**
This video is of a Complex Consonant Pattern Jeopardy game.

*Adaptable* **for Other Stages**

### 6.18 Jeopardy Game

In this game, four or five students recall and spell words that follow a particular pattern; for example, the final *ch* pattern.

**MATERIALS** Divide a poster board into 5-by-5-inch sections, as shown in Figure 6.18 and place clue cards in each space. The side of each card facing down holds a clue about a word in that category (with the answer); the side facing up shows an amount (100 to 400).

**PROCEDURES**
1. One player is the moderator or game host. The others roll a die to determine who goes first.
2. The game begins when the first player picks a category and an amount for the moderator to read ("I'll take short vowels for 100"). The moderator reads the clue and the player must respond by phrasing a question and spelling the word, as in the following example.

   *Moderator*: When struck, it produces fire.

   *Player*: What is a match? *M-a-t-c-h*.
3. If the answer is correct, the player receives the card and chooses another clue. (A player can only have two consecutive turns.) If the player misses, the player to the left may answer.
4. The game continues until all the clue cards are read and won or left unanswered. Players add their points, and the one with the highest amount wins.

   The following words could be used for a game reviewing *ch* and *tch*.

| Short Vowels | Long Vowels | N | R | Oddballs |
|---|---|---|---|---|
| stitch | beach | bench | march | much |
| watch | teach | lunch | perch | such |
| sketch | roach | branch | porch | rich |
| witch | coach | pinch | torch | which |

*Adaptable* **for Other Stages**

## 6.19 Vowel Rummy Card Game

Up to four students practice grouping short and long vowel words by pattern.

**MATERIALS** You need 35 to 45 cards. A good starting combination is five cards for each short vowel in the CVC pattern for a total of 25 cards, plus five cards for each long vowel in the CVCe pattern (except for long *e* because there are so few words in that category) for a total of 20 more cards. You can also include wild cards. Write the words in the top-left corner of the cards.

**PROCEDURES**

1. Five cards are dealt to each player and the rest are turned *face-down* in a deck. Players look in their hands for pairs, three of a kind, four of a kind, or five of a kind.

2. Each player has one chance to discard unwanted cards and draw up to four new cards from the deck to keep a hand of five cards. For example, a player might be dealt *bone, rope, that, wet, rake*. This player may want to discard *that, wet,* and *rake,* and draw three other cards to possibly create a better hand.

3. The possible combinations are one pair *(that, camp)*; two pairs *(that, camp, bone, rope)*; three of a kind *(bone, rope, rode)*; four of a kind *(bone, rope, rode, smoke)*; three of a kind plus a pair *(bone, rope, rode, hat, rat)*; or five of a kind.

4. Players lay down their hands to determine the winner of the round. The winner is determined in this order: Five of a kind (this beats everything), four of a kind, three of a kind plus a pair, two pairs, three of a kind, and finally one pair. In the case of a tie, players can draw from the deck until one player comes up with a card that breaks the tie.

5. Play continues by dealing another set of cards to the players. The player who wins the most rounds is the winner.

## 6.20 Declare Your Category!

This game for two to five players (three is optimal) works best with students who have some experience playing games. In this game, players guess the first player's category.

**MATERIALS** Create a deck of 45 word cards with a variety of vowels and vowel patterns. Make at least four cards with any one pattern.

**PROCEDURES**

1. Seven cards are dealt to each player and the remainder are placed *face-down* in a deck. Players lay out their seven cards face-up.

2. The first player turns up a key card from the deck (for example, *home*) and looks for a word in his or her hand to match in some way. It might have the same sound and/or spelling pattern (either *o-e* or VCe); for example, *soap, bone,* or *gave*. The match is laid down for all to see and the player announces, "Guess my category." Play moves to the next person, who must search his or her hand for a similar match. Players can pass when they want. The player who started the category keeps the sorting strategy a secret. Play keeps going until the last player to put a card down declares the category.

3. If the person who set up the category does not think the next player has put down an acceptable card, he or she can send a card back and give that player another chance. Mistakes are discussed at the end of each round.

4. The player who plays the last card has to declare the category to win and keep all the cards. If the player is wrong, the previous player gets a chance to declare the category.

5. At the end of each round, students are dealt enough cards to get them back to seven. The winner of the round turns up a card from the pile and makes up the next category.

6. Play continues until the deck is empty. The player with the most cards wins.

**VARIATIONS** Add wild cards to the pile to change categories in midstream. The person who establishes a new category must guess the original category correctly. This player becomes the new judge: "Your category was words with long *o* and the silent *e*. I am putting down my wild card and laying down *loan*. Guess my category." The rules of the game can be expanded to include semantic (for example, types of birds) and grammatical (for example, nouns) categories.

**6.21** Word Categories

This is a fast-moving word study game for a group of 3 to 8 players. Students review a variety of vowel patterns as they think of words that match a given pattern. They earn points only when their word is different from everyone else's so the goal is to think of less common answers. Here is an example of a completed sample game card after three rounds:

**MATERIALS** You will need a timer, pencils and a game card for each player. A copy of the sound boards (Beginning Consonants and Blends and Digraphs) found in Appendix C will help students think of words. A dictionary should be available for checking answers.

**PROCEDURES**
1. *The game is played in three rounds.* All players get the same game card.
2. *Playing: The timer is set for 1 minute (adjust as needed).* All players quickly fill in the first column of their game card, adding letters to the rimes or patterns to create a word. Answers must be real words that use the vowel pattern given. For example, *n*, *l*, *sl* or *tr* could be added to *ap*.
3. *Scoring:* Players take turns reading their answers aloud for each number. Words that are called aloud by other players should be checked off. Players get points for any words that do *not* match any other player's answer, earning one point for a unique answer. Record the score for unique answers at the bottom of the column of the answer sheet.
4. *Starting a new round:* Set the timer again; continue playing, filling in the next column with new answers.
5. *Winning the game:* After three rounds, players total the three scores on their game cards. The player with the highest score is the winner.
6. *Challenging answers:* While answers are being read, other players may challenge their acceptability. In this case the dictionary should be consulted to determine whether an answer is a real word.

**Enhanced eText**
**Teacher Resource:** Categories Game Boards for Units 1–6 and Blank Template To Make Your Own

---

**FIGURE 6.19  Sample Word Categories Game Card**

Word Category Game Board Unit 1

| **Word Categories: CVC & CVCe patterns** | | | | | |
|---|---|---|---|---|---|
| Name Henry | | | | | |
| | **Round 1** | | **Round 2** | | **Round 3** |
| 1 | trap | 1 | ✓ name | 1 | ✓ book |
| 2 | ✓ give | 2 | ✓ fill | 2 | ✓ line |
| 3 | ✓ joke | 3 | ✓ tube | 3 | glove |
| 4 | ✓ kick | 4 | ✓ rob | 4 | grape |
| 5 | ✓ rake | 5 | ✓ like | 5 | ✓ tune |
| 6 | ✓ duck | 6 | ✓ ship | 6 | ✓ base |
| 7 | ✓ sink | 7 | shack | 7 | ✓ rose |
| 8 | ✓ save | 8 | shock | 8 | bring |
| 9 | rot | 9 | ✓ hope | 9 | ✓ rash |
| 10 | ✓ shut | 10 | ✓ just | 10 | ✓ lime |
| Points | 2 | | 2 | | 3 |
| | | | | 7 | Total Points |

## 6.22 Homophone Win, Lose, or Draw

Four or more students work in teams to draw and guess each other's words in a game that resembles charades; a list of homophones can be found on page 477.

### PROCEDURES

1. Write homophone pairs on cards and shuffle.
2. Students divide into two equal teams, and one player from each team is selected as the artist for that round. The artist must draw a picture representing a given homophone, which requires understanding a homophone's spelling and meaning.
3. A card is pulled from the deck and shown simultaneously to the artists for both teams. As the artists draw, their teammates call out possible answers. When the correct word is offered, the artist calls on that team to spell both words in the pair.
4. A point is awarded to the team that provides the correct information first. The artist then chooses the next artist and play proceeds in the same fashion.

## 6.23 Homophone Rummy

This activity is suitable for two to six students. The object of the game is to get the most homophone pairs.

**MATERIALS** Prepare several decks of homophone pairs (52 cards, 26 pairs); a list of homophones can be found on page 477. Select words your students are familiar with. Write the words in the upper-left corner of the cards, as shown in Figure 6.20.

### PROCEDURES

1. Players are dealt seven cards and begin the game by checking their hands for already existing pairs. Pairs can be laid down in front of the player, who must give the meaning for each word or use it in a sentence that makes the meaning clear.
2. The remainder of the deck is placed in a central location and the first card is turned face-up beside it to form a discard pile.
3. The person on the left of the dealer goes first. Each player draws from either the deck or the discard pile. Any new pairs are laid down and defined. The player must then discard one card to end the turn. *Note:* If a card is taken from the discard pile, all the cards below are also taken and the top card must be used to make a pair.
4. A player can be challenged by another player who disagrees with the definitions. The person who challenges looks up the words in the dictionary. Whoever is right gets to keep the pair.
5. The game is over when one player has no cards left. That person yells, "Rummy!" Then the pairs are counted up to determine the winner.

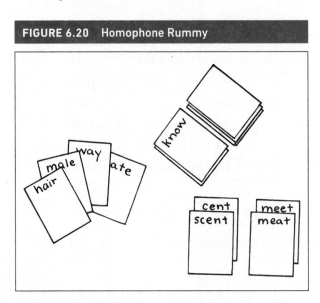

**FIGURE 6.20** Homophone Rummy

## 6.24 Hink Pinks

Hink Pinks is a traditional language game that involves a riddle answered by a pair of rhyming words; for example, "What do you call a chubby kitty or an obese feline? (*fat cat*). What do you call an angry father? (*mad dad*). What do you call a plastic pond? (*fake lake*)." Hinky Pinky usually demands two-syllable rhymes: What is a bloody tale? (*gory story*), whereas Hinkety Pinkety requires three-syllable answers: What is the White House? (*presidents' residence*). You can find lots more examples by searching online. Visual hink pinks are featured in the book *One Sun: A Book of Terse Verse*, by Bruce McMillan.

**FIGURE 6.21    Hink Pinks**

### PROCEDURES

1. Share examples of hink pinks and discuss the structure of the language or read *One Sun* with your students and talk about the riddles and photographs.
2. Brainstorm objects and possible adjectives that rhyme; for example, *pink/sink*, *bear/lair*, *sled/bed*. When students understand the concept, have them work in small groups or individually to think of their own hink pinks.
3. Challenge students to draw a picture to illustrate their hink pink (see Figure 6.21) or to write a riddle. These can be exchanged with a classmate.

## 6.25 Go Fish for R-controlled Vowels

This game for three or four players works like the traditional game of Go Fish. The goal is to make sets of four rhyming words and run out of cards to end the game.

**MATERIALS**    Create a single set of playing cards by copying the Go Fish cards onto card stock and cutting them apart.  A ready made version of this game is available on the WTW Digital website.

### PROCEDURES

1. Deal seven cards to each player and put the remaining deck in the middle to draw from.
2. The lead player asks another player for a match to a card in his or her hand. For example: *"Do you have a word that rhymes with fort?"* If the lead player receives a matching card they may then go again and ask the next player. Anytime a player does not have a matching card, he or she replies, *"Go fish"* and the lead player draws one card from the deck to end their turn.
3. When a player has a set of four matching rhyming words (such as *fort, sport, short,* and *port*) they lay the set down and read the words aloud.
4. Play continues around the circle until one player is out of cards. The player with the most sets is the winner.

## 6.26 Homophone Concentration

This game is for 2 to 4 players to review homophones after the words have been studied.

**MATERIALS**    Create cards by writing homophone pairs on sets of cardstock. A list of homophones can be found on page 477. Use no more than 18 pairs at a time or use fewer to save time.

### PROCEDURES

1. Shuffle the cards in a set and lay them face down in rows and columns.
2. Players take turns turning over two cards at a time. The goal is to turn over a homophone match such as *plane* and *plain* and remove them from the array. If a match is not made the cards are turned back over before the next players goes.
3. When players make a match they must provide the meaning of both words before picking them up as a pair. In giving definitions, players may use the actual word in the sentence to show the meaning or provide a synonym or definition. Pairs are placed in front of each player.

**Example**: A player turns over the words *plane* and *plain*. They can provide sentences like "He gave me a plain paper bag" and "The plane to New York took off on time." Or, the player could provide a definition or synonym like, "A vehicle that can fly" and "Something simple."

4. When a player makes a match she gets to go again. Then the next player has a turn.

5. The game ends when all the cards have been matched. The winner is the player with the most cards.

*Note:* A player can be challenged by someone disagreeing with her definitions. The person issuing the challenge looks up the words in the dictionary. Whoever is right gets to keep the pair.

**FIGURE 6.22** Homophone Concentration Cards

| mane | main | pain |
|------|------|------|
| pane | plane | plain |
| male | mail | pale |
| pail | waste | waist |
| sale | sail | bear |
| bare | break | brake |

## 6.27 Slap Jack for Diphthongs

This game for two players works like the traditional game of Slap Jack. The goal is to acquire the entire deck of cards.

**MATERIALS** Create a set of playing cards by copying the words featuring contrasting sounds *au* and *ou* (*caught* vs. *bought*), *ou* and *ow* (*shout* vs. *clown*), or *oo* (*boot* vs. *hoof*) onto card stock and cutting them apart.

**PROCEDURES**

1. Deal out all the cards face down in front of each player. The cards remain face down throughout the game.
2. At a signal such as calling "Slap Jack" the two players simultaneously turn over the top card in their deck. If the two words share the same vowel sound (such as *draw* and *fought*) the first player to slap their hand on the cards gets to claim them and move them to the bottom of their deck.
3. If the cards do not have the same vowel sound (such as *sauce* and *mouth*) the players turn over another set of cards on top of them. Whoever slaps the cards correctly takes all the cards below.
4. If a player slaps a set that does not match, the cards are given to the other player.
5. Play continues until one player has all the cards or time is called, and the player with the most cards is the winner.

**VARIATIONS:** Play Slap Jack for the different sounds of OO as well (*food, shook, cool,* and so on).

# Word Study for the Syllables and Affixes Stage

## Chapter 7: Syllables & Affixes STAGE

*WTW* Digital is a new online tool that accompanies this core text, and it was designed to help you implement word study in an engaging and interactive way. Resources for this chapter include:

- **Automatically scored qualitative spelling inventories** suggest each student's approximate stage of spelling development. Word study groups are also automatically generated based on inventory results.
- **Interactive sorts** that allow students to engage with word study in a digital environment
- **6 word study games** in a printable format that present fun activities for students to build their phonics, vocabulary, and spelling knowledge.

An access code for *WTW* Digital is included with each new copy of package ISBN: 9780135174623. Visit www.wtwdigital.pearson.com to get started.

Beginning in second or third grade for many students, and in fourth grade for most, cognitive and language growth supports movement into the syllables and affixes stage of word knowledge. Although students have been reading and writing words of more than one syllable for some time, during this stage they systematically study the generalizations that govern how syllables are joined. And though they might have studied how **affixes** (both **prefixes** such as *re-* or *un-* and **suffixes** such as *-ing* or *-ly*) affect word meaning, during this stage students also look at how suffixes might affect the spelling of the base word. Examining how affixes and base words combine supports students' learning how to figure out the meaning of many longer, unfamiliar words they encounter in their reading.

Many teachers find that there is much about the English writing system or **orthography** at this stage that is new to them as well as to their students. Your own curiosity about words and a willingness to dig deeper into the way words work will enable you to learn right along with your students. This chapter and supporting material will help you facilitate students' word explorations to help them discover the patterns of sound, spelling, and meaning that link thousands of words. This knowledge will help them read, write, and spell more effectively.

Before we talk in detail about the features of study in this stage, let's visit Sharon Radcliffe's fourth-grade classroom in mid-year. Ms. Radcliffe has a range of abilities in her classroom that is evident in both reading levels and spelling inventory results. She has a large group of 14 students who fall into the syllables and affixes stage, four students in the late within word pattern stage, and five students who are in derivational relations. She makes time to meet with each group on Monday while the other groups work independently. In the following vignette, Ms. Radcliffe meets with her syllables and affixes group at the front of the room for a 20-minute lesson while the rest of the students find comfortable places to read and discuss in the Book Club format (Raphael, Pardo, Highfield, & McMahon 2013). The syllables and affixes students are studying the final syllable (*ar/er/or*), which poses a challenge for spellers because it is pronounced the same, /ər/, across the different spellings.

Ms. Radcliffe begins her word study lesson using a directed spelling thinking activity (Zutell, 1996). She asks her students to spell three words, *dollar*, *faster*, and *actor*, as a way to stimulate discussion and set a purpose for the sort. Ms. Radcliffe asks students to share their spellings, encouraging a variety of answers, which include *doller*, *dollor*, *dollar*, *faster*, *acter*, and *actor*. Ms. Radcliffe then thinks out loud, "Hmmm . . . This is very interesting. We agree on how to spell the first syllable of each word, but we don't always agree about how to spell the final syllable. What makes this part hard?" Jason volunteers that the words sound the same at the end. "Do the rest of you agree?" Ms. Radcliffe asks and then adds, "Let's find out if this is true for other words as well."

Ms. Radcliffe has made a copy of the weekly word sheet and cut it apart to sort on the document camera. She selects several words for discussion whose meaning might not be clear (e.g., *blister* and *mayor*) and reviews the meanings of *lunar* and *solar* from their recent science unit. Next she asks, "How might we sort these words?" She takes several suggestions that include sorting by vowel patterns and when Sara suggests that they sort by the last two letters she responds, "Let's try that since we agreed that was the hard part of the word."

Ms. Radcliffe removes all the words except *dollar*, *faster*, and *actor*, which she underlines to use as key words for the sort. She then displays each word in turn, calling on a student to read it and tell her where to place it (the final sort is shown in Figure 7.1). To check the sort they read down each column to be sure they all have the same sound at the end. Ms. Radcliffe then asks the students, "What do you notice about these words now that we have sorted them?" Several students offer ideas and together they summarize by saying, "When we hear /ər/, the sound will not help us spell it, so we will have to concentrate on remembering whether it is spelled *er*, *or*, or *ar*."

**FIGURE 7.1**  Final *ar/er/or* Word Sort

| dollar | faster | actor |
| sugar | blister | doctor |
| grammar | jogger | tractor |
| solar | speaker | motor |
| lunar | skater | favor |
| collar | cleaner | editor |
| | poster | mayor |
| | freezer | author |
| | dreamer | |
| | bigger | |

Ms. Radcliffe hands out copies of the word sort and goes over the students' word study assignments for the week. She reminds them, "Cut apart and sort the words, and then write the word sort in your word study notebooks." While they work at their seats, Ms. Radcliffe meets with a different developmental group to get their weekly sort started. On other days, students work independently by doing a blind sort with a partner, sorting at home, and hunting for additional words in trade books. On Friday, Ms. Radcliffe gives them a spelling test of 10 words, but she also calls the group together to compile a list of the words they were able to find in their word hunts. This extensive list will be used to introduce the following week's lesson, in which students will discover that *er* is the most common way to spell the final sound, that it is always used to spell comparative adjectives (*faster, smaller, longer*), and that *er* and *or* are often used to spell agents or people who do things (*teacher, worker, author, sailor*).

Ms. Radcliffe's lesson promotes two key ideas of this stage. First, it demonstrates to students how much they already know about spelling a particular word—spelling is not an all-or-nothing affair. Usually spellers at this stage get most of the word correct, and teachers need to remind and reassure them about this. Second, it demonstrates to students what they need to focus on when they look at a word. Because they already know most of the word, they need to attend to the part that is still challenging.

# Literacy Development of Students in the Syllables and Affixes Stage

Students in the syllables and affixes stage of word knowledge are what Henderson (1990) called *intermediate readers*—students who are not yet mature or advanced readers. Reading skill during this stage of development can, on average, span several reading levels, from the second-grade level to the middle grades.

## Reading in the Syllables and Affixes Stage

The intermediate and middle school years are a time of expanding reading interests and fine-tuning of reading strategies. Students will be expected to read textbooks and other informational texts as classroom instruction shifts to a greater emphasis on content or disciplinary studies, a key focus in English/Language Arts standards. In previous developmental stages, the challenges posed by reading stem mostly from students' ability to identify words as they read about familiar topics. At the intermediate level, background knowledge and vocabulary become critical elements in comprehension as students explore new genres and topics.

During the syllables and affixes stage, students learn to look at words in a new way, not as single words with CVC, CVVC, or other vowel patterns, but as two or more units of sound and pattern as well as meaning. Breaking words into two or more syllabic units is a more sophisticated decoding strategy than the phonics instruction typically offered in the primary grades using consonants, blends, digraphs, and vowel patterns—elements that students master in the within word pattern stage. In the syllables and affixes stage, students operate within Ehri's **consolidated alphabetic phase** (2005, 2014) where they use larger chunks to decode, spell, and store words in memory. For example, a word like *unhappy* can be analyzed as three syllabic chunks (*un-hap-py*) or two **morphemic**, or meaning, chunks (*un-happy*). Word study in the syllables and affixes stage helps students learn where these syllable and morphemic breaks occur in words so that they can use the appropriate chunks to read, spell, and determine the meanings of multisyllabic words.

Students in the intermediate stage read with greater fluency than at the transitional stage. They have many words stored in memory for automatic retrieval and they quickly and accurately figure out many unfamiliar words. This ease of word identification helps them read with phrasing and expression. By the end of this stage students may read up to 140 words per minute in narrative texts (Hasbrouck & Tindal, 2006) and even faster while reading silently (Morris, 2013).

**Enhanced eText**
Video Example 7.1
This video is an overview of how students' literacy develops in this stage.

## Writing in the Syllables and Affixes Stage

Intermediate writers become increasingly confident and fluent in their writing and are able to work on longer pieces over many days. The ability to automatically spell most of the words they need for writing allows them to focus more attention on the meaning they are trying to convey. You are likely to hear "voice" in their writing and they are more aware of their audience. Intermediate writers can be expected to revise their written work and to edit it for spelling and punctuation accuracy.

Lexi's essay on the changes she would make to the Lincoln Middle School cafeteria exudes middle school bravado (see Figure 7.2). She touched on all things cool: sound systems, student choice, hamburgers and fries, and celebrities—all of which were sure to bring her the recognition she craved as "manager of the year." At the time, Lexi was a sixth grader in the later part of the syllables and affixes stage. She spelled *manager* correctly and incorrectly (MANAGAR) in the same essay and also confused the final syllables in other words, such as *radical* (RADACLE) and *music* (MUSICK). Vowel patterns in **accented syllables** were still not firm (AWSOME for *awesome*), and she was uncertain about the double consonants within base words containing an affix (INSTALATION for *installation*). After these syllable and affix issues were firmed up, Lexi was poised to study the **spelling–meaning connections** of the next stage of development—derivational relations—and to discover the reason DECESION is spelled with an *i* instead of an *e* (because it comes from the word *decide*).

## Vocabulary Learning in the Syllables and Affixes Stage

In this stage of literacy development, students' reading becomes the primary source of new vocabulary as they encounter more and more words in text whose meanings they do not know. This is especially true in disciplinary studies

**FIGURE 7.2   Lexi's Middle School Essay**

> If I could be the managar of the cafeteria at Lincoln Middle School I would make some awsome changes. The instalation of a sound system would be my first decesion. The kids could rotate bringing there own choice of musick. Then I would make radacle changes in the menu like we'd have hamburgers and fries and no rootine school menues. Then I'd send an invatation to Miley Cyrus to join us for lunch. If she acepts I'd get the Best Manager of the Year Award !

beyond third grade, such as science and social studies as students read informational books and textbooks. However, learning words from context cannot be left to chance; you need to take an active role in making sure that students' vocabularies are growing steadily. Understanding **academic vocabulary** is essential to success in school (Townsend, Filippini, Collins, & Biancarosa, 2012) and some instructional ideas are presented in this chapter. *Vocabulary Their Way* (Templeton et al., 2015) has entire chapters dedicated to teaching academic vocabulary.

# Orthographic Development in the Syllables and Affixes Stage

In previous chapters, systematic word study was limited to vowel and consonant patterns within single-syllable words to build a foundation for the multisyllabic words of intermediate word study, in much the same way that basic math facts build a foundation for long division. After students have this a systematic word study foundation, they are ready to begin studying multisyllabic words. Lexi's writing sample (Figure 7.2) shows that students in this stage spell most words correctly, making their writing quite readable, but they continue to make more advanced spelling errors.

Table 7.1 provides a summary of what students know; what they use but confuse; and what is still missing in the early, middle, and late syllables and affixes stage. For the most part, students know how to spell high-frequency words and vowel patterns in single-syllable words correctly. Spellings such as SHOPING and AMAZZING show us that students spell the *-ing* suffix but are not sure about the conventions of doubling and *e*-drop. The question of when to double also shows up in the spelling of two-syllable words where syllables meet—the **syllable juncture**— in KEPPER for *keeper* and BOTEL for *bottle*.

**TABLE 7.1**    **Characteristics of Syllables and Affixes Spelling**

| Gradations of Stage with Examples of Spelling | What Students Spell Correctly | What Students Use but Confuse | What Is Absent |
|---|---|---|---|
| *Early Syllables and Affixes*<br><br>SHOPING for *shopping*<br><br>AMAZZING for *amazing*<br><br>BOTEL for *bottle*<br><br>KEPER or KEPPER *for keeper* | Blends, digraphs, short vowels<br><br>Vowel patterns in one-syllable words<br><br>Complex consonant units in one-syllable words<br><br>High-frequency words | Consonant doubling and *e*-drop<br><br>Syllable juncture: open- and closed-syllable patterns | Few things are completely missing<br><br>Occasional deletion of reduced syllables |
| *Middle Syllables and Affixes*<br><br>SELLER for *cellar*<br><br>DAMIGE for *damage*<br><br>PERAIDING for *parading* | All the above plus:<br><br>Doubling and *e*-drop with inflectional endings<br><br>Syllable juncture: open- and closed-syllable patterns | Vowel patterns in accented syllables<br><br>Unaccented final syllables | Few things are completely missing<br><br>Doubled consonant for absorbed prefixes |
| *Late Syllables and Affixes*<br><br>CONFEDENT for *confident* | All the above plus:<br><br>Vowel patterns in accented syllables<br><br>Unaccented final syllables | Some suffixes and prefixes<br><br>Reduced vowels in unaccented syllables | Few things are completely missing<br><br>Doubled consonant for absorbed prefixes |

The syllables and affixes stage represents a new point in word analysis because there is more than one syllable to consider and each syllable may present a spelling problem. For example, students might spell the long vowel in the accented second syllable of *parading* with the *ai* pattern, as in PARAIDING. More likely, however, they will have problems with words such as BOTTEL for *bottle* and DAMIGE for *damage*. As the name of the stage suggests, in addition to syllables, students grapple with meaning units such as prefixes and suffixes (known collectively as *affixes*) and the idea that base words as morphemes or meaning units must retain their spellings when affixes are added. For example, in KEPER for *keeper*, the student fails to use his or her knowledge of the base word *keep*. In the sections that follow we describe the major features for instruction in the syllables and affixes stage.

Mrs. Wilson helps her students figure out the rules that govern the addition of *-ing*

## Base Words and Inflectional Endings

One category of suffixes is **inflectional endings**, such as *-s*, *-ed*, and *-ing*, that change the number and tense of the base word but do not change its meaning or part of speech. These endings also include the comparative forms *-er* and *-est*. Although students have encountered inflectional endings in oral language and reading since the preschool years, studying them systematically at this point introduces students to base words and suffixes as well as the rules that govern spelling changes.

**ADDING -S.** Probably the most common suffix students first learn is the plural, adding *-s* even when the sound it represents varies, as in *cats* (/s/) and *dogs* (/z/). However, plurals deserve to be addressed systematically in this stage to cover additional issues:

- Add *-es* when words end in *ch*, *sh*, *ss*, *s*, and *x*. When *-es* is added to a word, students can usually "hear" the difference because it adds another syllable to the word (*dish* becomes *dish-es*, unlike *spoons*).
- Change the *y* at the end of a word to *i* before adding *-es* when the word ends in a consonant + *y* (*baby* to *babies*) but not when it ends in a vowel + *y* (*monkeys*).
- Words may change spelling and pronunciation in the plural form. Some words with final *f* or *fe* change the *f* to *v* and add *es* (*wife* to *wives*, *wolf* to *wolves*). Other words take a new form (*goose* to *geese* and *mouse* to *mice*). And some words remain the same (*fish*, *sheep*, *deer*).

**ADDING -ED AND -ING.** One of the major challenges students face when adding *-ed* or *-ing* is whether to double the final letter of the base word. The basic doubling rule is that when a suffix beginning with a vowel is added to a base word containing a single vowel followed by a single consonant (e.g., *shop*), double the final consonant (e.g., *shopping*, *shopped*). This can be simplified as the *one-one-one rule*: one syllable, one vowel, one consonant—double. There are some exceptions such as words that end with *x* and *w*, which never double (*taxing*, *showed*), but the doubling rule is worth learning and has implications for syllable junctures, as described shortly. It takes time, however, for students to develop a firm understanding of it.

Rather than teaching rules, we suggest a series of word sorts that will allow students to discover the many principles at work. In Sort 1 of Figure 7.3, the students first sorted by words that double and those that do not, and then were asked to underline the base word. In Sort 2, sorting by the vowel pattern in the base word helped students discover that there are two conditions when the ending is simply added (CVVC words like *read* and CVCC words like *rest*) whereas only CVC words need to double. This will help clear up the confusion of *smelling* and *dressing*, words that students may initially place in the doubled column.

**FIGURE 7.3** Adding Inflectional Endings to Base Words

| Sort 1 | | Sort 2 | | |
|---|---|---|---|---|
| resting | jogging | CVVC | CVCC | CVC |
| reading | running | reading | resting | jogging |
| feeding | shopping | feeding | walking | running |
| walking | winning | sleeping | jumping | shopping |
| sleeping | planning | waiting | smelling | winning |
| jumping | skipping | raining | dressing | planning |
| waiting | sobbing | | | skipping |
| smelling | hugging | | | sobbing |
| dressing | snapping | | | snapping |

Table 7.2 summarizes the conditions that govern adding inflectional endings. The rules can get quite complicated, but when planning instruction, begin with the most common in the early syllables and affixes stage (numbers 1–5) and expect to reinforce these throughout the intermediate grades and even beyond in the case of two- and three-syllable words (where rules apply only if the final syllable is accented). Remember that it will take time for students to master these generalizations, and they should know the spellings of the base words before you ask them to think about how to add suffixes that require changing the base word.

## Compound Words

When students explore **compound words**, they learn different things. First, they learn how a word like *sun* can combine in different ways to form new words, as shown in Figure 7.4. This is an introduction to the combinatorial features of English words in building vocabulary. Second, studying compound words lays the foundation for explicit attention to syllables: Compound words often comprise two smaller words, each of which is a single syllable. Third, students reinforce their knowledge of the spellings of many high-frequency, high-utility words in English that are compound words (*someone*, *anything*). Look at Activity 7.8 on page 288 for specific ideas, such as illustrating words and brainstorming words that share the same base.

**TABLE 7.2** Changes to Base Words When Adding Inflectional Endings or Other Suffixes That Start with a Vowel

| Base Words | + ING | + ED or ER | + S |
|---|---|---|---|
| 1. CVVC, CVCC<br>Ex: *look, walk* | No change<br>Ex: *looking, walking* | No change<br>Ex: *looked, walked* | No change<br>Ex: *looks, walks* |
| 2. CVC*<br>Ex: *bat* | Double final letter<br>Ex: *batting* | Double final letter<br>Ex: *batted, batter* | No change<br>Ex: *bats* |
| 3. CVCe**<br>Ex: *skate* | Drop final *e*<br>Ex: *skating* | Drop final *e*<br>Ex: *skated, skater* | No change<br>Ex: *skates* |
| 4. Words that end in a consonant + *y*<br>Ex: *cry* | No change<br>Ex: *crying* | Change *y* to *i*<br>Ex: *cried, crier* | Change *y* to *i* and add *es*<br>Ex: *cries* |
| 5. Words that end in a vowel + *y*<br>Ex: *play* | No change<br>Ex: *playing* | No change<br>Ex: *played, player* | No change<br>Ex: *plays* |
| 6. Two-syllable words accented on second syllable<br>Ex: *admit, invite, apply, destroy* | Follow rules for 1–5<br>Ex: *admitting, inviting, applying, destroying* | Follow rules for 1–5<br>Ex: *admitted, invited, applied, destroyed, destroyer* | Follow rules for 1–5<br>Ex: *admits, invites, applies, destroys* |
| 7. Words that end in a *c*<br>Ex: *mimic* | Add a *k*<br>Ex: *mimicking* | Add a *k*<br>Ex: *mimicked* | No change<br>Ex: *mimics* |

*Words ending in *x* and *w* do not double (e.g., *boxed, chewed*). Words that end in *ck* avoid having to double a final *k* (*blocked, blocking*).

**Words that end in *ve* avoid having to double a final *v* (*loved, loving*).

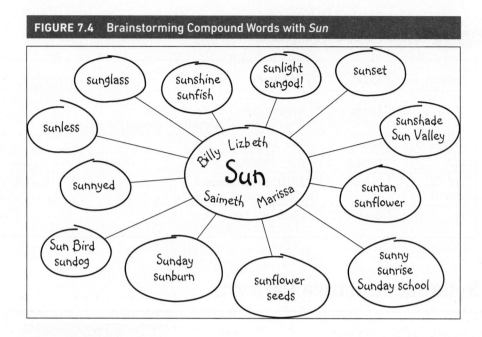

**FIGURE 7.4** Brainstorming Compound Words with *Sun*

## Open and Closed Syllables and Syllable Juncture

Why is *Tigger*, the name of the tiger from *Winnie the Pooh*, spelled with two *g*s? How do you pronounce *Caddie Woodlawn*? Answering these questions depends on whether the first syllable in the word is open or a closed. **Open syllables** (CV) end with a long vowel sound: *tiger*, *Katy*, *reason*. **Closed syllables** (CVC) contain a short vowel sound that is usually "closed" by two consonants: *Tigger*, *Caddie*, *rack*et.

**DOUBLING THE CONSONANT TO KEEP THE VOWEL SHORT.** Students are first introduced to the basics of open and closed syllables when they examine what happens when -*ed* and -*ing* are added to short and long vowel pattern words. If they write about how a rabbit moves along the ground (*hopping*) and do not double the *p*, they wind up with an entirely different meaning (*hoping*). The same confusion occurs in words like *riding* and *ridding* or *griped* and *gripped*. As Henderson (1985) explained, "The core principle of syllable juncture is that of doubling consonants to mark the short English vowel" (p. 65). Students learn that when they do not know whether to double the consonants at the juncture of syllables, they should listen to the vowel sound in the first syllable. If they hear a long vowel sound, the syllable is open and will not end with a consonant (*hu-man*). If they hear a short vowel sound, the odds are likely that the syllable is closed with an extra consonant (*mam-mal*). Knowing whether to double develops first through examining base words plus inflectional suffixes, and is later applied *within* base words: Because the vowel in the first syllable of *Tigger* is short, the *g* is doubled; because the vowel in the first syllable of *tiger* is long, the *g* is not doubled.

**SYLLABLE JUNCTURE PATTERNS.** Another way of describing what happens where syllables meet is through **syllable juncture patterns**, as shown in Table 7.3. For example, *hopping*, *Tigger*, and *stripping* illustrate the VCCV syllable juncture pattern for closed syllables; *hoping*, *tiger*, and *striping* illustrate the V/CV syllable juncture pattern for open syllables. These patterns are the most frequent. The third pattern, the closed VC/V pattern, with only a single consonant at the juncture after a short vowel (*nev-er*, *pan-ic*) occurs less frequently. The fourth pattern, the closed VCCCV pattern, includes words that have a consonant digraph or blend at the syllable juncture that cannot be separated (*ath-lete*, *hun-dred*). In the VV pattern, each vowel contributes a sound—the word is usually divided after the first long vowel sound (*cre-ate*, *li-on*) so it is another example of an open syllable.

**TABLE 7.3** Syllable Juncture Patterns

| Pattern | Type | Examples |
|---|---|---|
| VC/CV | Closed | *skipping, button, rubber* (doublets)<br>*chapter, window, garden* (two different consonants) |
| V/CV | Open | *lazy, coma, beacon* |
| VC/V | Closed | *river, robin, cover* |
| VCC/CV<br>VC/CCV | Closed | *father, athlete, pumpkin*<br>*pilgrim, instant, complain* |
| VV | Open | *create, riot, liar* |

# Contrasting Syllable Juncture Patterns

SAMPLE LESSON

1. **Introduce the sort.** Prepare a set of words such as those in Figure 7.5. Display the words in random order and read through them quickly. Compare the meanings of *dinner* and *diner* (you might eat dinner at a diner). You might add a simple drawing of a building and a plate of food to the word cards. Ask, *What do you notice about these words?* Take lots of ideas including the fact that they have two syllables and some have double letters. Pose the question, *Why do some words have double letters in the middle? Let's sort by those that do and those that don't and see what we can find out.*

2. **Sort.** Introduce the headers VCCV and VCV and compare to the key words *super* and *supper*. Explain, Supper *has two consonants in the middle and a vowel on each side so we can label the pattern in the middle of the word as VCCV. Super has one consonant in the middle with a vowel on each side so the pattern is VCV. Where will we put the word* dinner? Diner?

3. **Discuss.** After sorting the rest of the words say, *Let's read down each column. Use your eyes and ears to see how they are alike or different.* After reading down the column of words under VCV ask, *What did you notice about the words under super?* Take lots of answers and probe if necessary to focus attention on the vowel, *What do you notice about the vowel in the first syllable?* (It's long.) Then ask, *What do you notice about the words under supper?* Talk about how the vowel in the first syllable is short.

4. **Reflect and generalize.** Ask, *What did we learn about the words with double letters in the middle?*

(The vowel in the first syllable is short.) At this point you might explain that when the words with the VCCV pattern are divided into syllables, as in *sup-per*, the first syllable is called "closed" because it ends with consonant. When a VCV word like *super* is divided into syllables (su-per) the first syllable ends with a long vowel and is called "open".

5. **Extend.** Students should sort their own set of words and record them in their word study notebooks. In addition, ask them to write a generalization about open and closed syllables and the VCV and VCCV patterns. Students can apply their generalization by decoding unknown words like *rival* and *tuffet*. Ask them to work with a partner to generate a pronunciation and justification for the vowels sounds they used in the words. Students should also be assigned blind sorts with a partner as well as a word hunt.

**FIGURE 7.5** Introducing Syllable Juncture Patterns

| Sort 1 | |
|---|---|
| **VCCV** | **VCV** |
| super | supper |
| diner | dinner |
| tiger | happy |
| paper | penny |
| zero | rabbit |
| crazy | kitten |
| tiny | lesson |
| open | letter |

The sample lesson on the previous page shows how you can introduce syllable juncture patterns and open and closed syllables in a focused contrast. After sorting the words as shown in Figure 7.5 by the VCV and VCCV syllable juncture pattern, students are asked to think about the vowel sounds in the first syllable of words like *super* and *supper*.

**SYLLABLE TYPES.** Some teachers are familiar with, and may prefer, the terms **syllable types**, which focus on individual syllables rather than the syllable juncture. However, there is much overlap between the terms, and *open* and *closed* are used to describe both. There are six syllable types:

1. **Closed**: The syllable is "closed" with a consonant, usually, though not always indicating a short vowel sound as in *pan or panic.*
2. **Open**: The syllable is "open" because it ends with a long vowel sound as in *me* or *o-pen.*
3. **Vowel-Consonant-*e***: As in *make* or *pancake.*
4. **Vowel Team**: As in *team, cloud,* or *railroad.*
5. ***R*-controlled**: As in *mark, north,* or *airport.*
6. **Final Stable Syllable**: This includes the frequent "Consonant-*le*" pattern (*table, cycle, buckle*) as well as other common final unaccented syllables (*nation, creature, label*).

All but the final syllable type will be familiar to students who have completed the sorts in the within word pattern stage.

## Vowel Patterns in Accented Syllables

The vowel sounds and patterns students master in the within word pattern stage are reviewed and extended as they examine two syllable words in the syllables and affixes stage. For example, familiar long-*a* patterns are the focus in the sort in Figure 7.6 (*ai, ay,* and *a-e*). In most words of two or more syllables, one syllable is emphasized more than the others so students learn about **stress** or **accent** (we use those terms interchangeably) as a way to identify where these familiar patterns are likely to be found. As you read down each column of words in Figure 7.6 notice how the long a sound is clearly heard in the accented syllable.

## Unaccented Syllables

When students grasp the concept of an accented syllable they also learn about the other side of this concept, the **unaccented syllable**. The unaccented syllable is the one in which the spelling of the vowel is not clearly pronounced so students need to pay close attention to it. Recall how Ms. Radcliff focused her students' attention on the difficulty of spelling the final unaccented syllables in *dollar, faster,* and *actor* in the opening vignette. The vowel sound in this syllable is often represented by the **schwa**—the upside-down *e* in a dictionary pronunciation key (ə) that sounds something like /uh/. By the middle of the syllables and affixes stage, word study can focus on these unaccented final syllables:

**Enhanced eText**
**Video Example 7.2**
In this two-part video, Ms. Bruskotter meets with a small group of students in two sessions to study open and closed syllables.

**Enhanced eText**
**Video Example 7.3**
In the video, Ms. Bruskotter meets with her small groups for the second day of instruction in open and closed syllables.

**FIGURE 7.6** Common Long *a* Spellings in Two-Syllable Words

| complain | dismay | debate |
| raisin | crayon | bracelet |
| dainty | decay | parade |
| trainer | layer | mistake |
| sailor | today | escape |

### Introducing Accent or Stress

- Sorting students' names is a good way to introduce the concept of accent. When we pronounce a familiar name, where do we put the most emphasis? Which syllable seems to "sound louder" than the others? We pronounce Molly's name "**moll** ee," not "mo **lee**." We say "**jen** ifer," not "je **ni** fer" or "jenni **fer**."

- If students have trouble identifying the accented syllable, suggest that they try resting the back of their hand or their thumb lightly under their chin and feel how their jaw drops a bit more on the stressed syllable.

/əl/ as in *angle*, *angel*, *metal*, *civil*, and *fertile*
/ər/ as in *super*, *actor*, and *sugar*
/ən/ as in *sudden*, *human*, *basin*, *apron*, and *captain*
/chər/, /yər/, and /zhər/ as in *lecture*, *figure*, and *treasure*
/ĭt/ as in *jacket*, *edit*, and *climate*
/ē/ as in *money*, *cookie*, and *story*

When examining words with unaccented final syllables, you will find there is often no tidy generalization that governs the spelling and students may have to simply commit many of these words to memory. However, sometimes there are clues. For example, comparative adjectives are always spelled with *-er*, as in *smarter*, *faster*, and *taller*. (Sorting words by parts of speech as well as by spelling patterns is an important extension when studying words like these.) What is most useful for students to discover is that some spellings are simply more common than others. For example, more than 1,000 words end in *-le* but only about 200 end in *-el*. The ending *-er* is much more common than *-ar* or *-or*. An excellent follow-up to sorting these words is creating class lists based on word hunts that give students insight into the frequencies. Then they might use a "best guess" strategy when spelling an unfamiliar word.

## Learning about Accent or Stress

A number of reasons exist for why learning about accent or stress helps readers and spellers:

1. Different syllables or parts of words are more challenging to spell because they are either unaccented or receive less stress in a word so learning the language to talk about them can be beneficial. Identifying the vowel in unaccented syllables is one of the biggest challenges we all face as spellers. As our colleague Tom Gill explains to students, "You can't trust sound when your voice goes down."

2. Accent matters in the case of some **homographs**, words that are spelled the same but are pronounced differently according to which syllable is accented. Listen to the accent shift in the bolded syllables as you read these sentences:

   It is a good idea to re**cord** your expenses so you have a **rec**ord of them.

   Would you pre**sent** the **pres**ent to the guest of honor?

   The landfill might re**fuse** the **ref**use.

3. Learning about accent helps students pronounce new words when they check in the dictionary. Some dictionaries use apostrophes to show which syllables are accented, while others boldface the accented syllable. Show examples from classroom dictionaries and teach your students both systems. (Digital dictionaries help with pronunciation because students can click on the speaker icon to hear the correct pronunciation.)

4. In the derivational relations stage students will learn how the spelling of the schwa in the unaccented syllable can sometimes be explained in terms of meaning or parts of speech. The unaccented *-el* ending in *angel*, for example is stressed and the short *e* is clearly heard in the adjective *angelic*; the unaccented *-an* in *human* is accented and the long-*a* sound clearly heard in the adjective *humane*. The accented syllables in these related words often provide a clue to the spellings of unaccented syllables, as well as expanding students' vocabularies.

5. In English, words tend to be accented on the first syllable more than the second (unless the word begins with a prefix), but in other languages this is reversed. Talking about stress and sorting words by the accented syllable can be beneficial to students learning English. Mastering a new language means acquiring the proper "accent."

*for* **English Learners**

## Further Exploration of Consonants

Consonants continue to be revisited in more difficult words during this stage. Consider words like *circus* or *garbage*, in which *c* and *g* represent two different sounds. (They might be spelled phonetically as /sûr-kəs/ and /gär-bĭj/.) Generalizations about the spelling of hard and soft *g* and *c* reveal an underlying logic. As in one-syllable words, the sounds of *g* and *c* depend on the vowel that follows (*a*, *o*, and *u* follow the hard sound, whereas *e*, *i*, and *y* follow the soft sound), which results in some interesting spellings. Why is there a silent *u* in *tongue*? Without it, the *g* would become soft (/tunj/). The sound of /k/ can be spelled with *ck* (*shamrock*), *c* (*magic*), *x* (*index*), and *qu* (*antique*), and many words contain silent consonants such as *t* (*moisten*), *h* (*honest*), *k* (*knuckle*), and *gh* (*daughter*). Studying silent consonants foreshadows the in-depth study of spelling–meaning connections explored in the next stage, derivational relations, in which silent letters like the *t* in *moisten* can be explained by its connection to *moist*.

## Base Words and Simple Derivational Affixes

The groundwork for the study of base words and affixes is laid during the within word pattern stage when you talk about simple prefixes and suffixes in reading vocabulary. In the late syllables and affixes stage, students explore in depth how affixes combine with base words and word roots to create new words, and how to spell many of those words. This helps students analyze unknown words they encounter in their reading, leading to expansive and elaborate vocabularies.

**DERIVATIONAL AFFIXES.** Inflectional suffixes such as *-s*, *-ed*, and *-ing* do not significantly affect the meaning or part of speech of the base word to which they are attached; *helps*, *helped*, and *helping* are still verbs. However, **derivational affixes** (both prefixes such as *re-* and *un-* and suffixes such as *-ly* and *-less*) often do affect the meanings and grammatical functions of the bases to which they are attached. For example, adding *-ful*, *-ly*, or *-ness* to the base word *help* changes it from a verb to an adjective, adverb, or noun, as in *helpful*, *helpfully*, or *helpfulness*. Students benefit from learning about the meanings of derivational affixes as well as their role in changing the meaning and grammatical function of the base word.

**Enhanced eText**
**Video Example 7.4**
Ms. Bruskotter works with her whole class of fifth graders in these two videos. Students are first given words to use in an open sort.

**BASE WORDS AND ROOTS.** The terms *base word* and *root word* are often used interchangeably. We prefer using *base word* when referring to words that stand on their own after all prefixes and suffixes have been removed (*govern* in *government*; *agree* in *disagreement*). Base words such as these are also known as **free morphemes**. We use the term *root* to refer to a word part that remains after all prefixes and suffixes have been removed but usually is *not* itself a word that can stand alone (*vis* in *visible* and *spec* in *spectator*). These roots, also known as **bound morphemes**, usually come from Greek or Latin.

A sample lesson that introduces prefixes can be found in the box below. Unlike most sorts, we do not recommend talking about the meaning of words until *after* sorting. Although the lesson begins with a brief explanation of the terms base word and prefixes, open-ended questions are used throughout to elicit ideas from students about the meaning of words and prefixes. In this way the teacher avoids *telling* students things that the focused contrast reveals about the words.

**Enhanced eText**
**Video Example 7.5**
In this second video, Ms. Bruskotter's students sort on a white board in two different ways.

# Contrasting Prefixes

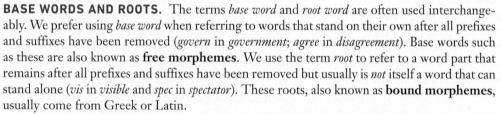

**SAMPLE LESSON**

1. **Introduce the sort.** Prepare a set of words such as those in Figure 7.7. Display the words in random order and read through them quickly. Save the discussion of word meanings until later. Ask, *What do you notice about these words?* Take lots of ideas. Remind students of the term *base word* used in the study of inflected endings, and then explain that these words all have *prefixes* added to the beginning of the base word.

2. **Sort.** Display *rebuild* and *unable* as key words and explain, *We will sort these words by the prefixes.* Model one or two and then with student help sort the rest of the words.

3. **Discuss.** Begin the discussion by saying, *Let's take a closer look at these words. What is the base word in* rebuild? (build) *When you* rebuild *something what do you do?* (Build it again). Generate a definition for each word using the base word (*recopy* means to copy again, and

so on) Then ask, *What is the same about all the words that begin with* re-? (They all mean to "do something again"). Repeat this with the words under *unable* and help students conclude that *un-* means "not" or the "opposite of."

4. **Reflect and generalize.** To summarize, ask, *What did you learn about prefixes in this sort?* (They are added to the beginning of base words and change the meaning of the word.) *What does the prefix* re- *mean?* Un-?

5. **Extend.** Students should sort their own set of words and record them in their word study notebooks. Word hunts will turn up more words including some such as *rescue* that looks like it might start with a prefix but has no base word. Challenge students to use two words from the sort in sentences such as *I am unable to rewrite the paper I lost.* Ask students to generate and define more words by adding *re-* and *un-* to base words such as *cover, finish, charge, lock, wrap,* and *plug.*

| FIGURE 7.7 | Simple Prefix Sort |
|---|---|
| rebuild | unable |
| recopy | unkind |
| refill | unfair |
| rewrite | uneven |
| review | unhappy |
| recycle | unsteady |
| reuse | unusual |
| remodel | unbeaten |

## TEACHING TIPS

### Exploring Suffixes

- Introduce suffixes through sorts in which students discover how the derivational suffixes affect the meanings of known words as well as parts of speech. For example, add *-y* to the noun *guilt* to produce the adjective *guilty*; adding *-ly* produces the adverb *guiltily*. Some derivational suffixes to study in this stage for both vocabulary and spelling include:

  *-er* as in *farmer* and *-or* as in *professor* (both denote "agents or someone or something who does something"; words of Latin origin use the *-or* spelling)

  *-y, -ly, -ful, -less,* and *-ness* (these suffixes generally change the meaning and part of speech, creating adjectives, adverbs, and nouns)

- Explore the **generative** aspect of combining prefixes and bases by constructing different words through combining and recombining prefix and base word cards or tiles in various ways: combine *dis-, re-, un-* with *able* and *order* to produce *disable, disorder, reorder,* and *unable.*

- Students should revisit the rules that govern e-drop and doubling as they add suffixes to base words. *Brave* becomes *bravely* with no change (the prefix *-ly* begins with a consonant), but when adding *-er* or *-est* (which begin with a vowel), the doubling rule applies, as in *flatter* and *flattest.* In addition, *y* must be changed to *i* before adding suffixes (*silly* to *sillier, silliest, silliness*). See Table 7.2 for a review of all the rules.

**Enhanced eText**
**Teacher Resource:** Sequence of Instruction for Core Affixes and Roots

# Word Study Instruction for the Syllables and Affixes Stage

Word study targeted to meet student needs can advance students' spelling knowledge, their vocabularies, and their strategies for figuring out unknown words in reading.

## Supporting Vocabulary Development

While vocabulary learning is important at all stages of development, it becomes an ever more important part of word study as children move into the upper grades when content related, or *disciplinary,* vocabulary is needed (Nagy & Townsend, 2012; Townsend, Barber, & Carter, in press; Zweirs, 2014). Some states' English Language Arts standards refer to the three tiers of vocabulary. After basic Tier 1 words, Tier 2 corresponds roughly to general academic vocabulary and Tier 3 is akin to domain-specific academic vocabulary (see Beck, McKeown, & Kucan, 2013). These words are often multisyllabic, and at first may be a challenge to pronounce, especially for students in the previous stage and in the beginning of this intermediate stage of reading. For example, students in this stage may struggle to read *analysis, analyze,* or *analytical* in which the accented syllable shifts.

Content area vocabulary instruction is usually a whole-class activity. It is important to remember that this vocabulary is often developmentally ahead of spelling vocabulary, so it is not appropriate to expect students to master the spelling of these words. You might add two-syllable words from a science unit on volcanoes (e.g., *mantle, pressure, pumice,* and *lava*) to sorts featuring syllable patterns and accent, but other words (e.g., *tectonically*) are not appropriate spelling words for students in the syllables and affixes stage. Many academic words are made up of complex Greek and Latin word parts that are studied in the next stage, derivational relations.

Student records prefix sort

Your own enthusiasm and curiosity about words is likely to enhance students' **word consciousness**—they develop a favorable attitude toward words and are curious about words and word learning (Blachowicz & Fisher, 2009; Scott, Skobel, & Wells, 2008; Templeton et al., 2015). Look for books about language to read to your students such as *Miss Alaineous: A Vocabulary Disaster* by Debra Frasier, *The Boy Who Loved Words* by Roni Schotter, *Frindle* by Andrew Clements, and *The Phantom Tollbooth* by Norton Juster.

**LEARNING FROM CONTEXT.** We want students to grow into independent word learners who acquire many words simply from extensive reading, but this does not happen automatically for most students. Many textbook authors try to provide a rich context to support new vocabulary and often highlight important new terms for the reader. However, an understanding of how to break unfamiliar words into morphemic parts (described next) supports vocabulary learning. Adams (1990) best emphasized this importance:

> Learning from context is a very important component of vocabulary acquisition. But this means of learning is available only to the extent that children bother to process the spelling—the orthographic structure—of the unknown words they encounter. Where they skip over an unknown word without attending to it, and often readers do, no learning can occur. (p. 150)

**MORPHEMIC ANALYSIS.** One of your most important responsibilities for word study instruction at this stage is to engage students in examining how important word elements—prefixes, suffixes, and base words—combine. This **morphemic analysis** is a powerful tool for vocabulary development and figuring out unfamiliar words during reading. Students' knowledge of morphology is related to reading comprehension and disciplinary knowledge and achievement (Carlisle, 2010; Nagy, 2007; Nagy, Berninger, & Abbott, 2006; Townsend et al., 2013).

You can show students directly how to apply this knowledge by modeling the following strategy for analyzing unfamiliar words that they cannot identify in their reading.

1. Examine the word for meaningful parts—base word, prefixes, or suffixes.
   - If there is a prefix or a suffix, take it off so you can find the base.
   - Look at the base to see if you know it or if you can think of a related word (a word that has the same base).

- Reassemble the word, thinking about the meaning contributed by the base, the suffix, and then the prefix. This should give you a more specific idea of what the word is.

2. Try out the meaning in the sentence; check whether it makes sense in the context of the sentence and the larger context of the text that you are reading.
3. If the word still does not make sense and is critical to the meaning of the overall passage, look it up in the dictionary.
4. Record the new word on a chart or in a word study notebook to be reviewed over time.

**Enhanced eText
Teacher Resource:**
"Break It Down"
Template

Take a look at how Ms. Radcliffe models this process for students in the box below, beginning with a familiar word and then extending the lesson to an unfamiliar word. Morphemic analysis will become one of the most effective means of developing and extending students' vocabulary knowledge so it is critical to model and reinforce this strategic approach often when

## Modeling Morphemic Analysis

Ms. Radcliffe says, "I've underlined one of the words in this sentence: *They had to* redo *the programs after they were printed with a spelling error.* What does *redo* mean? Yes, Chloe?"

"When you have to do something over again?"

"Okay! So you already had done something once, right?"

"Now, let's cover up this first part that we call a prefix [covers *re*]. What we have left is the base word *do*. Now, let's look at some other base words."

Ms. Radcliffe writes the words *join*, *tell*, and *write* on the board; then she writes the prefix *re-* in front of each base word as she pronounces the new word. "When we join the prefix *re-* to each base word, what happens? Can you tell me what these words now mean? We are going to be doing these things again— we can *rejoin* a group, *retell* a story, *rewrite* a paper." She then asks the students what they think the prefix *re-* means. After a brief discussion, she asks a student to look up the prefix in the dictionary to check their definitions.

Ms. Radcliffe's next step is to model this strategy with a word she is fairly certain the students do not yet know. She shows the following sentence on the overhead:

As they got closer to the front of the line, her friends had to *reassure* Hannah that the Big Thunder roller coaster ride was safe.

"Okay," Ms. Radcliffe proceeds, "I've underlined this word [pointing to *reassure*]. Any ideas what this word is?" Most students shake their heads; Kaitlyn frowns as she slowly pronounces "REE–sure." "Good try, Kaitlyn," Ms. Radcliffe responds. "You're trying to pronounce it, but it doesn't sound like a word we've

heard before. What about the beginning of the word, though? Could that be the prefix we've just been thinking about? Now look for the base word."

This prompt works for the students and they start trying to pronounce the base, *assure*, without the prefix *re-*. "Right," Ms. Radcliffe encourages. "You've taken off the prefix, *re-*, and are trying to figure out the base word. Any ideas?" Though a couple of students are pronouncing *assure* correctly, they are uncertain about its meaning.

Ms. Radcliffe continues: "Well, we know that, whatever *assure* means, the prefix *re-* means it's being done again! Let's look back at the sentence. Do you think Hannah can't wait to go on the roller coaster—or is she getting worried?" After some discussion with the students, Ms. Radcliffe talks about the base word, *assure*, and explains that Hannah's friends had probably already talked with her about how there had never been any accidents, and had helped Hannah to feel more confident—*assured* her—that Big Thunder was safe. (Most students are nodding their heads now, saying things such as "Oh, yeah, I've heard that word before.") As Hannah and her friends got closer to actually going on the roller coaster, however, they had to assure her again— *reassure* her. Ms. Radcliffe asks students to check the dictionary definition to confirm the meaning of the word (to remove doubts or fears).

Ms. Radcliffe summarizes: "Many times, by looking carefully at a word you don't know—looking for any prefixes, suffixes, and thinking about the base— you can get pretty close to the actual meaning of the word. Then ask yourself if this meaning makes sense in the sentence and text that you're reading."

encountering unfamiliar words. Students need plenty of opportunities to try it out under your guidance (Baumann et al., 2003). Encourage students to talk about their ideas as they apply the process so that you can encourage, facilitate, and redirect as necessary. It is also important to model what to do when the process does not yield an appropriate meaning for the unfamiliar word (e.g., analyzing *repel* into *re* + *pel* is not much help)—students should consult a dictionary.

**DICTIONARIES.** Always have available unabridged dictionaries and online dictionaries, as well as dictionaries that are published specifically for intermediate students. The *American Heritage Children's Dictionary* (grades 4 to 6) and the *American Heritage Student's Dictionary* (grades 5 to 9) are two dictionaries that are helpful at this stage. Attractive in format, they present definitions, word histories, and usage information in student-friendly language.

Dictionaries provide invaluable information for definitions and additional insights about words

Dictionaries are crucial for distinguishing alternative meaning of words and then determining the appropriate one. Look in the box below for an example of how Ms. Radcliff demonstrated how to use the resources in a dictionary.

Dictionaries can also provide helpful information about the history of a word and make explicit the interrelationships among words in the same meaning "families." Discussing dictionary entries illustrates how one word's entry can include information about words related in spelling and meaning; for example, the entry for *enhance* includes *enhancement*. Sections labeled "Usage Notes," "Synonyms," and "Word History" provide important information about the appropriateness of particular words and subtle but important differences among their meanings. Some entries contain stories that explain spellings and deepen understanding of important terms. See Activities 7.5 to 7.7 for ideas about teaching students how to use the dictionary.

## Using the Dictionary to Explore Alternate Meanings

While reading Robyn Montana Turner's biography of Faith Ringgold, Ms. Radcliffe focuses on the word *enhancing* in the sentence "Faith Ringgold decided to use cloth frames as a way of enhancing her art." Breaking the word into parts to pronounce the word does not seem to help because it is not in the students' speaking/listening vocabularies. Ms. Radcliffe talks about the context in which the word occurs; it may narrow the possibilities somewhat, but possible meanings suggested by the context include "protecting" or "showing."

Ms. Radcliffe underlines the word *enhancing* and explains that, to check the meaning of this word in the dictionary, they need to look up the base word, *enhance*. Reminding the students that they may need to watch out for changes in spelling when they are trying to figure out the base word for an unfamiliar word, she notes that the *e* is dropped when the *-ing* is added. Looking up a base word also helps to highlight the spelling of other forms of the word.

The students find that the dictionary definition for *enhance* is "to make greater, as in value, beauty, or reputation." Ms. Radcliffe has the students return to the sentence in the text and discuss which of these features they believe Faith Ringgold had in mind when she decided to use cloth frames. The students agree that, in the context of the sentence and the overall text, Faith Ringgold probably wanted to make her quilts more "beautiful."

**GRAPHIC ORGANIZERS.** A number of graphic organizer formats developed over the years have proven effective in helping engage students with new and/or difficult concepts that lead to understanding and deeper knowledge (Blachowicz & Fisher, 2009; Templeton et al., 2015). One key to the effectiveness of graphic organizers is their visual presentation of the relationships among target vocabulary and related concepts. Two examples provided in the activity section (7.1 and 7.2) of this chapter are *semantic maps* and *concept* (or *word*) *maps*. Discussion is critical when using graphic organizers in the classroom. As Stahl and Nagy (2006) observe, "The graphs and procedures are no more than structures to explain to students what particular words mean. It is the explanation, the talk, that is important" (p. 96).

**WORD SORTS AND VOCABULARY.** In most cases, vocabulary words from content areas should not be assigned as spelling words, but the word sorts you use to teach spelling generalizations likely contain words whose meanings should be explored, perhaps briefly, as Ms. Radcliffe did with *blister* and *mayor*. As part of your introductory routine, ask a student to look up a word and be ready to report to the group its meaning or multiple meanings. This is a good way to encourage regular dictionary use for an authentic reason. Avoid assigning students to look up long lists of words; instead, have students select several words each week to look up in the dictionary and then record definitions or other information (parts of speech, origins, and so on). Word study notebook routines can include illustrating five or more words or using them in sentences to demonstrate their meanings. You can assign words to students and then teach them how to share what they learned in either small groups or as a class activity.

**DOMAIN-SPECIFIC VOCABULARY INSTRUCTION.** Specialized vocabulary used in disciplinary studies is known as **domain-specific academic vocabulary.** For example, students will know the word *square* but it takes on a very specific meaning when used in mathematics as *square root*. Words from specific domains or content areas (*perpendicular* in geometry or *democratic process* in social studies) become increasingly important as students move through the grades. You will find these words in your district and state standards, and the curricula for the different subject areas. If there is a required textbook for a particular content area, it will usually reflect the important concepts and the domain-specific vocabulary that represent those concepts (usually bolded in text).

**GENERAL ACADEMIC VOCABULARY INSTRUCTION.** General academic vocabulary occurs across all disciplines (Coxhead, 2000; Gardner & Davies, 2013), and is related to students' school success (Townsend et al., 2012). Can you imagine any textbook without these general academic words: *however, analysis, comparison, establish, major, response,* or *structure*? General academic vocabulary is often the mortar that holds domain-specific vocabulary and concepts together, but many words are often difficult to define in isolation. Instead of trying to define words like *nevertheless, however, similar,* or *likewise,* use such terms repeatedly in meaningful contexts ("Let's look at how these ideas are similar, or alike").

Students can work in pairs to discuss the meaning of a few of these words and develop sentences to share with their classmates. In the next stage of development, students examine the Greek origin of words that begin with *ana-* to find that it is derived from "a loosening," or "breaking up," and possibly find other words. For now, learning this word family in its various contexts, and being comfortable with reading, writing, and talking about what the word *analyze* means is ideal. Furthermore, during this syllables and affixes stage, students may examine this word family for the meaning of different suffixes; for example, *-ed, -ly, -ic, -al*. These exercises increase students' exposure to general academic vocabulary in different contexts. See Teaching Tips on the next page.

**CONCEPT SORTS AND DISCIPLINARY LEARNING.** Concept sorts have been described in earlier chapters and are appropriate at all levels as a way to activate prior knowledge, generate interest in a topic, and develop academic vocabulary. For new vocabulary to "stick," students need multiple exposures to those words in multiple contexts (Beck, McKeown, & Kucan, 2013). Concept sorts provide that exposure and the process of categorizing helps students think about relationships

TEACHING TIPS

## Develop Academic Vocabulary

- Help students understand what functions the words serve—what the words ask readers to do (Flanigan, Templeton, & Hayes, 2012). For example, students may know that *establish* is a synonym for *set up* or *show*, but presenting this word in phrases helps students understand the nuances of meaning: to *establish an argument* is a more formal presentation of ideas than *to set up* or *show* an argument. There are other phrases that add depth to students' understanding of *establish*; for example, *establish the truth*, *establishment of the state of Israel*, and *established custom*.

- Text structures that compare and contrast, sequence, examine cause and effect, pose a problem, and/or present a resolution have their own general academic vocabulary associated with them. For example, phrases like *in contrast*, *on the other hand*, *likewise*, and *along the same lines* indicate a "compare and contrast" text structure. Take an excerpt from a text and model for students how to locate general academic vocabulary. You may want to begin with the lists prepared by Coxhead (2000; available online at https://www.victoria.ac.nz/lals/resources/academicwordlist/), or Gardner and Davies (2013; available online at https://corpus.byu.edu/coca/) to show them general academic vocabulary and how these words and phrases function to hold text together. After this modeling, ask students to work with partners to locate general academic vocabulary, create class charts of these words and phrases, and record these collections in their vocabulary notebooks. They can share their lists with the class and discuss how the general academic vocabulary indicates a particular text structure.

- Another way to familiarize students with the meaning of general academic vocabulary is to increase their exposure to related words or words that come from the same word family. By using dictionaries and other resources, students can find numerous related words that will clarify meanings. For example, when you look up *analyze* in a dictionary or an online source (e.g., OneLook), you find many members of the *analysis* word family including *analyzed*, *analyzing*, *analysis*, *analyst*, *analytic*, *analytical*, *analytically*, *analyses*, *psychoanalyst*, *microanalysis*, and *self-analysis*.

- To provide further depth and practice with vocabulary, use the list of phrases that can be found in OneLook and other references; for example, the word *courage* generated 122 phrases (see González-Fernández & Schmitt, 2017).

between words and their ideas. Concept sorts can be used in all content areas such as sorting geometric shapes in mathematics or sorting terms related to immigration in a social studies unit.

As an introduction to a study of the solar system, Mrs. Wilson helped her students brainstorm what they knew about planets and what they knew about stars. Taking some of their ideas, and adding more, she created a handout with phrases and examples that she gave students the next day to cut apart and sort in small groups. She encouraged the students to talk about each item and share what they knew in the group to support their decisions. She suggested that they set aside any items that they were not sure about. These were turned into questions such as "What are stars made of? Or "Do planets give off light?" Over the next few weeks, as students read books and articles, watched videos, and examined models and photographs, Mrs. Wilson reminded students of these questions and others to set a purpose for reading and discussing. At the end of the unit, Mrs. Wilson asked the students to sort again and this time everyone was able to sort accurately.

**Enhanced eText**
**Teacher Resource:**
Planets and Stars
Concept Sort

Concept sorts for planets and stars

**WHICH WORDS TO TEACH?** A common lament is that there are "so many words, so little time." Although most of your students' vocabularies grow through wide reading and discussion about that reading, you are still responsible for selecting words for students to tackle. Publishers of the textbooks, eBooks, and other curricular resources that you may be required to use have already selected and highlighted vocabulary and, while that is helpful, you still have a bit of work to do. The following questions will guide your decisions about which "target" or "key" vocabulary words to select when planning a unit of study and how to well address them (Templeton et al., 2015).

- *Which words are critical to address in depth before moving into the unit/selection?* What are the words that represent major concepts and for which students need to develop a deep understanding? Introduce and develop these at the beginning of the unit and before the reading, as well as during and after.
- *Which words are critical to address only briefly before moving into the unit/selection?* Students must know these words for the specific reading assignment, but do not require a deep understanding. Mention these words and provide brief definitions.
- *Which words are critical but might lend themselves to students' problem solving during their reading?* These words are important but students may figure them out through morphemic analysis and/or help from the context. Follow up on these words after the reading.

**TEACH VOCABULARY DIRECTLY.** Whether the words are domain specific, general academic vocabulary, or words you have selected from a core book you will be reading with your students, vocabulary needs to be taught directly. At the intermediate and middle grades, the following principles guide instruction:

- Activate background knowledge. Find out what students already know about a word, and remind them of related terms they may already know. For example, if you chose *solar*, you can explore their understanding of the terms *solar heat*, *solar system*, *solar eclipse*, and so on.
- Explain the meaning of the word, how it is used, and its relationship to other words that share similar meanings: *solarium*, *solar energy*, and so on.
- Ensure students have many exposures to words in meaningful contexts, both in and out of connected text. Display words and refer to them frequently.
- Use graphic organizers, charts, diagrams, or concept sorts to portray relationships among the words. Students can be actively involved in creating visual displays.
- Always be ready to include morphemic analysis as part of any vocabulary study. Look for words with structural elements such as syllables, base words, affixes, and the effects of affixes on the base words to which they are attached. For example, the word *renewable* can be analyzed as having a prefix that means "again," a familiar base word, and a suffix that creates an adjective.
- Discuss examples and non-examples. In the case of *solar*, important non-examples would relate to other words that share a similar spelling but have a different meaning: *sole*, *solitude*, *solitary*, *solidify*, and so on.

Actively involve students in the exploration of words to develop students' word consciousness, a positive attitude toward *learning* words and a curiosity *about* words.

## Systematic Word Study for Spelling

Too often, spelling instruction at the intermediate level and above lacks systematic attention to generalizations. Without a good understanding of the features that require instruction at this level, teachers in the upper grades often give students lists of spelling words from content areas that are really vocabulary words (*amphibian*, *vertebrates*, *metamorphosis*, *carnivore*). While such words are important for understanding content and concepts, they lack any common spelling features and may not be appropriate for students who are in different spelling stages.

## Sorting and Discussion in the Syllables and Affixes Stage

Throughout this chapter, we offer suggestions for planning and carrying out word study. There are a few cautions for you to consider during this upper-level word study.

**Students sort at their seats before a group discussion**

***Sorts are just a starting place.*** Students can often sort the words in a focused contrast easily by visual features (such as patterns for long a: *ai, ay, a-e*). How much learning takes place is questionable unless the teacher uses open-ended questions to help students develop generalizations that can be applied to unstudied words and reading. Weekly routines should include developing and writing a reflection, finding more examples, and using words in ways that explore meaning.

Many sorts during this stage hinge on making spelling–meaning connections. After the spelling aspect becomes apparent, have students try to figure out the meaning connection to the spelling. For this reason, we discuss ways for you to increase students' exposure to words that share a specific spelling–meaning connection. For example, think of how easy it is for students to sort words that begin with prefixes like *dis-, ex-* or *mis-*. What requires effort and thought and results in lasting learning is determining what the prefixes mean and how they change the meaning of the base word.

***Choosing words for focused contrasts.*** Consider the difficulty of the vocabulary in word sorts during this stage. It is likely that intermediate-grade students in the syllables and affixes stage can read many words whose meanings elude them so it is important to consider the semantic difficulty of the words as much as the spelling challenge when selecting words and features to study at this stage. For example, many of the words that follow the "*i* before *e* except after *c* or when sounded like *a* as in *neighbor* and *weigh*" rule may not be in the speaking vocabulary of elementary students (*conceive, perceive, conceited, receipt*). Selecting a few words whose meanings students might not know, or words that they only know tenuously, is fine, but do not overburden sorts with these words.

## The Word Study Lesson Plan in the Syllables and Affixes Stage

We recommend the basic word study lesson plans described in detail in Chapter 3. Teacher-directed sorts are a good way to introduce new features, but open sorts involve students in more active thinking. You may be skeptical about using word sorts with older students, but experience proves the value of sorts at this level. Even adults who are poor spellers enjoy and benefit from hands-on sorting activities (Massengill, 2006). Here is a review of the basic word study routines:

1. Introduce a new focused contrast by sorting in a group or have students sort individually. Either way, lead them in a discussion of the generalizations revealed by the sort as Ms. Radcliffe did at the beginning of this chapter. You should also discuss word meanings before or after (in the case of prefixes) sorting.
2. Have students sort their own set of words and check their sorts. Sorting the weekly words, not once, but four or five times across the week, is a valuable routine for students and should be at the heart of systematic developmental word study.
3. Blind sorts are very valuable but not appropriate for all focused contrasts. Include blind sorts with a partner when visual patterns (*-el* and *-le* or *-er,-ar,-or*) make the categories obvious but sound is not a clue. However, sorting words with prefixes (*re-* and *un-*) and suffixes (*-ful, -less,* and *-ness*) makes a blind sort too easy. Introduce a modified blind sort in

which the partner has to define a word without showing or saying it (that is, "This word means the opposite of *selfish*.")

4. Encourage students to clarify and summarize their understandings with oral and written reflections that describe what they learned from the sort. Model as needed to be sure students know how to construct these.

5. Use extension activities across the week to reinforce and broaden students' understandings. Activities include homework and working with partners in blind sorts, writing sorts, word hunts and timed sorts as described in Chapter 3. Games and other activities are another way to engage students in further exploration and review of the features they are learning in their sorts. Word study notebook activities are described on page 284.

# Sequence and Pacing of Word Study in the Syllables and Affixes Stage

For students in the elementary grades who have reached the syllables and affixes stage, there is less urgency than in earlier stages because they have mastered much of what is typically considered "phonics" (consonants, blends, digraphs, and vowels) and they can spell most single-syllable and high-frequency words. However, students still have much to learn about spelling, and knowing how to tackle unfamiliar multisyllabic words they encounter in reading.

## Sequence of Focused Contrasts

A sequence of spelling features based on what students do developmentally for this stage is presented in Table 7.4. In addition, the study of **generative morphology**, putting together the building blocks of base words, roots, and affixes to create new words, is explored through vocabulary study. Knowing the processes of word combination plays a powerful role in vocabulary development as well as spelling.

## Placement Using Spelling Inventories and Spell Check

**Enhanced eText**
**Video Example 7.6**
In this video, Ms. Bruskotter talks about how she assigns students to groups in her 5th grade classroom.

The Elementary Spelling Inventory (ESI) described in Chapter 2 and found in Appendix A helps identify students in the syllables and affixes stage. Some teachers find that the Upper-Level Spelling Inventory (USI) provides better information about students in the later part of the stage. If students appear to be in the late syllables and affixes or derivational relations stage on the ESI, be sure to move on to the USI. Use spell checks and Table 7.1 (see page 260) to more accurately identify what features students are ready to study—what they are using but confusing— to plan instruction.

At advanced spelling stages (both syllables and affixes and derivational relations) you may find students "leveling out" on their spelling inventory results; that is, they are instructional on a range of spelling features at the same time and few features are missing completely. This means that a strict sequence of instruction is not as important as in previous stages, and you can form larger groups for instructing certain features. For example, although prefixes are listed as being in the late syllables and affixes stage they can be introduced any time, as well as to students in early derivational relations.

**EARLY, MIDDLE, OR LATE PLACEMENT.** Identifying whether students are in the early, middle, or late part of the stage (see Table 7.4) will help you target where in the sequence of features to begin word study instruction. If in doubt about where to place students, remember it is best to take a step back and study earlier features that students may not fully understand even if they are spelling many words with those features correctly.

**Early.** Students early in this stage know how to spell the vowel patterns in most single-syllable words but make errors when adding inflectional endings, as in SHOPING for *shopping* and

**TABLE 7.4**    **Sequence of Focused Contrast for Syllables and Affixes**

| Patterns and Features | Examples |
|---|---|
| ***Early*** | |
| Plural endings -*s* and -*es* | *books/dishes* |
| Unusual plurals | *goose/geese, knife/knives, fish, sheep* |
| Inflectional endings: | |
| Sort by sound of -*ed* suffix | *walked* /t/, *wagged* /d/, *shouted* /əd/ |
| Doubling | *stopping, stopped* (CVC) |
| E-drop | *skating, skated* (CVCe) |
| No change | *walking, walked* (CVCC) and *nailing, nailed* (CVVC) |
| Change final *y* to *i* and add -*ed* or -*s* | *cried* (*y* after a consonant), *plays* (*y* after a vowel) |
| Irregular Verbs | *throw/threw, shine/shone* |
| Compound words | *pancake, sidewalk* |
| ***Middle*** | |
| Syllable juncture patterns | |
| VCCV doublet | *button, happy* |
| VCCV different consonants | *window, sister* |
| V/CV open with long vowel | *bacon, lazy* |
| VC/V closed with short vowel | *river, camel* |
| VCCCV blend or digraph | *pilgrim, tangle* |
| V/V | *giant, diet* |
| Vowel patterns in accented syllables: | |
| Common vowel patterns in accented syllable | *lonely, toaster, owner* |
| Less common and ambiguous vowels in accented syllables | *fountain, powder, laundry, awful, marble, prepare, repair, narrow* |
| Final unaccented syllables: | |
| /ər/ | *beggar, barber, actor* |
| /ən/ | *captain, human, frighten, basin, apron* |
| /əl/ | *angel, able, central, civil, fertile* |
| /chər/ and /zhər/ | *culture, measure, teacher* |
| Special consonants in two-syllable words | hard and soft *g* and *c* |
| | silent consonants (*written, knuckle, rhythm*) |
| | *ph* (*dolphin*), *gh* (*laughter, daughter*) |
| | *qu* (*question, antique*) |
| ***Late*** | |
| Simple prefixes and base words | *un-* (not–*unlock*), *re-* (again–*remake*), *dis-* (opposite–*dismiss*), *in-** (not–*indecent*), *non-* (not–*nonfiction*), *mis-* (wrong–*misfire*), *pre-* (before–*preview*), *ex-* (out–*exclude*), *uni-* (one–*unicycle*), *bi-* (two–*bicycle*), *tri-* (three–*tricycle*) |
| Suffixes | *-y* (adjective–like, tending, toward: *jumpy*), (*-ly* (adverb–like: *gladly*), *-er, -est* (comparatives), *-ful* (full: *graceful*), *-less* (without: *penniless*), *-ness* (condition: *happiness*), *-ment* (action, process, or *result* of an action or process: *excitement*), *-ion* (action, process, or *result* of an action or process: *action*) |
| Two-syllable homophones | *pedal, peddle* |
| Two-syllable homographs | *rebel, rebel* |

CARRYES for *carries*. They are ready to explore the "double, drop, or nothing" principles that govern the place where base word and inflection meet.

**Middle.** Students in the middle of the stage usually add inflectional endings correctly but make mistakes with syllable junctures within words and with unaccented final syllables, as in RIPPIN for *ripen* and BOTEL for *bottle*. They are ready to extend their understanding of doubling to syllable junctures within words as they study open and closed syllables. Vowel patterns that students learned in the within word pattern stage are reviewed within the accented syllable. After studying accented syllables, students in the middle of the syllables and affixes stage look at the final unstressed syllable and two-syllable homophones and homographs. They also examine some unusual consonant sounds and spellings.

**Late.** Students who are in the late phase of the stage can spell most words correctly in the syllables and affixes categories on the inventory. In word study, the focus is on simple prefixes and derivational suffixes that affect the meanings of familiar base words in straightforward ways (*rebuild, dislike*) as an introduction to the spelling–meaning connection that is the focus in the derivational relations stage. For a faster pace, students in middle grades or high school might skip this introduction and go to the sorts recommended for early derivational relations in which they review these affixes in more advanced words (*reconsider, discourage*).

**PACING AND EXTRA SUPPORT.** Normally, achieving students in the intermediate grades will take at least two years and more to progress through this stage. It may be tempting to rush students through the syllables and affixes stage into the derivational relations stage but they may not be ready for the more advanced vocabulary used in the word sorts. At the same time, students in the middle grades who are still in the syllables and affixes stage should be moved along at a steady pace and might skip the late features because they are covered again in early derivational relations. Students in the middle grades and high school who are still in the syllables and affixes stage may need the extra support suggested in *Words Their Way® with Struggling Readers: Word Study for Reading, Vocabulary and Spelling Instruction, Grades 4–12* (Flanigan, et al., 2011).

## Spelling Strategies

By the syllables and affixes stage, expectations for correct spelling include a large percentage of the words students use when writing. A good activity to do with students is to brainstorm a list of the many things they can do when they do not know how to spell a word they need for writing. A list can include the following:

> Listen for the sounds and spell as best you can
> Ask a friend or ask a teacher
> Look around the room or in books where the word might have occurred
> Write the word and then ask yourself if it looks right
> Think of a word that sounds like it (spell by analogy)
> Look it up in a dictionary

Help students to prioritize these options, and throughout this stage show them how to think of related words and see if there is a spelling–meaning connection they can make.

**HELP CHILDREN DEVELOP A SPELLING CONSCIENCE.** We want to create a desire in students to improve their spelling and have pride in what they can do correctly. There are several ways to do this (see Teaching Tips on the next page), keeping in mind there needs to be a balance between expectations for correct spelling and encouraging students to spell as best they can in order to write with real purpose.

**DOES IT LOOK RIGHT?** Intermediate readers have seen many words and can use the strategy of writing a word and then considering whether it looks right. Introduce this using the "Have-a-Go" sheet (see Activity 6.6 in Chapter 6), but as students progress, they can use the strategy less formally. They need only to write one or two attempts anywhere that is handy.

**TEACHING TIPS**

## How to Develop a Spelling Conscience

- Talk with students about *why* good spelling matters (to be sure readers can understand what we write; to give a good impression) and *when* it matters. Brainstorm with them a list of the kinds of writing that need to be correctly spelled.

- Meet with students during and after their independent writing time and talk about their spelling. Compliment them on the words they got right (or almost right) and ask them what they did. You may be surprised at the wide range of strategies they already use (Chandler, 1999). Talk about a few words that you think they might be able to add to their personal lists or dictionaries, or spell correctly with a bit more attention. For example, Ruth wrote, "The wind blue all through the night." The teacher began by saying, "You got that tough word *through*. How did you know that?" Ruth replied that when she spelled it as THRU that it did not look right so she found it in her spelling dictionary. Then the teacher pointed to the word *blue*. "That names the color but there is a homophone for the word you need. Let's check our homophone collection."

- Expect students at this stage to edit their written work for spelling errors but only after you take the time to teach spelling and editing strategies. Simply saying, "Read your paper and find your spelling mistakes," is not particularly helpful. Modeling is important; when you write for students, think aloud about spelling, and model spelling strategies as well as proofreading techniques such as rereading to check spelling. Occasionally, project a student's writing sample (with permission) and model with the class how you go about proofreading it using the tips on page 78 in Chapter 3.

**LOOK IT UP IN THE DICTIONARY.** Let's be honest: Few of us turn to a thick heavy dictionary to look up the spelling of a word if other resources are more easily available—like spell check or asking the person beside you. Still, we want students to practice this skill so that it is available to them. Spelling dictionaries contain lists of commonly used words without definitions so they are much easier to use. (See page 225 in Chapter 6 for a list of spelling dictionaries.) If you have students who are literate in a language other than English, they may find a bilingual dictionary handy. They can look up a word they know in their own language to find the English spelling.

*for* **English Learners**

**SPELL CHECK USING SOFTWARE.** Students who compose on the computer have access to spell check as a way to edit their work. Some educators and parents worry that using spell check discourages students from learning to spell. There is no evidence that this is true and besides, if word study is an ongoing part of your curriculum, then your students are getting the spelling instruction they need. After students reach the syllables and affixes stage, they should be spelling most words correctly. While they continue to create spellings for words they don't know in certain situations, such as journal writing, the process is less valuable. Learning how to use spell check for polished work is a useful skill.

# Assess and Monitor Progress in the Syllables and Affixes Stage

Involve students in the elementary grades in their own progress monitoring, which, as they track their progress over time, can be very motivating.

## Weekly Assessments and Spell Checks

Weekly spelling tests and unit assessments are described in Chapter 2 as a means by which you can monitor student progress. Call out 10 words each week, but also include some words that assess transfer of a feature (e.g., more words to which students must add -*ing* or -*ed*) or words from a previous week's sort to send the message that students are not just responsible for the set of words they sorted that week. When students make errors on these assessments, you can ask them to go back to their word study notebooks to review the generalizations they explored and then to analyze their errors in an attempt to determine why they misspelled Figure 7.8 shows two examples from a lesson on hard and soft *g*. In addition, review and grade students' word study notebooks once a week. (See Enhanced eText link to "Word Study Expectations Ms. Bruskotter's Fifth Grade" in Chapter 9, p. 347.)

| FIGURE 7.8 | Error Reflections | |
| --- | --- | --- |

| Word | Error | What went wrong |
| --- | --- | --- |
| guide | giude | I reversed the u and i. The u keeps the g from taking the soft j sound before an i. |
| iceberg | iceberge | Don't need an e on the end of this word because the sound is hard g, not the soft j sound. |

## Monitoring Progress

To assess retention over time, prepare an assessment that samples words from previous lessons, or use unit spell checks. Prepared spell checks can be found in Appendix B and in the supplement *WTW Word Sorts for Syllables and Affixes Spellers*. Use the assessments' results to determine whether students have met the goals listed on the goal-setting chart. We recommend that you meet with students individually to go over the spelling inventory you used to assess them and to identify where to begin the study of features listed on the chart.

Figure 7.9 is an example of the goal-setting chart for early syllables and affixes. After taking the spell check as a pretest, the score is recorded and correct responses checked off. A posttest is given after studying the feature, and again, the score is recorded and correct responses are checked off. When students score 90 to 100 percent on weekly tests and 80 to 100 percent on unit spell checks, that feature can be considered "mastered." If students do not meet these goals, you should consider whether they were appropriately placed for instruction or whether they got adequate practice each week with the words. It may be necessary to reteach using different sets of words or increase the number of times students sort their words during the week.

| FIGURE 7.9 | Goals for Early Syllables and Affixes | |
| --- | --- | --- |

| 18. Spell inflected endings (-ed, -ing, -s) | double _____ e-drop _____ nothing _____ change y to i _____ es _____ |
| --- | --- |
| Spell Check 18 | Pretest:     Date:     Posttest:     Date: |

# Word Study with English Learners in the Syllables and Affixes Stage

English learners in the syllables and affixes stage have mastered many of the basic phonics and spelling generalizations of English and are ready to study the more advanced features of this stage. However, many of the words used in sorts at this stage may be new vocabulary. For this reason, it is especially important to make word study a language-learning event. Words that are featured due to spelling issues should be defined and used in conversational speech as a part of every lesson. The suggestions in Chapter 6 to support English learners apply to this stage as well. (See also *Words Their Way with English Learners* by Helman, Bear, Templeton, Invernizzi, & Johnston, 2012; and *Teaching Reading and Writing: The Developmental Approach* by Templeton & Gehsmann, 2014.) Many features in the syllables and affixes stage may present some conceptual difficulty for English learners:

*for* **English Learners**

- Verb forms may be constructed differently in the native language, particularly inflected verbs. In Spanish, for example, the corresponding equivalent to the English *-ing* is often an infinitive used as an abstract noun (e.g., *To sleep is good for you*). As a result, English learners may have difficulty understanding English sentences that use the *-ing* form as the subject of the sentence (e.g., *Sleeping is good for you*) or perceiving the pronunciation of *-ing* or *-ed* at the ends of English words (Swan & Smith, 2001).
- Plurals may also be formed differently in the native language. Perceiving and producing the pronunciations of *-s* or *-es* at the end of a word may require explicit attention. It will also take some time to learn the small subset of English nouns, verbs, and adjectives that involve unusual internal spelling–sound changes (*knife/knives, leave/left, child/children*).
- In contrast to many other languages, English spellings are full of double letters that might puzzle English learners.
- The compounding and generative aspects of English may not occur in the native language. Compound words like *outsmart* or *windfall* may seem strange to English learners, especially when they are metaphoric (*headstrong*) rather than literal (*sundown*). Similarly, the common use of affixes and base words in English to generate new words may be rare in some languages.

Studying these features in detail is important in helping English learners not only learn the spellings and meanings of words but also understand *why* words work the way they do in English.

There are also commonalities to look for in other languages. Spanish shares many of the same Greek and Latin morphemic units as English and this includes the prefixes *pre-, re-, in-, dis-*, and *mis-*. It is easy to find cognates like *preparer, revisar,* and *intolerante* in cognate dictionaries, online, and in paper bilingual dictionaries, and these might be added to lists, charts, and word hunts. The number prefixes (*uni-, bi-*, and *tri-*) are also used in Spanish and many cognates can be found such as *biciclete* (bicycle) or *trío*.

**Enhanced eText**
**Video Example 7.7**
In this video, Ms. Bruskotter discusses her classroom organization based on the assessments and how she meets the special needs of EL students.

# Word Study Routines and Management

Organizing differentiated instructional-level groups for word study is challenging but will best serve students' needs, especially those who are below grade level or learning English. The key to finding time for meeting with small groups is establishing routines. When students learn weekly word study routines, they become responsible for completing much of their work independently (both in class and at home) or with partners, leaving you free to work with other small groups. Look for organization tips in Chapter 3 and Chapter 9.

**Enhanced eText**
**Video Example 7.8**
Ms. Bruskotter describes word study activities and her weekly schedule.

## Word Study Notebooks in the Syllables and Affixes Stage

Using word study notebooks in this stage continues to be an easy way to help you and your students manage the routines and organization of word study.

After pasting a sort into her word study notebook, this student has indicated the part of speech beside each one

**WORD STUDY NOTEBOOK ACTIVITIES.** Recording the weekly sort by writing words into the appropriate categories and writing a reflection are the basic word study notebook activities. In addition you may want to develop a list of activities from which you and your students select independent seatwork or homework. Some of these may be more appropriate at times than others, and some can be done to review previous lessons.

- Work with a partner to complete a blind writing sort. Write up the headers for the sort. One partner calls the words aloud and the other writes them in the correct category without seeing the word. Each word should be checked immediately and corrected if necessary. If using word with prefixes, which pose no problem in a blind sort, partners can offer a definition such as "use again" for *reuse.*
- Students complete a speed sort by sorting their words the day after a sort is introduced and record the time. They should sort again a day or two later and try to beat the first time.
- Words from word hunts can be added to categories.
- Select five words to look up in the dictionary. Record the multiple meanings you find for each word. (See other dictionary-related ideas at Activity 7.6)
- Select five words and use them in sentences or illustrate them to demonstrate meaning.
- Find words that have base words and underline the base word.
- Take a base word and add affixes to form other words (such as *reuse, misuse, useful, useless*)
- Break words into syllables and underline the accented syllables.
- Make appropriate words on your lists plural or add *-ing* or *-ed.*
- Circle or underline any prefixes or suffixes you find in the words on your list.
- Add a prefix and/or suffix, when possible, to words on your list.
- Sort your words by parts of speech or subject areas and record your sort.

**WORD STUDY NOTEBOOK ORGANIZATION.** With the increased emphasis on vocabulary learning, you may want to have your students divide their word study notebooks into two or three sections:

- In Tamara Barnen's class, the first section is titled "Word Study" and is a record of the work done with assigned sorts. This section includes written sorts, timed sorts and word hunts as well as reflections and other activities such as those described earlier that are follow-ups to the assigned sorts.
- The second section is called "Looking into Language" and contains lists of words related to themes and units, words categorized by parts of speech, graphic organizers, and semantic webs of content area studies. Students can create synonym and antonym wheels in their word study notebook, as shown in Figure 7.10.

**FIGURE 7.10   Synonym and Antonym Wheels**

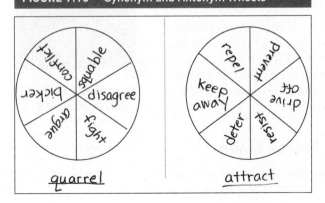

- Some teachers include a third section, called a "Personal Dictionary," in which students record words they frequently need to use in writing.
- Because these notebooks will be used constantly, many teachers recommend stiff-backed, stitched composition books. Other teachers have students use loose leaf paper inserted into either a 1½-inch, three-ring binder or a less expensive cardboard folder with three pre-inserted brads. Notebook paper, handouts and worksheets can be added at any time and place, making a notebook a more flexible choice.

# RESOURCES FOR IMPLEMENTING WORD STUDY *in Your Classroom*

You can find prepared sorts on at *WTW Digital* and in Appendix E. Appendix F has words listed by features that can be used to create your own focused contrasts or to modify the suggested sorts.

*Words Their Way®: Word Sorts for Syllables and Affixes Spellers 3rd edition* (Johnston, Invernizzi,

Bear, & Templeton, 2018) has more than 50 ready to use blackline masters. The focused contrasts are divided into nine units with spell checks and a monitoring form. Use the spell checks to better identify what students are ready to study and also for pre- and post-testing to monitor progress.

# ACTIVITIES for The Syllables and Affixes Stage

Several vocabulary activities are described first in this section followed by some dictionary activities. The remaining games and activities are designed to extend and reinforce the spelling features covered in this stage.

## Vocabulary Activities

Refer to vocabulary activities in Chapter 6 (Activities 6.1 to 6.5) that are also appropriate for this stage.

### 7.1 Semantic Maps

Semantic maps provide an excellent way to activate students' background knowledge on a topic by asking them to brainstorm words related to a topic, which gives you an idea of how much students already know. During or after the brainstorming session, organize the terms into categories. Keep the map posted and add new terms throughout the unit. "Rainforest Ecosystem" is the example used here.

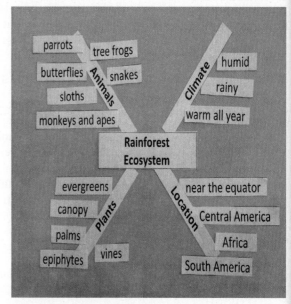

Semantic map for rainforest

### PROCEDURES

1. To kick off a unit, ask students what words or ideas they associate with rainforests. Record their ideas without too much comment and feel free to add a few more terms that were not mentioned but are important terms in the unit.

2. Talk with the students about different ways in which these words may be categorized and then arrange the words, with students' input, along the appropriate "leg" (category) of the map. This may lead students to think of more terms. As they talk and read further, they are growing their understanding of the new terms and their relationships to more familiar words and concepts. Have students make their own copy of the map as a follow-up activity and add to it over time.

3. Keep the maps posted throughout the unit, prominently displayed, and have students add terms as they move through the unit. Students may also decide that a particular term belongs to a different category, and if they can justify it, then they can move the term to the new category.

## 7.2 Concept Mapping

Concept or word maps focus on a specific term and visually represent its place in a conceptual hierarchy using guided questions. In Figure 7.11, the word *colony* is the focus. When you first present the map, the ovals are blank except for the headings: What is it? What is it like? What are some examples? What are some non-examples? As you discuss each question, fill the ovals with ideas offered by students

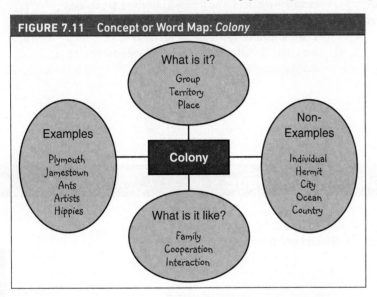

**FIGURE 7.11   Concept or Word Map:** *Colony*

What is it?
Group
Territory
Place

Examples
Plymouth
Jamestown
Ants
Artists
Hippies

Colony

Non-Examples
Individual
Hermit
City
Ocean
Country

What is it like?
Family
Cooperation
Interaction

**Enhanced eText**
**Teacher Resource:**
Concept Map Template

## 7.3 Vocabulary Jeopardy

Students enjoy playing the familiar Jeopardy game after brainstorming terms related to a study unit.

**MATERIALS**  Create vocabulary cards for a study unit. Start with the vocabulary students generate on their own, followed by a scan through texts and materials. Determine four to five categories, such as "What Comes Out of a Volcano?" with terms such as *pumice, sulfur, ash, lava,* and *molten rock.* With these cards, students make a Jeopardy game. (Activity 6.18 in Chapter 6 contains a sample game board.) Students write items on cards that relate to facts and concepts they have studied and write correct responses on the backside. For example, *Material that comes out of a volcano* could take responses that include *What is ash?* or *What is molten rock?* Teams of students play the game as a whole-class vocabulary review of the unit.

## 7.4 Word Roots

Examining how Greek and Latin roots combine with affixes helps students build their generative morphological knowledge. This examination builds on the earlier investigation of how base words combine with affixes and anticipates the study of derivationally related words in the next stage. This activity, adapted from Templeton and Gehsmann (2014), illustrates how the initial presentation and discussion of the Latin roots *vis/vid* and *dict* may be planned over the course of a week's instruction. See Table 7.5 for additional Greek and Latin roots to explore at this stage.

**PROCEDURES**
*Day 1.*

1. Share with the students that they'll begin looking at roots that come from Latin, and present the word *predict.*

   Ask the students what it means if they *predict* something. Then, ask them if they see a prefix in *predict* (pre). What does it mean? (before) Cover *pre-*, and tell the students that they're

**TABLE 7.5** Greek and Latin Roots: Generative Vocabulary Instruction at the Syllables and Affixes Stage

| Common Greek Roots | Common Latin Roots |
| --- | --- |
| *tele* (far, distant: *telegraph*) | *aud* (hear: *audible*) |
| *therm* (heat: *thermometer*) | *dict* (say: *predict*) |
| *photo* (light: *photograph*) | *spec* (look: *inspect*) |
| *gram* (thing that is written: *diagram*) | *vis/vid* (see: *vision, video*) |
| *graph* (writing: *digraph*) | *port* (carry: *portable*) |
| *meter, metr* (measure: *barometer, metric*) | *struct* (build: *structure*) |
| *micro* (small: *microscopic*) | *rupt* (break: *interrupt*) |
| *scop* (view, see: *telescopic*) | *fract* (break: *fracture*) |
| *phon* (sound: *homophone*) | *scrib/script* (write: *transcribe, transcription*) |
| *bio* (life: *biography*) | |
| *auto* (self: *autobiography*) | |

left with *dict*, which is not a word that can stand by itself, but which is the *root* of *predict*. Explain that *dict* comes from a Latin word that means "to say or speak," and that when we "predict" something [display the whole word] we *say* [point to *dict*] that something will happen *before* [point to *pre*] it actually happens.

If you feel your students don't need such an explicit walkthrough, after you present the word *predict* ask them what they think the root means. Then, ask them that if they *predict* that something will happen, what they think that means.

2. Display the words *vision* and *revision*. Discuss the meaning of *vision*, emphasizing that it has to do with "seeing." Then, ask the students about *revision*, and what's involved during the *revision* step in writing. Ask them to turn to a partner and talk about how they think *revision* has to do with "seeing." You are guiding them to the realization that, when they *revise* their writing, they are "seeing" [point to *vis*] it "again" [point to *re-*].

*Day 2.*

1. Display the words from Day 1, and ask the students how they defined *dict* and *vis*. Then, display the following words:

| | |
| --- | --- |
| visit | dictate |
| visor | dictionary |
| visibility | contradict |
| supervise | dictionary |

2. Ask the students to talk with a partner about how the meaning of each root works in each of these words. For example, how does the meaning of "say" or "speak" work in the word *dictionary*? When someone *supervises* you, what does that have to do with the meaning of "see"? Circulate around the room as your students are talking, then bring the whole class back together to share their ideas.

*Day 3.*

With *vis* or *dict* as a root, have students create a word using any of the prefixes and/or suffixes they have explored up to this point. In their word study notebook, have them write the word, a definition for it, and—if it can be illustrated—include an illustration. Be sure to follow up and have the students share their new words.

# Dictionary Skills for Syllables and Affixes Spellers

You should base instruction in the organization and use of the dictionary on a print version, but because of their ease of use, online dictionaries and dictionary apps have the potential to bring students more easily and engagingly into the exploration of words. Online versions of dictionaries include a "speaker"-type icon that, when clicked, provides a pronunciation of the word. For the upper elementary grades, some dictionaries include information about a word's origin in the entry. At the time of this writing, probably the best dictionary app for upper elementary students and beyond is the website "Vocabulary." It is part of a more expansive vocabulary instruction app—it provides accessible definitions, context sentences, and more important, morphologically related word families for most entry words.

## 7.5 Teaching the Dictionary

Model how to use a dictionary regularly as part of word study lessons, read-alouds, subject area lessons, or any time a question might arise that can be answered in a dictionary. Begin with a print version but move to electronic versions as well.

**PROCEDURES** Walk through the dictionary features with your students, projecting pages on a white board or screen. Introduce the many different kinds of information that they can find:

- Introductory pages addressing how to use the dictionary, including important terminology (e.g., guide words, entry words)
- Introduction of special features throughout the dictionary; boxes that address synonyms, morphology, word histories
- Pronunciation guides are discussed in the introduction and also usually appear on every other page in the dictionary
- Information presented in each word entry:

  Parts of speech
  Definitions with context sentences that help students make the important distinctions for multiple-meaning words
  Syllable breaks
  Accent or stress (sometimes with accent marks and sometimes with bolded letters)
  Inflected forms (e.g., *editing, edited*)

**MATERIALS** Here are some resources you might use in your classroom. Often schools have a set of dictionaries on a rolling cart, but having a few in your classroom is important. Consider a variety of dictionaries instead of multiple copies because then students can compare entries and features.

Online:

*Longman Dictionary of Contemporary English*
*Merriam-Webster Online Dictionary*
*Vocabulary.com*

Print:

*Longman dictionary of American English* (5th ed.). Pearson.
*The American Heritage children's dictionary*. Boston: Houghton Mifflin Harcourt.
Ayto, J. (2009). *Oxford school dictionary of word origins: The curious twists & turns of the cool and weird words we use*. Oxford: Oxford University Press.
Fine, E. H. (2004). *Cryptomania! Teleporting into Greek and Latin with the Cryptokids*. Berkeley, CA: Tricycle.

## 7.6 Weekly Word Study Notebook Dictionary Assignments

After students learn how to find information in a dictionary, be sure they get practice doing so by assigning activities such as these that require them to use the dictionary.

**PROCEDURES** Studying in weekly sorts suggests different assignments that students can complete in their word study notebooks, such as:

- To reinforce open and closed syllables, ask students to write 5–10 of the week's words according to the syllable breaks found in the dictionary (*tab-let, ta-ble*).
- Write 10 words and indicate where the accent falls on the stressed syllable. Homographs like *pro'duce* and *pro duce'* are interesting to look up.
- Find more words that begin with a certain prefix. Caution students to be sure the words do indeed contain a prefix. (e.g., *reappear* has the *re-* prefix meaning "again," but *reason* does not).
- Select 5–10 words to look up and record the definition(s). You might select these yourself or let students choose. Finding new definitions for polysemous words students already know makes this worthwhile. For example, students are likely to say they already know what *table* means (a piece of furniture) but of course it can mean other things, such as a chart or to put something aside.

## 7.7 Dictionary Bees

These drills are designed to help students develop skills in using the dictionary but keep them fast and fun. You can make these competitive or not. If one student is consistently the fastest make that student an announcer or referee so others can be first.

**MATERIALS** Every student should have an elementary dictionary.

**PROCEDURES** Here are several different drills:

- *How many turns?* Announce a word for everyone to find using the fewest number of page turns. Remind students to first think about where the word is likely to come in the alphabetic sequence and then to use guidewords at the top. Tell them to keep track of how many tries it takes. Model this for the students first, and then do it yourself at the same time they do; after a while they might beat you at the game! Students can work in teams—one keeps score of the number of times the page is turned by the other student.
- *Look up the spelling.* Announce a word that students are not likely to know how to spell (e.g., *legitimate* or *foreign*) and challenge them to find the word in the dictionary. The first one to find the word, write it on a white board or card, and hold up the written word is the winner. Even if students know how to spell the word, they cannot write it until they find the word.
- *Find information.* Write an unfamiliar word on the board (perhaps one from an upcoming unit in science or social studies) and challenge them to find the definition, part of speech, pronunciation, or origin.

# Spelling Activities

These activities and games are designed to reinforce the generalizations and memory for words found in sorting activities. Many of the games described in previous chapters are adaptable for use with the features studied in this stage:

*Adaptable* **for Other Stages**

- The Spelling Game (Activity 6.13, in Chapter 6) can be used with any feature, as it involves asking a player to spell a word before moving on the board. The word cards from any sort can be used as the playing cards for the game.

- Go Fish (5.29, in Chapter 5), and the Racetrack Game (6.12), "I'm Out" (6.14), Jeopardy (6.18), Declare Your Category! (6.20), and Homophone Rummy (6.23) in Chapter 6 work well with the many features in this stage that have three or more categories: syllable patterns, vowel patterns in stressed syllables, unaccented final syllables, silent consonants, hard and soft *g* and *c*, prefixes, suffixes, and so on.

### 7.8 Compound Word Activities

*Adaptable* **for Other Stages**

When asking students to spell compound words, consider the difficulty of the base words they use. *Cupcake* and *outfit* consist of two words that have common one-syllable patterns mastered in the within word pattern stage, but *cheeseburger* and *grandparent* include two-syllable words that students may find challenging to spell (*burger* and *parent*). Following are ways you can explore these words:

**PROCEDURES**
- Share some common compound words with the students (e.g., *cookbook* and *bedroom*). Discuss their meanings, pointing out how each word in the compound contributes to the meaning of the whole word. You might ask students to draw pictures for illustration. For example, a student might draw a horse and a shoe, and then a horseshoe.
- Using the compound word list in Appendix E, prepare word sorts that can be sorted in a variety of ways. The sort can focus on shared words (**head**light, **head**band, **head**ache, **head**phones versus **foot**ball, **foot**hill, **foot**print, **foot**step). You might also conduct concept sorts; for example, words that have to do with people (*anyone, someone, somebody, anybody*) or things we find outdoors (*sunlight, airplane, waterfall, airport*).
- Have students cut a set of compound words apart. Then challenge them to create as many new compound words as they can. Some words will be legitimate words (*mailbox*); others will be words that do not formally exist but could (*bookbox*). Have students share and discuss their words. Students might then write sentences using the pseudo-words and draw pictures that illustrate the meaning of each.
- Give students a word such as *fire, man, head, book,* or *rain* and challenge them to see how many related compound words they can brainstorm (*fireplace, firefighter, cookbook, bookmark, rainbow, raincoat*). Teams compete to see who can come up with the longest list of unique words. Let the team with the longest list read it aloud. Everyone checks off any word that another team has also thought of. Only words that no other team thinks of earn points. Repeat until every team has had a chance to read the words remaining on their list. Remember that each part of the word must stand alone as a free morpheme.
- Create a year-long class collection of compound words on a chart or in a section of word study notebooks. This collection can include hyphenated words (*good-bye, show-off, push-up,* and so on).

### 7.9 Double Scoop

This board game helps students review and master consonant doubling and *e*-drop when adding inflectional endings. It is appropriate for small groups of two to four students. You can find a ready-to-use version of this game at *WTW Digital*.

**MATERIALS** Prepare a game board as shown in Figure 7.12 and write sentences, such as the following examples, on small cards to go into a deck. You will also need playing pieces, a spinner or die, and a small white board or paper on a clipboard for writing answers under the categories of *e-Drop, Double,* and *No Change*.

| | |
|---|---|
| The bunny was *hopping* down the road. | I was *hoping* to get new shoes. |
| The cat is *sunning* herself on the chair. | He is *diving* into the pool. |
| Brittany *shopped* at her favorite store. | She *glided* across the ice. |

**PROCEDURES**

1. Players put their pieces on the sun to start. Player 2 (the reader) reads a sentence card and repeats the underlined word.
2. Player 1 (the writer) spells the underlined word under the correct heading on the white board or paper.
3. Player 2 checks the answer by comparing it with the sentence card. If it is correct, player 1 spins and moves that number of spaces on the playing board.
4. Play then moves to the next student, who must spell and sort the underlined word given by the next player. If there are only two players, they simply switch roles.
5. The first player to reach the double scoop of ice cream wins.

**FIGURE 7.12   Double Scoop Game Board**

### 7.10 Freddy, the Hopping, Diving, Jumping Frog

In this board game for two to four players, students review generalizations for adding *-ing*.

**MATERIALS**  Create a game board using one or more of the follow-the-path templates in Appendix F, or by arranging green circles in a path to represent lily pads much like the game board for the Hopping Frog game in Activity 5.30 in Chapter 5. On each space, write either *Double*, *e-Drop*, or *Nothing*. Prepare playing cards by writing a variety of words with *-ing* added until there is an equal number for each rule (e.g., *hopping*, *diving*, *jumping*). Use words that students have been sorting and add more words from the syllables and affixes word lists in Appendix F. You can also add penalty or bonus cards such as the following:

> You have the strongest legs. Jump ahead to the next lily pad.
> You are the fastest swimmer. Skip 2 spaces.
> Your croaking made me lose sleep. Move back 2 spaces.
> You ate too many flies. Move back 2 spaces.

**PROCEDURES**

1. Place playing cards face down and put playing pieces on the starting space.
2. Each player draws a card, reads the card aloud, and moves to the closest space that matches. For example, if the card says *hopping*, the player moves to the nearest space marked *Double*.
3. A player who draws a penalty or bonus card must follow the directions on the card.
4. The winner is the first to reach the home lily pad.

**VARIATIONS**  Players can draw for each other, read the word aloud, and the player whose turn it is must spell the word correctly before moving to the appropriate space. You can also prepare a set of words with uninflected forms on cards (*hop*, *jump*, *dive*), and have players write how the word should be spelled before moving to the appropriate place. Include an answer sheet with words in alphabetical order to check if there is disagreement.

### 7.11 Slap Jack

This card game for two people may be used to contrast open- and closed-syllable words as represented by any of the syllable spelling patterns (V/CV versus VCCV; V/CV versus VC/V). The object of the game is for one player to win all 52 cards. You can find a ready-to-use version of this game at *WTW Digital*.

*Adaptable* **for Other Stages**

**ACTIVITIES | SYLLABLES AND AFFIXES STAGE**

**MATERIALS** On 52 small cards, write the words that you want to be contrasted. For example, 26 words that follow the open-syllable VCV pattern (*pilot, human*) and 26 that follow the closed-syllable VCCV pattern (*funny, basket*); see word lists in Appendix G. Write the words on both ends of the cards so that neither player has to read the words upside down.

**PROCEDURES**
1. Deal the cards one at a time until the deck is gone. Players keep their cards face down in a pile in front of them.
2. Each player turns a card face up in a common pile at the same time. When two words with either open syllables or closed syllables are turned up together, the first player to slap the pile takes all the cards in the common pile and adds them at the bottom of his or her pile. Turning cards and slapping must be done with the same hand.
3. A player who slaps the common pile when there are not two open- or closed-syllable words must give both cards to the other player.
4. Play continues until one player has all the cards. If time runs out, the winner is the player with the most cards.

**VARIATIONS** Additional syllable juncture patterns may be added to the deck—for example, closed-syllable VCV (*cabin, water*) and VV (*riot, diet*). Word cards could be prepared for any feature that has two or three categories, such as inflected forms with -*ed* that players would slap when both words represent e-drop, double, or no change.

*Adaptable* **for Other Stages**

### 7.12 Word Study Uno

This game is a version of the popular card game for three to four players.

**MATERIALS** Create a deck of at least 30 word cards by writing words in the upper-left corners of tagboard rectangles or blank cards. Use words that represent at least four different patterns for a particular feature. For example, words like *gather, gentle, contest,* and *center*) would fall into four categories of hard *g*, soft *g*, hard *c*, and soft *c*. Also create 10 special cards: four "Wildcards," three "Skip" cards, and three "Draw 2" cards.

**PROCEDURES**
1. Deal five cards to each player. The remaining cards are placed in a deck face down and the top card is turned face up to start the discard pile.
2. Players take turns playing cards that match the pattern of the face-up card. For example, if the beginning card is *gentle,* the first player could put down *genius, gerbil, or ginger.*
3. Players can also play one of the special cards. The "Draw 2" card forces the next player to pick two cards from the pile without playing any cards. The "Skip" card indicates that the next player loses a turn. When a "Wild" card is played, the player can select the category.
4. A player who cannot put down any card must draw from the pile. If the draw matches the pattern of the face-up card, it can be played.
5. A player who has only one card remaining must yell, "Uno." If the player forgets, another player can tell the player with one card to draw another card.
6. The first player to run out of cards wins the game.

*Adaptable* **for Other Stages**

### 7.13 Pair Them Up

In this version of Memory or Concentration, students match up unusual plurals.

**MATERIALS** Create 11 sets of cards using word pairs such as the following: *wife/wives, leaf/leaves, life/lives, wolf/wolves, knife/knives, man/men, woman/women, mouse/mice, goose/geese, tooth/teeth, child/children.* Make one card each of *fish, sheep,* and *deer.*

**PROCEDURES**
1. Shuffle the cards and lay them all out face down in a 5-by-5 array.

2. Each player turns over two cards at a time. If the cards make a match, the player keeps them and turns over two more.

3. If *fish*, *sheep*, or *deer* are turned over, there is no match and the player automatically gets to keep the card and go again.

**VARIATIONS** Create a similar game for two-syllable homophones (*berry*, *bury*) or for irregular past-tense pairs: *sleep/slept, slide/slid, shine/shone, freeze/froze, say/said, think/thought*, and so on.

### 7.14 The Apple and the Bushel

The purpose of this board game is to give students added practice in differentiating between -*le* and -*el* endings.

**MATERIALS** Prepare the Apple and Bushel game board (see Figure 7.13) and word cards with words that end in -*el* and -*le* (*bushel, angel, apple, angle*).

**PROCEDURES**
1. Players draw for each other and read the word aloud.
2. Players must spell the word orally or in writing correctly and then move the marker to the nearest -*le* or -*el* ending that spells the word.
3. The game continues until one player reaches the bushel. (*Note*: To get in the bushel, an -*el* word must be drawn. A player who draws an -*le* word must move backward and continue playing from that space.)

**VARIATION** Add words that end with -*il* (*pencil*) and -*al* (*pedal*).

### 7.15 Prefix Spin

This game for two to four players reinforces the idea that prefixes and base words can be combined in different ways. Let students play this after they have sorted words with the featured prefixes. You can find a ready-to-use version of this game at *WTW Digital*.

**MATERIALS** Make a spinner using the directions in Appendix G. Divide the spinner into six sections and write each of these prefixes in a section: *mis-, pre-, un-, dis-,* and *re-* (use *re-* twice because it can be used in twice as many words as the others; see Figure 7.14). Prepare a deck of 24 cards with the following base words written on them: *judge, match, take, wrap, set, test, view, charge, pay, able, like, form, count, place, use, order, cover,* and *pack* (you can duplicate the last six to enlarge the deck; each can combine with three of the prefixes—for example, *misplace, replace,* and *displace*). Include paper and pencil for each player to record their matches. You may also want to include a list of allowable words to solve disputes. Matches include the following:

> miscount, misjudge, mismatch, misplace, mistake, misuse, prejudge, preset, pretest, preview, preform, preorder, prepay, recount, rematch, replace, retake, reuse, reset, retest, review, recharge, reform, reorder, repay, recover, repack, rewrap, unable, uncover, unlike, unpack, unwrap, discount, displace, discharge, disorder, disable, discover, dislike, disuse

**FIGURE 7.13** Apple and Bushel Game Board

**FIGURE 7.14** Prefix Spin

### PROCEDURES

1. Turn the base word cards face down in a deck in the center of the playing area. Turn up one card at a time.
2. The first player spins for a prefix (such as *un-*). If the prefix can be added to the base word to form a real word (such as *unwrap*), the player takes the card and records the whole word on paper.
3. If the first player spins a prefix that cannot be added (such as *dis-*), the next player spins and hopes to land on a prefix that will work with the base word. This continues until someone can form a word.
4. A new base word is turned up for the next player and the game continues.
5. The winner is the player who has the most base word cards at the end of the game.

### VARIATIONS

1. Use two spinners with suffixes written on the second one, such as *-s*, *-ed*, *-ing*, and *-able*. Award a bonus point when a player can use both the prefix and suffix with a base word, as in *replaceable* or *discovering*.
2. Make two sets of cards with the base words and pass out four words to each player that are laid out face up. Each player spins and tries to match the prefix with one of the words he or she has. A word that is successfully matched can be turned over in a point pile and another card drawn so the player always has four cards for possible matches. This works well with prefixes that might not be as common as the original five.

## 7.16 Feed the Alligator

This game for two or more players reviews words that end in unaccented final syllables. This example uses words that end in *-ain*, *-an*, *-in*, and *-on*. Ready-to-use versions of this game can be found on the website including one with final *-er*, *-ar*, *-or*, and *-ure* endings as well as one with *-le*, *-el*, *-il*, and *-al* endings.

### MATERIALS

- Write a variety of words ending in *-ain*, *-in*, *-an*, and *-en* without their final syllable on heavy paper or card stock to cut apart. On the back of each word card, write the correct ending for the word. For example, for the word *mountain*, one side of the card would have *mount-* and the other side would have *-ain*. On the back of each card also write a number from 1 to 3 in the corner, using 3 for harder words. You will need two or three cards with a picture of an alligator and a strip of paper or a card with the possible endings.
- Create a collection of dried beans, corn, or some other small objects that will be "food" for the alligator. Store these in a baggie or small container.

### PROCEDURES

1. Shuffle the word cards and arrange them face up in a deck. Place the card of possible endings (*ain*, *en*, *an*, *in*) next to it for reference. Player 1 looks at the first card and identifies which ending should be used to correctly complete the word and names the word. (Players can also be asked to write out the entire word.)
2. Player 1 then turns the card over to see whether he or she is correct. If correct, Player 1 takes the card, looks at the number on the card, and takes the number of beans or other objects indicated on the card.

3. If incorrect, the player may not take any food and must return the word card to the bottom of the deck to be used again.
4. Players who get an alligator card when it is their turn must feed the alligator and lose all their beans or other pieces.
5. When all the cards have been used, the player with the most beans left is the winner.

## 7.17 Follow the Leader

This game is for three or four players to review two-syllable words with long *a* or long *o*. The goal is to be the first to discard all of the cards in a hand.

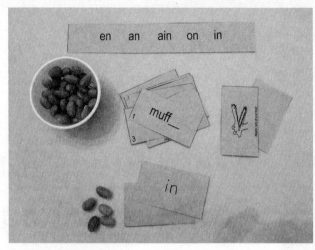

Feed the Alligator game

### MATERIALS

- Create a single set of playing cards.

### PROCEDURES

1. Shuffle the cards. Deal six cards to each player and put the remaining deck in the middle to draw from. The top card is turned over to start the game and this sets the pattern to be followed. For example, if the word is *rainbow*, other players must discard and read words with the *ai* pattern in the accented syllable.
2. Each player tries to lay down a card from their hand with the same vowel pattern and reads it aloud. If they do not have a word to match, they must draw a card from the deck. If the drawn card makes a match, they can discard it.
3. Players may elect to use a "Change It" card if they have one in their hand. When a "Change It" card is played, players can name a new pattern and play a card on it.
4. Play continues around the circle until one player is out of cards.

# Word Study for the Derivational Relations Stage

## Chapter 8: Derivational Relations STAGE

*WTW Digital* is a new online tool that accompanies this core text, and it was designed to help you implement word study in an engaging and interactive way. Resources for this chapter include:

- **Automatically scored qualitative spelling inventories** suggest each student's approximate stage of spelling development. Word study groups are also automatically generated based on inventory results.
- **30 interactive sorts** that allow students to engage with word study in a digital environment
- **4 word study games** in a printable format that present fun activities for students to build their phonics, vocabulary, and spelling knowledge.

An access code for *WTW Digital* is included with each new copy of package ISBN: 9780135174623. Visit www.wtwdigital. pearson.com to get started.

**D**erivational relations describes the type of word knowledge that more advanced readers and writers develop in the final stage. The term emphasizes how spelling and vocabulary knowledge at this stage grow primarily through understanding processes of *derivation*—from a single base word or word root, we *derive* related words by adding prefixes and suffixes. Though students start exploring these processes in the within word pattern and syllables and affixes stages, their understanding expands and becomes much more elaborate at the derivational relations stage. Exploring words at the derivational relations stage draws on extensive experiences in reading and writing. The word sorts that students do at this level, together with their exploration of words, generally have more to do with *vocabulary* development than simply spelling development.

We will visit the sixth- and seventh-grade classrooms of Jorge Ramirez and Kelly Rubero several times in this chapter. Here, Mr. Ramirez illustrates how a teacher can guide students to understand that a "silent" consonant in one word may often be explained by another word that is related in spelling and meaning, and in which the consonant is pronounced.

Mr. Ramirez randomly displays a number of words including *sign, columnist, muscle, solemn, crumb, hasten, muscular,* and *column.* He takes the time to talk about a few of the words before having the students sort them: "What do you notice about the words *sign* and *hasten*? What might make them hard to spell?" Students point out that there are silent letters. "Let's think about why those silent letters may be there." Mr. Ramirez writes *sign* on the board and says, "The spelling of the word *sign*—as when you *sign* a letter—contains a *g* even though you don't hear it. When you *sign* your name, what's that called?" (*signature*) He writes *signature* under the word *sign* and underlines the *g* in both words. He asks, "What do you notice? Right! We hear the *g* in *signature* but not in *sign*. Would you say that *sign* and *signature* are related in meaning?" Students usually have an "aha" moment when they see the words presented this way, one under the other, so that the letter sequence *sign* is obvious.

Mr. Ramirez displays the headers *silent consonant* and *sounded consonant* and says, "I am going to put *sign* under the heading 'silent consonant' and *signature* under the heading *sounded consonant*." He then writes the word *hasten* and asks, "What letter is silent in this word? Is there a word related to *hasten* and in which the *t* is sounded?" (*haste*) He writes *haste* underneath *hasten*, underlining the *t* in both words, and asks, "Where should I put *hasten*? (Under *silent consonant*) Where should *haste* go? (Under *sounded consonant*) Let's look for more word pairs and find the letter that is silent." With the students' help, he sorts the rest of the words.

As they sort, Mr. Ramirez talks about the meanings of some of the words. He knows that students may be unfamiliar with one of the words in a pair such as *solemn, solemnity* or *resign, resignation.* He tells the students, "If you know one of the words, that word may be a clue to the meaning of the unfamiliar word. For example, if you're unsure about *solemnity* you can take off the suffix, think of the meaning of the base, *solemn,* and it will be your clue to the meaning of *solemnity.*" In discussing *column,* he refers to a *column* in a newspaper or website—a *columnist* is the person who writes that *column.* The completed sort appears as follows:

| Silent consonant | Sounded consonant |
|---|---|
| **sign** | **signature** |
| bomb | bombard |
| soften | soft |
| muscle | muscular |
| crumb | crumble |
| fasten | fast |
| design | designate |
| column | columnist |
| resign | resignation |
| hasten | haste |
| solemn | solemnity |
| moisten | moist |

Mr. Ramirez has the students *reflect* by asking, "Why do many words like *sign* and *solemn* have silent letters? What can that tell us?" He is guiding the students to the realization that such spellings keep the meaning that the words share with related words— the silent letters can be heard in related words.

# Literacy Development of Students in the Derivational Relations Stage

We find students in the derivational relations stage beginning in the upper-elementary grades but most are in middle school and high school, and the stage continues through adulthood. Students at this level are fairly competent spellers, so the errors they make are "high level," requiring a more advanced foundation of spelling and vocabulary. However, misspellings such as INDITEMENT, ALLEDGED, IRELEVANT, and ACCOMODATE occur even among highly skilled and accomplished readers and writers. (Indeed, the persistence of such misspellings leads many adults to lament that, though they are good readers, they are "terrible" spellers!) Exploring the logic underlying the correct spellings of these words not only helps us learn and remember the correct spelling, but more important, leads to a deeper understanding and appreciation of how words work to represent meaning. This understanding and appreciation leads in turn to the growth and differentiation of concepts—to vocabulary development.

## Reading in the Derivational Relations Stage

Advanced, proficient readers have had extensive experience with reading, thinking about, and responding to texts across many genres. These experiences shape their knowledge about language and orthography (Reichle & Perfetti, 2003). The type of word knowledge that underlies advanced reading includes an ever-expanding conceptual foundation and the addition of words that represent these concepts. Advanced readers should explore further the Greek and Latin word elements that are the important morphemes out of which thousands of words are constructed (Crosson & McKeown, 2016; Mountain, 2015). This is a **generative process** (Templeton, 2011/2012; Templeton et al., 2015), and linguists estimate that 60 to 80 percent of English vocabulary is generated by combining bases, word roots, prefixes, and suffixes (Nagy & Anderson, 1984). More than 90 percent of science and technology vocabulary is generated through this process (Green, 2008). Students who understand this generative

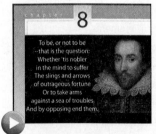

**Enhanced eText**
**Video Example 8.1**
Examine the Derivational Relations stage of spelling and the accompanying reading behaviors.

process are in a position to analyze and understand the unfamiliar domain-specific academic vocabulary they will encounter in the reading materials of middle school and high school. Reading is the primary means by which students gain access to these words; the words simply do not occur as often in oral language. The explicit, generative, and deep study of written vocabulary adds to students' reading experience and conceptual development.

Readers at the derivational stage develop their understanding of the "meaning" layer of orthography quite extensively. This understanding, based primarily on morphological knowledge, supports their perception and identification of multisyllabic words. During the reading process at this stage, in addition to the syllabic chunks that intermediate readers and students in the syllables and affixes stage find in longer words, the advanced reader picks up larger **morphemic** or meaning chunks as well (Taft, 2003; Templeton, 1992). For example, an intermediate reader attempting to read the word *morphology* analyzes it syllable by syllable, picking up the letter sequences *mor-pho-lo-gy*. The advanced reader likely picks up the meaning chunks in *morph-ology*, which cross syllable boundaries and offer insights into the meaning of the word (*morph* = structure, *ology* = study of).

> **FIGURE 8.1** Sixth-Grader's Response Journal
>
> At the end of Chapter 17, it said "as long as Rontu lived" - so that means he'll die before Karana leaves the island. I wonder when he dies, if she'll get a new pet. Maybe another wild dog. Every once in a while, the book gives you hints about things that will happen, just like this one. Sometimes this book is Eerrie with a capital E. Is this how you spell Eerrie?

**Enhanced eText**
**Video Example 8.2**
Middle school teacher Ms. Rubero discusses the reading interests of her students in the advanced stage of reading.

## Writing in the Derivational Relations Stage

Proficient writers have the potential to use the forms and functions—structures and purposes—of different genres. Together with their expanding vocabularies, this knowledge of form and function helps to inform their voice, which in turn guides their word choice when they write and revise. This understanding and sensitivity is often evident in their informal writing as well, such as in journals. Figure 8.1 presents an excerpt from a sixth-grader's response journal; her literature response group has been reading Scott O'Dell's *Island of the Blue Dolphins*. Her writing shows literary insights ("Every once in a while, the book gives you hints about things that will happen . . .") and a humorous stance ("Sometimes this book is Eerrie with a capital E").

## Vocabulary Learning in the Derivational Relations Stage

Through wide reading and study in specific content domains, students' growth in **general academic** or "Tier 2" vocabulary, as well as **domain-specific** or "Tier 3" vocabulary, accelerates dramatically at the derivational relations stage. It is important to note the distinction between *word-specific* and *generative* vocabulary instruction at this stage. There are effective activities for teaching a deep understanding of the concepts that specific words represent, which has been the traditional objective of vocabulary instruction (Beck, McKeown, & Kucan, 2013); for example, graphic organizers such as 4-square maps and vocabulary webs. It is at least equally important, however, to teach *about* words—the generative morphological processes by which meaningful word parts combine (Bowers & Kirby, 2010; Nagy, 2007; Templeton, 2011/2012; Templeton et al., 2015). Together with knowledge of an increasing number of Latin and Greek word parts, knowledge of generative processes helps students independently generate significant vocabulary growth. For example, knowledge of the

Students collecting words that illustrate frequently occurring Latin roots in middle school English class

Latin word root *gress*, meaning "move," together with knowledge of a few affixes, can generate an understanding of dozens of words, including *progress, progression, transgress, transgression, regress, regressive, aggressive*. This type of knowledge helps students independently figure out the meaning of thousands of words they will encounter throughout their lives. Although students are introduced to the base word/word root distinction during the syllables and affixes stage, their understanding of the generative features of Greek and Latin affixes and roots really takes off during the derivational relations stage.

# Orthographic Development in the Derivational Relations Stage

Table 8.1 summarizes some of the characteristics of spellers in this stage—what they know and what they use but confuse. At first glance, misspellings at the derivational relations stage appear similar to those at the syllables and affixes stage. Errors occur at the **syllable juncture** and with the vowel in unaccented or unstressed syllables. In contrast to the two-syllable words in which these errors occur at the syllables and affixes stage, however, derivational relations errors occur primarily in words of three or more syllables.

The Upper-Level Spelling Inventory (USI) is useful for collecting spelling errors for analysis and better identifying the spelling-meaning "landscape" that students are exploring. Specific spelling errors characteristic of this stage fall into three main categories:

1. Multisyllabic words often have **unaccented** syllables in which the vowel changes to the *schwa* sound, as in the second syllable of *opposition*. Remembering the base from which this word is derived (*oppose*) often helps students choose the correct vowel.

**TABLE 8.1**    **Characteristics of Derivational Relations Spelling**

| Gradations of Stage with Examples of Spelling | What Students Spell Correctly | What Students Use but Confuse | What Is Absent |
|---|---|---|---|
| *Early Derivational Relations*<br><br>CONFADENT for *confident*<br><br>MENTLE for *mentality* | Most words they use in writing<br><br>Vowel patterns in accented syllables<br><br>Doubling and e-drop at syllable juncture | Unaccented vowels in derivationally related pairs | *Note:* No features are completely absent. |
| *Middle Derivational Relations*<br><br>CRITISIZE for *criticize*<br><br>CLOROFIL for *chlorophyll*<br><br>CIRCUMFRENCE for *circumference*<br><br>ADAPTIBLE for *adaptable*<br><br>DOMINENCE for *dominance* | All the above plus:<br><br>Common Latin suffixes and prefixes<br><br>Same or similar spelling of most bases and word roots in related words | Other spelling-meaning connections<br><br>(criti*c*/criti*c*ize; perceive/perception)<br><br>Some Greek letter-sound relationships<br><br>Greek and Latin elements | |
| *Late Derivational Relations*<br><br>ILITERATE for *illiterate*<br><br>COMOTION for *commotion*<br><br>SUPRESSION for *suppression* | All the above | Advanced suffixes<br><br>Absorbed prefixes | |

2. Several suffixes have different spellings despite similar pronunciations. For example, *-tion* in *opposition* is easily confused with *-ian* (*clinician*) and *-sion* (*tension*), which sound the same.
3. Other errors occur in the feature known as an **absorbed** or **assimilated prefix**. The prefix in *opposition* originally comes from *ob*, but because the word root starts with the letter *p* (*pos*), the spelling has changed to reflect an easier pronunciation.

## The Spelling–Meaning Connection: Foundations of *Generative* Vocabulary Knowledge

The spelling–meaning connection is another way of referring to the generative understanding of words and the significant role that spelling knowledge plays in understanding and using morphology and in learning vocabulary (Rosenthal & Ehri, 2008; Templeton, 2011/2012). In this stage students systematically and comprehensively explore spelling–meaning relationships: The principle that words that are related in *meaning* are often related in *spelling* as well, despite changes in sound (Chomsky, 1970; Templeton, 1992, 2011/2012, 2012). This supports a powerful spelling strategy: If you do not know how to spell a word, try to think of a word that is similar in meaning and spelling that you *do* know how to spell. This strategy also applies to figuring out the meaning of unfamiliar words in reading and thereby expanding your vocabulary: If you are unsure of the meaning of a word, think words that are spelled alike and look for a meaning that is common across them. This consistency supports a powerful integration of spelling and vocabulary instruction.

Being aware of logical spelling–meaning connections that apply to most words in the English language results in far more productive and confident word learning than the traditional one-word-at-a-time approach—demonstrating the "teach someone *how* to fish" adage here as well. For example, a general academic vocabulary word like *paradigmatic* is better learned, understood, and retained when related to *paradigm*, which students may already know. The new word *paradigmatic*, in turn, now provides a helpful clue to remembering the silent *g* in *paradigm*. In the same way, *mnemonic* can be related to *amnesia* and *amnesty*, all of which have to do with memory.

*criticize* as CRITISIZE

*critic → criticize*

**Enhanced eText**
**Video Example 8.3**
Additional examples of how the spelling-meaning connection improves spelling are discussed.

**COMMON AFFIXES.** Students first explore the spelling–meaning connection when studying affixes in the syllables and affixes stage, and review it in derivational relations with more advanced vocabulary and additional affixes. Table 8.2 (pp. 315–316) presents the most frequently occurring prefixes and suffixes.

*Adding* -ion *to Words.* The suffix pronounced "shun" or "zhun" can be spelled several ways, as in *protec**tion***, *admi**ssion***, *musi**cian***, and *inva**sion***. Hundreds of words in English end with this suffix, which means "act, process, or the result of an act or process." Usually a verb is changed to a noun by adding *-ion*, as in *elect* to *election* or *create* to *creation*. In the case of *-ian* it means "person" (*clinician, dietician*). This suffix affects sounds in interesting ways—it sometimes causes a final consonant sound to alternate (as in *detect/detection*, in which the /t/ becomes /sh/) or a vowel to alternate (as in *decide/decision*).

The generalizations governing changes in spelling when this suffix is added are complex, but you can address them early in the derivational relations stage because there are so many familiar words to examine. To spell the /shən/ suffix, consider the ending of the base word. The following list summarizes the generalizations about this suffix and the order in which they can be introduced and explored.

1. Base words that end in *-ct* or *-ss*, just add *-ion* (*traction, expression*)
2. Base words that end in *-ic*, add *-ian* (*magic/magician*)
3. Base words that end in *-te*, drop the *e* and add *-ion* (*translate/translation*)
4. Base words that end in *-ce*, drop the *e* and add *-tion* (*reduce/reduction*)
5. Base words that end in *-de* and *-it*, drop those letters and add *-sion* or *-ssion* (*decide/decision, admit/admission*)
6. Sometimes *-ation* is added to the base word, which causes little trouble for spellers because it can be clearly heard (*transport/transportation*)

**FIGURE 8.2** Word Sort to Explore *–ion* Ending

| | | | |
|---|---|---|---|
| divide | division | produce | production |
| delude | delusion | reduce | reduction |
| deride | derision | introduce | introduction |
| allude | allusion | reproduce | reproduction |

In Figure 8.2, students first pair the base word (the verb) with its derivative (the noun) and then group the pairs by the spelling patterns to determine the generalization (for example, words ending in *de*, drop the *de* and add *sion*). Students should also look for the type of vowel or consonant alternations that have occurred.

**SOUND ALTERNATIONS.** Students at the derivational relations stage explore more directly how the sound of vowels and consonants change or alternate in related words. Despite these changes in sounds, the spelling often remains the same to preserve the meaning connection. For example, note the sound changes, but consistent spelling, in the bases of the words *allege/allegation* and *patriot/patriotic*.

**Consonant alternation.** As we saw in the opening vignette, consonants that are silent in one word are sometimes "sounded" in a related word, as in the words *sign*, *signal*, and *signature*. The pronunciation of consonants often changes when a suffix is added to words, as in the /t/ to /sh/ shift in *prevent/prevention*, /s/ to /sh/ in *compress/compression*, and /k/ to /sh/ in *magic/magician*. This phenomenon is known as **consonant alternation**.

Consonant alternation study begins with silent/sounded pairs such as *bomb/bombard, crumb/crumble, muscle/muscular, hasten/haste, soften/soft*. As students move through the grades, they will encounter more words that follow this pattern, thereby expanding their vocabularies (*column/columnist, solemn/solemnity, assign/assignation*). Rather than trying to remember the spelling of one silent consonant in one word, students learn the strategy: Try to think of a word related in spelling and meaning; you may get a clue from the consonant that is sounded.

**Vowel alternation.** In the pair *revise/revision*, the long *i* in the base word (*revise*) changes to a short *i* in the derived word (*revision*). **Vowel alternation** occurs in related words in which the spelling of the vowels remains the same despite an alternation or change in the sound represented by the spelling. These alternations occur as suffixes are added and the accented syllables change (e.g., *imPOSE / IMpoSItion*). Students benefit most from the study of vowel alternation patterns when these patterns are presented in a logical sequence. Begin by studying related words containing simple vowel alternations that change from long to short vowel sounds as suffixes are added, as in *nature* to *natural*, *sane* to *sanity*, and *divine* to *divinity*.

Next, students explore in depth the spelling of the **schwa**, the least-accented vowel sound in a word. As affixes are added to words, the accented syllables change—*conFIDE* to *CONfident*—and the change in accent influences the sound of the vowel. The long *i* changes to a schwa in *reside/resident*, *oppose/opposition*, and *invite/invitation*. In other words, the vowel changes from the short sound to the schwa: *allege/allegation*, *excel/excellent*, *habitual/habit*.

**Predictable spelling changes in vowels and consonants.** After students have systematically explored some base words and their derivational relatives that share the same spelling, they begin examining related words in which both the sound *and* spelling change. This change is predictable or occurs regularly in families. For example, the spelling change of the long *a* in *explain* from *ai* to a schwa in the derived word *explanation* is not the only word pair in which this type of change occurs; it also occurs in *exclaim/exclamation* and *proclaim/proclamation*. A similar change from long to short *e* occurs in *receive/reception* and *deceive/deception*. Students learn that, if the base word has the *ai* or *ei* spelling, the derived word's spelling is simply *a* or *e*. Students can examine these words after they understand the spelling–meaning patterns presented earlier.

Students first conduct a word sort in which each base word is paired with its derivative, and then sort the word pairs according to the specific spelling change that occurs. The following sort illustrates this feature:

| | | |
|---|---|---|
| receive/reception | exclaim/exclamation | detain/detention |
| conceive/conception | proclaim/proclamation | retain/retention |
| deceive/deception | reclaim/reclamation | |
| perceive/perception | acclaim/acclamation | |

Often *multiple* alternations occur in a group of related words. This insight might lead to an investigation of how many vowel and consonant alternations students can find within pairs of words, such as the following:

| | |
|---|---|
| ferocious | ferocity |
| diplomatic | diplomacy |
| specific | specificity |

What alternations can you spot? In *ferocious* and *ferocity*, for example, there is a long-to-short-*o* vowel alternation and a /sh/-/s/ consonant alternation.

**ADVANCED SUFFIX STUDY.** A handful of suffixes present occasional challenges even for advanced readers and writers. The adjective-forming suffix *-able/-ible* seems to be a classic for misspelling. However, there is a generalization that usually helps determine whether this suffix is spelled *-able* or *-ible*. Consider the following sort and look for the word root or base word from which each word is derived.

| | |
|---|---|
| dependable | credible |
| profitable | audible |
| agreeable | edible |
| predictable | visible |

If the suffix is attached to a base word or **free morpheme (***depend***)**, it is usually spelled *-able*; if it is attached to a word root or **bound morpheme (***cred***)**, it is usually spelled *-ible*. Base words that end in *e* usually drop the *e* and add *-able* (*desire/desirable*); however, soft *c* or *g* endings may be followed by *-ible*, as in *reducible*, and sometimes a final *e* is retained to keep the soft sound, as in *noticeable* and *manageable*. These investigations generate discussions of how taking words apart, or morphemic analysis, leads to roots and the words they generate. For example, the root *ten* (*stretch*) in *pretend, contend, tense, tent,* and *tendon*; the Latin root *facere* (*do* or *make*) in words with the root forms *fac, fic, fact,* and *fect*, as seen in words like *facile, beneficial, factory,* and *defect*.

Students can understand the connection between the suffixes *-ant/-ance* and *-ent/-ence* when pairs are examined: *brilliant/brilliance, confident/confidence*. Sound is no clue, but students learn that if they know the spelling of a word that ends in one of these suffixes, that word is a clue to the spelling of the suffix in the related word (Templeton, 1980).

Whether consonants are doubled when inflectional endings are added, in words like *committed* and *benefited*, is revisited in the derivational relations stage with words of more than one syllable. Mr. Ramirez provides a collection of words that double and words that do not, and challenges his students to figure out why.

"Okay, we've got a few words here to sort. What do you notice about these words? That's right, they all end in *-ed*. What do you notice about the base words?" Mr. Ramirez and his students discuss the fact that in some cases the final consonant has been doubled before adding *-ed*, and in others it has stayed the same. He has them sort the words into two columns by those features:

| | |
|---|---|
| excelled | edited |
| occurred | limited |
| submitted | orbited |
| referred | conquered |

Mr. Ramirez asks the students to work in pairs to talk about what they see and hear when they contrast the words in both columns. He encourages them to read the base words in each column several times. If no one brings up "accent" or "stress" as a possible explanation, he asks them to listen as he reads the base words in each column, emphasizing the accented syllable: ex**cel**, oc**cur**, sub**mit**, re**fer**. Then he reads **ed**it, **lim**it, **or**bit, **con**quer.

"I get it, I get it!" yells Silvio. "The accent is on a different syllable! When it is on the last syllable you have to double!"

Silvio has uncovered the generalization that Mr. Ramirez is working toward: if the last syllable of the base word is accented, double the final consonant before adding -ed (and -ing as well). If the last syllable is not accented, then do not double the final consonant.

Mr. Ramirez follows up the sort with a bit of history:

"Remember when Elsa brought in the British copy of *Harry Potter and the Goblet of Fire* that her grandma bought for her in England and we noticed how the spelling of some of the words was different than in American English? For example, there were a lot of doubled consonants that we don't have—*benefited* had two *t*s. Actually, in just about every situation where we in the United States do not double the final consonant, people in other English-speaking countries do. Do you know who we can blame for making it so that Americans have to think about whether or not to double? Would you believe it was Noah Webster? Yes! The man who brought us our first dictionary!

"Actually, what Webster wanted to do was make English spoken and written in the United States different from English spoken and written in Britain. When he did this, our country wasn't getting along too well with Britain—after all, we had fought a war to become independent not long before! So in his dictionary of American English—the first of its kind—Webster decided to change many spellings. One of the most obvious ways was to take out the *u* in words such as *honour* and *behaviour*." Mr. Ramirez writes these words on the board. "He also switched the *re* in words such as *theatre* and *centre*." He writes these on the board.

When students notice exceptions to this principle—when they see the spelling *travelled* or *benefitted*, for example—Mr. Ramirez asks them to check the dictionary. Though they will see the American spelling they will also see the alternative spelling, perhaps with the label *Brit* because final consonants like *l* are more likely to be doubled in British English whether they are accented or not. (By the way, Mr. Ramirez was able to work the information about Noah Webster into his lesson because he had recently read Joshua Kendall's *The Forgotten Founding Father*.)

The spelling–meaning connection explored through consonant and vowel alternations plays an important role in fine-tuning spelling knowledge and expanding students' vocabularies. After students understand how the principle operates in known words, they may explore how it applies in unknown words. For example, let's say a student understands, but misspells, the word *solemn* as SOLEM in his writing. Show him the related word *solemnity*. In so doing, you can address two important objectives. First, the reason for the so-called silent-*n* in *solemn* becomes clear—the word is related to *solemnity*, in which the *n* is pronounced. Second, because he already knows the meaning of *solemn*, he can understand the meaning of the new but related word *solemnity*. You have just used the spelling system to expand this student's vocabulary.

**Assimilated prefixes.** Students study prefixes first in the within word pattern stage, and explore them more systematically at the syllables and affixes stage. Some prefixes are obvious visual and meaning units that are easy to see and understand, as in *unlikely* or *inactive*. Students at the derivational relations stage examine a group of prefixes that is somewhat disguised, as in the word *illegal*. The only clue to the prefix is the doubled letters. Known as **assimilated, absorbed,** or "chameleon" prefixes, their spellings may pose a significant challenge for students because they depend on considerable prior knowledge about other basic spelling–meaning patterns, processes of adding prefixes to base words, and simple Greek and Latin roots. Most adults are unaware of how assimilated prefixes work, but understanding how to spot and interpret them will help students unpack the meanings of thousands of multisyllabic words as well as spell them correctly. This knowledge can also resolve many spelling dilemmas—such as how to spell *accommodate*, one of the most frequently misspelled words in the English language. See the box for an example of how to talk about these with students.

**Enhanced eText**
**Video Example 8.4**
Ms. Rubero introduces a sort to teach absorbed prefixes with her seventh-grade students who are in the early part of the derivational relations stage.

BACKGROUND | DERIVATIONAL RELATIONS STAGE

# Modeling How Assimilated Prefixes "Work" Within Words

SAMPLE LESSON

1. Use the following sort to explore the idea of assimilated prefixes. The words—including *inactive, illiterate, immature, improper,* and *irrational*—are first presented in a random list and students discuss their meanings (*immature* means "not mature," *improper* means "not proper," and so on). Students conclude that they all seem to mean "not" or "the opposite of." Ask how the words might be sorted. The following categories emerge:

   | | | | | |
   |---|---|---|---|---|
   | ineffective | illiterate | immature | irregular | impossible |
   | inorganic | illegal | immobile | irrational | impatient |
   | inactive | illogical | immortal | irrelevant | improper |
   | infinite | illegible | immodest | | |

2. Ask, "If all these prefixes mean the same thing, why do we spell them in different ways?" If students seemed puzzled, probe with "What do you notice about the base words in each column? (The spelling of the prefix seems to be related to the base word; *il-* is used before words starting with *l, im-* is used before words starting with *m,* and *ir-* before words starting with *r.*)

3. "Try saying *inmobile* or *inrelevant*. Does that feel kind of weird? Does your tongue kind of get stuck on the beginning of *mobile*? Though it's possible to pronounce them, it's definitely awkward—moving from the *n* to *m* in *inmobile* and the *n* to *r* in *inrelevant* is cumbersome."

4. Return to the question, "If all these prefixes mean the same thing, why do we spell them in different ways?" Students should now be able to explain that the particular spelling of the prefix *in-* often depends on the first letter of the base word because the pronunciation changed. If necessary, have them pronounce the words in the last column with both *in-* and *ip-* as the prefix (*inproper, ipproper,* and *improper*). They should agreed that *im-* worked best before base words starting with *p.* Explain that that the terms *assimilated* or *absorbed* are used to describe prefixes whose spellings have changed.

5. Have students look up the prefixes *ir-, im-,* and *il-* in an unabridged dictionary. They are usually listed as "variants of" or "assimilated forms" of *in-,* and linked to the original prefix *in-.* You may ask students to look up the words *absorb* and *assimilate* and talk about the different definitions for each word. They should see that the idea of "to make alike or similar" is most appropriate in this case.

6. Offer some background history to summarize: "Think about the word *immobile.* A long time ago, the prefix *in-* was combined with the word *mobile* to create a new word that meant 'not mobile.' Try pronouncing the word like it was pronounced when it first came into existence: **in**mobile. Over time it became easier for people to leave out the /n/ sound when pronouncing the word. The sound of the *n* became 'absorbed' or 'assimilated' into the /m/ sound at the beginning of the base word *mobile.* Before long, the spelling of the *n* changed to indicate this change in pronunciation—but it's important to remember that this letter didn't disappear. They knew it was necessary to keep the two letters in the prefix to indicate that it was still a prefix. If the last letter of the prefix had been dropped, then the meaning of the prefix might have been lost."

Primarily Latin in origin, assimilated or absorbed prefixes are widespread in English; an extensive list of assimilated prefixes with example words is provided in Appendix F. By the way, *accommodate* has two assimilated prefixes: the *d* in the prefix *ad-* is absorbed into the first letter sound of the second prefix *con-,* and the *n* in *con-* is absorbed into the first letter sound of the word root *-mod-* (literally, "to fit with"). Whenever there are double letters at the beginning of a multisyllabic word there is a good chance an assimilated prefix is present.

## Latin and Greek Word Parts

For purposes of vocabulary development, students begin to learn about Latin and Greek word parts—roots and affixes—before the derivational relations stage. At this stage, however, the advanced study of Latin and Greek word parts, along with spelling challenges, offers an incredibly rich terrain to explore, and extends through middle school, high school, and beyond.

Importantly, most significant vocabulary terms within specific academic domains comprise these Latin and Greek word parts.

**ROOTS AND STEMS** It is important to note that, over the years, educators and linguists have used different terms to refer to these word elements and to make distinctions between roots of Greek or Latin origin (Dale, O'Rourke, & Bamman, 1971; Henry, 2003; Moats, 2000; Templeton & Gehsmann, 2014). For example, roots of Greek origin are often labeled "combining forms," and those of Latin origin are simply "roots." This is to distinguish the flexibility of Greek elements from Latin elements. Greek roots such as *photo* ("light") and *graph* ("write") may combine in different places in words—at the beginning, middle, or end (tele**photo**, **graph**ic, **photograph**). Latin roots, on the other hand, tend to stay in one place, with prefixes and suffixes attached, as in *cred* ("believe") (**cred**ible, **cred**ence, and in**cred**ible). A number of Greek roots may stand alone as words, too (*auto, photo, bio*), whereas Latin roots rarely do. After students understand these word parts and how they work, it may be helpful—as well as interesting—to point out this distinction between Greek and Latin roots. You may also encounter the term **stem** or **stem-word**, which usually refers to a base word or an affixed word root to which additional affixes may be added. Here are some examples: *function* is a stem to which -*s*, -*ed*, or -*ing* may be added; *dysfunction* is also a stem to which these same inflectional endings may be added. As with so much of word study, we need to know the various terms and usages but must use them judiciously and consistently with our students so as not to overwhelm them with labels when they are first learning a concept.

Word roots nestle within longer words and are the meaningful anchor to which prefixes and suffixes may attach. Roots also follow the basic spelling–meaning premise that words with similar meanings are usually spelled similarly. It is important to point out to students that spellings *visually* represent the meanings of these elements and preserve the meaning relationships among words that at first may appear quite different. The consistent spelling of word roots is students' best clue to identifying them and examining how they function within words; for example, *spec* ("look") in in**spec**t, **spec**tator, and *dict* ("speak") in pre**dict** and in**dict**. Occasionally, the spelling of the roots may vary—both *vid* (in **vid**eo and e**vid**ent) and *vis* (in **vis**ible and tele**vis**ion) come from the Latin word *videre*, meaning "to see." Students may already have noted some of these variations. For example, ask them to think about how *receive* and *reception* are related in meaning. Students can now examine these words while attending to the meaning of the root within the related words (*ceiv* and *cep* both mean "take").

**FREQUENCY AND TRANSPARENCY** At the derivational relations stage, students will build on the understandings about Greek and Latin word parts developed during the syllables and affixes stage, reviewing those that occur with greatest frequency in the language and are most transparent in the words in which they occur. The sequence of instruction for Greek and Latin word parts is based on the abstractness of their meanings, from concrete to abstract (Templeton, 2004, 2012). For syllables and affixes learners, for example, the Greek roots *therm* (heat) and *tele* (far, distant) and the Latin roots *aud* (to hear), *rupt* (to break, burst), and *vis* (to see) are introduced and explored early in the sequence because their meaning is transparent or straightforward. (See Activity 7.4 in Chapter 7 that illustrates how to introduce word roots and how they combine with affixes.) The way in which other roots function within words is often not as transparent, so those roots are explored later, during derivational relations. For example, how the Latin roots *fer* (to carry) in *defer* and *spir* (to breathe) in *inspiration* behave are more abstract, or metaphorical. The Scope and Sequence presented in Table 8.2 (pp. 315–316) lists representative Greek and Latin roots to be addressed throughout the derivational relations stage. Additional Greek and Latin roots are provided in Appendix F and in "Greek and Latin: Paired Roots & Affixes." Also, see the links on page 306 for generative roots and affixes in specific domains.

Following is a sample lesson that illustrates what your exploration of Latin word roots might look like with derivational students who have already learned a number of roots and how they combine with affixes. Their exploration will now move more deeply into etymology; how to use dictionaries and websites to investigate word origins and etymologies is discussed on pages 310–312.

**Enhanced eText**
**Teacher Resource:**
Greek & Latin: Paired
Roots & Affixes

# Exploring How Word Roots "Work" within Words: The Latin Roots *man, scrib/script, fac, struc*

**SAMPLE LESSON**

**Generalization:** The Latin root *man* means "hand"; *scrib* or *script* means "to write"; *fac* means "to make"; *struc* means "to build, pile up."

1. **Introduce the sort.** Prepare a set of words such as those in Figure 8.3. Display the words in random order and have the students read through them. Ask, "How many roots do you see in these words?" If students reply "five," remind them of previous sorts in which the spelling of a root may have changed: Do they see that possibility in these words? How can they tell? (The spellings *scrib* and *script* are similar.)

2. **Sort.** Say, "With a partner, go ahead and sort the words into four "root" categories. Talk about what you think the meaning of each root might be. Then, check your ideas with the unabridged dictionary. You may find that the *Online Etymology Dictionary* will come in handy for at least one of these words!

3. **Discuss.** Ask, "Did you find that any words could be sorted into more than one root category?" (*manufacture* and *manuscript*). Follow up by "walking through" a few words for each root. Understanding how *man* and *scrib/script* work is usually straightforward—*manual* labor is working by hand, *manuscript* is writing by hand. Students will probably be quite curious about *manure*, however! Ask, "Did anyone try checking the etymology dictionary for the word *manure*? What did you find?" (*Manure* is actually closely related to *manual*: It evolved from a Middle English word that meant "to cultivate land," which in turn evolved from a Latin word that meant "to work with the hands," and this involved "putting dung on the soil.")

Pointing to the words *factory* and *manufacture*, ask whether anyone can determine the meaning of the root *fac*. If not, have them check the dictionary. "So, do you see how the meaning of "make" works in the words *factory* and *manufacture*? For *facsimile*, ask, "Do you see a familiar pattern in *facsimile*?" If they do not note it, remove *fac* so that *simile* remains. Ask, "What do you think *simile* might mean?" (For most students, this is the first time they become aware that "similar" is in *facsimile*). Ask, "Literally, then, what does *facsimile* mean?" (Make similar.) "So, if we send a *facsimile* of an original document to someone, what does that mean?" (Similar to the original document.)

4. **Pull out the words *prescribe, prescription, inscribe, and inscription*.** Ask, "In each of these words, what happens to the spelling when *-ion* is added?" (Changes to *pt*) "With your partner, see if you can come up with some other *scrib/script* words ending in *-ion*." (Some possibilities are *subscribe/subscription, describe/description, transcribe/transcription*.) This is an excellent opportunity for you to make explicit to students the following: "As we have seen with some other roots, this is another predictable spelling change when adding *-ion* to words with the root *scribe*. Add this to your chart of spelling changes when adding *–ion*."

5. **Reflect and extend:** In pairs or teams, have students select a group of additional words that share the same root (for example *manacle, manipulate, manage; circumscribe, describe; postscript, subscribe; faculty, facile*). They can apply their understanding by reading about the etymology of each; then select one to explain, in their own words, how the meaning evolved from the earliest form.

**FIGURE 8.3** Exploring How Word Roots "Work" Within Words: The Latin Roots *man, scrib/script, fac, struc*

| *man* | *scrib/script* | *fac* | *struc* |
|---|---|---|---|
| **manual** | **transcribe** | **factory** | **construct** |
| manuscript* | prescribe | artifact | construction |
| manicure | prescription | facsimile | structure |
| manufacture* | scribe | facilitate | restructure |
| manure | scribble | manufacture* | |
| | manuscript* | | |
| | transcription | | |

* Words may be sorted into more than one category

## RESOURCE CONNECTIONS

### Resources for Word Study: Greek and Latin Word Parts

Ayers, D. M. (1986). *English Words from Latin and Greek Elements* (2nd ed., revised by Thomas Worthen). Tucson: The University of Arizona Press.

Bear, D. R., Flanigan, K., Hayes, L., Helman, L., Invernizzi, M., Johnston, F. J., & Templeton, S. (2014). *Vocabulary Their Way: Words and Strategies for Academic Success.* Glenview, IL: Pearson.

Crutchfield, R. (1997). *English Vocabulary Quick Reference: A Comprehensive Dictionary Arranged by Word Roots.* Leesburg, VA: LexaDyne.

Danner, H., & Noel, R. (2004). *Discover It! A Better Vocabulary the Better Way* (2nd ed.). Occoquan, VA: Imprimis Books.

Fine, E. H. (2004). Illustrated by K. Donner. *Cryptomania: Teleporting into Greek and Latin with the Cryptokids.* Berkeley, CA: Tricycle Press.

Fry, E. (2004). *The Vocabulary Teacher's Book of Lists.* San Francisco: Jossey Bass.

Kennedy, J. (1996). *Word Stems: A Dictionary.* New York: Soho Press.

Moore, B., & Moore, M. (1997). *NTC's Dictionary of Latin and Greek Origins: A Comprehensive Guide to the Classical Origins of English Words.* Chicago: NTC Publishing Group.

Rasinski, T., Padak, N., Newton, R., & Newton, E. (2008). *Greek and Latin Roots: Keys to Building Vocabulary.* Huntington Beach, CA: Shell Education.

Templeton, S., Bear, D. R., Invernizzi, M., Johnson, F., Flanigan, K., Townsend, D. R., Helman, L., & Hayes, L. (2015). *Words Their Way: Vocabulary for Middle and Secondary Students* (2nd ed.). Boston: Pearson.

**Enhanced eText**
**Teacher Resource:**
Generative Roots and
Affixes in History/Social
Studies

**Enhanced eText**
**Teacher Resource:**
Generative Roots and
Affixes in Mathematics

**Enhanced eText**
**Teacher Resource:**
Generative Roots and
Affixes in Science

*for* **English learners**

## Spelling Strategies

Students in the derivational relations stage can use a range of strategies to spell unfamiliar words. The sixth grader whose writing appears in Figure 8.1 is certainly thinking about spelling in her final sentence—"Is this how you spell Eerrie?"—evidence of a spelling conscience. The proofreading tips described in Chapter 3 and strategies described in Chapter 7 apply in this stage as well. Specifically:

- Does the word look right?
- Can you think of another word that has a similar meaning and might even have part of this word in it?
- If you're not sure how to spell a word, how would you know which pattern to use? What would be your best try? Why?

As these questions suggest, at this level it is *not* helpful to tell students to "sound the word out"—it is primarily knowledge of spelling-meaning patterns and morphological relationships that students are learning to apply. It is especially important to remind students whose first language is not English and which may be spelled more phonemically about this—trying to rely on sound-letter correspondences at this level will frustrate their efforts.

# Word Study Instruction for the Derivational Relations Stage

The principles for instructing intermediate readers and writers also guide our instruction at the advanced level. As at the intermediate level, word study for advanced readers emphasizes actively exploring words and applying word knowledge to spelling, vocabulary development, and analyzing unknown words encountered in reading. In their reading and study, students deepen their skills in combining morphemic analysis with context as they independently learn many more words than are explicitly taught.

## Supporting Vocabulary Development

As we have noted, *generative* vocabulary instruction is the primary emphasis at this level, so we will examine the relationships between spelling and meaning in some depth. Word sorts addressing focused contrasts among derivationally related words continue to be an effective context in which this knowledge is developed. For example, when examining clues to the spelling of unaccented vowels in words such as *labor* and *acquisition*, students will examine the related words *laborious* and *acquire* in which the vowel is clearly accented. Such focused contrasts, while clarifying spelling, will also reveal the meaning of unfamiliar words such as *laborious* and *acquisition*. Spelling is improved while vocabulary is expanded!

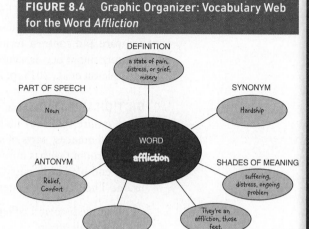

**FIGURE 8.4** Graphic Organizer: Vocabulary Web for the Word *Affliction*

**WORD-SPECIFIC INSTRUCTION: GENERAL ACADEMIC AND DOMAIN-SPECIFIC.**
Although focus in this chapter is primarily on generative vocabulary, it is important to remind you of the excellent approaches for word-specific instruction described in Chapter 7, including a number of graphic organizers. All of these may be adapted for the vocabulary that older students will be encountering.

**Graphic organizers.** Figure 8.4 offers an example of a vocabulary web for the word *affliction*, which takes on additional literal and figurative meanings over the course of the compelling narrative in *Al Capone Does My Shirts* (2004). Its first occurrence, early in the book, is used lightheartedly, sarcastically: "But at least I don't have those big feet, either. They're an affliction, those feet" (Choldenko, p. 8). Figure 8.5 offers an example of a 4-square map for the concept "abstract."

**Enhanced eText**
**Teacher Resource:**
4-Square Template

**Concept sorts and disciplinary learning.** As noted in previous chapters, concept sorts are an excellent framework for developing word-specific knowledge as well as relationships among the concepts that the words represent. They activate students' background knowledge and generate their interest in and questions about the topic. Based on the students' level of background knowledge, concept sorts may be closed or open, depending on whether categories are defined. Usually, the words to be sorted for a topic of study are the key academic and/or domain-specific vocabulary and important related words.

In her eigth-grade math class, for example, Dianna Townsend's unit addresses the standards on "Expressions and Equations" (Templeton et al., 2015). She focuses on the following terms:

| | |
|---|---|
| expression | slope |
| equation | unit rate |
| properties | similar triangles |
| integer exponents | origin |
| equivalent numerical expressions | intercept |
| square root | coordinates |
| cube root | vertical axis |
| rational number | linear equations |
| irrational number | distributive property |
| scientific notation | collecting like terms |
| proportional relationships | |

After students have initially explored and discussed the meanings over the course of several days, they can complete a "closed" concept sort: They would sort the terms into the categories "terms related to exponents," "terms related to graphs," and "terms related

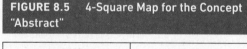

**FIGURE 8.5** 4-Square Map for the Concept "Abstract"

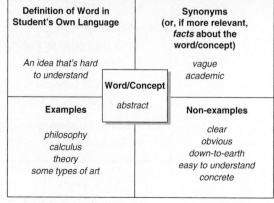

| Definition of Word in Student's Own Language | Synonyms (or, if more relevant, *facts* about the word/concept) |
|---|---|
| *An idea that's hard to understand* | *vague* *academic* |
| **Examples** | **Non-examples** |
| *philosophy* *calculus* *theory* *some types of art* | *clear* *obvious* *down-to-earth* *easy to understand* *concrete* |

Word/Concept: *abstract*

to solving equations." This concept sort provides an opportunity for students to examine relationships between these important terms. It could also be extended to ask students to compare and contrast terms within the categories. A follow-up question in the "exponent" category might be: "Is a cubed number an example of an integer exponent? Why or why not?" (Templeton et al., 2015, p. 204).

**DICTIONARIES.** Because students use dictionaries frequently in the derivational relations stage, ensure that they understand the features—pronunciation guides, multiple definitions, sample sentences, parts of speech, and so on (see Chapter 7). Have at least one dictionary in the classroom that has information about word origins. This information is usually in brackets at the end of a main entry. Online dictionaries, such as *OneLook* and *YourDictionary*, are also useful. The following materials should always be readily available to students:

- Intermediate and collegiate dictionaries: enough copies for six to eight students to work in a small group
- Thesaurus collection: enough for six to eight students in small-group and whole class study
- Several word origin (etymological) dictionaries and root books (see next section)

## RESOURCE CONNECTIONS

### Resources for Word-Specific Vocabulary Activities

Beck, I., McKeown, M., & Kucan, L. (2008). *Creating Robust Vocabulary: Frequently Asked Questions*. New York: Guilford.

Beck, I. L., McKeown, M. G., & Kucan, L. (2013). *Bringing Words to Life: Robust Vocabulary Instruction* (2nd ed.). New York: Guilford.

Blachowicz, C., & Fisher, P. (2009). *Teaching Vocabulary in All Classrooms* (4th ed.). Boston: Allyn & Bacon.

Blachowicz, C., Fisher, P., Ogle, D., & Watts-Taffe, S. (2013). *Teaching Academic Vocabulary, K–8: Effective Practices Across the Curriculum*. New York: Guilford.

Diamond, L., & Gutlohn, L. (2007). *Vocabulary Handbook*. Baltimore: Paul Brookes.

Flanigan, K., Hayes, L., Templeton, S., Bear, D. R., Invernizzi, M., & Johnston, F. (2011). *Words Their Way with Struggling Readers: Word Study for Reading, Vocabulary, and Spelling Instruction, Grades 4–12*. Boston: Pearson/Allyn & Bacon.

Nilsen, A. J., & Nilsen, D. L. F. (2004). *Vocabulary Plus High School and Up: A Source-Based Approach*. Boston: Allyn & Bacon.

Stahl, S., & Nagy, W. (2006). *Teaching Word Meanings*. Mahwah, NJ: Erlbaum.

Templeton, S., Bear, D. R., Invernizzi, M., Johnson, F., Flanigan, K., Townsend, D. R., Helman, L., & Hayes, L. (2015). *Vocabulary Their Way: Word Study with Middle and Secondary Students* (2nd ed.). Boston: Pearson.

Templeton, S., & Flanigan, K. (2014). Exploring Words with Advanced and Verbally Gifted Students. *Words Their Way: Vocabulary for Middle and High School* (Teacher Edition) (pp. T47–T51). Glenview, IL: Pearson.

Templeton, S., & Gehsmann, K. (2014). *Teaching Reading and Writing: The Developmental Approach (PreK–8)*. Boston: Pearson.

Zwiers, J. (2014). *Building Academic Language: Meeting Common Core Standards Across Disciplines, Grades 5-12* (2nd ed.). San Francisco, CA: Jossey-Bass.

Older students are often interested in the history of dictionaries. An excellent book that is accessible to many middle-grade advanced readers and writers is Joshua Kendall's *The Forgotten Founding Father: Noah Webster's Obsession and the Creation of an American Culture* (2010). Books that provide fascinating insights to share with students as they explore dictionaries more extensively are Simon Winchester's *The Professor and the Madman: A Tale of Murder, Insanity, and the Making of the Oxford English Dictionary* (1998) and *The Meaning of Everything: The Story of the Oxford English Dictionary* (2003).

Continue to model your own use and curiosity about dictionaries, including the serendipitous discoveries you can make—this helps develop your students' word consciousness. When looking up *graph*, for example, a note about *grafitti* caught seventh-grade teacher Kelly Rubero's eye and she was delighted to learn (and share with her students) that *graffiti* is an Italian plural form of *graffito* and both, like *graph*, are related to Greek *graphein* (to write). While electronic dictionaries are important and easy to use, one advantage of printed dictionaries is that students end up browsing the page and coming across other interesting facts about words.

Keep dictionaries handy when introducing word sorts so that students can check the accuracy of their morphological analyses. For example, after sorting words by the root *spect* and hypothesizing that it means "to look," students were unsure about how *speculate* fit that meaning. After looking at definitions and illustrative uses of *speculate* in several dictionaries they decided that one would be likely *to look* closely at something in the process of thinking about it or before taking a chance on buying it (Flanigan, Templeton, & Hayes, 2012).

**WORD ORIGINS.** Exploring dictionaries and the information they provide leads into the more sustained study of word origins. Exploring word origins and the processes of creating words provides a powerful knowledge base for learning vocabulary and spelling, as well as for facilitating more effective reading and writing. **Etymology**, the study of word origins and histories (from the Greek *etymon*, meaning "true sense of a word"), may develop into a lifelong fascination for many students. As you engage students in examining word roots and affixes, the groundwork is laid for more focused exploration of etymology and a lifelong love of word histories and vocabulary.

Students develop a real sense of how words work at this level as well as a general sense of how words can move through history. Ms. Rubero often reminds her students of the depth of their insights as they engage in this type of exploration during word study. She shares the handout *A (Very) Brief History of English* with students, which provides a general

**Enhanced eText**
**Teacher Resource:**
A (Very) Brief History of English

foundation for making sense of the more specific information they will find in etymological entries in dictionaries as well as the other resources presented here, particularly Shipley's *Origins of English Words* (2001). Such explorations invariably bring a wealth of additional words and relationships to students' attention. In Shipley, for example, the entry for *peter*, the original Indo-European root for "father," explains how the Romans created the name of the god *Jupiter* from the Greeks' *Zeus + peter*. Although all students benefit from these types of investigations, more verbally advanced students in the intermediate grades often become true "word nerds" after they are initiated. Studying word roots extends into the even more ancient Indo-European root forms (Templeton et al., 2015), a topic touched on briefly in the very last activity in this chapter.

Students explore origins and etymologies in selected reference resources

# Modeling How to Interpret Etymological Information

Proficient readers can explore more expansively the etymological information provided in dictionary entries and online etymological sites. Intermediate readers in the middle grades should certainly be exposed to this information, so you may address both developmental levels in a whole-class lesson addressing these entries. This "walk-through" focuses on helping students understand how information about the meaning and combination of the word parts contributes to the core meaning or sense of the word, as well as showing them what they should pay attention to, and what they may skim over.

In a unit on the American Civil War, *emancipation* is an important concept. Using the base word *emancipate* as an example, display the information for the word in the Etymology Online site to the class (Templeton, Johnston, Bear, & Invernizzi, 2019) and explain:

- There is a lot of information "up front" in this etymological entry that includes Latin phrases, but I want to get to the explanation of the word parts, so I'm skimming to where the word parts are mentioned. Here's the prefix *ex-*, which we've seen means "out," and the *e* at the beginning of *emancipate* is another way to spell this prefix.

- We then see another couple of Latin words; the last one [point to *manus*] means "hand."

- Then there's this other Latin word [point to *capere*], meaning "to take."

- Now we have all the parts, and what we do next is put their meanings together. Dictionaries don't do this for us; they only give us the history and leave the "putting together" to us!

- So, *emancipate* literally means "to take out of the hand."

- Point to the second paragraph in the entry and say, "Interestingly, it tells us here that the use of the word *emancipate* in the sense of 'slavery' came much later. But still, can you see how the literal meaning still applies? Slaves were 'taken out of their owner's hand.'"

You may decide to discuss the rest of the information in the entry for *emancipate* with the students—for example, how it included a sense of "ownership" in Roman times—but the "walk through" illustrated here is focused on helping students understand how information about the meaning and combination of the word parts contributes to the core meaning or sense of the word.

As with learning the purpose and use of any new tool, your students' application of this knowledge will take time—you will probably need to model such "walk throughs" many times. With time, however, you will be able to pull back from this more explicit guidance as your students develop the ability to use the tool of etymological entries independently.

## Resources for Word Study: Word Origins

Asimov, I. (1961). *Words from the Myths*. Boston: Houghton Mifflin. (The most readable and interesting resource of this kind, available on any website that sells out-of-print books; such as Daedalus-books and Alibris.)

Ayto, J. (1993). *Dictionary of Word Origins*. New York: Arcade. (Accessible for some students in the intermediate grades and most in the middle and secondary grades.)

Ayto, J. (2009). *Oxford School Dictionary of Word Origins: The curious twists & turns of the cool and weird words we use*. Oxford: Oxford University Press. (Excellent for elementary and middle grades.)

Cousineau, P. (2012). *The Painted Word: A Treasure Chest of Remarkable Words and Their Origins*; and (2010) *Word catcher: An odyssey into the world of weird and wonderful words*. Berkeley, CA: Viva Editions.

D'Aulaire, I., & D'Aulaire, E. (1980). *D'Aulaires' Book of Greek Myths*. New York: Doubleday. (Of interest to third graders and up; upper-intermediate reading level.)

Fisher, L. (1984). *The Olympians: Great Gods and Goddesses of Ancient Greece*. New York: Holiday House. (Of interest to third graders and up; third-grade reading level.)

Green, T. M. (2008). *The Greek and Latin Roots of English* (4th ed.). Lanham, MD: Rowman & Littlefield Publishers, Inc.

Jones, C. F. (1999). Illustrated by J. O'Brian. *Eat Your Words: A Fascinating Look at the Language of Food*. New York: Delacorte Press.

*Merriam-Webster New Book of Word Histories*. (1995). Springfield, MA: Merriam-Webster. (Of interest to most middle grade and secondary students.)

Robinson, S. (1989). *Origins* (Volume 1: *Bringing Words to Life*; Volume 2: *The Word Families*). New York: Teachers and Writers Collaborative. (Fascinating explorations for elementary students of selected Indo-European roots.)

Shipley, J. (2001). *The Origins of English Words*. Baltimore: Johns Hopkins University Press. (For teachers who are truly dedicated wordsmiths, Shipley's book is the ultimate source. A delightful read!)

Watkins, C. (2011). *The American Heritage Dictionary of Indo-European Roots* (3rd ed.). Boston: Houghton Mifflin Harcourt.

Although the spelling of a word may appear odd, understanding its origin provides the most powerful key to remembering the spelling. Knowing that so many words have come from mythology, literature, historical events, and famous figures provides important background knowledge for students' reading in the various subject matter domains. The books and websites listed in "Resource Connections: Resources for Word Study—Greek and Latin Elements" and "Resources for Word Study: Word Origins" also help. To stimulate students' curiosity about word origins, read aloud excerpts from such books when you have a few extra minutes. The resource links here provide introductory information you may share with students about Greek mythology, from which most Roman myths and legends derive, and words and their origins from Greek and Roman myths and legends.

Another way to add interest to studying word origins is to talk about words we imported from other countries. A significant number of words have recently come into American English from other contemporary languages, primarily Spanish (*quesadilla*, *chili con carne*) but some from French (*bistro*, *à la carte*) and Italian (*al fresco*, *cappuccino*) as well. As you may have guessed, such words initially turn up on our menus (Venezky, 1999). Given enough time, such "borrowed" words or "loanwords" become so familiar they don't strike us as foreign: *algebra* and *algorithm* from Arabic, *adventure* and *marine* from French, *husband* and *window* from Scandinavian, *canyon* and *ranch* from Spanish, *tomato* and *chocolate* from Native American languages. A popular classroom activity is to post a large world map on the wall and display words according to their country of origin. For example, where would you post the word *segue*?

**ONLINE RESOURCES.** The number of vocabulary- and word-themed websites seems to be increasing exponentially. Some of our favorites are listed in "Resource Connections: Online Resources about Words" (page 312). One in particular, *Visual Thesaurus*, offers significant potential for students' explorations. Users type in a word, and the word is then presented in a "thinkmap" web that displays the meaning relationships shared by the target word or concept and other terms. Clicking on any word in these web-based resources reveals definitions and examples in context, as well as a new web of relationships. Figure 8.6 shows the thinkmap for the word *tranquil*.

**Enhanced eText**
Teacher Resource: Greek Mythology: A Very Brief Primer

**Enhanced eText**
Teacher Resource: Words from Greek and Latin Myths & Legends

**FIGURE 8.6    Thinkmap for *tranquil***

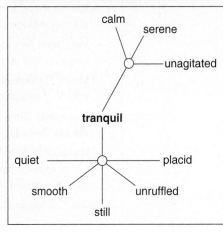

**Enhanced eText**
**Video Example 8.5**
English Language Arts teacher Ms. Amy Burton models and talks about how to set up an interactive, inquiry-based classroom that encourages students to take ownership of their word learning.

Clicking on the node above *tranquil* reveals the definition as it applies to individuals; clicking on the lower node describes *tranquil* in relation to a body of water. Figure 8.7 displays the thinkmap for *lithosphere*, an important term in a science unit on the four earth systems. Exploring the different nodes and the word or conceptual relationships they reveal provides students with a framework for exploring in breadth and depth an understanding of the lithosphere and its relationship to the other three earth systems, as well as their characteristics and functions. Another very helpful resource in the website is the "Vocabgrabber," an excellent tool for helping analyze the type, frequency, and relevance of the vocabulary in any text you use.

We must offer a cautionary note about any website that we recommend: although they are powerful tools, they do not know your students. *How* you use them and the information they provide ultimately rests on your judgment. For example, though "Vocabgrabber" will generate lists of important vocabulary words, *which* words you include is based on your judgment and knowledge of your students.

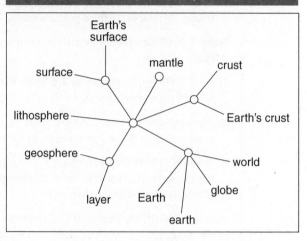

**FIGURE 8.7** Thinkmap for *lithosphere*

---

**RESOURCE CONNECTIONS**

### Online Resources about Words

Do an Internet search for the following resources:

- **Corpus of American English:** Continually updated, this is an invaluable online resource for locating related words in English. It may be used to search for the occurrence of words in different types of texts.

- **Etymology Online:** Useful for exploring word histories, this site includes accessible etymological information. The site's author, Douglas Harper, updates it on a regular basis.

- **OneLook:** A comprehensive dictionary website on which most of the major dictionaries are available. This site also has excellent search capabilities for locating words that contain specific roots and affixes, as well as words that relate to a particular concept.

- **WordWorks:** The educator who developed this website, Peter Bowers, shares lesson plans, lesson videos, and information about all aspects of English orthography; particularly strong are the morphological/etymological components.

- **Verbivore:** An excellent site for wordplay, containing many links to informative and engaging language and word sites.

- **Visual Thesaurus:** One of the most comprehensive interactive sites available. There is an annual subscription fee, but the benefits are more than worth the modest price.

- **Visuwords:** Similar in format to Visual Thesaurus, this site offers a more abbreviated web display. One significant feature is that, at the time of this writing, the site is free.

- **Wordsmith:** Subscribe for free and receive a new word in your inbox every day. Each week, words follow a particular theme. The categories of words discussed in this chapter—for example, eponyms and mythology—are represented.

# Exploring Spelling-Meaning Connections with Unfamiliar Words: Vowel Alternations—Long, Short, and Schwa

**SAMPLE LESSON**

In this sort students review the three vowel alternation patterns—long with short, long with schwa, and short with schwa. In addition, the teacher helps them think about figuring out unknown words that are related in spelling—and therefore meaning—to words they know. They should also come to realize that an unfamiliar word often explains the spelling of a known word. Figure 8.8 presents the completed sort.

1. Display the words in Figure 8.8 randomly, without the headers, and read through them quickly because some words may pose challenges for pronunciation. Ask, "What do you notice about these words?" Students should be able to offer a number of ideas. "How might we sort these words?" If students mention that there are base words and derived words that may be matched, begin with that.

2. Ask if there are any words whose meaning the students weren't sure about, and how we could figure them out. (Think of the meaning of word parts; check the dictionary.) If necessary, support their thinking—they may be familiar with *sufficient*, but may not know *suffice*. Discuss what *sufficient* means, then ask students "Based on the meaning of *sufficient*, therefore, what might *suffice* mean?" Discuss how *custodian* refers not just to an individual who keeps up the condition of a school—it has a broader application, referring to anyone or anything that holds custody of something. It may be an idea—for example, when a people are referred to as "custodians of democracy." Point out that the stressed syllable in the new word *triviALity* can help students remember the unaccented syllable in *trivial*.

3. Display the headers "Long to short," "Long to schwa," and "Short to schwa." Have students read the word pairs, paying attention to how the

vowel sound—usually the second—alternate within each pair. Then, model how to sort the key words: *wise - wisdom*. Ask what vowel sound they hear in *wise*? (Long) In *wisdom*? (Short) Place this word pair under the "Long to Short" header. Then sort *inspire-inspiration*: The long vowel in *inspire* changes to an unaccented "schwa" sound in *inspiration*, so this word pair would be placed under the "Long to Schwa" header. Ask, "How do the sounds change in *metal* and *metallic*? (The accented vowel in *metallic* is short *a* and in *metal* the *a* changes to the schwa sound.) "So we'll need to put the derived word *metallic* first and then the base word *metal*." You may continue to sort as a group, or ask students to sort independently or with a partner. After the sort is completed, read down each column to check for the appropriate changes.

4. If you have a larger group, an alternative way to begin this sort is to give students one word each and let them move around the room to find the person with the related word to make a pair. Then, have them work with their partner to decide into which category their word pair should be sorted. They should be ready to explain their rationale for sorting the way they did.

5. Ask follow-up questions such as, "What did you learn from the sort to help you spell words or figure out their meanings? What parts of the words might be tricky to spell?"

To extend this sort, you may want to take some time to examine other words that end like *democratic* and *democracy*. The suffixes *-crat* and *-cracy* mean "rule," and occur in words like *autocracy* (rule by one) and *aristocracy* (rule by the best). Students may also notice the short *a*-to-schwa alternation in the third syllable of *democratic* and *democracy*.

---

**FIGURE 8.8** Spelling-Meaning Sort with Unfamiliar Words: Vowel Alternations— Long, Short, and Schwa

| Long to Short | Long to Schwa | Short to Schwa |
|---|---|---|
| **wise wisdom** | **inspire inspiration** | **metallic metal** |
| decide decision | narrate narrative | triviality trivial |
| impede impediment | custodian custody | emphatic emphasis |
| suffice sufficient | mandate mandatory | democracy democratic |

## Systematic Word Study

As we have described, spelling-meaning—or morphological—patterns, including Latin and Greek word parts, will be your focus for systematic exploration. To reiterate our observation in Chapter 7: Your sorting and other activities are just a starting place—*discussion* and *reflection* are critical at this stage. Many of the critical questions presented in Table 3.2 (p. 65) apply at this level as well, particularly those that address affixes, bases, and roots. For example, "How did you figure that out? What word parts did you use? Did you think of other similar words to help you out? What were they? In your reading, which of these word roots do you see more frequently? What if we changed that prefix to another prefix? What would the word mean then?"

## Sequence

Table 8.2 presents a general sequence for word study in the derivational relations stage. Just as at the syllables and affixes stage, deciding what features to teach is often restricted by the difficulty of the word meanings rather than any problems with reading or spelling the words. For example, assimilated prefixes are examined later because many of the words that contain them will not occur with much frequency in the reading materials or be in the speaking vocabularies of most upper elementary students (e.g., *immunity* or *innumerable*). Although you can include some new vocabulary words in every sort at this level, there should still be a good number of familiar words from which students can begin to make generalizations, moving from the known to the unknown.

**EARLY/MIDDLE.** Students in the early stage of derivational relations have mastered most syllable juncture conventions, including spellings of most prefixes and suffixes and what happens when they are affixed to bases; they are working through the juncture conventions that govern the spelling of the frequent suffix *-ion* (*-tion*, *-sion*, *-ssion*). Occasionally, a common prefix may be misspelled, such as *permission* spelled PURMISSION by analogy with words such as *purchase*, or *destroy* spelled DISTROY because of the pronunciation of the first syllable and the frequency of the prefix *dis-*. Students in the early phase are also still learning how meaning is a clue to spelling unstressed vowels, such as not realizing that IMPASITION (*imposition*) is explained by the related word *impose*. By the middle phase, the spellings of prefixes and most suffixes are fairly locked in, as are the spellings of most bases and roots across morphologically related words (**compet**e/ **compet**itive/**compet**ition).

**LATE.** A few students in the upper-elementary grades may be in the late derivational relations stage, but many will not reach this stage until at least middle school and high school. Students at this phase can spell most new academic vocabulary words correctly when first encountering them. They use but confuse assimilated prefixes, however, as well as the suffixes *-able/-ible*, *-ant/-ent*, and *-ance/-ence*. As we have noted, this phase is not an "end" to development but rather part of an ongoing, fascinating journey.

Teacher models focused contrasts in several domain-specific terms before students sort

**TABLE 8.2** **Sequence of Word Study**

### AFFIXES: Prefix and Suffix Study

Review and explore affixes introduced during the syllables and affixes stage (*in-, un-, dis-, mis-, re-, ex-, pre-, -err, -est, -ful, -ness, -less, -ly, -ion*) in more advanced vocabulary.

*Additional Suffixes*

| | | |
|---|---|---|
| *-er/-or/-ian/-ist* | people who do or believe | defend**er**, creat**or**, guard**ian**, special**ist** |
| *-ary/-ory/-ery* | having to do with (whatever it is affixed to) | station**ary**, vict**ory**, machin**ery** |
| *-ity* | quality, condition | moral**ity** matur**ity** |
| *-al/-ic* | relating to, characterized by | fiction**al**, magnet**ic** |

*Additional Prefixes*

| | | | |
|---|---|---|---|
| *inter-* between | *anti-* against | *fore-* before | *sub-* under |
| *intra-* within | *ex-* out, former | *post-* after | *quadr-* four |
| *super-* over, greater | | *pro-* in front of, forward | *pent-* five |

### Spelling-Meaning Patterns

A number of suffixes affect the pronunciations of bases to which they are attached. These are examined in the context of consonant and vowel alternations and are the foundation of understanding the spelling-meaning connection: Words that are related in spelling are often related in meaning as well, despite changes in sound.

| Consonant Alternations | | Vowel Alternations | |
|---|---|---|---|
| Silent-Sounded | si**g**n/si**g**nal, condem**n** /condem**n**ation, soften/soft | Long-to-short | crime/criminal, ignite/ignition, humane/ humanity |
| /t/ to /sh/ | conne**ct**/conne**ct**ion, sele**ct**/sele**ct**ion | Long-to schwa | compete/competition, define/definition gene/genetic |
| /k/ to /sh/ | musi**c**/musi**c**ian, magi**c**/magi**c**ian | | |
| /k/ to /s/ | criti**c**/criti**c**ize, politi**c**al/politi**c**ize | | |
| /s/ to /sh/ | prejudi**c**e/prejudi**c**ial, offi**c**e/offi**c**ial | | |

#### Predictable Spelling Changes in Consonants and Vowels

| /t/ to /sh/ | permi**t**/permi**ss**ion, transmi**t**/transmi**ss**ion | /sh/ to /s/ | fa**c**ial/fa**c**e, expre**ss**ion/expre**ss** fero**c**ious/fero**c**ity |
|---|---|---|---|
| /t/ to /s/ | silen**t**/silen**c**e, absen**t**/absen**c**e | /d/ to /zh/ | explo**d**e/explo**s**ion deci**d**e/deci**s**ion |

### Latin and Greek Word Parts

In the context of more advanced words appropriate for this level, explore in greater depth the Latin and Greek roots and affixes first introduced during the syllables and affixes stage (see Table 7.5).

For example:

Latin — *dict* (say: *diction*), *aud* (hear: *auditory*) *vis* (see: *visible*) *spec* (look: *retrospect*) *port* (carry: *portable*)

Greek — *tele* (far, distant: *telegraph*) *photo* (light: *photograph*) *graph* (writing: *digraph*), *-crat/-cracy* (rule: *democracy*, rule by the people), *-logy* (science of: *geology*, science of the earth, studying the earth), *phon* (sound: *homophone*)

*(Continued)*

**TABLE 8.2**    **Sequence of Word Study** *(Continued)*

### Spelling-Meaning Patterns

Extend students' understanding of the range of spelling-meaning relationships that exist among words in the English language and of the value of understanding these relationships.

#### Vowel Alternations

| | |
|---|---|
| Schwa-to short | *local/locality, legal/legality, metal/metallic* |
| Long, Short, and Schwa | *suffice/sufficient, inspire/inspiration, emphatic/emphasis* |
| Vowel Alternation with Spelling Change | *explain/explanation, re**sume**/re**sump**tion* |
| | *re**ceive**/re**cep**tion* |
| Multiple Alternations | *pub**lic**/pub**lic**ity/pub**lic**ize, family/fami**liar**/fami**liar**ity* |
| | *spirit/spiritual/spirituality* |

#### Latin and Greek Word Parts

Begin to explore combinations of roots and affixes in which the original literal meaning has become extended to a more connotative or associative meaning. For example, *circumspect* (look around), *distract* (pull away), *emotion* (move out of), *fractious* (break), *manufacture* (make by hand), *prescribe* (write before), *prefer* (carry before), *educate* (lead out), *introvert* (to turn inward)

#### Advanced Suffix Study

| | |
|---|---|
| *-ant/-ance* | *fragr**ant**/fragr**ance**, domin**ant**/domin**ance*** |
| *-ent/-ence* | *depend**ent**/depend**ence**, flore**scent**/flore**scence*** |
| *-able/-ible* | *respect**able**, favor**able** versus vis**ible**, aud**ible*** |

#### Prefix Assimilation

| | |
|---|---|
| Prefix + base word | *in* (not) + *mobile* = **im**mobile (not mobile); *ad* (to) + *count* = **ac**count (to count) |
| Prefix + word root | *in* (into) + *merse* = **im**merse (to plunge into) *ad* (to) + *cept* (take) = **ac**cept (to take) |

#### Accent and Doubling

| | |
|---|---|
| Double | *preferred referred* |
| Don't Double | *preference reference* |

#### Latin and Greek Word Parts

Advanced examination of combinations within words that have resulted in more nuanced meanings. Though many words English were originally "the sum of their parts," a natural phenomenon is that, over time, the meaning that a word represents grows metaphorically. Consider how the literal meanings of the following words have evolved over time: *unify* (make one), *benediction* (speak well), *monotonous* (one tone), *quintessential* (fifth essence), *decimate* (punish every tenth), *hyperbole* (throw beyond), *inspiration* (breathe in), *privilege* (law affecting one person), *provocative* (call forth), *secede* (go apart), *tenuous* (stretch), *obliterate* (to write over letters).

#### Advanced Prefix Assimilation

Students have the appropriate vocabulary knowledge to examine this wide-ranging process across a number of other prefixes.

| | |
|---|---|
| *com-* "with, together" | **col**laborate (work with), **cor**relate (relate together), **con**fer (carry together) |
| *sub-* "under, beneath" | **suf**fer (bear under), **sup**port (carry from beneath), **suc**cumb (lie beneath), **sus**ceptible (to take up from under) |
| *dis-* "apart" | **dif**fuse (pour apart), **dif**fer (carry away from) |
| *ob-* "against, toward" | **op**ponent (put against), **oc**cur (run toward); **ap**pendage (to hang), **as**sign (to mark), **at**traction (to be drawn toward), **ac**commodate (to fit with) |
| *ad-* "to, toward" | |

TEACHING TIPS

**Fine-Tuning Instruction**

- *An important caution:* You may want to confirm that students who seem to be at the derivational stage based on the Elementary Spelling Inventory (ESI) are indeed at that level. Administering the Upper-Level Spelling Inventory (USI) more accurately identifies what features students need to study in the late syllables and affixes and early derivational relations stages.

- Although we suggest a sequence of study, you will probably find that most students can be instructed on a number of features at the same time, which allows some flexibility in terms of grouping and selecting topics of study.

# Assess and Monitor Progress in the Derivational Relations Stage

Students in the derivational relations stage generally are good spellers because they have already acquired a great deal of word knowledge. As we emphasize in this chapter, word study for these students focuses primarily on the generative aspects of morphology and how the structure of words is usually the key to their meanings. You should address meaning in assessments as well as spelling. When you do assess with a focus on spelling, you needn't call out all the words in a sort, but rather only 10 or 15. Every few weeks, administer a cumulative review consisting of selected words representing different elements and patterns.

## Ways to Assess

There are several ways to assess:

- Ask students to spell the words studied that week. This works well for endings such as *-ion*, *-ible/-able*, and *-ence/-ance*, in which sound is not a clue.
- Ask students to both spell and define words; definitions should be in their own words.
- Give students a base word and ask them to add suffixes, such as adding *-ion* to words like *separate* (*separation*), *invade* (*invasion*), and *commit* (*commission*). Use words that they have not sorted to test for understanding of generalizations.
- Ask students to generate words given a prefix, suffix, or root. For example, the root *tract* should yield words like *attract*, *traction*, and perhaps *tractor*.
- Ask students to generate a related word in which a consonant or vowel sound is heard. For example, "There is a silent letter in *moisten*. Write a related word in which you can hear the sound of the letter." (*moist*)
- Ask students to match elements to meaning, such as matching *hyper-* and *hypo-* to the meanings "over" and "under."
- Ask students to spell a word and then underline a prefix, suffix, or root and also define the element, such as *fracture* means "*break*."
- Provide a sentence and ask students to supply or select the target word, as in the following: He loved to learn *magic* tricks and wanted to become a _____.

You may also use the spell checks in Appendix B and *Words Their Way*®: *Word Sorts for Derivational Relations Spellers* (3rd ed.)

## Monitoring Progress

As in the syllables and affixes stage, students at this stage can monitor their own progress. However, there is less urgency in this stage because word study for derivational relations is typically spread out over the middle school and high school years and beyond—literally for the rest of their lives. Think about the word sorts you do with students at this level as supporting their vocabulary

**Enhanced eText**
**Video Example 8.6**
Examine the spelling development of three students in Ms. Rubero's middle school classroom from their midyear spelling performance on the Upper-Level Qualitative Spelling Inventory (USI).

knowledge, both word-specific and generative. Unlike earlier developmental stages, sorts at this level need not be one-week affairs. Rather, they often stretch across two and sometimes three weeks.

As at all stages, review and grade student vocabulary notebooks. Focus on the range of words collected during word hunts for particular patterns, the types of open sorts that are recorded, and how well new words have been collected and described. (See Templeton et al., 2015 for additional assessment ideas, including how to involve older students in effective self-assessments.)

## Word Study with English Learners in the Derivational Relations Stage

*for* **English Learners**

English learners have the potential to be *more* sensitive to words than monolingual speakers simply because they must be more analytical—of their home language as well as English—in order to understand the nature of spelling–sound–meaning relationships (Templeton, 2010). The study of **cognates** can be quite productive at the derivational relations stage and can also benefit native English speakers who might be learning Spanish, French, or German as a foreign language. Cognates are words in different languages that share similar structures/spelling and similar meanings because they share similar origins.

We know that a large number of words in English are derived from Latin; this is true for many other languages as well. You can see the spelling–meaning connection in *mater* (Latin), *madre* (Spanish), *mere* (French), *mutter* (German), and *mother* (English). Paying attention to cognates helps both English learners and native speakers of English see morphological similarities between their native language and their to-be-learned language. Just as with word sorts in English, sorting English and Spanish cognates offers opportunities for examining spelling–meaning relationships and grammatical features. For example, students may notice the common suffixes and their spellings that key different parts of speech in the example at the top of the next page (Nash, 1997):

**Enhanced eText**
**Teacher Resource:**
Selected English/
Spanish Cognates

### TEACHING TIPS

#### Exploring Cognates

- Opportunities for finding cognates abound in specific academic domains such as science (Bravo, Hiebert, & Pearson, 2005), math, and social studies (Templeton, 2010; Templeton et al., 2015). In science or math, for example, students may match and discuss what they notice about the following cognates:

| English | polygon | quadrilateral | hexagon | pentagon | triangle |
|---------|---------|---------------|---------|----------|----------|
| Spanish | polígono | cuadrilatero | hexágono | pentágono | triángulo |

- Word roots also offer a rich terrain for exploring cognates in other languages. Make it a point to look for cognates as you study the different Latin roots—*port* shows up in Spanish *importar* and *exportar* and means the same thing ("carry") as in *export* and *import*. Create a chart of cognates in your classroom that students can add to as they discover more words. While most cognates across languages have the same or similar meanings, it is also important to be aware of potential "false friends." For example, the Spanish word *suburbio* looks a lot like the English word *suburbia*, or *suburbs*, but the Spanish word *suburbio* refers to the slums (Swan & Smith, 2001). Likewise, the Spanish word *éxito* doesn't correlate with *exit* at all, but means "success." The following resource supports exploring words and patterns at the derivational relations level in Spanish, and supports extensive cognate study with English:

Helman, L., Bear, D. R., Invernizzi, M., Templeton, S., & Johnston, F. (2019). *Palabras a su paso—Derivaciones.* Glenview, IL: Pearson.

|  | *Nouns* | *Adjectives* | *Verbs* | *Adverbs* |
|---|---|---|---|---|
| English | alphabet | alphabetic | alphabetize | alphabetically |
| Spanish | alfabeto | alfabético | alfabetizar | alfabéticamente |
| English | favor | favorable | favor | favorably |
| Spanish | favor | favorable | favorecer | favorablemente |

# Word Study Routines and Management

Keep three basic points in mind regarding students' word study at this level (Templeton, 1989, 1992, 2012):

1. Words and word elements selected for study should be *generative*, which means that, when possible, teach about words in "meaning families." This highlights the awareness that particular patterns of relationships can be extended or generalized to other words. For example, being aware of the long-to-short vowel alternation pattern in words such as *compete* and *competitive* can generalize to words such as *reduce* and *reduction*.
2. The words that we initially select for students to explore through focused contrasts should be based on how obvious the relationship is. For example, focus on clear contrasts first using visibly related words, such as *represent/misrepresent*, before contrasting words that are less clearly related, such as *expose/exposition*.
3. There should be a balance of teacher-directed instruction with students' exploration and discussion. See ideas about how to foster thoughtful active discussions in Table 3.2 on page 65. For example: "What are some ways we could figure out the meaning of that word? How could we check?" "Tell me how your sorting went. What words were difficult? What were you sure of/unsure of? What problems did you come across in your sort?"

## Teacher-Directed Word Study Instruction

Opportunities for word study should take place all day long and in all domains as you pause to examine words, talk about unusual spellings (e.g., *pneumonia*), search for clues to meaning in words and in context, and look up and discuss words in the dictionary. But, as in other stages, students in the derivational relations stage still need in-depth systematic attention to features at their developmental level. We emphasize the importance of word study at this developmental level for middle and secondary students, especially if these students have not experienced this type of systematic word study in school prior to this time.

Additional words and lists are provided in Appendices E and F. Students should already be able to spell and define at least half of the words in a sort. With more advanced students, a larger proportion of the words included in sorts may be unfamiliar, but the students usually are able to infer the meanings because these words share similar meaning elements with the known words.

## Routines

Many of the routines and word study notebook activities described in previous chapters are still appropriate, but at this stage, exploring a particular group of words and the spelling–meaning patterns they represent offers a number of paths to take. For this reason, some teachers adopt a two-week schedule that includes a word study contract such as the one on page 360. Have students complete a selection of routines independently in school or for homework. Test them every two weeks and include an assessment of meaning as well as of spelling.

**Enhanced eText**
**Video Example 8.7**
Ms. Rubero discusses her weekly word study schedule.

**Enhanced eText**
**Video Example 8.8**
Ms. Rubero discusses the spelling and reading development of her students in her 7th and 8th grade classes.

## Extending Word Study Activities for Derivational Spellers

- **Word meanings** are very important so use routines that focus on this. For example, have students use the dictionary to look up and record definitions and word origins of a few selected words (not 20 at a time!). Have students use words in sentences to demonstrate their understanding of meaning, but invite them also to try illustrations or cartoons. These visual representations can be powerful mnemonics, as shown in Figure 8.9. Having students work cooperatively and letting them share their sentences or drawings is engaging.

- **Sorting** words into categories according to focused contrasts is still a powerful learning activity; however, some teachers rely more on writing words into categories than on cutting out words and sorting them physically.

- **Blind sorts** still work well when spelling is an issue (as in -*able* and -*ible* sorts or when working with the /shən/ ending), but do not pose much of a challenge when the sort features prefixes and roots. The blind sort can be modified so that instead of saying a word to sort, the leader offers a definition as in, "This word means 'to breath in.'" The partner would respond with *inhale* and indicate that it goes under the *in-* prefix heading.

**FIGURE 8.9** Illustrating Word Relationships

- **Word hunts** should extend over longer periods of time. In addition to words and features pulled from literary and informational texts, brainstorming additional words ("word hunts in the head") sometimes works well, and dictionaries can become a place for word hunts. Students can be taught to search online dictionaries by using an asterisk before and/or after the word part to get a list of words (e.g., *cian* will give you words that end with -*cian*; *hydr* will yield the hundreds of words that contain this root).

- **Word displays** provide an ongoing review as words turn up in reading and in class discussions; these can be added to categories started weeks before.

- **Explore etymologies.** As students research word histories, show them how to reference and read the entries in unabridged dictionaries and in the resources available for such exploration.

- **Games** are a valuable way to review words not only for a test, but also over time. At this level students can create many games themselves based on popular games like Concentration, Rummy, War, Slap Jack, Uno, Trivial Pursuit, and Jeopardy. Give them blank game board templates from Appendix G or card stock for playing cards and they can do the rest. While creating games, they will remember the words and come to understand the feature better.

## Word Study Notebooks in the Derivational Relations Stage

Word study notebooks are an integral part of students' word learning at this stage (Templeton et al., 2015). In this last stage of development, the word study notebooks may be called Vocabulary Notebooks. Students use the notebooks to record word sorts and add words to the sorts after going on word hunts.

**SETTING UP THE NOTEBOOK.** To begin, divide the notebooks into three sections:

1. *Word Study.* A weekly record of sorts, reflections, and homework, this is also the section to record words that consistently present spelling challenges. Thinking of related words is one way to help clarify spellings.

2. *Looking into Language.* Includes records of whole-group word study of related words, concept sorts, word webs, interesting word collections, investigations, and thematic words.

3. *New and Interesting Words.* Words that students encounter in their reading that really grab them (much as "golden lines" do in their reading) are *golden words.*

**COLLECTING WORDS.** Teach the following steps to help older students collect golden words:

- *Collect the word.* While reading, mark words that really grab you or that you find difficult. When you are through reading or studying, go back to these words.
- *Record the word and sentence.* Write the word, followed by the sentence in which it was used, the page number, and an abbreviation for the title of the book. (At times the sentence will be too long; write enough of it to give a clue to meaning.) Think about the word's meaning.
- *Look at word parts and think about their meanings.* Look at the different parts of the word—prefixes, suffixes, and base word or root word. Think about the meanings of the affixes and the base or root.
- *Record related words.* Think of other words that are like this word, and write them underneath the part of the word that is similar.
- *Use the dictionary.* Look the word up in the dictionary, read the various definitions, and record the one that applies to the word in the book you are reading. Look for similar words (both in form and meaning) above and below the target word and list them as well. Look at the origin of the word, and add it to your entry if it is interesting.
- *Review the words.*

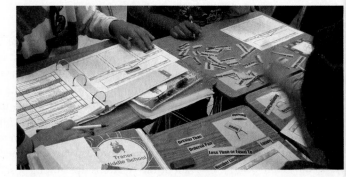

Sorting mathematical terms and expressions in middle school

## Recording Information about Words

SAMPLE LESSON

A realistic goal is to collect five to ten golden words a week. Students can record information about the word, as in the following example:

1. Collect the word: *orthography*.
2. Record the word and sentence: "English *orthography* is not crazy, and it carries the history of the word with it." p. 22, *Sounds of Language*.
3. Look at word parts and think about their meanings: *ortho/graph* (may have something to do with writing).
4. Record possible related words: *orthodontist, orthodox, graphics, orthopedics*.
5. Study the word in the dictionary, and record interesting information: "A method of representing the sounds of a language by letters; spelling." Origin: *ortho*—"correct;" *graph*—"writing."

Model how to think about making meaning connections among related words. For example, for *ortho*- say, "What does an *orthodontist* do? An orthodontist makes your teeth straight. And an *orthopedist*? An orthopedist makes your bones straight. And indeed when we look in the dictionary, *ortho*- means straight or correct."

*Words Their Way: Vocabulary for Middle and Secondary Students* (2nd edition) by Templeton, Bear, Invernizzi, Johnston, Flanigan, Townsend, Helman, and Hayes (2015) provides background and a wealth of instructional support for students at this level, including engaging ways of developing and fully using word study/vocabulary notebooks. You should find this resource especially helpful for derivational level students at the intermediate grades, extending the types of activities and instruction presented in this chapter. In addition, you may find that it extends your own knowledge base as well and provides you with the confidence to explore words more deeply with your students.

**Enhanced eText**
**Video Example 8.9**
English Language Arts teacher Ms. Amy Burton works with her middle school students to pique their curiosity about words.

## Word Consciousness

When you consistently model the exploration of and curiosity about words—*word consciousness*—it becomes part of students' learning repertoires. Your modeling extends to providing concrete opportunities for students to reflect on and value interesting words. Dedicate a space on a bulletin board where students can write interesting words—you may comment on them and generate discussion. Students may also write interesting words on slips and deposit them in a "Words We Treasure" box. From time to time, words are pulled out and students use them in sentences or in a broader conversation. Word consciousness becomes a mindset. Students who develop word consciousness become lifelong wordsmiths and almost automatically wonder about the relationships among words in general, and about a particular word specifically; for example, does the similarity in spelling between *ap**plaud**/**plaud**it* and *****mor**dant/**mor**sel* capture underlying meaning relationships? (Yes!) When you share this type of awareness and curiosity, you nourish the continual growth of vocabulary and conceptual networks.

Word Consciousness—Developing deeper appreciation of words by depositing favorites in "Words We Treasure"

# RESOURCES FOR IMPLEMENTING WORD STUDY *in Your Classroom*

In addition to Appendices E and F, the following resources offer sample sorts and lists of words for other sorts or to modify the sorts that are suggested.

*Words Their Way®: Word Sorts for Derivational Relations Spellers* (3rd ed.) (Templeton, Johnston, Bear, & Invernizzi, 2019) has two levels, "Basic" and "Advanced" Derivational Relations. Prepared sorts are divided into twelve units of study with assessments. These assessments tap both spelling and morphological or vocabulary knowledge (e.g., matching prefixes or word roots with their meanings).

*Words Their Way®: Vocabulary for Middle and Secondary Students* (2ⁿᵈ ed.) (Templeton, Bear, Invernizzi, Johnston, Flanigan, Townsend, Helman, & Hayes, 2015) offers guided walk-throughs in the appendices that address the concrete-to-abstract

spelling–meaning continuum and Greek/Latin roots. These are particularly useful for working with middle-grade and secondary students.

*Palabras a su paso—Derivaciones* (Helman, Bear, Invernizzi, Templeton, & Johnston, 2019) provides a complete curriculum of word study with prepared materials. This resource supports exploring words and patterns at the derivational relations level in Spanish and supports extensive cognate study with English.

*Words Their Way™: Vocabulary for Middle and High School* (Bear, Flanigan, Hayes, Helman, Invernizzi, Johnston, & Templeton, 2014). This resource addresses general academic and domain-specific vocabulary for the middle and secondary grades, as well as generative strategies that emphasize morphological analysis and etymology.

## ACTIVITIES for the Derivational Relations Stage

# Vocabulary Activities

Vocabulary activities presented here are divided into two parts: *Generative* and *Word-Specific* (beginning on p. 331).

# Generative

### 8.1 Break It Down

Conduct this as a group activity or as a game (Flanigan et al., 2011). Beginning with words the students have already studied, provide sentences containing each word. Using the following questions, each group analyzes—breaks down—a word and then justifies how their derived meaning fits in the context of the sentence. Later, after students have applied these questions with known words, extend to unfamiliar words. This way of thinking about words deepens the strategy for analyzing unfamiliar words they encounter when they are reading independently (Chapter 7).

1. How many meaning parts do you see in the word? (Write the word, circle the root or base word, underline affixes.)
2. Do you see any prefixes or suffixes? What do they mean?
3. What do the roots or base words mean?
4. What do you think the word means? Can you make up your own definition?
5. Does this meaning fit the sentence where you found the word?

### 8.2 Operation Examination

This game asks students to examine the changes to the root word when various spellings of the suffix /shun/ are added to the base word. The goal is to be the first player to run out of cards.

**MATERIALS** A ready-made version of this game is available at *WTW Digital*. You will need the following *cue cards*:

Just add *-ion*; Drop the *e* and add *-ion*; Drop the *e* and add *-ation*; Change *y* to *i* and add *-ication*; Change the *d* to *s* and add *-ion*; Just add *-ation*

Write the following words in the upper-left corner of a card to create a single deck of playing cards:

*expression discussion collection subtraction invention suggestion prevention digestion protection affection impression rejection operation creation decoration illustration imitation donation explosion erosion invasion conclusion expansion division provision information relaxation temptation expectation imagination organization reservation starvation quotation civilization invitation confirmation exploration identification application purification notification*

**PROCEDURES**
1. Put the cue cards (such as "drop a final *e* and add *-ion*") into one deck facedown. Deal the rest of the cards out to the players making sure that everyone gets the same number. The rest are set aside.
2. The first player turns over a cue card. All the players look for words in their hand that fit the criteria. For example, if the cue card says, "change the *d* to *s* and add *-ion*," players look for matches such as *explosion* and *expansion* and remove them from their hands.

**Enhanced eText**
**Video Example 8.10**
Ms. Rubero discusses how she chooses words for vocabulary study and how the students explore them.

**Enhanced eText**
**Teacher Resource:**
Break it Down Template

3. The matches are displayed faceup and if any are contested the player must justify their decision by naming the base word and how it changed. For example, "The base word was *explode* so the *d* was changed to an *s* when *-ion* was added to make *explosion*."

4. The next player turns over a new cue card and again students look for all possible matches and pull them from their hands.

5. The winner is the player who runs out of cards first.

*Adaptable* **for Other Stages**

**Enhanced eText**
Teacher Resource:
Root Tree Template

**FIGURE 8.10    Word Tree: Words That Grow from Base Words and Roots**

## 8.3  Words That Grow from Base Words and Word Roots

In this whole-class or small-group activity, students see directly how words "grow." It builds on and extends the understanding, begun during the syllables and affixes stage, of how word elements combine.

**MATERIALS** You will need a drawing of a tree (see Figure 8.10).

**PROCEDURES**
1. Decide on a base word or a word root to highlight. Begin with more frequently occurring words; over time, move to less frequently occurring roots.
2. Write the base word or word root at the bottom of the tree, and think of as many forms as possible.
3. Write the different forms on individual branches.
4. Display the word tree in the classroom for several days and encourage students to think of, find, and record more derived words. At the end of the week wipe them off and begin again by introducing a new base or word root.

**VARIATIONS** After making the words, students may use them individually in sentences and/or discuss their meanings. Confirm with the dictionary.

**Enhanced eText**
**Video Example 8.11**
Ms. Rubero conducts a whole-class lesson to study the root *tract*.

Students contributing words to the word root tree for *tract* (to pull, to draw)

## 8.4 Latin Jeopardy

A total of six students can be involved in this game:

- 3 students are contestants
- 1 student is the host, and is in charge of the answers and questions
- 1 student is the scorekeeper
- 1 student is the judge in case of the need to question a decision

You may also divide the whole class into two teams.

**MATERIALS** A ready-made version of this game can be found at *WTW Digital* or you can make a copy of the Jeopardy boards in Figures 8.11 and 8.12, enlarging them as much as possible. These can be used in different ways:

Option 1:

- Use paper squares to cover the individual clues, and use a smartboard to project the game board.

Option 2:

- Enlarge and print the Jeopardy boards and cut apart the board into clues. Write the point value on the back of each clue. The clues can then be placed in a pocket chart or taped on the board or wall, showing only the side with the point value. During the game, you will turn the requested square over and read the clue. Set up the roots as headers.

**Enhanced eText**
**Video Example 8.12**
On Day 2 of a seventh-grade, whole-class vocabulary lesson, students continue to study the root *tract* and they add more words to their root trees.

**FIGURE 8.11** Latin Root Jeopardy Game Board

| LATIN ROOT JEOPARDY | | | | |
|---|---|---|---|---|
| SPECT (to look) | FORM (shape) | PORT (to carry) | TRACT (draw or pull) | DICT (to say, speak) |
| 100<br>One who watches; an onlooker | 100<br>One "form" or style of clothing such as is worn by nurses | 100<br>Goods brought into a country from another country to be sold | 100<br>Adjective: having power to attract; alluring; inviting | 100<br>A book containing the words of a language explained |
| 200<br>The prospect of good to come; anticipation | 200<br>One who does not conform | 200<br>One who carries burdens for hire | 200<br>A powerful motor vehicle for pulling farm machinery, heavy loads | 200<br>A speaking against, a denial |
| 300<br>To regard with suspicion and mistrust | 300<br>To form or make anew; to reclaim | 300<br>To remove from one place to another | 300<br>The power to grip or hold to a surface while moving, without slipping | 300<br>A blessing often at the end of a worship service |
| 400<br>Verb: to esteem<br>Noun: regard, deference<br>Literally: to look again | 400<br>To change into another substance, change of form | 400<br>To give an account of | 400<br>An agreement: literally, to draw together | 400<br>1An order proclaimed by an authority |
| 500<br>Looking around, watchful, prudent | 500<br>Disfigurement, spoiling the shape | 500<br>A case for carrying loose papers | 500<br>To take apart from the rest, to deduct | 500<br>To charge with a crime |

FIGURE 8.12   Double Latin Root Jeopardy

| LATIN ROOT DOUBLE JEOPARDY | | | | |
|---|---|---|---|---|
| CRED (to believe) | DUCT (to lead) | FER (to bear, carry) | PRESS (to press) | SPIR (to breathe) |
| 200 A system of doing business by trusting that a person will pay at a later date for goods or services | 200 A person who directs the performance of a choir or an orchestra | 200 (Plants) able to bear fruit; (Animals) able or likely to conceive young | 200 A printing machine | 200 An immaterial intelligent being |
| 400 A set of beliefs or principles | 400 To train the mind and abilities of | 400 To carry again; to submit to another for opinion | 400 Verb: to utter; Noun: any fast conveyance | 400 To breathe out: to die |
| 600 Unbelievable | 600 To enroll as a member of a military service | 600 To convey to another place, passed from one place to another | 600 To press against, to burden, to overpower | 600 To breathe through; to emit through the pores of the skin |
| 800 Verb, prefix meaning "not"; word means to damage the good reputation of | 800 The formal presentation of one person to another | 800 Endurance of pain; distress | 800 State of being "pressed down" or saddened | 800 To breathe into; to instruct by divine influence |
| 1000 An adjective, prefix ac, word means officially recognized | 1000 An artificial channel carrying water across country | 1000 Cone bearing, as the fir tree | 1000 To put down, to prevent circulation | 1000 To plot; to band together for an evil purpose |

**PROCEDURES**   The game consists of two rounds: Jeopardy and Double Jeopardy.

1. The game is modeled after the *Jeopardy* television game. The clue is in the form of an answer and players must phrase their response in the form of a question:

   Answer clue: Coming from the Latin root *tract*, it means "a machine for pulling heavy loads."

   Question response: What is *tractor*?

2. Determine who goes first. The player selects a category and point value. The host uncovers the clue and reads it aloud.

3. The first player responding correctly adds the point amount of the question to his or her total or gets to keep the card that was turned over. He or she then chooses another category and point amount. An incorrect answer means that the points are subtracted.

4. The winner is the one with the most points.

**VARIATIONS**

1. Add rounds of Double Jeopardy and Final Jeopardy. When it is time for the Final Jeopardy question, players see the category, but not the answer. They then decide how many of their points they will risk. When they see the answer, they have 30 seconds to write the question. If they are correct, they add the number of points they risked to their total; if incorrect, that number of points is subtracted from their total.

2. Alternate from one player to the next, or from one team to the next, rather than who shouts out the response first. If one player misses, the other team gets a chance to respond. If they are correct, they also get another turn.

3. Include Daily Doubles: The number of points for an answer is doubled and, if correct, added to the player's score; if incorrect, the doubled number of points is subtracted from the player's score.

4. Develop a Vocabulary Jeopardy to accompany a study unit. Generate vocabulary cards from the unit that fit into four or five categories (e.g., "Food Groups" or "Habitats"). Write questions that relate to facts and concepts studied on cards. Teams of students play the game as a whole-class vocabulary review of the unit.

**FIGURE 8.13   Word Part Shuffle Cards**

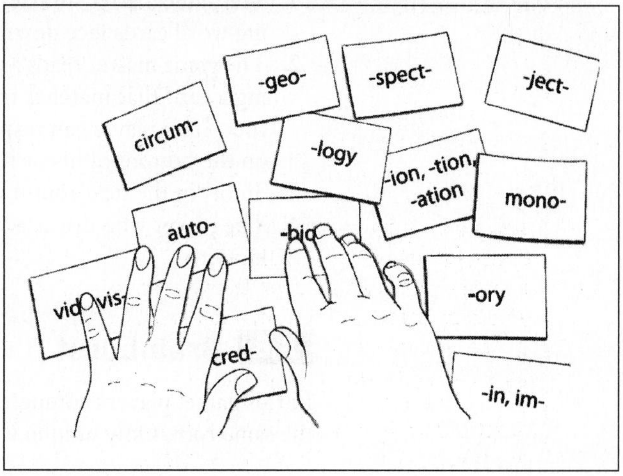

## 8.5   Word Part Shuffle

Word Part Shuffle is a noncompetitive word-building activity (Moloney, 2008). A group of students receives a stack of cards consisting of most of the most generative prefixes, suffixes, and bases/word roots (see Figure 8.13). The group first creates words that may be found in a standard dictionary. Then the group coins a new word, using as many of the cards as they can. They create a definition for the new word and then share with other groups. Kara Moloney created a deck of these cards with color-coded margins indicating prefix, suffix, or base/root, which is available at *https://verbumnosvocat.com*.

## 8.6   Quartet

Many games can be played with a deck of word cards made into suits of four. This game is much like "Go Fish," except the object is to collect and lay down a suit of four cards (or a quartet).

**MATERIALS**   Create 10 to 12 suits of four cards, composed of words that share a common root; for example, *biology, biography, biome, antibiotic*. Write the words at the top left so students can read the words when holding cards in their hands. A ready-made version of this game can be found at *WTW Digital*.

**PROCEDURES**

1. Each player is dealt seven cards; the rest are put in a deck. Each player looks through his or her cards for words in the same suit.

2. The first player turns to the next and asks for a particular root: "Give me any cards with the *bio* root." If the second player has any cards with the requested root, the player must give them up and the first player gets to go again. If the second player does not have any matches, he or she responds, "Draw one" and the first player draws from the deck.

3. Play proceeds in a clockwise fashion. When a player has a complete suit of four cards, he or she may lay them down. The player who has the most suits at the end—when someone runs out of cards—is the winner.

## 8.7   It's All Greek to Us

In this card game, the deck is composed of words derived from Greek roots. Three to five players may participate, one of whom will serve as game master, and hold and read definition cards.

**MATERIALS**   Using the list of Greek roots and derived words in Appendix F, prepare ten definition cards that consist of a root and definition, such as *derm* ("skin"). For each root, create four or more word cards (*epidermis, dermatology, taxidermist, hypodermic, pachyderm*). Write these words at the top so they can be seen when held in the hand.

### PROCEDURES

1.  The game master shuffles the word cards, deals ten cards per player, and places the remaining word cards face down.
2.  The game master reads a definition card and lays it down face up. All players who are holding a card that matches the definition read it and place it below the corresponding Greek root. If no player can respond to the definition, the game master places the definition card on the bottom of his or her cards for rereading later in the game.
3.  To begin the next round, a new definition card is laid down.
4.  The player who discards all ten word cards first is the winner and becomes the next game master.

### 8.8 Brainburst

In this game, players compete to brainstorm as many words as they can that are derived from the same root. Only unique words earn points.

**MATERIALS** Write different roots on cards—such as *graph*, *phon*, *scope*, *aud*, *dict*, *port*, *tract*, *struct*, *spect*—roots that can generate a wide variety of possible derivations. Each team or player needs a pencil and sheet of paper. You will need a timer and a standard dictionary (condensed dictionaries may not have enough words).

### PROCEDURES

1.  Select one card and announce the root. Set the timer for two to three minutes. Each player or team tries to think of as many words as possible derived from that root.
2.  When the timer goes off, players draw a line under their last words and count the number they have.
3.  The player with the longest list reads the list aloud. If another player has the same word, it is crossed off of everyone's list. Any words that are not on another list (unique words) are checked.
4.  Each player in turn reads aloud any words that no one else has called to determine whether he or she has a unique word. Disputes should be settled with the help of a dictionary.
5.  The player or team with the most unique words is the winner of the round.

**VARIATIONS** This game can also be played with prefixes (*ex-*, *sub-*, *pre-*, *post-*, and so on) and suffixes (*-ible*, *-able*, *-ant*, *-ent*, and so on).

### 8.9 Joined at the Roots

This concept sort is an effective extension of students' exploration of Latin and Greek word roots. It is appropriate for individuals, partners, or small groups.

**MATERIALS** You will need a word sort board, word cards, and vocabulary notebook.

### PROCEDURES

1.  Model how to place words with appropriate roots under a particular category; for example, "Speaking and Writing," "Building/Construction," "Thinking and Feeling," and "Movement." Then involve students in the categorization.
2.  After students grasp how this categorization scheme works, they can work in small groups or in pairs. Each group or pair takes a different category and sorts words whose roots justify their membership in that category.
3.  Have students write lists in vocabulary notebooks, and bring them to the larger group to share and discuss. (*Note:* Several of the words to be sorted may be placed under different categories.) Following are some examples of categories and a few illustrative words:

| Speaking and Writing | Building/ Construction | Thinking and Feeling | Government | Movement | Travel |
|---|---|---|---|---|---|
| autobiography | technology | philanthropy | economy | synchrony | astronaut |
| photograph | construct | philosophy | demagogue | fracture | exodus |
| catalogue | tractor | attraction | politics | | |
| emphasis | | | | | |

## 8.10 Root Webs

Root webs like the one in Figure 8.14 are a graphic way to represent the links among words derived from a common root.

**PROCEDURES**

1. Choose a set of common roots, such as *photo-*, *geo-*, *aqua-*, and *astro-*.
2. Model a web for students, as they complete their own webs in their vocabulary notebooks. After students understand how to create the root webs, they can do them independently or in small groups.
3. Brainstorm related words. Students should use dictionaries to locate roots, verify their meanings, find their origins, and search for related words.
4. Honor all suggestions. Eliminate words that do not fit the meaning of a root. Lead students to examine parts and meaning.

**VARIATIONS** A progressive root web provides the context for a more systematic walk-through of how words are generated from a common word root. Figure 8.15 is an example of a completed progressive web for the root *ject*, meaning "throw." Walk through each addition of an affix on one strand of the web, writing the derived word and discussing its meaning with students. Invite students to complete the other strands, discussing the meaning of each derived word with the class. This model can then be used with other roots by students who work in pairs or small groups.

## 8.11 Identifying the Meanings of Word Roots

Given a series of words that share the same root, students analyze the words to determine the meaning of the root. Each group of three words can be finished with one of the words provided. For example, in item 1 of the first grouping, students look for which of the three words—*introspection*, *interrupt*, or *distract*—contains the same root as *spectator*, *inspect*, and *prospector* (*introspection*). In the next sentence, they write what they believe the root *spect* means. In the third sentence, they decide which of the remaining words—*interrupt* or *distract*—contains the

*Adaptable* **for Other Stages**

**FIGURE 8.14** "Root Web" in Student's Vocabulary Notebook

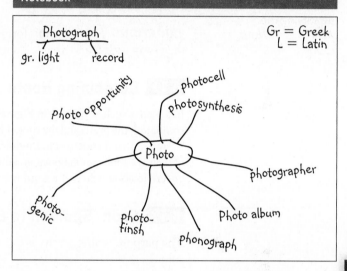

**FIGURE 8.15** Progressive Root Web

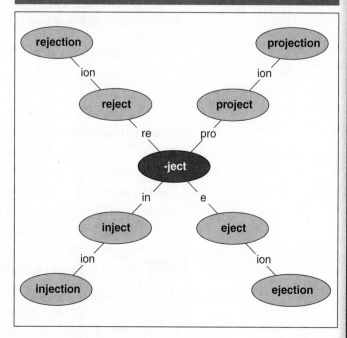

**FIGURE 8.16** Matrix of Roots and Prefixes

|  | duce/duc/duct | port | spect | dict | tract |
|---|---|---|---|---|---|
| in/im | X | X | X |  |  |
| trans |  |  |  |  |  |
| ex |  |  | X |  | X |
| pre |  |  |  | X |  |
|  | induce | import | inspect | predict | extract |
|  |  |  | expect |  |  |

same root as *corrupt*, *disrupt*, and *eruption*, and so on. This is an excellent activity for students to work on in pairs.

**VARIATIONS** Following this format, groups of students can construct their own exercises and then swap with other groups. Appendix F has additional roots.

## 8.12 Combining Roots and Affixes

In a matrix such as the one in Figure 8.16, students indicate with an *X* words that can be made by combining the prefix and the root. Then they write the words below. A variation is to indicate with a "?" words that do not exist in English, but could. Students may write these words in a special section of their vocabulary notebooks, creating a definition and using each in a sentence. When students are uncertain about whether a word is an actual word in English, they may check it in the dictionary.

## 8.13 From Spanish to English—A Dictionary Word Hunt

The purpose of this activity is to expand students' vocabularies through discovering relations among *cognates*.

*for* **English learners**

**PROCEDURES**

1. Look through a Spanish–English dictionary to find words in Spanish that remind you of words in English. Briefly note the definition or synonym (see Nash, 1997).
2. With an English dictionary, find words that share the same root or affix. Write these related words in your vocabulary notebook.
3. Record findings in the vocabulary notebook and create a class chart.

Following are sample entries on a class chart of cognates that one group of students collected in this activity.

| Spanish (Translation) | English Relations | Spanish Relations |
|---|---|---|
| presumir (boast) | presume, presumption, presumptuous | presunción, presumido |
| extenso (extensive) | extend, extension | extensivo, extender |
| nocturno (nightly) | nocturnal, nocturne | noche, noctámbulo |
| polvo (powder) | pulverize (from Latin *pulvis*, meaning "dust") | polvillo, polvorear |

## 8.14 Words That Grow from Indo-European Roots

The Indo-European (IE) language, spoken almost 8,000 years ago, is a "mother" language to more than half of the world's languages (Watkins, 2011). This is one reason why the etymological information included for many entries in the *American Heritage Dictionary* (2012) includes not only the Latin or Greek roots from which they came but also their Indo-European root. Exploring these roots provides fascinating insights for students at the derivational level. You may want to begin this exploration with the more concrete roots and activities provided in the "Origins" two-volume series by Sandra Robinson and her colleagues (1989). Using an Indo-European root such as *dhreu*, which meant "to fall," students come to appreciate how some of our English words with that root developed—*drop, droop, drip, drizzle*—as well as the more figurative meanings of *drowsy* and *dreary*.

**Enhanced eText**
**Teacher Resource:**
The Indo-European Language (Briefly)

After students understand how the meanings of more common English words evolved from their Indo-European roots, you can extend their exploration to roots that have generated both transparent and more opaque meanings, words that occur most often in general academic and domain-specific vocabulary (Templeton, 2015).

**MATERIALS**  Have Watkins' *American Heritage Dictionary of Indo-European Roots* (2011) on hand (also available online) as well as Shipley's *Origins of English Words* (2001). Different groups of students may be assigned different Indo-European roots to examine.

**PROCEDURES**  Each group selects English words derived from the root that they believe are good examples of how the "core" meaning of the Indo-European root functions in those words. Then they construct a word tree like they did with Latin and Greek roots (see Figure 8.10). Figure 8.17 shows a word tree growing from the Indo-European root -*genə*-, which means "to give birth, beget; with derivatives referring to aspects and results of procreation and to familial and tribal groups" (Watkins, 2011, p. 27).

Much of the activity's value lies in the discussion that surrounds the students' investigation. For example, first students wonder how *gentle* came from a root having to do with giving birth or beginning something. Then, when they check the etymological information in the *American Heritage Dictionary*, they find that *gentle* comes from a Middle English word *gentil*, which in turn came from French. It meant "courteous," coming in turn from Latin *gentilis*, meaning "of the same clan." The students now understand the part of the Indo-European meaning of -*genə*- having to do with "familial and tribal groups." They discuss how you would be courteous to others who were in the same clan—the group you began your life with. Generative forms add up quickly, including *gentle, genteel, gently, gentleman, genealogy, gentry, generic, genus*, and *hydrogen* to name a few. Students should be able to see into words with *gen* and begin to think of meaning connections. Students can dig as deeply as they want, and 10 to 15 minutes at a time is usually enough time for a whole class or small group examination.

Students at this level are aware of how the spelling in related words sometimes changes (having examined, for example, pairs such as *exclaim/exclamation, proclaim/proclamation*). When they see the many different words that have evolved from a single Indo-European root they will notice how the spelling of the root has often changed. For example, the *e* in *gen* has fallen away in the word *cognate*, but *gn* still functions as a meaningful root. Students may realize that so many cognates in different languages were, in a sense, "born together" (*co + gen*) because they came from the same Indo-European root!

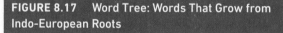

**FIGURE 8.17  Word Tree: Words That Grow from Indo-European Roots**

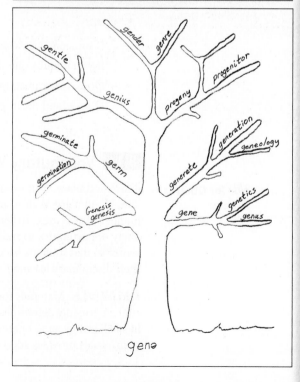

# Word-Specific

## 8.15 Well-Crafted Questions

Well-crafted questions are easy to create and involve students in demonstrating their ability to apply new vocabulary in various contexts (Beck, McKeown, & Kucan; Templeton et al., 2015). The following three "frames" for generating questions provide examples that start with teacher-created questions. These serve as springboards for oral discussions or as part of a written assessment/activity. As students become familiar with these frames for generating questions, they can create and share their own examples.

**Frame 1: Generate Situations.** Create a prompt that requires your students to apply the vocabulary word in a situation or to a person.

- "Tell about a time when you were *crestfallen*. Be sure to explain why your example illustrates the word."
- "Describe how someone would act *furtively*. Be sure to also explain why someone might act this way."
- "Think about someone who is an *aristocrat*. Write about why someone would be called an aristocrat."

Create more challenging situations with less common uses of the word. For example:

- "The teacher *lavishly* praised the student for her efforts on the exam. What do you think the teacher thought about the student's work? Why?"
- "Full of *consternation*, the student stared at the theorem in his geometry book. How do you think the student felt about class that day? Why?"

**Frame 2: Relationships.** Identify pairs of words that are semantically similar. Students will discuss how these words are similar as well as how they are different—this type of thinking focuses your students' attention on the subtle *nuances* of word meanings. Students may also provide examples and nonexamples of the target words.

- "Tell how *fervor* and *enraptured* are alike. Now tell how these words are different."
- "Consider these two descriptions. Which is an example of *impassively* and which is a non-example: A girl telling her friends about her 16th birthday party on Saturday night. A boy counting his tips as he does every day at the end of the lunch shift."
- "Give an example of someone who is *entranced*. Now give a *non*example of entranced."

**Frame 3: Yes/No Items.** Create a series of yes/no items that probe both the word's use in context as well as its definition. Ask students to explain or justify their yes/no answer with follow-up questions such as: Why? What makes you say that? Why wouldn't that word work here?

- *ecstatic*

  - "If someone just won first place in a dance competition, might that person be *ecstatic*?"
  - "If you found a one-dollar bill while walking to school, would you be *ecstatic*?"
  - "Does *ecstatic* mean you feel extremely happy?"
  - "Does *ecstatic* mean you feel indifferent?"

## 8.16 Vocabulary Wall

*Adaptable* **for Other Stages**

The Vocabulary Wall extends students' focus on words to the exploration of their meanings. The Vocabulary Wall is an essential classroom resource and provides the foundation for a number of activities. To learn general academic and domain-specific vocabulary, students need many opportunities to *read* that vocabulary. Vocabulary walls place essential words front and center so that students have many opportunities to read the words that are most important for their disciplinary learning.

**MATERIALS** Materials for vocabulary walls, such as the words themselves and technical and student-friendly definitions and graphic support, can be created by students. This may be done in small groups or as homework or extra credit assignments. Involving students in the creation of materials provides additional opportunities for them to practice with the words.

**PROCEDURES**

1. Choosing words: For any content area or discipline, identifying both discipline-specific academic words and general academic words is essential. Here are the types of words that may be included on classroom vocabulary walls:

   * Key words from the content area that will be relevant all year
   * Key words from the content area that relate to the current unit
   * General academic words that support understanding of the key words

   Students should be an active part in the process of developing word lists for vocabulary walls. After a few classes of introductory activities in a unit, they may work together to create a list of key general academic and domain-specific words they believe are most relevant to the unit of study they are about to begin (see Activity 8.20).

2. Creating the physical vocabulary wall: Students should also be involved in this part of the process.

   Not all middle school teachers have their own classroom, and this is a challenge for using vocabulary walls. There are two possible ways this may be addressed: The first is digital. If you have a smartboard, a doc cam, or an overhead projector, keep your lists on a flash drive or on transparencies and "post" them on a regular basis. The second solution is a portable. Have students use the front and back covers of their Vocabulary Notebooks as individual vocabulary walls. Another option is to laminate a set of vocabulary wall cards to be passed out at the beginning of each class.

3. Using the vocabulary wall: Possibilities for using vocabulary walls are endless. Here are a few that may be used on a daily basis:

   * Recognize students when they notice their peers or their teachers using vocabulary wall words, or when they notice the words in instructional materials. The teacher might keep a running tally on the board, or students may do so in their notebooks.
   * Require that students accurately use vocabulary wall words in their writing, from exit slips to essays.
   * Students have to respond to each other and to the teacher using vocabulary wall words.
   * As described earlier, have students keep Vocabulary Notebooks in which they record information about important words. Such information might be concept maps, morphological information, and/or graphics. Students can record new information based on classroom discussions that have occurred involving vocabulary wall words.

4. Following are possible entry and exit slip prompts using vocabulary wall words:

   * Write down the words _____, _____, and _____ from our vocabulary wall. With a partner, write down everything you think you know about them.
   * Here are two questions we'll be discussing today. Which vocabulary wall words do you think will be most important in addressing these questions?
   * Choose two vocabulary wall words and explain the relationship between them.
   * Write down one new thing you learned today and use at least two of our vocabulary wall words.
   * Which vocabulary wall words were the most important in our lesson today?

**Enhanced eText**
**Teacher Resource:**
Concept Map Template

## 8.17 The Synonym/Antonym Continuum

This activity encourages students to think about the subtle differences between word meanings as they work with antonyms and synonyms.

**MATERIALS** Think of opposites like *hot/cold, brave/frightened, old/young, lazy/energetic,* and so on. Use a thesaurus to find synonyms for each word in the pair and write them on cards or in a list.

*Adaptable* **for Other Stages**

**PROCEDURES** Have students arrange the words along a continuum. At the ends of the continuum are the antonyms (words that are most opposite in meaning). Next to each of these words,

**FIGURE 8.18** Poster for Laissez-Faire

> **laissez faire**
> /lay-zay fair/
> definition: noninterference, lack of government intervention
> origin: French laisser - to let + faire - to do
> example: The teacher had a laissez faire attitude about chewing gum in school.

students decide where to place synonyms (words that are closest to the meaning of the opposite words) and so on until all words are used.

For example, the words *balmy*, *frigid*, *chilly*, *boiling*, *frozen*, *tepid*, *hot*, *cool*, and *warm* can be arranged this way:

*frigid frozen chilly cool tepid balmy warm hot*

Students can first work individually and then compare their continua with one another. They should discuss differences and provide rationales for why they arranged particular words the way they did. The dictionary is the final judge of any disagreements. Encourage students to add other words, like *sweltering*, *steamy*, *balmy*, and so on, by brainstorming or using a thesaurus or dictionary. Give students a word pair of opposites and send them to a thesaurus to create a list of words. They can then order them as described previously or present them to another team to order.

### 8.18 You Teach the Word

*Adaptable* **for Other Stages**

The vocabulary demands of content domains are significant. One way to handle these is to assign one word to each student, who then becomes responsible for teaching that word to the rest of the class. Ask each student to create a small poster to add to a class word wall, such as the one in Figure 8.18, that includes a definition, a synonym and/or antonym, an etymology, a sentence, or an illustration. Students can share their posters, but also encourage them to think of creative ways to help each other learn the word, such as by acting it out. For more advanced students, see the "Word Museum" project in Templeton et al. (2015).

### 8.19 Vocabulary Cards

As shown in Figure 8.19, vocabulary cards may be used for the most important key concepts/vocabulary in a specific selection or in a unit of study—those that represent the "big ideas."

1. Model how to make these cards so that students will then be able to construct their own. The key vocabulary word will be on the front and the definition on the back. For students who are studying influential African-Americans in the 19th and 20th centuries, for example, model how to construct a card for the word *inspiration*, a key concept in this study, an example of which occurs in the text *Let It Shine: Stories of Black Women Freedom Fighters* (Pinkney, 2009). Because this text is a historical narrative, there are not always the types of straightforward in-text definitions students will find, for example, in science and mathematics texts. So, you will read aloud the paragraph in which the word occurs, mentioning that it provides a rich context for suggesting the meaning of the word. Then, reread the sentence in which the word occurs: "Mary McLeod Bethune visited jails, slum houses, and hospitals, where she offered comfort and *inspiration* by leading people in prayer or singing a hymn" (p. 43). Discuss what students believe the word means, then check in the dictionary—a number of definitions are offered; discuss which one best fits the meaning in *Let It Shine*. ("A person or thing that moves the intellect or emotions.")

2. As students construct their own cards, they should select the definition from the text if it is clear, include the sentence in the text that uses the word, or both. For narrative texts in which the meaning is less clear, students may then check a glossary or dictionary. For general and domain-specific vocabulary terms, they should be encouraged to generate their own examples that illustrate the concept, as in the student's example for the mathematical term *expression* (Figure 8.19).

3. As students learn how to use different types of graphic organizers, they may also include these formats on the back of the cards—as, for example, a "4-square" design (see p. 307).

**FIGURE 8.19   Vocabulary Cards**

Front of Card

**inspiration**

Front of Card

**expression**

Back of Card

A person or thing that moves the intellect or emotions

"Mary McLeod Bethune visited jails, slum houses, and hospitals, where she offered comfort and *inspiration* by leading people in prayer or singing a hymn."

Back of Card

TD: a group of symbols that make a mathematical statement

MD: a group of numbers and symbols doing some math together (like with + or / ) and  there is no equal sign

Example: 4x- 7

TD = Technical Definition      MD = My Definition

## 8.20  Clue Review with Vocabulary Cards

Using vocabulary cards in Clue Review affords students opportunities to review and reinforce their knowledge of definitions in a motivating and easy-to-use format across a range of contexts (Flanigan et al., 2011).

1. Pair the students: One will be "clue giver" and the other "hot seat."
2. The student on the "hot seat" shuffles the deck of vocabulary cards. Without looking, she places the first card on her forehead with the front of the card with the vocabulary term showing and the back of the card against her forehead.
3. The clue giver gives the "hot seat" a clue—for example, for "inspiration" the clue giver says, "When you make someone feel really good, help them deal with problems."
4. If "hot seat" correctly identifies the word, she moves on to the next vocabulary card. If not, the clue giver offers additional clues. If partners cannot identify the word, the clue giver flips the card over and they review the definition.
5. The aim is to get as many vocabulary cards correct without needing to check definitions.
6. After going through the words once, the partners switch roles. This ensures that both students will have the opportunity to provide definitions in their own words.

Tips for "Clue Review":

- Clues must relate to important features of the concept. For example, students might try "rhymes with *perspiration*" for *inspiration*—that doesn't count!
- Occasionally you may partner more proficient with less proficient students. More proficient students will be the first clue giver, providing a language model for their partner.
- Switch pairs from time to time so that students will hear different ways of defining the same word.
- Homework assignments may involve another family member as a partner—a parent, grandparent, or sibling.

**ACTIVITIES I DERIVATIONAL RELATIONS STAGE**

**FIGURE 8.20** Semantic Feature Analysis

|  | Cannot Stand Alone | Comes Before a Base Word or Root Word | Usually Comes from Greek or Latin | Can Stand Alone | Comes After Base Word or Word Root |
|---|---|---|---|---|---|
| Prefix | + | + | + | – | – |
| Base word | – | – | ? | + | – |
| Affix | + | ? | + | – | ? |
| Suffix | + | – | + | – | + |
| Word root | + | – | + | – | – |

## 8.21 Semantic Feature Analysis

This analysis (Anders & Bos, 1986) engages students in examining words and definitions in relation to each other.

### PROCEDURES

1. Write the words to be examined down the left margin of a matrix. (In this example, the words are *prefix*, *base word*, *affix*, *suffix*, and *word root*.) Then write the features of these words across the top. When you introduce this activity to students, list these features yourself. Later, after students understand how the analysis works, they have them suggest the features that will be listed.
2. Discuss the matrix with the whole class or with small groups. Students mark each cell with one of the following symbols: a plus sign (+) indicates a definite relationship between the word and a feature; a minus sign (–) shows the word does not have that feature; and a question mark (?) says that students feel they need more information before responding.
3. After students complete the matrix, point out (1) they now *really* know how much they know about each word, and (2) they also know what they still need to find out (Templeton, 1997). Figure 8.20 illustrates a semantic feature analysis completed by a group of sixth-grade students under a teacher's guidance to clarify the meanings of word study terms.

## 8.22 Finding Critical Vocabulary and Concepts

We teach students how to locate key vocabulary and concepts in new units of study by showing them how we select and organize the vocabulary.

**PROCEDURES** Part I. Find Critical Vocabulary in *Informational Texts*

1. Find the "building blocks." What are the key domain-specific vocabulary and concepts in the unit? See if there are lists of terms at the opening and closing of the chapter. Look through the unit for bolded terms, key dates, tables, and figures.
2. Find signal words and phrases. These are general academic words and phrases that cue you to the type of pattern or relationship the writer is using (for example *As a result*; *If...then*; *the problem is...*).
3. Find a few key "blocks" for in-depth exploration. These will often be domain-specific words that are examples of *generative* vocabulary—they include roots, prefixes, suffixes you have been exploring or plan to explore. Select "anchor" words and word parts like *Civil War* for the root *civ* ("citizen"), *populism* for the root *popul/pub* ("people"), *assimilation* for the suffix *-ion* ("act or process of").

Students beginning collaborative selection of critical vocabulary for literature unit

**FIGURE 8.21** Vocabulary Overview for Unit on "The American West"

| Domain-Specific Vocabulary | | General Academic Vocabulary And Language | Generative Vocabulary |
|---|---|---|---|
| **Native Americans** <br> • Buffalo <br> • Horse <br> • **Assimilation** <br> • Dawes Act <br> • Reservation <br> • Americanization <br> • Wounded Knee Massacre <br> • Custer's Last Stand <br> • Sitting Bull <br> • George Armstrong Custer <br><br> **Farmers/Sodbusters** <br> • Homesteaders <br> • Homestead Act of 1862 <br> • Great Plains <br> • Exodusters <br> • Bonanza Farms <br> • Debt <br> • **Populism** <br> • Bryan's "Cross of Gold" | **Cowboys/Ranchers** <br> • Transcontinental Railroad <br> • Longhorn <br> • Chisholm Trail <br> • Long Drive <br> • Abilene <br> • Barbed Wire <br> • "Wild Bill" Hickok <br> • "Calamity" Jane <br><br> **Miners** <br> • **Boomtown** <br> • 49er's /Gold Rush | **Problem/Solution** <br> The problem is . . . <br> The dilemma is . . . <br> The hardship is . . . <br> If . . . then, <br> The question . . . answer <br> . . . so that . . . <br> Despite . . . <br> . . . faced with . . . <br> . . . overcome . . . <br> When confronted <br> with . . . <br> As a result, <br> For example, <br> To illustrate, <br> In spite of . . . | • **Populism** <br> **POPUL/PUB** –"people" <br> population <br> populate/ <br> **overpopulated** <br> populace <br> popular <br> popularity <br> **populist** <br> public <br> republic <br> publicize <br> publicity <br> **publish** <br> **publication** <br> • **Assimilation** <br> **-ION** – "act or process of" <br> reproduction <br> division <br> delusion <br> **publication** <br> production <br> reduction |

The overview shown in Figure 8.21 shows the result of applying these three steps for a unit on "The American West" that we created (Flanigan et al., 2017). Share the first few overviews you create with your students so they will have these models. They can then work in pairs or small groups to create their own overviews. They may also follow these three steps when they create handouts for their own vocabulary presentations.

Part II. Find Critical Vocabulary in *Narrative Texts*

1. Look for special or unique words, phrases, concepts, and sentences.
2. Note character descriptions, figurative language (simile, metaphor, personification), symbolism, nuances in how words are used, themes, special graphics (italics, boldface).
3. Record key events, people, places, and dates.

## 8.23 Word Challenge: Words from Myths and Legends

Prerequisite: Students must be familiar with the content selected, such as Greek and Roman myths and legends.

**MATERIALS** At least 20 word cards with questions—4 categories selected such as Science, Art, Timely Events, or Everyday Words

**Directions:**

Object of the game: To earn the most points by correctly answering questions within the category selected.

Example Questions from **Science**:

Q: What is a word that comes from the Cyclops, a monstrous giant with an eye in his forehead?

A: *cyclone*

**Enhanced eText**
**Teacher Resource:**
Greek Mythology: A
Very Brief Primer

**Enhanced eText**
**Teacher Resource:**
Words from Greek
and Roman Myths &
Legends

Q: What is a word that comes from Sol, the Roman god of the sun?

A: *solar*

Q: What is a word that comes from Hydra, the nine-headed water serpent slain by Hercules?

A: *hydraulics*

Example Questions from **Music**:

Q: What is a word that comes from the Muses, Zeus' nine daughters?

A: *music*

Q: What is a word that comes from Polyhymnia, the muse of religious music?

A: *hymn*

Q: What is a word that comes from Mnemosyne, the mother of the Muses?

A: *mnemonic*

Example Questions from **Timely Events**:

Q: What is a word that comes from Janus, the two-faced god of doors?

A: *January*

Q: What is a word that comes from Nox, the goddess of darkness of night?

A: *nocturnal*

Q: What is a word that comes from Chronos, the god of time?

A: *chronological*

Example Questions from **Everyday Words**:

Q: What is a word that comes from Terra, the goddess of earth?

A: *terrarium*

Q: What is a word that comes from Oceanus, the god of water?

A: *ocean*

Q: What is a word that comes from Clotho, who was pictured as spinning all the threads that represent life?

A: *clothes*

*Other words from different areas/categories:*

Science: *hygiene, iris, cosmos, Pluto, Jupiter, Uranus, Mars, Venus, Mercury, Earth, Saturn, Neptune, cyclone, aurora, lunar, solar, hydraulics, terrestrial, terrain, geography, geology, volcano, hydrate, iridescent*

Timely Events: *Easter, dawn, January, March, chronological, the Olympics, nocturnal, June, Valentine's Day* (Cupid)

Arts: *music, calliope, hymn, museum, Orpheum, muse*

Everyday Words: *giant, cosmetics, ocean, chaos, atlas, furious, clothes, cereal, lethargic, panic, pomegranate, mnemonic, panacea, salute, tantalize, lethal, nectarine, ambrosia, echo, narcissism, mortal, clue, labyrinth, terrace, titanic*

## 8.24 Eponyms: Places, Things, Actions

**Eponyms** are words that refer to places, things, and actions that are named after an individual (from Greek *epi-* for "after" + *noma* for "name"). Students' interest in word origins is often sparked by finding out where such words originate. As these words are discovered, they can be recorded in the "Looking into Language" section of the vocabulary notebook and/or displayed on a bulletin board.

Following is a sampler of common eponyms:

| | |
|---|---|
| *Bloomers* | Amelia Bloomer, an American feminist in the late nineteenth century |
| *Boycott* | Charles Boycott, whose servants and staff refused to work for him because he would not lower their rents |
| *Diesel* | Rudolph Diesel, a German engineer who invented an alternative engine to the slow-moving steam engine |
| *Ferris wheel* | G. W. C. Ferris, designer of this exciting new ride for the 1893 World's Fair in Chicago |
| *Guillotine* | Joseph Guillotin, a French physician and the inventor of the device |
| *Leotard* | Jules Leotard, a French circus performer who designed his own trapeze costume |
| *Magnolia* | Pierre Magnol, French botanist |
| *Pasteurize* | Louis Pasteur, who developed the process whereby bacteria are killed in food and drink |
| *Sandwich* | John Montagu, the Earl of Sandwich, who requested a new type of meal |
| *Sax* | Antoine Joseph Sax, Belgian instrument maker, designer, and builder of the first saxophone |

The following resources include lists and information about eponyms:

Freeman, M. S. (1997). *A New Dictionary of Eponyms*. New York: Oxford University Press.

Marciano, J. (2009). *Anonyponymous: The Forgotten People behind Everyday Words*. New York: Bloomsbury.

Terban, M. (1988.) *Guppies in Tuxedos: Funny Eponyms*. New York: Clarion.

# Spelling Activities

## 8.25 Which Suffix?

This activity is an excellent follow-up to previous work with base words, word roots, and suffixes. It is appropriate for individuals, buddies, or small groups. The suffixes included are *-tion/-sion*, *-ible/-able*, *-ence/-ance*, and *-ary/-ery*. (See lists for these suffixes in Appendix F.)

**MATERIALS** You will need a word sort board, word cards, and a vocabulary notebook.

**PROCEDURES**

1. Decide how many suffix pairs to place at the top of the word sort board. (Note that several of the words to be sorted may be placed under different suffixes; for example, *permit: permissible, permission.*) Each card has the base word written on one side and the same word with allowable suffixes on the other side.
2. Mix up the word cards and place the deck with base words faceup. The students in turn choose the top card and decide in which suffix category it belongs.
3. After all the cards are placed, have students record in their vocabulary notebooks what they think is the correct spelling of the word.
4. After recording all the words, students turn over the cards to self-check the correct spelling.

**VARIATIONS** Students can work as buddies to explore a particular suffix "team" (e.g., *-tion* and *-sion*) to see what generalization(s) may underlie the use of a suffix.

## 8.26 Defiance or Patience?

The game Defiance (if using the *ant/ance/ancy* family), or Patience (if using the *ent/ence/ency* family), is for three to five players. The object of the game is to make as many groups of two, three, or four cards of the same derivation as possible and to run out of cards first.

**MATERIALS** Using words from the lists in Appendix F, create a deck of 52 cards with suits of two, three, or four words (e.g., *attend, attendance,* and *attendant* is a set of three, and *radiate, radiant, radiance,* and *radiancy* for a set of four). Write each word across the top of a card, and your deck is prepared.

**PROCEDURES**

1. Each player is dealt five cards from the deck. The player to the left of the dealer begins the game. The player may first lay down any existing groups of two, three, or four held in his or her hand. This player then may ask any other player for a card of a certain derivation in his or her own hand: "Matthew, give me all of your *resistance*." (This could result in gaining *resistance, resistant, resistancy,* or *resist*.)

2. If a player does not have cards with the requested feature, he or she responds, "Be Defiant" (or "Be Patient," depending on which game is being played).

3. At this point, the requesting player must draw another card from the deck. If the card is of the same family he or she is looking for, the player lays down the match and continues asking other players for cards. If the card is not a match, play passes to the person on the left and continues around the circle in the same manner. If the drawn card makes a match in the asking player's hand but was not in the group requested, he or she must hold the pair in hand until his or her turn comes up again. Of course, this means there is a risk of another player taking the pair before the next turn.

4. Play ends when one of the students runs out of cards. The player with the most points wins.

5. Players may play on other people's card groups, laying related cards down in front of themselves, not in front of the player who made the original match.

6. Scoring is as follows.

| Singles played on other people's matches | 1 point |
|---|---|
| Pairs | 2 points |
| Triples | 6 points |
| Groups of four | 10 points |
| First player to run out of cards | 10 points |

**VARIATIONS**

1. Play a version called "Defy My Patience" that mixes sets of words from both lists to create an *ent/ant* deck.

2. "Challenge My Patience or Defy My Challenge." In this version, during scoring, before everyone throws down his or her hand, students should secretly write additional words that have not been played for groups they have laid down. Before hands are revealed, students share these lists and an additional point is added to the player's score for each related word he or she wrote. Any player who doubts the authenticity of a word claimed by an opponent may challenge the word. The challenger loses a point if the word is valid or gains a point if it is not. The player, likewise, counts the word if it is valid or loses a point if the challenger proves him or her wrong.

3. Encourage students to develop their own derivational families to add to this game, or another feature to substitute for the *ant/ent* contrast.

### 8.27 Assimile

This game can be played by two to six players. A ready-made copy can be found at *WTW Digital*.

**MATERIALS** The game board is modeled after a *Monopoly* board (see Figure 8.22). You will also need dice, game playing pieces, a deck of prefixes that can be assimilated (*ad-, sub-, in-, ex-, com-, ob-*), a deck of base words that can take assimilated prefixes (e.g., base words such as *company* [*accompany*] or *mortal* [*immortal*]), and a set of chance cards. The chance cards are similar to the base word cards but should be written on cards of a different color. Players will need a sheet of paper and pencil or pen to use in spelling words.

## PROCEDURES

1. Players will need a pencil and paper to spell words.
2. Shuffle and then place word cards face down around the perimeter of the board, one for each space.
3. Place the remaining cards face down to serve as the draw pile.
4. Choose a particular prefix to focus on, and place this card faceup in the center of the board.
5. Players roll dice to see who goes first. The player with the highest total rolls again and moves the number of spaces on the board.
6. Upon landing on a particular space, the word card is turned up, and the player has to determine whether or not this word can be assimilated to the prefix in the center of the board.

   - **If the word can be assimilated to the prefix**, the player attempts to both say *and* spell the word correctly. A player who is able to correctly say and spell the word receives one point and is also allowed another turn. The word card is removed and retained by the player. A card from the deck is drawn to replace it.
   - If the word can be assimilated, but the player spells the word incorrectly, the card is turned back over to be played later in the game.
   - **If the word cannot be assimilated to the prefix**, it is placed on the bottom of the draw pile to be used later. The player then replaces the card on the perimeter of the board with a new card from the draw pile, and also places a new prefix card on top.

7. If the player unable to come up with a word (for whatever reason), play moves to the next player.

**FIGURE 8.22    Assimile Game Board**

The game is over when all the cards that can be played are played, and the player with the most correctly spelled words is the winner.

**VARIATIONS**   A separate set of Community Chest cards using all the original assimilated prefixes can be placed in the middle of the board, from which players can draw after each round of turns. This ensures that all prefixes are studied. (Community Chest cards will have the prefixes *ad-*, *in-*, *com-*, *ob-*, *sub-*, *ex-*, and *dis-*.) With this method, the word cards that cannot be played with one particular prefix are turned facedown until they can be played.

## 8.28  Rolling Prefixes

Players must be familiar with all types of assimilated prefixes to play this card game.

**MATERIALS**   Create a deck of 32 word cards of assimilated prefixes (eight sets of four). Each group of four should consist of a mixed sort from each of the seven sets of assimilated prefixes: *ad-*, *in-*, *com-*, *ob-*, *sub-*, *ex-*, and *dis-*. One set must be a "wild set" (words with the aforementioned prefixes).

## PROCEDURES

1. Each player is dealt eight cards—three cards to each player on the first round, two cards to each player on the second round, and three cards to each player on the third round.
2. The player on the dealer's left starts the game by putting a card faceup in the center of the table. It does not matter what the card is; the player must read the word and state the prefix.

3. The next player to the left and the others that follow attempt to play a card of the same suit (having the same prefix) as the first one put on the table. Players must read their word and state the prefix.

4. If everybody follows suit, the cards in the center of the table are picked up after all the players have added their cards, and put to the side. No one scores.

5. The game continues in the same fashion until someone is unable to follow suit. When this occurs, the player can look through his or her hand for a "wild card" and play it, changing the suit for the following players.

6. A player may change suit in this manner at any point in the game if he or she so chooses. For example, a player may play the word *collide* (prefix *com-*), and the next player may either play a *com-* prefix word (such as *concoct*) or a word with *com* elsewhere in the word, such as *accommodate*. If the player chooses *accommodate*, the prefix the following player must concentrate on is *ad-* or a form of *ad-*.

7. A player who is unable to follow suit must pick up the center deck of cards. The player who picks up the cards begins the next round. The game continues this way until someone runs out of cards.

## VARIATIONS

- At first, players may not want to state the original prefix of the words.
- Make multiple decks of assimilated prefixes, allowing for variation.
- Instead of ending the game after one person runs out of cards, the game can continue by the winner of the first round receiving one point for each card that the other players hold in their hands at the end of the round.

# 9

## Implementation of Word Study Instruction: Schedules, Routines, Materials, and Effective Practices

# chapter 9

# Implementation of Word Study Instruction: Schedules, Routines, Materials, and Effective Practices

This final chapter presents the best routines and schedules we know of to organize and manage the word study activities in this book. Having now become familiar with the stages and word study activities, you are certainly asking lots of questions about implementation, questions like:

- What does a word study classroom look like?
- How do I differentiate instruction in small groups?
- What exactly do students do on different days?
- How much time do we spend on word study each day?
- When I'm with one group, what are the others doing?
- Do I need to meet with each group each day?
- How can I make weekly spelling checks reflect the thinking I want them to do and not just rote memorization?
- When or how often should I change group membership?
- Where should my students store their word cards?

These frequently asked questions and more about schedules, routines, materials, and practices are answered in this chapter.

From our experiences teaching, working with teachers and doing research, we have obtained a good sense of what makes for lively and successful word study (Ganske, 2017; Gehsmann, Millwood, & Bear, 2012; Gehsmann & Bear, 2014a).

# Ten Indicators of Effective Word Study Instruction

Here is a list of 10 indicators of effective word study instruction from the *Words Their Way Observation Tool* (Bear, Invernizzi Templeton, Johnston, & Helman, 2019). This chapter focuses on several of these indi- cators, and also shows how to schedule and organize word study activities you've learned in Chapters 3–8.

1. *Grouping:* The word study grouping is differentiated and developmentally appropriate.
2. *Materials:* The word study materials are professionally prepared, well organized, and accessible.
3. *Teacher talk:* The teacher's talk scaffolds students' thinking, learning, and self-correction.
4. *Student-to-student talk:* The word study activities facilitate conversation among students working in smaller groups or partnerships.
5. *Extension and transfer:* Students extend and transfer their learning about how words work to other reading and writing activities.
6. *Instructional routines:* There is evidence of weekly routines.
7. *Reflection:* The teacher helps the students develop and articulate hypotheses about how words work.
8. *Word Study Notebook:* Students' thinking about words is evident in their word study folders or notebooks.
9. *Engagement:* Students are purposefully engaged in thinking about the sound, spelling, meaning, and use of words in reading and writing contexts.
10. *Teacher knowledge and classroom management:* The teacher is knowledgeable about the content of the lesson and manages the lesson well.

In the following sections, you will read examples from Ms. Bruskotter's classroom (the teacher you met in Chapter 7) for some of the 10 indicators of effective practices. Several of these indicators have to do with asking students open-ended questions to reflect on their learning. "What do you notice about these words?" is a question we often hear in classrooms where there is plenty of talking, learning, and thinking going on. You can find a list of guiding questions in Table 3.2.

*Grouping.* Ms. Bruskotter's organization of both small groups and whole class illustrates how to differentiate word study developmentally and by instructional goals in an intermediate grade classroom. As you can see in Table 9.1, this fifth-grade classroom had four distinct word study groups ranging from the letter name–alphabetic stage to middle syllables and affixes. Most students knew two languages, and four students were newcomers learning English. Word study included activities to help students clarify some of the properties of English (like the *s*-blends, which do not exist in Spanish), some difficult consonant digraphs, open and closed syllables, domain-specific and general academic vocabulary, and bilingual texts.

## Teacher Talk, Student-to-Student Talk, and Reflection

Ms. Bruskotter was expert at asking open-ended questions that encouraged extended responses—questions that can't be answered yes or no, or in one word. She often asked students to tell each other what they were learning: "Turn to a neighbor and tell your neighbor what you think an open syllable is." "Work with a partner to sort the words." "Use the dictionaries to find the prefixes you have been studying." "Why do you want to put *humor* in that column?"

Walls of words: Dfferentiated word study charts

## Weekly Routines, Word Study Notebooks, and Extension and Transfer

Ms. Bruskotter posted a weekly schedule with activities that were adaptable for each word study group. During the literacy block students made entries in their word study notebooks, played word study games, and worked with partners in a blind writing sort or word hunt. Toward the end of the first quarter, the class brainstormed a list of expectations for their behavior in word study that they reviewed occasionally.

**TABLE 9.1**  Range of Development in Ms. Bruskotter's Fifth Grade Classroom

| Range of Development in Ms. Bruskotter's Fifth Grade Classroom | | | | |
|---|---|---|---|---|
| Spelling Stages → | Letter Name-Alphabetic | Within Word Pattern | Syllables and Affixes | |
| Number of students in January | 5 | 7 | 8 | 7 |
| Reading Stages → | Beginning | Transitional | Intermediate | |

# Teacher Knowledge and Classroom Management

Like many intermediate grade teachers, Ms. Bruskotter conducted both small group and whole-class word study lessons. The small group lesson focused on developmental spelling and the whole-class instruction featured vocabulary lessons on topics such as affixes. The differences between whole-class and small-group word study are described in the following two descriptions of word study lessons.

Student hunting for words in a familiar book

**A DIFFERENTIATED, SMALL GROUP LESSON.** With students in the middle of the syllables and affixes stage, Ms. Bruskotter taught a lesson about open and closed syllables based on the *Words Their Way* supplement, *Word Sorts for Syllables and Affixes Spellers* (Johnston, Invernizzi, Bear, Templeton, 2018). She picked up with their discussion from the previous week when they studied the VC/CV doublet in *tun/nel*, the VC/CV in *chap/ter*, and the V/CV in the open syllable in *fe/ver*. After the review, Ms. Bruskotter introduced the new material—the VC/V pattern as in words like *nev/er*, and *vis/it*. They proceeded with a teacher-directed word sort and the lesson closed with a reflection in which the students concluded that the VCV juncture pattern can be both open and closed. The students were instructed to come back the next day having completed three word study notebook activities:

- Copied the sort into their word study notebooks
- Collected five additional words that fit the patterns
- Written a rationale for why they sorted each column the way they did

On day two, Ms. Bruskotter began with the sort, and then asked students to share the words they found on their word hunts. Their entries can be seen in the columns they created on the whiteboard.

| **V/CV** *long* | **VV/CV** *long* | **VC/V** *short* |
|---|---|---|
| bacon | sealer | level |
| timer | season | liver |
| climber | feeler | giver |
| rival | | |

Students were asked to reflect: "What are your thoughts about these words? Are you noticing any patterns? What is unusual about *climber*?" In a review of what they had learned, she asked: "Where is the syllable going to break, where's the juncture?"

**A WHOLE CLASS WORD STUDY LESSON.** Ms. Bruskotter began a series of lessons on understanding affixes, a core standard for fifth graders. In Video Examples 9.4 and 9.5, you will see that one group examines the easier suffixes (*-er, -ar,* and *-or,* and *-ly* ) while another group studies the more complex suffixes *-ous* and *-tion*. Conceptually, everyone learns what an affix is, but the examples were differentiated developmentally.

Toward the end of the first quarter, the class brainstormed a list of expectations for their behavior in word study that they reviewed occasionally. A schoolwide intervention program was used to identify students in need of small group tiered intervention. Ms. Conner, a Title I teacher, pushed in to teach during the morning literacy period to teach students in the letter name–alphabetic stage who were far below grade level.

**Enhanced eText**
**Teacher Resource:**
Daily Word Study
Class Work Schedule
Developed by
K. Bruskotter

**Enhanced eText**
**Video Example 9.1**
Ms. Bruskotter discusses her classroom organization based on the assessments.

Small group word study of two-syllable word patterns

**Enhanced eText**
**Teacher Resource:**
Word Study
Expectations
Ms. Bruskotter's Fifth
Grade

Whole class word study to categorize prefixes and suffixes

In this description of Ms. Bruskotter's word study, there were eight indicators of an effective word study program. We will return to the indicators of effective instruction at the end of this chapter to think about plans for professional development in word study.

# Word Study Schedules and Routines

Regular word study promotes fluent reading and writing and vocabulary knowledge—critical goals for academic success. However, finding time each day for word study can be a challenge. In this section, we present ideas for organizing in the primary grades, upper-elementary, middle, and secondary classrooms. You will need to adapt the schedules given the logistics of your teaching and the setting and structure of your day

Some teachers conduct word study lessons as part of their reading groups. Other teachers work with two to three separate word study groups and may rotate their students from small-group work in a circle area to individual seatwork and workstation or center times. Still others use a block of time that incorporates differentiated word study. Some teachers meet with students in a workshop routine with word study groups meeting two or three times a week to discuss their sorts and word study notebook reflections.

**Enhanced eText**
**Video Example 9.2**
In these videos, Ms. Bruskotter meets with a small group of students in two sessions to study open and closed syllables.

**Enhanced eText**
**Video Example 9.3**

## How to Begin a Word Study Program

For students who are unfamiliar with categorizing and sorting in word study activities, and for teachers who are hesitant about implementing a brand-new organizational scheme, here are some recommendations about how to gradually transition into fully differentiated word study.

1. *Begin with whole group activities to teach routines.* Start with just one to three weeks of whole-class sorts that will be relatively easy for everyone in the class. Use teacher-directed closed sorts (described in Chapter 3) for maximum support so you can model and offer explicit directions. Show students how to cut words out quickly and neatly and teach them the basic routines that you want them to use throughout the week. Role-play buddy activities such as blind sorts or writing sorts by having students observe as you partner with a student, demonstrating how to lead the sort and take turns. Activities such as draw and label or cut and paste are good for primary grade students and can be done independently at their seats and centers after they are modeled and practiced.

2. *Introduce the sorting process with relatively easy material and teacher-directed closed sorts.* Here are examples for a few stages. With emergent learners use objects or pictures and just two categories in a closed concept sort (such as animals/not animals or animals/birds). When they are familiar with the sorting process, introduce sound sorts such as two rhyming categories or two initial sounds for early beginning letter name–alphabetic word study. Students in the within word pattern stage who are new to sorting may be ready to study the CVVC pattern but can start with an easier sort by short and long vowels with the teacher.

3. *Teach students how to talk about the sorts.* Table 3.2 offers lots of questions to guide student discussion but if students have trouble responding to your open-ended questions, model your own thinking with phrases like "I notice that . . . " or "I learned that . . . ." Ask students to begin their reflections the same way and give them the language to formulate statements until they can do it for themselves. ("This week we learned about how two-syllable words sometimes have double letters in the middle and short vowel sounds in the first syllable.") Ask students to turn and talk to a partner before sharing in the group to increase verbal interactions.

4. *Begin to differentiate.* After routines are well established, begin to work with two and then three groups of students. Because students in the lowest group need the most help, create that group first as the other students continue to work together. Then split that group. Observe how students sort, how they do on spell checks, and how they work together to modify groups as needed.

5. *Introduce open, student-centered sorts.* Model how to do open sorts by thinking aloud as you sort before you assign them to students. Students can sort independently or with partners, but bring them together to talk about the sort at least briefly.

With experience, students gain skill and independence which makes it easier for you to manage the groups; see Tables 9.2, 9.4, and 9.5 on pages 350, 354, and 355, respectively.

## Develop a Word Study Schedule

When scheduling word study in your classroom, consider the following principles:

- *Develop a familiar weekly routine with daily activities.* Routines will save you planning time, ease transitions, and make the most of the instructional time you devote to word study. We describe several weekly schedules to suggest ideas to create your own schedules. Include routines for word study at home as well. When parents know what to expect every evening, they are more likely to see that the work gets done.
- *Schedule time for group work with the teacher.* Students at the same developmental level should work with you for directed word study. During this time introduce the sorts and lead discussions that help students develop and test hypotheses and reach conclusions. Chapter 2 offers guidelines on grouping students for instruction.
- *Practice time.* An important decision to make in scheduling word study activities over the course of a week is to include adequate practice time. If students have been placed appropriately but are not scoring 90% or better on weekly spelling tests it may be that they need more practice time with the words.
- *Plan time for students to sort independently and with partners.* Students need time to sort through words on their own and make decisions about their attributes. Build this independent work into seatwork and center activities. Word study also lends itself nicely to many cooperative activities. Working together in pairs and in groups allows students to learn from each other.
- *Keep it short.* Word study should be a regular part of daily language arts, but it need not take up a great deal of time. Teacher-led introductory lessons take the most time, but subsequent activities take little time and do not require a lot of supervision after students understand the routines. For example, try a quick word hunt through already-read pages following a guided reading lesson. Other word study activities fit easily into odd bits of time during the day. Students can play spelling games right before lunch or sort their words one more time before they pack up to go home.

## Organizing Word Study in the Primary Grades

In grades 1 to 3 there are several common configurations for word study sessions. You may want to integrate them into reading lessons, make them part of a circle, seat, center rotation, or set aside a word study block on one day of the week with shorter follow-up sessions on subsequent days. Resource teachers can also be responsible for word study.

**Enhanced eText**
Video Example 9.4
Ms. Bruskotter works with her whole class of fifth graders in these two videos. Students are first given words to use in an open sort and then they sort on a whiteboard in two different ways.

**Enhanced eText**
Video Example 9.5

**WORD STUDY AS AN INTEGRATED PART OF THE READING GROUP.** Because orthographic knowledge, spelling, and reading development are so closely aligned, it makes good sense for word study instruction to occur as an extension of the reading group whenever possible. You can move quite seamlessly from the reading lesson into word study by asking students to look back through certain pages to find words that contain features you want to introduce or review. For example, after a shared reading of *The Cat on the Mat* (by B. Wildsmith), go back and find words in the *at* family. After reading a chapter in *Frindle* (by A. Clements), ask students to find words that end in *-ed* as an introduction to a unit on inflectional endings. You may spend 10 minutes on reading and 15 minutes to introduce a new word study sort but on subsequent days, you may only spend three to five minutes on word study and the rest on reading. Much of the word study would be completed as individual or partner activities that are completed in centers or at students' seats, or for homework. This organizational setup is efficient and integrates word study into the total reading and language arts program. An example can be found in the box on the next page.

**CIRCLE-SEAT-CENTER ROTATION FOR WORD STUDY GROUPS.** The Circle-Seat-Center rotation shown in Table 9.2 works well if your word study groups are separate from the reading groups. Create and post a schedule for students to follow that you review at the beginning of the day. Introduce a new sort during **circle time** to a group of students who are at the same developmental level. Half of the remaining students work independently or in buddy pairs for **seatwork**, while the other half work at stations for **center time**. After about 25 minutes, the groups rotate. Students at the centers join you at the circle table, students who were working at their seats go to the centers, and students who had been with you return to their seats to work independently or with buddies. Counting transition time, three word study groups rotate through all three instructional formats in about an hour. This organization scheme works well when the entire morning is devoted to reading and language arts. Of course, if you have classroom assistants or aides they can have their own circle time or supervise students at seats or centers. These push-in teachers may include language specialists and Title I teachers and may make it possible to have additional groups.

In Table 9.2, you see an Evaluation and Break period. This is a time to reflect on students' self-assessment, something that you see on page 354 in the Teaching Tips box titled "Three Questions to Teach Self-Reflection."

**TABLE 9.2**  **Circle-Seat-Center Schedule**

| | | 9:00–9:25 | 9:25–9:30 | 9:30–9:55 | 9:55–10:00 | 10:00–10:25 | | |
|---|---|---|---|---|---|---|---|---|
| Whole-Class Review of Schedule & Activities | Group 1 | Circle | Evaluation and Break | Seat | Evaluation and Break | Center | Evaluation and Break | Whole-Class Activities |
| | Group 2 | Center | | Circle | | Seat | | |
| | Group 3 | Seat | | Center | | Circle | | |

## How to Launch into Word Study at the Close of a Small-Group Reading Lesson

Mrs. McGill is finishing up with her small reading group, and she wanted to link their study of *r*- and *l*-blends to words they just read in context as well as new vocabulary and concepts. The students in this group have been reading books about bats and they just finished reading a nonfiction book called *Bats Around the World*.

Mrs. McGill decides to use a variation of the List, Group, and Label activity (Lenski, Wham, and Johns, 1999; ReadingRockets, 2015) to launch a discussion of what the students learned from this book. Instead of listing random ideas or words, she displays an assortment of words she intentionally selected from the text they just read. She asks students to write the words in their notebooks into groups according to what they just read about bats. After referring back to the book and consulting with their partners, her students share their groupings and their labels. They agree that they learned about bats' body parts (*hands, fingers, wings, skin, toes*), about what they eat (*frogs, flowers, insects, fruits*) and about what bats do (*cling, catch, hang, sleep, eat, hear, smell*)—and these phrases were used to label the word groups, as follows:

| bat body parts | what bats eat | what bats do |
|---|---|---|
| hands | frogs | cling |
| fingers | flowers | catch |
| wings | insects | hang |
| skin | fruits | sleep |
| toes | | eat |
| | | hear |
| | | smell |

Mrs. McGill then asks students to turn and talk to their partners about how bats *cling*, what they cling to, and why. She also asks them to look back in their books to find the sentence that tells how fruit bats help people (*After eating fruit, the bats drop the seeds*). Mrs. McGill writes the words *cling* and *fruit* on the dry erase board and reminds students that they have been contrasting the spelling of words that begin with two consonants, called consonant blends, versus those that start with just one consonant. Mrs. McGill then asks students to skim back through their books to see how many *r*- and *l*-blend words they can find and to write them under the words *cling* and *fruits* in their word study notebooks. The students find the following examples from their reading:

| | |
|---|---|
| cling | fruit |
| flowers | trees |
| sleep | drop |
| clinging | frogs |
| flying | great |
| fly | |

Mrs. McGill sends her students back to their seats with a page of *r*- and *l*-blend words to cut apart and sort. Finding exemplars before the teacher gives out the words builds deeper learning.

**WORD STUDY BLOCK.** Some teachers set aside a separate word study block on Mondays to meet with each developmental group and then schedule a short follow-up each day of the week. Some students may be cutting and sorting their words at the same time the teacher is meeting with small groups. On other days students will engage in follow-up activities, doing the same activities but with different words. This organizational plan works well when you want everyone to be doing the same thing at the same time, yet allows for differentiation of instruction within the word study block.

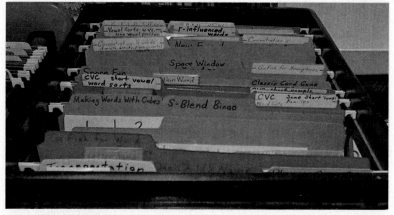

Many teachers keep sorts and games in crates and color-coded by features

**INDIVIDUALIZED WORD STUDY IN INTERVENTION SETTINGS.** Resource teachers who work with small groups of students identified with special needs may have only short sessions with mixed-ability groups, making it challenging to include word sorting. However, these are usually the very students who need differentiated word study the most! In these settings we recommend that you have appropriate sorts selected and cut out in advance. Many resource teachers prepare folders of sorts that are used from year-to-year. The headers are glued into place and the pictures or words are stored in an envelope. Students might complete follow-up activities under your supervision on other days of the week, or they might take their sorts back to the classroom and engage in the same activities as their classmates using their own word cards.

## Schedules for Students Working with Picture Sorts

Betty Lee, a *Washington Post* Teacher of the Year, introduced her emergent to letter name–alphabetic spellers to picture sorts at circle time while other students worked at centers or at their seats. She organized the word study activities in a five-day schedule, as summarized in Table 9.3. This schedule can be modified to three days for a faster pace when reviewing initial consonants at the beginning of first grade, or for moving through the large number of blends and digraphs.

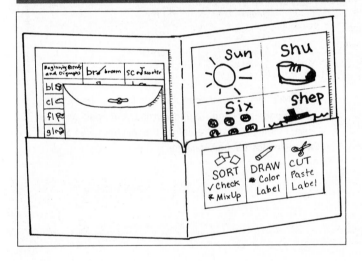

**FIGURE 9.1** Pocket Folder for Organizing Materials

Figure 9.1 shows an individual pocket folder used to keep materials organized and guide students through the daily routines. Students can keep their cut-out pictures in the envelope until they are pasted down or discarded. Each folder has a **soundboard** (one of three sound charts that can be found in Appendix C) to use as a reference and a record of progress. Students simply color the boxes lightly with crayon to indicate which sounds they have worked with.

**MONDAY—PICTURE SORT.** Ideally, the choice of initial sounds is based on what students are reading. You may start by finding words in the text that begin with particular letters as described in the whole-to-part plan in Chapter 4. In small groups, model a picture sort with a letter as a header to help students develop a strong association between the beginning sound of a word and the letter or letters that represent it. Each picture is named and compared with the

**TABLE 9.3** Schedules for Word Study with Pictures

| Betty Lee's 5-Day Schedule | | | | |
| Monday | Tuesday | Wednesday | Thursday | Friday |
| --- | --- | --- | --- | --- |
| Introduce picture sort in circle time and re-sort for seatwork | Re-sort in circle time. Draw and label for seatwork | Re-sort, paste, and label for seatwork | Word hunts in circle or center time | Games and activities in centers<br><br>(continue into the next week) |
| **3-Day Schedule** | | | | |
| Introduce picture sort in circle time and re-sort for seatwork | Re-sort and Word Hunt in circle time<br>Draw and label for seatwork | Re-sort, paste, and label for seatwork<br><br>Games in centers | | |

key picture to listen for sounds that are the same. The sort might be repeated several times in the circle as a group or with partners. During their center or seat time, students do the same picture sort again on their own or with a partner. See Chapter 4 for more ideas about sorting pictures.

**TUESDAY—DRAW AND LABEL.** Students sort again and then extend the feature through drawing and labeling activities that ask them to think of other words that have the same beginning sound, as in Figure 3.12 on page 72. Encourage students to write as much of the word as they can, using developmental spelling to label their drawing.

**WEDNESDAY—CUT AND PASTE.** After re-sorting, students can paste the picture sort into categories and label them. Or, they can look through old catalogs and magazines for pictures that begin with a particular sound. These pictures are cut out, pasted into categories or into an alphabet book (as described in Activity 4.25 in Chapter 4), and labeled. Assess these spellings to judge student progress in hearing and representing sounds.

**THURSDAY—WORD AND PICTURE HUNTS.** Under your direction, students reread nursery rhymes and jingles, and look for words that begin with the same sounds they have been categorizing all week. You can then add the words to a chart. Students can also go for word hunts in alphabet books or picture dictionaries as a circle or center activity. Keep a variety on hand to teach students rudimentary research skills. Their findings can be recorded as an additional draw and label activity.

**FRIDAY—GAME DAY AND ASSESSMENT.** Introduce games and activities related to the sort and then keep them available for several weeks in centers. Children delight in the opportunity to play board or card games and other fun activities for practice and review. Assessment at this level is primarily informal as the teacher watches for automaticity and accuracy during sorting and how well students label pictures or use initial sounds in writing.

## Schedule for Students Working with Word Sorts

The next schedule works well for children who are readers and able to spell entire words. This can be students in the middle to late letter name–alphabetic stage all the way up to derivational relations, so this is the basic schedule for most teachers. Sorting words in a variety of contexts and completing assignments in word study (WS) notebooks comprise most of the activities in the schedule summarized in Table 9.4. The exact routines you do each day throughout the week may vary depending on time and preferences, but we do recommend re-sorting for several days and including the blind sort on Wednesday or Thursday for students working with vowel patterns.

**Enhanced eText**
**Video Example 9.6**
Ms. Flores conducts a small group lesson with students in the middle of the Within Word Pattern stage of spelling.

**MONDAY—INTRODUCE THE SORT.** Words are introduced and sorted according to one of the levels of support described in Table 3.1 on page 59. Many teachers like to keep each group's attention on one set of word cards used for modeling and guided practice. Then, students sort their own words individually in the group, at their seats, and for homework. Repeat this procedure with the next group, focusing on a different feature. Each group has different words, depending on the students' stage of development. After meeting with a second and third group, circulate around the room to check in with students sorting at their desks.

If you do not want to take a large block of time on Monday to do all the introductory small-group sorts, spread them across the week by meeting with one group a day on Monday, Tuesday, and Wednesday, with each group's independent work operating on an "offset" schedule (see Table 9.5). In such a schedule, students in the earliest stages of development get the most practice, but everyone does similar activities by Thursday and Friday. Some teachers prefer to give all groups a five-day schedule but begin and end on different days of the week.

**TUESDAY—PRACTICE THE SORT, REFLECTION, INITIAL SPEED SORT, AND WRITING SORT.** Students sort again at their seats. Encourage students to "say it and lay it." That means that they read the words as they sort. Circulate through the classroom and ask students to read the columns of words and explain their thinking in preparation for writing a reflection.

**Enhanced eText**
**Teacher Resource:**
Ms. Kiernan's Word Study Schedule

## Three Questions to Teach Self-Reflection

These three questions are part of a gradual release of responsibility to encourage student self-reflection and responsibility for learning. This exercise also informs the teacher as to how students' learning progressed.

Notice in Table 9.2 that there is a brief period for students to assess their learning and activity level before moving to another activity. In the primary grades these evaluation and break periods are maybe two to three minutes and may include singing a song or a movement activity. But over time, these periods may include some discussion using the following questions. Betty Lee used the following questions with first-grade students as they got ready to rotate in the circle–seat–center configuration, and she posted them on the wall for reference:

1. *Did you finish your work?* This first question asks students to think about the nature and complexity of the task.

2. *Did you do the best you could?* This question asks students to look at themselves to see if they were ready to complete the task, and to consider their level of engagement.

3. *What did you do when you were through?* This third question is designed for students to think about what they might do if they complete an assignment early.

Over the first several weeks of school, develop a number of activities for when students are through, like writing in their reading response journals, and writing reflections in their word study notebooks.

In the intermediate and secondary grades, students may stay in small groups a whole class period, and the teacher may travel among the groups to pose similar questions for self-reflection. In the intermediate grades, students may complete contracts or self-assessment forms. Often in these grades students have plenty of projects to work on after the assigned word study or vocabulary activities are completed.

Students can also bring their words to sort under your supervision in a brief session or as part of a reading group. Ask students to write a reflection to summarize or discuss the generalization about the features being studied. Assign students a writing sort for seatwork or for homework. Speed sorts might also be planned for Tuesday. Students are sure to show improvement when they do a speed sort later in the week.

**WEDNESDAY—BLIND SORTS AND WRITING SORTS.** Students work in pairs to do blind sorts. After each partner has had a turn to lead the sort, the pair might do a blind writing sort in which partners take turns calling words aloud for the other to write into categories. This can also be an assignment at home. Students can complete other word study notebook activities such as illustrating a few words, writing a generalization about word patterns in their word sorts, writing or finding phrases using the vocabulary at Onelook, the online reference, writing a few words in sentences, etc.

**TABLE 9.4** Suggested Schedule for Students Who Sort Words

| Monday | Tuesday | Wednesday | Thursday | Friday |
|---|---|---|---|---|
| Introduce sort and supervise individual sort | Re-sort<br><br>Record sort<br><br>Write a summary or reflection<br><br>First speed sort | Re-sort<br><br>Blind sort<br><br>Word study notebook assignments | Re-sort<br><br>Word hunt<br><br>Second speed sort | Assessment and games<br><br>(Games continue into the next week as seat or center activities) |

**TABLE 9.5**   "Offset" Weekly Plan

|  | Day 1 | Day 2 | Day 3 | Day 4 | Day 5 |
|---|---|---|---|---|---|
| *Group 1* | Meet with teacher | Re-sort<br>Record sort | Blind sort<br>WS* notebook | Re-sort<br>Word hunt | Testing and games |
| *Group 2* | Sort independently | Meet with teacher<br>Record sort | Blind sort<br>WS notebook | Re-sort<br>Word hunt | Testing and games |
| *Group 3* |  | Sort independently | Meet with teacher<br>Record sort | Re-sort<br>Word hunt | Testing and games<br>or blind sort and<br>test on next day |

\* WS = Word Study

**THURSDAY—SECOND SPEED SORT AND WORD HUNTS.** Thursday is a good day to sort for speed as students try to beat their times from earlier in the week. Conduct word hunts in groups, with partners, or individually. All students in the class can be engaged at the same time by convening in their respective groups. Circulate from group to group to comment and listen in on students' discussions during the word hunt. Ask group members to provide reasons for the agreed word groupings. Afterward, students record words from the hunt in their word study notebooks. Students can find additional examples to add to their notebooks from the books they are reading at home.

Small group writing sort

**FRIDAY—GAMES AND ASSESSMENT.** Although games can be played any time, Fridays might be when new games are introduced. Games from previous weeks provide ongoing review and you need not provide a game for every sort. Students pair up with partners or join small groups according to their developmental levels during center time or a designated word study time. Friday is also the traditional day for assessment.

## Assessments and Grading

There are many types of assessment, and both the content and format are dependent on the students' developmental levels. For a broader perspective, some schools have renamed spelling as "word study," and made it clear to students and families that the grade is a combination of

Students enjoy playing games to practice and review words and generalizations

phonics, spelling, and vocabulary assignments and activities. Several ways to assess and grade are discussed in this section.

**GRADING FORMS.** Some teachers are expected to assign grades for spelling, or spelling may be averaged into a language arts or writing grade. Such a grade should include more than an average of Friday test scores. The word study grading form in Table 9.6 offers a more holistic assessment using a form that can be adapted for different grade levels. You may also want to ask students to assess themselves. There are a variety of ways presented here to assess progress and grade students' word study and spelling.

**TRADITIONAL SPELLING TESTS.** A traditional spelling test is an easy way to assess and sends an important message that students are responsible for mastering the words they have sorted during the week. If you have two or three groups, simply call one word in turn for each group. Students will recognize the words they have studied over the week and rarely lose track. It is not necessary to call out every word studied during the week; ten words is probably enough. If students have been appropriately placed and engaged in a variety of activities throughout the week, they should score well on the Friday test, 90% or better.

If scores are low, consider why this is so. Was the feature too difficult? Were the words selected too difficult? Did the students get enough practice? Should you revisit the feature? Group membership may also change depending on a given student's success.

**BONUS WORDS.** Many teachers call out some bonus or transfer words that were not among the original list to see whether students can generalize the orthographic principles to new words. In this way the generalization is emphasized, as opposed to rote memorization of a given

**TABLE 9.6**    **Grading Form for Word Study**

NAME _____     GRADING PERIOD _____

|  | Excellent Effort | Good Effort | Needs Improvement |
|---|---|---|---|
|  |  |  |  |
| ***Weekly Word Study*** |  |  |  |
| Word sorts |  |  |  |
| Word Study notebook |  |  |  |
| Partner work |  |  |  |
| Final tests |  |  |  |
| ***Editing Written Work*** |  |  |  |
| Spells most words correctly |  |  |  |
| Finds misspelled words to correct |  |  |  |
| Assists others in editing work |  |  |  |
| Uses a variety of resources to correct spelling |  |  |  |
| A = Excellent work in most areas |  |  |  |
| B = Good work in most areas |  |  |  |
| C = Needs improvement in most areas |  |  |  |
| Recommended Grade ____ |  |  |  |

Comments:

list of words. You might prompt students in the case where two or more patterns are possible by saying something like, "If you know how to spell *train*, then you can spell *brain*."

**WRITING SORTS.** It is particularly effective to conduct the spelling test as a writing sort, having students write each word as it is called out into the category where it belongs. Award one point for correct category placement and one point for correct spelling. See Chapter 3 for further directions for writing sorts.

**PROGRESS MONITORING AND GOALSETTING.** Use the progress-monitoring materials described in Chapter 2 and also available in the word sort supplements and in Appendix B. The goalsetting form is a great way for students to record progress and take responsibility for making their own learning goals.

**PROGRESS**
••••••••••••••••
**MONITORING**

**WORD STUDY NOTEBOOKS.** Word study notebooks provide formative assessments. When you look at a word study notebook you can see if students sorted accurately, if they were able to find words that fit the pattern, and if their understanding of the sort is evident in their written reflections. Over three days you may want to collect the word study notebooks and review them for the basic activities outlined here: word sort copied into notebook, additional words from the word hunt, and a written reflection. If you assign students to illustrate words, look up words in the dictionary, write sentences, and so on, these would also be included as part of the grade.

## Creating Word Study Groups

The realities of classroom organization and management have us return to the discussion we began on grouping in the assessment chapter, Chapter 2. Generally, we recommend no more than three developmental groups to keep things manageable. This may necessitate some compromises but remember that students will still be closer to their developmental level than in a traditional program where one list of words is assigned to all students.

After administering and scoring the spelling assessments from Chapter 2, you may not see a neat or straightforward way to create three groups. The guiding question then can become: *"What if I can't fit all my students into 3 groups?"* Here are several possible scenarios that may offer you solutions when grouping issues arise.

**SCENARIO ONE.** Combine adjacent developmental groups.

Late letter name-alphabetic spellers who have not completely mastered short vowels can be combined with early within word pattern spellers who review short vowels when they are first introduced to long vowels. Students still should to be able to read the majority of the words they are studying.

Another example of combining adjacent developmental groups addresses the spelling of long vowel patterns. Combine a middle to late within word pattern group studying long vowel patterns with a syllables and affixes group starting to look at long vowel patterns in accented syllables. While students in the within word pattern stage focus on long vowel patterns in single syllable words (*frame, claim, stay*) the students in the syllables and affixes stage focus on similar sounds and patterns in the accented syllable of two-syllable words (*awake, complain, delay*).

**SCENARIO TWO.** Utilize other staff.

Literacy and reading specialists, Title I teachers, special educators, and English language teachers are the most common staff members who push in to classrooms and can run their own word study groups. Teacher aides can start out by shadowing you during small group time and supervising follow-up activities before assuming responsibility for their own groups.

**SCENARIO THREE.** Divide a large group into two.

Beginning as early as second grade, you may find that there may be up to two-thirds of your students in the same stage of development. In this scenario, the teacher may have a large group demonstration lesson followed by small group time to have opportunities for more student interaction. For example, in Ms. Rabenstein's second-grade classroom, 17 of the 24 students in the class were in the latter part of the within word pattern stage. At a pocket chart, she showed students the sort and then she divided the 17 into two groups of 9 and 8 and met with them separately to supervise their sorting and help them summarize their learning.

**SCENARIO FOUR.** Teach with a grade level colleague.

You may find that a teaching neighbor is experiencing the same problem you have with uneven grouping. Two teachers, Ms. Nomura and Ms. Olds, were able to consolidate their groups: Ms. Olds took a few of Ms. Nomura's students from the derivational stage, and Ms. Nomura combined some of Ms. Olds' students in the syllables and affixes stage with her students. The two teachers coordinated their schedules to make this possible.

## Word Study Schedules in the Intermediate and Secondary Grades

Because middle and secondary English classes are not usually as heterogeneous developmentally as elementary classrooms, students are more likely to have similar word study needs. Still, the typical middle or secondary English teacher plans some word study instruction for students in at least two different stages of word knowledge. In addition, some word study activities are more conceptual and can be presented whole class, whereas instruction can be more developmental in small group sessions as described in Ms. Bruskotter's class.

You may find that a third of the intermediate and secondary students in a class are significantly delayed in their learning and need intensive literacy instruction and opportunities for success in school. Word study is often a significant part of their intervention program. If you work with students reading below grade level in middle school or high school, we recommend *Words Their Way with Struggling Readers: Word Study for Reading, Vocabulary, and Spelling Instruction, Grades 4–12* (Flanigan, Hayes, Templeton, Bear, Invernizzi, & Johnston, 2011) as a resource.

Another point to consider is that it is less important for students in the upper stages to physically sort word cards, although students at this level still enjoy the hands-on sorting. Often the sorts are quite easy with obvious visual clues—anyone can sort words by their prefixes, like *un-*, *re-*, *pre-*, and *anti-* without much attention or thought. Instead, sorts can be conducted in writing, using a format in which students write the words listed at the top or bottom of the sheet into the appropriate category. Other word study activities may also be conducted as paper-and-pencil tasks and organized in a word study section of a three-ring binder, or in a word study notebook.

**SCHEDULES IN INTERMEDIATE AND SECONDARY GRADES.** Students in middle and high school may change classes every 50 minutes, or if the school uses block scheduling, every 1 hour and 40 minutes. Either way, the constraints of periods or blocks limit the way word study is conducted. In a five-day weekly schedule that you see in Table 9.7, there are the teacher-guided whole-class and small group activities in the *Teaching Focus* column and more independent activities in the *Key Student Activities* column. There are many opportunities for work with classmates.

Many intermediate and secondary teachers find that a two-week cycle works well in which the teacher meets with small groups three times a week. Students have more time to work with a set of words and word hunts can go on for days instead of taking time on a particular day. The 90-minute block over two weeks provides plenty of time for small group word study sessions and small group, partner, and whole group meetings for teaching the English curriculum. More time allows deeper explorations of words and their connections with other words—including connections to other content areas (Flanigan, Templeton, & Hayes, 2012). For example, words containing the Latin root *ver* (meaning "to turn") as in *adversary* and *adverse circumstances* in English will appear in math (*convergent*, *adverse angles*), science (*vertebra*, *adverse reaction*), and history (*controversy*) (Hayes, 2014).

**TABLE 9.7**    **Weekly Word Study Schedule**

### Teacher-Guided Teaching Focus

| Day | Teaching Focus | | Key Student Activities, Partner and Individual |
|-----|----------------|---------------|-----|
| | **Whole Class** | **Small Group** | |
| Day 1 | Introduce vocabulary<br>Use words in context | Introduce sort | • Word study Self-assessment<br>• Vocabulary self-collection<br>• Vocabulary brainstorming<br>• Practice sort |
| Day 2 | Use words in context<br>Word hunt<br>Enter vocabulary in word study notebook<br>In-depth exploration of a few words (2-3 words) | Practice sort, check notebooks and reflection | • Share words from self-collection and locate several key vocabulary terms in text<br>• Concept organization of vocabulary with concept sorts, maps, or charts<br>• Group sort with student participation and teacher scaffolding<br>• Add related words to word study notebooks<br>• Consult etymologies and explore online resources |
| Day 3 | Continued In-depth exploration of a few words (2-3 words)<br>Share deep studies | Share word hunts, discuss exceptions, practice sort | • Make word study notebook entry of new information from shared study<br>• Speed sort<br>• Buddy concept sort<br>• Play one or two rounds of word study games |
| Day 4 | Share in-depth explorations<br>Prepare vocabulary reflections | Share word study notebook and develop group chart | • Word hunts for related words<br>• Prepare written reflections on vocabulary<br>• Play word study games |
| Day 5 | Share vocabulary reflections<br>Assessment Planning | Complete chart and assessment | • Review reflections of vocabulary learning with a partner or in a small group<br>• Update word study self-assessment with a partner<br>• Assess, including basic and extended options |

**STUDENT CONTRACTS IN INTERMEDIATE AND SECONDARY GRADES.** One way to organize word study instruction in secondary classrooms is by using contracts or individualized assignment plans. However, you still need time to meet with students in groups to introduce new activities and word features to categorize in sorts, provide corrective feedback, and discuss generalizations (Templeton et al., 2015). The word study grading form can also serve as a contract that involves students' self-assessments; see Table 9.8.

One- or two-week contracts are particularly useful at the intermediate and secondary levels. Students plan with you in advance to complete certain assignments in different areas, turn in that work by a certain date, and self-assess. Table 9.8 shows a sample student contract that is easily adaptable. Based on a point system, students can keep track of their activities divided into three groups: Required, Explore Spelling, and Explore Meaning. Student contracts "spell out" exactly what is expected for each assignment and how much they have to do to earn various grades. The feature to study may be determined by the goal-setting and self-assessment charts described in Chapter 2.

**WORKSHOPS IN INTERMEDIATE AND SECONDARY GRADES.** Reading and the English language arts are often taught in readers' workshop environments in the upper grades, in which students may be reading self-selected books as part of literature circles (Daniels, 2002), workshops or book clubs (Atwell, 2014; Calkins, 2001; Raphael, Pardo, Highfield, & McMahon, 2013). The workshop environment allows you to meet with groups and individuals to give direct instruction in word study and provide feedback as necessary.

**Enhanced eText**
**Teacher Resource:**
Student Weekly Grading Form and Vocabulary Contract

**Enhanced eText**
**Teacher Resource:**
Vocabulary Self-Assessment Template

**TABLE 9.8** Sample Student Work Contract

## WORD STUDY CONTRACT

**Name** _____ **Date** _____

**Feature of Study** _____

**Directions**: Select activities to earn up to 100 points toward your word study grade. Complete all written work in your word study notebook and turn in along with this contract for final grading.

|  |  |
|---|---|
| **Required Activities**<br>____ Sort, record, and reflect (30 pts) | ____ Work with a partner to complete at least one spelling activity.<br>Partner signs here: _____ |
| **Explore Spelling** (10 pts each)<br>____ Repeat sort 2 times<br>____ Blind sort with partner<br>____ Blind writing sort with partner<br>____ Play a game with partner | ____ Sort a different way and record<br>____ Word hunt (find at least 5 words)<br>____ Speed sorts<br>    Record times: _____ |
| **Explore Meaning** (20 pts each—select at least one)<br>____ Define 7 words<br>____ Use 7 words in sentences<br>____ Illustrate 7 words<br>____ Create a comic strip using 5 words<br>____ Complete a word tree or root web | ____ Brainstorm or hunt for additional words<br>____ Report etymologies for 7 words<br>____ Make up new words and define them<br>____ Create your own game<br>____ Other<br>**Total Points** _____ **Test Grade** _____ |

**WORD STUDY IN OTHER CONTENT AREAS.** In middle and high school, vocabulary instruction should be coordinated with other teachers so that domain-specific vocabulary can be intertwined in your word study instruction (Bear et al., 2014; Templeton et al., 2015). Generative vocabulary processes should be addressed, incorporating the Greek and Latin roots and affixes that occur across all disciplines as well as those that occur primarily in specific content areas (Templeton et al., 2015). At least quarterly, teachers might meet to share the key vocabulary and concepts, as well as roots and affixes, that will be taught. By sharing responsibility for teaching vocabulary, the number of exposures to words that students encounter enhances their vocabulary. This deepens their knowledge of words and their understanding of nuances in vocabulary.

## Communicate with Families

Word study at home provides valuable additional practice and opportunities to communicate with families. Here are some activities to encourage word study at home with parents and other family members who often include grandparents, and older siblings.

**SEND A LETTER OR CHECKLIST HOME.** A letter such as the one shown in Figure 9.2 is a good way to describe the weekly schedule and encourage families to become involved in their children's word study. A checklist such as the one in Figure 9.3 can be sent home with an extra copy of the words for the week stored in an envelope or plastic zip bag. You might allow students to choose two or three activities, and more options can be added to the checklist occasionally, such as using a small number of words in sentences.

**FIGURE 9.2    Sample Parent and Family Letter**

Dear Parents and Families,

Your child will be bringing home a collection of spelling or word study words weekly that have been introduced in class. Each night of the week your child is expected to do a different activity to ensure that these words and the spelling principles they represent are mastered. These activities have been modeled and practiced in school, so your child can teach you how to do them.

**Monday** Remind your child to *sort the words* into categories like the ones we did in school. Your child should read each word aloud during this activity. Ask your child to explain to you why the words are sorted in a particular way. Ask your child to sort them a second time as fast as possible. You may want to time him or her.

**Tuesday** Do a *blind sort* with your child. Lay down a word from each category as a header and then read the rest of the words aloud. Your child must indicate where the word goes without seeing it. Lay it down and let your child move it if he or she is wrong. Repeat if your child makes more than one error.

**Wednesday** Assist your child in doing a *word hunt*, looking in a book they have already read for words that have the same sound, pattern, or both. Try to find two or three for each category.

**Thursday** Do a *writing sort* to prepare for the Friday test. As you call out the words in a random order, your child should write them in categories. Call out any words your child misspells a second or even third time.

Thank you for your support. Together we can help your child make valuable progress!

Sincerely,

**FIGURE 9.3    Word Study Homework Checklist**

**Word Study at Home**                          Name _____

Check off the activities you complete and return this to your teacher.

____ Sort the words into the same categories you did in school.

____ Write the words into categories.

____ Blind sort with someone at home.

____ Write the words into categories as someone calls them aloud.

____ Hunt for more words that fit the categories and write them here:

                                    Parent's Signature _____

**ACTIVITIES FOR HOME.**  Word study activities by stage for families and parents are presented throughout *Words Their Way for Parents, Tutors, and School Volunteers* (Picard, et al., 2018). Many of the same word study activities assigned in school can be done at home for additional practice.

**SHOW PARENTS THAT SPELLING IS A PART OF THE READING AND WRITING PROGRAM.**  Parents are typically firm believers in the importance of spelling because it is such a visible sign of literacy. Unfortunately, developmental spelling is often misunderstood, and parents mistakenly associate the acceptance of developmental spelling with lack of instruction and an "anything goes" expectation regarding spelling. Be clear to parents that their children will be held accountable for what they have been taught. Because of the concentration on students making generalizations and transferring what they learn to reading and writing, word study holds students to high standards. Word study activities at home, especially when recorded in a word study notebook, help parents see what is being taught in phonics, spelling, and

**Enhanced eText**
**Video Example 9.7**
Learn how word study is part of a family literacy program.

## Word Study at Home

Here are some tips for involving parents and families with word study.

- At family night or whenever convenient, show parents how to do a blind sort or play easy games such as "memory" or concentration.
- Provide students with two copies of the weekly sort so that one can go home.
- You and your students might produce a brief video that demonstrates a few word study activities that can be done at home, and then share with parents via a website or social media.
- Talk to students about how they can teach their parents and siblings about the feature or patterns they are studying. Several activities are easy to teach family members, including concentration or memory, timing for speed sorts, and word hunts.
- Allow students to check out games to take home to play with their parents or other family members.
- For the parents and families of older students, show ways to explore vocabulary and make entries in word study notebooks using free online dictionaries or etymologies.

Child and parent play a word study board game at home

vocabulary. You can use the scope and sequence of the features in Table 3.4 to reassure parents that their children are being held accountable for the phonics and spelling features they have already been taught. Let families know that we want students to use their best judgment to spell what they have not been taught.

**HUNTING FOR INTERESTING WORDS AT HOME.** *Who has heard or found an interesting word?* This question embodies the curiosity you want students to have about words. Teach students and parents to be on the lookout for interesting words in what they read and hear at school and at home. It can start with their own names and the names of the streets and cities where they live. Activities with families in hunting for words can include semantic maps and vocabulary webs, and in upper grades, looking online at various dictionaries and etymological resources like the online resources presented in Chapter 8.

# Prepare Materials: Sorts, Games, Apps, and Storage

The materials you need for word study will include word sorts and games that match the developmental levels of your students. Digital sorting activities and software to make materials are expanding, and we present guidelines to help ensure that good materials are chosen.

## Prepare Sorts

Word study does not require a great monetary investment because the basic materials are already available in most classrooms. Access to a copier and plenty of unlined paper will get you well on your way.

**SORTS FOR STUDENTS.** Copies of prepared word sorts or picture sorts as shown in Figure 9.4 are available in the *Words Their Way* supplements for each stage listed on page 85, and online at *WTW Digital*. Word study handouts can also be created using the pictures, word lists, and templates in the appendices, the Create Your Own feature online, or by using the tables format on your computer and setting all margins at 0 inches.

Some teachers make manila sorting folders for seat or cener work such as the ones you see on page 77. File folders are divided into columns with key words or pictures for headers glued in place. Words or pictures for sorting are stored in the folder in library pockets or plastic bags and students sort directly on the folder. You may want to avoid laminating as it makes the sorting surface slippery, unless you anticipate heavy use. After the folders are developed, you can individualize word study fairly easily by pulling out the folders that target the exact needs of your students.

| **FIGURE 9.4** | **Sample Word Study Handouts** |
| --- | --- |

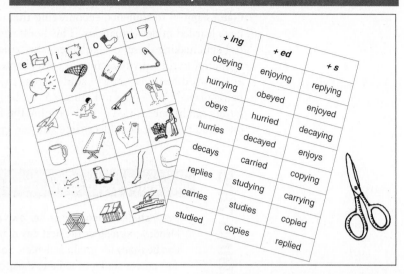

| + ing | + ed | + s |
| --- | --- | --- |
| obeying | enjoying | replying |
| hurrying | obeyed | enjoyed |
| obeys | hurried | decaying |
| hurries | decayed | enjoys |
| decays | carried | copying |
| replies | studying | carrying |
| carries | studies | copied |
| studied | copies | replied |

**SORTS FOR TEACHER MODELING.** For group time you will need your own set of pictures or words that students can see as you direct a sort. In small groups you may simply use the same cut-out words students have as you model on a table or rug. For larger groups you may want to model sorts using a pocket chart with enlarged pictures and words. Classroom technology such as document cameras, interactive whiteboards, tablets, and applications like the *WTW Digital* materials, offer other ways to introduce and model the sort in groups.

Pictures stored in library pockets are ready to use

Many pre-K and kindergarten teachers like to have a prepared set of pictures ready to use. Make sets of pictures by copying the sorts at the *WTW Digital* or the pictures in Appendix C (enlarge these at least 50%) onto card stock that is quite durable; laminating and coloring the pictures is optional. One or more sets of these pictures can be stored by beginning sounds or by vowel sounds, in library pockets or in envelopes. They can then be used for small-group work or for individual sorting assignments. For example, you may find that you have one student who needs work on digraphs. You can pull out a set of /ch/ and /sh/ pictures, mix them together, and then challenge the student to sort them into columns using the pocket as a header. The sound boards in Appendix B can be copied, cut apart, and used to label the picture sets.

Teacher involves students in modeling a sort on an interactive whiteboard

**DIGITAL SORTING ACTIVITIES.** Digital sorts for each stage are available on the *WTW Digital* website and you can create your own as well. These digital sorts are checked and timed, which makes them good for extra practice. Generally, we recommend that you introduce students to sorts using paper sorts or an interactive whiteboard. Then students can repeat the sorts with the cut-out words, computers, or handheld devices. The sample sorts and word lists in Appendixes E and F can be used with a variety of software to create eSorts (Zucker & Invernizzi, 2008). The *Words Their Way Classroom* program with its digital component includes developmental sorts to broadcast to students for their computers and tablets or display on an interactive whiteboard (Bear et al., 2019).

## Prepare Word Study Games for Extension and Practice

Games appeal to students, encouraging them to practice in more depth and apply what they have learned in new situations. This book contains many games to create, and you will want to begin making these to supplement the basic word or picture sorts. Look for games marked "generic" in the activity section of each chapter first, as many of them can be used with a variety of word features you will study across the year. For example, the Follow-the-Path game being played by the boys in Figure 9.5 can be laminated before labeling the spaces so that new letters can be substituted as they become the focus of study. Label the spaces with a washable overhead projector pen. Over time you can create more specific games. See Appendix G and

**Enhanced eText**
**Video Example 9.8**
Ms. Kiernan demonstrates how to teach students the tricks of cutting and pasting word and picture cards.

### Managing Word Sorts in the Classroom

- Every student needs his or her own sort. Have the handouts ready first thing Monday morning or the first day of the sort so students can cut apart the sorts and be ready for group activities. Sometimes you will want to assign an open sort before students come to the group for discussion. Other times you may prefer to distribute the handouts after the group introduction and assign students to cut them apart at their seats for follow-up activities.

- Eliminate the borders of prepared sorts by enlarging it about 10 percent before copying to reduce cutting time and paper waste.

- Show students how to use markers or crayons to draw three vertical lines down the backside of their paper to distinguish their word cards from others in case they should end up on the floor or get mixed up in some way. Students can be assigned different colors. Older students may initial their words or mark them in some other unique way. Younger students can be asked to simply scribble over the back of their paper before cutting, but model how to do this quickly, setting a time limit if necessary so they do not spend too much time coloring.

- Model how to cut words apart efficiently using three long vertical cuts before stacking them and cutting them horizontally. Take the time to teach these cutting routines explicitly so that students complete them quickly and independently.

- Find storage and file folders for the sorts. Words or pictures can be stored in an envelope or plastic bag that is reused. Previous sorts can be collected in a pocket or envelope in the back of word study notebooks, with new word study sheets in envelopes in a pocket or envelope with a brad in the front of their word study notebooks.

- Sometimes the cut-up words and pictures are kept for review, sometimes they are pasted into a notebook or onto paper, and sometimes they may be simply discarded. Pasting and labeling pictures is a good activity for emergent and letter-name spellers. However, after students are in the within word pattern stage, studying long vowels, many teachers discontinue pasting sorts. Older students can quickly write the sorts into their word study notebooks, and the experience of writing the words into categories is helpful.

- Prepare ready-to-use sorts. With younger students or when cutting is too time-consuming you may want to have prepared sets of pictures and words already cut for sorting. Resource teachers who have limited time to work with students often create word and picture card sets that can be reused from year to year. These can be copied onto cardstock for greater durability.

*WTW Digital* for templates and directions to make spinners. Three copies of the same game can be made to serve an entire group. In professional learning communities (PLCs) teachers may trade off coming to team meetings with enough folders and templates and game cards to create several copies of a new game they have found.

## Choosing Apps for Word Study

With the myriad of new applications and software available for students, it is important to have in mind guidelines for choosing word study applications. Some applications are attractive and fun to play but may not offer much in the way of actual learning.

These questions can guide you in selecting the appropriate digital word study to use with your students:

- Is the application or game developmentally appropriate?
- Can students read the words or name the pictures?
- Can they complete the activity quickly with high accuracy?
- Are students asked to think about words and generalizations?
- Are students given feedback to help them understand their errors?
- Does learning generalize to similar patterns and in different contexts, including their writing?

There are engaging applications to reinforce the alphabet, songs, rhyming, and letter-sound correspondence but often the software does not provide actual *instruction* for students who need it. Many applications have a poor mix of tasks that do not properly guide students, and often emphasize rote memorization without deeper examinations or reflection. You might add directions to the activities that correct for any deficiencies. For example, remind students to say the words aloud, and ask them to write the words into categories in their word study notebooks.

**FIGURE 9.5    Follow-the-Path Game for Initial Consonants**

Student sorts and writes the sort in word study notebook

**TABLE 9.9**  Word Study Materials

| From the Supply Room | From the Bookstore | From the Copy Room | Digital Resources |
|---|---|---|---|
| Scissors | Alphabet books and word books | Copy paper for sorts | Digital timer |
| Card stock; index cards to cut in fourths for blank word cards | Phonics readers, books for word hunts | Photocopied picture cards | Online access to *WTW Digital* |
| Word study notebooks; paper and brads; 1½-inch, 3-ring notebooks. | Dictionaries | Photocopied word cards | Access to online dictionaries and etymologies |
| Manila folders | Homophone books | Student sound boards | Applications for spelling and phonics activities and games |
| Game board materials such as spinners and dice | Etymological dictionary | Photocopied game templates | Access to spinner app |
| Stopwatches | Word histories | Poster sound boards | Online timers |
| Library pockets or bags to hold sorts | | | Applications to use as digital word study notebooks |
| Chart paper | | | Interactive smartboard |

Look for applications to make word study materials and extension activities:

- Create a puzzle: *Stick Around*
- Explain your sort: *Doceri*, *EducCreations*, and *Tellagami*
- Make a word map: *Popplet*
- Sentence writing: *Explain Everything*
- Spelling and word meaning practice: *Spelling City*, *Quizlet*, *My Spelling Test Spelling Notebook*, and *Notability*

## Prepare Your Room

Classroom space is needed for group work, individual work, and partner work. Separate areas for word sorting and discussion are convenient to convene a group on the floor or at tables in one part of the classroom while other students continue to work at their desks or in other areas of the room.

Individual sorting and partner work can be done just about anywhere but some teachers set up centers or workstations for sorting or playing games. A digital or mechanical timer is needed for speed sorts and can be placed in a word study center. Many teachers also post chart-sized sound boards and baggies of previous sorts in this word study area. Table 9.9 summarizes materials you might need, depending on the age and range of developmental word knowledge in your classroom.

# Effective Word Study Practices for Implementation

Thus far in this chapter, we have presented schedules, word study routines, and ideas for grouping and classroom organization and materials. In this concluding section we revisit the "Ten Indicators of Effective Word Study Instruction" that began this chapter to suggest key practices for continued professional development in teaching word study.

These questions can guide your thinking as we distill word study into effective word study practices for implementation:

- What do I concentrate on first?
- How can teachers support each other to implement word study?
- How can we implement word study at the school, and district levels?
- What are some models of professional development?

We have asked these types of questions nearly every day of our professional lives. The ideas and materials in this book and on the *WTW Digital* website make implementation easier and more efficient, but still, it takes practice to learn this approach. Be patient and build the support you need.

Second grade team teachers meet to discuss word study groups and activities

## Pace Your Implementation

The pace at which you implement word study will depend on many factors, including your teaching responsibilities, students' experience with word study, and your access to materials. Earlier, we discussed several ways to gradually transition to word study:

- Begin with whole group activities to teach routines.
- Introduce the sorting process and word study activities.
- Teach students how to talk about the sorts.
- Begin to differentiate.
- Introduce open sorts.

Particularly at the beginning of a school year, you have plenty to do to get to know students, and they, you and the daily routine. This gives time the first two weeks to teach students basic word study activities. While you show students how to sort, you will have time to administer a spelling inventory and analyze the results so that you can begin to select from available materials. In a nutshell, that's how to begin. The more you and students have experienced word study, the easier it is to begin differentiating by developmental levels.

## Indicators of Effective Word Study Instruction

Earlier, we introduced ten indicators of effective practices with examples from Ms. Bruskotter's fifth-grade classroom. These indicators describe effective word study instruction (Gehsmann & Bear, 2014a) and as you implement the practices that underlie these indicators in your classroom, we are confident that your teaching will be successful.

The indicators can be grouped into two types: Organizing Instruction and Student Reflection and Interaction. Considering the indicators this way, you can begin to see where you want to prioritize your work in implementing word study in your classroom.

**GROUP I: ORGANIZING INSTRUCTION.** Six of the indicators fit within this group:

1. Differentiated word study grouping
2. Preparation and organization of materials
3. Extension and transfer to reading and writing
4. Instructional routines for daily and weekly activities
5. Notebook use
6. Teacher knowledge and classroom management

These organizing practices begin with the assessment process described in Chapter 2 to determine what word study groups you have. Then focus on sorting routines and activities in Chapter 3 and the schedules and organizational tips in Chapter 9. Of course, you will need to dig deeply into the stage chapters that match students' development. These chapters guide you to specific activities and materials.

If you are using a core program or a supplemental spelling program, it is likely that you can use the materials and the activities there for much of the word study. To differentiate, follow the directions in Chapter 3 on how to make word lists and activities easier or harder. For perhaps 25% or more of your students, you will need to shift to other materials that include word study at a different stage altogether. For example, if the word study in the core program is focusing on long vowels, and you have a group of letter name–alphabetic spellers, they will need to go to other materials to study short vowels.

An important aspect is the teacher's knowledge about students' languages and literacies. This topic is discussed in detail in *Words Their Way with English Learners* (Helman et al., 2nd ed., 2014). Each new language will send you on a search for resources to learn about the particular language and for assessments and observations to understand how literate students are in other languages.

**GROUP II: STUDENT REFLECTION AND INTERACTION.** Four indicators address successful practice:

1. Teacher talk to scaffold student thinking and clarify concepts
2. Student-to-student talk is substantial
3. Student reflection to show student understanding
4. Engagement in activities

Word study is an act of discovery with students. Observing how students learn the word study generalizations presented in this book is a stimulating part of our professional development. The activities and guiding questions in word study (see Table 3.2) helps us to learn with and from students.

Now that we are better at providing the materials students need, we are reminded of the importance of student reflection. You can have the very best materials but still have an ineffective program. Discussion with classmates in small groups is essential to word study learning because it involves dialogue and thinking. Such discussion should lead to generalizations and new insights into language that come in the reflection part of every lesson. The written reflections in word study notebooks ensures that every student takes part. Talking and writing to explain what they are learning cements students' knowledge. What makes word study an approach and not just a program is the student-directed approach to learning that is full of engaging student talk.

## Professional Development

The tenth indicator is teacher knowledge and professional development. This raises questions such as, "What can we do to grow over time?" "What does professional development look like for word study?" "How can I grow as an individual and with my colleagues?"

Consider the knowledge base you want to have. Are there experts available to consult with and observe? For most teachers, spelling has been a separate, unrelated activity from reading and word knowledge. Integrating phonics, spelling, and vocabulary is a goal for many schools that is addressed over a few years. It takes time to educate a staff, administrators, students, and families. There are many ways to grow professionally in your knowledge of word study.

**PROFESSIONAL LEARNING COMMUNITIES (PLCs).** In PLCs, teachers may choose two indicators from group one and two above, individually or as a group, to concentrate on for a quarter. This may involve reviewing key chapters and videos, visiting each other's classrooms, meeting to discuss assessments and grouping, and "make and talk" sessions to discuss word study while making three copies of a game. Likewise, in book study groups, teachers may begin with the opening chapters and then turn to the chapters and videos that match the development of their students. Sometimes group members go and hunt up other *Words Their Way* resources, depending on the students and their development.

**Enhanced eText**
Video Example 9.9
In Part I, Ms. Simeral is an instructional literacy coach meeting with the second-grade teachers.

**Enhanced eText**
Video Example 9.10
In Part II, teachers from Part I discuss word study with English learners.

**COACHING.** A coach or literacy specialist can give feedback and marshal resources for word study. A coach may begin by helping to score and interpret the inventories, gather materials, and coordinate staff and volunteers to push in during the literacy block. The literacy coach may also push in class to model activities and, depending on responsibilities, teach a small group of students.

**ENGAGING ADMINISTRATORS.** Without administrators' active involvement in word study, the program has faint chance of being successful schoolwide. This means that principals need to attend the training to have a thorough understanding of the integrated approach to teaching phonics, vocabulary, and spelling, and they need to understand developmental and differentiated instruction. The administrator will also benefit from using an observation guide like the one discussed above.

School leaders have thought of many other ways to involve themselves in word study. Schoolwide activities can include "word of the day" announcements, spelling bees, and posting videos of word study games on the school's website. Family word study nights can be set up in the all-purpose room where each of five long cafeteria tables contains word study activities for a particular stage, and together families rotate among the tables to see how materials change developmentally.

**JOIN PROFESSIONAL COMMUNITIES.** We need professional contacts within our school, district, and area. Professional groups like the International Literacy Association and the National Council for Teachers of English provide opportunities to meet colleagues, share ideas, and learn the latest in practice and research at local, state, and national conferences. Publications such as the journal *The Reading Teacher* are another way to keep in touch with new ideas.

**VISIT US ONLINE.** Learning is ongoing. We have answered the questions that opened this chapter, but fascinating new questions and situations arise all the time. In addition to visiting *WTW Digital*, we welcome you to visit our websites where we share what we are learning.

Donald R. Bear Website: www.donaldrbear.com
Shane Templeton Website: www.shanetempleton.com

**Enhanced eText**
**Video Example 9.11**
Ms. Nielsen Dunn, a district literacy coordinator, discusses how *Words Their Way* assessments and supplements are used in the district.

**Enhanced eText**
**Video Example 9.12**
Ms. Nielsen Dunn discusses professional development at the district and school levels.

# Appendices

The Appendices provide many of the materials you will need in your classroom. Appendix A has assessment tools to identify stages and form groups for instruction. Appendix B has copies of assessments designed to monitor progress and for student goalsetting. Other Appendices contain pictures, sample sorts, word lists, and templates that you can use to create your own word study activities.

**Enhanced eText Teacher Resources:** When using the Pearson eText, certain headers in the table of contents below will be highlighted as clickable links. These links provide access to printer-friendly PDFs of materials found in the appendices.

## Qualitative Spelling Checklist

Student _____   Observer _____

Use this checklist to analyze students' uncorrected writing and to locate their appropriate stages of spelling development. There are three gradations within each stage—early, middle, and late. Words in parentheses are examples.

The spaces for dates at the top of the checklist are used to follow students' progress. Check when certain features are observed in students' spelling. When a feature is always present check "Yes." The last place where you check "Often" corresponds to the student's stage of spelling development.

Dates: _____   _____   _____

| **Emergent Stage** | | | |
|---|---|---|---|
| *Early* | | | |
| • Does the child scribble on the page? | Yes ____ | Often ____ | No ____ |
| • Are letter-like forms arranged linearly? | Yes ____ | Often ____ | No ____ |
| *Middle* | | | |
| • Are there random letters and numbers used in pretend writing? (4BT for *ship*) | Yes ____ | Often ____ | No ____ |
| *Late* | | | |
| • Are key sounds used in syllabic writing? (/s/ or /p/ for *ship*) | Yes ____ | Often ____ | No ____ |
| **Letter Name–Alphabetic** | | | |
| *Early* | | | |
| • Are salient sounds represented? (BD for *bed*) | Yes ____ | Often ____ | No ____ |
| • Are blends and digraphs represented partially? (SP for *ship*) | Yes ____ | Often ____ | No ____ |
| *Middle* | | | |
| • Are there logical vowel substitutions with a letter name strategy? (FLOT for *float*, BAD for *bed*) | Yes ____ | Often ____ | No ____ |
| *Late* | | | |
| • Are some consonant digraphs and blends spelled correctly? (**ship**, **when**, **fl**oat) | Yes ____ | Often ____ | No ____ |
| • Are short vowels spelled correctly? (*bed, ship, when, lump*) | Yes ____ | Often ____ | No ____ |
| • Is the *m* or *n* included in front of other consonants? (*lump, stand*) | Yes ____ | Often ____ | No ____ |
| **Within Word Pattern** | | | |
| *Early* | | | |
| • Are long vowels in single-syllable words used but confused? (FLOTE for *float*, TRANE for *train*) | Yes ____ | Often ____ | No ____ |
| • Are the most common consonant digraphs and blends spelled correctly? (**sled**, **dream**, **fright**) | Yes ____ | Often ____ | No ____ |
| *Middle* | | | |
| • Are common vowel words spelled correctly, but some long vowel spelling and other vowel patterns used but confused? (SPOYL for spoil) | Yes ____ | Often ____ | No ____ |
| *Late* | | | |
| • Are complex consonants spelled correctly? (s*peck*, swi*tch*, smu*dge*) | Yes ____ | Often ____ | No ____ |
| • Are most diphthongs and R-influenced vowels spelled correctly? (s*poil*, che*wed*, s*erving*) | Yes ____ | Often ____ | No ____ |
| **Syllables & Affixes** | | | |
| *Early* | | | |
| • Are inflectional endings added correctly to base words? (rain**ing**, walk**ed**, chew**ed**, shower) | Yes ____ | Often ____ | No ____ |
| *Middle* | | | |
| • Are junctures between syllables spelled correctly? (ca*ttle*, ce*llar*, ca*rries*, bo*ttle*) | Yes ____ | Often ____ | No ____ |
| *Late* | | | |
| • Are unaccented final syllables spelled correctly? (bot*tle*, fortu*nate*, civi*lize*) | Yes ____ | Often ____ | No ____ |
| • Are prefixes and suffixes spelled correctly? (fav*or*, rip*en*, cell*ar*, color*ful*) | Yes ____ | Often ____ | No ____ |
| **Derivational Relations** | | | |
| *Early* | | | |
| • Are most polysyllabic words spelled correctly? (*fortunate, memorial*) | Yes ____ | Often ____ | No ____ |
| • Are most reduced vowels in unaccented syllables in derived words spelled correctly? (*confident, civilize, category*) | Yes ____ | Often ____ | No ____ |
| *Middle* | | | |
| • Are Greek and Latin elements spelled correctly? (**circum**ference, **medic**inal, **chlor**ine) | Yes ____ | Often ____ | No ____ |
| *Late* | | | |
| • Are assimilated prefixes spelled correctly? (**il**literate, **cor**respond, **suc**ceed) | Yes ____ | Often ____ | No ____ |

# General Directions for Administering the *Words Their Way* Inventories

Students should not study the words before a test. Assure students that they will not be graded on this activity, and that they will be helping you plan for their needs. Introduce the assessment to students; for example:

> *I am going to ask you to spell some words. Spell them the best you can. Some of the words may be easy to spell; some may be difficult. When you do not know how to spell a word, spell it the best you can.*

Ask students to number their paper (or prepare a numbered paper for kindergarten or early first grade). Call each word aloud and repeat it. Say each word naturally, without emphasizing phonemes or syllables. Use it in a sentence, if necessary, to be sure students know the exact word. Sample sentences are provided along with the words. After administering the inventory, many of us like to write the correct word beside the incorrect spelling. In this way, we can show parents the types of errors their child has made. Complete a Feature Guide for each paper and staple the spelling to the guide. To create a class profile use either the Class Composite Form or the Spelling-by-Stage Classroom Organization Chart to complete your assessment.

*WTW Digital* has its own directions for having students listen to the words and enter the spelling digitally. These inventories are scored automatically and groups for instruction are suggested. Error Guide forms for the Primary and Elementary Inventories are available at *WTW Digital*.

## Scoring the Inventory Using the Feature Guides

1. To score by hand, make a copy of the appropriate Feature Guide (PSI p. 377, ESI p. 381, USI pp 384-385) for each student. Draw a line under the last word used if you called fewer than the total number and adjust the possible total points at the bottom of each feature column.
2. Score the words by checking off the features spelled correctly that are listed in the cells to the right of each word. For example, if a student spells *bed* as BAD, she gets a check in the initial *b* cell and the final *d* cell, but not for the short vowel. Write in the vowel used (*a*, in this case), but do not give any points for it. If a student spells *train* as TRANE, she gets a check in the initial *tr* cell and the final *n* cell, but not for the long vowel pattern. Write in the vowel pattern used (*a–e* in this case), but do not give any points for it. Put a check in the "Correct" column if the word is spelled correctly. Do not count reversed letters as errors but note them in the cells. If unnecessary letters are added, give the speller credit for what is correct (e.g., if *bed* is spelled BEDE, the student still gets credit for representing the consonants and short vowel), but do not check "Correct" spelling.
3. Add the number of checks under each feature and across each word, double-checking the total score recorded in the last cell. Modify the ratios in the last row depending on the number of words called aloud.

## Interpreting the Results of the Spelling Inventory

1. Look down each feature column to determine instructional needs. Students who miss only one (or two, if the features sample 8 to 10 words) can go on to other features. Students who miss two or three in a feature column need some review work; students who miss more than three need careful instruction on this feature. If a student did not get any points for a feature, earlier features need to be studied first.

2. Determine a developmental stage by noting where students first make two or more errors under the stages listed in the shaded box at the top of the Feature Guide and circle the stage.
3. Use power scores or total number correct as a guide to calling the stage. Refer to Table 2.2, "Power Scores and Estimated Stages" in Chapter 2.

## Using the Classroom Composite and Spelling-by-Stage Classroom Organization Chart

1. Staple each Feature Guide to the student's spelling paper and arrange the papers in rank order from highest to lowest total points or use raw scores.
2. List students' names in this rank order in the left column of the appropriate Classroom Composite (PSI p. 378, ESI p. 382, USI p. 386) and transfer each student's total feature scores from the Feature Guide to the Classroom Composite. If you did not call out the total word list, adjust the numbers on the Possible Points row of the Classroom Composite.
3. Highlight cells where students make two or more errors on a particular feature to get a sense of your students' needs and to form groups for instruction.
4. You may prefer to form groups using the Spelling-by-Stage Classroom Organization Chart (p. 379). List each student under the appropriate spelling stage (the stage circled on the Feature Guide) and determine instructional groups.

*Note:* See Chapter 2 for more detailed directions on choosing, administering, scoring, and interpreting the inventories, as well as using them to form instructional groups.

# Primary Spelling Inventory (PSI)

The Primary Spelling Inventory (PSI) is used in kindergarten through third grade. The 26 words are ordered by difficulty to sample features of the letter name–alphabetic to within word pattern stages. Call out enough words so that you have at least five or six misspelled words to analyze. For kindergarten students or other emergent readers, you may only need to call out the first five words. In late kindergarten and early first-grade classrooms, call out at least 15 words so that you sample digraphs and blends; use the entire list for late first, second, and third grades. If any students spell more than 20 words correctly, you may want to use the Elementary Spelling Inventory.

Using the following list, call out the spelling word, then the sample sentence, then repeat the spelling word.

1. fan          I could use a fan on a hot day.    *fan*
2. pet          I have a pet cat who likes to play.    *pet*
3. dig          He will dig a hole in the sand.    *dig*
4. rob          A raccoon will rob a bird's nest for eggs.    *rob*
5. hope         I hope you will do well on this test.    *hope*
6. wait         You will need to wait for the letter.    *wait*
7. gum          I stepped on some bubble gum.    *gum*
8. sled         The dog sled was pulled by huskies.    *sled*
9. stick        I used a stick to poke in the hole.    *stick*
10. shine       He rubbed the coin to make it shine.    *shine*
11. dream       I had a funny dream last night.    *dream*
12. blade       The blade of the knife was very sharp.    *blade*
13. coach       The coach called the team off the field.    *coach*
14. fright      She was a fright in her Halloween costume.    *fright*
15. chewed      The dog chewed on the bone until it was gone.    *chewed*
16. crawl       You will get dirty if you crawl under the bed.    *crawl*
17. wishes      In fairy tales wishes often come true.    *wishes*
18. thorn       The thorn from the rosebush stuck me.    *thorn*
19. shouted     They shouted at the barking dog.    *shouted*
20. spoil       The food will spoil if it sits out too long.    *spoil*
21. growl       The dog will growl if you bother him.    *growl*
22. third       I was the third person in line.    *third*
23. camped      We camped down by the river last weekend.    *camped*
24. tries       He tries hard every day to finish his work.    *tries*
25. clapping    The audience was clapping after the program.    *clapping*
26. riding      They are riding their bikes to the park today.    *Riding*

# Words Their Way Primary Spelling Inventory Feature Guide

Student's Name _____  Teacher _____  Grade _____  Date _____

Words Spelled Correctly: ____ /26  Feature Points: ____ /56  Total: ____ /82  Spelling Stage: _____

| SPELLING STAGES → | EMERGENT LATE | EARLY | MIDDLE | MIDDLE | LATE | EARLY | LATE | EARLY | | |
|---|---|---|---|---|---|---|---|---|---|---|
| | | LETTER NAME–ALPHABETIC | | | | WITHIN WORD PATTERN | | SYLLABLES AND AFFIXES | | |
| Features → | Consonants Initial | Consonants Final | Short Vowels | Digraphs | Blends | Common Long Vowels | Diphthongs, R-influenced, and Ambiguous Vowels | Inflected Endings | Feature Points | Words Spelled Correctly |
| 1. fan | f | n | a | | | | | | | |
| 2. pet | p | t | e | | | | | | | |
| 3. dig | d | g | i | | | | | | | |
| 4. rob | r | b | o | | | | | | | |
| 5. hope | h | p | | | | o-e | | | | |
| 6. wait | w | t | | | | ai | | | | |
| 7. gum | g | m | u | | | | | | | |
| 8. sled | | | e | | sl | | | | | |
| 9. stick | | | i | | st | | | | | |
| 10. shine | | | | sh | | i-e | | | | |
| 11. dream | | | | | dr | ea | | | | |
| 12. blade | | | | | bl | a-e | | | | |
| 13. coach | | | | ch | | oa | | | | |
| 14. fright | | | | | fr | igh | | | | |
| 15. chewed | | | | ch | | | ew | -ed | | |
| 16. crawl | | | | | cr | | aw | | | |
| 17. wishes | | | | sh | | | | -es | | |
| 18. thorn | | | | th | | | or | | | |
| 19. shouted | | | | sh | | | ou | -ed | | |
| 20. spoil | | | | | | | oi | | | |
| 21. growl | | | | | | | ow | | | |
| 22. third | | | | th | | | ir | | | |
| 23. camped | | | | | | | | -ed | | |
| 24. tries | | | | | tr | | | -ies | | |
| 25. clapping | | | | | | | | -pping | | |
| 26. riding | | | | | | | | -ding | | |
| **Totals** | /7 | /7 | /7 | /7 | /7 | /7 | /7 | /7 | /56 | /26 |

Teacher _____     School _____     Grade _____     Date _____

## Words Their Way Primary Spelling Inventory Classroom Composite

| SPELLING STAGES → | EMERGENT LATE | EARLY | LETTER NAME–ALPHABETIC MIDDLE | MIDDLE | LATE | WITHIN WORD PATTERN EARLY · MIDDLE | LATE | SYLLABLES AND AFFIXES EARLY | | |
|---|---|---|---|---|---|---|---|---|---|---|
| Students' Names ↓ | Consonants Initial | Final | Short Vowels | Digraphs | Blends | Common Long Vowels | Diphthongs, R-influenced, and Ambiguous Vowels | Inflected Endings | Correct Spelling | Total Rank Order |
| Possible Points | 7 | 7 | 7 | 7 | 7 | 7 | 7 | 7 | 26 | 82 |
| 1. | | | | | | | | | | |
| 2. | | | | | | | | | | |
| 3. | | | | | | | | | | |
| 4. | | | | | | | | | | |
| 5. | | | | | | | | | | |
| 6. | | | | | | | | | | |
| 7. | | | | | | | | | | |
| 8. | | | | | | | | | | |
| 9. | | | | | | | | | | |
| 10. | | | | | | | | | | |
| 11. | | | | | | | | | | |
| 12. | | | | | | | | | | |
| 13. | | | | | | | | | | |
| 14. | | | | | | | | | | |
| 15. | | | | | | | | | | |
| 16. | | | | | | | | | | |
| 17. | | | | | | | | | | |
| 18. | | | | | | | | | | |
| 19. | | | | | | | | | | |
| 20. | | | | | | | | | | |
| 21. | | | | | | | | | | |
| 22. | | | | | | | | | | |
| 23. | | | | | | | | | | |
| 24. | | | | | | | | | | |
| 25. | | | | | | | | | | |
| 26. | | | | | | | | | | |
| Highlight for instruction* | | | | | | | | | | |

*Highlight students who miss more than 1 on a particular feature; they will benefit from more instruction in that area.

# Spelling-by-Stage Classroom Organization Chart

| SPELLING STAGES → | EMERGENT | | | LETTER NAME—ALPHABETIC | | | WITHIN WORD PATTERN | | | SYLLABLES AND AFFIXES | | | DERIVATIONAL RELATIONS | | |
|---|---|---|---|---|---|---|---|---|---|---|---|---|---|---|---|
| | EARLY | MIDDLE | LATE | EARLY | MIDDLE | LATE | EARLY | MIDDLE | LATE | EARLY | MIDDLE | LATE | EARLY | MIDDLE | LATE |
| CHAPTERS IN *WORDS THEIR WAY* | CHAPTER 4 | | | CHAPTER 5 | | | CHAPTER 6 | | | CHAPTER 7 | | | CHAPTER 8 | | |

# Elementary Spelling Inventory (ESI)

The Elementary Spelling Inventory (ESI) covers more stages than the PSI. You can use it as early as first grade, particularly if a school system wants to use the same inventory across the elementary grades. The 25 words are ordered by difficulty to sample features of the letter name–alphabetic to derivational relations stages. Call out enough words so that you have at least five or six misspelled words to analyze. If any students spell more than 20 words correctly, use the Upper-Level Spelling Inventory to get a more accurate estimate of a student's ability; at the upper level, the ESI can overestimate the stage.

1. bed      I hopped out of bed this morning.   *bed*
2. ship      The ship sailed around the island.   *ship*
3. when      When will you come back?   *when*
4. lump      He had a lump on his head after he fell.   *lump*
5. float      I can float on the water with my new raft.   *float*
6. train      I rode the train to the next town.   *train*
7. place      I found a new place to put my books.   *place*
8. drive      I learned to drive a car.   *drive*
9. bright      The light is very bright.   *bright*
10. shopping      She went shopping for new shoes.   *shopping*
11. spoil      The food will spoil if it is not kept cool.   *spoil*
12. serving      The restaurant is serving dinner tonight.   *serving*
13. chewed      The dog chewed up my favorite sweater yesterday.   *chewed*
14. carries      She carries apples in her basket.   *carries*
15. marched      We marched in the parade.   *marched*
16. shower      The shower in the bathroom was very hot.   *shower*
17. bottle      The glass bottle broke into pieces on the tile floor.   *bottle*
18. favor      He did his brother a favor by taking out the trash.   *favor*
19. ripen      The fruit will ripen over the next few days.   *ripen*
20. cellar      I went down to the cellar for the can of paint.   *cellar*
21. pleasure      It was a pleasure to listen to the choir sing.   *pleasure*
22. fortunate      It was fortunate that the driver had snow tires.   *fortunate*
23. confident      I am confident that we can win the game.   *confident*
24. civilize      The researchers tried to civilize the wild cat to live with others.   *civilize*
25. opposition      The coach said the opposition would be tough.   *opposition*

# Words Their Way Elementary Spelling Inventory Feature Guide

Student's Name _____

Words Spelled Correctly: _____ / 25   Feature Points: _____ / 62   Total: _____ / 87

Teacher _____   Grade _____   Date _____

Spelling Stage: _____

| Features → | Consonants Initial (EMERGENT LATE) | Consonants Final (LETTER NAME–ALPHABETIC EARLY) | Short Vowels (MIDDLE) | Digraphs (MIDDLE) | Blends (LATE) | Common Long Vowels (WITHIN WORD PATTERN EARLY/MIDDLE) | Diphthongs and R-influenced Vowels (LATE) | Inflected Endings (SYLLABLES AND AFFIXES EARLY) | Syllable Junctures (MIDDLE) | Unaccented Final Syllables (MIDDLE) | Advanced Suffixes (LATE) | Bases or Roots (DERIVATIONAL RELATIONS EARLY) | Feature Points | Words Spelled Correctly |
|---|---|---|---|---|---|---|---|---|---|---|---|---|---|---|
| 1. bed | b | d |  |  |  |  |  |  |  |  |  |  |  |  |
| 2. ship |  | p | i | sh |  |  |  |  |  |  |  |  |  |  |
| 3. when |  |  | e | wh |  |  |  |  |  |  |  |  |  |  |
| 4. lump | l |  | u |  | mp |  |  |  |  |  |  |  |  |  |
| 5. float |  | t |  |  | fl | oa |  |  |  |  |  |  |  |  |
| 6. train |  | n |  |  | tr | ai |  |  |  |  |  |  |  |  |
| 7. place |  |  |  |  | pl | a-e |  |  |  |  |  |  |  |  |
| 8. drive |  | v |  |  | dr | i-e |  |  |  |  |  |  |  |  |
| 9. bright |  |  |  |  | br | igh |  |  |  |  |  |  |  |  |
| 10. shopping |  |  | o | sh |  |  |  | pping |  |  |  |  |  |  |
| 11. spoil |  |  |  |  | sp |  | oi |  |  |  |  |  |  |  |
| 12. serving |  |  |  |  |  |  | er | ving |  |  |  |  |  |  |
| 13. chewed |  |  |  | ch |  |  | ew | ed |  |  |  |  |  |  |
| 14. carries |  |  |  |  |  |  | ar | ies | rr |  |  |  |  |  |
| 15. marched |  |  |  | ch |  |  | ar | ed |  |  |  |  |  |  |
| 16. shower |  |  |  | sh |  |  | ow |  |  | er |  |  |  |  |
| 17. bottle |  |  |  |  |  |  |  |  | tt | le |  |  |  |  |
| 18. favor |  |  |  |  |  |  |  |  | v | or |  |  |  |  |
| 19. ripen |  |  |  |  |  |  |  |  | p | en |  |  |  |  |
| 20. cellar |  |  |  |  |  |  |  |  | ll | ar |  |  |  |  |
| 21. pleasure |  |  |  |  |  |  |  |  |  |  | ure | pleas |  |  |
| 22. fortunate |  |  |  |  |  |  | or |  |  |  | ate | fortun |  |  |
| 23. confident |  |  |  |  |  |  |  |  |  |  | ent | confid |  |  |
| 24. civilize |  |  |  |  |  |  |  |  |  |  | ize | civil |  |  |
| 25. opposition |  |  |  |  |  |  |  |  |  |  | tion | pos |  |  |
| **Totals** | /7 | /7 | /5 | /6 | /7 | /5 | /7 | /5 | /5 | /5 | /5 | /5 | /62 | /25 |

# Words Their Way Elementary Spelling Inventory Classroom Composite

| SPELLING STAGES → | EMERGENT LATE | LETTER NAME-ALPHABETIC MIDDLE | MIDDLE | LATE | WITHIN WORD PATTERN EARLY | MIDDLE LATE | EARLY | SYLLABLES AND AFFIXES MIDDLE | MIDDLE | LATE | DERIVATIONAL RELATIONS EARLY | | |
| --- | --- | --- | --- | --- | --- | --- | --- | --- | --- | --- | --- | --- | --- |
| Students' Names | Consonants | Short Vowels | Digraphs | Blends | Common Long Vowels | Diphthongs and R-influenced Vowels | Inflected Endings | Syllable Junctures | Unaccented Final Syllables | Advanced Suffixes | Bases or Roots | Correct Spelling | Total Rank Order |
| Possible Points → | 7 | 5 | 6 | 7 | 5 | 7 | 5 | 5 | 5 | 5 | 5 | 25 | 87 |
| 1. | | | | | | | | | | | | | |
| 2. | | | | | | | | | | | | | |
| 3. | | | | | | | | | | | | | |
| 4. | | | | | | | | | | | | | |
| 5. | | | | | | | | | | | | | |
| 6. | | | | | | | | | | | | | |
| 7. | | | | | | | | | | | | | |
| 8. | | | | | | | | | | | | | |
| 9. | | | | | | | | | | | | | |
| 10. | | | | | | | | | | | | | |
| 11. | | | | | | | | | | | | | |
| 12. | | | | | | | | | | | | | |
| 13. | | | | | | | | | | | | | |
| 14. | | | | | | | | | | | | | |
| 15. | | | | | | | | | | | | | |
| 16. | | | | | | | | | | | | | |
| 17. | | | | | | | | | | | | | |
| 18. | | | | | | | | | | | | | |
| 19. | | | | | | | | | | | | | |
| 20. | | | | | | | | | | | | | |
| 21. | | | | | | | | | | | | | |
| 22. | | | | | | | | | | | | | |
| 23. | | | | | | | | | | | | | |
| 24. | | | | | | | | | | | | | |
| 25. | | | | | | | | | | | | | |
| 26. | | | | | | | | | | | | | |
| Highlight for instruction* | | | | | | | | | | | | | |

*Highlight students who miss more than 1 on a particular feature; they will benefit from more instruction in that area.

# Upper-Level Spelling Inventory (USI)

You can use the Upper-Level Spelling Inventory (USI) in upper elementary, middle school, high school, and postsecondary classrooms. The 31 words are ordered by difficulty to sample features of the within word pattern to derivational relations spelling stages. With normally achieving students, you can administer the entire list, but you may want to stop when students misspell more than eight words and are experiencing noticeable frustration. If any students misspell five of the first eight words, use the ESI to more accurately identify within word pattern features that need instruction.

1. switch — We can switch television channels with a remote control. *switch*
2. smudge — There was a smudge on the mirror from her fingertips. *smudge*
3. trapped — He was trapped in the elevator when the electricity went off. *trapped*
4. scrape — The fall caused her to scrape her knee. *scrape*
5. knotted — The knotted rope would not come undone. *knotted*
6. shaving — He gave up shaving to grow a beard. *shaving*
7. squirt — Don't let the ketchup squirt out of the bottle too fast. *squirt*
8. pounce — My cat likes to pounce on her toy mouse. *pounce*
9. scratches — We had to paint over the scratches on the car. *scratches*
10. crater — The volcano crater was filled with bubbling lava. *crater*
11. sailor — When he was young, he wanted to go to sea as a sailor. *sailor*
12. village — My Granddad lived in a small seaside village. *village*
13. disloyal — Traitors are disloyal to their country. *disloyal*
14. tunnel — The rockslide closed the tunnel through the mountain. *tunnel*
15. humor — You need a sense of humor to understand his jokes. *humor*
16. confidence — With each winning game, the team's confidence grew. *confidence*
17. fortunate — The driver was fortunate to have snow tires on that winter day. *fortunate*
18. visible — The singer on the stage was visible to everyone. *visible*
19. circumference — The length of the equator is equal to the earth's circumference. *circumference*
20. civilization — We studied the ancient Mayan civilization last year. *civilization*
21. monarchy — A monarchy is headed by a king or a queen. *monarchy*
22. dominance — The dominance of the Yankees baseball team lasted for several years. *dominance*
23. correspond — Many students correspond through e-mail. *correspond*
24. illiterate — It is hard to get a job if you are illiterate. *illiterate*
25. emphasize — I want to emphasize the importance of trying your best. *emphasize*
26. opposition — The coach said the opposition would give us a tough game. *opposition*
27. chlorine — My eyes were burning from the chlorine in the swimming pool. *chlorine*
28. commotion — The audience heard the commotion backstage. *commotion*
29. medicinal — Take cough drops for medicinal purposes only. *medicinal*
30. irresponsible — It is irresponsible not to wear a seat belt. *irresponsible*
31. succession — The firecrackers went off in rapid succession. *succession*

# Words Their Way Upper-Level Spelling Inventory Feature Guide

Student's Name _____  Teacher _____  Grade _____  Date _____

Words Spelled Correctly: _____ /31   Feature Points: _____ /68   Total: _____ /99   Spelling Stage: _____

| SPELLING STAGES → | WITHIN WORD PATTERN | | | SYLLABLES AND AFFIXES | | | DERIVATIONAL RELATIONS | | | | |
| | EARLY | MIDDLE | LATE | EARLY | MIDDLE | LATE | EARLY | MIDDLE | LATE | | |
| Features → | Blends and Digraphs | Vowels | Complex Consonants | Inflected Endings and Syllable Juncture | Unaccented Final Syllables | Affixes | Reduced Vowels in Unaccented Syllables | Greek and Latin Elements | Assimilated Prefixes | Feature Points | Words Spelled Correctly |
|---|---|---|---|---|---|---|---|---|---|---|---|
| 1. switch | sw | | tch | | | | | | | | |
| 2. smudge | sm | u | dge | | | | | | | | |
| 3. trapped | tr | | | pped | | | | | | | |
| 4. scrape | | a-e | scr | | | | | | | | |
| 5. knotted | | o | kn | tted | | | | | | | |
| 6. shaving | sh | | | ving | | | | | | | |
| 7. squirt | | ir | squ | | | | | | | | |
| 8. pounce | | ou | ce | | | | | | | | |
| 9. scratches | | a | tch | es | | | | | | | |
| 10. crater | cr | | | t | er | | | | | | |
| 11. sailor | | ai | | | or | | | | | | |
| 12. village | | | | ll | age | | | | | | |
| 13. disloyal | | oy | | | al | dis | | | | | |
| 14. tunnel | | | | nn | el | | | | | | |
| 15. humor | | | | m | or | | | | | | |
| 16. confidence | | | | | | con | fid | | | | |
| 17. fortunate | | | | | ate | | | fortun | | | |
| 18. visible | | | | | | ible | | vis | | | |
| 19. circumference | | | | | | ence | | circum | | | |
| 20. civilization | | | | | | | liz | civil | | | |
| **Page Subtotals** | /5 | /9 | /7 | /8 | /7 | /4 | /2 | /4 | /0 | /46 | /20 |

(continued)

# Words Their Way Upper-Level Spelling Inventory Feature Guide (Continued)

Student's Name _____  Teacher _____  Grade _____  Date _____

Words Spelled Correctly: _____ /31    Feature Points: _____ /68    Total: _____ /99    Spelling Stage: _____

| SPELLING STAGES → | WITHIN WORD PATTERN | | | SYLLABLES AND AFFIXES | | | DERIVATIONAL RELATIONS | | | | |
| | EARLY | MIDDLE | LATE | EARLY | MIDDLE | LATE | EARLY | MIDDLE | LATE | | |
| Features → | Blends and Digraphs | Vowels | Complex Consonants | Inflected Endings and Syllable Juncture | Unaccented Final Syllables | Affixes | Reduced Vowels in Unaccented Syllables | Greek and Latin Elements | Assimilated Prefixes | Feature Points | Words Spelled Correctly |
|---|---|---|---|---|---|---|---|---|---|---|---|
| 21. monarchy | | | | | | | | arch | | | |
| 22. dominance | | | | | | ance | min | | | | |
| 23. correspond | | | | | | | res | | rr | | |
| 24. illiterate | | | | | ate | | | | ll | | |
| 25. emphasize | | | | | | size | | pha | | | |
| 26. opposition | | | | | | | pos | | pp | | |
| 27. chlorine | | | | | | ine | | chlor | | | |
| 28. commotion | | | | | | tion | | | mm | | |
| 29. medicinal | | | | | al | | | medic | | | |
| 30. irresponsible | | | | | | ible | res | | rr | | |
| 31. succession | | | | | | sion | | | cc | | |
| **Page Subtotals** | /0 | /0 | /0 | /0 | /2 | /6 | /4 | /4 | /6 | /22 | /11 |
| **Totals** | /5 | /9 | /7 | /8 | /9 | /10 | /6 | /8 | /6 | /68 | /31 |

## Words Their Way Upper-Level Spelling Inventory Classroom Composite

Teacher _____  School _____  Grade _____  Date _____

| SPELLING STAGES → | WITHIN WORD PATTERN | | | SYLLABLES AND AFFIXES | | | DERIVATIONAL RELATIONS | | | | |
| --- | --- | --- | --- | --- | --- | --- | --- | --- | --- | --- | --- |
| | EARLY | MIDDLE | LATE | EARLY | MIDDLE | LATE | EARLY | MIDDLE | LATE | | |
| Students' Names ↓ | Blends and Digraphs | Vowels | Complex Consonants | Inflected Endings and Syllable Juncture | Unaccented Final Syllables | Affixes | Reduced Vowels in Unaccented Syllables | Greek and Latin Elements | Assimilated Prefixes | Correct Spelling | Total Rank Order |
| **Possible Points** | 5 | 9 | 7 | 8 | 9 | 10 | 6 | 8 | 6 | 31 | 99 |
| 1. | | | | | | | | | | | |
| 2. | | | | | | | | | | | |
| 3. | | | | | | | | | | | |
| 4. | | | | | | | | | | | |
| 5. | | | | | | | | | | | |
| 6. | | | | | | | | | | | |
| 7. | | | | | | | | | | | |
| 8. | | | | | | | | | | | |
| 9. | | | | | | | | | | | |
| 10. | | | | | | | | | | | |
| 11. | | | | | | | | | | | |
| 12. | | | | | | | | | | | |
| 13. | | | | | | | | | | | |
| 14. | | | | | | | | | | | |
| 15. | | | | | | | | | | | |
| 16. | | | | | | | | | | | |
| 17. | | | | | | | | | | | |
| 18. | | | | | | | | | | | |
| 19. | | | | | | | | | | | |
| 20. | | | | | | | | | | | |
| 21. | | | | | | | | | | | |
| 22. | | | | | | | | | | | |
| 23. | | | | | | | | | | | |
| 24. | | | | | | | | | | | |
| 25. | | | | | | | | | | | |
| 26. | | | | | | | | | | | |
| 27. | | | | | | | | | | | |
| **Highlight for instruction*** | | | | | | | | | | | |

*Highlight students who miss more than 1 on a particular feature if the total is between 5 and 8. Highlight those who miss more than 2 if the total is between 9 and 10.

# McGuffey Qualitative Spelling Inventory

The words on these lists have been selected as representative of the words students are expected to master at different grade levels. The features are consistent with the developmental progression established for word knowledge.

## Directions

**Step 1.**  Establish a starting point. Begin with the spelling list that matches the grade level. First grade and kindergarten teachers begin with level I.

**Step 2.**  Call the words, use them in a sentence, and then repeat the word. Students write the words in a horizontal column. Kindergartners and first graders might be given paper with boxes for writing or blank paper rather than lined paper.

**Step 3.**  Collect the papers and check them. Determine a percentage score for each child. Words spelled with reversals are accepted as correct. Make a list of students who scored above 50% and those who scored below 50%.

**Step 4.**  Test again on the next day. Students who scored above 50% should be given the next higher level. Students who scored below 50% should be given the next lower level. In working with intermediate grade students, you may find it useful to call out only half the words on a list. When students score greater than 80%, you may want to move to a more advanced list.

**Step 5.**  Again check the papers. Continue to test until every child has scored above or below 50% so that you can establish an instructional level for everyone. The last level at which a student scores between 50% and 90% is his or her instructional level. For example, if Mary scores 30% on level III but 65% on level II, then she is clearly instructional at level II.

**Step 6.**  Create a class roster by listing scores achieved by each student at all levels. Circle the instructional level scores. This will allow you to form groups for instruction.

**Step 7.**  Examine the spelling errors of students in the groups you form. Errors will give you ideas about the features that students are ready to study.

## McGuffey Qualitative Inventory of Word Knowledge

| Level I | Level II | Level III | Level IV | Level V | Level VI | Level VII | Level VIII |
|---------|----------|-----------|----------|---------|----------|-----------|------------|
| bump | batted | find | square | enclosed | absence | illiteracy | meddle |
| net | such | paint | hockey | piece | civilize | communicate | posture |
| with | once | crawl | helmet | novel | accomplish | irresponsible | knuckle |
| trap | chop | dollar | allow | lecture | prohibition | succeed | succumb |
| chin | milk | knife | skipping | pillar | pledge | patience | newsstand |
| bell | funny | mouth | ugly | confession | sensibility | confident | permissible |
| shade | start | fought | hurry | aware | official | analyze | transparent |
| pig | glasses | comb | bounce | loneliest | inspire | tomatoes | assumption |
| drum | hugging | useful | lodge | service | permission | necessary | impurities |
| hid | named | circle | fossil | loyal | irrelevant | beret | pennant |
| father | pool | early | traced | expansion | conclusion | unbearable | boutique |
| track | stick | letter | lumber | production | invisible | hasten | wooden |
| pink | when | weigh | middle | deposited | democratic | aluminum | warrant |
| drip | easy | real | striped | revenge | responsible | miserable | probable |
| brave | make | tight | bacon | awaiting | accidental | subscription | respiration |
| job | went | sock | capture | unskilled | composition | exhibition | reverse |
| sister | shell | voice | damage | installment | relying | device | Olympic |
| slide | pinned | campfire | nickel | horrible | changeable | regretted | gaseous |
| box | class | keeper | barber | relate | amusement | arisen | subtle |
| white | boat | throat | curve | earl | conference | miniature | bookkeeping |
|  | story | waving | statement | uniform | advertise | monopoly | fictional |
|  | plain | carried | collar | rifle | opposition | dissolve | overrate |
|  | smoke | scratch | parading | correction | community | equipped | granular |
|  | size | tripping | sailor | discovering | advantage | solemn | endorse |
|  | sleep | nurse | wrinkle | retirement | cooperation | correspond | insistent |
|  |  |  | dinner | salute | spacious | emphasize | snorkel |
|  |  |  | medal | treasure | carriage | scoundrel | personality |
|  |  |  | tanner | homemade | presumption | cubic | prosperous |
|  |  |  | dimmed | conviction | appearance | flexible |  |
|  |  |  | careful | creature | description | arctic |  |

# Emergent Assessments

## Directions for the Emergent Assessment

These informal assessments are designed to complement the ongoing assessment you do as you observe students daily. They can be used as pre-assessments or post-assessments to monitor growth, group students, and guide instruction. We offer assessments for alphabet, phonological awareness, letter–sounds, students' writing, spelling, concepts of print, and concept of word. These assessments are also available in *Words Their Way PreK-K* and in the supplemental book, *Words Their Way, Letter and Picture Sorts for Emergent Spellers*.

In a number of instances, benchmark scores, which are based on the *Phonological Awareness Literacy Screening for Kindergartners (PALS-K)* (Invernizzi, Juel, Swank, & Meier, 2007), are reported for alphabet knowledge, phonological awareness, spelling, and concept of word. These benchmark measures from PALS have been tested on a very large sampling of children and have been found to be reliable and valid (http://pals.virginia.edu).

The *Emergent Assessment Summary Sheet* on page 397 should be copied for each student. While this form compiles most of the data you might collect about a student, there are additional forms for some tasks: *Concepts about Print* (p. 407) and the *Kindergarten Spelling Inventory*, p. 406. The Emergent Class Record (p. 405) can be used to compile information about your entire class.

## Alphabet Assessments

There are a number of things to know about the alphabet, beginning with the ability to recite the letters in order and to name the letters while pointing letters in and out of order in both upper- and lowercase. The sounds related to the letters are covered in later assessments.

### Alphabet Recitation and Tracking

Students who know the alphabet song and can handle *lmnop* in a punctuated fashion can be assessed to see who can point accurately as they sing or recite the letters using an alphabet strip.

**Directions:** Display an alphabet strip and say, *Touch and name each letter*. Record results on the *Assessment Summary Sheet* on page 397. Note who tracks accurately and can self-correct if they get off track.

### Alphabet Recognition

Note the ease with which students are able to identify letters when presented randomly. Do they respond quickly and confidently, or do they hesitate and perhaps recite the alphabet to help them recall the name of the letter? Only immediate recognition should be scored as correct. Students who score at least 16 on uppercase letters are likely to know a number of lowercase letters, so administer the lowercase alphabet recognition task as well.

**Directions:** To assess students' alphabet recognition when letters are presented out of order, pull students aside individually. Use a copy of page 398 for uppercase (or capitals) and page 399 for lowercase. Say, *Put your finger on each letter and say the name of the letter. Skip the letter if you do not know its name.* As each child points to and names the letters, record responses on the Assessment Summary Sheet.

Indicate substitutions by writing in what the student says. If the child identifies *O* as "zero" or *I* as "one," ask what letter it could be. Expect that reversals will be common with young children learning the lowercase letters, but mark these as errors.

**Benchmarks**: According to statewide PALS data in Virginia, at the beginning of kindergarten, on average, most students know the names of 20 lowercase letters and know 14 letter sounds. At the end of kindergarten, students on average know almost all the lowercase letters

(25 of the 26) and most letter sounds (24 of 26) (Invernizzi & DeCoster, 2016). Based on the PALS-PreK data, students who know more than nine lowercase letters often know many letter sounds and can benefit from further study of beginning consonant sounds through picture sorts.

### Alphabet Production

If students seem to know most letters, you can ask them to write the alphabet without looking at a model to assess how well they can produce the letter forms. Note if they write capitals or lowercase or both. There is no form for this. Staple results to the *Assessment Summary Sheet*.

## Phonological Assessments

A number of phonological awareness assessments are available, starting with large units such as syllables and ending with the smallest phoneme units. Some of these tasks involve pictures and ask the student to identify the words or sound units while others are oral and ask students to produce a word or segment the sound unit.

### Syllables

**1-A Syllable Sort with Pictures:** Administer this task individually and use the numbers to set up the categories. There is one demonstration picture (kitten). Provide corrective feedback for the next picture but count it as one of 10 items.

**Directions:** Make a copy of the sort on page 400 and cut it apart. Say, *Here are the numbers 2, 3, and 4.* Lay down the numbers as headers for the sort. Pull out the picture of the kitten and clap as you say, *Listen, kit-ten. When I say* kitten *I hear two syllables so I will put this under the number 2.* Pull out the picture of the motorcycle and say, *Listen to the syllables in* motorcycle: *mo-tor-cy-cle. Can you clap the syllables? How many syllables do you hear?* (Provide feedback but count the number of claps as right or wrong.) Say, *Now it is your turn. You are going to name the picture and clap the syllables. Then put the picture under the number of syllables.*

From now on, name the pictures as needed but leave it up to the child to clap the syllables. Because young children may not know their numerals, listen carefully to the claps and give credit when they clap correctly but put a picture under the wrong number. Count the number of correct responses in the next 10 choices. Enter scores on the *Emergent Assessment Summary Sheet*.

| 2 | 3 | 4 |
|---|---|---|
| kitten | kangaroo | motorcycle |
| zipper | umbrella | thermometer |
| turtle | newspaper | watermelon |
| pencil | ladybug | |

**1-B Syllables Segmentation** (Oral Production task): This assessment is done without pictures using the words listed after the following directions.

**Directions:** Say, *I am going to say a word and break it into syllables as I clap. Listen,* zip-per. Break the word zip-per as you clap each syllable. *Zipper has two syllables. Let me show you another one. I will say the word slowly and break it into syllables:* yes-ter-day (clap for each syllable). *I hear three syllables. Now I want you to do the same thing. I will say a word. You break it into syllables and clap for each syllable.* Record the number correct on the individual summary sheet. If the child cannot do the first few items, do not continue.

1. peppermint (3)    2. birthday (2)    3. kindergarten (4)    4. table (2)

5. October (3)    6. funny (2)    7. whisper (2)    8. celebrate (3)

### Rhyme

**2-A Rhyme Identification:** Make a copy of the assessment on page 401 for each student. Fold it in half so that only one side shows at a time. You can conduct this individually or in small groups but begin with a demonstration using the unnumbered item with pictures of a *duck*, *ball*, and *truck*. This can also be administered individually using pictures cards as manipulatives. Enlarge the form on page 401 about 10% and cut apart the pictures. Present children with three pictures at a time and ask them to match the ones that rhyme. Enter scores on the *Emergent Assessment Summary Sheet*.

**Directions:** Give each student a copy of the assessment folded in half. Explain, *We are going to be looking for rhyming words. In each space there are three pictures. Two of them rhyme and one does not. Let's do one together. Put your finger on the picture of the* duck. *Next to the duck is a* ball *and a* truck. *What are the two things that rhyme? Listen:* duck, ball, truck. *Which ones rhyme or sound the same at the end?* (Pause for responses) Duck *and* truck *rhyme. Circle the two pictures that rhyme.* Help students complete the sample item.

*Now you will mark the others on your own. Do not say your answers aloud so everyone can do their own thinking. Look at the bear, the keys, and the cheese. Circle the two things that rhyme. Listen:* bear, keys, cheese. *Which two rhyme?* Name the pictures each time for students to be sure they use the correct labels and guide them in the completion of this assessment. Enter scores on the *Emergent Assessment Summary Sheet*.

The picture words used in the Rhyme Identification assessment are as follows.

| | | | | | |
|---|---|---|---|---|---|
| * <u>duck</u> | ball | <u>truck</u> | **5.** <u>bug</u> | <u>rug</u> | cat |
| **1.** bear | <u>keys</u> | <u>cheese</u> | **6.** <u>snake</u> | <u>cake</u> | fish |
| **2.** <u>bed</u> | <u>bread</u> | sock | **7.** feet | <u>pan</u> | <u>man</u> |
| **3.** <u>mop</u> | jar | <u>shop</u> | **8.** <u>clock</u> | <u>rock</u> | fan |
| **4.** box | <u>bell</u> | <u>shell</u> | **9.** <u>star</u> | glass | <u>car</u> |

**2-B Rhyme Production:** There are two practice items for this oral task.

**Directions:** Say, *I am going to ask you to think up some rhyming words. Listen while I do one. The word is* jump. *I need to think of a word that rhymes with* jump. Jump – bump. *Can you think of one? What else would rhyme with* jump? Give feedback such as *Yes,* dump *rhymes with* jump). *Let's try another one. The word is* rock. *What rhymes with* rock? Rock *and* sock *rhyme. Can you think of one?* Give feedback. If child is successful continue with the assessment: *Listen to the word I say. Tell me a word that rhymes with it.* Record responses on the individual summary sheet. Accept nonsense words such as *gat* for *cat*.

| | | | | | | | |
|---|---|---|---|---|---|---|---|
| **1.** cat | | **2.** back | | **3.** wet | | **4.** hop |
| **5.** bug | | **6.** will | | **7.** king | | **8.** tap |

### Alliteration

**3-A: Beginning Sounds Match:** Make a copy of the assessment on page 402 for each student. You can conduct this individually or in small groups. Do not do it immediately after the rhyme assessment because students will find it confusing to shift their attention to the beginning of words after listening to the ends. Enter scores on the *Emergent Assessment Summary Sheet*. By the end of kindergarten students should complete seven out of eight correctly.

**Directions:** Give each student a copy of the assessment form. Begin by modeling the first item. *We are going to find pictures that begin with the same sound. Let's do one together. Put your finger on the sun. Say the word* sun. *Now look at the pictures beside the sun. Say them with me:* book, soap, jet. *Which one begins with the same sound as* sun? Sun *and* soap *begin with the same sound. Sun and* soap *begin with /s/. (Say the sound, not the letter.) Circle the picture of the soap because it begins the same as sun.* Help students complete the practice item.

*You are going to do the rest by yourself. I'll name the pictures and you circle the one that starts with the same sound as the first picture.* Name the rest of the pictures for students to be sure they use the correct labels and guide them in the completion of this assessment. Say the words naturally and do not overly elongate the initial sound. Correct responses are underlined in the following table.

| | | | |
|---|---|---|---|
| * sun | book | <u>soap</u> | jet |
| **1.** nose | fan | kite | <u>nine</u> |
| **2.** rabbit | <u>rug</u> | dog | leaf |
| **3.** lamp | cat | toes | <u>log</u> |
| **4.** watch | <u>web</u> | zero | van |
| **5.** belt | kitten | yo-yo | <u>bird</u> |
| **6.** pie | <u>pig</u> | ball | gum |
| **7.** zebra | key | <u>zipper</u> | hand |
| **8.** dog | jet | leaf | <u>desk</u> |

**3-B. Segment Initial Sound:** In this oral task children are asked to segment the first sound in a given word. There are two practice items.

**Directions:** Say, *I am going to say a word and listen for the first sound. The word is* five. *I say the word slowly and listen for the first sound: fffffffive.* Five *starts with /f/ (Say the sound, not the letter.) You try one. Say the word* wet. *What is the first sound you hear in* wet? Give feedback and assistance as needed. *Now it is your turn; I will say a word. Then you say the word again and tell me the first sound you hear.* Say each of the following words naturally. Do not draw out the first sound. Record the number correct on the individual summary sheet. If the child cannot do the first few items, do not continue.

**1.** soap      **2.** duck      **3.** mouse      **4.** fire

**5.** book      **6.** jump      **7.** give      **8.** nose

## Phonemes

Children in the emergent stage are not expected to segment all the sounds in a word, but this is included here just to round out the phonological assessments. Do not attempt this unless students have been successful at segmenting initial sounds.

**4. Segment Sounds with Counters:** For this task you will need four chips, blocks, or some other counters for the child to push for each sound. Do not name letters, only say the sounds.

**Directions:** Say, *I am going to say a word and listen for all the sounds. As I say the word and break it into sounds, I will push a counter for each sound I hear. The word is* toe. */t/ -/oooo/. I hear two sounds in* toe *so I push two counters, one for /t/ and the other for /o/. Let me do another one. The word is* stop. *Sssss-t-ooooo-p. I hear four sounds in* stop *so I'll push four counters: /s/-/t/-/o/-/p/. Now it's your turn. I will say a word. Then you say the word and break it into sounds as you push a counter for each sound.*

Say each of the following words naturally. Do not break them into sounds. Record the number correct on the individual summary sheet. If the child cannot do the first few items, do not continue.

**1.** sun (3)      **2.** zoo (2)      **3.** mat (3)      **4.** nest (4)

**5.** hoe (2)      **6.** flag (3)      **7.** rug (3)      **8.** sled (4)

## Beginning Consonant Sounds and Letters

In this assessment (see pages 403 and 404 for the two-page form) students are given a letter and told to circle the picture that begins with that letter. If students score at least 4 on the first page, continue to the second page. Do this assessment with students who know at least half of their alphabet letters.

**Directions**: Give each students a copy of the assessment form, Say, *We are going to find pictures that begin with certain letters. Let's do one together. Put your finger on the letter* m. *Circle the picture that starts with the sound the* m *makes*: kite, man, soap. *Which begins with* m? *(Say the letter.) Yes*, man *begins with* m, *so circle it.*

Help students complete the sample item. Then name the rest of the pictures for students to be sure they use the correct labels and guide them in the completion of this assessment. Enter the number correct on the *Emergent Assessment Summary Sheet*. The picture words used in the Beginning Consonant Sounds assessment are as follows. Correct responses are underlined.

**Beginning Consonant Sounds (1)**

| | | | |
|---|---|---|---|
| * **Mm** | kite | <u>man</u> | soap |
| 1. **Pp** | <u>pig</u> | moon | gum |
| 2. **Ss** | block | cap | <u>sink</u> |
| 3. **Nn** | bowl | <u>nest</u> | dog |
| 4. **Ff** | sock | <u>foot</u> | cat |
| 5. **Gg** | <u>game</u> | seal | rabbit |
| 6. **Kk** | <u>rug</u> | <u>king</u> | mouse |
| 7. **Ll** | bun | car | <u>leaf</u> |
| 8. **Ww** | <u>watch</u> | zoo | bird |

**Beginning Consonant Sounds (2)**

| | | | |
|---|---|---|---|
| 9. **Tt** | map | <u>tack</u> | rope |
| 10. **Cc** | zipper | pan | <u>cat</u> |
| 11. **Yy** | bat | <u>yo-yo</u> | fork |
| 12. **Bb** | <u>bird</u> | sheep | mop |
| 13. **Dd** | sled | <u>door</u> | horse |
| 14. **Jj** | <u>jump</u> | bag | comb |
| 15. **Rr** | lamp | fish | <u>rock</u> |
| 16. **Hh** | cake | <u>hill</u> | needle |

**Benchmarks.** By the end of kindergarten students should be able to identify the correct response in 6 of 8 (for assessment 1) or 14 of 16 (for both).

## Observe Students' Writing

Students' independent writing offers information about their knowledge of letter-sound relationships that can be recorded on the individual *Qualitative Spelling Checklist for Emergent and Letter–Name Alphabetic Stages* on page 373. It can be used to capture the change from scribbling to letter-like forms to random letters that characterize developmental changes in the early emergent stage. *The Emergent Class Record* on page 405 can be used in preschool and kindergarten to create a class profile based on your observation of student writing. The information you collect from students' efforts to write daily in journals or labeling pictures should be used to corroborate what you find when you administer a spelling inventory. If students are not using any letter–sound correspondences in their writing, even when prompted to "Write the sounds you hear," you may decide not to administer a spelling assessment until later in the year.

## Kindergarten Spelling Inventory (KSI)

We have included the Kindergarten Spelling Inventory (KSI) as a resource to better understand what alphabetic clues your students may or may not be using in their writing. A form is provided on page 406 to duplicate for each student. Note that the bottom half of the form should be folded up so that it is out of sight while students are writing the words. The KSI gives you information about students' abilities to segment phonemes (that is, break words into sounds) and choose phonetically acceptable letters to represent the beginning, middle, or ending sounds of simple short vowel words. The KSI is adapted from the PALS-K Assessment (Invernizzi, Juel, Swank, & Meier, 2007).

- You will be asking students to spell only five words. Students are not to study these words because doing so invalidates the goal of finding out what they truly know about phonics and spelling. Do *not* pre-teach these words and do *not* have them displayed during testing.
- To prepare students for this assessment you should conduct several lessons in which students are introduced to the idea of "spelling the best they can." If you are doing Write With activities, students should have seen you model how to say words slowly to listen for sounds and match those sounds to letters.
- Most teachers find it easiest to administer this assessment in small groups. Seat students so that they cannot see the papers of their classmates. Manila folders sat on end can provide a screen.
- Model *mat* as a practice item, helping students to focus on the letter sounds by stretching out or repeating the sounds made by the letters. Sounds are indicated in the directions between slash marks / /. Do not demonstrate the sounding-out process beyond the *mat* example. You may prompt students by saying, "What else do you hear? Do you hear any other sounds in the word ___?"
- Observe the students' writing. If you are not sure about the intended letter due to poor letter formation, ask the student what letter he or she has written or ask the student to point to the letter he or she meant to write on the alphabet strip. To help with scoring, write the intended letters above the student's attempt.

**Directions:** *Say, We're going to spell some words. I'll go first. The word I want to spell is* mat. *I am going to begin by saying the word slowly. MMM-AAA-TTT. Now I'm going to think about each sound I hear. Listen. MMM. I hear an /m/ sound so I will write down the letter* m. *MMM-AAA. After the /m/, I hear an /ah/ sound, so I will write down the letter* a. *MMM-AAA-TTT. At the end of the word, I hear a /t/ sound, so I will write down the letter* t.

Give each student a form with the bottom folded up. Say, *Now I want you to spell some words. Put down a letter for each sound you hear. You can use the alphabet strip at the top of your sheet if you forget how to make a letter. I will say each word and give you time to spell it.* Name each of the following words for the students to spell but do not isolate or elongate the sounds. A picture of each word is next to the line where it should be written to provide additional support for identifying the word you are saying.

**1.** nap    **2.** kid    **3.** log    **4.** jet    **5.** gum

**Scoring:** Please note that scoring is based on phonetically acceptable letter-sound matches because we are interested in whether students are able to segment the individual phonemes and choose a phonetically logical letter to represent each one. A phonetically logical letter may have the sound of the phoneme in the letter name itself. For example, the spelling of HKN for *chicken* is logical because the letter name "aitch" contains the /ch/ sound at the beginning of the word chicken, and so on. It is possible to see more than one phonetic representation for each sound. For example, the letter name "jay" also contains the /ch/ sound at the beginning of the word *chicken*. Read more about these logical substitutions in *Words Their Way*.

- Compare students' spelling to the boxes on the scoring grid at the bottom of the page and put a check in boxes that match the student's response. Only one check per column is possible for each word. Leave a box blank if there are no matches and proceed to the next column.
- Static reversals, where the student writes a mirror image of a single letter (e.g., Я for R), and self-corrections are *not* counted as errors.
- Count the number of boxes checked in each column and record on the bottom line labeled "Spelling Feature Analysis." Add all points and record this total in the column marked "Total Phonetically Acceptable." There is a space on the *Emergent Assessment Summary Sheet* for this score.

**Benchmarks:** A score of 12 out of 15 is the benchmark for the end of kindergarten.

Students in middle to late kindergarten who are spelling beginning and ending sounds most of the time and including some vowels are in the Letter Name–Alphabetic stage. They may be given the *Primary Spelling Inventory* (PSI). It does not give credit for logical substitutions that indicate a child's ability to segment phonemes and assign a phonetically acceptable letter.

## Concepts about Print Assessments

Make a copy of the *Concepts about Print (CAP) Assessment* form on page 407. Staple this to each student's *Emergent Assessment Summary Sheet*.

### Name Writing

You can learn a lot by assessing students' attempts to write their name.

**Directions:** Provide a sheet of unlined paper and say, *Draw a picture of yourself and then write your name.* If children respond that they do not know how to write their name, encourage them to "do the best they can," or "pretend." Before collecting the papers ask children to point out their name on the paper and, if they have letters, ask them to identify them. Record scores on the CAP assessment form to track children's development over time.

### Writing Sample

Writing samples collected from children can be analyzed in a manner similar to name writing. Assign points and record on the CAP assessment form.

### During Reading

Check off concepts children understand by posing questions during read alouds or shared reading. For individual assessments, sit down with one child at a time using a simple book that has at least one question. Explain that you are going to be reading the story but you will ask him or her to help. Sample questions and directives are in the following list and you can record responses on the CAP assessment form.

1. What do people do with this? (hold up a book)
2. Show me the front of this book (hand book to child with spine facing them).

3. Where is the title of the book?
4. Where would I start reading? Here or here? (Point to the print and picture).
5. Where would I go next? (Point to the end of a sentence that continues below.
6. Where is the top of the page? Where is the bottom of the page?
7. Point to one word on this page.
8. Show me the first letter in that word. Show me the last letter in that word.
9. Can you find the letter *T*? (Substitute any other letter).
10. Can you show me a capital letter? A lowercase letter?
11. Can you show me a sentence?
12. Can you show me a period?
13. Can you show me a question mark?

## Concept of Word Assessments

Children's ability to accurately track or point to the words of something they have memorized is easily assessed in daily classroom activities when you ask them to point as they read. The following are some guidelines about how to do this more formally. A scoring rubric for "Humpty Dumpty" is provided, but a blank form is also provided on page 411 so you can do this with any short text that students have memorized.

### Tracking Memorized Lines of Print

**Directions:** Teach a rhyme such as "Humpty Dumpty" as a whole class activity until children have memorized it. Then make a printed copy of the rhyme (page 409) or write it on a chart or sentence strips and present it so that all can see. Explain, *This time as I say the rhyme I am going to point to the words.* Model saying the rhyme slowly enough to point to each word. Then ask the students to say it along with you as you point again.

Assess concept of word with one child at a time. Provide a copy of the poem for the student to read (page 409). Make a copy of the assessment form (page 408 or 411) for each student to use for scoring. If you are not sure whether children have memorized the poem, have them recite it using the pictures as prompts before they are asked to read it. Say, *Read* Humpty Dumpty *to me and point to the words as you read.*

Note whether the student has accurately tracked each line, and use the rubric to score each child's efforts from 0 to 6 for each line. Score each line of the rhyme and then compute an average. Transfer this to the *Assessment Summary Sheet* and check "Developing," "Rudimentary," or "Firm."

Scoring is as follows:

*Developing COW*

0. No left to right directionality established. May go right to left or change directions.
1. Points left to right but pointing seems vague or random with no consistent units
2. Points to a letter for each syllable or rhythmic beat
3. Points to words for each rhythmic beat or syllable getting offtrack

*Rudimentary COW*

4. Points accurately to words but gets off track on two- or three-syllable words
5. Self-corrects when offtrack.

*Firm COW*

6. Points accurately

### Recognizing Words in Context

Students who are beginning to develop a concept of word can be asked to identify words in context, using their memory for the rhyme as support.

**Directions**: Point to the selected words on the child's copy of "Humpty Dumpty" (they are underlined on the teacher recording sheet), and say, *Can you tell me this word?* Give one point for each word that is correctly identified. Note strategies used by students. Did they reread to figure out the word or name it immediately? You might ask, *How did you know that word?* They may say something like, "I knew it was *horses* because it started with *h*."

### Word List Reading or Recognition in Isolation

If students' concept of word score is 4 or better, you can also assess recall of words in isolation. Children in the emergent stage are not likely to be able to identify words in isolation, but this is part of assessing a full concept of word.

**Directions:** Use the list of words from page 410 for "Humpty Dumpty" or create a similar list if you are using a different rhyme. Point to each word in turn, and ask students to say the words they can read in the list. Note correct responses on the right-hand side of the COW assessment form and then transfer scores to the *Emergent Assessment Summary Sheet*.

**Observations:** Use the space at the bottom of the recording form to write in any observations you made. How readily does child identify words in context? What strategies are used when the word is not identified immediately? When reading words in lists do errors resemble the word—such as reading *house* for *horse* or *pet* for *put*?

**Benchmarks**: At the beginning of kindergarten most children in the early emergent stage will score 1–3 on concept of word and will identify few, if any, words even in context. By the end of kindergarten most students will have at least a rudimentary concept of word and score 4 to 5 (Pointing to words but occasionally getting offtrack). They will be slow and hesitant about identifying words you point to but will know some of them. Students who consistently score 5–6 have a full concept of word and are probably in the letter name–alphabetic stage of spelling. They should be able to identify nearly all words quickly in context (6 of 7) and will identify most of the words in the list (7 of 10).

### References

Invernizzi, M., Juel, C., Swank, L., & Meier, J. (2007). *Phonological Awareness Literacy Screening-Kindergarten (PALS-K)*. Charlottesville: University of Virginia Printing.

Invernizzi, M. & DeCoster, J. (2016). 2015–2016 PALS-K "Screening Results in the Commonwealth of Virginia: Technical Report prepared for the Virginia Department of Education." University of Virginia.

# Emergent Assessment Summary Sheet

Name _____ Date _____ Teacher _____

---

## Alphabet:

Tracking Observations:

| Alphabet Recognition: Capitals | Alphabet Recognition: Lowercase |
|---|---|
| M P S O X N A F G K L | m p s o x n a f g k l t |
| T U C Y B I V D J E Q R | t u c y b i v d j e q r |
| Z H W   Number Correct ____ /26 | z h w   Number Correct ____ /26 |

## Phonological Awareness:

1-A  Syllable Sort ____ /12          1-B  Syllable Segmentation ____ /8

2-A  Rhyme Identification ____ /9          2-B  Rhyme Production ____ /8 (Record responses below.)

| 1. cat _____ | 2. back _____ | 3. wet _____ | 4. hop _____ |
|---|---|---|---|
| 5. bug _____ | 6. will _____ | 7. king _____ | 8. tap _____ |

3-A  Beginning Sound Match ____ /8          3-B  Segment Initial Sound ____ / 8

4. Segment Sounds with Counters ____ /8

## Phonics and Spelling:

Beginning Consonant Sounds and Letters ____ /16

Kindergarten Spelling Inventory (Use separate assessment form and summarize below.)

| Initial Phonemes ____ /5 | Middle Phonemes ____ /5 | Final Phonemes ____ /5 | Total Phonetically Acceptable ____ /15 |
|---|---|---|---|

## Concepts about Print: See separate assessment form.

## Concept of Word in Text: Use separate form and record final scores here.

Tracking Score Average ____ / 6          Developing (0-3) ____ Rudimentary (4-5) ____ Firm (6) ____

Word Recognition in Context ____ / 6          Word Recognition in Isolation ____ / 10

Observations:

M P S O X

N A F G K

L T U C Y

B I V D J

E Q R Z H

W

# Alphabet Recognition: Lowercase

m p s o x

n a f g k

l t u c y

b i v d j

e q r z h

w

# Syllable Sort with Pictures

| 2 : | 3 ∴ | 4 ∷ |
|---|---|---|
| | | |

Copyright © 2020 Pearson Education, Inc. Reproduction is permitted for classroom use only.

Rhyme Identification with Pictures

Name _____    Date _____

|     |     |     |     |     |
|-----|-----|-----|-----|-----|
| *   | 1   | 2   | 3   | 4   |
|     | 5   | 6   | 7   | 8   | 9 |

*Practice item

# Alliteration—Beginning Sound Match

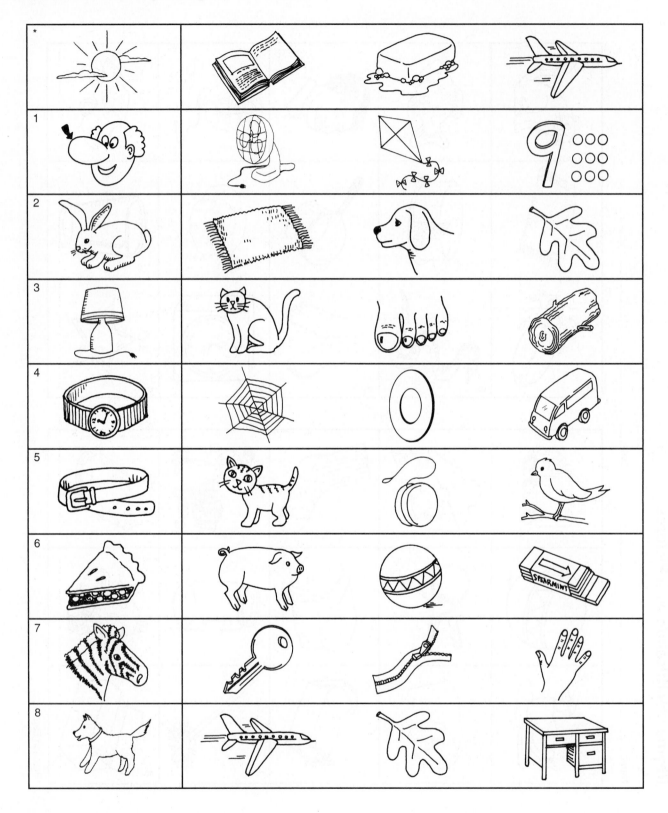

# Beginning Consonant Sounds and Letters

| | | | | |
|---|---|---|---|---|
| * | Mm | | | |
| 1 | Pp | | | |
| 2 | Ss | | | |
| 3 | Nn | | | |
| 4 | Ff | | | |
| 5 | Gg | | | |
| 6 | Kk | | | |
| 7 | Ll | | | |
| 8 | Ww | | | |

**Beginning Consonant Sounds and Letters (continued)**

| | | | |
|---|---|---|---|
| 9 <br> **Tt** | | | |
| 10 <br> **Cc** | | | |
| 11 <br> **Yy** | | | |
| 12 <br> **Bb** | | | |
| 13 <br> **Dd** | | | |
| 14 <br> **Jj** | | | |
| 15 <br> **Rr** | | | |
| 16 <br> **Hh** | | | |

# Emergent Class Record

## Class Record to Assess Emergent and Letter Name–Alphabetic Stage Spelling, Pre-Kindergarten–Kindergarten

*Directions: Check boxes or date entries over several observations. A check minus (√–) indicates features used occasionally. A check plus (√+) indicates consistent use.*

Teacher _____ Class _____ Grade _____ Date(s) _____

| SPELLING STAGES → | Emergent Stage | | | | | | Letter Name–Alphabetic Stage | | | | |
|---|---|---|---|---|---|---|---|---|---|---|---|
| | Early | Middle | | Late | | Early | | | Middle | | Late |
| ↓ Name of Student / Spelling Features → | Random Marks | Linear Scribbles | Letter-like Writing | Random Letters | Beginning Consonants | Final Consonants | Logical Vowel Substitutions* | Consonant Digraphs | Consonant Blends | | Correct Short Vowels |
| | | | | | | | | | | | |
| | | | | | | | | | | | |
| | | | | | | | | | | | |
| | | | | | | | | | | | |
| | | | | | | | | | | | |
| | | | | | | | | | | | |
| | | | | | | | | | | | |
| | | | | | | | | | | | |
| | | | | | | | | | | | |
| | | | | | | | | | | | |
| | | | | | | | | | | | |
| | | | | | | | | | | | |
| | | | | | | | | | | | |
| | | | | | | | | | | | |
| | | | | | | | | | | | |

\* Logical vowel substitutions show how a student would use a letter name strategy to spell long vowels (as in HOP for *hope*) or short vowels (PAT for *pet* or DEG for *dig*)

# Kindergarten Spelling Inventory

Name_____     Date _____

ABCDEFGHIJKLMNOPQRSTUVWXYZ
abcdefghijklmnopqrstuvwxyz

1. _____

2. _____

3. _____

4. _____

5. _____

*Adapted from PALS Quick Checks, University of Virginia*

Fold here - - - - - - - - - - - - - - - - - - - - - - - - - - - - - - - - - - - - - - - - - - - - - - - - - - - - - - - - - -

## Scoring Grid

|  | Beginning | Middle | Ending |  |
|---|---|---|---|---|
| 1. nap | n | a | p | |
|  | | e | b | # phonetically acceptable |
| 2. kid | k | i | d | |
|  | c or g | e | t | # phonetically acceptable |
| 3. log | l | o | g | |
|  | | i | k | # phonetically acceptable |
| 4. jet | j | e | t | |
|  | g | a | d | # phonetically acceptable |
| 5. gum | g | u | m | |
|  | k or c | o | | # phonetically acceptable |

| Spelling Feature Analysis | Number of Beginning Phonemes | Number of Middle Phonemes | Number of Ending Phonemes | Total Phonetically Acceptable |
|---|---|---|---|---|
|  | /5 | /5 | /5 | /15 |

# Concepts about Print Assessment

Name _____ Teacher _____ Year _____

## Name Writing Assessment:
Ask the child to draw a picture and write his or her name. Assign a point or check for all features that apply.

| Dates | Name separate from drawing | Linear | Separate units | Letter-like forms | First letter | At least half of letters | All letters | Left to right with no reversals | Names letters | Total points |
|---|---|---|---|---|---|---|---|---|---|---|
| 1. | | | | | | | | | | |
| 2. | | | | | | | | | | |
| 3. | | | | | | | | | | |
| 4. | | | | | | | | | | |

## Writing Assessment:
Evaluate independent writing samples. Assign a point or check for all features that apply.

| Dates | Identified as writing | Message assigned | Linear orientation | Separate symbols | Symbol salad | Salient sounds | Beginning and ending sounds | Some vowels | Spaces between words | Total points |
|---|---|---|---|---|---|---|---|---|---|---|
| 1. | | | | | | | | | | |
| 2. | | | | | | | | | | |
| 3. | | | | | | | | | | |
| 4. | | | | | | | | | | |

## During Reading:
Assign a point or check for concepts child knows.

| Dates | What is a book for? | Front and back | Title | Where to start reading | Where to go next | Top and bottom | Word | First and last letter | Find a letter | Capital and Lowercase | Sentence | Period | Question mark | Total points |
|---|---|---|---|---|---|---|---|---|---|---|---|---|---|---|
| 1. | | | | | | | | | | | | | | |
| 2. | | | | | | | | | | | | | | |
| 3. | | | | | | | | | | | | | | |
| 4. | | | | | | | | | | | | | | |

Concepts about Print Sort number correct _____

# Concept of Word in Text: Recording Form for Humpty Dumpty

Name_____ Date _____ Teacher_____

| | Pointing | Word ID | Word List |
|---|---|---|---|
| <u>Humpty</u> Dumpty sat on a <u>wall</u> | | (2) | on |
| Humpty Dumpty had a <u>great</u> fall | | (1) | Humpty |
| All the <u>king's</u> horses | | (1) | put |
| And all the king's <u>men</u> | | (1) | horses |
| Couldn't <u>put</u> Humpty together again | | (1) | sat |
| | | | men |
| | | | king's |
| | | | wall |
| | | | had |
| | | | fall |
| **Totals** | / 6 | / 6 | / 10 |
| **COW-T:** Developing      Rudimentary      Firm | | | |

**Scores for pointing:** Score each line of the poem and compute the total.

| | | |
|---|---|---|
| Developing | 0 | No left-to-right directionality established. May go right to left or change directions. |
| | 1 | Points left to right, but pointing is vague or random with no consistent units. |
| | 2 | Points to a letter for each syllable or rhythmic beat. |
| | 3 | Points to words for each rhythmic beat or syllable, getting off track. |
| Rudimentary | 4 | Points to words accurately, but gets off track on two- or three-syllable words. |
| | 5 | Points to words accurately. Gets off track, but self-corrects. |
| Firm | 6 | Points to words accurately. |

**Scores for word recognition in context:** Point to underlined words on the child's copy. Put a check for each one named correctly.

**Scores for word recogniton in isolation**: Ask the child to read from the list of words. Put a check for each correct one. Write in substitutions.

**Totals:** Compute the totals and circle the COW-T level.

**Observations:**

Name_____     Date/Story Number_____

# Humpty Dumpty

Humpty Dumpty sat on a wall.

Humpty Dumpty had a great fall.

All the king's horses

And all the king's men

Couldn't put Humpty together again!

on

Humpty

put

horses

sat

men

king's

wall

had

fall

# Concept of Word in Text: Recording Form Template

Name_____ Date_____ Teacher_____

|  | Pointing | Word ID | Word List |
|---|---|---|---|
|  |  |  |  |
|  |  |  |  |
|  |  |  |  |
|  |  |  |  |
|  |  |  |  |
|  |  |  |  |
|  |  |  |  |
|  |  |  |  |
|  |  |  |  |
|  |  |  |  |
| **Totals** | / 6 | / 6 | / 10 |
| **COW-T:** Developing    Rudimentary    Firm | | | |

**Scores for pointing**: Score each line of the poem and compute the total.

Developing    0    No left-to-right directionality established. May go right to left or change directions.

                 1    Points left to right, but pointing is vague or random with no consistent units.

                 2    Points to a letter for each syllable or rhythmic beat.

                 3    Points to words for each rhythmic beat or syllable, getting off track.

Rudimentary   4    Points to words accurately, but gets off track on two- or three-syllable words.

                 5    Points to words accurately. Gets off track, but self-corrects.

Firm              6    Points to words accurately.

**Scores for word recognition in context:** Point to underlined words on the child's copy. Put a check for each one named correctly.

**Scores for word recogntion in isolation**: Ask the child to read from the list of words. Put a check for each correct one. Write in substitutions.

**Totals:** Compute the totals and circle the COW-T level.

**Observations:**

# Directions for Using Progress Monitoring / Goal Setting Charts

The following charts are examples you can use to help monitor student progress and guide your conferences with specialists, parents, and students. Charts for early letter name to early derivational relations are provided. Slightly different spell checks and monitoring forms are available in the companion word sort books where they serve as unit tests.

**SETTING GOALS.** Use results from one of the inventories to determine a stage and to select the chart that is most appropriate. You can fine-tune your assessment and set goals by using the spell checks in the section that follows to more exactly determine where in a stage a student is in and what features the student needs to study. Students are generally ready to study a feature when they score 40% to 70% on a pretest. Record the date and score for the pretest and check off the specific features that were correct. Put an x beside any feature not spelled correctly and determine a score expressed as a ration (3/10) or a percentage (30%).

**INVOLVE STUDENTS IN GOAL SETTING.** Setting goals and monitoring their own progress can be motivating for students. We recommend that you meet with students individually and share the results of the inventory or spell checks to set goals. The charts help student define a set of goals that are within reach—within their zone of proximal development. This is especially helpful for students who are struggling in the area of spelling and may feel overwhelmed with all they need to learn.

**MEETING GOALS.** Use the spell checks as a posttest to determine whether students have mastered the features covered in the sorts and met learning goals. You can also give a delayed posttest several weeks later to assess retention. Record the date and the score on the chart. Check the targeted sounds or patterns spelled correctly and put an x by any missed (use different colors for pretest and posttest). All the sounds or patterns in a given feature category may not be tested every time (all the word families for example). But a sample can be considered sufficient. In general no more than 2 out of 10 (80%) should be missed to move on to a new category of features, although a lower criterion may be acceptable for features that will be reviewed in future sorts.*

---

* Goal setting charts were not developed for Middle and Late DR because mastery of many features such as Greek and Latin combining forms continues throughout adulthood. Knowing the meaning of words is the goal rather than the spelling of the word.

# Progress Monitoring Charts

## Letter Name – Alphabetic Monitoring Charts

Name _____ Teacher _____ Date _____

### Goals for Early Letter Name – Alphabetic

| 1. Know initial consonants | b _____ c _____ d _____ f _____ g _____ h _____ j _____ k _____<br><br>l _____ m _____ n _____ p _____ r _____ s _____ t _____ v _____<br><br>w _____ y _____ z _____ |
|---|---|
| Spell Check 1 | Pretest:　　　　Date:　　　　Posttest:　　　　Date: |
| 2. Identify same-vowel word families | at _____ an _____ ad _____ ap _____ ag _____<br><br>op _____ ot _____ og _____ et _____ eg _____ en _____<br><br>ug _____ ut _____ un _____ ig _____ ip _____ ill _____ |
| Spell Check 2 | Pretest:　　　　Date:　　　　Posttest:　　　　Date: |

### Goals for Middle Letter Name – Alphabetic

| 3. Know initial digraphs | sh _____ ch _____ th _____ wh _____ |
|---|---|
| Spell Check 3 | Pretest:　　　　Date:　　　　Posttest:　　　　Date: |
| 4. Know initial blends | st _____ sp _____ sk _____ sm _____ sc _____ sn _____ sw _____<br><br>sl _____ pl _____ cl _____ fl _____ bl _____ gl _____<br><br>cr _____ fr _____ br _____ gr _____ pr _____ tr _____ dr _____<br><br>qu _____ tw _____ |
| Spell Check 4 | Pretest:　　　　Date:　　　　Posttest:　　　　Date: |
| 5. Spell CVC word families | at _____ ot _____ it _____ an _____ un _____ in _____<br><br>ad _____ ed _____ ab _____ ob _____ ag _____ og _____ |
| 6. Spell CVCC word families | ig _____ ug _____ eg _____ ill _____ ell _____ all _____<br><br>ick _____ ack _____ ock _____ uck _____ ish _____ ash _____ ush _____ |
| Spell Check 5 | Pretest:　　　　Date:　　　　Posttest:　　　　Date: |
| Spell Check 6 | Pretest:　　　　Date:　　　　Posttest:　　　　Date: |

### Goals for Late Letter Name – Alphabetic*

| | |
|---|---|
| 7. Identify short vowels | ă _____ ĕ _____ ĭ _____ ŏ _____ ŭ _____ |
| 8. Spell simple CVC words | ă _____ ĕ _____ ĭ _____ ŏ _____ ŭ _____ |
| 9. Spell short vowels with blends and digraphs | ă _____ ĕ _____ ĭ _____ ŏ _____ ŭ _____ |
| Spell Check 7 | Pretest:          Date:          Posttest:          Date: |
| Spell Check 8 | Pretest:          Date:          Posttest:          Date: |
| Spell Check 9 | Pretest:          Date:          Posttest:          Date: |
| 10. Spell short vowels with preconsonantal nasals | ing _____ ang _____ ong _____ ung _____ amp _____ ump _____<br><br>imp _____ ant _____ int _____ ent _____ unt _____ and _____<br><br>end _____ ank _____ ink _____ unk _____ |
| Spell Check 10 | Pretest:          Date:          Posttest:          Date: |
| 11. Spell simple R-influenced vowels | ar _____ or _____ |
| Spell Check 11 | Pretest:          Date:          Posttest:          Date: |

*Short vowels and r-influenced vowels will be reviewed in the within word pattern stage so complete mastery is not needed before moving on to the study of long vowels.

# Within Word Pattern Monitoring Charts

Name _____ Teacher _____ Date _____

## Goals for Early Within Word Pattern

| | |
|---|---|
| 12. Spell short vowels and long vowels in CVCE | ă _____ a_e _____ ĭ _____ i_e _____<br><br>ŏ _____ o_e _____ ŭ _____ u_e _____ |
| 13. Spell long vowels in CVCE and CVVC patterns | a_e _____ ai _____ ee _____ ea _____ ea _____<br><br>oo _____ o_e _____ oa _____ u_e _____ ui _____ |
| Spell Check 12 | Pretest:          Date:          Posttest:          Date: |
| Spell Check 13 | Pretest:          Date:          Posttest:          Date: |
| 14. Spell other or less common long vowel patterns | ay _____ ow _____ igh _____ ue _____ ew _____ igh _____<br><br>i-e _____ y _____ |
| Spell Check 14 | Pretest:          Date:          Posttest:          Date: |

## Goals for Middle Within Word Pattern

| | |
|---|---|
| 15. Spell r-influenced vowel patterns | ar _____   air _____   are _____ war _____ er _____   ear _____<br><br>eer _____   ere _____   or _____   oar_____   ore _____   oor _____<br><br>wor _____   ur _____   ure _____   ir _____   ire _____ |
| Spell Check 15 | Pretest:          Date:          Posttest:          Date: |
| 16. Spell ambiguous vowels | oi _____ oy _____ oo _____ oo _____ aw _____ au _____ al _____<br><br>ou _____ ow _____ o _____ wa _____ |
| Spell Check 16 | Pretest:          Date:          Posttest:          Date: |

## Within Word Pattern Monitoring Charts

Name _____ Teacher _____ Date _____

### Goals for Late Within Word Pattern

| 17. Spell complex consonant units | kn _____ wr _____ gn _____ hard & soft g and c _____ |
| --- | --- |
| | scr _____ str _____ spr _____ spl _____ shr _____ thr _____ squ _____ |
| | -ce _____ -se _____ -ve _____ -ge _____ -dge _____ -tch _____ |
| Spell Check 17 | Pretest:          Date:          Posttest:          Date: |

## Syllable and Affixes Monitoring Charts

Name _____ Teacher _____ Date _____

### Goals for Early Syllables and Affixes

| 18. Spell inflected endings (ed, ing, s) | double _____      e-drop _____      nothing _____<br><br>change y to i _____ es _____ |
|---|---|
| Spell Check 18 | Pretest:      Date:      Posttest:      Date: |

### Goals for Middle Syllables and Affixes

| 19. Spell syllable juncture patterns | V-CV _____   VCCV _____   VC-V _____   VCCCV _____   VV _____ |
|---|---|
| Spell Check 19 | Pretest:      Date:      Posttest:      Date: |
| 20. Spell long vowel patterns in accented syllables | a-e / ai / ay _____      e-e / ea / ee _____   i -e / igh / _____<br><br>o-e / oa / ow _____      oo / u-e/ ew _____ |
| Spell Check 20 | Pretest:      Date:      Posttest:      Date: |
| 21. Spell ambiguous and r-influenced vowels in accented syllables | ou / ow _____         oy / oi _____      au / aw / al _____<br><br>ar / are / air _____   or / ore _____   war / wor / wa _____<br><br>er / ir / ur _____      eer / ear / _____ |
| Spell Check 21 | Pretest:      Date:      Posttest:      Date: |
| 22-23. Spell unaccented final syllables | -le _____ -el _____ -al _____ -il _____ -er _____ -or _____ -ar _____<br><br>-ure _____ -en _____ -on _____-ain _____ -in _____<br><br>-et _____ -it _____ -ate _____ -y _____ -ie _____ -ey _____ |
| Spell Check 22 | Pretest:      Date:      Posttest:      Date: |
| Spell Check 23 | Pretest:      Date:      Posttest:      Date: |
| 24. Spell special consonants in two syllable words | Hard & soft g and c _____ -ce _____ -ss _____ -ge _____ -age _____<br><br>gu _____ -gue _____ -ck _____ -ic _____ -ix _____ qu _____<br><br>silent consonants _____ ph _____ gh _____ |
| Spell Check 24 | Pretest:      Date:      Posttest:      Date: |

### Goals for Late Syllables and Affixes

| 25. Spell and explain the meaning of simple prefixes | re _____ un _____ dis _____ mis _____ pre _____ ex _____ non _____<br><br>in _____ fore _____ uni _____ bi _____ tri _____ |
|---|---|
| 26. Spell simple suffixes | -y _____ -ly _____ -ily _____ -er/-ier _____ -est/-iest _____<br><br>-ness _____ -ful _____ _less _____ |
| Spell Check 25 | Pretest:        Date:        Posttest:        Date: |
| Spell Check 26 | Pretest:        Date:        Posttest:        Date: |

# Early Derivational Relations Monitoring Chart

Name _____ Teacher _____ Date _____

**Goals for Early Derivations Relations**

| 27. Spell and explain the meaning of prefixes | un _____ in _____ pre _____ re _____ non _____ ex _____<br><br>dis _____ mis _____ post _____ com _____ pro _____ de _____<br><br>sub _____ en _____ |
|---|---|
| Spell Check 27 | Pretest:    Date:    Posttest:    Date: |
| 28. Spell derivational suffixes | -y/-ly/-ily _____ -er / -ier _____ -est / -iest _____ -ian _____<br><br>-ist _____ -ary / -ery / -ory _____ -ty / -ity _____<br><br>-al / -ial / -ic _____ -ous / -ious _____ -en / -ize / -ify _____ |
| 29. Spell –ion endings | -tion _____ -sion _____ -cian _____ -ation _____ |
| Spell Check 28 | Pretest:    Date:    Posttest:    Date: |
| Spell Check 29 | Pretest:    Date:    Posttest:    Date: |

# Spell Checks

Spell checks can be used as pretests to place students for instruction and/or as posttests to assess students to determine their mastery of a feature. A delayed posttest might also be given 3–6 weeks after studying a feature to assess retention over time. Students should not be asked to restudy these words prior to a posttest. Two forms are provided here. Use the progress monitoring/goal setting charts on pages 413 to 419 for record keeping. Students are generally ready to study a feature when they score 40% to 70% on a pretest. Posttest scores should be at least 80% to move on to the next feature. When features are reviewed later in the stage, you can set a lower criterion for moving on.* There are links to student forms for spell checks that involve pictures. Otherwise students can simply number a paper and write the words as they are called aloud.

## Letter Name–Alphabetic Spell Checks

**Enhanced eText**
Teacher Resource:
Spell check for Initial
Consonants Form
A and B

1. **Initial Consonants:** Make a copy of the form with pictures for each student. Use *boy* (or *five*) as a practice item. Say, *Listen as I name the first picture—boy. The first sound in* boy *is /b/ so write a B under the picture.* Boy *begins with B. Now you write the first letter in each word as I name it.* Students can be asked to spell the entire word if you would like to gather more information but only the initial sound is counted. The criterion to move on is 17 out of 19.

| Form A | | Form B | |
|---|---|---|---|
| 1. tire | 11. rose | 1. moon | 11. pie |
| 2. mouse | 12. yawn | 2. dime | 12. cone |
| 3. gum | 13. cake | 3. kick | 13. gate |
| 4. key | 14. zoo | 4. boat | 14. seal |
| 5. sun | 15. horn | 5. hand | 15. toast |
| 6. jeep | 16. nails | 6. watch | 16. ring |
| 7. lamp | 17. wall | 7. leaf | 17. yarn |
| 8. pan | 18. ball | 8. jump | 18. zebra |
| 9. fork | 19. van | 9. vest | 19. fire |
| 10. desk | | 10. nest | |

**Enhanced eText**
Teacher Resource:
Spell Check for Same
Vowel Word Families
Form A and B

2. **Same-Vowel Word Families:** Make a copy of the form with pictures for each student. Name each picture and ask students to circle the correct word. The criterion to move on is at least 6 of 10 because these are reviewed later.

| Form A | | Form B | |
|---|---|---|---|
| 1. bat | 6. mad | 1. rat | 6. nut |
| 2. mop | 7. bag | 2. jog | 7. ten |
| 3. run | 8. pot | 3. cap | 8. fan |
| 4. jug | 9. wig | 4. hot | 9. zip |
| 5. pill | 10. peg | 5. wet | 10. bug |

Note: The focus of this assessment is really on whether students get the beginning and ending consonants. The medial short vowels may not be mastered at this point.

3. **Initial Digraphs:** Make a copy of the form with pictures for each student. Name each picture and ask students to write the sound they hear at the beginning. If students write the entire word, only the beginning digraph is counted. The criterion to move on is at least 5 of 6.

**Enhanced eText**
Teacher Resource:
Spell Check for
Digraphs

| **Form A** | | **Form B** | |
|---|---|---|---|
| 1. shirt | | 1. shop | |
| 2. chick | | 2. chair | |
| 3. whistle | | 3. whisker | |
| 4. thermos | | 4. think | |
| 5. shelf | | 5. whip | |
| 6. chin | | 6. chief | |

4. **Initial Blends:** Make a copy of the form with pictures for each student. Name each picture. Students can write only the initial blend or spell the entire word, but only the blend is counted. The criterion to move on is at least 17 of 20. You may want to give credit for either sc or sk for *skip, scout, scale,* and *skunk* because sound provides no clue as to which blend is correct.

**Enhanced eText**
Teacher Resource:
Spell Check for Blends
form A and B

| **Form A** | | | **Form B** | | |
|---|---|---|---|---|---|
| 1. grapes | 11. spear | | 1. sponge | 11. skunk | |
| 2. quilt | 12. sleeve | | 2. twist | 12. drill | |
| 3. smoke | 13. twelve | | 3. snow | 13. plant | |
| 4. stool | 14. track | | 4. prize | 14. grill | |
| 5. swan | 15. blouse | | 5. block | 15. swing | |
| 6. plane | 16. skip | | 6. stamp | 16. brush | |
| 7. bread | 17. fry | | 7. clouds | 17. scale | |
| 8. fly | 18. crack | | 8. smell | 18. crib | |
| 9. drip | 19. glove | | 9. quack | 19. truck | |
| 10. clock | 20. scout | | 10. float | 20. frog | |

5. **Mixed-Vowel Word Families in CVC Words:** Call words aloud for students to write on their own paper (no form is provided). The criterion to move on is at least 8 out of 10.

| **Form A** | | | **Form B** | | |
|---|---|---|---|---|---|
| 1. dot | 6. led | | 1. fat | 6. pan | |
| 2. run | 7. rob | | 2. bun | 7. hug | |
| 3. bit | 8. wag | | 3. pad | 8. cab | |
| 4. win | 9. jog | | 4. fed | 9. wig | |
| 5. bad | 10 rug | | 5. job | 10. leg | |

6. **Mixed-Vowel Word Families in CVCC Words:** Call words aloud for students to write on their own paper. The criterion to move on is at least 8 out of 10.

| **Form A** | | | **Form B** | | |
|---|---|---|---|---|---|
| 1. bill | 6. wish | | 1. fill | 6. rush | |
| 2. sack | 7. rock | | 2. pick | 7. hall | |
| 3. lick | 8. fall | | 3. cash | 8. tuck | |
| 4. hush | 9. rash | | 4. lock | 9. rack | |
| 5. fell | 10. luck | | 5. sell | 10. fish | |

**Enhanced eText**
Teacher Resource:
Spell Check for Short
Vowels form A and B

7. **Short Vowels:** Make a copy of the form with pictures for each student. Name each picture and ask students to write the missing vowel. The criterion to move on is at least 8 out of 10.

| **Form A** | | | **Form B** | | |
|---|---|---|---|---|---|
| 1. sun | 6. sled | | 1. cut | 6. pet |
| 2. flag | 7. can | | 2. map | 7. hat |
| 3. box | 8. lock | | 3. pop | 8. mop |
| 4. lid | 9. bib | | 4. dig | 9. hill |
| 5. rug | 10. net | | 5. bun | 10. bed |

8. **Short Vowels in CVC Words:** Call words aloud. The criterion to move on is at least 8 out of 10.

| **Form A** | | | **Form B** | | |
|---|---|---|---|---|---|
| 1. jam | 6. cab | | 1. ham | 6. map |
| 2. set | 7. fed | | 2. vet | 7. leg |
| 3. lid | 8. bit | | 3. rid | 8. him |
| 4. fox | 9. hot | | 4. box | 9. pop |
| 5. hug | 10. nut | | 5. rug | 10. rut |

9. **Short Vowels with Blends and Digraphs:** Call words aloud. The criterion to move on is at least 8 out of 10.

| **Form A** | | | **Form B** | | |
|---|---|---|---|---|---|
| 1. path | 6. crab | | 1. math | 6. cram |
| 2. west | 7. fret | | 2. best | 7. sled |
| 3. ship | 8. lift | | 3. chill | 8. gift |
| 4. soft | 9. slob | | 4. boss | 9. drop |
| 5. much | 10. plus | | 5. such | 10. dust |

10. **Preconsonantal Nasals and Short Vowels:** Call words aloud for students to spell. The criterion to move on is at least 8 out of 10.

| **Form A** | | | **Form B** | | |
|---|---|---|---|---|---|
| 1. bring | 6. tent | | 1. rung | 6. stump |
| 2. camp | 7. thank | | 2. lamp | 7. send |
| 3. hunt | 8. dump | | 3. print | 8. plant |
| 4. blend | 9. sang | | 4. think | 9. long |
| 5. wink | 10. hand | | 5. limp | 10. junk |

11. **R-controlled A and O:** Call words aloud for students to spell. The criterion to move on is at least 5 out of 6.

| **Form A** | | **Form B** | |
|---|---|---|---|
| 1. yard | | 1. sort |
| 2. fort | | 2. word |
| 3. dark | | 3. card |
| 4. horn | | 4. born |
| 5. work | | 5. part |
| 6. jar | | 6. form |

# Within Word Pattern Spell Checks

Posttest scores should be at least 80% to move on to the next feature. When features are reviewed later in the stage, you can set a lower criterion for moving on.

### 12. Long Vowels and Review of Short Vowels in CVC and CVCe

| Form A | | | Form B | | |
|---|---|---|---|---|---|
| 1. fast | 6. lick | | 1. last | 6. spill |
| 2. mice | 7. tame | | 2. cute | 7. truck |
| 3. joke | 8. rude | | 3. woke | 8. take |
| 4. spot | 9. bus | | 4. nice | 9. robe |
| 5. rake | 10. vote | | 5. flop | 10. game |

### 13. CVCe and CVVC Patterns

| Form A | | | Form B | | |
|---|---|---|---|---|---|
| 1. chain | 6. leaf | | 1. brain | 6. blame |
| 2. stone | 7. place | | 2. tune | 7. teach |
| 3. keep | 8. soap | | 3. goat | 8. sleep |
| 4. head | 9. suit | | 4. slope | 9. bread |
| 5. spoon | 10. cube | | 5. tooth | 10. fruit |

### 14. Less Common Long Vowel Patterns

| Form A | | | Form B | | |
|---|---|---|---|---|---|
| 1. stay | 6. say | | 1. tray | 6. true |
| 2. slow | 7. glue | | 2. grow | 7. row |
| 3. chew | 8. mow | | 3. stew | 8. shy |
| 4. sky | 9. few | | 4. cry | 9. fine |
| 5. night | 10. white | | 5. bright | 10. high |

### 15. R-influenced Vowels

| Form A | | | Form B | | |
|---|---|---|---|---|---|
| 1. bare | 6. cheer | | 1. chair | 6. clerk |
| 2. germ | 7. wire | | 2. dirt | 7. sharp |
| 3. fear | 8. burst | | 3. storm | 8. warm |
| 4. heard | 9. cure | | 4. world | 9. roar |
| 5. worm | 10. store | | 5. pure | 10. near |

### 16. Ambiguous Vowels

| Form A | | | Form B | | |
|---|---|---|---|---|---|
| 1. join | 6. fault | | 1. spoil | 6. mouth |
| 2. stood | 7. cloud | | 2. hook | 7. bald |
| 3. joy | 8. clown | | 3. claw | 8. frown |
| 4. draw | 9. wand | | 4. toy | 9. wasp |
| 5. root | 10. cross | | 5. caught | 10. frost |

### 17. Complex Consonants

| Form A | | | Form B | | |
|---|---|---|---|---|---|
| 1. knob | 6. fence | | 1. wrong | 6. tease |
| 2. scrape | 7. shrink | | 2. sprain | 7. gym |
| 3. stretch | 8. leave | | 3. squish | 8. fudge |
| 4. through | 9. cent | | 4. guest | 9. switch |
| 5. guess | 10. judge | | 5. dance | 10. splash |

## Syllables and Affixes Spell Checks

Students are generally ready to study a feature when they score 40% to 70% on a pretest. Post-test scores should be at least 80% to move on to the next feature. When features are reviewed later in the stage, you can set a lower criterion for moving on.

### 18. Inflected Endings: ed, ing, and s

| Form A | | | Form B | | |
|---|---|---|---|---|---|
| 1. dripping | 6. moved | | 1. dragging | 6. dries |
| 2. passed | 7. stepped | | 2. missed | 7. lived |
| 3. winked | 8. brushes | | 3. blinked | 8. dropped |
| 4. waving | 9. spied | | 4. ashes | 9. fried |
| 5. cries | 10. mailed | | 5. sailed | 10. shaving |

### 19. Syllable Juncture Patterns (CV-C, C-VC, CVVC, CVVVC, VV): Do not count unaccented errors in final syllables.

| Form A | | | Form B | | |
|---|---|---|---|---|---|
| 1. paper | 6. lazy | | 1. crazy | 6. complete |
| 2. river | 7. wagon | | 2. puppy | 7. diet |
| 3. rabbit | 8. pumpkin | | 3. follow | 8. skimmed |
| 4. penny | 9. riot | | 4. never | 9. finish |
| 5. chapter | 10. winning | | 5. letter | 10. winter |

### 20. Long Vowels in Accented Syllables: Count only the spelling in the accented syllables.

| Form A | | | Form B | | |
|---|---|---|---|---|---|
| 1. explain | 6. rooster | | 1. complain | 6. owner |
| 2. season | 7. confuse | | 2. reduce | 7. shampoo |
| 3. payment | 8. mistake | | 3. maybe | 8. parade |
| 4. decide | 9. fifteen | | 4. polite | 9. reason |
| 5. lonesome | 10. extreme | | 5. suppose | 10. thirteen |

### 21. Ambiguous and R-influenced Vowels in Accented Syllables: Count only the accented vowel and not unaccented final syllables

| Form A | | | Form B | | |
|---|---|---|---|---|---|
| 1. loyal | 6. sincere | | 1. poison | 6. perform |
| 2. lawyer | 7. repair | | 2. coward | 7. severe |
| 3. powder | 8. appear | | 3. laundry | 8. ignore |
| 4. counter | 9. worry | | 4. market | 9. furnish |
| 5. faucet | 10. person | | 5. declare | 10. county |

### 22. Unaccented Final Syllables: Students should be able to spell the entire word correctly.

| Form A | | | Form B | | |
|---|---|---|---|---|---|
| 1. table | 6. sugar | | 1. bottle | 6. slower |
| 2. cover | 7. future | | 2. spider | 7. dollar |
| 3. total | 8. evil | | 3. travel | 8. nature |
| 4. faster | 9. creature | | 4. flavor | 9. metal |
| 5. level | 10. doctor | | 5. pencil | 10. treasure |

### 23. More Unaccented Syllables

| Form A | | | Form B | | |
|---|---|---|---|---|---|
| 1. hidden | 6. private | | 1. mitten | 6. cabin |
| 2. rocket | 7. ribbon | | 2. bargain | 7. orbit |
| 3. monkey | 8. captain | | 3. pocket | 8. brownie |
| 4. dizzy | 9. habit | | 4. donkey | 9. parties |
| 5. movie | 10. copies | | 5. cherry | 10. dragon |

### 24. Special Consonants

| Form A | | | Form B | | |
|---|---|---|---|---|---|
| 1. central | 6. traffic | | 1. gentle | 6. frantic |
| 2. office | 7. frequent | | 2. practice | 7. banquet |
| 3. manage | 8. answer | | 3. package | 8. wrestle |
| 4. guilty | 9. nephew | | 4. compass | 9. orphan |
| 5. vague | 10. enough | | 5. complex | 10. gentle |

### 25. Simple Prefixes:
Call words aloud and ask student to spell them and write a brief definition. For example, *uniform* means one form, and *quadrangle* means a shape with four sides. Definitions can include the root word and should show an understanding of the meaning of the prefix. Must spell and define for credit.

| Form A | Form B |
|---|---|
| 1. disloyal "not loyal" | 1. disable " not able" |
| 2. mistreat "treat badly" | 2. mismatch "badly matched" |
| 3. preview "Look at before" | 3. preheat "heat before" |
| 4. extend "to stick out" | 4. exclude "leave out" |
| 5. incorrect "not correct" | 5. uniform "one form" |
| 6. forecast "to tell before" | 6. foresee "see before" |
| 7. rewrite "to write again" | 7. unkind "not kind" |
| 8. unfair "not fair" | 8. nonfat " without fat" |
| 9. triangle "three angles" | 9. bisect "cut in two" |
| 10. nonstop "without stopping" | 10. retell "tell again" |

### 26. Simple Suffixes:
The criterion for moving on is at least 5 out of 6.

| Form A | Form B |
|---|---|
| 1. hotter | 1. hottest |
| 2. dirtier | 2. easier |
| 3. penniless | 3. happiness |
| 4. easily | 4. noisily |
| 5. prettiest | 5. nicely |
| 6. careful | 6. painful |

# Early Derivational Relations Spell Checks

Students are generally ready to study a feature when they score 40% to 70% on a pretest. Post-test scores should be at least 80% to move on to the next feature. When features are reviewed later in the stage, you can set a lower criterion for moving on.

27. **Prefixes:** Call words aloud and ask student to spell them and write a brief definition. For example, *dishonest* means not honest, and *forefathers* are family who come before you. Definitions can include the root word and should show an understanding of the meaning of the prefix. Must spell and define for credit.

| Form A | | Form B | |
|---|---|---|---|
| 1. prehistoric "before history" | | 1. predict "to say before" | |
| 2. posttest "test that comes after" | | 2. submerge "to put under" | |
| 3. subtitle "title that is under" | | 3. compound "things together | |
| 4. companion "someone with you" | | 4. provide "to have for someone" | |
| 5. promote "to put forward" | | 5. entrust "to trust in someone" | |
| 6. endanger "to put in danger" | | 6. export "to take out" | |
| 7. exterior "outside" | | 7. insane "not sane" | |
| 8. inhabit "to live in a place" | | 8. delete "to take away" | |
| 9. defrost "to take way the frost" | | 9. misfortune "bad luck" | |
| 10. misleading "to be led wrong" | | 10. inhale "to breathe in" | |

28. **Derivational Suffixes:** Call words aloud for students to spell.

| Form A | | Form B | |
|---|---|---|---|
| 1. messier | 6. civilize | 1. fearfulness | 6. directory |
| 2. ordinary | 7. emptiness | 2. fancier | 7. harmonize |
| 3. purify | 8. glorious | 3. logical | 8. studious |
| 4. musical | 9. tutorial | 4. beautify | 9. industrial |
| 5. shiniest | 10. humidity | 5. fancier | 10. minority |

29. **The suffix /shun:** Call words aloud. The criterion to move on is 5 out of 6 or better.

| Form A | Form B |
|---|---|
| 1. selection | 1. connection |
| 2. discussion | 2. confession |
| 3. musician | 3. electrician |
| 4. prevention | 4. adoption |
| 5. invasion | 5. expansion |
| 6. purification | 6. notification |

## Sound Board for Beginning Consonants and Digraphs

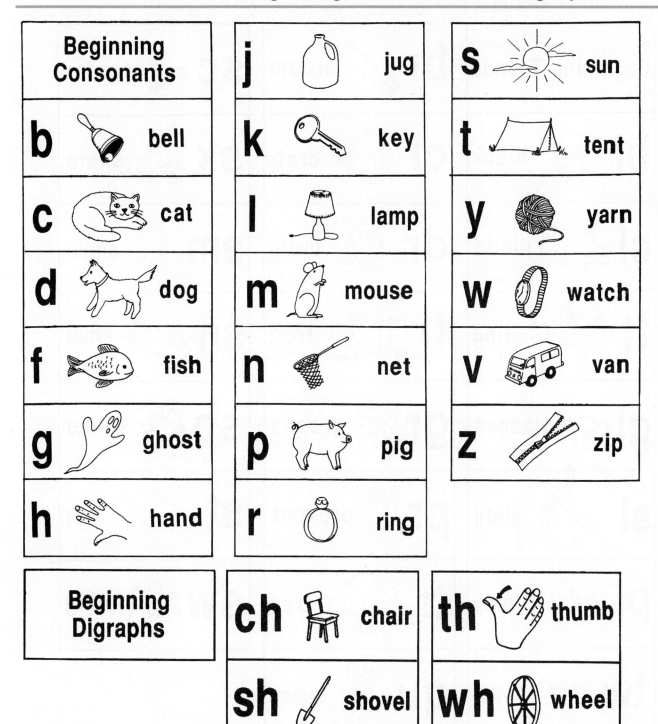

| Beginning Consonants | | |
|---|---|---|
| **b** bell | **j** jug | **s** sun |
| **c** cat | **k** key | **t** tent |
| **d** dog | **l** lamp | **y** yarn |
| **f** fish | **m** mouse | **w** watch |
| **g** ghost | **n** net | **v** van |
| **h** hand | **p** pig | **z** zip |
| | **r** ring | |

| Beginning Digraphs | | |
|---|---|---|
| | **ch** chair | **th** thumb |
| | **sh** shovel | **wh** wheel |

# Sound Board for Beginning Blends

| Beginning Blends | | |
|---|---|---|
| **bl** block | **br** broom | **sc** scooter |
| **cl** cloud | **cr** crab | **sk** skate |
| **fl** flag | **dr** drum | **sm** smile |
| **gl** glasses | **fr** frog | **sn** snail |
| **sl** slide | **gr** grapes | **sp** spider |
| **pl** 2+1=3 plus | **pr** present | **st** star |
| **tw** twins | **tr** tree | **sw** swing |
| | **qu** queen | |

# Sound Board for Long and Short Vowels

| Short Vowels | | Long Vowels | | | |
|---|---|---|---|---|---|
| ă | cat | ā | cake | ā | tray |
| | | | | ā | rain |
| ĕ | bed | ē | feet | ē | leaf |
| ĭ | pig | ī | kite | ī | light |
| ŏ | sock | ō | bone | ō | soap |
| ŭ | cup | ū | tube | | |

You can use the pictures that follow in a number of ways. For example, you can use them like clip art to create picture sorts. Refer to Chapters 4 and 5 for suggested contrasts for picture sorts or create your own. Simply make copies of the pictures you need (combining two, three, or four sounds) and glue them randomly onto a template, such as the one in Appendix G on page 501. You will probably want to enlarge the pictures about 50 percent and insert labels from the sound board boxes as headers. You may also want to make a complete set of pictures for modeling, small-group work, or centers. Glue or copy pictures to card stock, and perhaps color them, and laminate the card stock for durability. Use the pictures for games and other activities as well.

Pictures are grouped by beginning consonants, digraphs, blends, short vowels, and long vowels. The following list will help you find pictures for rhyme sorts, word families, additional short vowels, and long vowels. The picture names in bold type are in either the short or long vowel picture section, whereas the others can be found by their beginning sounds.

## Long Vowel Picture Rhymes

| | | | | | | | |
|---|---|---|---|---|---|---|---|
| **tape** | **game** | **soap** | **beach** | deer | **slide** | fire | |
| **cape** | **frame** | **rope** | **peach** | spear | **bride** | tire | |
| | | | | | | | |
| **vine** | **bone** | **toad** | pear | **moon** | **seal** | **cube** | **bead** |
| **nine** | **cone** | **road** | chair | spoon | **heel** | **tube** | **read** |
| | | | | | | | |
| **suit** | gate | **snake** | **glue** | jeep | school | **peas** | king |
| **fruit** | plate | **cake** | **shoe** | sheep | stool | **cheese** | ring |
| **flute** | skate | **rake** | zoo | sleep | spool | **keys** | sting |
| | | lake | two | sweep | | | |
| | | | | | | | |
| **hive** | **rose** | **coat** | **three** | **hay** | **cane** | **pie** | **whale** |
| **five** | **nose** | **boat** | **bee** | **pay** | **rain** | **tie** | **tail** |
| **dive** | **toes** | **goat** | **knee** | pray | **chain** | **fly** | **mail** |
| **drive** | hose | **float** | tree | tray | **plane** | cry | snail |
| | | **note** | key | play | **train** | fry | sail |
| | | | **pea** | | | | pail |
| | | | | | | | nail |
| | | | | | | | Scale |

*Note:* More long vowel pictures can be found among initial sounds: paint, vase, shave, blade, flame, grapes, braid, leaf, leash, steam, seal, key, wheel, sleeve, teeth, queen, dream, bike, dice, dime, kite, smile, prize, climb, price, globe, snow, comb, ghost, smoke, toast, flute.

# Short Vowel Picture Rhymes

| | | | | | | | |
|---|---|---|---|---|---|---|---|
| glass | lamp | four | bus | trunk | duck | switch | mitten |
| grass | stamp | door | plus | skunk | truck | witch | kitten |
| | | | | | | | |
| **vest** | **wig** | car | **leg** | **cut** | **sun** | | |
| chest | **pig** | jar | egg | **hut** | **bun** | | |
| nest | **dig** | star | peg | **nut** | **run** | | |
| | | | | | | | |
| wall | **box** | hook | **pup** | jump | **bug** | | |
| saw | **fox** | book | **cup** | stump | **jug** | | |
| claw | socks | | | | **rug** | | |
| | | | | | | | |
| **hen** | **bed** | kick | **gum** | dog | **pot** | **fin** | net |
| **men** | **sled** | stick | drum | log | **dot** | **pin** | jet |
| ten | shed | chick | plum | jog | **hot** | chin | **pet** |
| pen | bread | brick | thumb | frog | **cot** | twin | vet |
| | | | | | | | |
| **bag** | **can** | **cat** | king | **sock** | **shell** | | |
| **rag** | **man** | **bat** | ring | **rock** | **bell** | | |
| **wag** | **fan** | **hat** | wing | **lock** | **well** | | |
| flag | pan | mat | sting | **clock** | smell | | |
| tag | van | bat | swing | block | | | |
| | | | | | | | |
| **cap** | **mop** | **zip** | **jack** | **mug** | **pill** | | |
| **map** | **hop** | **lip** | **sack** | **bug** | **hill** | | |
| **nap** | **top** | **rip** | **pack** | **jug** | **mill** | | |
| trap | **pop** | ship | shack | **tug** | spill | | |
| clap | chop | whip | quack | **rug** | drill | | |
| snap | shop | skip | track | plug | grill | | |
| | stop | clip | crack | | | | |
| | | drip | | | | | |
| | | flip | | | | | |

*Note:* Bolded words may be found in vowel pictures. More short vowel pictures can be found among initial sounds: gas, ham, mask, match, glass, crab, sad, trash, desk, check, belt, web, dress, fish, six, bridge, swim, crib, flip, kiss, kit, twin, cup, gum, tub, brush.

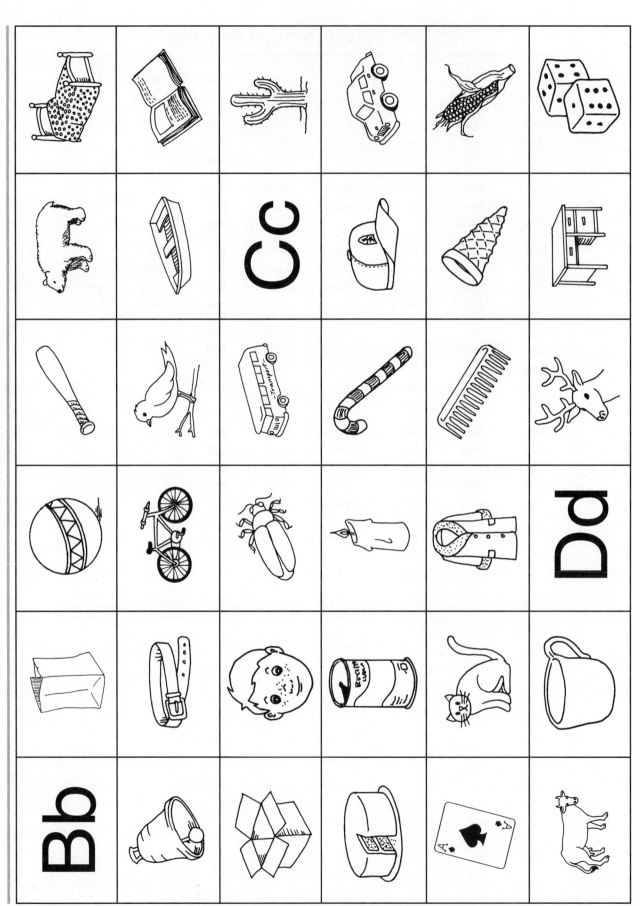

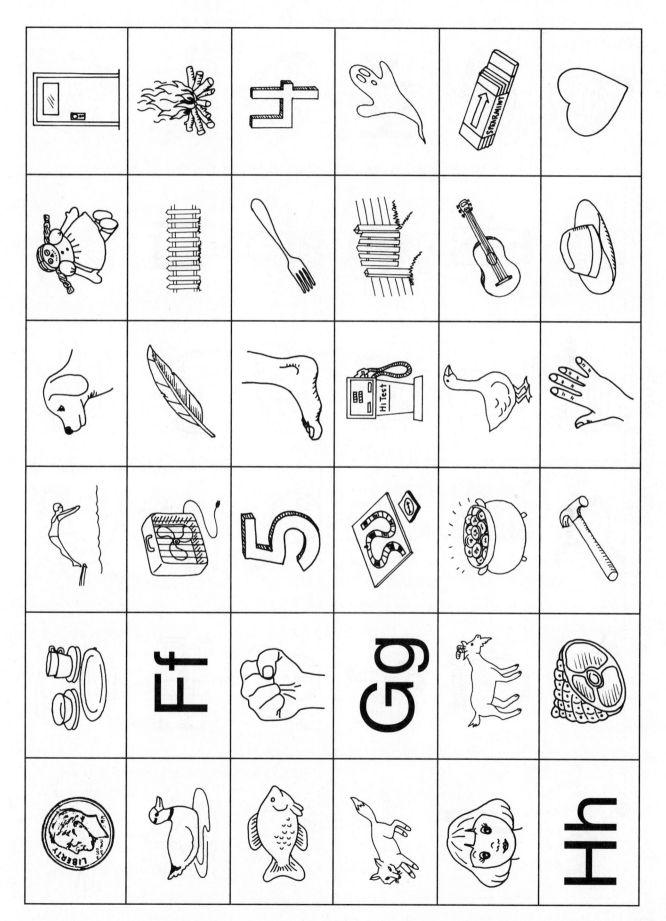

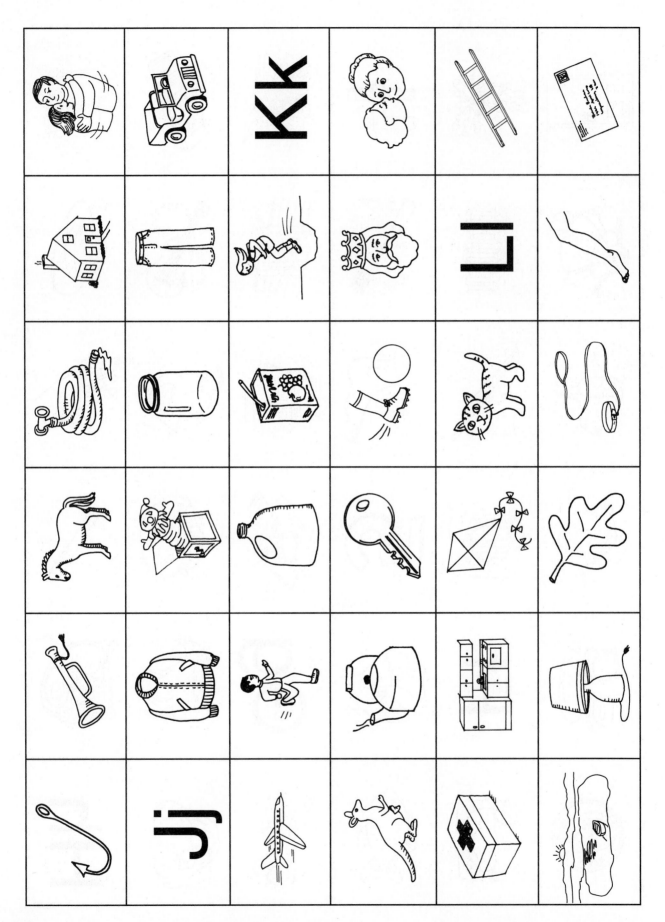

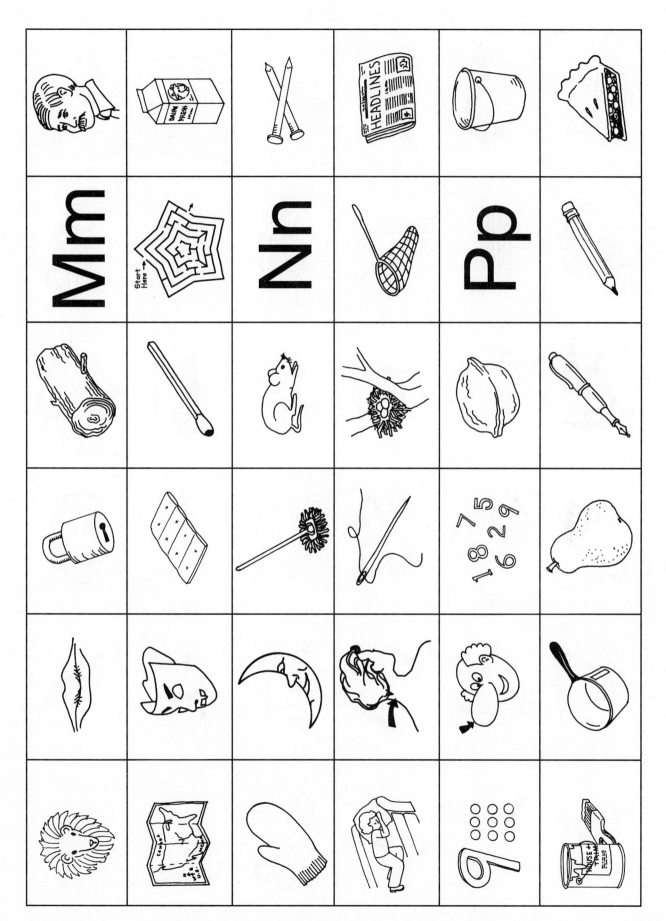

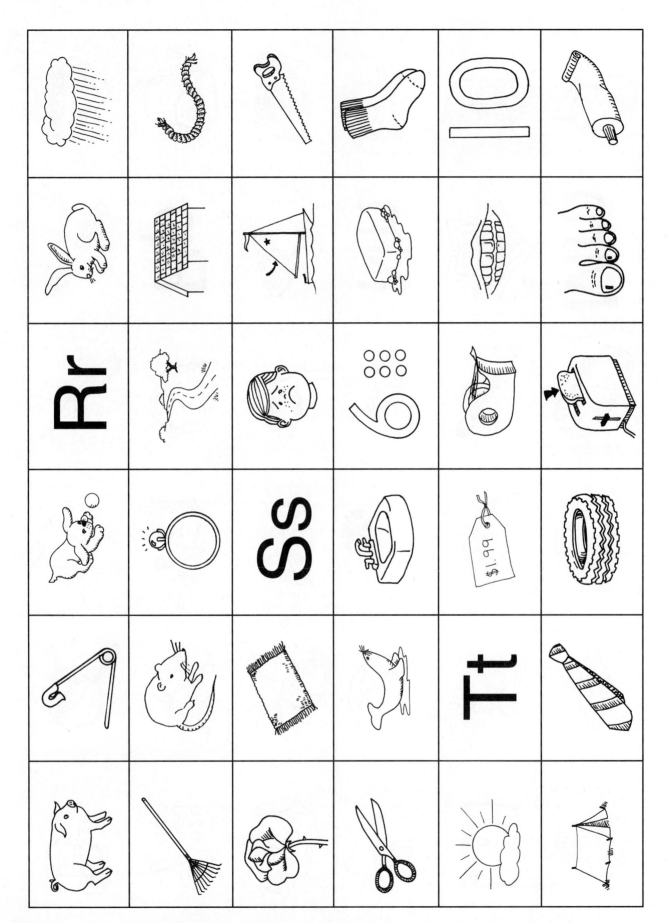

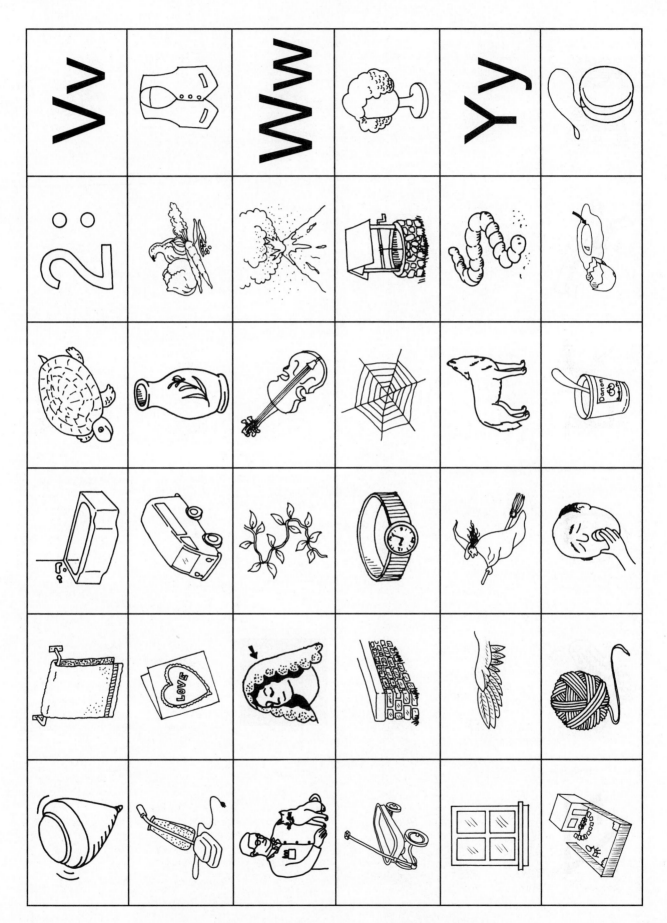

# Initial Digraphs

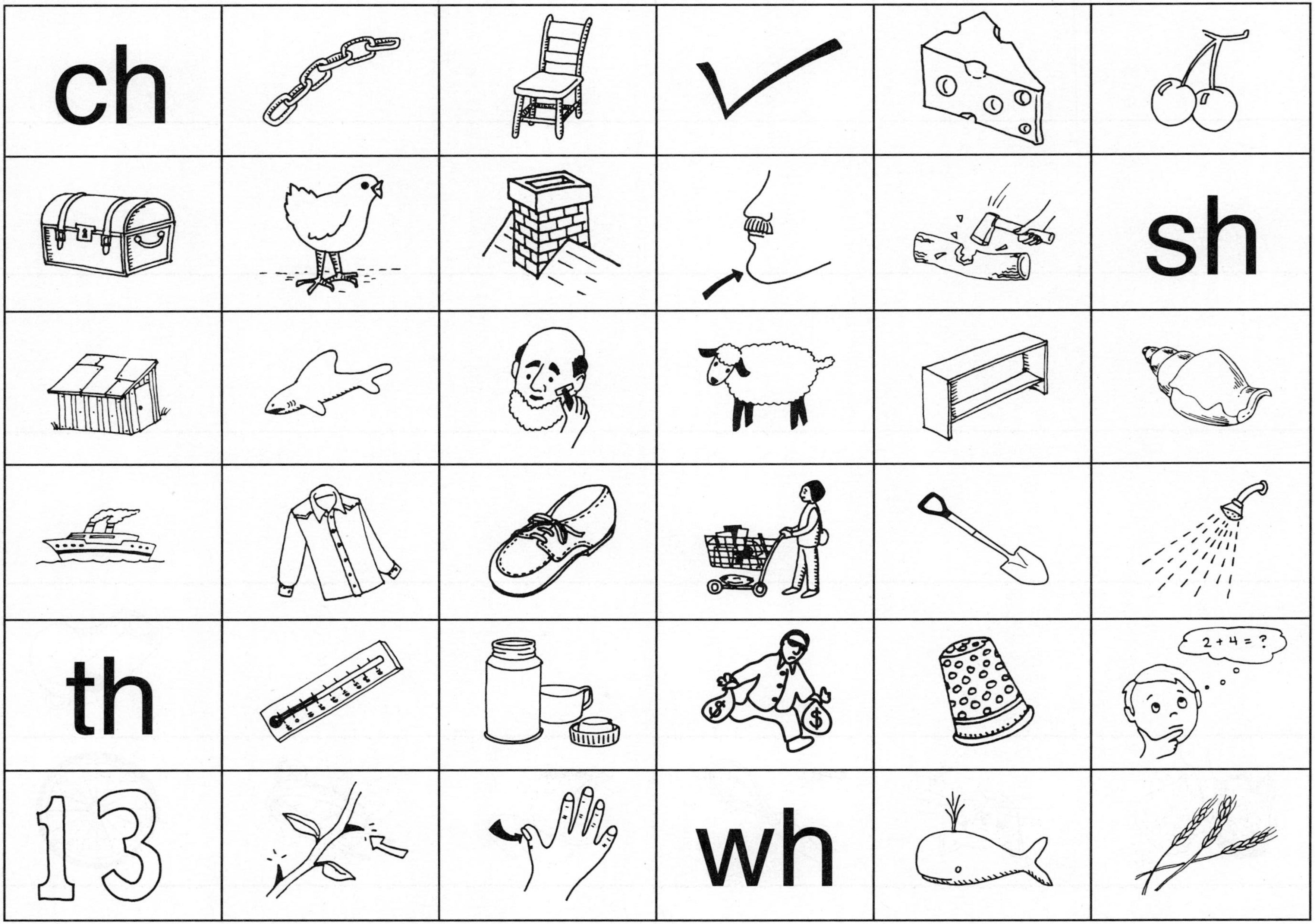

| | | | | | |
|---|---|---|---|---|---|
| | | | | | |
| | | | | | |
| | | | | | |
| | | | | | |
| | | | | | |
| | | | | | |

Initial Blends

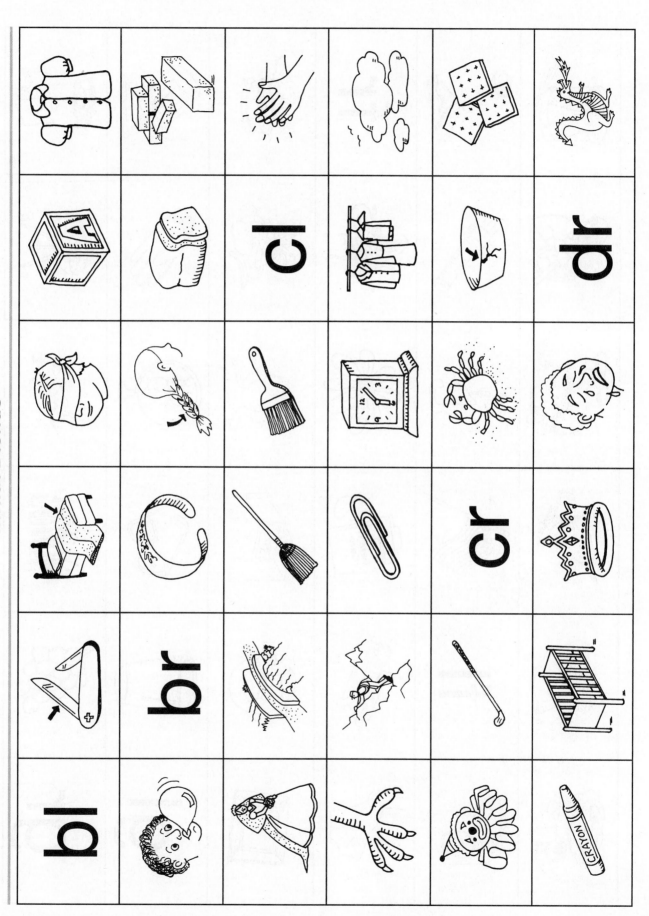

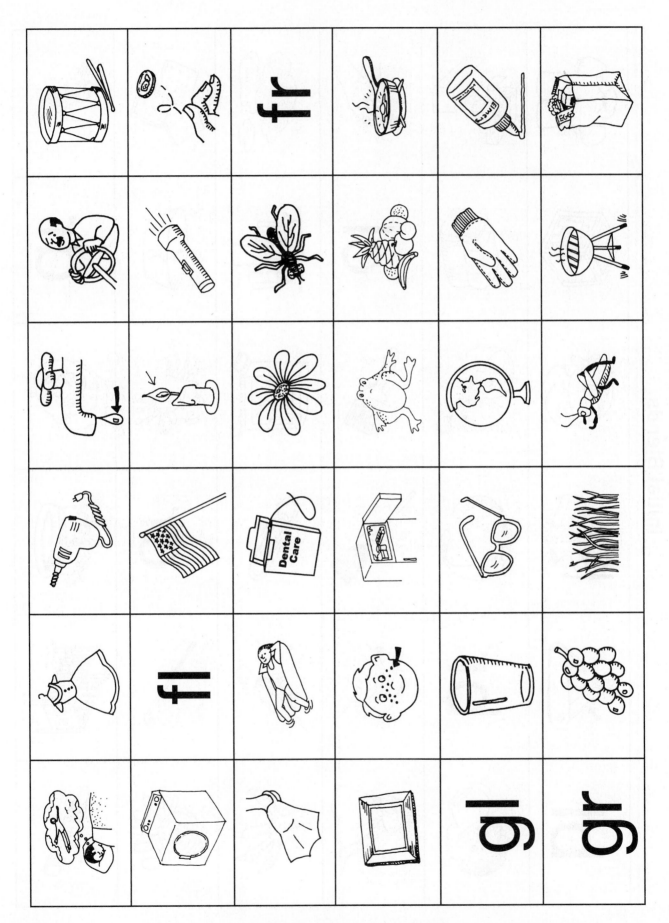

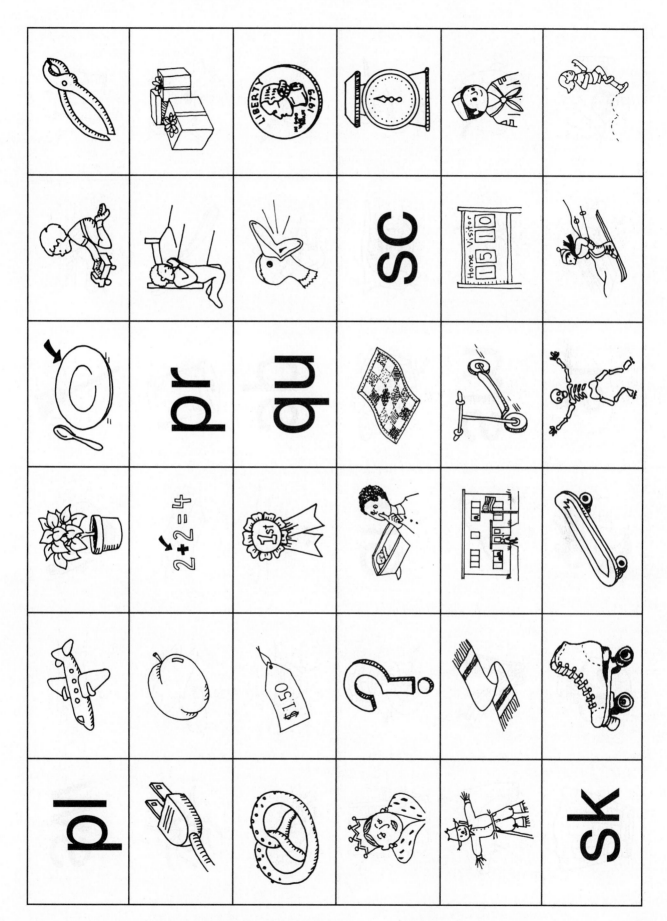

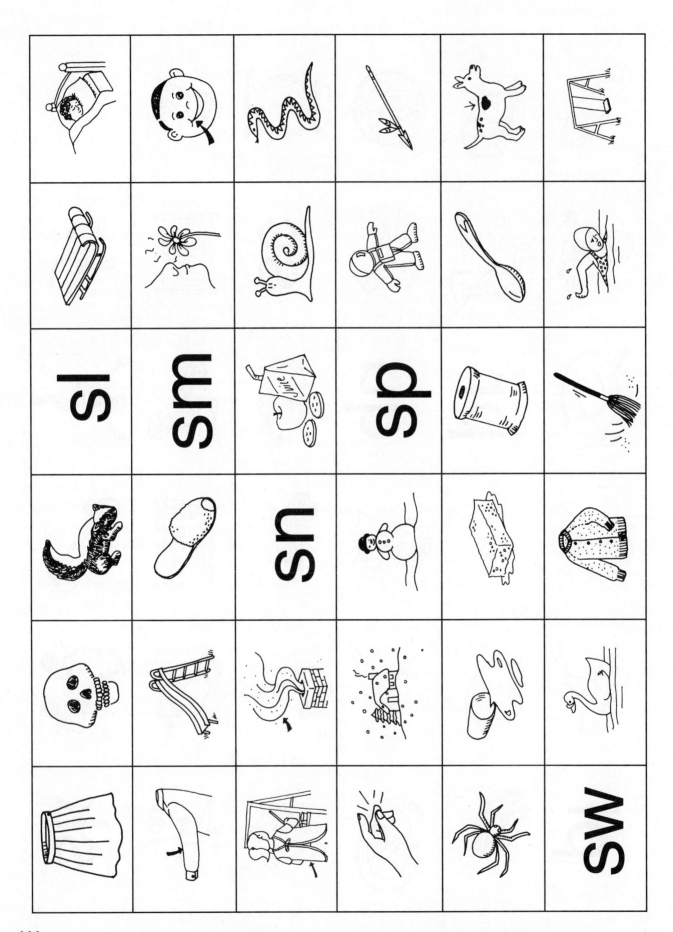

|  |  |  | tw |  |  |
| --- | --- | --- | --- | --- | --- |
|  | STOP |  |  |  |  |
|  |  |  |  |  |  |
| 25¢ |  |  |  | 20 |  |
| st |  |  |  | 12 |  |
|  |  | tr |  |  |  |

Medial Vowels

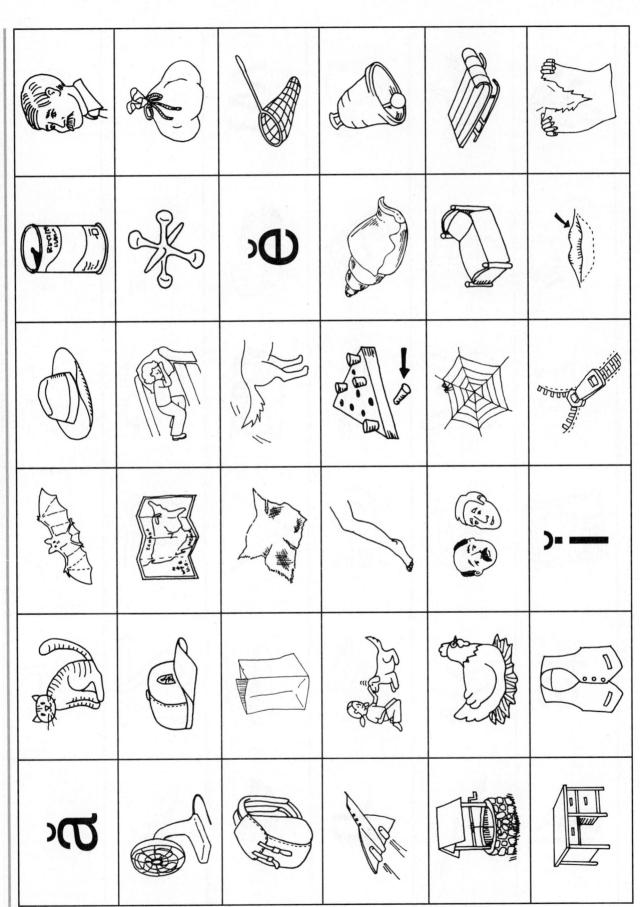

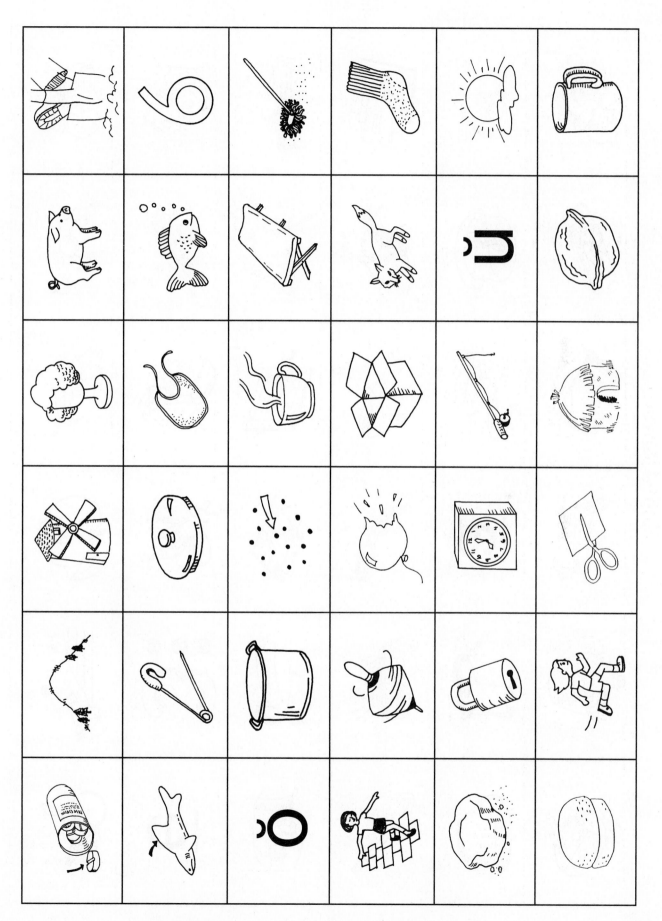

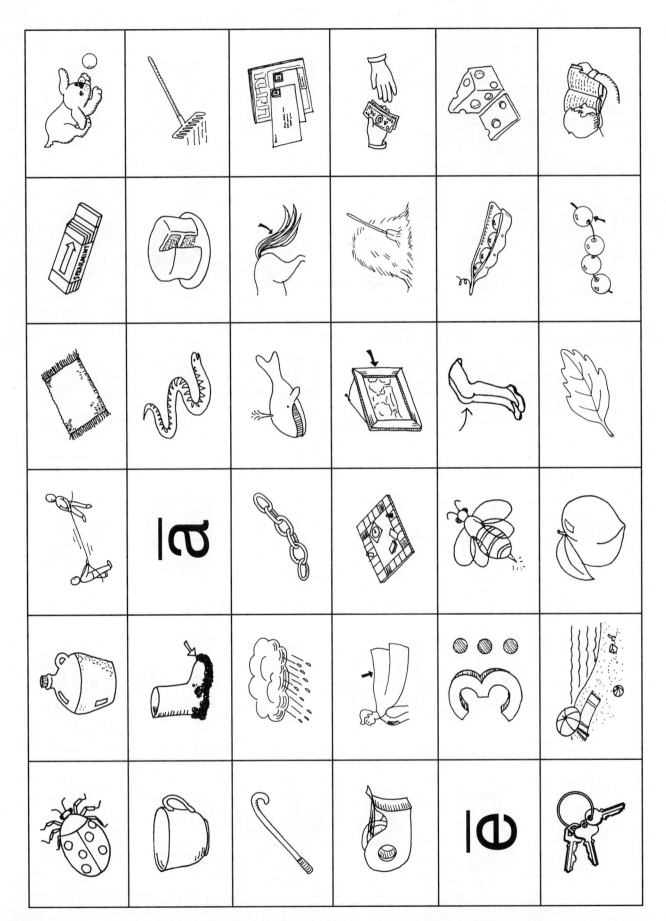

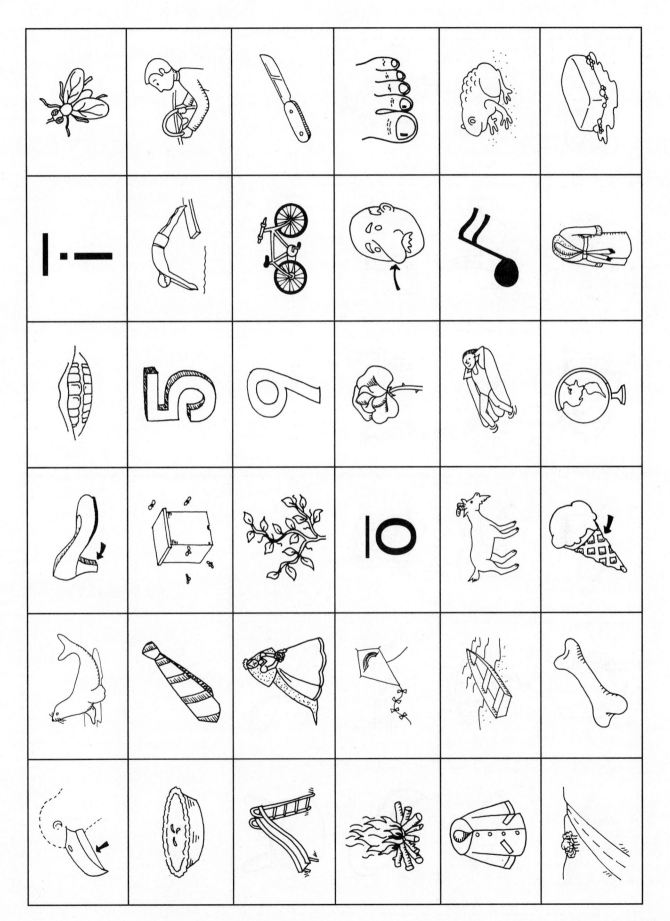

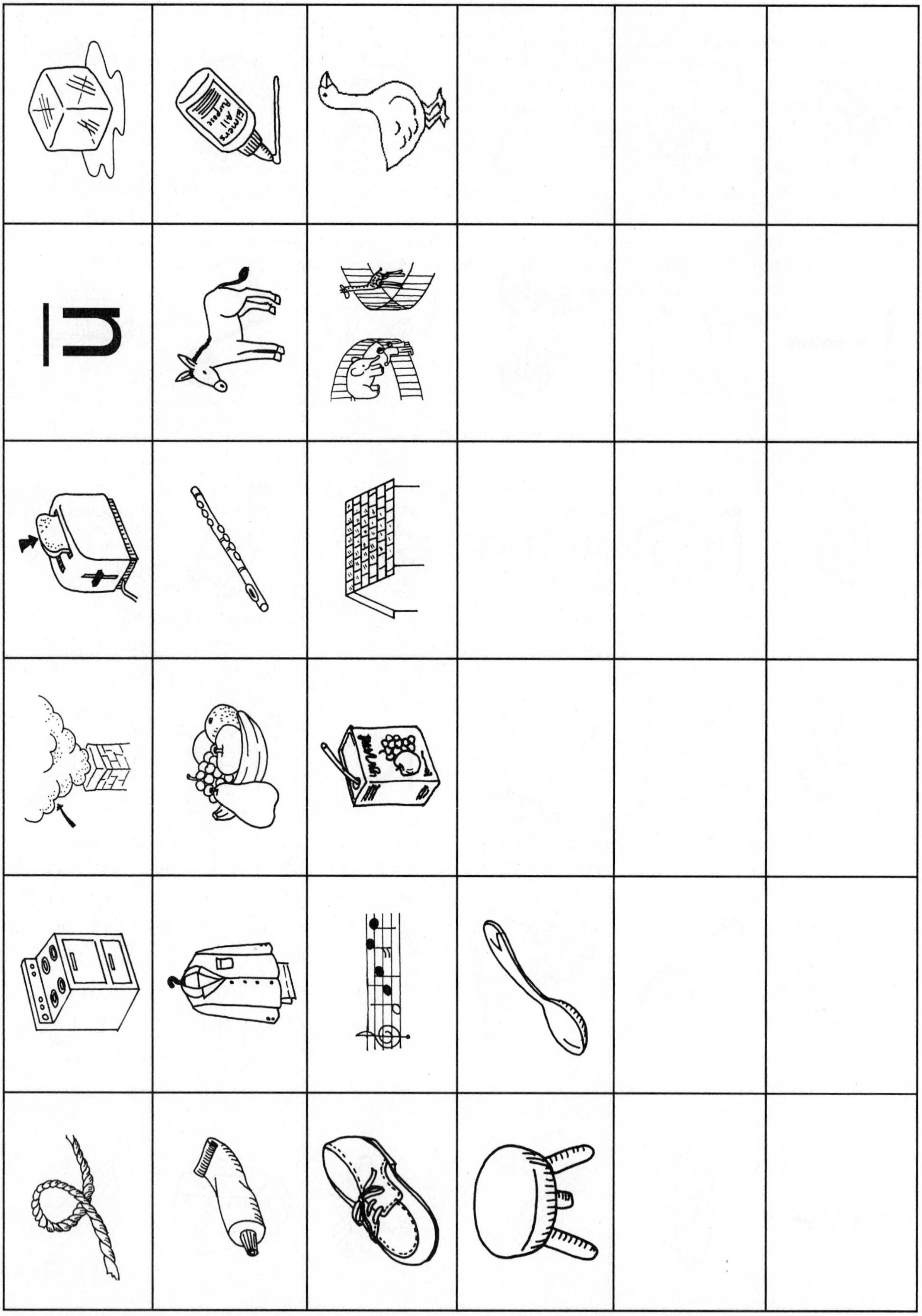

The sample word sorts on the following pages offer you ideas about the kinds of focused contrasts that are designed to explore a feature. Prepare word sorts for your students by writing the words on a template such as the one in Appendix G on page 501. Be sure to write the words on the template randomly so that students can make their own discoveries as they sort. Consider the following information when using these sorts.

- These sorts are not intended to be a sequence for all students. Chapter 2 will help you match your students to the spelling stages. Each instruction chapter contains additional suggestions about the pacing and sequencing of word study for each stage. Choose appropriate sorts from among those presented here.
- This is not an exhaustive list of sorts, but it does give you a starting point for creating your own. You can adapt these sorts by adding, deleting, or substituting words that are more appropriate for your students. Word lists are provided in Appendix F.

# Letter Name–Alphabetic Focused Contrasts

Letter name–alphabetic spellers will also need to study initial consonants, digraphs, blends, and short vowels with picture sorts. Use the pictures in Appendix D to create these sorts and refer to Chapter 5, Table 5.5, for a scope and sequence.

## Same Short Vowel Word Families

| **1.** Short *a* | | **2.** More Short *a*'s | | | **3.** Short *i* | | **4.** More Short *i*'s | | | |
|---|---|---|---|---|---|---|---|---|---|---|
| cat | man | sad | cap | bag | sit | big | pin | pill | rip | sick |
| bat | can | mad | tap | rag | bit | wig | win | will | lip | pick |
| sat | pan | dad | map | wag | hit | pig | fin | fill | hip | lick |
| fat | ran | had | nap | tag | fit | dig | thin | hill | zip | kick |
| mat | fan | pad | lap | flag | kit | fig | chin | mill | dip | tick |
| rat | van | | rap | | quit | | | bill | | chick |
| hat | Tan | | | | | | | kill | | |

| **5.** Short *o* | | **6.** More Short *o*'s | | | **7.** Short *e* | | | | **8.** Short *u* | | | | |
|---|---|---|---|---|---|---|---|---|---|---|---|---|---|
| not | hop | job | lock | dog | pet | ten | bed | bell | cut | tub | bug | fun | duck |
| got | pop | rob | rock | log | net | hen | red | tell | nut | rub | rug | bun | luck |
| hot | mop | cob | sock | frog | met | pen | fed | well | hut | cub | dug | run | suck |
| lot | cop | mob | dock | fog | set | men | led | fell | but | club | jug | sun | truck |
| pot | stop | blob | clock | jog | jet | then | sled | shell | shut | | hug | gun | tuck |
| dot | shop | sob | block | | bet | when | | | | | tug | | |
| shot | | | | | get | | | | | | | | |

# Mixed Short Vowel Word Families

### 9. Short *a, i, u*

| | | |
|---|---|---|
| man | pin | fun |
| can | win | run |
| fan | fin | sun |
| ran | thin | bun |
| than | grin | gun |
| plan | chin | |
| van | skin | |

### 10. Short *a, i, o, u*

| | | | |
|---|---|---|---|
| cat | sit | not | cut |
| mat | fit | hot | mutt |
| hat | hit | got | nut |
| sat | kit | pot | but |
| rat | bit | rot | hut |
| that | pit | cot | shut |
| | quit | dot | |

### 11. Short *a, i, e*

| | | | |
|---|---|---|---|
| bag | big | pill | bell |
| rag | wig | will | sell |
| wag | pig | hill | tell |
| flag | jig | fill | well |
| tag | dig | bill | fell |
| snag | fig | spill | shell |
| | | drill | smell |

### 12. Families with *ck*

| | | | | |
|---|---|---|---|---|
| back | sick | lock | duck | neck |
| sack | lick | rock | suck | peck |
| tack | pick | sock | tuck | deck |
| jack | tick | dock | truck | speck |
| pack | kick | clock | | |
| black | chick | block | | |

### 13. Preconsonantal Nasals

| | | | |
|---|---|---|---|
| camp | jump | band | sink |
| lamp | dump | hand | pink |
| ramp | hump | sand | think |
| stamp | stump | land | wink |
| damp | lump | stand | drink |

### 14. Families Ending in *sh*

| | | |
|---|---|---|
| mash | fish | mush |
| cash | dish | hush |
| trash | wish | rush |
| rash | swish | gush |
| dash | | brush |
| crash | | |
| flash | | |

# Short Vowels in CVC Words

### 15. Short *a, o*

| | | |
|---|---|---|
| cat | not | * |
| bag | job | was |
| mad | top | for |
| pan | fox | |
| pat | got | |
| cab | top | |
| jam | not | |

### 16. Short *e, u*

| | | |
|---|---|---|
| pet | but | * |
| bell | sun | put |
| red | cup | push |
| yes | mud | |
| let | cut | |
| ten | hug | |
| beg | duck | |
| | gum | |

### 17. Short *a, i, o*

| | | |
|---|---|---|
| hat | big | pop |
| fan | six | rock |
| cab | lip | box |
| tax | did | mom |
| bat | dig | stop |
| back | zip | lock |
| | will | hop |
| | win | hot |

### 18. All Short Vowels

| | | | | |
|---|---|---|---|---|
| can | let | hit | sock | hug |
| that | fed | fish | mop | luck |
| lap | met | fill | dot | run |
| last | web | six | box | bus |
| sack | fell | this | rob | pup |
| | wet | sick | | bun |
| | | wig | | rug |

### 19. Short Vowels with Digraphs

| | | |
|---|---|---|
| that | ship | when |
| chat | chill | check |
| than | whip | shed |
| shall | this | shell |
| shack | whiz | then |
| chap | chip | them |
| wham | thin | |
| | thick | |

### 20. Two-Step Sort with Blends and Short Vowels

**a.** Initial consonant and blends

| | | | | |
|---|---|---|---|---|
| rack | tack | dug | trick | drum |
| rag | tag | dip | track | drill |
| rash | tap | duck | trash | drag |
| rug | tick | | trap | drug |
| rip | | | trip | drip |
| | | | truck | |

**b.** Short vowels

| | | |
|---|---|---|
| tack | tick | truck |
| tap | trip | drum |
| trash | drill | dug |
| drag | dip | rug |
| rack | rip | duck |
| rag | trick | drug |
| rash | drip | |
| trap | | |

**21. Two-Step Sort with Blends and Short Vowels**

**a.** Blends

| | | |
|---|---|---|
| cram | slip | spill |
| crab | slid | spin |
| crash | slap | spot |
| crib | clock | snap |
| brag | blob | |
| brat | flag | |
| grip | flop | |
| | flock | |

**b.** Vowels

| | | |
|---|---|---|
| crab | clip | trot |
| cram | slid | drop |
| brag | spill | spot |
| brat | grip | flop |
| slap | slip | clock |
| crash | spin | blob |
| flag | crib | flock |
| snap | twig | |

**22. Two-Step Sort with Presconsonantal Nasals and Short Vowels**

**a.** Preconsonantal Nasals

| | | | | |
|---|---|---|---|---|
| sang | camp | pant | pink | sand |
| king | lamp | plant | think | land |
| sing | stamp | print | junk | |
| swing | limp | hunt | trunk | |
| sting | jump | want | | |
| sung | bump | | | |

**b.** Short Vowels

| | | | |
|---|---|---|---|
| sang | king | jump | * |
| camp | limp | sung | want |
| sand | print | bump | |
| lamp | pink | junk | |
| pant | sing | hunt | |
| land | think | trunk | |
| plant | swing | skunk | |
| stamp | sting | | |

*Note:* Oddballs are in columns marked with asterisks.

# Within Word Pattern Focused Contrasts

**23.** Short/Long *a*

| | | |
|---|---|---|
| hat | name | * |
| jack | date | have |
| ask | race | what |
| slap | plane | |
| fast | cape | |
| lamp | page | |
| flag | same | |
| pass | safe | |
| path | gave | |
| glad | gate | |

**24.** Short/Long *a*

| | | |
|---|---|---|
| cap | lake | rain |
| last | wave | wait |
| plan | late | nail |
| sat | tape | gain |
| flat | bake | fail |
| tax | base | pail |
| | shade | plain |
| | made | sail |
| | maze | |
| | sale | |

**25.** Long *a* Patterns

| | | | |
|---|---|---|---|
| same | mail | day | * |
| whale | pain | say | said |
| flake | train | play | have |
| grape | paid | may | |
| stage | brain | pay | |
| grade | snail | stay | |
| chase | chain | clay | |
| shave | tail | | |
| tale | waist | | |
| waste | | | |

**26.** Short/Long *e*

| | | |
|---|---|---|
| well | week | she |
| step | peel | he |
| west | weed | we |
| men | peek | me |
| bed | speed | |
| help | keep | |
| belt | pee | |

## 27. Short/Long e

| best | green | mean | * |
|------|-------|------|---|
| left | wheel | team | been |
| neck | sheet | deal | head |
| bell | need | reach | |
| bled | bleed | beach | |
| yet | teeth | steam | |
| | creep | clean | |
| | speed | bean | |

## 28. Short/Long e

| mess | head | neat |
|------|------|------|
| rest | dead | meal |
| bell | deaf | speak |
| kept | breath | meat |
| nest | death | treat |
| shell | dread | sneak |
| vest | bread | heat |

## 29. Short/Long i

| dish | hike | * |
|------|------|---|
| chip | ride | give |
| kick | ripe | live |
| whip | nice | |
| twin | white | |
| miss | dime | |
| pick | fine | |
| rich | life | |

## 30. Short/Long i

| clip | mine | try | * |
|------|------|-----|---|
| win | price | fly | eye |
| trick | spine | shy | buy |
| gift | lime | why | bye |
| list | wife | sky | |
| mitt | vine | dry | |
| thick | five | | |
| swim | | | |

## 31. Short/Long o

| lock | home | * |
|------|------|---|
| odd | slope | move |
| crop | note | gone |
| shot | hose | some |
| clock | vote | |
| shock | joke | |
| knob | smoke | |
| slot | hope | |
| | choke | |

## 32. Long-o Patterns

| rope | road | blow | * |
|------|------|------|---|
| woke | boat | grow | now |
| close | soap | know | cow |
| stone | soak | slow | |
| bone | moan | throw | |
| phone | loaf | snow | |
| broke | coach | low | |
| hole | load | bow | |
| vote | toast | flow | |

## 33. Short/Long u

| bun | June | blue | * |
|-----|------|------|---|
| fuss | cute | glue | truth |
| luck | rule | clue | |
| lump | tube | due | |
| trust | tune | true | |
| plum | huge | | |
| crust | cube | | |

## 34. Long u Patterns

| rude | fruit | new | * |
|------|-------|-----|---|
| crude | suit | chew | fuel |
| flute | juice | drew | build |
| mule | bruise | knew | |
| fume | cruise | stew | |
| chute | | few | |
| dune | | dew | |
| use | | brew | |

## 35. Less Common Long a

| hay | prey | eight | break |
|------|------|-------|-------|
| tray | they | weigh | great |
| stray | obey | vein | steak |
| pray | hey | veil | |
| sway | | freight | |
| play | | sleigh | |
| | | neigh | |

## 36. r-Influenced a

| car | care | chair | * |
|------|------|-------|---|
| star | share | pair | bear |
| bark | bare | hair | |
| card | mare | air | |
| far | rare | | |
| dark | scare | | |
| arm | hare | | |
| start | | | |

## 37. Less Common Long e

| greed | chief | these | * |
|-------|-------|-------|---|
| speech | field | scene | vein |
| greet | brief | theme | friend |
| creek | grief | eve | seize |
| fleet | shriek | | |
| geese | piece | | |
| cheese | thief | | |
| | niece | | |

## 38. r-Influenced e

| her | near | cheer | bear | * |
|------|------|-------|------|---|
| fern | clear | deer | pear | heart |
| germ | dear | sneer | wear | |
| jerk | year | queer | swear | |
| herb | spear | peer | | |
| herd | beard | | | |
| perch | | | | |

## 39. Long i Patterns

| kite | might | mind |
|------|-------|------|
| bride | night | wild |
| write | right | kind |
| spice | bright | blind |
| hide | light | find |
| wipe | tight | child |
| mice | sight | mild |
| | grind | |

## 40. r-Blends/ r-Influenced i

| grin | third | hire |
|------|-------|------|
| bring | shirt | tire |
| drip | dirt | fire |
| grill | bird | wire |
| trick | skirt | tired |
| drink | girl | |
| brick | | |
| crib | | |

### 41. Ambiguous/Long *o*

| | | | |
|---|---|---|---|
| soft | roll | ghost | * |
| moth | cold | most | son |
| cost | stroll | host | from |
| cross | mold | post | |
| cloth | scold | | |
| lost | fold | | |
| toss | told | | |
| frost | folk | | |
| long | | | |

### 42. *r*-Influenced *o*

| | | | |
|---|---|---|---|
| for | more | door | * |
| born | store | poor | your |
| short | chore | floor | |
| porch | tore | | |
| storm | shore | | |
| north | score | | |
| fort | wore | | |
| torch | swore | | |

*Note:* Oddballs are marked with asterisks.

### 43. Other Long *u*

| | | |
|---|---|---|
| gloom | new | who |
| bloom | grew | to |
| roost | crew | too |
| smooth | flew | two |
| scoop | blew | |
| school | stew | |
| mood | dew | |
| pool | knew | |

### 44. *r*-Influenced *u*

| | | |
|---|---|---|
| hurt | cure | heard |
| turn | pure | learn |
| church | sure | earn |
| burst | lure | pearl |
| curl | | yearn |
| purr | | earth |
| purse | | search |

### 45. *r*-Blends/Vowels

| | |
|---|---|
| grill | girl |
| trap | tarp |
| crush | curl |
| fry | first |
| price | purse |
| track | dark |
| brag | bark |
| drip | dirt |
| frog | fort |

### 46. *r*-Influenced Vowels

| | | |
|---|---|---|
| car | her | for |
| shark | first | short |
| farm | bird | corn |
| hard | burn | horn |
| card | word | scorn |
| yard | worm | torn |
| scar | world | |
| march | dirt | |
| | jerk | |

### 47. *ck, k, ke*

| | | |
|---|---|---|
| lick | leak | like |
| lack | seek | lake |
| tack | soak | take |
| snack | sleek | snake |
| stuck | weak | stake |
| stick | week | strike |
| whack | croak | wake |

### 48. CVCe Sorts across Vowels

| | | | |
|---|---|---|---|
| cave | drive | drove | huge |
| crane | while | those | fume |
| taste | smile | throne | prune |
| stage | twice | phone | chute |
| trade | crime | wrote | flute |
| waste | guide | quote | mule |

### 49. CVVC across Vowels

| | | | |
|---|---|---|---|
| road | team | rain | * |
| boast | stream | strain | board |
| coach | sweet | claim | great |
| groan | queen | waist | |
| throat | peach | faith | |
| toast | thief | praise | |
| roast | peace | strain | |
| | | trail | |

## Ambiguous Vowels and Complex Consonants

### 50. Diphthongs

| | | | |
|---|---|---|---|
| toy | coin | town | sound |
| boy | foil | clown | mouth |
| joy | boil | brown | scout |
| | spoil | gown | round |
| | noise | frown | couch |
| | point | howl | loud |

### 51. More Diphthongs

| | | |
|---|---|---|
| row | owl | out |
| snow | growl | found |
| blown | drown | shout |
| flown | crown | cloud |
| grown | plow | south |
| thrown | fowl | foul |
| | prowl | doubt |

### 52. Ambiguous Vowels

| | | | |
|---|---|---|---|
| salt | hawk | fault | * |
| bald | draw | caught | fought |
| chalk | lawn | cause | ought |
| stall | raw | taught | |
| false | crawl | sauce | |
| small | claw | haul | |
| walk | paw | pause | |

### 53. Words Spelled with *w*

| | | |
|---|---|---|
| watch | war | wrap |
| swamp | warn | wreck |
| swan | warm | write |
| wand | dwarf | wrist |
| swat | swarm | wren |
| wash | wart | wrong |

### 54. Complex Consonants

| | | | |
|---|---|---|---|
| scram | straight | shrank | square |
| scrape | strange | shrink | squawk |
| scratch | stretch | shred | squint |
| screech | strict | shrunk | squash |
| screw | string | shriek | squeeze |
| screen | strong | shrimp | squirt |
| scrap | | | |

### 55. *tch* and *ch*

| | | |
|---|---|---|
| catch | reach | * |
| witch | coach | rich |
| patch | peach | such |
| fetch | roach | |
| hutch | screech | |
| itch | beach | |
| switch | pouch | |
| ditch | | |
| latch | | |

### 56. *dge* and *ge*

| | |
|---|---|
| badge | page |
| ridge | stage |
| edge | huge |
| fudge | rage |
| bridge | cage |
| judge | |
| hedge | |
| lodge | |

### 57. Hard and Soft *c* and *g* across Vowels

| | | | | |
|---|---|---|---|---|
| cave | coat | cute | cent | cyst |
| camp | coast | cup | cell | gym |
| cast | cost | cue | cease | |
| gave | gold | gum | gem | |
| gain | golf | gush | germ | |
| gasp | goof | | | |

### 58. *ce, ge, ve, se*

| | | | |
|---|---|---|---|
| dance | charge | glove | cheese |
| chance | large | give | please |
| prince | wedge | curve | tease |
| fence | dodge | shove | loose |
| since | ridge | live | choose |
| voice | edge | above | |
| juice | change | have | |

## Concept Sorts

### 59. What Lives in Water?

| Yes | No |
|---|---|
| frog | toad |
| fish | lizard |
| whale | zebra |
| sea turtle | tortoise |
| clam | elephant |
| crab | horse |

### 60. Edible Plants

| Grain | Fruit | Vegetable |
|---|---|---|
| wheat | apples | carrots |
| oats | peaches | beans |
| rice | berries | lettuce |
| rye | pears | cucumber |
| barley | bananas | cabbage |
| | oranges | beets |

### 61. Animal Attributes

| Fish | Bird | Mammal |
|---|---|---|
| scale | feather | hair |
| eggs | eggs | born alive |
| gills | lungs | lungs |
| heart | heart | heart |
| fins | wings | legs |

### 62. States

| East | West | North | South |
|---|---|---|---|
| Virginia | California | Maine | Florida |
| Delaware | Nevada | Vermont | Mississippi |
| Maryland | Utah | New York | Texas |
| | Arizona | | Alabama |

### 63. Geometry Terms

| Shapes | Lines | Measurements |
|---|---|---|
| triangle | ray | perimeter |
| rhombus | angle | degrees |
| square | line | diameter |
| rectangle | right angle | circumference |
| parallelogram | obtuse angle | area |
| isosceles triangle | | radius |

# Syllables and Affixes Focused Contrasts

## Inflected Endings (*ed* and *ing*), Consonant Doubling, and Plurals

### 64. Sort for Sound of *ed*

| /t/ | /id/ | /d/ |
|-----|------|-----|
| trapped | waited | played |
| mixed | dotted | mailed |
| stopped | patted | boiled |
| chased | treated | raised |
| cracked | traded | tried |
| walked | ended | filled |
| asked | handed | seemed |

### 65. Plural Words (*s* and *es*)

| | | | |
|---|---|---|---|
| cows | boxes | buses | dishes |
| chicks | mixes | glasses | benches |
| farms | axes | dresses | watches |
| fences | foxes | passes | lashes |
| gates | | gases | churches |
| horses | | guesses | ashes |
| | | | brushes |

### 66. Plurals with *y*

| | |
|---|---|
| babies | plays |
| carries | monkeys |
| ponies | boys |
| bodies | trays |
| pennies | donkeys |
| worries | enjoys |
| daddies | turkeys |
| berries | valleys |

### 67. Base Words + *ed* and *ing*

| | | |
|---|---|---|
| jump | jumped | jumping |
| hike | hiked | hiking |
| dress | dressed | dressing |
| wait | waited | waiting |
| stop | stopped | stopping |
| pass | passed | passing |
| live | lived | living |
| wag | wagged | wagging |

### 68. Adding *ing* (double and *e*-drop)

| | |
|---|---|
| batting | baking |
| shopping | skating |
| bragging | biting |
| hopping | hoping |
| humming | sliding |
| begging | waving |
| skipping | moving |
| swimming | caring |

### 69. Adding *ed* (double, nothing)

| | | |
|---|---|---|
| slipped | picked | traded |
| grabbed | called | baked |
| stopped | tracked | wasted |
| wagged | peeled | liked |
| tripped | watched | stared |
| knotted | cheered | waved |
| rubbed | talked | skated |
| whizzed | dreamed | tasted |

### 70. Adding *ing* (double, *e*-drop, nothing)

| | | | | |
|---|---|---|---|---|
| trimming | diving | pushing | floating | * |
| running | riding | jumping | raining | mixing |
| popping | sliding | finding | sleeping | taxing |
| dragging | driving | kicking | boating | |
| wagging | wasting | wanting | waiting | |
| quitting | whining | munching | cheering | |

### 71. Past Tense Verbs

| | | | |
|---|---|---|---|
| kneel | knelt | chase | chased |
| teach | taught | mix | mixed |
| bring | brought | walk | walked |
| deal | dealt | bake | baked |
| sweep | swept | shop | shopped |
| send | sent | | |
| think | thought | | |
| lend | lent | | |
| drink | drank | | |

## Syllable Juncture

### 72. Compound Words

| | | | |
|---|---|---|---|
| landfill | downtown | backyard | homework |
| homeland | downstairs | backbone | homemade |
| wasteland | lowdown | backpack | hometown |
| landlord | downcast | backward | homeroom |
| landslide | downfall | bareback | homesick |
| landscape | downpour | flashback | |
| landmark | breakdown | piggyback | |
| mainland | countdown | paperback | |

### 73. VCCV at Juncture (same/different)

| | |
|---|---|
| button | market |
| sunny | garden |
| yellow | signal |
| happy | member |
| happen | basket |
| sitting | center |
| fellow | plastic |
| matter | tablet |

### 74. Syllable Juncture (VCCV, open VCV)

| | |
|---|---|
| tablet | baby |
| napkin | human |
| happen | music |
| winter | fever |
| foggy | silent |
| tennis | duty |
| sudden | writer |
| fossil | rival |

### 75. VCV Open and Closed

| | | |
|---|---|---|
| meter | petal | * |
| human | rapid | water |
| secret | punish | busy |
| paper | magic | |
| lazy | shiver | |
| even | comet | |
| major | river | |
| climate | clever | |
| crater | proper | |
| clover | liquid | |
| bacon | | |

### 76. Closed VCCV/Open VCV

| | | |
|---|---|---|
| funny | picture | pilot |
| summer | expert | navy |
| pretty | until | nature |
| dollar | forget | music |
| butter | napkin | spoken |
| gossip | canyon | frozen |
| letter | sister | spider |
| pattern | army | student |
| | number | |

### 77. Closed/Open with Endings

| | | |
|---|---|---|
| sadden | dusting | sliding |
| chipped | rented | shining |
| matted | helping | named |
| scarred | sifted | scaring |
| winner | faster | rider |
| biggest | longest | tamest |
| running | walker | moping |

### 78. VCC/CV, VC/CCV, and V/V

| | | | |
|---|---|---|---|
| athlete | pilgrim | create | * |
| pumpkin | control | poet | cruel |
| English | complete | riot | |
| kingdom | children | trial | |
| mushroom | monster | lion | |
| halfway | kitchen | diet | |
| | hundred | | |

# Unaccented Syllables

### 79. *le* and *el*

| | | |
|---|---|---|
| fable | camel | * |
| angle | angel | pencil |
| little | model | journal |
| rattle | gravel | |
| settle | motel | |
| cattle | bushel | |
| nibble | level | |
| turtle | pretzel | |
| table | travel | |
| middle | | |

### 80. *er, ar, or*

| | | |
|---|---|---|
| bigger | burglar | doctor |
| freezer | grammar | favor |
| dreamer | collar | author |
| faster | dollar | editor |
| blister | lunar | tractor |
| jogger | solar | motor |
| speaker | | mayor |
| skater | | |
| smaller | | |

### 81. *er, ar, or*

| Comparatives | Agents | Things |
|---|---|---|
| sweeter | worker | cellar |
| thinner | teacher | meter |
| smarter | waiter | river |
| slower | voter | pillar |
| younger | actor | anchor |
| gentler | beggar | vapor |
| steeper | barber | trailer |
| cheaper | skater | flower |

### 82. Final *en/on/in/ain*

| | | | |
|---|---|---|---|
| broken | dragon | cousin | mountain |
| hidden | weapon | cabin | captain |
| heaven | apron | napkin | fountain |
| chosen | ribbon | pumpkin | curtain |
| children | gallon | | certain |
| eleven | cotton | | |

### 83. Unaccented First Syllables

| | | |
|---|---|---|
| again | decide | beyond |
| away | design | begin |
| another | defend | between |
| aloud | debate | behave |
| agree | depend | before |
| afraid | | beside |
| awoke | | |

### 84. /j/ Sound

| | | |
|---|---|---|
| carriage | budget | magic |
| voyage | agent | engine |
| message | angel | region |
| postage | gorgeous | fragile |
| village | danger | margin |
| storage | legend | logic |
| sausage | pigeon | |
| savage | dungeon | |
| courage | gadget | |

### 85. Changing *y* to *i*

| | | |
|---|---|---|
| cry | cries | cried |
| hurry | hurries | hurried |
| party | parties | partied |
| empty | empties | emptied |
| baby | babies | babied |
| reply | replies | replied |
| supply | supplies | supplied |
| carry | carries | carried |
| fry | fries | fried |

### 86. *y* Words by Part of Speech

| Long *i* | | Long *e* | |
|---|---|---|---|
| Verb | Noun | Adjective | Adverb |
| try | celery | happy | happily |
| certify | candy | pretty | correctly |
| apply | gypsy | guilty | clearly |
| occupy | quarry | angry | safely |
| rely | country | silly | horribly |
| | cemetery | | hourly |
| | category | | certainly |
| | copy | | sensibly |

### 87. Words with *ure* and *er (ture, sure, cher)*

| | | | |
|---|---|---|---|
| capture | measure | archer | * |
| creature | treasure | butcher | injure |
| fracture | pleasure | preacher | failure |
| mixture | closure | stretcher | |
| pasture | leisure | teacher | |
| texture | | rancher | |
| future | | | |
| nature | | | |

# Vowel Patterns in Accented Syllables

### 88. Patterns for Long *a*

| | | |
|---|---|---|
| debate | explain | layer |
| mistake | dainty | dismay |
| amaze | trainer | payment |
| parade | complain | crayons |
| engage | acquaint | hooray |
| bracelet | raisin | decay |
| estate | refrain | betray |
| escape | painter | |

### 89. Patterns for Long *u* and *o*

| | | | |
|---|---|---|---|
| rooster | useful | toaster | suppose |
| cartoon | refuse | oatmeal | decode |
| scooter | amuse | approach | remote |
| balloon | reduce | loafer | erode |
| noodle | conclude | rowboat | tadpole |
| | pollute | goalie | lonesome |
| | perfume | | explode |

### 90. Patterns for Long *e* and *i*

| | | | | * |
|---|---|---|---|---|
| needle | reason | polite | highway | |
| succeed | eager | decide | lightning | sweater |
| fifteen | increase | advice | delight | believe |
| thirteen | defeat | invite | tonight | |
| canteen | season | surprise | resign | |
| steeple | conceal | survive | | |

### 91. Long *u* in Stressed Syllable

| | |
|---|---|
| bu' gle | a muse' |
| future | compute |
| ruby | confuse |
| rumor | reduce |
| tulip | perfume |
| tuna | pollute |
| tutor | salute |
| super | excuse |
| pupil | abuse |
| ruler | include |

### 92. Diphthongs *oi* and *oy*

| | |
|---|---|
| moisture | joyful |
| appoint | boycott |
| poison | royal |
| turquoise | soybean |
| moisten | oyster |
| pointless | voyage |
| broiler | annoy |
| embroider | enjoy |
| rejoice | destroy |
| noisy | employ |
| avoid | |
| pointed | |

### 93. Diphthongs *ou* and *ow*

| | | * |
|---|---|---|
| county | flower | |
| council | allow | double |
| lousy | brownie | |
| fountain | vowel | |
| mountain | shower | |
| scoundrel | towel | |
| counter | tower | |
| around | chowder | |
| bounty | coward | |
| mouthful | drowsy | |
| | powder | |
| | power | |

### 94. Spelling the *er* Sound in Accented and Unaccented Syllables

| | | | |
|---|---|---|---|
| cer'tain | re verse' | sur prise' | lan'tern |
| person | observe | perhaps | concert |
| thirsty | alert | survive | modern |
| service | prefer | surround | western |
| hurry | emerge | | govern |
| turkey | | | |

---

*Note:* Oddballs are in columns marked with asterisks.

## Affixes

### 95. Prefixes

| | | |
|---|---|---|
| unfair | retell | disagree |
| unable | replay | disappear |
| uncover | retrain | disgrace |
| unkind | return | disarm |
| undress | reuse | disorder |
| unplug | research | disobey |
| unequal | regain | disable |
| uneven | reword | displaced |
| unpack | rebuild | disloyal |
| unusual | remodel | dishonest |

### 96. More Prefixes

| | | |
|---|---|---|
| preschool | explode | misspell |
| preview | exceed | mistreat |
| prevent | expose | misplace |
| preheat | explore | misuse |
| prefix | exile | misbehave |
| prepare | expand | mistake |
| predict | exclaim | |

### 97. Number Prefixes

| | | |
|---|---|---|
| unicycle | bicycle | tricycle |
| unison | biweekly | trilogy |
| unicorn | bisect | triangle |
| unique | bilingual | tripod |
| uniform | biplane | triple |
| universe | bifocals | trio |
| | | triplets |

### 98. Suffixes

| | | |
|---|---|---|
| sunny | slowly | happily |
| rainy | quickly | angrily |
| foggy | sadly | nosily |
| guilty | calmly | busily |
| bossy | bravely | drily |
| dirty | hardly | daintily |
| messy | strangely | gaily |
| wordy | weakly | greedily |

### 99. More Suffixes

| | | |
|---|---|---|
| darkness | harmless | colorful |
| kindness | fearless | faithful |
| illness | homeless | dreadful |
| weakness | restless | thankful |
| freshness | ageless | thoughtful |
| hardness | mindless | painful |
| blindness | helpless | |

# Derivational Relations Focused Contrasts

## Adding Suffixes

### 100. Adding *-ion*

| ct + -ion | | ss + -ion | |
|---|---|---|---|
| act | action | express | expression |
| distinct | distinction | impress | impression |
| select | selection | process | procession |
| extinct | extinction | depress | depression |
| predict | prediction | success | succession |
| subtract | subtraction | profess | profession |
| contract | contraction | discuss | discussion |
| affect | affection | | |

**101.** *e*-Drop + *-ion*

| *te* + *-ion* | | *ce* + *-ion* | | *se* + *-ion* | |
|---|---|---|---|---|---|
| educate | education | induce | induction | expulse | expulsion |
| congratulate | congratulation | introduce | introduction | convulse | convulsion |
| create | creation | produce | production | repulse | repulsion |
| decorate | decoration | deduce | deduction | | |
| generate | generation | reproduce | reproduction | | |
| imitate | imitation | reduce | reduction | | |
| fascinate | fascination | | | | |
| complicate | complication | | | | |
| separate | separation | | | | |

**102.** *-sion* and Spelling Changes

| *t* to *s* + *-sion* | | *de*-drop, + *-sion* | |
|---|---|---|---|
| commit | commission | explode | explosion |
| transmit | transmission | collide | collision |
| permit | permission | conclude | conclusion |
| emit | emission | persuade | persuasion |
| omit | omission | erode | erosion |
| regret | regression | delude | delusion |
| remit | remission | include | inclusion |
| | | divide | division |
| | | intrude | intrusion |

**103.** *e*-Drop + *-ation* or *-ition*

| *e*-drop + *-ation* | | *e*-drop + *ition* | |
|---|---|---|---|
| admire | admiration | compose | composition |
| determine | determination | define | definition |
| explore | exploration | dispose | disposition |
| combine | combination | oppose | opposition |
| declare | declaration | expose | exposition |
| inspire | inspiration | decompose | decomposition |
| organize | organization | | |
| examine | examination | | |
| perspire | perspiration | | |

**104.** *-ible* and *-able*

| base + *-able* | root + *-ible* |
|---|---|
| dependable | audible |
| expendable | edible |
| breakable | visible |
| agreeable | feasible |
| predictable | terrible |
| remarkable | possible |
| readable | legible |
| profitable | plausible |
| perishable | horrible |
| punishable | tangible |
| laughable | credible |

**105.** *-able* after *e*

| *e*-drop | soft *ce/ge* | hard *c/g* |
|---|---|---|
| presumable | changeable | navigable |
| desirable | manageable | amicable |
| usable | peaceable | despicable |
| lovable | serviceable | impeccable |
| deplorable | noticeable | applicable |
| comparable | | |
| excusable | | |

**106.** Assimilated Prefix Sort

| *com-* | *ad-* | *in-* |
|---|---|---|
| compound | adverse | inactive |
| conform | affair | irresponsible |
| colleague | affront | immature |
| compact | assemble | irrational |
| context | affirm | immortal |
| correlate | arrange | illogical |
| constrain | acclaim | innumerable |
| | admit | illegal |

## Vowel Alternations and Reduced Vowels in Unaccented Syllables

**107.** Vowel Alternations in Related Pairs

| Long *a* to Short *a* | Long *a* to Schwa |
|---|---|
| cave/cavity | major/majority |
| humane/humanity | narrate/narrative |
| nation/national | relate/relative |
| volcano/volcanic | famous/infamous |
| grave/gravity | able/ability |
| nature/natural | native/nativity |
| insane/insanity | educate/educable |
| flame/flammable | proclaim/proclamation |
| profane/profanity | stable/stability |

**108.** Vowel Alternations in Related Pairs

| Long *e* to Short *e* | Long *e* to Schwa |
|---|---|
| serene/serenity | compete/competition |
| brief/brevity | repeat/repetition |
| proceed/procession | remedial/remedy |
| recede/recession | |
| succeed/succession | |
| conceive/conception | |
| receive/reception | |

**109.** Vowel Alternations in Related Pairs

| Long *i* to Short *i* | Long *i* to Schwa |
|---|---|
| resign/resignation | invite/invitation |
| sign/signal | define/definition |
| divine/divinity | reside/resident |
| divide/division | recite/recitation |
| revise/revision | deprive/deprivation |
| deride/derision | admire/admiration |
| criticize/criticism | inspire/inspiration |
| arise/arisen | preside/president |

**110.** Vowel Alternations in Related Pairs

| Long to Short | Long to Schwa | Schwa to Short |
|---|---|---|
| induce/induction | compose/composition | metal/metallic |
| seduce/seduction | propose/proposition | brutal/brutality |
| reduce/reduction | impose/imposition | local/locality |
| produce/production | expose/exposition | spiritual/spirituality |
| telescope/telescopic | harmonious/harmony | vital/vitality |
| microscope/microscopic | compete/competition | fatal/fatality |
| prescribe/prescription | serene/serenity | total/totality |
| | | final/finality |
| | | original/originality |

## Roots to Contrast

**111.** Greek Roots

| | |
|---|---|
| autograph | telegram |
| automatic | telepathy |
| autobiography | telegraph |
| autonomy | televise |
| automobile | telephone |
| autonomous | teleconference |

## Greek and Latin Roots (contrast three or four at a time)

| | | | | | | | |
|---|---|---|---|---|---|---|---|
| judge | traction | suspect | visual | formulate | credit | portable | dictate |
| adjudicate | contract | spectator | visionary | uniform | incredible | porter | contradict |
| judgment | attract | inspect | vision | reform | discredit | reporter | prediction |
| judicial | intractable | respect | vista | transform | creed | portfolio | verdict |
| prejudice | subtraction | spectacular | visible | deformed | credulous | export | dictionary |
| judicious | tractor | inspector | revise | nonconformist | accredit | import | dictator |
| prejudicial | contraction | spectacles | television | | | | diction |
| judiciary | protractor | disrespect | supervise | | | | |
| | distraction | expectation | | | | | |
| | | circumspect | | | | | |

| | | | | | | | |
|---|---|---|---|---|---|---|---|
| conduct | fertile | pressure | respiration | hypodermic | hydrophobia | ecology | astrology |
| induct | refer | express | spirit | hypodermis | hydrology | economy | astronomer |
| educate | transfer | depression | expire | hypothermia | hydrogen | ecosystem | astronaut |
| introduction | suffer | suppress | perspire | hypotension | hydroplane | | asterisk |
| produce | conifer | impression | inspiration | | hydrofoil | | |
| reduce | conference | oppressive | conspire | | | | |
| induction | | | | | | | |

## Creating Your Own Word Sort Sheets

The following lists of words are organized by features students need to study in the letter name–alphabetic through derivational relations stages. The words are generally grouped by frequency and complexity. For example, under short *a*, the early part of the list offers words most likely encountered by first graders (*am*, *ran*, *that*). The latter part of the list contains words that may be more obscure in meaning and spelled with blends or digraphs (*yam*, *brass*, *tramp*). Fry's 300 instant words listed on page 467 are the most frequent words and should be included in beginner sorts.

The lists include possible exceptions or oddballs that can be added to sorts. Sometimes the oddballs you include will be true exceptions (such as *said* in a sort with long-*a* patterns), but other times oddballs may represent a less common spelling pattern, such as *ey* representing long *a* in *prey* and *grey*.

Prepare word sorts to use with students by deciding on a focused contrast such as different long-*a* patterns. You may want to write headers at the top such as patterns labels (that is, *a-e*, *ai*, *ay*) and select the most familiar word as a keyword. For an open sort that challenges students to determine their own categories, omit these headers and keywords. Select the words from the list and write them into a template such as the one on 503 in Appendix G. We recommend that you enlarge the template about 5 to 8 percent before writing in the words neatly. Be sure to insert the words randomly so students can make their own discoveries as they sort. Many people find it easy to create computer-generated word sort sheets using the "table" function in a word processing program. First, set the margins all around at 0.5 inches, and then insert a table that is three columns by six to eight rows. Save the blank template to use again. Type words into each cell, leaving a blank line above and below each word. After typing in all the words, "select" the entire table and click the "center" button. Choose a simple font (Ariel and Geneva work well) and a large font size (26 works well). After creating the sort, save it using a name that identifies the focused contrast, such as "Short Vowels: a, o, e." Here are some reminders and tips about creating your own word sorts.

1. Use focused contrasts that will help students form their own generalizations about how words work. Use a collection of 15 to 25 words so that there are plenty of examples to consider.
2. Contrast at least two, and up to four, patterns or sounds in a sort. There are many sample sorts in Appendix E to give you ideas.

   **Examples of sound sorts:**
   Contrast short *o* and long *o*.
   Contrast the sound of *ear* in *learn* and in *hear*.
   Contrast the sound of *g* in *guest* and *gym*.

   **Examples of pattern sorts:**
   Contrast long *o* spelled with *oa*, *o-e*, and *ow*.
   Contrast words that end with *or*, *er*, and *ar*.
   Contrast words that double a consonant before *-ing* with those that do not.

   **Examples of meaning sorts:**
   Contrast words derived from *spect* and *port*.
   Contrast words with prefixes *sub*, *un*, and *trans*.

3. Consider whether you want to underline keywords or create headers for the sort. Your decision will depend on the level of support you feel your students need, as described in Chapter 3.
4. In most sorts, include up to three oddballs when possible—words that have the same sound or pattern but are not consistent with the generalization that governs the other words. For

example, in a long-*o* sort, with words sorted by the *oa*, *o-e*, and *ow* patterns, the exceptions might include the words *now* and *love* because they look like they would have the long-*o* sound but do not. The best oddballs are high-frequency words students already know from reading. These are listed under *Oddballs* in the word lists in this appendix.

5. Words in a sort can be made easier or harder in a number of ways:

   - Common words such as *hat* or *store* are easier than uncommon words such as *vat* or *boar*. It is important to use words students know from their own reading in the letter name–alphabetic and within word pattern stages to make sorts easier. This is less important when you get to syllables and affixes and derivational relations stages in which words sorts can help to extend a student's vocabulary.
   - Add words with blends, digraphs, and complex consonant units (for example, *ce*, *dge*, or *tch*) to make words harder. *Bat* and *blast* are both CVC words, but *blast* is harder to read and spell.
   - Adding more oddballs to a sort makes the sort harder. But don't use oddballs students are not likely to know (like *plaid* in a long-*a* sort for students early in the within word pattern stage).

# 300 Instant High-Frequency Words

**First Hundred**

| | | | | | |
|---|---|---|---|---|---|
| a | can | her | many | see | us |
| about | come | here | me | she | very |
| after | day | him | much | so | was |
| again | did | his | my | some | we |
| all | do | how | new | take | were |
| an | down | I | no | that | what |
| and | eat | if | not | the | when |
| any | for | in | of | their | which |
| are | from | is | old | them | who |
| as | get | it | on | then | will |
| at | give | just | one | there | with |
| be | go | know | or | they | work |
| been | good | like | other | this | would |
| before | had | little | our | three | you |
| boy | has | long | out | to | your |
| but | have | make | put | two | |
| by | he | man | said | Up | |

**Second Hundred**

| | | | | | |
|---|---|---|---|---|---|
| also | color | home | must | red | think |
| am | could | house | name | right | too |
| another | dear | into | near | run | tree |
| away | each | kind | never | saw | under |
| back | ear | last | next | say | until |
| ball | end | leave | night | school | upon |
| because | far | left | only | seem | use |
| best | find | let | open | shall | want |
| better | first | live | over | should | way |
| big | five | look | own | soon | where |
| black | found | made | people | stand | while |
| book | four | may | play | such | white |
| both | friend | men | please | sure | wish |
| box | girl | more | present | tell | why |
| bring | got | morning | pretty | than | year |
| call | hand | most | ran | these | |
| came | high | mother | read | thing | |

**Third Hundred**

| | | | | | |
|---|---|---|---|---|---|
| along | didn't | food | keep | sat | though |
| always | does | full | letter | second | today |
| anything | dog | funny | longer | set | took |
| around | don't | gave | love | seven | town |
| ask | door | goes | might | show | try |
| ate | dress | green | money | sing | turn |
| bed | early | grow | myself | sister | walk |
| brown | eight | hat | now | sit | warm |
| buy | every | happy | o'clock | six | wash |
| car | eyes | hard | off | sleep | water |
| carry | face | head | once | small | woman |
| clean | fall | hear | order | start | write |
| close | fast | help | pair | stop | yellow |
| clothes | fat | hold | part | ten | yes |
| coat | fine | hope | ride | thank | yesterday |
| cold | fire | hot | round | third | |
| cut | fly | jump | same | those | |

Copyright © 2000 Edward B. Fry. Used with permission.

# Word Lists

## *a* Families

| *at* | *ad* | *ag* | *an* | *ap* | *ab* | *am* | *all* | *ar* | *art* |
|---|---|---|---|---|---|---|---|---|---|
| at* | had* | bag | man* | cap | cab | am** | all* | bar | cart |
| cat | bad | rag | than** | lap | dab | dam | ball** | car | dart |
| bat | dad | sag | ran** | gap | jab | ham | call** | far** | mart |
| fat | mad | wag | can* | map | nab | ram | tall | jar | part |
| hat | pad | nag | fan | nap | lab | jam | fall | par | tart |
| mat | sad | flag | pan | rap | tab | clam | hall | star | start |
| pat | rad | brag | tan | yap | blab | slam | mall | | chart |
| rat | glad | drag | van | tap | crab | cram | wall | | smart |
| sat | lad | shag | plan | zap | scab | wham | small | | |
| that* | | snag | clan | clap | stab | swam | stall | | |
| flat | | lag | scan | flap | grab | yam | | | |
| brat | | tag | | slap | slab | gram | | | |
| chat | | | | trap | | | | | |
| gnat | | | | chap | | | | | |
| | | | | snap | | | | | |
| | | | | wrap | | | | | |
| | | | | strap | | | | | |

| *and* | *ang* | *ash* | *ack* | *ank* | *amp* | *ast* | *ant* | *atch* | *ass* |
|---|---|---|---|---|---|---|---|---|---|
| hand** | bang | bash | back** | bank | camp | fast | ant | batch | mass |
| band | fang | cash | pack | sank | damp | cast | pant | catch | pass |
| land | hang | dash | jack | tank | lamp | past | chant | hatch | class |
| sand | sang | gash | rack | yank | ramp | last** | slant | latch | grass |
| brand | rang | hash | lack | blank | champ | mast | grant | match | brass |
| grand | clang | mash | sack | plank | clamp | vast | plant | patch | glass |
| stand** | | rash | tack | crank | cramp | | | snatch | bass |
| strand | | sash | black** | drank | stamp | | | scratch | |
| | | lash | quack | prank | tramp | | | | |
| | | trash | crack | spank | scamp | | | | |
| | | crash | track | thank | | | | | |
| | | smash | shack | | | | | | |
| | | slash | snack | | | | | | |
| | | clash | stack | | | | | | |
| | | flash | | | | | | | |

## More Short-*a* Words

| | | | | | | *Oddballs* | |
|---|---|---|---|---|---|---|---|
| as* | wax | bath | fact | draft | ranch | want** | saw** |
| has* | ask | path | mask | shaft | grasp | what* | laugh |
| gal | yak | task | bask | craft | plant | was* | |
| pal | tax | calf | raft | staff | shall** | | |
| gas | math | half | lamb | graph | branch | | |

*Occurs in first 100 instant words.

**Occurs in second 100 instant words.

## e Families

| et | en | ed | ell | eg | ess | eck | est | end | ent |
|----|-----|-----|------|-----|-------|-------|-------|-------|-------|
| get* | men** | red** | tell** | beg | less | deck | best** | end** | bent |
| let** | den | bed | bell | peg | mess | neck | nest | bend | dent |
| bet | hen | fed | cell | leg | guess | peck | pest | lend | cent |
| met | ten | led | fell | keg | bless | wreck | rest | mend | lent |
| net | pen | wed | jell | | dress | speck | test | send | rent |
| pet | then* | bled | sell | | press | check | vest | tend | sent |
| set | when* | fled | well | | stress | fleck | west | blend | tent |
| wet | wren | sled | shell | | | | chest | spend | vent |
| vet | Ben | shed | smell | | | | jest | trend | went |
| fret | Ken | shred | spell | | | | crest | | scent |
| jet | | | swell | | | | guest | | spent |
| yet | | | dwell | | | | | | |

## More Short-e Words

| | | | | | | | | Spelled ea | |
|----|------|------|--------|-------|-------|--------|--------|--------|--------|
| yes | gem | pep | left** | melt | self | etch | clench | read** | death |
| web | them* | step | kept | pelt | shelf | fetch | drench | head | breath |
| egg | hem | held | slept | knelt | fresh | sketch | tempt | bread | dread |
| elm | stem | help | wept | | flesh | wretch | tenth | dead | deaf |
| next** | | desk | swept | | | stretch | debt | lead | wealth |
| | | | | | | | | tread | health |
| | | | | | | | | spread | breast |
| | | | | | | | | thread | threat |

## Short-i Families

| it | id | ig | in | ill | im | ip | ick | ink | int | itch | ing |
|-----|------|------|------|-------|------|------|-------|--------|-------|--------|--------|
| it* | did* | big** | in* | will* | dim | dip | lick | link | mint | itch | king |
| bit | hid | dig | fin | dill | him* | hip | kick | mink | lint | pitch | ping |
| fit | lid | fig | pin | fill | Jim | lip | pick | pink | hint | ditch | sing |
| hit | kid | jig | tin | hill | Kim | nip | sick | sink | print | hitch | ring |
| lit | bid | pig | din | kill | rim | rip | tick | rink | glint | witch | wing |
| pit | rid | rig | win | gill | Tim | sip | slick | wink | flint | switch | thing** |
| sit | slid | wig | bin | mill | trim | tip | quick | think** | | | bring** |
| kit | skid | zig | thin | pill | brim | zip | trick | blink | | | sling |
| wit | | twig | twin | till | swim | whip | chick | drink | | | sting |
| skit | | | chin | bill | slim | clip | flick | stink | | | swing |
| spit | | | shin | drill | whim | flip | brick | clink | | | spring |
| slit | | | spin | grill | grim | slip | stick | shrink | | | string |
| quit | | | grin | chill | skim | skip | thick | | | | cling |
| | | | | skill | | drip | click | | | | fling |
| | | | | spill | | trip | prick | | | | wring |
| | | | | still | | chip | | | | | |
| | | | | thrill | | ship | | | | | |
| | | | | quill | | snip | | | | | |
| | | | | | | strip | | | | | |

## More Short-i Words

| | | | | | | | | | | | Oddballs |
|------|--------|------|------|------|--------|------|------|-------|-------|-------|--------|
| if* | his* | mix | mitt | crib | cliff | rich | film | risk | swift | disc | child |
| is* | this* | six | hiss | fish | stiff | wind | tilt | brisk | inch | sixth | mind |
| with* | which* | fix | kiss | dish | lift | fist | limp | sift | pinch | fifth | find** |
| wish** | live** | whiz | milk | swish | gift | inn | limb | shift | | | climb |

### Short-*o* Families

| ot | | ob | og† | op | ock | ong | oss |
|---|---|---|---|---|---|---|---|
| not* | blot | bob | dog | cop | cock | long* | boss |
| got** | slot | cob | bog | hop | dock | bong | toss |
| hot | plot | job | fog | pop | lock | gong | moss |
| jot | shot | rob | hog | mop | mock | song | loss |
| lot | spot | gob | jog | top | rock | strong | gloss |
| pot | knot | mob | log | slop | sock | throng | cross |
| cot | trot | sob | clog | flop | tock | | |
| dot | | snob | frog | drop | block | | |
| | | blob | | shop | clock | | |
| | | glob | | stop | flock | | |
| | | knob | | crop | smock | | |
| | | throb | | plop | shock | | |
| | | | | prop | stock | | |

### More Short-*o* Words

| | | | | | *Ambiguous Sounds of o†* | | | *Oddballs* | |
|---|---|---|---|---|---|---|---|---|---|
| box** | rod | prod | fond | notch | on* | lost | moth | of* | for* |
| ox | sod | odd | bond | romp | off | cost | cloth | won | from* |
| fox | god | mom | blond | stomp | loft | frost | broth | son | cold |
| pox | plod | con | gosh | prompt | soft | doll | golf | front | post |

### *u* Families

| ut | ub | ug | um | un | ud | uck | ump | ung |
|---|---|---|---|---|---|---|---|---|
| but* | cub | bug | bum | run** | bud | buck | bump | sung |
| cut | hub | dug | gum | fun | mud | duck | jump | rung |
| gut | rub | hug | hum | gun | stud | luck | dump | hung |
| hut | tub | jug | sum | bun | thud | suck | hump | lung |
| nut | club | mug | plum | sun | | tuck | lump | swung |
| rut | grub | rug | slum | spun | | yuck | pump | clung |
| jut | snub | tug | scum | stun | | pluck | rump | strung |
| shut | stub | slug | chum | | | cluck | plump | slung |
| strut | scrub | plug | drum | | | truck | stump | sprung |
| | shrub | drug | strum | | | stuck | thump | wrung |
| | | snug | | | | | clump | flung |
| | | | | | | | slump | stung |
| | | | | | | | grump | |

| uff | unk | ush | ust | unch | umb |
|---|---|---|---|---|---|
| buff | bunk | gush | must** | bunch | dumb |
| cuff | hunk | hush | just* | hunch | numb |
| huff | junk | mush | gust | lunch | crumb |
| muff | sunk | rush | dust | munch | thumb |
| ruff | chunk | blush | bust | punch | plumb |
| puff | drunk | brush | rust | crunch | |
| fluff | flunk | crush | crust | brunch | |
| stuff | skunk | flush | trust | | |
| snuff | shrunk | slush | | | |
| scuff | stunk | | | | |
| gruff | slunk | | | | |
| bluff | trunk | | | | |

†These words do not have a short *o* in some dialects, but instead are pronounced as "aw."

**More Short-*u* Words**

|  |  |  |  |  | ul‡ | ou = u | o = u | o-e =u | Oddballs |
|---|---|---|---|---|---|---|---|---|---|
| up* | much* | buzz | gull | hunt | gulp | tough | of* | come* | put* |
| us* | such** | fuzz | dull | grunt | bulge | rough | does | some* | push |
| pup | plus | tusk | mutt | stunt | bulk | touch | son | none | bush |
| cup | thus | dusk | butt | shucks | gulf | young | ton | done | truth |
| bus | fuss | husk | tuft |  | sulk |  | won | love |  |
|  |  |  |  |  | pulse |  | from* | dove |  |
|  |  |  |  |  |  |  | front | glove |  |

**Long-*a* Words**

**CVCe** (*a-e*)

| | | | | |
|---|---|---|---|---|
| made** | ate | wake | tame | ape |
| name** | gate | fake | fame | gape |
| same | hate | shake | flame | grape |
| came** | late | brake | blame | drape |
| make* | date | flake | lame | trace |
| take* | sale | base | lane | grace |
| bake | male | vase | plane | space |
| cake | tale | chase | cane | waste |
| lake | whale | race | crane | paste |
| age | pale | lace | rate | taste |
| cage | fade | place | fate | haste |
| page | wade | pace | crate | sake |
| face | shade | state | grate | quake |
| gave | grade | plate | bathe | drake |
| save | trade | skate | cave | phase |
| wave | shape | rage | grave | jade |
| tape | cape | stage |  | blade |
| safe | mate |  |  |  |

**C V VC** (*ai*)

| | | | |
|---|---|---|---|
| pane | rain | wait | snail |
| vane | pain | bait | frail |
| mane | tail | gain | praise |
| slate | nail | vain | trail |
| scale | mail | main | strait |
| stale | sail | plain | saint |
| gaze | pail | chain | quaint |
| daze | rail | stain | strain |
| blaze | fail | drain | faith |
| graze | jail | grain | straight |
| haze | gain | brain | raise |
| range | main | aim |  |
| change | train | claim |  |
| strange | aid | ail |  |
|  | paid | aide |  |
| *Oddballs* |  |  | *Oddballs* |
| have* | maid | raid | said* |
| dance | laid | paint | again* |
| chance | braid | waist | their* |

**C V V Open** (*ay*)

| |
|---|
| day |
| jay |
| may** |
| play** |
| say** |
| stay |
| way** |
| clay |
| gray |
| pray |
| tray |
| slay |
| *Oddballs* |
| they* |
| prey |
| grey |

**C V VC** (*ei*)

| |
|---|
| eight |
| neigh |
| rein |
| weigh |
| weight |
| eighth |
| freight |
| reign |
| veil |
| sleigh |
| beige |
| heir |
| vein |
| *Oddballs* |
| break |
| great |
| steak |

## Long-e Words

| CV CVV Open | CVCe | C V VC | | | | | | | | ie | |
|---|---|---|---|---|---|---|---|---|---|---|---|
| *-e, -ee* | *e-e* | *ea* | | | | *ee* | | | | *ie* | *Oddballs* |
| me* | eve | read** | beak | east | leave** | seem** | kneel | spree | geese | thief | been* |
| he* | scene | sea | leak | feast | weave | feed | steel | screen | cheese | chief | seize |
| be* | scheme | eat* | weak | least | flea | feel | keep | greet | sneeze | grief | suite |
| she* | theme | beat | peak | clean | peace | feet | deep | sheet | breeze | brief | vein |
| we* | these** | seat | lean | steal | please** | beet | beep | greed | freeze | yield | weird |
| the* | | meat | heal | knead | cease | meet | seep | reef | sleeve | field | their |
| see* | | mean | real | sneak | crease | seen | jeep | breed | | shield | friend** |
| bee | | bean | deal | creak | grease | week | sheep | keen | | niece | dead |
| wee | | seal | meal | steam | squeal | peek | sleep | teeth | | piece | head |
| tree** | | tea | heap | dream | league | seed | | queen | | shriek | deaf |
| flee | | pea | leap | cream | breathe | need | heel | eel | | pier | steak |
| glee | | bead | seam | scream | | peep | reel | sweep | | siege | great |
| three* | | neat | each** | stream | | beef | peel | creep | | grieve | break |
| knee | | team | teach | plead | | week | speed | steep | | fierce | |
| free | | beam | beach | knead | | seek | bleed | sleet | | fiend | |
| | | lead | reach | beast | | weed | cheek | street | | priest | |
| | | ear** | peach | treat | | deed | sweet | fleet | | | |
| | | | | squeak | | green | sleek | speech | | | |
| | | | | | | wheel | creek | preen | | | |

‡These words have a slightly different *u* sound before the *l*.

## Long-i Words

| CVCe | | | | | | CVV-Open | CV-Open | VCC | |
|---|---|---|---|---|---|---|---|---|---|
| *i-e* | | | | | | *ie* | *y/ye* | *igh* | |
| like* | five** | while** | wide | white** | tribe | lie | my* | high** | find** |
| bike | mine | ice | slide | quite | scribe | pie | by* | night** | kind** |
| dime | fine | mice | pride | write | stride | tie | why** | right** | mind |
| time | nine | nice | tide | spite | stripe | die | fly | light | climb |
| hide | vine | rice | glide | site | strike | | cry | might | child |
| ride | shine | mile | wipe | lice | spine | *Oddballs* | sky | bright | wild |
| side | drive | file | pipe | spice | whine | buy | try | fight | mild |
| line | dive | pile | swipe | slice | prime | guy | dry | sigh | blind |
| live | hive | smile | spike | twice | chime | live** | shy | tight | grind |
| kite | life | wise | lime | price | fife | give* | sly | flight | hind |
| size | ripe | rise | crime | guide | knife | eye | spry | fright | sign |
| bite | hike | wife | pine | prize | thrive | | dye | sight | bind |
| | | | | | | | lye | slight | wind |
| | | | | | | | rye | thigh | rind |

## Long-o Words

| CVCe | | | | C V VC | | | CV Open | C V V | VCC | |
|---|---|---|---|---|---|---|---|---|---|---|
| *o-e* | | | | *oa* | | | *o* | *ow* | *oCC* | |
| home** | wove | rove | slope | boat | foam | float | go* | bow | old* | both** |
| nose | drove | cove | lope | coat | roam | coach | no* | know* | gold | most** |
| hole | dome | stove | lone | goat | goal | roach | so* | show | hold | folk |
| rope | globe | whole | stroke | road | coal | throat | ho | slow | cold | roll |
| robe | cone | sole | throne | toad | loaf | toast | yo-yo | snow | told | poll |
| note | zone | wrote | quote | load | coax | coast | | crow | fold | stroll |
| hose | role | choke | clothe | soap | whoa | boast | *oe* | blow | mold | scroll |
| hope | stole | broke | phone | oat | loan | roast | toe | glow | sold | post |
| vote | doze | poke | | oak | moan | cloak | woe | grow | bold | ghost |
| code | froze | smoke | | soak | groan | croak | doe | sow | scold | host |
| mole | pose | yoke | | whoa | moat | loaves | hoe | low | bolt | comb |
| pole | chose | spoke | | | | | foe | tow | colt | |
| joke | those | tone | | | | | | flow | jolt | |
| stone | close | shone | | | | | | own** | volt | |

| *Oddballs* | | | | | | | *Oddballs* | | | |
| one* | love | some* | | broad | | | to* | flown | tomb | |
| done | dove | come* | | | | | do* | throw | | |
| none | glove | move | | | | | who* | thrownt | | |
| gone | prove | lose | | | | | two* | blown | | |
| once | shove | whose | | | | | shoe | grown | | |
| | | | | | | | broad | bowl | | |
| | | | | | | | sew | | | |

## Long-u Words

| CVCe | | C V VC | C V V | C V VC | | | C V V | | Oddballs |
|---|---|---|---|---|---|---|---|---|---|
| *u-e* | | *ui* | *ue* | *oo – /u_/* | | | *ew* | | *Oddballs* |
| use** | nude | fruit | blue | too** | goof | goose | new* | brew | do* |
| cute | crude | suit | due | zoo | soon** | scoop | dew | stew | you* |
| rude | dune | bruise | clue | moo | noon | school** | chew | crew | to* |
| rule | flute | cruise | glue | boot | moon | spoon | drew | whew | two* |
| mule | fume | juice | true | root | room | tooth | few | screw | build |
| tune | chute | | flue | food | zoom | shoot | flew | threw | built |
| June | mute | | hue | mood | boom | smooth | knew | shrewd | guide |
| tube | plume | | cue | tool | loom | roost | grew | strewn | truth |
| cube | prune | | sue | cool | bloom | proof | | | through |
| duke | muse | | fuel | fool | gloom | stool | | | guilt |
| huge | spruce | | cruel | pool | loop | spook | | | suite |
| dude | | | | roof | troop | brood | | | |

**Ambiguous Vowels**

| al | au | aw | | o | | ough | w + a |
|---|---|---|---|---|---|---|---|
| tall | caught | saw** | gnaw | on* | loss | cough | wash |
| wall | taught | paw | thaw | off | cross | ought | wand |
| mall | pause | law | caw | dog | gloss | fought | wasp |
| talk | sauce | draw | bawl | frog | cloth | bought | watt |
| walk | fault | claw | awe | log | moth | thought | swap |
| calm | haunt | dawn | drawn | fog | broth | brought | swat |
| palm | launch | lawn | crawl | bog | soft | trough | watch |
| bald | because** | yawn | shawl | hog | loft | | |
| halt | fraud | fawn | sprawl | lost | golf | | /w/ + a |
| salt | haul | hawk | squawk | cost | bong | | squash |
| small | maul | raw | straw | frost | song | | squat |
| stall | jaunt | gawk | scrawl | boss | long* | | squad |
| stalk | gaunt | | | toss | strong | | |
| chalk | | | | moss | throng | | Oddballs |
| waltz | *Oddballs* | | | | | | was* |
| false | aunt | | | | | | want** |
| scald | laugh | | | | | | |

| oo‡ | | ow | | ou | | oi | oy |
|---|---|---|---|---|---|---|---|
| book** | | how* | drown | out* | house** | coin | boy* |
| look** | | now | frown | our* | about* | join | toy |
| good* | | cow | crown | loud | mouse | oil | joy |
| cook | | down* | crowd | ouch | foul | foil | enjoy |
| took | | bow | fowl | cloud | mouth | soil | soy |
| foot | | wow | scowl | proud | shout | boil | ploy |
| wood | | town | prowl | count | pout | coil | |
| hook | | gown | growl | round | scout | point | |
| shook | | brown | vow | sound | snout | joint | |
| stood | | clown | | found** | stout | hoist | |
| wool | | owl | | pound | sprout | moist | |
| crook | | howl | | mound | pouch | toil | |
| hood | | sow | | bound | couch | broil | |
| soot | | plow | | hound | crouch | voice | |
| hoof | | | | wound | drought | noise | |
| brook | | | | ground | doubt | choice | |
| nook | | | | | | | |

| *Oddballs* | | | | *Oddballs* |
|---|---|---|---|---|
| blood | | | | could** |
| flood | | | | would* |
| | | | | should** |
| | | | | touch |
| | | | | young |
| | | | | cough |
| | | | | tough |
| | | | | through |
| | | | | rough |

## *r*-Influenced Vowels

| *ar* | | *ar + e* | *are* | *air* | *ear /ee/* | *eer* | *er* | *ear /@/* | *Oddballs* |
|------|------|----------|-------|-------|-----------|-------|------|-----------|-----------|
| far** | dart | carve | care | fair | ear** | deer | her* | heard | very* |
| car | start | large | bare | hair | near** | cheer | fern | earth | their* |
| jar | bark | starve | dare | pair | hear | steer | herd | learn | there* |
| star | shark | barge | share | stair | dear** | queer | jerk | earn | were* |
| card | lark | charge | stare | flair | year** | jeer | term | search | here* |
| hard | scar | | mare | chair | fear | sneer | germ | pearl | where** |
| yard | mar | *Oddballs* | flare | lair | tear | peer | stern | yearn | heart |
| art | barb | are* | glare | | clear | | herb | | bear |
| part | harp | war | rare | | beard | | per | | wear |
| cart | sharp | warm | scare | | gear | | perk | | swear |
| bar | snarl | | hare | | spear | | perch | | pear |
| arm | scarf | | snare | | shear | | clerk | | hearth |
| harm | charm | | blare | | smear | | nerve | | |
| dark | arch | | fare | | | | serve | | |
| park | march | | square | | | | verse | | |
| spark | smart | | | | | | swerve | | |
| yarn | chart | | | | | | | | |

| *ur* | *ure* | *ir* | *ire* | *or* | *ore* | *our* | *oar* | *w + ar* | *w + or* |
|------|-------|------|-------|------|-------|-------|-------|----------|----------|
| fur | sure** | girl** | fire | or* | more** | your* | roar | warm | work* |
| burn | cure | first** | tire | for* | store | four** | soar | war | word |
| turn | pure | bird | wire | born | shore | pour | boar | ward | world |
| curl | lure | dirt | hire | corn | bore | mourn | coarse | wharf | worm |
| hurt | | stir | sire | horn | chore | court | hoarse | quart | worth |
| curb | *ur-e* | sir | | worn | score | fourth | board | swarm | worse |
| church | curve | fir | *ier* | cord | sore | gourd | | warp | |
| burst | nurse | skirt | drier | cork | before* | source | *oor* | wart | |
| surf | curse | third | pliers | pork | wore | course | door | warn | |
| churn | urge | birth | flier | fort | tore | | poor | | |
| burr | purse | firm | crier | short | swore | *Oddballs* | floor | | |
| purr | | shirt | | nor | | our* | | | |
| lurch | | twirl | *iar* | ford | | flour | | | |
| lurk | | swirl | liar | lord | | hour | | | |
| spur | | chirp | briar | storm | | scour | | | |
| hurl | | thirst | friar | porch | | sour | | | |
| blur | | squirm | | torch | | | | | |
| blurt | | squirt | | force | | | | | |
| | | | | north | | | | | |
| | | | | horse | | | | | |
| | | | | forth | | | | | |
| | | | | scorn | | | | | |
| | | | | chord | | | | | |
| | | | | forge | | | | | |
| | | | | gorge | | | | | |

## Complex Consonants

| ch | tch | Cch | | Hard g | | Soft g | dge | Cge |
|---|---|---|---|---|---|---|---|---|
| teach | catch | ranch | arch | frog | guide | huge | edge | range |
| reach | patch | branch | march | drug | guard | cage | ledge | change |
| beach | hatch | lunch | starch | twig | guilt | age | hedge | barge |
| peach | latch | bunch | search | flag | guess | page | wedge | charge |
| coach | match | munch | perch | shrug | guest | stage | pledge | large |
| speech | watch | punch | lurch | gave | ghost | rage | badge | forge |
| couch | ditch | bench | church | game | | orange | ridge | gorge |
| crouch | pitch | clench | birch | gain | | gem | bridge | surge |
| pouch | witch | trench | torch | gauge | *Oddballs* | germ | lodge | bulge |
| screech | switch | wrench | porch | gone | get* | gene | dodge | strange |
| pooch | fetch | drench | scorch | goat | girl** | gym | judge | sponge |
| | sketch | pinch | | gold | gift | gyp | budge | plunge |
| *Oddballs* | clutch | finch | | goose | gear | giant | fudge | hinge |
| rich | scratch | hunch | | goof | geese | gist | smudge | merge |
| such | stretch | mulch | | golf | | | trudge | lounge |
| much* | stitch | gulch | | gulp | | | grudge | |
| which* | twitch | launch | | gull | | | | |
| | blotch | | | gust | | | | |
| | | | | gulf | | | | |

| Hard c | Soft c | ce | se /z/ | se /s/ | -ze | -z | -ve | Voiceless th | Voiced th |
|---|---|---|---|---|---|---|---|---|---|
| card | cell | rice | wise | cease | size | buzz | love | bath | bathe |
| cave | cent | face | chose | dense | haze | fizz | dove | cloth | clothe |
| cast | cease | place | close | false | doze | jazz | shove | booth | soothe |
| cause | cinch | brace | phase | geese | prize | frizz | glove | loath | loathe |
| caught | cyst | slice | muse | goose | froze | quiz | have* | teeth | teethe |
| couch | cite | price | those | loose | graze | quartz | give* | breath | breathe |
| core | | truce | these** | moose | blaze | waltz | move | | seethe |
| coin | | trace | prose | mouse | gauze | | weave | *Silent w* | |
| coast | | since | cause | nurse | seize | | leave | write | *Silent k* |
| cost | | fence | noise | purse | freeze | | curve | wrist | know* |
| coach | | peace | pause | sense | sneeze | | nerve | wrap | knew |
| cough | | juice | raise | tense | snooze | | serve | wrong | knee |
| curb | | niece | tease | rinse | breeze | | twelve | wreck | knit |
| curl | | voice | cheese | verse | maize | | solve | wring | knock |
| curve | | sauce | please | chase | bronze | | prove | who* | knife |
| cult | | once | poise | close | wheeze | | sleeve | whole | knight |
| cuff | | hence | browse | blouse | squeeze | | | | knob |
| | | force | choose | house** | | | | *Silent g* | knot |
| | | ounce | bruise | pulse | | | | gnaw | |
| | | dance | cruise | lapse | | | | gnome | *Silent b* |
| | | chance | | worse | | | | gnat | crumb |
| | | prince | | hoarse | | | | gnash | comb |
| | | fleece | | glimpse | | | | gnu | limb |
| | | piece | | | | | | | thumb |
| | | bounce | | | | | | *Silent h* | climb |
| | | source | | | | | | ghost | lamb |
| | | choice | | | | | | honest | herb |
| | | fierce | | | | | | rhino | tomb |
| | | | | | | | | rhyme | numb |
| | | | | | | | | hour | |

**Homophones**

| | | | | |
|---|---|---|---|---|
| be/bee | hey/hay | serial/cereal | Mary/marry/merry | browse/brows |
| blue/blew | made/maid | cheap/cheep | great/grate | bred/bread |
| I/eye/aye | male/mail | days/daze | seem/seam | guessed/guest |
| no/know | nay/neigh | dew/do/due | knew/new | rest/wrest |
| here/hear | oh/owe | doe/dough | stair/stare | beech/beach |
| to/too/two | pail/pale | heel/heal | hour/our | real/reel |
| hi/high | pair/pear/pare | horse/hoarse | rough/ruff | peel/peal |
| new/knew/gnu | peek/peak/pique | ho/hoe | poor/pour | team/teem |
| see/sea | reed/read/Reid | in/inn | haul/hall | leak/leek |
| there/they're/their | so/sew/sow | need/knead | piece/peace | sees/seas |
| bear/bare | root/route | lone/loan | ant/aunt | sheer/shear |
| by/buy/bye | shone/shown | we/wee | flair/flare | feet/feat |
| deer/dear | aid/aide | ring/wring | mist/missed | hymn/him |
| ate/eight | add/ad | peddle/petal/pedal | mane/main | whit/wit |
| for/four/fore | break/brake | straight/strait | wail/whale/wale | scents/cents/sense |
| our/hour | cent/sent/scent | pole/poll | died/dyed | tents/tense |
| red/read | flee/flea | earn/urn | manor/manner | gilt/guilt |
| lead/led | creak/creek | past/passed | pier/peer | knit/nit |
| meat/meet | die/dye | sweet/suite | Ann/an | tic/tick |
| plane/plain | fair/fare | ore/or | tacks/tax | sight/site/cite |
| rode/road/rowed | hair/hare | rain/reign/rein | cash/cache | rye/wry |
| sail/sale | heard/herd | role/roll | rap/wrap | style/stile |
| stare/stair | night/knight | sole/soul | maze/maize | might/mite |
| we'd/weed | steel/steal | seller/cellar | air/heir | climb/clime |
| we'll/wheel | tail/tale | shoo/shoe | bail/bale | fined/find |
| hole/whole | thrown/throne | soar/sore | ail/ale | side/sighed |
| wear/ware/where | fir/fur | steak/stake | prays/praise | tide/tied |
| one/won | waist/waste | some/sum | base/bass | vice/vise |
| flower/flour | week/weak | tow/toe | faint/feint | awl/all |
| right/write | we've/weave | vein/vane/vain | wade/weighed | paws/pause |
| your/you're | way/weigh | medal/metal/meddle | wave/waive | born/borne |
| lye/lie | wait/weight | wrote/rote | knave/nave | chord/cord |
| its/it's | threw/through | forth/fourth | whet/wet | foul/fowl |
| not/knot | vail/veil/vale | tea/tee | sell/cell | mall/maul |
| gate/gait | aisle/I'll/isle | been/bin | bell/belle | mourn/morn |
| jeans/genes | ball/bawl | board/bored | bowled/bold | rot/wrought |
| time/thyme | beat/beet | course/coarse | bough/bow | bald/balled |
| son/sun | bolder/boulder | boy/buoy | | |

## Compound Words by Common Base Words

We have limited the list here to words that have base words across a number of compound words.

| | | | | | |
|---|---|---|---|---|---|
| aircraft | checkbook | foothold | homesick | snowman | raincoat |
| airline | cookbook | footlights | homespun | fireman | raindrop |
| airmail | scrapbook | footnote | homestead | gentleman | rainfall |
| airplane | textbook | footprint | homework | handyman | rainstorm |
| airport | buttercup | footstep | horseback | policeman | roadblock |
| airtight | butterfly | footstool | horsefly | salesman | roadway |
| anybody | buttermilk | barefoot | horseman | nightfall | roadwork |
| anymore | butterscotch | tenderfoot | horseplay | nightgown | railroad |
| anyone | doorbell | grandchildren | horsepower | nightmare | sandbag |
| anyplace | doorknob | granddaughter | horseshoe | nighttime | sandbar |
| anything | doorman | grandfather | racehorse | overnight | sandbox |
| anywhere | doormat | grandmother | sawhorse | outbreak | sandpaper |
| backboard | doorstep | grandparent | houseboat | outcast | sandpiper |
| backbone | doorway | grandson | housefly | outcome | sandstone |
| backfire | backdoor | haircut | housewife | outcry | seacoast |
| background | outdoor | hairdo | housework | outdated | seafood |
| backpack | downcast | hairdresser | housetop | outdo | seagull |
| backward | downhill | hairpin | birdhouse | outdoors | seaman |
| backyard | download | hairstyle | clubhouse | outfield | seaport |
| bareback | downpour | handbag | doghouse | outfit | seasick |
| feedback | downright | handball | greenhouse | outgrow | seashore |
| flashback | downsize | handbook | townhouse | outlaw | seaside |
| hatchback | downstairs | handcuffs | landfill | outline | seaweed |
| paperback | downstream | handmade | landlady | outlook | snowball |
| piggyback | downtown | handout | landlord | outnumber | snowflake |
| bathrobe | breakdown | handshake | landmark | outpost | snowman |
| bathroom | countdown | handspring | landscape | outrage | snowplow |
| bathtub | sundown | handstand | landslide | outright | snowshoe |
| birdbath | touchdown | handwriting | dreamland | outside | snowstorm |
| bedrock | eyeball | backhand | farmland | outsmart | somebody |
| bedroom | eyebrow | firsthand | homeland | outwit | someone |
| bedside | eyeglasses | secondhand | highland | blowout | someday |
| bedspread | eyelash | underhand | wasteland | carryout | somehow |
| bedtime | eyelid | headache | wonderland | cookout | somewhere |
| flatbed | eyesight | headband | lifeboat | handout | something |
| hotbed | eyewitness | headdress | lifeguard | hideout | sometime |
| sickbed | shuteye | headfirst | lifejacket | workout | underline |
| waterbed | firearm | headlight | lifelike | lookout | undergo |
| birthday | firecracker | headline | lifelong | overall | underground |
| birthmark | firefighter | headlong | lifestyle | overboard | undermine |
| birthplace | firefly | headmaster | lifetime | overcast | underwater |
| birthstone | firehouse | headphones | nightlife | overcome | watercolor |
| childbirth | fireman | headquarters | wildlife | overflow | waterfall |
| blackberry | fireplace | headstart | lighthouse | overhead | watermelon |
| blackbird | fireproof | headstrong | lightweight | overlook | waterproof |
| blackboard | fireside | headway | daylight | overview | saltwater |
| blackmail | firewood | airhead | flashlight | playground | windfall |
| blacksmith | fireworks | blockhead | headlight | playhouse | windmill |
| blacktop | backfire | figurehead | moonlight | playmate | windpipe |
| bookcase | bonfire | homeland | spotlight | playpen | windshield |
| bookkeeper | campfire | homemade | sunlight | playroom | windswept |
| bookmark | football | homemaker | mailman | playwright | downwind |
| bookworm | foothill | homeroom | doorman | rainbow | headwind |

478

## Plurals

| ch + es | sh + es | ss + es | x + es | y + s | Change y to i + es | | | | f to ves |
|---------|---------|---------|--------|-------|--------------------|---|---|---|----------|
| arches | bushes | bosses | foxes | plays | flies | babies | daisies | stories | wives |
| watches | dishes | classes | boxes | stays | fries | berries | guppies | buddies | knives |
| coaches | flashes | glasses | taxes | trays | cries | bodies | ladies | sixties | leaves |
| couches | brushes | crosses | axes | donkeys | tries | bunnies | parties | | loaves |
| inches | ashes | guesses | mixes | monkeys | skies | cities | pennies | *Oddballs* | lives |
| peaches | wishes | kisses | | jockeys | spies | copies | ponies | goalies | wolves |
| notches | crashes | passes | s + es | turkeys | dries | counties | supplies | taxies | calves |
| lunches | leashes | dresses | gases | volleys | | fairies | puppies | movies | elves |
| switches | lashes | | buses | valleys | | duties | bullies | cookies | scarves |
| churches | | | | enjoys | | armies | hobbies | | selves |
| branches | | | | obeys | | fairies | spies | | shelves |
| benches | | | | decays | | skies | | | |

## Verbs for Inflected Ending Sorts

| VCC | C V VC | | e-Drop | | C V C Words That Double | | | Don't Double | Irregular Verbs |
|-----|--------|---|--------|---|------------------------|---|---|--------------|-----------------|
| help | act | need | live** | dance | stop | drip | grab | level | see/saw |
| jump | add | wait | time | glance | pat | fan | hug | edit | fall/fell |
| want** | crash | boat | name | hike | sun | flop | jam | enter | feel/felt |
| ask | crack | shout | bake | hire | top | grin | kid | exit | tell/told |
| back** | block | cook | care | serve | hop | grip | log | limit | grow/grew |
| talk | bowl | head | close | score | plan | mop | map | suffer | know/knew |
| call** | count | meet | love | solve | pot | plod | nap | appear | draw/drew |
| thank | brush | peek | move | sneeze | shop | rob | nod | complain | blow/blew |
| laugh | bump | bloom | smile | trace | trip | shrug | pin | explain | throw/threw |
| trick | burn | cool | use** | trade | bet | sip | dip | repeat | find/found |
| park | climb | cheer | hate | vote | cap | skin | dim | attend | drink/drank |
| pick | camp | clear | hope | drape | clap | skip | rub | collect | sink/sank |
| plant | curl | dream | ice | fade | slip | slam | beg | | hear/heard |
| rock | dash | float | joke | graze | snap | slap | blur | **Double** | break/broke |
| start | dust | flood | paste | praise | spot | snip | bud | admit | hold/held |
| bark | farm | fool | phone | scrape | tag | sob | chip | begin | stand/stood |
| work** | fold | join | prove | shave | thin | strip | chop | commit | build/built |
| walk | growl | lean | race | shove | trap | wrap | crop | control | ring/rang |
| yell | hunt | mail | scare | snare | trot | zip | strum | excel | sing/sang |
| wish** | kick | nail | share | cause | tug | brag | swap | forbid | sweep/swept |
| guess | land | moan | skate | cease | wag | chug | swat | forget | sleep/slept |
| turn | learn | scream | stare | pose | drop | hem | | omit | keep/kept |
| smell | nest | pour | taste | quote | drum | jog | *Oddballs* | permit | drive/drove |
| track | lick | sail | wave | rove | whiz | mob | box** | rebel | shine/shone |
| push | lock | trail | carve | blame | flap | plot | fix | refer | feed/fed |
| miss | melt | zoom | | | flip | prop | wax | | bleed/bled |
| paint | point | | | | scar | blot | row | **e-Drop** | lay/laid |
| wash | print | | | | skim | chat | chew | arrive | pay/paid |
| wink | quack | | | | slug | scan | sew | escape | say/said |
| rest | reach | | | | stab | slop | show | excuse | speak/spoke |
| | | | | | throb | | snow | nibble | send/sent |
| | | | | | | | | rattle | buy/bought |
| | | | | | | | | refuse | bring/brought |
| | | | | | | | | amuse | tear/tore |
| | | | | | | | | ignore | wear/wore |
| | | | | | | | | retire | |

### Pairs to Contrast

| | |
|--------|---------|
| hoping | hopping |
| taping | tapping |
| pining | pinning |
| griping | gripping |
| striping | stripping |
| moping | mopping |
| waging | wagging |

## Syllable Juncture

| VCCV Doublet | VCCV | | VCV Open | V VCV Open | VCV Closed | V V | V C C C V |
|---|---|---|---|---|---|---|---|
| pretty** | after* | campus | over** | season | never** | create | constant |
| better** | under** | frantic | open** | reason | present** | riot | dolphin |
| blizzard | number | magnet | baby | peanut | cabin | liar | laughter |
| blossom | chapter | mascot | writer | leader | planet | fuel | pilgrim |
| button | pencil | sandal | basic | sneaker | finish | poem | instant |
| cabbage | picnic | pretzel | even | easy | robin | diary | complain |
| copper | basket | splendid | bacon | floated | magic | cruel | hundred |
| cottage | cactus | kidnap | chosen | waiter | limit | trial | monster |
| dipper | canyon | wisdom | moment | needed | manage | diet | orchard |
| fellow | capture | goblet | human | reading | prison | neon | orphan |
| foggy | center | goblin | pilot | | habit | lion | purchase |
| follow | window | tonsil | silent | *Oddballs* | punish | poet | complete |
| common | compass | finger | vacant | cousin | cover | giant | athlete |
| funny | contest | subject | navy | water | promise | chaos | kitchen |
| happen | costume | walnut | music | busy | closet | idea | children |
| mammal | doctor | velvet | female | | camel | video | inspect |
| message | picture | injure | robot | | cavern | meteor | pumpkin |
| office | plastic | welcome | crater | | comet | violin | English |
| pattern | public | chimney | climate | | dozen | annual | kingdom |
| sudden | problem | trumpet | duty | | finish | casual | bottle |
| tennis | reptile | twenty | famous | | habit | radio | mumble |
| traffic | rescue | umpire | fever | | honest | alien | sandwich |
| tunnel | sentence | | final | | level | piano | actress |
| valley | seldom | | flavor | | lever | area | enchant |
| village | fabric | | humid | | lizard | mosaic | congress |
| hollow | helmet | | labor | | modern | | ostrich |
| dessert | husband | | legal | | oven | | subtract |
| butter | lumber | | local | | palace | | pitcher |
| hammer | master | | pirate | | timid | | stretcher |
| attic | napkin | | private | | panic | | control |
| gallon | dentist | | program | | rapid | | mushroom |
| rabbit | blanket | | recent | | visit | | thimble |
| gallop | tablet | | rumor | | solid | | |
| lesson | bandit | | siren | | wagon | | |
| banner | wonder | | solar | | vanish | | |
| kitten | index | | spiral | | topic | | |
| ribbon | insect | | crazy | | travel | | |
| mitten | Sunday | | bonus | | study | | |
| bonnet | elbow | | lazy | | seven | | |
| bottom | enter | | paper | | rigid | | |
| cotton | whimper | | secret | | polish | | |
| fossil | winter | | hero | | legend | | |
| gossip | signal | | zero | | banish | | |
| muffin | sister | | spider | | gravel | | |
| puppet | temper | | tiger | | tragic | | |
| yellow | thunder | | rodent | | | | |
| | | | super | | | | |
| | | | bonus | | | | |
| | | | tulip | | | | |
| | | | sequel | | | | |

## *a* Patterns in Accented Syllables

| Long *a* VCV Open Accent in 1st | Long-*a* Accent in 1st | Long-*a* Accent in 2nd | Short *a* in VCCV Accent in 1st | Short *a* in VCW Accent in 1st | *ar* Accent in 1st | *air* Accent in 1st | *arr/are* Accent in 1st |
|---|---|---|---|---|---|---|---|
| baby | rainbow | complain | attic | wagon | artist | stairway | marry |
| nation | painter | contain | hammer | cabin | marble | fairway | parrot |
| vapor | raisin | explain | batter | planet | garden | airport | narrow |
| skater | railroad | remain | happen | magic | party | dairy | carrot |
| lazy | daisy | terrain | mammal | habit | carpet | haircut | sparrow |
| bacon | dainty | exclaim | valley | camel | pardon | fairy | narrate |
| wafer | sailor | refrain | cabbage | habit | market | airplane | barrel |
| raven | straighten | campaign | traffic | rapid | tardy | chairman | carry |
| famous | failure | regain | pattern | panic | harvest | prairie | parent |
| fatal | tailor | obtain | scatter | panel | parka | | careful |
| navy | waiter | maintain | ballot | palace | charter | | barely |
| basic | traitor | decay | daddy | cavern | larva | **Accent in 2nd** | barefoot |
| flavor | mailbox | dismay | gallop | manage | garland | repair | |
| data | maybe | delay | massive | vanish | parcel | despair | **Accent in 2nd** |
| crater | player | portray | napkin | travel | barber | unfair | prepare |
| savor | crayon | mistake | basket | satin | starchy | impair | compare |
| raking | mayor | parade | fabric | tragic | charter | affair | beware |
| labor | payment | amaze | plastic | falcon | garlic | | aware |
| vacant | prayer | replace | master | shadow | margin | | declare |
| radar | layer | dictate | cactus | chapel | hardly | | |
| hazel | crayfish | crusade | chapter | facet | partner | | |
| favour | bracelet | debate | canyon | radish | bargain | | |
| | pavement | behave | capture | tavern | carbon | | |
| | basement | cascade | tadpole | statue | farther | | |
| | baseball | escape | ambush | | jargon | | |
| | grateful | disgrace | lantern | **Broad *a* VCV** | scarlet | | |
| *oddballs* | graceful | erase | scamper | bravo | parlor | | |
| any* | safety | essay | canvas | father | sharpen | | |
| many* | statement | foray | package | drama | sparkle | | |
| water | wakeful | invade | tablet | water | target | | |
| | mayhem | insane | lather | plaza | tarnish | | |
| | painless | sustain | | llama | harbor | | |
| | ailment | betray | | squalid | partial | | |
| | | evade | | | marshal | | |
| | | disdain | | **Broad *a* in VCCV** | martyr | | |
| | *Oddballs* | | | swallow | carton | | |
| | again* | | | wallet | darling | | |
| | captain | *Oddballs* | | wallow | varnish | | |
| | bargain | obey | | waffle | | | |
| | postage | survey | | waddle | *Oddballs* | | |
| | | | | wallop | toward | | |
| | | | | | lizard | | |

# e Patterns in Accented Syllables

| Long e VCV Open Accent in 1st | Long-e Accent in 1st | Long-e Accent in 2nd | Long-ie Accent in 1st | Short e in VCCV Accent in 1st | Short e in VCV Accent in 1st | er = ur Accent in 1st | eer/ear/ere Accent in 1st |
|---|---|---|---|---|---|---|---|
| even | needle | succeed | briefly | better | medal | person | eerie |
| female | freedom | indeed | diesel | letter | metal | perfect | deerskin |
| fever | freezer | fifteen | | fellow | level | nervous | cheerful |
| zebra | breezy | thirteen | **Accent in 2nd** | tennis | lever | sermon | earache |
| legal | cheetah | canteen | believe | message | never | serpent | fearful |
| meter | steeple | agree | achieve | penny | debit | hermit | earmuff |
| recent | tweezers | degree | retrieve | beggar | denim | thermos | spearmint |
| depot | beetle | between | relief | pencil | lemon | kernel | yearbook |
| cedar | feeble | proceed | besiege | dentist | melon | perky | dreary |
| detour | greedy | asleep | apiece | center | memo | permit | bleary |
| veto | sweeten | delete | relieve | helmet | pedal | sherbet | clearly |
| prefix | beaver | supreme | belief | reptile | petal | gerbil | nearby |
| tepee | eager | trapeze | | rescue | seven | mermaid | hearsay |
| decent | easy | compete | **Long-ei Accent in 1st** | seldom | clever | certain | teardrop |
| preview | easel | extreme | either | sentence | credit | merchant | weary |
| prefix | season | stampede | ceiling | temper | senate | version | merely |
| evil | reason | deplete | leisure | twenty | tenor | servant | nearly |
| zenith | reader | recede | seizure | welcome | epic | verbal | clearing |
| | feature | convene | neither | velvet | relic | mercy | dearest |
| **VV** | creature | mislead | weirdo | pesky | | verdict | spearmint |
| neon | meaning | disease | | | **Short ea** | | |
| create | eastern | increase | **Accent in 2nd** | | feather | **ear = ur** | **Accent in 2nd** |
| area | bleachers | defeat | receive | | heavy | early | career |
| idea | cleaner | repeat | perceive | | steady | earnings | appear |
| video | eager | conceal | receipt | | ready | earthworm | overhear |
| | treaty | ideal | deceive | | leather | pearly | endear |
| | neatly | reveal | conceive | | weather | earnest | adhere |
| | peanut | ordeal | caffeine | | pleasant | yearning | austere |
| | weasel | appeal | receipt | | sweater | rehearse | revere |
| | greasy | mislead | receive | | healthy | research | severe |
| | beacon | obese | deceit | | weapon | earthquake | sincere |
| | beagle | esteem | conceited | | sweaty | learner | interfere |
| | eagle | redeem | | | heaven | | |
| | measles | retreat | | | heather | | |
| | | ordeal | | | meadow | | |
| | | decree | | | measure | | |
| | | complete | | | treasure | | |
| | | | | | breakfast | | |
| | *Oddballs* | *Oddball* | | | | | |
| | people | mischief | | | | | |
| | hearty | heifer | | | | | |
| | pretty | forfeit | | | | | |
| | cherry | | | | | | |
| | leopard | | | | | | |
| | heifer | | | | | | |
| | neighbor | | | | | | |
| | reindeer | | | | | | |

## *i* Patterns in Accented Syllables

| Long *i* VCV Open Accent in 1st | Long-*i* Accent in 1st | Long-*i* Accent in 2nd | Short *i* in VCCV Accent in 1st | Short *i* in VCV Accent in 1st | *ir* Accent in 1st | *ire* Accent in 1st | *y* = /ĭ/ Accent in 1st |
|---|---|---|---|---|---|---|---|
| pilot | ninety | polite | into** | finish | thirty | tiresome | typist |
| silent | driveway | surprise | kitten | limit | firmly | firefly | dryer |
| diner | sidewalk | decide | dipper | river | dirty | direful | flyer |
| writer | iceberg | advice | slipper | lizard | birthday | | tyrant |
| tiger | lively | survive | mitten | timid | thirsty | **Accent in 2nd** | hydrant |
| siren | mighty | combine | dinner | visit | birdbath | require | bypass |
| pirate | slightly | arrive | silly | given | circle | rehire | nylon |
| private | frighten | invite | skinny | city | circus | attire | stylish |
| spiral | lightning | describe | ribbon | sliver | stirring | inquire | rhyming |
| biker | highway | divide | pillow | civil | firmly | expire | python |
| spider | brightly | excite | dizzy | digit | virtue | desire | cycle |
| visor | higher | provide | chilly | prison | stirrup | perspire | tryout |
| minus | nightmare | confide | bitter | wizard | twirler | admire | cyclone |
| rival | tighten | recline | minnow | quiver | skirmish | inspire | hybrid |
| bison | fighter | ignite | blizzard | figure | circuit | entire | hyphen |
| item | highlight | despite | tissue | | irksome | acquire | stylish |
| friday | sightsee | oblige | mixture | | whirlpool | retire | skyline |
| sinus | blindfold | divine | fifty | | chirping | | hygiene |
| slimy | kindness | tonight | picnic | | flirting | | tycoon |
| icy | climber | resign | picture | | squirrel | | |
| climax | wildcat | design | chimney | | | | **Accent in 2nd** |
| idol | wildlife | delight | frisky | | | | defy |
| | | guitar | windy | | | | July |
| **V V** | | rewind | signal | | | | apply |
| lion | | unkind | sister | | | | rely |
| dial | | behind | whimper | | | | imply |
| diet | | beside | finger | | | | supply |
| riot | | inside | winter | | | | reply |
| pliers | | recite | kidnap | | | | deny |
| diary | | collide | jigsaw | | | | |
| vial | | advise | window | | | | *y* = /ī/ Accent in 1st |
| triumph | | confine | blister | | | | crystal |
| friar | | | fiction | | | | hymnal |
| liar | | | listen | | | | pygmy |
| trial | | | scissors | | | | rhythm |
| violin | | | | | | | symbol |
| client | | | | | | | system |
| science | | | | | | | sylvan |
| violet | | | | | | | cynic |
| | | | | | | | physics |
| *Oddballs* | | | | | | | cymbal |
| machine | | | | | | | |
| liter | | | | | | | |
| mirror | | | | | | | |
| pizza | | | | | | | |
| spirit | | | | | | | |
| busy | | | | | | | |
| women | | | | | | | |

## o Patterns in Accented Syllables

| Long o VCV Open Accent in 1st | Long-o Accent in 1st | Long-o Accent in 2nd | Short o in VCCV Accent in 1st | Short o in VCV Accent in 1st | or Accent in 1st | wor Accent in 1st | ore/oar/our Accent in 1st |
|---|---|---|---|---|---|---|---|
| robot | lonely | alone | foggy | robin | morning** | worker | boredom |
| pony | lonesome | explode | follow | closet | forty | worry | shoreline |
| chosen | hopeful | erode | copper | comet | stormy | worthy | scoreless |
| donate | homework | awoke | blossom | promise | story | worship | hoarsely |
| motor | closely | decode | cottage | honest | corner | | coarsely |
| soda | goalie | enclose | common | modern | border | **war/quar** | hoarding |
| notice | loafer | dispose | office | solid | torment | warning | sources |
| sofa | coaster | suppose | hollow | topic | forest | warden | fourteen |
| frozen | toaster | compose | nozzle | volume | fortress | warrior | pouring |
| local | coastal | remote | bottle | body | shortage | wardrobe | mournful |
| moment | soapy | unload | comma | novel | torrent | quarrel | foursome |
| rodent | roadway | approach | cotton | profit | tortoise | quarter | courtroom |
| grocer | owner | afloat | hobby | promise | portrait | reward | |
| potion | bowling | below | yonder | comic | forfeit | | **Accent in 2nd** |
| ocean | rowboat | bestow | popcorn | logic | shorter | | before* |
| rotate | snowfall | aglow | contest | proper | order | | ignore |
| hoping | lower | disown | costume | novice | normal | | restore |
| stolen | mower | enroll | doctor | | northern | | explore |
| solar | slowly | behold | bonfire | **Short-o /u/** | forward | | galore |
| poem | towboat | revolt | bother | oven | corncob | | aboard |
| | soldier | almost | cobweb | onion | chorus | | ashore |
| | poster | expose | conquer | shovel | florist | | adore |
| | hostess | oppose | problem | monkey | boring | | |
| | postage | console | posture | mother | sporty | | |
| | smolder | | monster | nothing | hornet | | |
| | molten | **Long o V V** | congress | smother | organ | | |
| | molding | poet | collar | wander | morsel | | |
| | folder | poem | volley | dozen | mortal | | |
| | oatmeal | boa | goblin | stomach | orbit | | |
| | | oasis | | | orchard | | |
| **Long o Unaccented** | | coerce | **Oddballs** | | | | |
| yellow | | | dolphin | | **Accent in 2nd** | | |
| pillow | | **Oddballs** | stomach | | report | | |
| shadow | | hotel | Europe | | record | | |
| mellow | | only** | sorry | | perform | | |
| willow | | | | | inform | | |
| hollow | | | | | afford | | |
| fellow | | | | | reform | | |
| sparrow | | | | | absorb | | |
| follow | | | | | abhor | | |
| window | | | | | adorn | | |
| | | | | | distort | | |
| | | | | | endorse | | |

**u Patterns in Accented Syllables**

| Long *u* VCV Open Accent in 1st | Long-*u* Accent in 1st | Long-*u* Accent in 2nd | Short *u* in VCCV Accent in 1st | Short *u* in VCV Accent in 1st | *ur* Accent in 1st | *ure* Accent in 2nd | V V |
|---|---|---|---|---|---|---|---|
| super | useful | amuse | supper | punish | sturdy | secure | fuel |
| music | Tuesday | misuse | button | suburb | purpose | assure | cruel |
| ruby | juicy | confuse | funny | pumice | further | endure | annual |
| tuna | chewy | reduce | sudden | study | hurry | impure | casual |
| truly | dewdrop | conclude | tunnel | | purple | mature | usual |
| pupil | jewel | dilute | puppet | *Oddballs* | turtle | unsure | dual |
| rumor | pewter | exclude | buddy | cougar | furnish | obscure | duel |
| human | skewer | include | butter | beauty | Thursday | manure | fluent |
| humid | sewage | pollute | fuzzy | cousin | blurry | brochure | duet |
| future | poodle | excuse | guppy | | turkey | insure | |
| tutor | rooster | resume | ugly | | current | disturb | |
| tumor | moody | compute | husband | | purchase | | |
| futile | doodle | abuse | lumber | | burger | | |
| student | noodle | perfume | number | | furry | | |
| tuba | scooter | protrude | public | | murky | | |
| tulip | toothache | salute | Sunday | | mural | | |
| unit | neutral | dispute | thunder | | surfer | | |
| ruler | sewer | askew | trumpet | | burden | | |
| | feudal | assume | umpire | | bureau | | |
| | | immune | under** | | burrow | | |
| | | consume | hundred | | curfew | | |
| | | accuse | mumble | | hurdle | | |
| | | intrude | lucky | | jury | | |
| | | pollute | hungry | | murmur | | |
| | | review | bucket | | turnip | | |
| | | cartoon | bundle | | burner | | |
| | | raccoon | public | | gurgle | | |
| | | lagoon | custom | | burglar | | |
| | | shampoo | juggle | | curtain | | |
| | | balloon | luster | | during | | |
| | | baboon | publish | | further | | |
| | | cocoon | suffer | | murder | | |
| | | maroon | yummy | | surplus | | |
| | | tattoo | | | | | |

# Ambiguous Vowels in Accented Syllables

| Accent in 1st | Accent in 1st | Accent in 1st | Accent in 1st | Accent in 1st | Accent in 1st | Accent in 1st | Accent in 1st |
|---|---|---|---|---|---|---|---|
| *oy/oi* | *oo* | *ow* | *ou* | *ou = short u* | *au* | *aw* | *al* |
| voyage | poodle | powder | county | trouble | saucer | awful | also** |
| loyal | foolish | power | counter | double | author | awkward | always |
| joyful | rooster | flower | thousand | southern | August | lawyer | almost |
| boycott | scooter | prowler | fountain | couple | autumn | awesome | halter |
| royal | | coward | mountain | cousin | laundry | awfully | salty |
| soybean | **Accent** | tower | council | touched | caution | gnawing | balky |
| oyster | **in 2nd** | drowsy | lousy | younger | faucet | gawking | balmy |
| moisture | balloon | brownie | scoundrel | youngster | sausage | flawless | calmly |
| poison | cartoon | rowdy | bounty | moustache | auction | drawing | falter |
| noisy | shampoo | chowder | boundary | nervous | haunted | jawbone | halting |
| pointed | baboon | vowel | founder | famous | cauldron | lawless | hallway |
| toilet | caboose | dowdy | doubtful | country | gaudy | tawny | waltzing |
| ointment | cocoon | towel | southeast | | daughter | yawning | alter |
| | harpoon | shower | voucher | *ou = long u* | jaunty | clawed | asphalt |
| **Accent** | igloo | cowboy | cloudy | coupon | naughty | brawny | walnut |
| **in 2nd** | platoon | powwow | flounder | toucan | slaughter | bawdy | walrus |
| annoy | raccoon | drowning | trousers | youthful | trauma | gnawed | |
| enjoy | typhoon | trowel | | cougar | pauper | | *Oddballs* |
| employ | papoose | | **Accent** | crouton | nausea | *Oddball* | laughed |
| destroy | maroon | **Accent** | **in 2nd** | souvenir | | drawer | all right |
| ahoy | tattoo | **in 2nd** | about* | | | | balloon |
| appoint | lagoon | allow | without | **Accent** | **Accent** | | gallon |
| avoid | | | around | **in 2nd** | **in 2nd** | | |
| exploit | | | announce | routine | because** | | |
| rejoice | | | profound | acoustics | exhaust | | |
| | | | surround | bouquet | assault | | |
| *Oddballs* | | | | | applause | | |
| porpoise | | | | | | | |
| tortoise | | | | | | | |
| turquoise | | | | | | | |

## Final Unaccented Syllables

| al | il/ile | el | le | | et | it |
|---|---|---|---|---|---|---|
| normal | stencil | model | fiddle | scribble | target | profit |
| central | April | angel | little* | people** | basket | audit |
| crystal | civil | barrel | able | hurdle | blanket | bandit |
| cymbal | council | bagel | ample | hustle | bucket | credit |
| dental | evil | bushel | angle | juggle | budget | digit |
| fatal | fossil | camel | ankle | jungle | carpet | edit |
| feudal | gerbil | cancel | apple | kettle | closet | exit |
| final | lentil | channel | battle | knuckle | comet | habit |
| focal | nostril | chapel | beagle | maple | cricket | hermit |
| formal | pencil | diesel | beetle | middle | faucet | limit |
| global | peril | flannel | bottle | needle | fidget | merit |
| journal | pupil | funnel | bramble | noodle | gadget | orbit |
| legal | tonsil | gravel | bridle | noble | hatchet | rabbit |
| mammal | | hazel | bubble | paddle | helmet | spirit |
| medal | docile | jewel | buckle | pebble | hornet | summit |
| mental | facile | kennel | bundle | pickle | jacket | unit |
| metal | fertile | kernel | bugle | purple | locket | visit |
| nasal | fragile | label | candle | puzzle | magnet | |
| naval | futile | level | castle | riddle | vomit | |
| neutral | hostile | morsel | cattle | saddle | planet | *-ate* |
| oval | missile | nickel | cable | sample | poet | climate |
| pedal | mobile | novel | chuckle | settle | puppet | private |
| petal | sterile | panel | circle | single | racket | senate |
| plural | | parcel | cradle | steeple | scarlet | pirate |
| rascal | | quarrel | cripple | struggle | secret | chocolate |
| rival | | ravel | cuddle | stumble | skillet | |
| royal | | satchel | cycle | tackle | sonnet | *Oddball* |
| rural | | sequel | dimple | tickle | tablet | biscuit |
| sandal | | shovel | doodle | title | thicket | |
| scandal | | shrivel | double | triple | toilet | |
| signal | | squirrel | eagle | trouble | trumpet | |
| spiral | | swivel | fable | twinkle | velvet | |
| tidal | | tinsel | freckle | turtle | wallet | |
| total | | towel | fumble | waffle | diet | |
| vandal | | travel | gamble | whistle | market | |
| vital | | tunnel | gargle | wrinkle | pocket | |
| vocal | | vessel | gentle | muscle | quiet | |
| local | | vowel | grumble | simple | rocket | |
| coastal | | | handle | temple | violet | |
| | | | idle | wrestle | | |
| | | *Oddballs†* | rattle | ripple | | |
| | | motel | rifle | huddle | | |
| | | hotel | sprinkle | dribble | | |
| | | | brittle | straddle | | |
| | | | crinkle | stubble | | |
| | | | gurgle | | | |
| | | | humble | | | |
| | | | pimple | | | |
| | | | puddle | | | |
| | | | sparkle | | | |

†accented on the final syllable

## More Final Unaccented Syllables

| er | | | er Agents | er Comparatives | ar | or | |
|---|---|---|---|---|---|---|---|
| other* | poster | bother | butcher | bigger | beggar | color** | rumor |
| under** | printer | center | robber | cheaper | burglar | actor | mirror |
| better** | shower | copper | swimmer | cleaner | scholar | author | horror |
| never** | timber | finger | runner | farther | cellar | doctor | humor |
| over** | toaster | power | drummer | quicker | cedar | editor | meteor |
| mother** | trouser | powder | jogger | slower | cheddar | mayor | motor |
| another** | ladder | proper | dreamer | younger | collar | neighbor | razor |
| banner | counter | quiver | dancer | older | cougar | sailor | scissors |
| blister | crater | roller | speaker | flatter | dollar | tailor | splendor |
| border | cancer | rubber | teacher | plainer | grammar | traitor | sponsor |
| clover | cider | sander | skater | lighter | hangar | tutor | terror |
| cluster | scorcher | saucer | marcher | darker | lunar | visitor | tractor |
| fiber | ledger | scooter | shopper | weaker | solar | donor | tremor |
| freezer | stretcher | shaver | racer | stronger | molar | armor | vapor |
| liter | pitcher | weather | grocer | wilder | polar | error | cursor |
| litter | answer | silver | barber | sweeter | sugar | favor | honor |
| lumber | blender | | peddler | cooler | nectar | anchor | tumor |
| manner | flower | | plumber | braver | pillar | | harbor |
| spider | | | ranger | | liar | | |
| sister | | | usher | | | | |
| brother | | | voter | | | | |
| father | | | catcher | | | | |
| lather | | | baker | | | | |

| /chər/ | | | /shər/ | /yər/ | /zhər/ | /jər/ |
|---|---|---|---|---|---|---|
| culture | nurture | mixture | pressure | failure | leisure | conjure |
| capture | rapture | moisture | fissure | manicure | measure | injure |
| creature | sculpture | picture | reassure | figure | closure | procedure |
| denture | stature | pasture | | | pleasure | |
| feature | stricture | posture | | senior | treasure | |
| fixture | texture | puncture | | junior | enclosure | |
| fracture | tincture | nature | | warrior | exposure | |
| future | torture | furniture | | | composure | |
| gesture | venture | miniature | | | disclosure | |
| juncture | adventure | premature | | | | |
| lecture | departure | signature | | Oddballs | | |
| injure | | | | danger | | |

| ain | an | en Verb | en Noun | en Adjective | in | on | |
|---|---|---|---|---|---|---|---|
| captain | human | frighten | chicken | golden | basin | apron | bacon |
| certain | organ | sharpen | children | open** | cabin | button | carton |
| curtain | orphan | shorten | garden | rotten | cousin | cannon | cotton |
| fountain | slogan | sweeten | kitten | spoken | margin | common | gallon |
| mountain | urban | thicken | mitten | sunken | pumpkin | dragon | lemon |
| villain | woman | widen | women | swollen | raisin | wagon | lesson |
| bargain | | deafen | heaven | wooden | robin | pardon | prison |
| chieftain | | flatten | oxygen | broken | dolphin | person | poison |
| | | lengthen | siren | hidden | muffin | reason | ribbon |
| | | open** | linen | chosen | penguin | season | weapon |
| | | | eleven | stolen | satin | salmon | |
| | | | | | napkin | | |

## More Unaccented syllables

| /ij/ | | /is/ | | /ē/ = ey | /ē/ = ie | /ē/ = y | |
|------|------|------|------|------|------|------|------|
| voyage | sausage | justice | furnace | chimney | cookie | very* | berry |
| bandage | cabbage | practice | surface | donkey | movie | pretty** | body |
| village | rummage | service | palace | turkey | brownie | early | beauty |
| message | savage | office | necklace | jockey | genie | crazy | drowsy |
| cottage | passage | crevice | menace | valley | goalie | candy | empty |
| wreckage | image | notice | grimace | volley | sweetie | daisy | guilty |
| courage | marriage | novice | terrace | journey | zombie | forty | tidy |
| storage | manage | bodice | | honey | birdie | envy | treaty |
| luggage | sewage | police | | money | eerie | worry | carry |
| damage | language | | *Oddballs* | jersey | bootie | gravy | bossy |
| postage | package | tennis | lettuce | pulley | rookie | sorry | trophy |
| garbage | | basis | porpoise | hockey | pinkie | dizzy | stingy |
| hostage | partridge | iris | tortoise | galley | prairie | cherry | bury |
| storage | knowledge | crisis | | monkey | | funny | easy |
| shortage | cartridge | axis | | alley | | happy | story |
| | porridge | | | | | hurry | Icy |

## Prefixes and Suffixes

| mis- | pre- | re- | un- | dis- | in ("not") | non- |
|------|------|-----|-----|------|------------|------|
| misbehave | precook | rebound | unable | disable | incomplete | nonsense |
| misconduct | predate | recall | unafraid | disagreeable | incorrect | nonstop |
| miscount | prefix | recapture | unarmed | disappear | indecent | nonfiction |
| misdeed | pregame | recharge | unbeaten | disarm | indirect | nonfat |
| misfit | preheat | reclaim | unbroken | discharge | inexpensive | nonprofit |
| misgivings | prejudge | recopy | uncertain | disclose | inflexible | nondairy |
| misguide | premature | recount | unclean | discolor | informal | nonstick |
| misjudge | prepay | recycle | unclear | discomfort | inhuman | nonviolent |
| mislay | preschool | reelect | uncommon | discontent | injustice | nonskid |
| mislead | preset | refill | uncover | discover | insane | nonstandard |
| mismatch | preteen | refinish | undone | dishonest | invalid | |
| misplace | pretest | reform | unequal | disinfect | invisible | de- |
| misprint | preview | refresh | unfair | dislike | inept | deflate |
| misspell | prewash | relearn | unkind | disloyal | | defrost |
| mistake | predict | remind | unlike | disobey | in ("in" or "into") | deprive |
| mistreat | precede | remodel | unlock | disorder | income | decrease |
| mistrust | prehistoric | renew | unpack | displace | indent | delete |
| misuse | prepare | reorder | unreal | disregard | indoor | deport |
| mischief | prevent | repay | unripe | disrespect | inset | detract |
| | precaution | reprint | unselfish | distaste | insight | deficient |
| | preschool | research | unstable | distrust | inside | degrading |
| | prenatal | restore | unsteady | disgrace | inlaid | denounce |
| | prescribe | retrace | untangle | | inmate | depleted |
| | | return | untie | | ingrown | deprived |
| | | review | unwrap | | inboard | detached |
| | | rewrite | unbutton | | inland | deviate |
| | | rebuild | uneven | | infield | deodorant |
| | | report | unhappy | | inflate | decongestant |
| | | recall | unopened | | inhale | dehydrated |
| | | refuel | unheated | | insert | desegregated |
| | | reject | unattached | | inspect | decaffeinated |
| | | reassure | unplanned | | inspire | demerits |
| | | reconsider | unplug | | intake | |

## More Prefixes

| uni- | bi- | tri- | fore- | sub- | ex- | en- |
|------|-----|------|-------|------|-----|-----|
| unicorn | biceps | triangle | forearm | subset | expel | enable |
| unicycle | bicycle | triple | forecast | subtract | express | endanger |
| uniform | bifocals | triceps | foretell | subdivide | explore | enact |
| unify | bilingual | triceratops | foresee | subgroup | exceed | enclose |
| union | binoculars | tricycle | foresight | submerge | excerpt | encourage |
| unique | bisect | trilogy | forehand | submarine | exclaim | enforce |
| unison | biweekly | trio | forehead | submerse | exclude | enjoy |
| universal | biannual | trivet | foreman | submit | excrete | enslave |
| universe | | triplets | forethought | subway | exhale | enlarge |
| | | tripod | foreshadow | subtotal | exile | enlist |
| | | triad | forepaw | subtitle | expand | enrage |
| | | trinity | foremost | sublet | explode | enrich |
| | | trident | forefathers | subsoil | exit | enroll |
| | | triathlon | | subject | extend | entrust |
| | | trillion | | | exempt | |
| | | | | | exhaust | |

### -ly

| | |
|---|---|
| badly | nightly |
| barely | safely |
| bravely | friendly |
| closely | gladly |
| costly | lonely |
| cruelly | nearly |
| deadly | quickly |
| loudly | quietly |
| proudly | slowly |
| smoothly | surely |
| kindly | lively |
| nicely | |

*Change y to i*

noisily
lazily
angrily
busily
easily
happily
luckily
daily
gaily
bodily
readily
steadily

### -y =/e/

breezy
bumpy
chilly
choppy
cloudy
dirty
dusty
easy
floppy
frosty
gloomy
greasy
grouchy
gritty
noisy
rainy
sandy
soapy
snowy
stormy
sweaty
thirsty
windy
dressy
skinny
speedy
floppy
lucky
grubby

### -fy =/i/

unify
classify
falsify
simplify
fortify
horrify
manify
purify

### -er/-est

blacker/blackest
bigger/biggest
bolder/boldest
braver/bravest
calmer/calmest
closer/closest
cheaper/cheapest
cleaner/cleanest
cooler/coolest
colder/coldest
smaller/smallest
thinner/thinnest
fewer/fewest
finer/finest
hotter/hottest
harder/hardest
sadder/saddest
newer/newest
quicker/quickest
lighter/lightest
louder/loudest
larger/largest
meaner/meanest

*Change y to i*

funnier/funniest
noisier/noisiest
prettier/prettiest
dirtier/dirtiest
easier/easiest
juicier/juiciest
lazier/laziest
luckier/luckiest
busier/busiest
crazier/craziest
heavier/heaviest
clumsier/clumsiest

### -less

ageless
breathless
careless
ceaseless
endless
helpless
homeless
lawless
painless
powerless
priceless
reckless
spotless
tasteless
useless
fearless
lifeless
speechless
thankless
cloudless
fruitless
jobless
scoreless
sleeveless
pointless
restless
worthless

*Change y to i*

penniless
pitiless
merciless

### -ful

careful
cheerful
colorful
fearful
graceful
harmful
hopeful
lawful
peaceful
playful
powerful
tasteful
thoughtful
truthful
useful
wasteful
wonderful
youthful
beautiful
armful
dreadful
respectful
faithful
grateful
hateful
helpful
joyful
painful
skillful
thankful
wishful
fretful

### -ness

awareness
closeness
coolness
darkness
firmness
goodness
openness
ripeness
sickness
sharpness
stiffness
stillness
thinness
weakness
moistness
vastness
dullness
kindness
dampness
blindness
tenderness
eagerness

*Change y to i*

dizziness
emptiness
laziness
readiness
fussiness
happiness
ugliness
clumsiness
liveliness

## Special Consonants

| Hard g | Soft g | Hard c | Soft c | Final c | que | k / ke | ph | Silent Letters |
|--------|--------|--------|--------|---------|-----|--------|-----|----------------|
| gadget | genie | cabin | city | attic | antique | namesake | trophy | wrinkle |
| gallon | genius | cafe | cider | music | unique | cupcake | dolphin | wreckage |
| gallop | genre | cactus | civil | topic | clique | earthquake | orphan | wriggle |
| gamble | general | campus | cinder | zodiac | opaque | forsake | phonics | wryly |
| garage | gentle | candle | clinic | clinic | critique | keepsake | gopher | wrestle |
| gully | gerbil | canyon | circle | comic | physique | mistake | nephew | answer |
| golden | gesture | cavern | circus | cynic | mystique | pancake | phantom | |
| gossip | giant | carpet | citric | toxic | brusque | provoke | pheasant | knuckle |
| guilty | ginger | cable | cedar | panic | conquer | slowpoke | phony | knowledge |
| gorilla | giraffe | comma | celery | picnic | boutique | turnpike | physics | |
| gopher | gypsy | copy | cement | classic | | evoke | triumph | gnaw |
| gather | gyrate | cozy | census | critic | **x** | homework | photo | gnarl |
| gutter | gently | cocoa | center | elastic | relax | embark | telephone | gnome |
| guitar | gender | comet | cereal | exotic | complex | landmark | alphabet | gnostic |
| gobble | | coffee | ceiling | frantic | index | network | | gnu |
| goggles | | corner | certain | graphic | perplex | berserk | | |
| gaily | | county | cycle | hectic | reflex | | | ghetto |
| gallery | | cubic | cynic | garlic | vortex | | | ghastly |
| | | cuddle | cymbal | fabric | vertex | | | ghoul |
| *Oddballs* | | culprit | cyclist | frolic | prefix | | | |
| giggle | | curtain | cyclone | logic | phoenix | | | honest |
| geyser | | custom | cylinder | drastic | annex | | | honor |
| gecko | | concern | cellar | scenic | | | | rhombus |
| | | concert | | basic | **ck** | | | rhyme |
| | | cancel | | plastic | attack | | | rhythm |
| | | cancer | | public | gimmick | | | shepherd |
| | | | | traffic | hammock | | | |
| | | | | arctic | ransack | | | solemn |
| | | | | mystic | padlock | | | column |
| | | | | skeptic | potluck | | | autumn |
| | | | | metric | hemlock | | | condemn |
| | | | | mimic | carsick | | | |
| | | | | | haddock | | | castle |
| | | | | | | | | thistle |
| | | | | | | | | whistle |
| | | | | | | | | fasten |
| | | | | | | | | listen |
| | | | | | | | | often* |
| | | | | | | | | soften |
| | | | | | | | | moisten |
| | | | | | | | | |
| | | | | | | | | daughter |
| | | | | | | | | naughty |
| | | | | | | | | height |
| | | | | | | | | weight |
| | | | | | | | | freight |
| | | | | | | | | assign |
| | | | | | | | | design |
| | | | | | | | | resign |

## Alternations and Reduced Vowels in Unaccented Syllables

| Silent to Sounded Consonant | Long to Short | Long to Schwa | Short to Schwa |
|---|---|---|---|
| bomb/bombard | cave/cavity | able/ability | metallic/metal |
| column/columnist | flame/flammable | famous/infamous | academy/academic |
| soften/soft | grave/gravity | major/majority | malice/malicious |
| crumb/crumble | nature/natural | native/nativity | periodic/period |
| debt/debit | athlete/athletic | prepare/preparation | emphatic/emphasis |
| damn/damnation | please/pleasant | relate/relative | celebrate/celebrity |
| design/designate | crime/criminal | stable/stability | democratic/democracy |
| fasten/fast | decide/decision | compete/competition | excel/excellent |
| hasten/haste | revise/revision | combine/combination | perfection/perfect |
| hymn/hymnal | wise/wisdom | define/definition | critic/criticize |
| malign/malignant | know/knowledge | invite/invitation | habit/habitat |
| moisten/moist | episode/episodic | recite/recitation | mobility/mobile |
| muscle/muscular | assume/assumption | reside/resident | prohibit/prohibition |
| resign/resignation | produce/production | compose/composition | geometry/geometric |
| sign/signal | convene/convention | expose/exposition | |
| condemn/condemnation | volcano/volcanic | custodian/custody | |
| | serene/serenity | pose/position | |
| | ignite/ignition | social/society | |
| | humane/humanity | | |
| | divide/division | | |

## Adding /shun/ to Base Words

| ct + ion | ss + ion | t + ion | d, de to sion | e-drop + ion | it to ission |
|---|---|---|---|---|---|
| action | expression | assertion | explosion | creation | admission |
| subtraction | oppression | digestion | decision | decoration | omission |
| distinction | possession | invention | division | generation | permission |
| election | profession | suggestion | invasion | imitation | submission |
| prediction | confession | adoption | conclusion | illustration | transmission |
| extinction | compression | insertion | intrusion | indication | |
| detection | obsession | congestion | protrusion | translation | e-drop + tion |
| selection | digression | prevention | allusion | congratulation | production |
| rejection | impression | distortion | collision | frustration | introduction |
| reaction | discussion | exhaustion | evasion | operation | reduction |
| connection | aggression | eruption | erosion | location | reproduction |
| distraction | depression | exception | seclusion | vibration | deduction |
| objection | procession | desertion | persuasion | circulation | seduction |
| infection | recession | | expansion | pollution | |
| instruction | | t + ation | ascension | dictation | be to p + tion |
| protection | c + ian | adaptation | suspension | hesitation | description |
| conviction | magician | temptation | exportation | donation | prescription |
| correction | musician | presentation | consultation | devotion | inscription |
| detection | optician | indentation | | graduation | subscription |
| abstraction | logician | plantation | | migration | transcription |
| inspection | clinician | infestation | | navigation | |
| injection | diagnostician | lamentation | | isolation | |
| reflection | electrician | confrontation | | | |
| | politician | expectation | | | |
| | technician | | | | |

## Vowel Alternations with Change in Accent When Adding Suffixes

| Schwa to Short with ity | Long to Short with cation | Long to Schwa with ation |
|---|---|---|
| mental/mentality | apply/application | declare/declaration |
| general/generality | certify/certification | degrade/degradation |
| moral/morality | clarify/clarification | prepare/preparation |
| brutal/brutality | classify/classification | admire/admiration |
| central/centrality | gratify/gratification | combine/combination |
| eventual/eventuality | imply/implication | define/definition |
| personal/personality | notify/notification | deprive/deprivation |
| neutral/neutrality | purify/purification | derive/derivation |
| original/originality | modify/modification | incline/inclination |
| normal/normality | unify/unification | invite/invitation |
| mental/mentality | simplify/simplification | recite/recitation |
| formal/formality | multiply/multiplication | compile/compilation |
| equal/equality | magnify/magnification | perspire/perspiration |
| vital/vitality | specify/specification | explore/exploration |
| legal/legality | verify/verification | |
| local/locality | qualify/qualification | |
| hospital/hospitality | identify/identification | |
| personal/personality | justify/justification | |
| | beautify/beautification | |

## Adding the Suffix able/ible

| Root Word + ible | Base Word + able | e-drop + able | y to i + able |
|---|---|---|---|
| audible | affordable | achievable | variable |
| credible | agreeable | admirable | reliable |
| edible | allowable | adorable | pliable |
| eligible | avoidable | advisable | pitiable |
| feasible | breakable | believable | justifiable |
| gullible | comfortable | comparable | identifiable |
| horrible | dependable | conceivable | deniable |
| invincible | expandable | consumable | enviable |
| legible | favorable | debatable | remediable |
| plausible | laughable | deplorable | |
| possible | payable | desirable | *Drop ate in Base* |
| terrible | preferable | disposable | tolerable |
| visible | predictable | excitable | vegetable |
| indelible | profitable | lovable | operable |
| intangible | punishable | notable | navigable |
| compatible | reasonable | pleasurable | abominable |
| combustible | refillable | recyclable | negotiable |
| responsible | remarkable | valuable | educable |
| defensible | respectable | | estimable |
| divisible | transferable | *ce/ge + able* | irritable |
| plausible | | manageable | appreciable |
| tangible | | enforceable | |
| accessible | | noticeable | |
| | | changeable | |

## Adding *ant/ance/ancy* and *ent/ence/ency*

| | |
|---|---|
| hesitant/hesitance/hesitancy | competent/competence/competency |
| abundant/abundance/abundancy | dependent/dependence/dependency |
| relevant/relevance/relevancy | emergent/emergence/emergency |
| extravagant/extravagance/extravagancy | equivalent/equivalence/equivalency |
| malignant/malignance/malignancy | excellent/excellence/excellency |
| petulant/petulance/petulancy | expedient/expedience/expediency |
| radiant/radiance/radiancy | lenient/lenience/leniency |
| brilliant/brilliance/brilliancy | resident/residence/residency |
| defiant/defiance | resilient/resilience/resiliency |
| reluctant/reluctance | convenient/convenience |
| exuberant/exuberance | different/difference |
| fragrant/fragrance | diligent/diligence |
| instant/instance | evident/evidence |
| elegant/elegance | impatient/impatience |
| vigilant/vigilance | independent/independence |
| resistant/resistance | patient/patience |
| significant/significance | innocent/innocence |
| tolerant/tolerance | intelligent/intelligence |
| observant/observance | obedient/obedience |
| resistant/resistance | indulgent/indulgence |
| | violent/violence |

## Using *ary, ery,* and *ory*

| ary | ery | ary with Schwa | ery with Schwa | ory | ory with Schwa |
|---|---|---|---|---|---|
| customary | very | anniversary | artery | allegory | compulsory |
| fragmentary | cemetery | boundary | bribery | auditory | cursory |
| extraordinary | stationery | documentary | celery | category | directory |
| hereditary | confectionery | elementary | discovery | dormitory | memory |
| imaginary | | glossary | gallery | explanatory | satisfactory |
| legendary | | salary | grocery | inventory | theory |
| literary | | summary | machinery | observatory | victory |
| military | | burglary | mystery | territory | history |
| missionary | | diary | nursery | circulatory | memory |
| necessary | | infirmary | scenery | derogatory | accessory |
| ordinary | | auxiliary | surgery | laboratory | compulsory |
| revolutionary | | documentary | drapery | mandatory | victory |
| secretary | | rudimentary | forgery | respiratory | |
| solitary | | | misery | | |
| stationary | | | | | |
| temporary | | | | | |
| vocabulary | | | | | |
| primary | | | | | |
| dictionary | | | | | |

## Accent in Polysyllabic Words

| First Syllable | | | Second Syllable | | | Third Syllable |
|---|---|---|---|---|---|---|
| anything | cantaloupe | aptitude | December | asparagus | whoever | constitution |
| somebody | comedy | architect | November | attorney | accountant | population |
| beautiful | customer | artery | October | computer | agility | planetarium |
| families | engineer | avalanche | September | election | amphibian | Sacramento |
| grandfather | evidence | calculator | uncommon | endurance | apprentice | Tallahassee |
| january | forestry | camera | unusual | executive | deliver | understand |
| libraries | generator | carpenter | unwanted | erosion | remember | imitation |
| wednesday | improvise | everything | protection | ignition | whenever | regulation |
| wonderful | iodine | colorful | reduction | judicial | tomorrow | California |
| populate | meteorite | gasoline | romantic | mechanic | abilities | definition |
| acrobat | navigator | everywhere | unable | banana | apartment | diagnosis |
| amateur | average | hamburger | providing | department | companion | hippopotamus |
| | | | vacation | important | condition | irrigation |
| | | | | | | Mississippi |
| | | | | | | declaration |
| | | | | | | exclamation |

## Prefixes

| anti ("against") | auto ("self") | circum ("around") | inter ("between") | intra ("within") | mal ("bad") |
|---|---|---|---|---|---|
| antifreeze | autograph | circumference | interact | intramural | malice |
| antidote | automation | circumvent | intercede | intravenous | malignant |
| antitoxin | autobiography | circumstance | interfere | intrastate | maltreated |
| antibiotic | automobile | circumspect | interloper | | malpractice |
| anticlimactic | autocrat | circumscribe | interchange | | maladjusted |
| antisocial | autonomy | circumlocution | interject | | malnutrition |
| antigen | autopsy | circumnavigate | interrupt | | malcontent |
| antipathy | | | intercede | | malfunction |
| antiseptic | | | intercom | | malady |
| | | | international | | |
| | | | interlocking | | |
| | | | intermission | | |
| | | | international | | |
| | | | intermural | | |

| peri ("around") | post ("after") | pro ("before," "forward") | | super ("higher") | trans ("across, beyond, through") |
|---|---|---|---|---|---|
| perimeter | posterior | proceed | profile | superpower | transfer |
| period | posterity | propel | promotion | supervision | transport |
| periphery | posthumous | produce | prohibit | supermarket | transmit |
| periscope | postpone | progress | procreate | supernatural | transplant |
| peripatetic | postscript | provide | propitious | superman | translate |
| periodontal | postmortem | program | pronounce | supersede | translucent |
| | postgraduate | projector | promulgate | supersonic | transparent |
| | postmeridian | protective | propensity | superstition | transform |
| | postseason | proclaim | proficient | superficial | transient |
| | postdated | profess | protracted | supercilious | transcend |
| | | | | | transact |

## Number-Related Prefixes (see also *uni*, *bi*, and *tri* under "More Prefixes" on page 490)

| mon, mono | cent | mil | oct | poly | semi | multi |
|---|---|---|---|---|---|---|
| monarchy | centigrade | million | octagon | polygon | semiannual | multitude |
| monastery | centimeter | millimeter | octopus | polygamy | semicolon | multiply |
| monogram | centipede | milligram | October | polychrome | semicircle | multicolored |
| monologue | centennial | millennium | octave | polyhedron | semisolid | multipurpose |
| monorail | century | millionaire | octahedron | polyglot | semiconscious | multicultural |
| monotone | percent | | octogenarian | polyester | semifinal | multimedia |
| monotonous | bicentennial | *deca/deci* | octane | polygraph | semiweekly | multiplex |
| monolith | | decade | | polymath | semiprecious | multifaceted |
| monopoly | *sex/hex* | December | *pent* | polymers | | multivitamin |
| monochrome | sextant | decahedron | pentagon | polyp | *quad* | multifarious |
| monogamy | sextuplets | decagon | pentameter | polytechnic | quadrangle | multiplication |
| | hexagon | decimal | pentacle | | quadrant | |
| | | decathlon | | | quarter | |

## Assimilated or Absorbed Prefixes

| in ("not") | il | im | | ir |
|---|---|---|---|---|
| inaccurate | illogical | immature | impure | irrational |
| inefficient | illegal | immaterial | impaired | irreconcilable |
| inoperable | illiterate | immobile | impartial | irreparable |
| insecure | illegible | immodest | impossible | irregular |
| innumerable | illicit | immoderate | impediment | irrelevant |
| inactive | illustrious | immoral | imperfect | irreplaceable |
| inappropriate | illegitimate | immortal | impersonal | irresistible |
| incompetent | illuminate | immovable | improper | irresponsible |
| indecent | | immigrant | impractical | irreversible |
| | | immediate | | irradiate |
| | | immerse | | Irreligious |

| sub ("under" or "lower") | | suf | sup | sur |
|---|---|---|---|---|
| subversion | subatomic | suffix | supplant | surreal |
| subterranean | subcommittee | suffuse | suppliant | surrender |
| suburban | subdivision | suffer | support | surrogate |
| substitute | submarine | suffice | supposition | surreptitious |
| substandard | subconscious | sufficient | suppress | |
| subsidize | subcontractor | suffocate | supplicant | *suc* |
| subclass | subjugate | | supplement | succumb |
| sublease | subscribe | | | succeed |
| subscript | subscription | | | success |
| subtract | submarine | | | succinct |
| subdue | submit | | | successive |

## More Assimilated Prefixes

| com ("with" or "together") | col | con | cor | co |
|---|---|---|---|---|
| common | collection | conspire | correlate | coagulate |
| community | collide | concert | corroborate | coexist |
| combination | collision | connect | correct | coalition |
| committee | collage | congress | correspond | coauthor |
| company | collaborate | congestion | corrupted | coeducational |
| comply | colleague | congregation | corrugated | cohabit |
| compress | collapse | conclude | | cohesion |
| compound | collusion | condense | | cohort |
| companion | collate | construct | | coincide |
| compact | collateral | constellation | | cooperate |
| complete | colloquial | connote | | coordinate |
| comrade | collect | | | |
| combine | | | | |

| ad ("to" or "toward") | at | ac | af | al | ap | as | ar |
|---|---|---|---|---|---|---|---|
| adjacent | attend | accompany | affinity | alliance | approach | assemble | arrange |
| adjoining | attune | acceptable | affable | alliteration | approximate | associate | arrest |
| addicted | attract | access | affection | allowance | appropriate | assimilate | array |
| adhesive | attach | accident | affluence | allusion | apprentice | assent | arrive |
| adjacent | attack | accommodate | affiliate | alleviate | apprehend | assault | arrogant |
| adaptation | attain | accomplish | affricative | allotment | appreciate | assertion | |
| additional | attention | accumulate | affirmation | | application | assessment | |
| adjective | attempt | accelerate | | an | applause | assume | |
| adjust | attitude | acquisition | ag | annex | appetite | assiduous | |
| admire | attribute | acquire | aggregate | annihilate | appendix | assistance | |
| admission | attrition | acquisitive | aggravate | announce | appear | assuage | |
| advocate | | | aggression | annul | appeal | assumption | |
| | | | aggrieved | annotate | | | |

| dis ("not" or "opposite of" or "apart") | | dif | ex ("out or "from") | | ef |
|---|---|---|---|---|---|
| disadvantage | disarray | difficult | extract | explode | efface |
| dissatisfied | disconcerted | diffusion | excavate | excrete | effect |
| disillusioned | discharged | different | exceed | exhume | efferent |
| disaster | disclaimer | diffidence | exception | extinct | efficiency |
| disability | disconsolate | | excerpt | expand | effrontery |
| disagreeable | discouraged | | excursion | extend | effusive |
| disseminate | disregard | | exhale | exclude | effort |
| disappoint | disenchanted | | exile | exhaust | effront |
| discern | disoriented | | expansion | extension | effluent |
| disdain | | | expenditure | explosion | effervescent |
| | | | exclaim | | |
| | | | | | ec |
| | | | | | ecstasy |
| | | | | | eccentric |
| | | | | | ecclesiastical |

| ob ("to," "toward," or "against") | | | op | of | oc |
|---|---|---|---|---|---|
| oblong | obscure | obscure | opponent | offend | occurrence |
| objection | observant | oblique | opposite | offensive | occasion |
| obligation | obstruction | obstacle | opportunity | offering | occupation |
| obliterate | obstreperous | obsolete | opposition | offense | occupy |
| oblivious | obstinate | obnoxious | oppress | officious | occlude |

## Greek Roots

| | |
|---|---|
| *aer* | "air" aerate, aerial, aerobics, aerodynamic, aeronautics, aerosol, aerospace |
| *arch* | "rule, chief" monarchy, anarchy, archangel, archbishop, archetype, architect, hierarchy, matriarch, patriarch |
| *aster, astr* | "star" aster, asterisk, asteroid, astrology, astronomy, astronaut, astronomical, astrophysics, disaster |
| *bi, bio* | "life" biology, biography, autobiography, biopsy, symbiotic, biodegradable, antibiotic, amphibious, biochemistry |
| *centr* | "center" center, central, egocentric, ethnocentric, centrifuge, concentric, concentrate, eccentric |
| *chron* | "time" chronic, chronicle, chronological, synchronize, anachronism |
| *cosm* | "world" cosmic, cosmology, cosmonaut, cosmopolitan, cosmos, microcosm |
| *crat* | "rule" democrat, plutocrat, bureaucrat, idiosyncratic, technocrat |
| *crit* | "judge" critic, criticize, critique, criterion, diacritical, hypocrite |
| *cycl* | "circle" cycle, bicycle, cyclone, tricycle, unicycle, recycle, motorcycle, cyclical, encyclopedia |
| *dem* | "people" demagogue, democracy, demographics, endemic, epidemic, epidemiology |
| *derm* | "skin" dermatologist, epidermis, hypodermic, pachyderm, taxidermist, dermatitis |
| *geo* | "earth, land" geology, geophysics, geography, geothermal, geocentric, geode |
| *gram* | "to write" diagram, program, telegram, anagram, cryptogram, epigram, grammar, monogram |
| *graph* | "to write" graph, paragraph, autograph, digraph, graphics, topography, biography, bibliography, calligraphy, choreographer, videographer, ethnography, phonograph, seismograph, lexicographer |
| *homo* | "same" homophone, homograph, homosexual, homogeneous |
| *hydra* | "water" hydra, hydrant, hydrate, hydrogen, hydraulic, hydroelectric, hydrology, hydroplane, hydroponics, anhydrous, hydrangea, hydrophobia |
| *logo* | "word, reason" logic, catalogue, dialogue, prologue, epilogue, monologue |
| *logy* | "study of" biology, geology, ecology, mythology, pathology, psychology, sociology, theology, genealogy, etymology, technology, zoology |
| *meter* | "measure" centimeter, millimeter, diameter, speedometer, thermometer, tachometer, altimeter, barometer, kilometer |
| *micro* | "small" microscope, microphone, microwave, micrometer, microbiology, microcomputer, microcosm |
| *ortho* | "straight, correct" orthodox, orthodontics, orthography, orthodontists, orthopedic |
| *pan* | "all" pandemic, panorama, pandemonium, pantheon, Pan-American |
| *path* | "feeling, suffer" sympathy, antipathy, apathetic, empathize, pathogen, pathologist, pathetic, pathos, osteopath |
| *ped* | "child" (see Latin *ped* for "foot") pedagogy, pediatrician, pedophile, encyclopedia |
| *phil* | "loving" philosophy, philharmonic, bibliophile, Philadelphia, philanderer, philanthropy, philatetic, philter |
| *phobia* | "fear" phobia, acrophobia, claustrophobia, xenophobia, arachnophobia, agoraphobia |
| *phon* | "sound" phonics, phonograph, cacophony, earphone, euphony, homophone, microphone, telephone, xylophone, saxophone, phoneme, symphony |
| *photo* | "light" photograph, telephoto, photocopier, photographer, photosynthesis, photocell, photogenic, photon |
| *phys* | "nature" physics, physical, physician, physiology, physique, astrophysics, physiognomy, physiotherapy |
| *pol* | "city" politics, police, policy, metropolis, acropolis, cosmopolitan, megalopolis, Minneapolis |
| *psych* | "spirit, soul" psyche, psychology, psychoanalyst, psychiatry, psychedelic, psychosis, psychosomatic, psychic |
| *scope* | "see" microscope, periscope, scope, telescope, stethoscope, gyroscope, horoscope, kaleidoscope, stereoscope |
| *sphere* | "ball" sphere, atmosphere, biosphere, hemisphere, ionosphere, stratosphere, troposphere |
| *tech* | "build, art, skill" technical, technician, technology, polytechnic |
| *tele* | "far" telecast, telegraph, telegram, telescope, television, telethon, teleconference, telepathy |
| *therm* | "heat" thermal, geothermal, thermometer, thermonuclear, thermos, thermostat, thermodynamic, exothermic |
| *typ* | "to beat, to strike" typewriter, typist, typographical, archetype, daguerreotype, prototype, stereotype, typecast |
| *zo* | "animal" zoo, zoology, protozoan, zodiac, zoologist |

## Latin Roots

| | |
|---|---|
| *aud* | "hear" audio, auditorium, audience, audible, audition, inaudible, audiovisual |
| *bene* | "well" benefactor, benevolent, beneficial, benefit, benign, benefactress, benediction |
| *cand, chand* | "shine" candle, chandelier, incandescent, candelabra, candid, candidate |
| *cap* | "head" captain, capital, capitol, capitalize, capitulate, decapitate, per capita, captivity |
| *cide* | "cut, kill" incise, incision, concise, circumcise, excise, fungicide, herbicide, pesticide, insecticide, suicide, homicide, genocide |
| *clud, clos, clus* | "shut" close, closet, disclose, enclose, foreclose, conclude, exclude, exclusive, preclude, occlude, seclude, seclusion, recluse |

| | |
|---|---|
| *cogn* | "know" recognize, incognito, cognizant, cognition, recognizance |
| *corp* | "body" corpse, corporal, corporation, corpus, corpulent, incorporate, corpuscle |
| *cred* | "trust, believe" credit, credible, credentials, incredible, accredited, credulous |
| *dent, don't* | "tooth" dentist, dentures, orthodontist, indent |
| *dic, dict* | "speak" dictate, diction, dictionary, predict, verdict, benediction, contradict, dedicate, edict, indict, jurisdiction, valedictorian, dictation |
| *doc* | "teach" documentary, indoctrinate, doctorate, doctor, docent, docile, doctrine |
| *duc, duct* | "lead" abduct, conductor, deduct, aqueduct, duct, educate, educe, induct, introduction, reduce, reproduce, viaduct |
| *equa, equi* | "equal" equal, equality, equation, equator, equity, equivalent, equilibrium, equivocate, equidistant, equinox |
| *fac, fec* | "do" factory, manufacture, faculty, artifact, benefactor, confection, defect, effect, facile, facilitate, facsimile, affect, affection |
| *fer* | "carry" ferry, transfer, prefer, reference, suffer, vociferous, inference, fertile, differ, conifer, conference, circumference |
| *fid* | "trust" fidelity, confidant, confidence, diffident, infidelity, perfidy, affidavit, bona fide, confidential |
| *fin* | "end" final, finale, finish, infinite, definitive |
| *flex, flect* | "bend, curve" flex, flexible, inflexible, deflect, reflection, inflection, circumflex, genuflect |
| *flu* | "flow" fluid, fluent, influx, superfluous, affluence, confluence, fluctuate, influence |
| *form* | "shape" conform, deform, formal, formality, format, formation, formula, informal, information, malformed, platform, reform, transform, uniform |
| *grac, grat* | "thankful" grace, gratuity, gracious, ingrate, congratulate, grateful, gratitude, ingratiate, persona non grata, gratify |
| *grad, gress* | "go, step" graduate, gradual, gradient, grade, retrograde, centigrade, degraded, downgrade, digress, aggressive, congress, egress, ingress, progress, regress, transgression |
| *ject* | "throw" eject, injection, interject, object, objection, conjecture, abject, dejected, projection, projectile, projector, reject, subjective, trajectory |
| *jud* | "judge" judge, judgment, prejudice, judiciary, judicial, adjudge, adjudicate, injudicious |
| *junct* | "join" junction, juncture, injunction, conjunction, adjunct, disjunction |
| *langu, lingu* | "tongue" language, bilingual, linguistics, linguist, linguine, lingo |
| *lit* | "letter" literature, illiterate, literal, literacy, obliterate, alliteration, literary |
| *loc, loq* | "speak" elocution, eloquent, loquacious, obloquy, soliloquy, ventriloquist, colloquial, interlocutor |
| *mal* | "bad" malady, malignant, maladroit, malaria, malcontent, malicious, malign, maladjusted, malevolent, malfunction, malnourished, malpractice |
| *man* | "hand" manual, manufacture, manicure, manuscript, emancipate, manacle, mandate, manipulate, manage, maneuver |
| *mem* | "memory, mindful" remember, memory, memorize, memorial, memorandum, memento, memorabilia, commemorate |
| *min* | "small" diminish, mince, minimize, minute, minuscule, minus, minor, minnow, minimum |
| *miss, mit* | "send" transmission, remission, submission, admit, transmit, remit, submit, omit, mission, missile, demise, emission, admission, commission, emissary, intermission, intermittent, missionary, permission, promise |
| *mob, mot* | "move" mobile, motion, motor, remote, automobile, promote, motivate, motel, locomotion, immobile, emotion, demote, commotion |
| *pat* | "father" paternal, patrimony, expatriate, patron, patronize |
| *ped* | "foot" pedal, pedestal, pedicure, pedigree, biped, centipede, millipede, moped, impede, expedite, orthopedic, pedestrian, quadruped |
| *pens, pend* | "hang" appendage, appendix, pending, pendulum, pension, suspended, suspense, compensate, depend, dispense, expend, expensive, pensive, stipend, impending, pendant |
| *port* | "carry" porter, portfolio, portage, portable, export, import, rapport, report, support, transport, comportment, deport, important, portmanteau |
| *pos, pon* | "put, place" pose, position, positive, apropos, compose, composite, compost, composure, disposable, expose, impose, imposter, opposite, postpone, preposition, proponent, proposition, superimpose, suppose |
| *prim, princ* | "first" prime, primate, primer, primeval, primitive, prima donna, primal, primary, primogeniture, primordial, primrose, prince, principal, principality, principle |
| *quir, ques* | "ask" inquire, require, acquire, conquer, inquisition, quest, question, questionnaire, request, requisite, requisition |
| *rupt* | "break" rupture, abrupt, bankrupt, corrupt, erupt, disrupt, interrupt |

| | |
|---|---|
| *sal* | "salt" salt, saline, salary, salami, salsa, salad, desalinate |
| *sci* | "know" science, conscience, conscious, omniscience, subconscious, conscientious |
| *scrib, script* | "write" scribble, script, scripture, subscribe, transcription, ascribe, describe, inscribe, proscribe, postscript, prescription, circumscribe, nondescript, conscription |
| *sect, seg* | "cut" bisect, dissect, insect, intersect, section, sector, segment |
| *sent, sens* | "feel" sense, sensitive, sensory, sensuous, sentiment, sentimental, assent, consent, consensus, dissent, resent, sensation |
| *sequ, sec* | "follow" sequel, sequential, consequence, consecutive, non sequitur, persecute, second, sect, subsequent |
| *son* | "sound" sonic, sonnet, sonorous, unison, ultrasonic, assonance, consonant, dissonant, resonate, sonate |
| *spec, spic* | "see" spectacle, spectacles, spectacular, specimen, prospect, respect, retrospective, speculate, suspect, suspicion, aspect, auspicious, circumspect, inspector, introspection |
| *spir* | "breathe" spirit, respiration, perspire, transpire, inspire, conspire, aspirate, dispirited, antiperspirant |
| *sta, stis* | "stand" stable, state, station, stationary, statistic, statue, stature, status, subsist, assist, consistent, desist, insistent, persistent, resist |
| *stru* | "build" construct, instruct, destruction, reconstruction, obstruct |
| *tain, ten* | "hold" detain, obtain, pertain, retain, sustain, abstain, appertain, contain, entertain, maintain |
| *tang, tact* | "touch" tangible, intangible, tangent, contact, tactile |
| *tend, tens* | "stretch" distend, tendon, tendril, extend, intend, intensify, attend, contend, portend, superintendent |
| *term* | "end" term, terminal, terminate, determine, exterminate, predetermine |
| *terra* | "earth" terrain, terrarium, terrace, subterranean, terrestrial, extraterrestrial, Mediterranean, terra cotta, terra firma |
| *tort, torq* | "twist" contort, distort, extort, torture, tortuous, torque |
| *tract* | "pull" tractor, traction, contract, distract, subtract, retract, attract, protracted, intractable, abstract, detract |
| *vac* | "empty" vacant, vacuum, evacuate, vacation, vacuous, vacate |
| *val* | "strong, worth" valid, valiant, validate, evaluate, devalue, convalescent, valedictorian, invalid |
| *ven, vent* | "come" vent, venture, venue, adventure, avenue, circumvent, convention, event, intervene, invent, prevent, revenue, souvenir, convenient |
| *vers, vert* | "turn" revert, vertex, vertigo, convert, divert, vertical, adverse, advertise, anniversary, avert, controversy, conversation, extrovert, introvert, inverse, inverted, perverted, reverse, subvert, traverse, transverse, universe, versatile, versus, vertebra |
| *vid, vis* | "see" video, vista, visage, visit, visual, visa, advise, audiovisual, envision, invisible, television, supervise, provision, revision, improvise |
| *voc* | "call" vocal, vociferous, evoke, invoke, advocate, avocation, convocation, equivocal, invocation, provoke, revoke, vocabulary, vocation |
| *vol, volv* | "roll" revolve, evolve, involve, volume, convoluted, devolve |

## Game Boards

This appendix contains templates for picture and word sorts as well as games. Figures G.1 through G.8 are templates that you can use to create some of the games described throughout the book. Note that there are two sides for each game board. When the two sides are placed together, they form a continuous track or path. These games can be adapted for different features and levels. Here are some general tips for creating the games.

1. Photocopy the game boards (enlarge slightly) and mount them on colored manila file folders, making them easy to create and store. Place game materials, such as spinners, word cards, or game markers, in plastic bags or envelopes labeled with the name of the game and stored in the folder. You might mark the flip side of word cards in some way so that lost cards can be returned to the correct game. Rubber stamp figures work well.
2. When mounting a game board in a folder, be sure to leave a slight gap (about an eighth of an inch) between the two sides so that the folder will still fold. If you do not leave this gap, the paper will buckle. Trim the sheets of paper so the two new sides line up neatly, or cut around the path shape and line up the two pieces of the pathway.
3. Various objects (buttons, plastic discs, coins, and bottle caps) can be used for game markers or pawns that the students will move around the board. Flat objects store best in the folders, or you may want to put a collection of game markers, dice, and spinners in a box. Store the box near the games, and students can take what they need.
4. Add pizazz to games with pictures cut from magazines or old workbooks, stickers, comic characters, clip art, and so on. Rubber stamps, your drawings, or students' drawings can be used to add interest and color. Create catchy themes such as Rabbit Race, Lost in Space, Through the Woods, Mouse Maze, Rainforest Adventure, and so forth.
5. Include directions and correct answers (when appropriate) with the game, stored inside along with playing pieces or glued to the outside of the folder.
6. Label the spaces around the path or track according to the feature you want to reinforce, and laminate the board for durability. If you want to create open-ended games that can be adapted to a variety of features, laminate the path before you label the spaces. Then you can write in letters or words with a washable overhead pen and change them as needed. Permanent marker can also be used and removed with hairspray or fingernail polish remover.
7. Add interest to the game by labeling some spaces with special directions (if you are using a numbered die or spinner) or add cards with special directions to the deck of words. Special directions can offer the students a bonus in the form of an extra turn or a penalty such as losing a turn. These bonus or penalty directions can tie in with your themes. For example, in the Rainforest Adventure, the player might forget a lunch and be asked to go back to the starting space. Keep the reading ability of your students in mind as you create these special directions.

## Spinners

Many of the word study games described in this book use a game spinner. Figure G.8 provides simple directions for making a spinner.

# Template for Picture Sorts

| | | | |
|---|---|---|---|
| | | | |
| | | | |
| | | | |
| | | | |
| | | | |

# Template for Word Sorts

|  |  |  |
|---|---|---|
|  |  |  |
|  |  |  |
|  |  |  |
|  |  |  |
|  |  |  |
|  |  |  |
|  |  |  |
|  |  |  |

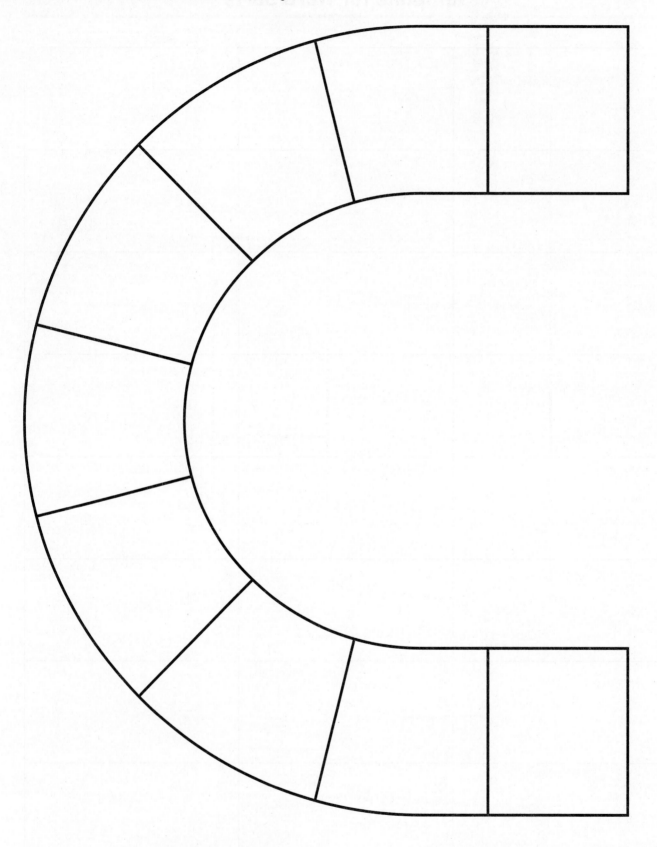

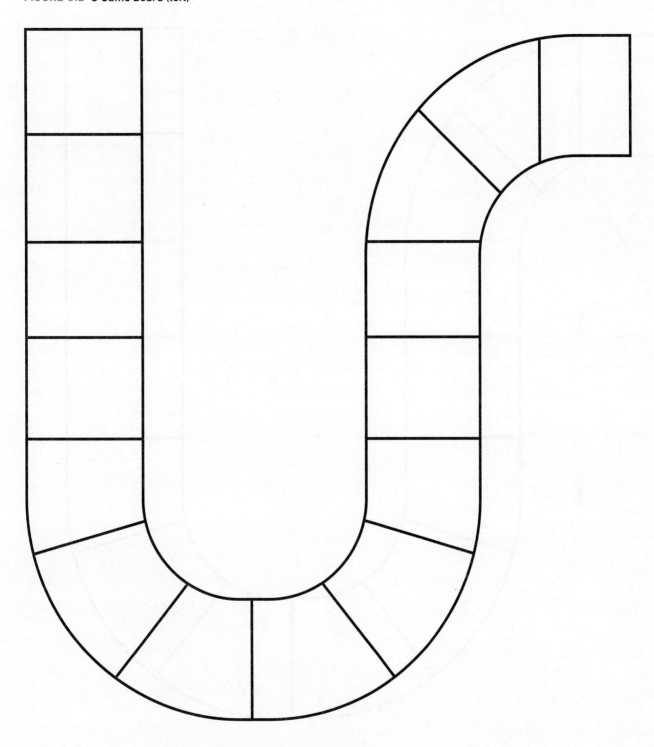

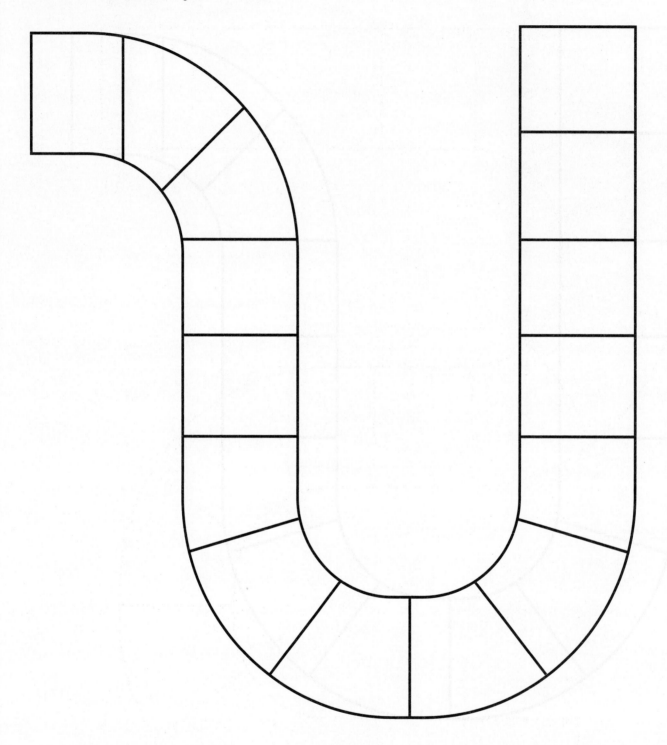

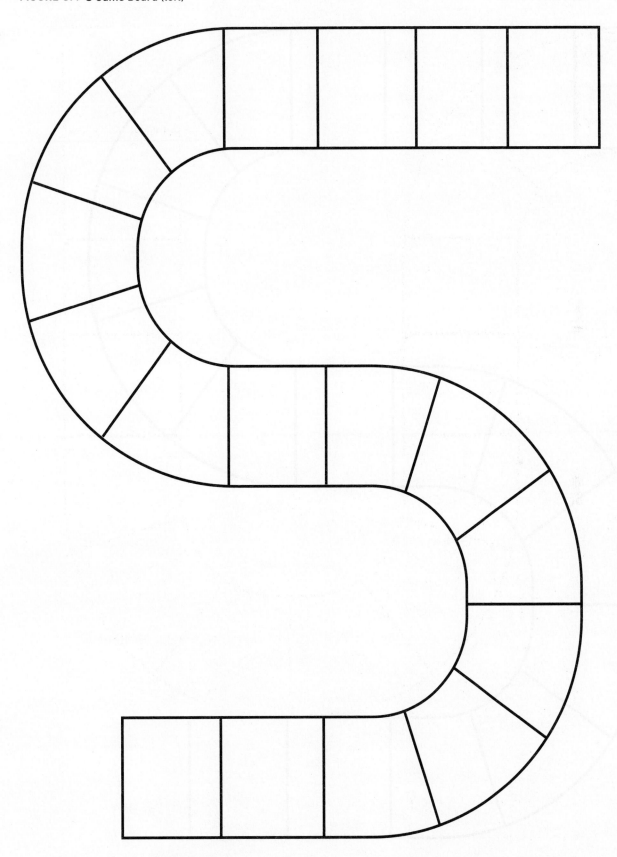

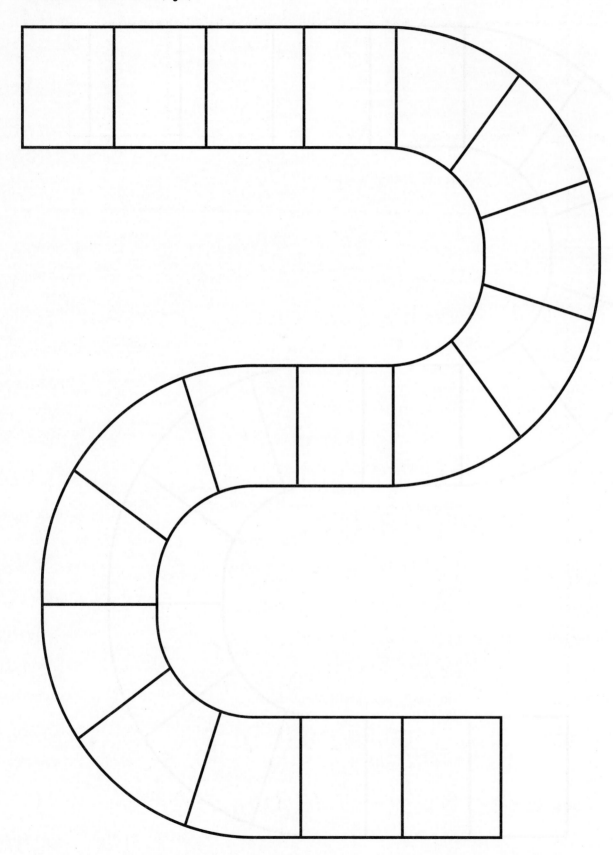

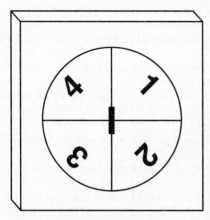

1. Glue a circle 3" to 4" in diameter onto a square of heavy cardboard or foamcore that is about 5" square. Square spinner bases are easier to hold than round ones.

2. Cut a narrow slot in the center of the circle with the point of a sharp pair of scissors or a razor blade.

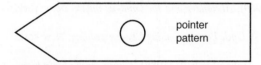

pointer pattern

3. Cut the pointer from soft plastic (such as a milk jug) and make a clean round hole with a hole punch.

4. A washer, either a metal one from the hardware store or one cut from the same plastic as the spinner, helps the pointer move freely.

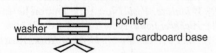

washer — pointer
— cardboard base

5. Push a paper fastener through the round hole of the pointer, the washer, and the slot in the spinner base. Flatten the legs, leaving space for the pointer to spin easily. Put a piece of tape over the flattened legs of the paper fastener.

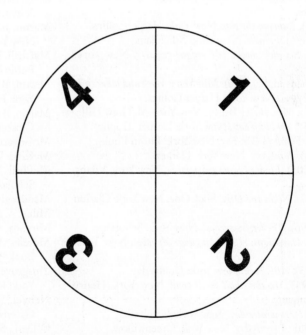

## Children's Literature

Azarian, M. (1981). *A farmer's alphabet*. Boston: David Godine.

Baker, K. (2010). *LMNO Peas*. San Diego, CA: Beach Lane Books.

Barnes, D. (2008). *Ruby and the Booker Boys series*. New York: Scholastic.

Base, G. (1986). *Animalia*. New York: Harry Abrams.

Bayer, J. (1984). *A, My name is Alice*. Illustrated by Steven Kellogg. New York: Dial.

Berenstain, S., & Berenstain, J. (1971). *The Berenstain's B book*. New York: Random House.

Bluemie, E. (2012). *How do you wokka-wokka?* Somerville, MA: Candlewick.

Blume, J. (1971). *Freckle juice*. New York: Yearling.

Blume, J. (2003). *Superfudge*. New York: Penguin.

Brett, J. (2003). *Town mouse, country mouse*. New York: Putnam.

Bruna, D. (1978). *B is for bear*. New York: Price Stern Sloan.

Brown, M. (2013). *Marisol McDonald and the clash bash: Marisol McDonald y la fiesta sin igual*. New York: Lee and Low. (Latino; bilingual; story).

Cameron, P. (1961). *I can't, said the ant*. New York: Putnam Publishing.

Carle, E. (1974). *My very first book of shapes*. New York: HarperCollins.

Carle, E. (1987). *Have you seen my cat?* New York: Scholastic.

Carle, E. (2007). *Eric Carle's ABC*. New York: Grosett and Dunlap.

Carle, E (2007). *Eric Carle's opposites*. New York: Grosset and Dunlop.

Christelow, E. (1989). *Five little monkeys jumping on the bed*. Boston: Clarion Books.

Cleary, B. (1968). *Ramona the pest*. New York: HarperCollins.

Clements, A. (1996). *Frindle*. New York: Atheneum.

Cole, J. (1993). *Six sick sheep: 101 tongue twisters*. New York: Morrow.

Cole, J., & Calmenson, S. (1990). *Miss Mary Mack and other children's street rhymes*. New York: Harper Collins.

Cowley, J. (1997). *Mrs. Wishy Washy*. New York: McGraw Hill.

Crews, D. (1995). *Ten black dots*. New York: Harper Trophy.

Dahl, R. (1988). *Fantastic Mr. Fox*. New York: Puffin Books.

Degan, B. (1983). *Jamberry*. New York: Harper.

Dewdney, A. (2005). *Llama Llama red pajama*. New York: Viking Juvenile.

English, K. (2007). *Nikki and Deja*, Book One. New York: Clarion Books

Ernst, L. C. (1996). *The letters are lost*. New York: Scholastic.

Fain, K. (1993). *Handsigns: A sign language alphabet*. New York: Scholastic.

Falls, C. B. (1923). *ABC book*. New York: Doubleday.

Fleming, D. (1993). *In the small small pond*. New York: Henry Holt and Company.

Florian, D. (1987). *A winter day*. New York: Scholastic.

Florian, D. (1990). *A beach day*. New York: Greenwillow.

Folsom, M. (2005). *Q is for duck: An alphabet guessing game*. Berkeley, CA: Sandpiper.

Frasier, D. (2007). *Miss Alaineus: A vocabulary disaster*. Berkeley, CA: Sandpiper.

Freeman, D. (1968). *Corduroy*. New York: Viking Juvenile Books.

Gág, W. (1933). *The ABC bunny*. New York: Coward-McCann.

Galdone, P. (1973). *The three billy goats gruff*. New York: Clarion Books.

Galdone, P. (2006). *The little red hen*. Boston: Clarion.

Garten, J. (1994). *The alphabet tale*. New York: Greenwillow.

Gray, K (2014). *Frog on a log?* New York: Scholastic

Guarina, D. (1989). *Is your mama a llama?* Illustrated by Steven Kellogg. New York: Scholastic.

Grimes, N. (2010). *Dyamonde Daniel series*. New York: Puffin Books.

Hague, K. (1984). *Alphabears: An ABC book*. New York: Holt, Rinehart & Winston.

Heller, R. (1993). *Chickens aren't the only ones*. New York: Putnam.

Hoban, T. (1978). *Is it red? Is it yellow? Is it blue?* New York: Greenwillow Books.

Hoban, T (1990). *Exactlty the opposite*. New York: Greenwillow Books.

Horenstein, H. (1999). *Arf! Beg! Catch! Dogs from A to Z*. New York: Scholastic.

Hutchins, P. (2005). *Rosie's walk*. Fullerton, CA: Aladdin.

Jay, A. (2005). *ABC: A child's first alphabet book*. New York: Dutton Juvenile.

Juster, N. (1961/2005). *The phantom tollbooth*. New York: Yearling.

Knutson, B. (2013). *Love and roast chicken: A trickster tale from the Andes mountains*. Minneapolis: Learner Books.

Langstaff, J. (1974). *Oh, a hunting we will go*. New York: Atheneum.

Lewis, B. & Lewis, A. (2016). *My alphabet animals: Learning letters and sounds with critters from A to Z*. Heritage Press Early Learning Education Books

Lewis, K. (2006). *My truck is stuck*. New York: Disney Hyperion.

Lionni, L. (1969). *Alexander and the wind-up mouse*. New York: Pantheon.

Look, L. (2004). *Uncle Peter's amazing Chinese wedding*. New York: Atheneum.

Martin, B., & Archambault, J. (1989). *Chicka chicka boom boom*. New York: Simon & Schuster.

Marshall, E., & Marshall, J. (1994). *Fox and his friends*. New York: Puffin Books.

Martin, B. (1970). *Brown bear, brown bear, what do you see?* New York: Henry Holt.

Martin, B (1998). *Here are my hands*. New York: Henry Holt.

McCloskey, R. (1948). *Blueberries for Sal*. New York: Puffin Books.

McGovern, A. (1996). *Stone soup*. New York: Scholastic.

McKissack, P. (1986). *Flossie and the fox*. New York: Dial.

McPhail, D. (1989). *David McPhail's animals A to Z*. New York: Scholastic.

Meddaught, (1992). *Martha speaks*. Boston: Houghton Mifflin.

Milne, A. A. (2009). *Winnie the Pooh*. New York: Dutton Juvenile.

Miranda, A. (2001). *Alphabet fiesta*. New York: Turtle Books.

Morales, Y. (2013). *Niño wrestles the world*. New York: Roaring Book Press.

Musgrove, M. (1976). *Ashanti to Zulu: African traditions*. New York: Dial.

Neitzel, S. (1994). *The jacket I wear in the snow*. New York: Greenwillow.

O'Dell, S. (2010). *Island of the blue dolphins*. Berkeley CA: Sandpiper.

Paparone, P. (1995). *Five little ducks*. New York: Scholastic.

Raffi, C. (1976). *Singable songs for the very young*. Universal City, CA: Troubadour Records.

Raffi, C. (1985). *One light, one sun*. Universal City, CA: Troubadour Records.

Raffi, C. (1999). *Down by the bay*. New York: Crown Books.

Rathman, P. (1994). *Good night, Gorilla*. New York: Scholastic.

Rathman, P. (1999). *10 minutes till bedtime*. New York: Scholastic.

Ratisseau, S. (2014). *Jumping joy: A book about jump rope rhymes.* Seattle, WA: Laughing Elephant.

Rinker, S. D. (2011). *Goodnight, goodnight, construction site.* San Francisco, CA: Chronicle Books.

Rodgers, G. (2014). *Chufki rabbit's big bad bellyache: A trickster tale.* El Paso, TX: Cinco Puntos Press.

Roth, S. L., & Abouraya, K. L. (2012). *Hands around the library: Protecting Egypt's treasured books.* New York: Dial.

Rowling, J. K. (2000). *Harry Potter and the goblet of fire.* New York: Scholastic.

Schotter, R. (2006). *The boy who loved words.* New York: Schwartz & Wade.

Scieszka, J. (1992). *The good, the bad, and the goofy.* New York: Viking Press.

Seuss, Dr. (1963). *Dr. Seuss's ABC.* New York: Random House.

Seuss, Dr. (1965). *Hop on pop.* New York: Random House.

Seuss, Dr. (1974). *There's a wocket in my pocket.* New York: Random House.

Shannon, G. (1996). *Tomorrow's alphabet.* New York: Greenwillow.

Sharmat, M. (1980). *Gregory the terrible eater.* New York: Four Winds Press.

Shaw, N. (1986). *Sheep in a jeep.* Boston: Houghton Mifflin.

Slate, J. (1996). *Mrs. Bindergarten gets ready for kindergarten.* New York: Scholastic.

Sierra, J., & Sweet, M. (2005). *Schoolyard rhymes: Kids' own rhymes for rope jumping, hand clapping, ball bouncing, and just plain fun.* New York: Knopf.

Slepian, J., & Seidler, A. (1967). *The hungry thing.* New York: Follett.

Slepian, J., & Seidler, A. (1990). *The hungry thing returns.* New York: Scholastic.

Slobodkina, E. (1947). *Caps for sale.* New York: Harper Trophy.

Sobel, J. (2006). *B is for bulldozer.* New York: HMH Books for Young Readers.

Steig, W. (1978). *Amos and Boris.* New York: Farrar, Straus and Giroux.

Stevens, J. (1995). *Tops and bottoms.* Boston: Houghton Mifflin.

*The tree* (A First Discovery Book). (1992). New York: Cartwheel Books.

Thomas, J. (2009). *Rhyming Dust Bunnies,* San Diego: Beach Lane Books.

Tyron, L. (1991). *Albert's alphabet.* New York: Atheneum.

Wagener, G. (1991). *Leo the lion.* New York: New York: HarperCollins.

Wallner, J. (1987a). *City mouse–country mouse.* New York: Scholastic.

Wallner, J. (1987b). *The country mouse and the city mouse and two more mouse tales from Aesop.* New York: Scholastic.

Wells, N. (1980). *Noisy Nora.* New York: Dial Press.

White, E. B. (1945). *Stuart Little.* New York: Harper Row.

Williams, M. (2003). *Don't let the pigeon drive the bus.* New York: Hyperion books.

Williams, M. (2004). *Knuffle Bunny.* New York: Hyperion books.

Williams, S. (1989). *I went walking.* New York: HMH for Young Readers.

Wilson, K. (2002). *Bear snores on.* New York: Little Simon.

Wilson, K. (2003). *Bear wants more.* New York: Little Simon.

Wilson, K. (2006). *Bear's new friend.* New York: Little Simon.

Wilson, K. (2012). *Bear says thanks.* New York: Little Simon.

Wilson, S. (2003). *Nap in a lap.* New York: Henry Holt.

Wildsmith, B. (1982). *The cat on the mat.* New York: Oxford Press.

Wood, A. (1995). *Silly Sally went to town.* Boston, MA: Houghton Mifflin Harcourt.

Woodson, J. (2012). *Each kindness.* New York: Nancy Paulsen Books.

Zuckerman, A. (2009). *Creature ABC.* San Francisco, CA: Chronicle Books.

# Bibliography of Word Study Books

Aboff, M. (2008). *If you were a prefix.* Chicago: Picture Window.

Allen, M. S., & Cunningham, M. (1999). *Webster's new world rhyming dictionary.* New York: Simon & Schuster.

*The American heritage book of English usage: A practical and authoritative guide to contemporary English.* (1996). Boston: Houghton Mifflin.

Asimov, I. (1961). *Words from the myths.* Boston: Houghton Mifflin.

Asimov, I. (1959). *Words of science, and the history behind them.* Boston: Houghton Mifflin.

Asimov, I. (1962). *Words on the map.* Boston: Houghton Mifflin.

Ayers, D. M. (1986). *English words from Latin and Greek elements* (2nd ed. revised by Thomas Worthen). Tucson, AZ: The University of Arizona Press.

Ayto, J. (2009). *Oxford school dictionary of word origins: The curious twists & turns of the cool and weird words we use.* Oxford: Oxford University Press.

Ayto, J. (1993). *Dictionary of word origins.* New York: Arcade

Balmuth, M. (2009). *The roots of phonics: A historical introduction,* revised edition. Baltimore: Brookes Publishing.

Barretta, G. (2010). *Dear Deer: A book of homophones.* Square Fish

Barretta, G. (2011). *Zoola palooza: A book of homographs.* New York: Henry Holt.

Barretta, G. (2018). *The bat can bat: A book of true homonyms.* New York: Henry Holt.

Barretta G. (2018). *The bass plays the bass and other homographs.* New York: Henry Holt.

Bear, D. R., Invernizzi, M., Johnston, F., & Templeton, S. (2019). *Words their way: Letter and picture sorts for emergent spellers* (3rd ed.). New York, NY: Pearson.

Beck, I., McKeown, M., & Kucan, L. (2008). *Creating robust vocabulary: Frequently asked questions.* New York: Guilford.

Beck, I. L., McKeown, M. G., & Kucan, L. (2013). *Bringing words to life: Robust vocabulary instruction* (2nd ed.). New York: Guilford.

Black, D. C. (1988). *Spoonerisms, sycophants and sops: A celebration of fascinating facts about words.* New York: Harper & Row.

Blachowicz, C., & Fisher, P. (2009). *Teaching vocabulary in all classrooms* (4th ed.). Boston: Allyn & Bacon.

Blachowicz, C., Fisher, P., Ogle, D., & Watts-Taffe, S. (2013). *Teaching academic vocabulary, K–8: Effective practices across the curriculum.* New York: Guilford.

Byson, B. (1990). *The mother tongue: English and how it got that way.* New York: Morrow.

Byson, B. (1994). *Made in America: An informal history of the English language in the United States.* New York: Morrow.

Ciardi, J. (1980). *A browser's dictionary: A compendium of curious expressions and intriguing facts.* New York: Harper & Row.

Cleary, B. (2007). *How much can a bare bear bear: What are homonyms and homophones?* Minneapolis: Millbrook.

Cleary, B. (2012). *I'm and won't, they're and don't: What's a contraction?* Minneapolis: Millbrook.

Cleary, B. (2013). *Thumbtacks, earwax, lipstick, dipstick: What is a compound word?* Minneapolis: Millbrook.

Cleary, B. (2015). *Pre- and re-, mis- and dis-: What is a prefix?* Minneapolis: Millbrook.

Cleary, B. (2016). Ful- and -less, -er and -ness: What is a suffix? Minneapolis: Millbrook.

Collis, H. (1981). *Colloquial English.* New York: Regents Pub.

Collis, H. (1986). *101 American English idioms.* New York: McGraw Hill.

Cousineau, P. (2010). *Word catcher: An odyssey into the world of weird and wonderful words.* Berkeley, CA: Viva Editions.

Cousineau, P. (2012). *The painted word: A treasure chest of remarkable words and their origins.* Berkeley, CA: Viva Editions.

Crutchfield, R. (1997). *English vocabulary quick reference: A comprehensive dictionary arranged by word roots.* Leesburg, VA: LexaDyne.

Crystal, D. (1987). *The Cambridge encyclopedia of language.* New York: Cambridge University Press.

Crystal, D. (2012). *Spell it out: The curious, enthralling, and extraordinary story of English spelling.* New York, NY: Picador/St. Martin's Press.

Cummings, D. W. (1988). *American English spelling.* Baltimore: Johns Hopkins University Press.

Danner, H., & Noel, R. (2004). *Discover it! A better vocabulary the better way* (2nd ed.). Occoquan, VA: Imprimis Books.

D'Aulaire, I., & D'Aulaire, E. (1980). *D'Aulaires' book of Greek myths.* New York: Doubleday.

Editors of the American Heritage Dictionaries. (2008). *Curious George's dictionary.* Boston: Houghton Mifflin Harcourt.

Editors of the American Heritage Dictionaries. (2009). *The American Heritage first dictionary.* Boston: Houghton Mifflin Harcourt.

Fine, E. H. (2004). Illustrated by K. Donner. *Cryptomania: Teleporting into Greek and Latin with the Cryptokids.* Berkeley, CA: Tricycle Press.

Fisher, L. (1984). *The Olympians: Great gods and goddesses of ancient Greece.* New York: Holiday House.

Freeman, M. S. (1997). *A new dictionary of eponyms.* New York: Oxford University Press.

Folsom, M. (1985). *Easy as pie: A guessing game of sayings.* New York: Clarion.

Franlyn, J. (1987). *Which is witch?* New York: Dorset Press.

Fry, E. (2004). *The vocabulary teacher's book of lists.* San Francisco: Jossey Bass.

Fry, E. B., & Kress, J. E. (2006). *The reading teacher's book of lists* (5th ed.). San Francisco: Jossey-Bass.

Funk, C. E. (1948). *A hog on ice and other curious expressions.* New York: Harper & Row.

Funk, C. E. (1955). *Heavens to Betsy and other curious sayings.* New York: Harper & Row.

Funk, W. (1954). *Word origins and their romantic stories.* New York: Grosset & Dunlap.

Green, T. M. (2008). *The Greek and Latin roots of English* (4th ed.). Lanham, MD: Rowman & Littlefield Publishers, Inc.

Gwynne, F. (1970). *The king who rained.* New York: Simon & Schuster.

Gwynne, F. (1976). *A chocolate moose for dinner.* New York: Simon & Schuster.

Gwynne, F. (1980). *A sixteen hand horse.* New York: Simon & Schuster.

Gwynne, F. (1988). *A little pigeon toad.* New York: Simon & Schuster.

Harrison, J. S. (1987). *Confusion reigns.* New York: St. Martin's Press.

Heacock, P. (1989). *Which word when?* New York: Dell.

Heller, R. (1987). *A cache of jewels and other collective nouns.* New York: Grosset & Dunlap.

Heller, R. (1988). *Kites sail high.* New York: Grosset & Dunlap.

Heller, R. (1989). *Many luscious lollipops: A book about adjectives.* New York: Grosset & Dunlap.

Heller, R. (1990). *Merry-go-round: A book about nouns.* New York: Grosset & Dunlap.

Heller, R. (1991). *Up, up and away: A book about adverbs.* New York: Grosset & Dunlap.

Heller, R. (1995). *Behind the mask: A book about prepositions.* New York: Grosset & Dunlap.

Hoad, T. F. (1986). *The concise Oxford dictionary of English etymology.* New York: Oxford University Press.

Johnston, F., Bear, D., Invernizzi, M., & Templeton, S. (2018). *Words their way: Word sorts for letter name–alphabetic spellers* (3rd ed.). New York: Pearson.

Johnston, F., Invernizzi, M., Bear, D. R., & Templeton, S. (2018). *Words their way: Word sorts for syllables and suffixes spellers* (3rd ed.). New York: Pearson.

Jones, C. F. (1999). Illustrated by J. O'Brian. *Eat your words: A fascinating look at the language of food.* New York: Delacorte Press.

Kennedy, J. (1996). *Word stems: A dictionary.* New York: Soho Press.

Kinsley, C. (1980). *The heroes.* New York: Mayflower.

Kress, J. E. (2002). *The ESL teacher's book of lists.* San Francisco, CA: John Wiley & Sons.

Lewis, N. (1983). *Dictionary of correct spelling.* New York: Harper & Row.

Lipton, J. (1991). *An exaltation of larks.* New York: Penguin.

Loewen, N. (2007). *If you were a homonym or a homophone.* Chicago: Picture Window Books.

Maestro, G. (1983). *Riddle romp.* New York: Clarion.

Maestro, G. (1984). *What's a frank frank? Easy homograph riddles.* New York: Clarion.

Maestro, G. (1985). *Razzle-dazzle riddles.* New York: Clarion.

Maestro, G. (1986). *What's mite might? Homophone riddles to boost your word power.* New York: Clarion.

Maestro, G. (1989). *Riddle roundup: A wild bunch to beef up your word power.* New York: Clarion.

Marciano, J. (2009). *Anonyponymous: The forgotten people behind everyday words.* New York: Bloomsbury.

*Merriam-Webster children's dictionary.* (2008). New York: DK Publishing.

*Merriam-Webster new book of word histories.* (1995). Springfield, MA: Merriam-Webster.

Moore, B., & Moore, M. (1997). *NTC's dictionary of Latin and Greek origins: A comprehensive guide to the classical origins of English words.* Chicago: NTC Publishing Group.

Nash, R. (1991). *NTC's dictionary of Spanish cognates thematically organized.* Chicago: NTC Publishing Group.

Nilsen, A. J., & Nilsen, D. L. F. (2004). *Vocabulary plus high school and up: A source-based approach*. Boston: Allyn & Bacon.

Nilsen, A. J., & Nilsen, D. L. F. (2004). *Vocabulary plus K-8: A source-based approach*. Boston: Allyn & Bacon.

Partridge, E. (1984). *Origins: A short etymological dictionary of modern English*. New York: Greenwich House.

Pei, M. (1965). *The story of language*. Philadelphia: Lippincott.

Presson, L. (1996). *What in the world is a homophone?* Hauppauge, NY: Barron's.

Presson, L. (1997). *A dictionary of homophones*. New York: Barron's.

Pulvner, R. (2012). *Happy endings, A story about suffixes*. New York: Holiday House.

Randall, B. (1992). *When is a pig a hog? A guide to confoundingly related English words*. New York: Prentice Hall.

Rasinski, T., Padak, N., Newton, R., & Newton, E. (2008). *Greek and Latin roots: Keys to building vocabulary*. Huntington Beach, CA: Shell Education.

Robinson, S. R. (1989). *Origins, Volume 1: Bringing words to life*. New York: Teachers & Writers Collaborative.

Robinson, S. R., with Lindsay McAuliffe (1989). *Origins, Volume 2: The word families*. New York: Teachers & Writers Collaborative.

Room, A. (1992). *NTC's dictionary of word origins*. Lincolnwood, IL: National Textbook.

Safire, W. (1984). *I stand corrected: More on language*. New York: Avon.

Sarnoff, J., & Ruffins, R. (1981). *Words: A book about word origins of everyday words and phrases*. New York: Charles Scribner's Sons.

Scarry, R. (1998). *Best word book ever*. New York: Random House.

Schleifer, R. (1995). *Grow your own vocabulary: By learning the roots of English words*. New York: Random House.

*The Scholastic dictionary of synonyms, antonyms, homonyms*. (1965). New York: Scholastic.

Scragg, D. G. (1974). *A history of English spelling*. Manchester, England: Manchester University Press.

Shaskan, T.S. (2008). *If you were a compound word*. Chicago: Picture Window Books.

Shipley, J. T. (1967). *Dictionary of word origins*. Lanham, MD: Rowman & Littlefield.

Shipley, J. (2001). *The origins of English words*. Baltimore: Johns Hopkins University Press.

Stahl, S., & Nagy, W. (2006). *Teaching word meanings*. Mahwah, NJ: Erlbaum.

Templeton, S., Johnston, F., Bear, D., & Invernizzi, M. (2019). *Words their way: Word sorts for derivational relations spellers* (3rd ed.). New York, NY: Pearson.

Terban, M. (1982). *Eight ate: A feast of homonym riddles*. New York: Clarion.

Terban, M. (1983). *In a pickle and other funny idioms*. New York: Clarion.

Terban, M. (1984). *I think I thought and other tricky verbs*. New York: Clarion.

Terban, M. (1986). *Your foot's on my feet! And other tricky nouns*. New York: Clarion.

Terban, M. (1987). *Mad as a wet hen! And other funny idioms*. New York: Clarion.

Terban, M. (1988a). *The dove dove: Funny homograph riddles*. New York: Clarion.

Terban, M. (1988b). *Too hot to hoot: Funny palindrome riddles*. New York: Clarion.

Terban, M. (1991). *Hey, hay! A wagonful of funny homonym riddles*. New York: Clarion.

Terban, M. (1992). *Funny you should ask: How to make up jokes and riddles with wordplay*. New York: Clarion.

Venesky, R. (1970). *The structure of English orthography*. The Hague: Mouton.

Venezky, R. L. (1999). *The American way of spelling: The structure and origins of American English orthography*. New York: Guilford Press.

Watkins, C. (2011). *The American Heritage Dictionary of Indo-European Roots, Third Edition*. Boston: Houghton Mifflin Harcourt.

*Webster's dictionary of word origins*. (1992). New York: Smithmark.

Weiner, S. (1981). *Handy book of commonly used American idioms*. New York: Regents Pub.

Winchester, S. (1998). *The professor and the madman: A tale of murder, insanity, and the making of the Oxford English dictionary*. New York: HarperCollins.

Winchester, S. (2003). *The meaning of everything: The story of the Oxford English Dictionary*. New York: Oxford University Press.

Zwiers, J. (2014). *Building academic language: Meeting Common Core Standards across disciplines, Grades 5-12* (2nd ed.). San Francisco, CA: Jossey-Bass.

# Glossary

**absorbed (assimilated) prefixes**   Prefixes in which the spelling and sound of the consonant has been absorbed into the spelling and sound at the beginning of the base or root to which the prefix is affixed (e.g., *ad + tract = attract*).

**academic vocabulary**   Academic vocabulary includes domain-specific vocabulary found in content area, specialized, disciplinary texts (e.g., *dendrite* in biology, *coordinates* and *equilateral* in geometry, *electoral college* in government), as well as general academic vocabulary used across content areas and disciplines (e.g., *analyze, define, factors, method, principle*).

**accented/stressed syllable**   The syllable in a word that receives more emphasis when spoken and usually has a clearly pronounced vowel sound. Compare to *unaccented syllable*.

**affix**   Most commonly a suffix or prefix attached to a base word, stem, or root.

**affixation**   The process of attaching a word part, such as a prefix or suffix, to a base word, stem, or root.

**affricate/affricates**   A speech sound produced when the breath stream is stopped and released at the point of articulation, usually where the tip of the tongue rubs against the roof of the mouth just behind the teeth, such as when pronouncing the final sound in the word *such* or the beginning sound in the word *trip*. Includes the sounds for /ch/, /sh/, /j/, and /tr/.

**alliteration**   The occurrence in a phrase or line of speech of two or more words having the same beginning sound; e.g., *Big burly bears bashed berry baskets*.

**alphabetic**   A writing system containing characters or symbols representing individual speech sounds.

**alphabetic layer**   The first layer of word study instruction, focusing on letter–sound correspondences. Old English was phonetically regular to a great extent.

**alphabetic principle**   The concept that letters and letter combinations are used to represent phonemes in orthography. See also *orthography*; *phoneme*.

**ambiguous vowels**   A vowel sound represented by a variety of different spelling patterns (e.g., the /ä/ sound in *cause, lawn, false,*) or vowel patterns that represent a wide range of sounds (e.g., the *ou* in *cough, through*, and *could*).

**analytic phonics**   Phonics instruction that begins with whole words that are divided into their elemental parts through phonemic, orthographic, and morphological analysis. See *synthetic phonics*.

**articulated/articulation**   Sounds are physically shaped in the mouth during speech using the tongue, teeth, lips, and the roof of the mouth. Some mistakes are made in spelling based on similarities in articulation (e.g., *tr* for *dr*).

**assimilated prefixes**   See *absorbed (assimilated) prefixes*.

**automaticity**   Refers to the speed and accuracy of word recognition and spelling. Automaticity is the goal of word study instruction and frees cognitive resources for comprehension.

**base word**   A word to which prefixes and/or suffixes are added. For example, the base word of *unwholesome* is *whole*. See *free morphemes*.

**blends**   A phonics term for an orthographic unit of two or three letters at the beginning or end of words that are blended together. There are *l*-blends such as *bl*, *cl*, and *fl*; *r*-blends such as *gr*, *tr*, and *pr*; *s*-blends such as *pc*, *scr*, and *squ*; and final blends such as *ft*, *rd*, and *st*. Every sound represented in a blend is pronounced, if only briefly.

**blind sort**   A word sort done with a partner in which students who are responsible for sorting cannot see the word. They must instead attend to the sounds and sometimes visualize the spelling pattern to determine the category.

**blind writing sort**   A variant of a blind sort in which one student (or teacher) names a word without showing it to another student, who must write it in the correct category under a key word.

**bound morphemes**   Meaning units of language (morphemes) that cannot stand alone as a word. *Respected* has three bound morphemes: *re+spect+ed*. Compare to *free morphemes*.

**build, blend, and extend**   *Build* new words by providing a rime unit (*-ime*) then name words for students to spell by changing the initial letter (*dime, crime, shine*). *Blend* the words by writing the vowel pattern and substitute different beginning letters to create new words for students to read. *Extend* involves spelling and reading words that were not part of the original word study lesson but follow the same spelling feature.

**center time**   Work completed independently in prepared areas within a classroom.

**choral reading**   Oral reading done in unison with another person or persons.

**circle time**   Group work conducted under the teacher's direction.

**classroom composite**   A classroom profile that organizes students into instructional groups by features to be taught within each stage.

**closed sorts**   Word or picture sorts based on predetermined categories. Compare to *open sorts*.

**closed syllable**   A syllable that ends with or is "closed" by a consonant sound. In polysyllabic words, a closed syllable contains a short vowel sound that is closed by two consonants (e.g., *rabbit, racket*). Compare to *open syllable*.

**cognates**   Words in different languages derived from the same root. They are the same or similar in spelling and share the same or similar meanings.

**complex consonant patterns**   Consonant units occurring at the end of words determined by the preceding vowel sound. For example, a final *tch* follows the short vowel sound in *fetch* and *scotch*, whereas a final *ch* follows the long vowel sound in *peach* and *coach*. Other complex consonant patterns include final *ck* (*pack* vs. *peak*) and final *dge* (*badge* vs. *cage*).

**compound words**   Words made up of two smaller words. A compound word may or may not be hyphenated, depending on its part of speech.

**concept of word in text (COW-T)**   The ability to match spoken words to printed words, as demonstrated by the ability to point to, or track, the words of a memorized text while reading.

**concepts about print (CAP)**   Understandings about how books are organized (front-to-back page turning, titles, illustrations), how print is oriented on the page (top to bottom, left to right), and features of print such as punctuation and capitalization.

**concept sorts**   A categorization task in which pictures, objects, or words are grouped by shared attributes or meanings to develop concepts and vocabulary.

**consolidated alphabetic phase**   Ehri's fourth phase of word recognition, in which readers use patterns, chunks, and other word parts to figure out unfamiliar words.

**consonant alternation**   The process in which the pronunciation of consonants changes in the base or root of derivationally related words while the spelling does not change (e.g., the silent-to-sounded *g* in the words *sign* and *signal*; the /k/ to /sh/ pattern in the words *music* and *musician*).

**consonant blend**   See *blends*.

**consonant digraph**   See *digraph*.

**consonants**   Letters that are not vowels (*a*, *e*, *i*, *o*, and *u*). Whereas vowel sounds are thought of as musical, consonant sounds are known for their noise and the way in which air is constricted as it is stopped and released or forced through the vocal tract, mouth, teeth, and lips.

**continuant sound/continuants**   A consonant sound, such as /sssss/ that can be prolonged as long as the breath lasts without distorting the sound quality. Includes the consonant sounds for /f/, /l/, /m/, /n/, /r/, /s/, /v/, /w/, and /th/. See *stop consonants*.

**cut and paste activities**   A variation of picture sorting in which students cut out pictures from magazines or catalogs and paste them into categories.

**derivational affixes**   Affixes added to base words that affect the meaning (*sign*, **re**sign; *break*, *break**able***) and/or part of speech (*beauty*, *beaut**iful***). Compare to *inflected/inflectional endings*.

**derivational relations**   The last stage of spelling development, in which spellers learn about derivational relationships preserved in the spelling of words. *Derivational* refers to the process by which new words are created from existing words, chiefly through affixation, and the development of a word from its historical origin. *Derivational constancy* refers to spelling patterns that remain the same despite changes in pronunciation across derived forms. For example, *bomb* retains the *b* from *bombard* because of its historical evolution.

**developmental level**   An individual's stage of spelling development: emergent, letter name–alphabetic, within word pattern, syllables and affixes, or derivational relations.

**developmental spelling**   Spelling that reflects the current word knowledge of students who spell "as best they can." See also *invented spelling*.

**dialogic reading**   An approach to reading aloud that is designed to stimulate oral language and dialogue while enhancing students' ability to retell stories.

**digraph**   Two letters that represent one sound. There are consonant digraphs and vowel digraphs, though the term most commonly refers to consonant digraphs. Common consonant digraphs include *sh*, *ch*, *th*, and *wh*. Consonant digraphs at the beginning of words are *onsets*.

**diphthong**   A complex speech sound beginning with one vowel sound and moving to another within the same syllable. The *oy* in *boy* is a diphthong, as is the *ou* in *cloud*.

**directionality**   The left-to-right direction used for reading and writing English.

**domain-specific academic vocabulary**   See *academic vocabulary*.

**draw and label activities**   An extension activity for a picture sort in which students draw pictures of things that begin with the sounds under study. The pictures are drawn in the appropriate categories and labeled with the letter(s) corresponding to that sound.

**echo reading**   Oral reading in which the student echoes or imitates the reading of the teacher or partner to offer support for beginning readers and to model fluency.

**emergent**   A period of literacy development ranging from birth to beginning reading. This period precedes the letter name–alphabetic stage of spelling development.

**eponyms**   Places, things, and actions that are named after an individual.

**etymology**   The study of the origin and historical development of words.

**extensions**   Activities that extend the word study lesson to new words that have similar spelling features and to reading and writing them in context.

**feature analysis**   More than scoring words right and wrong, feature analyses provide a way of interpreting students' spelling errors by considering their knowledge of specific orthographic features such as consonant blends or short vowels. Feature analyses inform teachers what spelling features to teach.

**feature guide**   A tool used to classify students' errors within a hierarchy of orthographic features. Used to score spelling inventories to assess students' knowledge of specific spelling features at their particular stage of spelling development and to plan word study instruction to meet individual needs.

**final consonant blends**   see *blends*

**focused contrasts**   A set of deliberately targeted spelling features that can be compared, contrasted, and categorized according to sound, pattern, or meaning.

**free morphemes**   Meaning units of language (morphemes) that stand alone as words. (*Workshop* has two free morphemes: *work* and *shop*.) Compare to *bound morphemes*.

**frustration level**   A dysfunctional level of instruction where there is a mismatch between instruction and what an individual is able to grasp. This mismatch precludes learning and often results in frustration.

**full alphabetic readers/phase**   Ehri's third phase of word recognition, in which readers are able to sound out words using letter–sound correspondences or phonics they know.

**general academic vocabulary**   See *academic vocabulary*.

**generative**   The approach to word study that emphasizes spelling and morphological principles that apply to *many* words, as opposed to an approach that focuses on individual words. Generative instruction addresses the combination of base words, Greek and Latin word roots, and affixes in order to *generate* students' understanding of how most words in the English language work.

**headers** Words, pictures, or other labels used to designate categories for sorting.

**high-frequency words** Words that make up roughly 50 percent of any text—those that occur most often (e.g., *the, was, were, is*).

**homographs** Words that are spelled alike but have different pronunciations and different meanings (e.g., "*tear* a piece of paper" and "to shed a *tear*"; "*lead* someone along" and "the element *lead*").

**homonyms** Words that share the same spelling but have different meanings (tell a *yarn*, knit with *yarn*). See *homographs*; *homophones*; *polysemous*.

**homophones** Words that sound alike, are spelled differently, and have different meanings (e.g., *bear* and *bare*, *pane* and *pain*, and *forth* and *fourth*).

**idiomatic expression** An expression, word, or phrase that has a figurative meaning that is different from the literal meaning of the individual words (i.e. *headstrong*, and *dime a dozen*).

**independent level** That level of academic engagement in which an individual works independently, without need of instructional support. Independent-level behaviors demonstrate a high degree of accuracy, speed, ease, and fluency.

**Indo-European (IE) root** More than half of the world's languages were influenced by Indo-European, a language spoken more than 7,000 years ago. The origin of most roots in a language may be traced to Indo-European. For example, the IE root *bhel*, meaning "blow, swell" gave rise to the English words *ball*, *balloon*, and *bold*.

**inflected/inflectional endings** Suffixes that change the verb tense (*walks, walked, walking*) or number (*dogs, boxes*) of a word.

**instructional level** A level of academic engagement in which instruction is comfortably matched to what an individual is able to grasp. See also *zone of proximal development (ZPD)*.

**interactive read-alouds** A reading format to support emergent reading where the teacher reads aloud to the students and invites discussion and other participation.

**interactive writing** A cooperative instructional strategy whereby a text is composed with student input and the writing is done largely by the students under supervision to create an accurately spelled final version. It can be used to model writing strategies and concepts about print.

**invented spelling** Also known as spelling "as best you can"; allows students to write even before they can read during the emergent stage. See also *developmental spelling*.

**key pictures** Pictures placed at the top of each category in a picture sort. Key pictures act as headers for each column and can be used for analogy.

**key words** Words placed at the top of each category in a word sort. Key words act as headers for each column and can be used for analogy.

**kinetic reversal** An error of letter order (PTE for *pet*).

**known words** Words that can be pronounced immediately without having to resort to sounding them out. See *sight words*.

**language experience approach** An approach to teaching reading in which students dictate to a teacher, who records their language. Dictated accounts can then be used as familiar reading materials.

**lax** Lax vowels are commonly known as the short vowel sound. Short vowel sounds are produced by relaxing the vocal cords. See *tense vowels*.

**letter name–alphabetic spelling stage** The second stage of spelling development, in which students represent beginning, middle, and ending sounds of words with phonetically accurate letter choices, often based on the sound of the letter name itself, rather than learned letter–sound associations. The letter name *h* (aitch), for example, produces the /ch/ sound, and is often selected to represent that sound (HEP for *chip*).

**lexical quality** The mental representation of a word's pronunciation, meaning, and use. The quality of this representation, when merged with the word's spelling, supports fluency and comprehension.

**liquids** The consonant sounds for /r/ and /l/, which, unlike other consonant sounds, do not obstruct air in the mouth. The sounds for /r/ and /l/ are more vowel-like in that they do not involve direct contact between the lips, tongue, and the roof of the mouth as other consonants do. Instead, they "roll around" in the mouth, as if liquid.

**long vowels** Every vowel (*a, e, i, o,* and *u*) has two sounds, commonly referred to as "long" and "short." The long vowel sound "says its letter name" and frequently are paired with other vowels as in *bake* and *beak*. See *tense vowels*.

**meaning layer** The third layer of English orthography, including meaning units or morphemes such as prefixes, suffixes, and word roots. These word elements were acquired primarily during the Renaissance, when English was overlaid with many words of Greek and Latin derivation. See *morphemes*.

**meaning sorts** A type of word sort in which the categories are determined by semantic categories or by spelling–meaning connections.

**memory reading** An accurate recitation of text accompanied by fingerpoint reading.

**miscellaneous category** A column for placing words that do not appear to fit any of the targets contrasts in a picture or word sort. See *oddball*.

**mock linear** A kind of pretend writing where children beginning to approximate the broader contours of the writing system, starting with the linear arrangement of print.

**morphemes (or morphemic)** Meaning units in the spelling of words, such as the suffix *-ed*, which signals past tense, or the root *graph* in the words *autograph* or *graphite*. See also *bound morphemes*; *free morphemes*.

**morphemic analysis** The process of analyzing or breaking down a word in terms of its meaning units or morphemes (e.g., *in-struct-or*).

**morphology** The study of word parts related to syntax and meaning.

**nasals** A sound, such as /m/, /n/, or /ng/, produced when the air is blocked in the oral cavity but escapes through the nose. The first consonants in the words *mom* and *no* represent nasal sounds.

**oddballs** Words that do not fit the targeted feature in a sort.

**onset** The initial consonant(s) sound of a single syllable or word. The onset of the word *sun* is /s/. The onset of the word *slide* is /sl/. See *rimes*.

**open sorts** A type of picture or word sort in which the categories for sorting are left open. Students sort pictures or words into groups according to the students' own judgment. See *closed sorts*.

**open syllable** Syllables that end with a long-vowel sound (e.g., *la-bor, sea-son*). Compare to *closed syllable*.

**orthography** The writing system of a language—specifically, the correct sequence of letters, characters, or symbols.

**other vowels** Vowels that are neither long nor short and include *r*-influenced vowels and diphthongs, such as *oy* or *ou*.

**partial alphabetic readers/phase** Ehri's second phase of word recognition, in which students use partial clues, primarily initial consonants, to identify words. Also known as *selective cue stage*.

**pattern** A letter sequence that functions as a unit to represent a sound (such as *ai* in *rain, pain,* and *train*) or a sequence of vowels and consonants, such as the consonant-vowel-consonant (CVC) pattern in a word such as *rag* or at a syllable juncture such as the VCCV pattern in *button*.

**pattern layer** The second layer or tier of English orthography, in which patterns of letter sequences, rather than individual letters themselves, represent vowel sounds. This layer of information was acquired during the period of English history following the Norman invasion. Many of the vowel patterns of English are of French derivation.

**pattern sort** A word sort in which students categorize words according to similar spelling patterns.

**personal readers** Individual books of reading materials for beginning readers. Group experience charts, dictations, rhymes, and short excerpts from books comprise the majority of the reading material.

**phoneme** The smallest unit of speech that distinguishes one word from another. For example, the *t* of *tug* and the *r* of *rug* are phonemes.

**phoneme segmentation** The process of dividing a spoken word into the smallest units of sound within that word. The word *bat* can be divided or segmented into three phonemes: /b/, /ă/, /t/.

**phonemic awareness** The ability to consciously isolate, identify, and manipulate individual phonemes in a spoken language. Phonemic awareness is often assessed by the ability to tap, count, or push a penny forward for every sound heard in a word like *cat*: /k/, /ă/, /t/.

**phonetic** Representing the sounds of speech with a set of distinct symbols (letters), each denoting a single sound. See also *alphabetic principle*.

**phonics** The systematic relationship between letters and sounds.

**phonics readers** Beginning reading books written with controlled vocabulary that contain recurring phonics elements. Also called decodable texts.

**phonograms** Often called *word families*, phonograms end in rimes that vary only in the beginning consonant sound to make a word. For example, *back, sack, black,* and *track* are phonograms with the rime *-ack*.

**phonological awareness** An awareness of various speech sounds such as syllables, rhyme, and individual phonemes.

**phonology** Literally "the study of sound," linguists use this term to refer to the largely tacit or subconscious knowledge that underlies the ability to speak—to pronounce speech sounds and assign stress to syllables and words as well as rising and falling intonation in phrases and sentences.

**picture sort** A categorization task in which pictures are sorted into categories by sound or by meaning. Pictures cannot be sorted by pattern.

**polysemous (or polysemy)** The characteristic of words to have multiple meanings; derived from *poly-* ("many") + *sem-* the Latin root referring to "meaning").

**power score** The total number of words spelled correctly on a spelling inventory. Used as a rough estimate of overall spelling stage.

**pre-alphabetic readers phase** Ehri's first phase of word recognition, in which students use nonalphabetic clues, like word length or distinctive print, to identify words. Also known as *logographic*.

**preconsonantal nasals** Nasals that occur before consonants, as in the words *bump* or *sink*. The vowel is nasalized as part of the air escapes through the nose during pronunciation. See also *nasals*.

**predictable text** Text for beginning readers with repetitive language patterns, rhythm and rhyme, and illustrations that make it easy to read and remember.

**prefix** An affix attached at the beginning of a base word or word root that changes the meaning of the word.

**prephonetic** Writing that bears no correspondence to speech sounds; literally, "before sound." Prephonetic writing occurs during the emergent stage and typically consists of random scribbles, mock linear writing, or hieroglyphic-looking symbols.

**pretend reading** A paraphrase or spontaneous retelling told by students as they turn the pages of a familiar story book.

**print referencing** The practice of referring to features of print such as punctuation, capital letters, directionality, and so forth as a way to teach students concepts about print. See also *concepts about print (CAP)*.

**prosodic/prosody** The musical qualities of language, including intonation, expression, stress, and rhythm, that contribute to fluency.

**reduced vowel** A vowel occurring in an unstressed syllable. See also *schwa*.

**rimes** A unit composed of the vowel and any following consonants within a syllable. For example, the rime unit in the word *tag* is *ag*. See also *onset*.

**r-influenced (r-controlled) vowels** In English, *r* colors the way the preceding vowel is pronounced. For example, compare the pronunciation of the vowels in *bar* and *bad*. The vowel in *bar* is influenced by the *r*.

**root word/roots** Words or word parts, often of Latin or Greek origin, that are often combined with other roots to form words such as *telephone* (*tele* and *phone*). See also *stem*.

**salient sound** A prominent sound in a word or syllable that stands out because of the way it is made or felt in the mouth.

**schwa**  A vowel sound in English that often occurs in an unstressed syllable, such as the /uh/ sound in the first syllable of the word *above*.

**seatwork**  School work that is completed at the student's own desk. Seatwork is usually on a student's independent level and is usually assigned for practice. See also *independent level*.

**semantics**  Knowledge of the meaning underlying words.

**semiphonetic**  Writing that demonstrates *some* awareness that letters represent speech sounds (literally, "part sound"). Beginning and/or ending consonant sounds of syllables or words may be represented, but medial vowels are usually omitted (e.g., ICDD for *I see Daddy*). Semiphonetic writing occurs at the end of the emergent stage or the very outset of the early letter name–alphabetic stage.

**shared reading**  An activity in which the teacher prereads a text and then invites students to join in on subsequent readings.

**short vowels**  Every vowel (*a, e, i, o*, and *u*) has two sounds, commonly referred to as "long" and "short." The vocal cords are more relaxed when producing the short vowel sound than the long vowel sound. Because of this, short vowel sounds are often referred to as *lax*. The five short vowels can be heard at the beginning of these words: *apple, Ed, igloo, octopus*, and *umbrella*. Compare to *long vowels*.

**sight words/sight word vocabulary**  Printed words stored in memory by the reader that can be read immediately, "at first sight," without having to use decoding strategies. See *known words*.

**sound board**  Charts used by letter name–alphabetic spellers that contain pictures and letters for the basic sound–symbol correspondences (e.g., the letter *b*, a picture of a bell, and the word *bell*).

**sound sort**  Sorts that ask students to categorize pictures or words by sound as opposed to visual patterns.

**speed sorts**  Pictures or words that are sorted under a timed condition. Students try to beat their own time.

**spelling-by-stage classroom organization chart**  A classroom composite sheet used to place students in a developmental spelling stage and form groups.

**spelling inventories**  Assessments that ask students to spell a series of increasingly difficult words used to determine what spelling features students know or use but confuse, as well as a specific developmental stage of spelling.

**spelling–meaning connections**  Words that are related in meaning often share the same spelling despite changes in pronunciation from one form of the word to the next. For example, the word *sign* retains the *g* from *signal* even though it is not pronounced, thus "signaling" the meaning connection through the spelling.

**static reversal**  A handwriting error that is the mirror image of the intended letter (*b* for *d*, or *p* for *d*).

**stem**  This usually refers to a base or word root together with any derivational affixes that have been added, and to which inflectional endings may be added.

**stop consonants**  A consonant sound such as /t/ that is formed by briefly obstructing air in the vocal track followed by a puff of air; stop consonant sounds (/b/, /d/, /g/, /k/, /p/, and /t/) cannot be prolonged without distorting the sound.

**stressed/accented syllable**  The syllable in a word that is given an added emphasis when spoken and marked with bold letters or accent marks in the dictionary (e.g., ap' ple or **ap** ple).

**structural analysis**  The process of determining the pronunciation and/or meaning of a word by analyzing word parts, including syllables, base words, and affixes.

**suffix**  An affix attached at the end of a base word or word root.

**syllable juncture**  The transition from one syllable to the next. Sometimes this transition involves a spelling change such as consonant doubling or dropping the final *-e* before adding *-ing*.

**syllable juncture patterns**  The alternating patterns of consonants (C) and vowels (V) that surround the point where syllables meet. For example, the word *rabbit* follows a VCCV syllable pattern at the point where the syllables meet (i.e. *rab̲b̲it*).

**syllables**  Units of spoken language that consist of a vowel that may be preceded and/or followed by several consonants. Syllables are units of sound and can often be detected by paying attention to movements of the mouth. Syllabic divisions indicated in the dictionary are not always correct because the dictionary will always separate meaning units regardless of how the word is pronounced. For example, the proper syllable division for the word *naming* is *na-ming*; however, the dictionary divides this word as *nam-ing* to preserve the *ing*.

**syllables and affixes stage**  The fourth stage of spelling development, which coincides with intermediate reading. Syllables and affixes spellers learn about the spelling changes that often take place at the point of transition from one syllable to the next. Frequently this transition involves consonant doubling or dropping the final *-e* before adding a suffix.

**synchrony**  Occurring at the same time. In this book, stages of spelling development are described in the context of reading and writing behaviors occurring at the same time.

**syntax**  Knowledge underlying the ability to arrange words into phrases and sentences.

**synthetic phonics**  Phonics instruction that begins with individual sounds and the blending of those sounds to form words. See *analytic phonics*.

**teacher-directed sorts**  An explicit word study lesson in which the teacher models and leads students through the sorting process, offers explanations, and facilitates a discussion about the features and the meaning of words.

**tense vowels**  A vowel sound that is commonly known as the long vowel sound. Long vowel sounds are produced by tensing the vocal cords. (See *lax vowels*)

**tracking**  The ability to fingerpoint read a text, demonstrating concept of word in text. See *concept of word in text (COW-T)*.

**unaccented/unstressed syllable**  The syllable in a word that gets little emphasis and may have an indistinct vowel sound, such as the first syllable in *about*, the second syllable in *definition*, or the final syllables in *doctor* or *table*. See also *schwa*.

**unvoiced (or voiceless)**  A sound that, when produced, does not cause the vocal cords to vibrate. For example, the *t* in *at* is unvoiced. Voiced/voiceless consonant contrasts include these pairs: [/p/ /b/], [/t/ /d/], [/k/ /g/], [/ch/ /j/], [/f/ /v/], [/s/ /z/]. In most languages, vowels are voiced.

**voice pointing**   A strategy used by emergent readers to identify a word in a memorized rhyme or familiar text. They go back to the beginning of the text and start reciting it in their heads (or out loud) while mentally pointing to each word as it is recited until they arrive at the word in question.

**voiced**   A sound that, when produced, vibrates the vocal cords. The letter sound of *d* in *add*, for example, vibrates the vocal cords. Compare to *unvoiced*.

**vowel**   A speech sound produced by the easy passage of air through a relatively open vocal tract. Vowels form the most central sound of a syllable. In English, vowel sounds are represented by the following letters: *a, e, i, o, u,* and sometimes *y*. Compare to *consonants*.

**vowel alternation**   The process in which the pronunciation of vowels changes in the base or root of derivationally related words, while the spelling does not change (e.g., the long-to-short vowel change in the related words *crime* and *criminal*; the long-to-schwa vowel change in the related words *impose* and *imposition*).

**vowel digraphs**   A phonics term for pairs of vowels that represent a single vowel sound (such as *ai* in *rain*, *oa* in *boat*, *ue* in *blue*). Compare to *digraph*.

**vowel marker**   A silent letter used to indicate the sound of the vowel. In English, silent letters are used to form patterns associated with specific vowel sounds. Vowel markers are usually vowels, as the *i* in *drain* or the *a* in *treat*, but they can also be consonants, as the *l* in *told*.

**whole-to-part model**   A technique for fostering early literacy development using the shared reading of a whole texts followed activities involving the parts (sentences, words, letters, and sounds).

**within word pattern spelling stage**   The third stage of spelling development, which coincides with the transitional period of literacy development. Within word pattern spellers have mastered the basic letter–sound correspondences of written English and they grapple with letter sequences that function as a unit, especially long-vowel patterns that include silent letters.

**word**   A unit of meaning. A word may be a single syllable or a combination of syllables. A word may contain smaller units of meaning within it. In print, a word is separated by white space. In speech, several words may be strung together in a breath group. For this reason, it takes a while for young students to develop a clear concept of word. See also *concept of word in text (COW-T)*.

**word bank**   A collection of known words harvested from frequently read beginning reading materials. Word bank words are written on small cards and stored for review and use in word study games and word sorts.

**word cards**   Words written on 2-by-1-inch pieces of cardstock or paper.

**word consciousness**   An attitude of curiosity and attention to words critical for vocabulary development.

**word families**   Phonograms or words that share the same rime. (For example, *fast, past, last,* and *blast* all share the *ast* rime.) In the derivational relations stage, *word families* refers to words that share the same root or origin, as in *spectator, spectacle, inspect,* and *inspector*. See *phonograms; rimes*.

**word hunts**   A word study activity in which students go back to texts they have previously read to hunt for other words that follow the same spelling features examined during the word or picture sort.

**word knowledge**   A constellation of linguistic information about words and the concepts they represent. Such information includes a concept of what a word is (as opposed to a phrase or a letter), word meanings, pronunciations, the way words are used in sentences and texts, and all the connotations and concepts that might be associated with a word. All of this linguistic information is reflected in the word's spelling. See *lexical quality*.

**word operations**   A process of exchanging spelling features in various word positions to make new words. Consonants, blends, and digraphs are exchanged for other consonants at the beginning or end of words (e.g., *make-bake-brake-flake; mad-math-mash-mask*), or vowels or vowel patterns are exchanged in the middle (e.g. *drive-drove; give-gave; braid-breed*).

**word root**   See *root word/roots*.

**word sort**   A basic word study routine in which students group words into categories. Word sorting involves comparing and contrasting within and across categories. Word sorts are often cued by key words placed at the top of each category.

**word study**   A learner-centered, conceptual approach to instruction in phonics, spelling, word recognition, and vocabulary, based on a developmental model.

**word study notebooks**   Notebooks in which students write their word sorts into columns and add other words that follow similar spelling patterns throughout the week. Word study notebooks may also contain lists of words generated over time, such as new vocabulary, homophones, cognates, and so on.

**writing sorts**   An extension activity in which students write the words they have sorted into categories.

**zone of proximal development (ZPD)**   A term coined by the Russian psychologist, Vygotsky, referring to the ripe conditions for learning something new. A person's ZPD is that zone that is neither too hard nor too easy. The term is similar to the concept of *instructional level*.

# References

Adams, M. J. (1990). *Beginning to read: Thinking and learning about print*. Cambridge, MA: MIT Press.

Anders, P., & Bos, C. (1986). Semantic feature analysis: An interactive strategy for vocabulary development and text comprehension. *Journal of Reading, 29*, 610–616.

Armbruster, B. B., Lehr, F., & Osborn, J. (2001). *Put reading first: The research building blocks for teaching children to read*. Washington, DC: The Partnership for Reading.

Atwell, N. (2014). *In the middle* (3rd ed.). Portsmouth, NH: Heinemann.

Avineri, N., Johnson, E., Brice-Heath, S., McCarty, T., Ochs, E., Kremer-Sadlik, T., ... & Alim, H. S. (2015). Invited forum: Bridging the "language gap". *Journal of Linguistic Anthropology, 25*(1), 66–86.

Babayigit, S. (2014). The relations between word reading, oral language, and reading comprehension in children who speak English as a first (L1) and second language (L2): a multigroup structural analysis. *Reading and Writing, 28*: 527–544. doi: 10.1007/s11145-014-9536-x

Bahr, R. H., Silliman, E. R., & Berninger, V. (2009). What spelling errors have to tell about vocabulary learning. In C. Wood & V. Connelly (Eds.), *Contemporary perspectives on reading and spelling* (pp. 177–210). London: Routledge.

Ball, E. W., & Blachman, B. A. (1988). Phoneme segmentation training: Effect on reading readiness. *Annals of Dyslexia, 38*, 208–225.

Barrentine, S. J. (1996). Engaging with reading through interactive read-alouds. *The Reading Teacher, 50*, 36–42.

Baumann, J. F., Edwards, E. C., Font, G., Tereshinski, C. A., Kame'enui, E. J., & Olejnik, S. (2003). Teaching morphemic and contextual analysis to fifth-grade students. *Reading Research Quarterly, 37*(2), 150–176.

Bear, D. (1982). *Patterns of oral reading across stages of word knowledge*. Unpublished manuscript, University of Virginia, Charlottesville.

Bear, D. (1989). Why beginning reading must be word-by-word. *Visible Language, 23*(4), 353–367.

Bear, D. (1991a). Copying fluency and orthographic development. *Visible Language, 25*(1), 40–53.

Bear, D. (1991b). "Learning to fasten the seat of my union suit without looking around": The synchrony of literacy development. *Theory into Practice, 30* (3), 149–157.

Bear, D. (1992). The prosody of oral reading and stage of word knowledge. In S. Templeton & D. Bear (Eds.), *Development of orthographic knowledge and the foundations of literacy: A memorial Festschrift for Edmund H. Henderson* (pp. 137–186). Hillsdale, NJ: Lawrence Erlbaum.

Bear, D. R., Caserta-Henry, C., & Venner, D. (2004). *Personal readers and literacy instruction with emergent and beginning readers*. Berkeley, CA: Teaching Resource Center.

Bear, D. R., Flanigan, K., Hayes, L., Helman, L., Invernizzi, L., Johnston, F., & Templeton, S. (2014). *Words their way: Vocabulary for middle and high school*. Boston: Pearson.

Bear, D. R., & Helman, L. (2004). Word study for vocabulary development: An ecological perspective on instruction during the early stages of literacy learning. In J. F. Baumann & E. J. Kame'enui (Eds.), *Vocabulary instruction: Research to practice* (pp. 139–158). New York: Guilford Press.

Bear, D. R., Invernizzi, M., Johnston, F., & Templeton, S. (2018). *Words their way: Letter and picture sorts for emergent spellers* (3rd ed.). Boston: Pearson.

Bear, D. R., Invernizzi, M., Templeton S., Johnston, F., Helman, L. A. (2019). *Words Their Way Classroom*. Glenview, IL: Pearson Schools.

Bear, D. R., Negrete, S., Cathey, S. (2012). Developmental literacy instruction with struggling readers across three stages. *New England Journal of Reading, 48*(1), 1–9.

Bear, D., & Templeton, S. (1998). Explorations in developmental spelling: Foundations for learning and teaching phonics, spelling and vocabulary. *The Reading Teacher, 52*, 222–242.

Bear, D., Templeton, S., Helman, L., & Baren, T. (2003). Orthographic development and learning to read in different languages. In G. Garcia (Ed.), *English learners: Reaching the highest level of English literacy* (pp. 71–95). Newark, DE: International Reading Association.

Beck, I., McKeown, M., & Kucan, L. (2008). *Creating robust vocabulary: Frequently asked questions*. New York: Guilford.

Beck, I. L., McKeown, M. G., & Kucan, L. (2013). *Bringing words to life: Robust vocabulary instruction* (2nd ed.). New York: Guilford Press.

Beers, J. W., & Henderson, E. H. (1977). A study of developing orthographic concepts among first grade children. *Research in the Teaching of English, 11*, 133–148.

Berninger, V. W., Abbott, R. D., Nagy, W., & Carlisle, J. (2009). Growth in phonological, orthographic, and morphological awareness in grades 1 to 6. *Journal of Psycholinguistic Research, 39*(2), 141–163.

Biemiller, A. (1970). The development of the use of graphic and contextual information as children learn to read. *Reading Research Quarterly, 6*, 1, 75–96.

Biemiller, A. (2001). Teaching vocabulary: Early, direct, sequential. *American Educator, 25*(1), 24–28.

Biemiller, A. (2004). Teaching vocabulary in the primary grades: Vocabulary instruction needed. In J. F. Baumann & E. J. Kame'enui (Eds.), *Vocabulary instruction: Research to practice* (pp. 28–40). New York: Guilford Press.

Biemiller, A. (2005). Size and sequence in vocabulary development: Implications for choosing words for primary grade vocabulary instruction. In E. H. Hiebert & M. L. Kamil (Eds.), *Teaching and learning vocabulary: Bringing research to practice* (pp. 223–242). Mahwah, NJ: Lawrence Erlbaum.

Biemiller, A. (2010). *Words worth teaching: Closing the vocabulary gap*. Columbus, OH: McGraw-Hill SRA.

Bissex, G. L. (1980). *Gnys at wrk: A child learns to read and write*. Cambridge, MA: Harvard University Press.

Blachman, B. A. (1994). What we have learned from longitudinal studies of phonological processing and reading, and some unanswered questions: A response to Torgeson, Wagner, and Rashotte. *Journal of Learning Disabilities, 27,* 287–291.

Blachman, B. A. (2000). Phonological awareness. In M. L. Kamil, P. B. Mosenthal, D. P. Pearson, & R. Barr (Eds), *Handbook of reading research, Volume III,* pp. 483–502. Mahwah, NJ: Lawrence Erlbaum.

Blachowicz, C., & Fisher, P. J. (2009). *Teaching vocabulary in all classrooms* (4th ed.). Boston: Allyn & Bacon.

Blackwell-Bullock, R., Invernizzi, M., Drake, A. E., & Howell, J. L. (2009). A concept of word in text: An integral literacy skill. *Reading in Virginia, 31,* 30–35.

Bowers, P. N., & Kirby, J. R. (2010). Effects of morphological instruction on vocabulary acquisition. *Reading and Writing: An Interdisciplinary Journal, 23*(5), 515–537.

Bravo, M. A., Hiebert, E. H., & Pearson, P. D. (2005). Tapping the linguistic resources of Spanish/English bilinguals: The role of cognates in science. In R. K. Wagner, A. E. Muse, & K. R. Tannenbaum (Eds.), *Vocabulary acquisition: Implications for reading comprehension* (pp. 140–156). New York: Guilford Press.

Brown, K. J. (2003). What do I say when they get stuck on a word? Aligning teachers' prompts with students' development. *The Reading Teacher, 56*(8), 720–733.

Bryant, P., Nunes, T., & Bindman, M. (1997). Backward readers' awareness of language: Strengths and weaknesses. *European Journal of Psychology of Education, 12*(4), 357–372.

Button, K., Johnson, M. J., & Furgerson, P. (1996). Interactive writing in a primary classroom. *The Reading Teacher, 49,* 446–454.

Cabell, S. Q., Tortorelli, L. S., & Gerde, H. K. (2013). How do I write . . . ? Scaffolding preschoolers' early writing skills. *The Reading Teacher, 66*(8), 650–659.

Calkins, L. (2001). *The art of teaching reading.* New York: Longman.

Cantrell, R. J. (2001). Exploring the relationship between dialect and spelling for specific vocalic features in Appalachian first-grade children. *Linguistics and Education, 12*(1), 1–23.

Carlisle, J. F. (2010). Effects of instruction in morphological awareness on literacy achievement: An integrative review. *Reading Research Quarterly, 45*(4), 464–487.

Carpenter, K. (2010). *The relationships among concept sorts, storybook reading, language-based print awareness, and language proficiency in the vocabulary learning of kindergarten children.* Unpublished doctoral dissertation, University of Nevada, Reno.

Cartwright, K. B. (2006). Fostering flexibility and comprehension in elementary students. *The Reading Teacher, 59:* 628–634. doi: 10.1598/RT.59.7.2

Cartwright, K. B. (Ed.). (2008). *Literacy processes: Cognitive flexibility in learning and teaching.* New York: Guilford Press.

Cartwright, K. B. (2010). *Word Callers: Small-group and one-to-one interventions for children who read but don't comprehend.* Portsmouth, NH: Heinemann.

Cartwright, K. B. (2012). Insights from cognitive neuroscience: The importance of executive function for early reading development and education. *Early Education & Development, 23*(1), 24-36. doi:10.1080/10409289.2011.615025

Cathey, S. S. (1991). *Emerging concept of word: Exploring young children's abilities to read rhythmic text.* Doctoral dissertation, University of Nevada, Reno, NV, UMI #9220355.

Chall, J. S. (1983/1996). *Stages of reading development.* New York: McGraw-Hill.

Chandler, K. (1999) *Spelling inquiry: How one elementary school caught the mnemonic plague.* Portland, ME: Stenhouse.

Chomsky, C. (1970). Reading, writing, and phonology. *Harvard Educational Review, 40*(2), 287–309.

Chomsky, C. (1971). Write first read later. *Childhood Education, 47,* 296–299.

Clarke, L. K. (1988). Invented versus traditional spelling in first graders' writing: Effects on learning to spell and read. *Research in the Teaching of English, 22,* 281–309.

Clay, M. (1975). *What did I write?* Exeter, NH: Heinemann.

Clay, M. M. (1979). *Stones: The concepts about print test.* Portsmouth, NH: Heinemann.

Clay, M. (2009). *An observation survey of early literacy achievement* (2nd ed). Portsmouth, NH: Heinemann.

Clay, M. M. (1991). Introducing a new storybook to young readers. *The Reading Teacher, 45,* 264–273.

Conrad, N. J. (2008). From reading to spelling and spelling to reading: Transfer goes both ways. *Journal of Educational Psychology, 100*(4), 869–878.

Corriveau, K. H., Goswami, U. (2009). Rhythmic motor entrainment in children with speech and language impairments: tapping to the beat. *Cortex, 45*(1), 119–130.

Coxhead, A. (2000). A new academic word list. *TESOL Quarterly, 34,* 213–238.

Crosson, A. C., & McKeown, M. G. (2016). Middle school learners' use of Latin roots to infer the meaning of unfamiliar words. *Cognition and Instruction, 34*(2), 148–171. DOI: 10.1080/0737000.2016.1145121

Cunningham, A. E., Stanovich, K. E., & West, R. F. (1994). Literacy environment and the development of children's cognitive skills. In E. M. H. Assink (Ed.), *The developing body and mind. Literacy acquisition and social context* (pp. 70–90). Oxford, England: Harvester Wheatsheaf/Prentice Hall.

Cunningham, P. (2013). *Phonics they use: Words for reading and writing* (6th ed.) Boston, MA: Pearson.

Dale, E., O'Rourke, J., & Bamman, H. (1971). *Techniques of teaching vocabulary.* Palo Alto, CA: Field Educational Publications.

Daniels, H. (2002). *Literature circles: Voice and choice in book clubs and reading groups.* Portland ME: Stenhouse Publishers.

Delpit, L. D. (1988). The silenced dialogue: Power and pedagogy in educating other people's children. *Harvard Educational Review, 58,* 280–298.

Dixon, L.Q., Zhao, J., & Joshi, R. M. (2012). One dress, two dress: Dialectical influence on spelling of English words among kindergarten children in Singapore. *System, 40,* 214–225.

Dolch, E. W. (1942). *Better spelling.* Champaign, IL: The Garrard Press.

Dorr, R. E. (2006). Something old is new again: Revisiting language experience. *The Reading Teacher, 60*(2), 138–146.

Doyle, G. B., & Bramwell, W. (2006). Promoting emergent literacy and social–emotional learning through dialogic reading. *The Reading Teacher, 59*(6), 554–564.

Duffy, G. (2014). *Explaining reading: A resource for teaching concepts, skills and strategies* (3rd ed.). New York: Guilford Press.

Ehri, L. C. (1997). Learning to read and learning to spell are one and the same, almost. In C. A. Perfetti, L. Rieben, & M. Fayol (Eds.), *Learning to spell: Research, theory, and practice across languages* (pp. 237–269). Mahwah, NJ: Lawrence Erlbaum.

Ehri, L. (2000). Phases of acquisition in learning to read words and implications for teaching. *British Journal of Educational Psychology: Monograph Series, 1,* 7–28.

Ehri, L. C. (2005). Learning to read words: Theory, findings, and issues. *Scientific Studies of Reading, 9*(2), 167–188.

Ehri, L. C. (2006). Alphabetics instruction helps children learn to read. In R. M. Joshi & P. G. Aaron (Eds.), *Handbook of orthography and literacy* (pp. 649–678). Mahwah, NJ: Lawrence Erlbaum.

Ehri, L. C. (2014). Orthographic mapping in the acquisition of sight word reading, spelling memory, and vocabulary learning. *Scientific Studies of Reading, 18*(1), 5–21.

Ehri, L. C., & Wilce, L. S. (1980). Do beginning readers learn to read function words better in sentences or lists? *Reading Research Quarterly, 15,* 675–685.

Ehri, L. C., & Roberts, T. (2006). The roots of learning to read and write: Acquisition of letters and phonemic awareness. In D. K. Dickinson & S. B. Neuman (Eds.), *Handbook of early literacy research* (vol. 2, pp. 113–131). New York: Guilford Press.

Ehri, L. C., Satlow, E., & Gaskins, I. (2009). Grapho-phonemic enrichment strengthens keyword analogy instruction for struggling young readers. *Reading & Writing Quarterly, 25*(2–3), 162–191.

Elkonin, D. B. (1973). U.S.S.R. In J. Downing (Ed.), *Comparative reading.* New York: Macmillan.

Ferreiro, E., & Teberosky, A. (1982). *Literacy before schooling.* Portsmouth, NH: Heinemann.

Fisher, D., & Frey, N. (2008). *Better learning through structured teaching: A framework for gradual release of responsibility.* Alexandria, VA: Association for Supervision and Curriculum Development.

Flanigan, K. (2006). "Daddy, where did the words go?": How teachers can help emergent readers develop a concept of word in text. *Reading Improvement, 43*(1), 37–49.

Flanigan, K. (2007). A concept of word in text: A pivotal event in early reading acquisition. *Journal of Literacy Research, 39*(1), 37–70.

Flanigan, K., Hayes, L., Templeton, S., Bear, D. R., Invernizzi, M., & Johnston, F. (2011). *Words their way with struggling readers: Word study for reading, vocabulary, and spelling instruction, grades 4–12.* Boston: Allyn & Bacon.

Flanigan, K., Templeton, S., & Hayes, L. (2012). What's in a word? Using content vocabulary to generate growth in general academic vocabulary knowledge. *Journal of Adolescent and Adult Literacy, 56*(2), 132–140. doi: 10.1002/JAAL.00114

Ford, K., Invernizzi, M. & Huang, F. (2018). The effects of orthographic complexity on Spanish spelling in grades 1-3. *Journal of Reading & Writing, 31,* 5,1063–1081. https://doi.org/10.1007/s11145-018-9828-7

Ford, K., & Invernizzi, M. (2009). *Phonological Awareness Literacy Screening for Kindergarteners in Spanish* (PALS español-K). Charlottesville, VA: University of Virginia.

Fry, E. (1980). The new instant word list. *The Reading Teacher, 34,* 284–289.

Fuchs, L. S., Fuchs, D., & Maxwell, L. (1988). The validity of informal reading comprehension measures. *Remedial & Special Education, 9*(2), 20–28.

Ganske, K. (1999). The developmental spelling analysis: A measure of orthographic knowledge. *Educational Assessment, 6,* 41–70.

Ganske, K. (2017). Lesson Closure: An Important Piece of the Student Learning Puzzle. *The Reading Teacher* 71.1: 95–100.

Ganske, K., & Jocius, R. (2013) Small-group word study: Instructional conversations or mini-interrogations? *Language Arts, 19,* 23–39.

Gehsmann, K., & Bear, D. (2014a). *Words Their Way™ Classroom Observation Tool.* Upper Saddle River, NJ: Pearson Education, Inc.

Gehsmann, K. M., Millwood, K., & Bear, D. R. (2012, December). *Validating a classroom observation tool for studying developmental word study instruction.* Presentation at the 62nd annual conference of the Literacy Research Association, San Diego, CA.

Gehsmann, K., Spichtig, A., & Tousley, E. (2018). Validating an online assessment of developmental word knowledge in grades 5–8. *Literacy Research: Theory, Method, and Practice, 20,* 1–14. DOI: 10.1177/2381336917718834

Gehsmann, K., & Templeton, S. (2013). Foundational skills. In L. M. Morrow, T. Shanahan, & K. K. Wixson (Eds.), *Teaching with the Common Core Standards for English Language Arts: PreK–2* (pp. 67–84). New York: Guilford Press.

Genishi, C. & Dyson, A. H. (2009). *Children, language, and literacy: Diverse learners in diverse times.* New York: Teachers College Press.

Gibson, J. J., & Yonas, P. M. (1968). A new theory of scribbling and drawing in children. In *The analysis of reading skill: A program of basic and applied research* (Final Report, Project No. 5-1213, Cornell University and the U.S. Office of Education, pp. 335–370). Ithaca, NY: Cornell University.

Gill, C. (1980). *An analysis of spelling errors in French.* Unpublished doctoral dissertation. University of Virginia.

Gill, C. H., & Scharer, P. L. (1996). Why do they get it on Friday and misspell it on Monday: Teachers inquiring about their students as spellers. *Language Arts, 73,* 89–96.

Gill, J. T. (1992). Focus on research: Development of word knowledge as it relates to reading, spelling, and instruction. *Language Arts, 69*(6), 444–453.

González-Fernández, B., & Schmitt, N. (2017). Vocabulary acquisition. In Lowe, S. and Sato, M. (Eds). *The Routledge Handbook of Instructed Second Language Acquisition,* 280–298.

Goswami, U. (2008). Reading, complexity, and the brain. *Literacy, 42*(2), 67–74.

Goswami, U., Gerson, D., & Astruc, L. (2010). Amplitude envelope perception, phonology and prosodic sensitivity in children with developmental dyslexia. *Reading and Writing, 23*(8), 995–1019.

Graham, S., Harris, K. R., & Fink, B. (2000). Is handwriting causally related to learning to write? Treatment of handwriting problems in beginning writers. *Journal of Educational Psychology, 92*(4), 620–633.

Graham, S., McKeown, D., Kiuhara, S., & Harris, K. (2012). A meta-analysis of writing instruction for students in the elementary grades. *Journal of Educational Psychology, 104* (4), 879–896.

Green, T. M. (2008). *The Greek and Latin roots of English* (4th ed). Lanham, MD: Rowman & Littlefield Publishers.

Hamre, B. K., Downer, J. T., Jamil, F. M., Piant, R. C. (2012). Enhancing teachers' intentional use of effective interactions with children. In R. C. Pianta (Ed.), *Handbook of early childhood education* (pp. 507–532). NY: Guilford Press.

Hanna, P. R., Hanna, J. S., Hodges, R. E., & Rudorf, H. (1966). *Phoneme-grapheme correspondences as cues to spelling improvement.* Washington, DC: United States Office of Education Cooperative Research.

Harré, R., & Moghaddam, F. (Eds.). (2003). *The self and others: Positioning individuals and groups in personal, political, and cultural contexts.* Westport, CT: Praeger.

Harris, M. L., Schumaker, J. B., & Deshler, D. D. (2011). The effects of strategic morphological analysis instruction on the vocabulary performance of secondary students with and without disabilities. *Learning Disability Quarterly, 34*(1), 17–33.

Harste, J. C., Woodward, V. A., & Burke, C. L. (1984). *Language stories and literacy lessons.* Portsmouth, NH: Heinemann.

Hart, B., & Risley, T. R. (1995). *Meaningful differences in the everyday experience of American children.* Baltimore: Paul C. Brookes.

Hasbrouck, J., & Tindal, G. A. (2006). Oral reading fluency norms: A valuable assessment tool for reading teachers. *The Reading Teacher, 59*(7), 636–644.

Hayes, L. (2014). "Reimagining the classroom." In Bear, D. R., Flanigan, K., Hayes, L., Helman, L., Invernizzi, M., Johnston, F. J., Templeton, S. *Words Their Way^{TM} Vocabulary for Middle and High School* (pp. T-34–T39). Glenview, Il: Pearson.

Helman, L. (2004). Building on the sound system of Spanish. *The Reading Teacher, 57,* 452–460.

Helman, L. A. (Ed.). (2009). *Literacy development with English learners: Research-based instruction in grades K–6.* New York: Guilford Press.

Helman, L., Bear, D. R., Invernizzi, M., Templeton, S., & Johnston, F. (2009). *Words their way: Emergent sorts for Spanish-speaking English learners.* Boston: Allyn & Bacon.

Helman, L., Bear, D. R., Invernizzi, M., Templeton, S., & Johnston, F. (2009). *Words their way: Letter name-alphabetic sorts for Spanish-speaking English learners.* Boston: Allyn & Bacon.

Helman, L. A., Bear, D. R., Templeton, S., Invernizzi, M., & Johnston, F. (2012). *Words their way with English learners* (2nd ed.). Boston: Pearson/Allyn & Bacon.

Helman, L., Bear, D. R., Invernizzi, M., Templeton, S., & Johnston, F. (2013). *Palabras a su paso: El estudio de palabras en acción- Etapa alfabética.* Glenview, IL: Pearson.

Helman, L., Bear, D. R., Invernizzi, M., Templeton, S., & Johnston, F. (2013). *Palabras a su paso-Derivaciones.* Glenview, IL: Pearson.

Helman, L., Delbridge, A., Parker, D., Arnal, M., & Jara Mödinger, L. (2016). Measuring Spanish orthographic development in private, public, and subsidised schools in Chile. *Assessment in Education: Principles, Policy & Practice 23*(3), 327–352. http://dx.doi.org/10.1080/0969594X.2015.1038217.

Henderson, E. H. (1981). *Learning to read and spell: The child's knowledge of words.* DeKalb: Northern Illinois Press.

Henderson, E. H. (1990). *Teaching spelling* (2nd ed.). Boston: Houghton Mifflin.

Henderson, E. H., & Beers, J. (Eds.). (1980). *Developmental and cognitive aspects of learning to spell.* Newark, DE: International Reading Association.

Henderson, E. H., & Templeton, S. (1986). The development of spelling ability through alphabet, pattern, and meaning. *Elementary School Journal, 86,* 305–316.

Henry, M. (1988). Beyond phonics: Integrated decoding and spelling instruction based on word origin and structures. *Annals of Dyslexia, 38,* 258–275.

Henry, M. (2003). *Unlocking literacy: Effective decoding and spelling instruction.* Baltimore: Paul H. Brookes.

Hiebert, E. H. (2005). In pursuit of an effective, efficient vocabulary curriculum for elementary students. In E. H. Hiebert & M. L. Kamil (Eds.), *Teaching and learning vocabulary: Bringing research to practice* (pp. 243–263). Mahwah, NJ: Lawrence Erlbaum.

Honig, A. S., & Shin, M. (2001). Reading aloud with infants and toddlers in child care settings: An observational study. *Early Childhood Education Journal, 28*(3), 193–197.

Huang, F. L., Tortorelli, L. S. & Invernizzi, M. (2014). An investigation of factors associated with letter-sound knowledge at kindergarten entry. *Early Childhood Research Quarterly, 29*(2), 182–192.

International Literacy Association (2018) "Explaining Phonics Instruction." Position Paper. https://www.literacyworldwide.org/docs/default-source/where-we-stand/ila-explaining-phonics-instruction-an-educators-guide.pdf

Invernizzi, M. (1992). The vowel and what follows: A phonological frame of orthographic analysis. In S. Templeton & D. Bear (Eds.), *Development of orthographic knowledge and the foundations of literacy: A memorial Festschrift for Edmund H. Henderson* (pp. 106–136). Hillsdale, NJ: Lawrence Erlbaum.

Invernizzi, M. (2002). Concepts, sounds, and the ABCs: A diet for a very young reader. In D. M. Barone & L. M. Morrow (Eds.), *Literacy and young children* (pp. 140–157). New York: Guilford Press.

Invernizzi, M. (2009). Virginia's Early Intervention Reading Initiative (EIRI) and Response to Intervention (RtI). *Reading in Virginia, 36–39.*

Invernizzi, M. (2017). The role of developmental word knowledge in achieving literacy. *Michigan Reading Journal, 49*(2), 48–52.

Invernizzi, M., Abouzeid, M., & Gill, T. (1994). Using students' invented spellings as a guide for spelling instruction that emphasizes word study. *Elementary School Journal, 95*(2), 155–167.

Invernizzi, M., & Hayes, L. (2004). Developmental-spelling research: A systematic imperative. *Reading Research Quarterly, 39,* 2–15.

Invernizzi, M., & Hayes, L. (2010). Word recognition. In D. Allington & A. McGill-Franzen (Eds.), *Handbook of reading disabilities.* Newark, DE: International Reading Association.

Invernizzi, M., Juel, C., Swank, L., & Meier, J. (2015). *Phonological Awareness Literacy Screening for Kindergartners* (PALS-K). Charlottesville, VA: University Printing Services.

Invernizzi, M., Juel, C., Swank, L., & Meier, J. (2008). *Phonological Awareness Literacy Screening–Kindergarten (PALS-K): Technical Reference.* Charlottesville, VA: University of Virginia.

Invernizzi, M., Justice, L., Landrum, T., & Booker, K. (Winter, 2005). Early literacy screening in kindergarten: Widespread implementation in Virginia. *Journal of Literacy Research, 36,* 479–500.

Invernizzi, M., Meier, J., & Juel, C. (2003). *PALS 1–3 Phonological Awareness Literacy Screening* (4th ed.). Charlottesville, VA: University Printing Services.

Invernizzi, M. A. & Tortorelli, L.S. (2013). Phonological awareness and alphabet knowledge: The foundations of early reading. In M. Mallette & D. Barone (Eds.), *Best Practices in Early Literacy Instructions.* New York, NY: Guilford.

Invernizzi, M., & Worthy, J. W. (1989). An orthographic-specific comparison of the spelling errors of LD and normal children across four levels of spelling achievement. *Reading Psychology, 10,* 173–188.

Invernizzi, M., & Buckrop, J. (2018). Reconceptualizing Alphabet Learning and Instruction. In C. M. Cassano, & S. M Dougherty (Eds.), *Pivotal Research in Early Literacy: Foundational Studies and Current Practices* (pp. 85–111). New York: Guilford Press.

James, W. (1958). *Talks to teachers on psychology and to students on some of life's ideals.* New York: Norton. (Original work published 1899.)

Johnston, F. R. (1998). The reader, the text, and the task: Learning words in first grade. *The Reading Teacher, 51,* 666–675.

Johnston, F. R. (2000). Word learning in predictable text. *Journal of Educational Psychology, 92,* 248–255.

Johnston, F. R. (2001). The utility of phonic generalizations: Let's take another look at Clymer's conclusions. *The Reading Teacher, 55,* 132–143.

Johnston, F. R. (2003, December). *The Primary Spelling Inventory: Exploring its validity and relationship to reading levels.* Paper presented at the National Reading Conference, Scottsdale, AZ.

Johnston, F., Invernizzi, M., Bear, D. R., & Templeton, S. (2018). *Words their way: Word sorts for syllables and affixes spellers* (3rd ed.). Boston: Pearson.

Johnston, F., Invernizzi, M., Helman, L., Bear, D. R., & Templeton, S. (2015). *Words Their Way for PreK and Kindergarten.* Boston: Pearson.

Johnston, F., Invernizzi, M., Juel, C., & Lewis-Wagner, D. (2009). *Book buddies: A tutoring framework for struggling readers.* New York: Guilford Press.

Johnston, P. H. (2004) *Choice words: How our language affects children's learning.* Portland, ME.: Stenhouse.

Johnston, P. H. (2012). *Opening minds: Using language to change lives.* Portland, ME: Stenhouse.

Jones, C. D., Clark, S. K., & Reutzel, D. R. (2013). Enhancing alphabet knowledge instruction: Research implications and practical strategies for early childhood educators. *Early Childhood Education Journal, 41*(2), 81–89.

Juel, C., Biancarosa, G., Coker, D., & Deffes, R. (2003). Walking with Rosie: A cautionary tale of literacy instruction. *Educational Leadership, 60*(7), 12–18.

Justice, L. M. (2006). *Communication sciences and disorders: An introduction.* Upper Saddle River, NJ: Pearson/Merrill/Prentice Hall.

Justice, L. M., & Ezell, H. K. (2004). Print referencing: An emergent literacy enhancement technique and its clinical applications. *Language, Speech, and Hearing Services in Schools, 35,* 185–193.

Justice, L. M., Kaderavek, J. N., Fan, X., Sofka, A., & Hunt, A. (2009). Accelerating preschoolers' early literacy development through classroom-based teacher child story book reading and explicit print referencing. *Language, Speech, & Hearing Services in Schools, 40,* 67–85.

Justice, L. M., & Pullen, P. (2003). Promising interventions for promoting emergent literacy skills: Three evidence-based approaches. *Topics in Early Childhood Special Education, 23,* 99–113.

Justice, L. M., & Sofka, A. E. (2010). *Engaging children with print: Building early literacy skills through quality read alouds.* New York: Guilford Press.

Kim, Y., Petscher, Y., Foorman, B., & Zhou, C. (2010). The contributions of phonological awareness and letter name knowledge to letter-sound acquisition—a cross-classified multilevel model approach. *Journal of Educational Psychology, 102,* 313–326.

Kirk, C., & Gillon, G. T. (2009). Integrated morphological awareness intervention as a tool for improving literacy. *Language, Speech, and Hearing Services in Schools, 40*(2), 341–351.

Kuchirko, Y. (2017). On differences and deficits: A critique of the theoretical and methodological underpinnings of the word gap. *Journal of Early Childhood Literacy,* 1468798417747029. doi: 10.1177/1468798417747029

Labbo, L. D. (2004). Author's computer chair [Technology in Literacy Department]. *The Reading Teacher, 57*(7), 688–691.

Labbo, L. D., Eakle, A. J., & Montero, M. K. (2002, May). Digital Language Experience Approach: Using digital photographs and software as a Language Experience Approach innovation. *Reading Online, 5*(8). http://www.readingonline.org/electronic/elec_index.asp?HREF=labbo2/index.html

Lane, H. B., & Allen, S. A. (2010). The vocabulary-rich classroom: Modeling sophisticated word use to promote word consciousness and vocabulary growth. *The Reading Teacher, 63*(5), 362–370.

Lenski, S. D., Wham, M. A., & Johns, J. L. (1999). *Reading & Learning Strategies for Middle & High School Students.* Kendall/Hunt Publishing Co., 4050 Westmark Drive, PO Box 1840, Dubuque, IA 52004–1840.

Lerer, S. (2007). *Inventing English: A portable history of the language.* New York: Columbia University Press.

Liberman, I., & Shankweiler, D. (1991). Phonology and beginning reading: A tutorial. In L. Rieben & C. Perfetti (Eds.), *Learning to read: Basic research and its implication.* Hillsdale, NJ: Lawrence Erlbaum.

Liberman, I. Y., Shankweiler, D., & Liberman, A. M. (1989). "The alphabetic principle and learning to read." *Meeting of the International Academy for Research on Learning Disabilities, Oct, 1986, Northwestern U, Evanston, IL, U.S.* The University of Michigan Press.

Lobo, Y. B., & Winsler, A. (2006). The effects of a creative dance and movement program on the social competence of Head Start preschoolers. *Social Development, 15*(3), 501–519.

Lundberg, I., Frost, J., & Peterson, O. (1988). Effects of an extensive program for stimulating phonological awareness in preschool children. *Reading Research Quarterly, 23,* 267–284.

Mages, W. K. (2008). Does creative drama promote language development in early childhood? A review of the methods and measures employed in the empirical literature. *Review of Educational Research, 78*(1), 124–152.

Marzano, R. J. (1992). *A different kind of classroom: Teaching with dimensions of learning.* Alexandria, VA: ASCD.

Massengill, D. (2006). Mission accomplished . . . It's learnable now: Voices of mature challenged spellers using a Word Study approach. *Journal of Adolescent and Adult Literacy, 49*(5), 420–431.

McCabe, A. (1997). *Chameleon readers: All kinds of good stories.* New York: Webster/McGraw-Hill.

McCabe, A. & Bliss, L. S. (2003). *Patterns of narrative discourse: A multi-cultural, life span approach.* Boston: Allyn & Bacon.

McCracken, M. J., & McCracken, R. A. (1995). *Reading, writing, and language* (2nd ed.). Winnipeg, Canada: Peguis.

McGee, L. M., & Richgels, D. J. (2011). *Literacy's beginnings: Supporting young readers and writers* (6th ed.). Boston, MA: Pearson.

McKeown, M. G., & Curtis, M. E. (Eds.). (2014). *The nature of vocabulary acquisition.* Psychology Press.

Mesmer, H. A., Cunningham, J. W., & Hiebert, E. H. (2012). Toward a theoretical model of text complexity for the early grades: Learning from the past, anticipating the future. *Reading Research Quarterly, 47*(3), 235–258.

Mesmer, H. A. E., & Williams, T. O. (2015). Examining the role of syllable awareness in a model of concept of word: Findings from preschoolers. *Reading Research Quarterly, 50*(4), 483–497.

Mesmer, H. A. & Duke, N. (2016). https://www.literacyworldwide.org/blog/literacy-daily/2016/06/23/teach-ldquo-sight-words-rdquo-as-you-would-other-words

MetaMetrics. (2013). The Lexile framework for reading. Durham, NC: Author.

Miles, K. P., & Ehri, L. C. (2017). Learning to Read Words on Flashcards: Effects of Sentence Contexts and Word Class in Native and Non-native English-Speaking Kindergartners. *Early Childhood Research Quarterly, 41*, 103–113.

Miles, K.P., Rubin, G.B., & Frey, S.G. (2018). Rethinking Sight Words. *The Reading Teacher, 71*(6), 715–726. https://doi.org/10.1002/trtr.1658.

Moats, L. (2000). *Speech to print: Language essentials for teachers.* Baltimore: Paul H. Brookes.

Moloney, K. (2008). *"I'm not a big word fan": An exploratory study of ninth-graders' language use in the context of word consciousness-oriented vocabulary instruction.* Unpublished doctoral dissertation, University of Nevada, Reno.

Morgan, R. K., & Meier, C. R. (2008). Dialogic reading's potential to improve children's emergent literacy skills and behavior. *Preventing School Failure, 52*, 11–16.

Morris, D. (1981). Concept of word: A developmental phenomenon in the beginning reading and writing process. *Language Arts, 58*(6), 659–668.

Morris, D. (1992). Concept of word: A pivotal understanding in the learning-to-read process. In S. Templeton, & D. R. Bear (Eds.), *Development of orthographic knowledge and the foundations of literacy: A memorial Festschrift for Edmund H. Henderson* (pp. 53–77). Hillsdale, NJ: Lawrence Erlbaum Associates.

Morris, D. (1993). The relationship between children's concept of word in text and phoneme awareness in learning to read: A longitudinal study. *Research in the Teaching of English, 27*(2), 133–154.

Morris, D. (1999). *The Howard Street tutoring manual* (2nd ed.). New York: Guilford Press.

Morris, D. (2013). *Diagnosis and correction of reading problems* (2nd ed.). New York: Guilford Press.

Morris, D., Blanton, L., Blanton, W. E., Nowacek, J., & Perney, J. (1995). Teaching low-achieving spellers at their "instructional level." *The Elementary School Journal, 96*(2), 163–177.

Morris, D., Blanton, L., Blanton, W., & Perney, J. (1995). Spelling instruction and achievement in six elementary classrooms. *The Elementary School Journal, 96*, 145–162.

Morris, D., Bloodgood, J. W., Lomax, R. G., & Perney, J. (2003). Developmental steps in learning to read: A longitudinal study in kindergarten and first grade. *Reading Research Quarterly, 38*, 302–328.

Mountain, L. M. (2015). Recurrent prefixes, roots, and suffixes. *Journal of Adolescent & Adult Literacy, 58*(7), 561–567. doi:10.1002/jaal.394

Nagy, W. (2007). Metalinguistic awareness and the vocabulary-comprehension connection. In R. K. Wagner, A. E. Muse, & K. R. Tannenbaum (Eds.), *Vocabulary acquisition: Implications for reading comprehension* (pp. 52–78). New York: Guilford Press.

Nagy, W., & Anderson, R. C. (1984). How many words are there in printed school English? *Reading Research Quarterly, 19*, 304–330.

Nagy, W., Berninger, V. W., & Abbott, R. D. (2006). Contributions of morphology beyond phonology to literacy outcomes of upper elementary and middle-school students. *Journal of Educational Psychology, 98*, 134–147.

Nagy, W., Berninger, V., Abbott, R., Vaughan, K., & Vermeulen, K. (2003). Relationship of morphology and other language skills to literacy skills in at-risk second-grade readers and at-risk fourth-grade writers. *Journal of Educational Psychology, 95*(4), 730–742.

Nagy, W., & Townsend, D. (2012). Words as tools: Learning academic vocabulary as language acquisition. *Reading Research Quarterly, 47*(1), 91–108.

Nash, R. (1997). *NTC's dictionary of Spanish cognates thematically organized.* Chicago: NTC Publishing Group.

National Early Literacy Panel. (2008). *Report on a synthesis of early predictors of reading.* Louisville, KY: National Institute of Family Literacy.

National Reading Panel (NRP). (2000). *Teaching children to read: An evidence-based assessment of the scientific research literature on reading and its implications for reading instruction.* Washington, DC: National Institute of Child Health and Human Development.

Neuman, S. B., & Roskos, K. (2012). More than teachable moments: Enhancing oral vocabulary instruction in your classroom. *The Reading Teacher, 66*(1), 63–67.

Neuman, S. B. & Wright, T. (2014). The magic of words: Teaching vocabulary in the early childhood classroom. *American Educator, 38*, 4–13.

Nunes, T., & Bryant, P. (2006). *Improving literacy by teaching morphemes.* London: Routledge.

Nunes, T., & Bryant, P. (2009). *Children's reading and spelling: Beyond the first steps.* London: Wiley-Blackwell.

Ouellette, G. P., & Sénéchal, M. (2008). A window into early literacy: Exploring the cognitive and linguistic underpinnings of invented spelling. *Scientific Studies of Reading, 12*(2), 195–219.

Palmer, J., & Invernizzi, M. (2014). *No more phonics and spelling worksheets.* Portsmouth, NH: Heinemann.

Papandropoulou, I., & Sinclair, H. (1974). What is a word? *Human Development, 17*(4), 241–258.

Parry, J., & Hornsby, D. (1988). *Write on: A conference approach to writing.* Portsmouth, NH: Heinemann.

Pasquarella, A., Chen, X., Gottardo, A., Geva, E. (2014). Cross-language transfer of word reading accuracy and fluency in Spanish-English and Chinese-English bilinguals: Script-universal and script-specific processes. *Journal of Educational Psychology, 107*(1), 96–110.

Pearson, P. D., & Gallagher, M. (1983). The instruction of reading comprehension. *Contemporary Educational Psychology, 8,* 317–344.

Pense, K. L., & Justice, L. M. (2008). *Language development from theory to practice.* Upper Saddle River, NJ: Pearson/Merrill/Prentice Hall.

Perfetti, C. A. (2007). Reading ability: Lexical quality to comprehension. *Scientific Studies of Reading, 11,* 357–383.

Perfetti, C., Beck, I., Bell, L., & Hughes, C. (1987). Phonemic knowledge and learning to read are reciprocal. *Merrill-Palmer Quarterly, 33,* 283–319.

Piasta, S. B., & Wagner, R. K. (2010). Developing early literacy skills: A meta-analysis of alphabet learning and instruction. *Reading Research Quarterly, 45*(1), 8–38.

Picard, M., Meadows, A., Invernizzi, M. A., Johnston, F., Bear, D. R. (2018). *Words their Way for parents and tutors.* Boston, MA: Allyn & Bacon.

Pressley, M. (2006). *Reading instruction that works: The case for balanced teaching* (3rd ed.). New York: Guilford Press.

Pufpaff, L. (2009). A developmental continuum of phonological sensitivity skills. *Psychology in the Schools, 46*(7), 679–691.

Pullen, P. C., & Justice, L. M. (2003). Enhancing phonological awareness, print awareness, & oral language skills in preschool children. *Intervention in School & Clinic, 39*(2), 87–98.

Raphael, T. E., Pardo, L. S., Highfield, K., & McMahon. (2013). *Book club: A literature-based curriculum* (2nd ed.). Lawrence, MA: Small Planet Communications, Inc.

Rawlins, A., & Invernizzi, M. (2019). Reconceptualizing sight words: Building an early reading vocabulary. *The Reading Teacher.* doi: 10.1002/trtr.1789

Rayner, K., Foorman, B. R., Perfetti, C. A., Pesetsky, D., & Seidenburg, M. S. (2001). How psychological science informs the teaching of reading. *Psychological Science in the Public Interest, 2,* 31–74.

Read, C. (1971). Pre-school children's knowledge of English phonology. *Harvard Educational Review, 41*(1), 1–34.

Read, C. (1975). *Children's categorization of speech sounds in English.* Urbana, IL: NCTE Research Report No. 17.

ReadingRockets, 2015 *Readers: Word Study for Reading, Vocabulary, and Spelling Instruction, Grades 4–12.*

Reichle, E. D., & Perfetti, C. A. (2003). Morphology in word identification: A word-experience model that accounts for morpheme frequency effects. *Scientific Studies of Reading, 7*(3), 219–237.

Robinson, S. R. (1989). *Origins, Volume 1: Bringing words to life.* New York: Teachers & Writers Collaborative.

Rosenthal, J., & Ehri, L. (2008). The mnemonic value of orthography for vocabulary learning. *Journal of Educational Psychology,* 100(1), 175–191. Retrieved from Education Abstracts (H. W. Wilson) database.

Sawyer, D. J., Lipa-Wade, S., Kim, J., Ritenour, D., & Knight, D. F. (1997). *Spelling errors as a window on dyslexia.* Paper presented at the 1997 annual convention of the American Educational Research Association, Chicago.

Sawyer, D. J., Wade, S., & Kim, J. K. (1999). Spelling errors as a window on variations in phonological deficits among students with dyslexia. *Annals of Dyslexia, 49,* 137–159.

Schlagal, R. (1992). Patterns of orthographic development into the intermediate grades. In S. Templeton & D. Bear (Eds.), *Development of orthographic knowledge and the foundations of literacy: A memorial Festschrift for Edmund H. Henderson* (pp. 31–52). Hillsdale, NJ: Lawrence Erlbaum.

Schlagal, R. (2013). Best practices in spelling and handwriting. In S. Graham, C. A. MacArthur, & J. Fitzgerald (Eds.), *Best practices in writing instruction* (2nd ed., pp. 257–283). New York: Guilford Press.

Schmitt, N. (2014). Size and depth of vocabulary knowledge: What the research shows. *Language Learning, 64*(4), 913–951.

Scott, J. A., Skobel, B. J., & Wells, J. (2008). *The word-conscious classroom: Building the vocabulary readers and writers need.* New York: Scholastic.

Sharp, A. C., Sinatra, G. M., & Reynolds, R. E. (2008). The development of children's orthographic knowledge: A microgenetic perspective. *Reading Research Quarterly, 43*(3), 206–226.

Shipley, J. T. (2001). *The origins of English words.* Baltimore, MD: The Johns Hopkins University Press.

Sinclair, E. M., McCleery, E. J., Koepsell, L., Zuckerman, K. E., & Stevenson, E. B. (2018). Home literacy environment and shared reading in the newborn period. *Journal of Developmental & Behavioral Pediatrics, 39*(1), 66–71.

Smith, S. B., Simmons, D. C., & Kame'enui, E. J. (1995). *Synthesis of research on phonological awareness: Principles and implications for reading acquisition* (Tech. Rep. No. 21). Eugene, OR: University of Oregon, National Center to Improve the Tools of Educators.

Snow, C. E., Burns, M. S., & Griffin, P. (Eds.). (1998). *Preventing reading difficulties in young children.* Washington, DC: National Academy Press.

Spear-Swerling, L., & Sternberg, R. J. (Contributor) (1997). *Off track: When poor readers become "learning disabled."* Boulder, CO: Westview Press.

Stauffer, R. (1980). *The language-experience approach to the teaching of reading* (2nd ed.). New York: Harper & Row.

Stever, E. (1976). Dialectic and socioeconomic factors affecting the spelling strategies of second-grade students. *Dissertation Abstracts International, 37*(07A), 4120. (University Microfilms No. AAG7700149.)

Sterbinsky, A. (2007). *Words their way spelling inventories: Reliability and validity analyses.* Memphis, TN: University of Memphis Center for Research in Educational Policy. http://assets.pearsonschool.com/asset_mgr/current/201034/Reliability_and_Validation_Study_Report.pdf.

Strickland, D., & Morrow, L. (1989). Environments rich in print promote literacy behavior during play. *Reading Teacher, 43,* 178–179.

Sulzby, E. (1986). Writing and reading organization. In W. H. Teale & E. Sulzby (Eds.), *Emergent literacy: Writing and reading* (pp. 50–89). Norwood, NJ: Abex.

Swan, M., & Smith, B. (2001). *Learner English: A teacher's guide to interference and other problems* (2nd ed.). New York: Cambridge University Press.

Taft, M. (2003). Morphological representation as a correlation between form and meaning. In E. G. H. Assink & D. Sandra (Eds.), *Reading complex words: Cross language studies* (pp. 113–137). New York: Kluwer Academic.

Temple, C. S. (1978). *An analysis of spelling errors in Spanish.* Unpublished doctoral dissertation, University of Virginia.

Templeton, S. (1979). Spelling first, sound later: The relationship between orthography and higher order phonological knowledge in older students. *Research in the Teaching of English, 13,* 255–264.

Templeton, S. (1980). Logic and mnemonics for demons and curiosities: Spelling awareness for middle- and secondary-level students. *Reading World, 20,* 123–130.

Templeton, S. (1983). Using the spelling/meaning connection to develop word knowledge in older students. *Journal of Reading, 27*(1), 8–14.

Templeton, S. (1989). Tacit and explicit knowledge of derivational morphology: Foundations for a unified approach to spelling and vocabulary development in the intermediate grades and beyond. *Reading Psychology, 10,* 233–253.

Templeton, S. (1992). Theory, nature, and pedagogy of higher-order orthographic development in older children. In S. Templeton & D. Bear (Eds.), *Development of orthographic knowledge and the foundations of literacy: A memorial Festschrift for Edmund H. Henderson* (pp. 253–278), Hillsdale, NJ: Lawrence Erlbaum.

Templeton, S. (1997). *Teaching the integrated language arts* (2nd ed.). Boston: Houghton Mifflin.

Templeton, S. (2002). Effective spelling instruction in the middle grades: It's a lot more than memorization. *Voices from the Middle, 9*(3), 8–14.

Templeton, S. (2003). Spelling. In J. Flood, D. Lapp, J. R. Squire, & J. M. Jensen (Eds.), *Handbook of research on teaching the English language arts* (2nd ed., pp. 738–751). Mahwah, NJ: Lawrence Erlbaum.

Templeton, S. (2004). The vocabulary-spelling connection: Orthographic development and morphological knowledge at the intermediate grades and beyond. In J. F. Baumann & E. J. Kame'enui (Eds.), *Vocabulary instruction: Research to practice* (pp. 118–138). New York: Guilford Press.

Templeton, S. (2008). Foreword. *Curious George's Dictionary.* Boston, MA: Houghton Mifflin Harcourt.

Templeton, S. (2010). Spelling–meaning relationships among languages: Exploring cognates and their possibilities. In L. Helman (Ed.), *Literacy development with English learners: Research-based instruction in grades K–6* (pp. 196–212). New York: Guilford Press.

Templeton, S. (2011/2012). Teaching and learning morphology: A reflection on generative vocabulary instruction. *Journal of Education, 192*(2/3), 101–107.

Templeton, S. (2012). The vocabulary-spelling connection and generative instruction: Orthographic development and morphological knowledge at the intermediate grades and beyond. In J. F. Baumann & E. J. Kame'enui (Eds.), *Vocabulary instruction: Research to Practice* (2nd ed., pp.116–138). New York: Guilford Press.

Templeton, S. (2015). Learning, reading, and writing words closely and deeply: The archaeology of thought. In Sisk, D. A. (Ed.), *Accelerating and extending literacy for diverse learners: Using culturally responsive teaching* (pp. 105–120). Lanham, MD: Rowman & Littlefield.

Templeton, S., & Bear, D. (Eds.). (1992). *Development of orthographic knowledge and the foundations of literacy: A memorial Festschrift for Edmund H. Henderson.* Hillsdale, NJ: Lawrence Erlbaum.

Templeton, S., & Bear, D. R. (2011). Phonemic awareness, word recognition, and spelling. In T. Rasinski (Ed.), *Developing reading instruction that works* (pp. 153–178). Bloomington, IN: Solution Tree Press.

Templeton, S., Johnston, F., Bear, D., & Invernizzi, M. (2019). *Words their way: Word sorts for Derivational Relations spellers* (3rd Ed.). New York, NY: Pearson.

Templeton, S. & Bear, D. R. (2018). Word study, research to practice: spelling, phonics, meaning. In D. Lapp & D. Fisher (Eds.). *Handbook of research on teaching the English language arts* (4th ed.) (pp. 207–232). New York: Routledge/Taylor & Francis.

Templeton, S., Bear, D. R., Invernizzi, M., Johnson, F., Flanigan, K., Townsend, D. R., Helman, L., & Hayes, L. (2015). *Vocabulary their way: Word study with middle and secondary students* (2nd ed.). Boston: Pearson.

Templeton, S., Bear, D. R., Johnston, F., & Invernizzi, M. (2010). *Vocabulary their way: Word study for middle and secondary students.* Boston: Pearson/Allyn & Bacon.

Templeton, S., & Gehsmann, K. (2014). *Teaching reading and writing: The developmental approach (preK-8).* Boston: Pearson.

Templeton, S., & Ives, R. T. (2007). The nature and development of spelling. In B. Guzetti (Ed.), *The encyclopedia of early childhood literacy education* (pp. 111–122). Westport, CT: Praeger.

Templeton, S., & Morris, D. (2000). Spelling. In M. Kamil, P. Mosenthal, P. D. Pearson, & R. Barr (Eds.), *Handbook of reading research* (vol. 3, pp. 525–543). Mahwah, NJ: Lawrence Erlbaum.

Templeton, S., & Spivey, E. M. (1980). The concept of "word" in young children as a function of level of cognitive development. *Research in the Teaching of English, 14*(3), 265–278.

Therrien, W. J. (2004). Fluency and comprehension gains as a result of repeated reading: A meta-analysis. *Remedial and Special Education, 25,* 4, 252–261.

Townsend, D., Filippini, A., Collins, P., & Biancarosa, G. (2012). Evidence for the importance of academic word knowledge for the academic achievement of diverse middle school students. *Elementary School Journal, 112*(3), 497–518.

Treiman, R. (1985). Onsets and rimes as units of spoken syllables: Evidence from children. *Journal of Educational Psychology, 77*(4), 417–427.

Treiman, R. Stothard, S. E., & Snowling, M. J. (2013). Instruction matters: Spelling of vowels by children in England and the U.S. *Reading and Writing: An Interdisciplinary Journal, 26,* 473–487.

Treiman, R., & Broderick, V. (1998). What's in a name: Children's knowledge about the letters in their own names. *Journal of Experimental Child Psychology, 70,* 97–116. doi:10.1006/jecp.1998.2448

Treiman, R., & Kessler, B. (2004). The case of case: Children's knowledge and use of upper and lowercase letters. *Applied Psycholinguistics, 25,* 413–428.doi:10.1017/S0142716404001195

Tunmer, W. E. (1991). Phonological awareness and literacy acquisition. In L. Rieben & C. A. Perfetti (Eds.), *Learning to read: Basic research and its implications* (pp. 105–120). Hillsdale, NJ: Lawrence Erlbaum.

Turbil, J. (2000) Developing a spelling conscience. *Language Arts, 77*, 209–216.

Uhry, J. K. (1999). Invented spelling in kindergarten: The relationship with finger-point reading. *Reading and Writing: An Interdisciplinary Journal, 11*(5–6), 441–464.

Uhry, J. K. (2002). Finger-point reading in kindergarten: The role of phonemic awareness, one-to-one correspondence, and rapid serial naming. *Scientific Studies of Reading, 6*(4), 319–342.

Upward, C., & Davidson, G. (2011). *The history of English spelling*. Chichester, West Sussex: John Wiley & Sons.

Vasquez, V. M. (2014). Negotiating critical literacies with young children. New York: Routledge.

Venezky, R. L. (1999). *The American way of spelling: The structure and origins of American English orthography*. New York: Guilford Press.

Viise, N. (1994). *Feature word spelling lists: A diagnosis of progressing word knowledge through an assessment of spelling errors*. Unpublished doctoral dissertation, University of Virginia.

Viise, N. (1996). A study of the spelling development of adult literacy learners compared with that of classroom children. *Journal of Literacy Research, 28*(4), 561–587.

Vygotsky, L. S. (1962). *Thought and language*. Cambridge, MA: MIT Press.

Ward, A. (2009). *A formative study investigating interactive reading activities to develop kindergartners' science vocabulary*. Unpublished dissertation, University of Virginia.

Warley, H. P., Invernizzi, M. A., & Drake, E. A. (2015). Sight Word Learning: There's More to it than Meets the Eye. *Reading in Virginia, 40*.

Wasik, B. A., Bond, M. A., & Hindman, A. (2006). The effects of a language and literacy intervention on Head Start children and teachers. *Journal of Educational Psychology, 98*(1), 63–74.

Watkins, C. (2011). *The American heritage dictionary of Indo-European roots* (3rd ed.) Boston: Houghton Mifflin Harcourt.

Welsch, J., Sullivan, A., & Justice, L. (2003). That's my letter: What preschoolers' name writing representation can tell us about emergent literacy knowledge. *Journal of Literacy Research, 35*(2), 757–776.

White, T. G., Sowell, J., & Yanagihara, A. (1989). Teaching elementary students to use word-part clues. *The Reading Teacher, 42*, 302–308.

Whitehurst, G. J. (1979). Meaning and semantics. In G. J. Whitehurst & B. J. Zimmerman (Eds.), *The functions of language and cognition* (pp. 115–139). New York: Academic Press.

Whitehurst, G. J., Arnold, D. S., Epstein, J. N., Angell, A. L., Smith, M., & Fiscehl, J. E. (1994). A picture book reading intervention in day care and home for children from low-income families. *Developmental Psychology, 30*, 679–689.

Williams, C. (2018) Learning to write with interactive writing instruction. *The Reading Teacher, 71, 523–532.*

Worthy, M. J., & Invernizzi, M. (1989). Spelling errors of normal and disabled students on achievement levels one through four: Instructional implications. *Bulletin of the Orton Society, 40*, 138–149.

Worthy, M., & Viise, N. M. (1996). Morphological, phonological and orthographic differences between the spelling of normally achieving children and basic literacy adults. *Reading and Writing: An Interdisciplinary Journal, 8*, 138–159.

Wylie, R. E., & Durrell, D. D. (1970). Teaching vowels through phonograms. *Elementary English, 47*, 787–791.

Yang, M. (2005). Development of orthographic knowledge among Korean children in grades 1 to 6. (Doctoral dissertation, University of Virginia). *Dissertation Abstracts International, 66/05*, 1697.

Young, K. (2007). Developmental stage theory of spelling: Analysis of consistency across four spelling-related activities. *Australian Journal of Language and Literacy, 30*(3), 203–220.

Zeno, S. M., Ivens, S. H., Millard, R. T., & Duvvuri, R. (1996). *The educator's word frequency guide*. New York: Touchstone Applied Science Associates.

Ziegler, J. C., & Goswami, U. (2005). Reading acquisition, developmental dyslexia, and skilled reading across languages: A psycholinguistic grain size theory. *Psychological Bulletin, 13*(1), 3–29.

Zucker, T.A., & Invernizzi, M. (2008). eSorts and digital extensions of word study. *The Reading Teacher, 61*(8), 654–658. doi:10.1598/RT.61.8.7

Zutell, J. (1996). The directed spelling thinking activity (DSTA): Providing an effective balance in word study instruction. *The Reading Teacher, 50*, 98–107.

Zwiers, J. (2014). *Building academic language: Essential practices for content classrooms*. San Francisco: Jossey-Bass.